HANDBOOK OF ASEAN AND REGIONAL COOPERATION

12th Summit & Beyond

HANDBOOK OF ASEAN AND REGIONAL COOPERATION

12th Summit & Beyond

Edited by

Dr. Prabhas Chandra Sinha

PENTAGON PRESS

HANDBOOK OF ASEAN AND REGIONAL COOPERATION
12th Summit & Beyond

First Published 2007

ISBN 81-8274-276-5

Published by

PENTAGON PRESS
A-38, Hauz Khas, New Delhi-110016 (India)
Phones: 011-41656996/7/8, 41517091
Telefax: 011-41656997
email: pentagonpress@airtelbroadband.net

Sales Office:
Flat # 105-106, 4262, St. # 3
Ansari Road, Darya Ganj, New Delhi-110002
Phones: 011-41563901/2, 23287705
Website: www.pentagon-press.com

Printed at New Elegant Printers, New Delhi.

PREFACE

This handbook has been edited keeping in mind the overall picture of the "Association of South East Asian Nations (ASEAN)," its recent programmes, plans of action, roadmaps, protocols and global partnership initiatives, thus setting out a comprehensive future strategy for the region. The implementation of the strategy continues along these suggested guidelines for various priority sectors at national, regional and global levels. To facilitate readers, three major categories of priority sectors have been identified. First category includes national sectors such as transport, travel and tourism, with focus on automotive industry, air travel, etc. Second category focuses on resource-based sectors such as fisheries, agro-based, rubber-based and wood-based industries. The third and the final category includes other socio-economic and industry oriented sectors such as e-ASEAN, electronics, textiles, apparels and healthcare.

The countries belonging to South East Asia, including Brunei Darussalam, Burma/Myanmar, Cambodia/Kampuchea, Indonesia, Laos, Malaysia, Philippines, Singapore, Thailand and Vietnam, have a total population of more than 512 million. Three countries, namely Burma, Cambodia and Laos are classified by the UN as Least-Developed Countries. In politico-security terms, the increased stability of the region is due to the efforts of the ASEAN Forum. In economic terms, the ASEAN countries form about 2% of the world's Gross Domestic Products (GDP). The region is a major trade and investment zone for many developed nations and regions of the world such as USA and EU, and hence a basic background information has been provided herein.

Regional cooperation initiatives in the said region have been quite substantial, particularly since the establishment of ASEAN (Association of South-East Asian Nations) in 1967. The efforts undertaken by ASEAN for regional integration have been put on a fast track since 1990s, with the establishment of ASEAN Free Trade Area (AFTA) and ASEAN Investment Area (AIA). In addition, the so-called "Initiative for ASEAN Integration", its protocols and guidelines have been result oriented. Also, the Bali Concord II of 2003 envisaged the creation of the ASEAN Economic Security and Socio-Cultural Communities by 2010.

This *"Handbook of ASEAN and Regional Cooperation: 12th Summit & Beyond"* provides readers with an introductory overview of contemporary situation with respect to making ASEAN a successful body. The upcoming 2007 Cebu ASEAN Summit in Philippines has been discussed including its agenda, plan of action and future vision of co-operation among ASEAN Community by 2020. The agreement reached at 2005 Kuala Lumpur ASEAN Summit has also been documented and reflected upon. The 2004 Valentine ASEAN Summit has been covered in detail with an outline of "Action Programme" for the coming future. The ASEAN+3 and the community's socio-cultural and security plan of action have been dealt with comprehensively. The handbook also covers in a great length the priority sectors' integration issue and outlines required strategy, in particular, against trafficking in women and children. Besides, it focuses on the dispute settlement mechanism practiced in cases of bilateral or multilateral disputes.

As such a general analysis gives readers a chance to evaluate the value of ASEAN and their interaction pattern globally. Special mention has been made about ASEAN-Japan, ASEAN-Korea, ASEAN-China and ASEAN-Russia relationship. The extent and pattern of cooperation between ASEAN and South Asia, especially SAARC (South Asian Association for Regional Cooperation) and India as well as ASEAN and the European Union have also been discussed. The obvious interdependence with other major nations and regions of the world and the emerging partnership, henceforth, have been the major concerns of this work. Finally, the handbook supported by an extensive bibliography provides deep insight into the summits and negotiations recently taken place among ASEAN and other important world nations.

—Editor

Contents

PART III

ASEAN SECTORAL INTEGRATION PROTOCOLS AND ROADMAPS

ACRONYM

AADCP	ASEAN Aquaculture Development and Coordinating Programme
AADCP-RPS	ASEAN-Australia Development Cooperation Programme Regional Partnership Scheme
AAECP	ASEAN-Australia Economic Cooperation Programme
AAF	ASEAN Automotive Federation
AAM	ASEAN Airlines Meeting
AAPSIP	ASEAN-Australia Postharvest System Improvement Programme
AARNET	ASEAN-AVRDC Regional Network for Vegetable Research and Development
AASROC	Asian-African Sub-Regional Organizations Conference
ABAC	ASEAN Business Advisory Council
ABAPAST	Advisory Body on ASEAN Plan of Action on Science and Technology
ABASF	Advisory Body of the ASEAN Science Fund
ABF	ASEAN Business Forum
ACBC	ASEAN-China Business Council; AFTA-CER Business Council
ACCICG	AFTA-CER CEP Implementation and Coordination Group
ACCORD	ASEAN and China Cooperative Operations in Response to Dangerous Drugs
ACCSM	ASEAN Conference on Civil Service Matters
ACCSQ	ASEAN Consultative Committee for Standards and Quality
ACCTC	ASEAN Coordinators of Customs Training Centre
ACDM	ASEAN Committee on Disaster Management
ACE	ASEAN Centre for Energy; ASEAN Committee on Education

ACECA	ASEAN-Canada Economic Cooperation Agreement
ACEDAC	ASEAN Centre for the Development of Agricultural Cooperatives
ACF	ASEAN Cultural Fund
ACFTA	ASEAN-China Free Trade Area
ACJCC	ASEAN-China Joint Cooperation Committee
ACP	ASEAN Cooperation Plan
ACSOC	ASEAN-China Senior Officials Consultation
ACTC	ASEAN Center for Combating Transnational Crime; ASEAN Common Technical Dossiers
ACTS	ASEAN Cargo Transport Study
ACTRs	ASEAN Common Technical Requirements
ACTT	ASEAN Communication Team for Tourism
ACW	ASEAN Committee on Women
ACWGDC	ASEAN-China Working Group on Development Cooperation
ADB	ASEAN Development Bank
ADCF	ASEAN Development Cooperation Forum
ADCG	ASEAN Datacom Coordinating Group
ADGICM	ASEAN Directors-General of Immigration Departments and Consular Affairs Division
ADPC	ASEAN Agriculture Development Planning Centre; ASIAN Disaster Preparedness Centre
AEBF	ASEAN Energy Business Forum
AEC	ASEAN Economic Community
AEEAP	ASEAN Environmental Education Action Plan
AEEMTRC	ASEAN-EC Energy Management Training and Research Centre
AEG	ASEAN Experts Group
AEGCD	ASEAN Expert Group on Communicable Diseases
AEGDM	ASEAN Expert Group on Disaster Management
AEGFS	Adhoc Expert Group on Food Safety
AEGM	ASEAN Experts Group on Minerals
AEIC	ASEAN Earthquake Information Centre
AEM	ASEAN Economic Ministers' Meeting
AEMC	ASEAN-European Community Management Centre
AEMEC	ASEAN Economic Ministers on Energy Cooperation

AEMM	ASEAN-European Union Ministerial Meeting
AENRIC	ASEAN Environmental and Natural Resources Information Centre
AEP	ASEAN Environmental Partnership
AERISRP	ASEAN Plus Three Emerging and Resurging Infections Surveillance and Response Programme
AERR	ASEAN Emergency Rice Reserve
AEY	ASEAN Environment Year
AF	ASEAN Foundation
AFAS	ASEAN Framework Agreement on Services
AFC	ASEAN Food Conference
AFDM	ASEAN Finance and Central Bank Deputies
AFDM-WG	ASEAN Finance and Central Bank Deputies Working Group
AFEEC	ASEAN Forum on Energy and Efficiency and Conservation
AFF	ASEAN Fisheries Federation
AFFA	ASEAN Federation of Forwarders Association
AFHB	ASEAN Food Handling Bureau
AFMA	ASEAN Federation of Mining Association
AFMM	ASEAN Finance Ministers' Meeting
AFOC	ASEAN Forum on Coal
AFPIC	ASEAN Forest Product Industry Club
AFPHTC	ASEAN Fisheries Postharvest Technology Centres
AFSIS	ASEAN Food Security Information System
AFSRB	ASEAN Food Security Reserve Board
AFTA	ASEAN Free Trade Area
AFTEX	ASEAN Federation of Textile Industries
AGBEP	ASEAN Business/Economic Graduate Programme
AHEWS	ASEAN Agricultural Hazards Early Warning System
AHIA	ASEAN Heads of Investment Agencies
AHMM	ASEAN Health Ministers' Meeting
AHRN	Asian Harm Reduction Network
AHPISA	Animal Health and Production Information System in ASEAN
AHPR	ASEAN Declaration on Heritage Parks and Reserves
AHSOM	ASEAN Heads of Statistical Offices Meeting

AHTN	ASEAN Harmonised Tariff Nomenclature
AIA	ASEAN Investment Area
AIBC	ASEAN-India Business Council
AIC	ASEAN Insurance Commissioner
AICO	ASEAN Industrial Cooperation Scheme
AIDA	ASEAN-India Digital Archive Project
AIDAB	Australian International Development Assistance Board
AIFM	ASEAN Institute Forest Management
AIFOCOM	ASEAN Inter-Parliamentary Organization Fact Finding Committee to Combat the Drug Menace
AIJSCC	ASEAN-India Economic Linkage Task Force
AIJV	ASEAN Industrial Joint Venture
AIMS	ASEAN Interconnection Masterplan Study
AIPA	ASEAN Intellectual Property Association
AIPO	ASEAN Inter-Parliamentary Organization
AIR	ASEAN Investment Report
AIRM	ASEAN Insurance Regulators' Meeting
AIT	ASEAN Institute of Technology
AITRI	ASEAN Insurance Regulators' Meeting
AJCCEP	ASEAN-Japan Committee on Comprehensive Economic Partnership
AJCEP	ASEAN-Japan Closer Economic Partnership
AJCEPEG	ASEAN-Japan Closer Economic Partnership Expert Group
AJCGM	ASEAN-Japan Consultative Group Meeting
AJDF	ASEAN-Japan Development Fund
AJSTD	ASEAN Journal for Science and Technology Development
AJUT	ASEAN-Japan Urban Transportation
AKECOP	ASEAN-Korea Environment Cooperation
ALIA	ASEAN Legal Information Authority
ALMM	ASEAN Labour Ministers' Meeting
AMAF	ASEAN Ministerial Meeting on Agriculture and Forestry
AMBDC	ASEAN Mekong Basin Development Cooperation
AMCA	ASEAN Ministers Responsible for Culture and Arts
AMC	Australian Managing Contractor
AMCs	ASEAN Member Countries

AMEICC	AEM-MITI Economic and Industrial Cooperation Committee
AMEM	ASEAN Ministers on Energy Meeting
AMG	Alliance for Mutual Growth
AMM	ASEAN Ministerial Meeting
AMME	ASEAN Ministerial Meeting on the Environment
AMMH	ASEAN Ministerial Meeting on Haze
AMMTC	ASEAN Ministerial Meeting on Transnational Crime
AMMST	ASEAN Ministerial Meeting on Science and Technology
AMO	ASEAN Macroeconomic Outlook
AMRDPE	ASEAN Ministers on Rural Development and Poverty Eradication
AMRI	ASEAN Ministers Responsible for Information
AMRI-TWC	ASEAN Ministers Responsible for Information Technical Working Group
AMRSW	ASEAN Ministers Responsible for Social Welfare
AMSAT	Australian Marince Science and Technology Pty. Limited
AMST	ASEAN Ministers for Science and Technology
ANDIN	ASEAN Newsletter on Disaster Management Information Network
ANEX	ASEAN News Exchange
ANWRA	ASEAN Network of Water Resource Agencies
ANZEC	ASEAN-New Zealand Economic Cooperation Programme
ANZCERTA	Australia-New Zealand Closer Economic Relations Trade Agreement
ANZECP	ASEAN-New Zealand Economic Cooperation Programme
APCASO	ASEAN-New Zealand Joint Management Committee
APBSD	ASEAN Policy Blueprint for SME Development
APCS	ASEAN Promotional Centre on Information, Culture and Tourism in Seoul
APCTs	ASEAN Promotional Chapters for Tourism
APDRTC	ASEAN Poultry Disease Research and Training Center
APEC	Asia Pacific Economic Cooperation
APERC	Asia Pacific Energy Research Centre

APHCN	ASEAN Plant Health Cooperation Network
APJSCC	ASEAN-Pakistan Joint Sectoral Cooperation Committee
APNSW	Asia Pacific Network of Sex Workers
APRIS	ASEAN Project for Regional Integration Support
APRTC	ASEAN Poultry Research and Training Centre
ARC	ASEAN Research Centre
ARCBC	ASEAN Regional Centre for Biodiversity Conservation
ARCSTC	ASEAN-Russia Commission on Scientific and Technological Cooperation
ARDCMR	ASEAN Regional Development Centre for Mineral Resources
ARF	ASEAN Regional Forum
ARF ISMCTTC	ASEAN Regional Forum Inter-Sessional Meeting on Counter Terrorism and Transnational Crime
ARISPA	ASEAN ISP Association
ARIX	ASEAN Regional Internet Exchange
ARPDM	ASEAN Regional Programme in Disaster Management
ARWGTEC	ASEAN Russia Working Group on Trade, Economic Cooperation
ARYDEC	ASEAN Rural Youth Development Centre
ASAP	ASEAN Services Access Platform
ASC	ASEAN Security Community
	ASEAN Standing Committee
ASCC	ASEAN Socio-cultural Community
ASCHN	ASEAN Sub-Committee on Health and Nutrition
ASCLA	ASEAN Sub-Committee on Labour Affairs
ASCOE	ASEAN Sub-Committee on Education
ASLOM	ASEAN Senior Labour Officials Meeting; ASEAN Senior Law Officials Meeting
ASNEM	ASEAN Specialized Meteorological Centre
	ASEAN Network for Environment Management
ASNET-RESED	ASEAN Network for Rapid Exchange of Strong Earthquake Data
ASOD	ASEAN Senior Officials on Drugs
ASOEN	ASEAN Senior Officials on the Environment
ASOF	ASEAN Senior Officials on Forestry
ASOMM	ASEAN Senior Officials' Meeting on Minerals

ASP	ASEAN Surveillance Process
ASP-5	ASEAN Sub-Regional Programme for the Fifth Cycle
ASPEN	ASEAN Strategic Plan of Action on the Environment
ASTICK	ASEAN Science and Technology Community for Innovation, Competitiveness and Knowledge
ASTNET	ASEAN Science and Technology Information Network
ASTU	ASEAN Surveillance Technical Support Unit
ASTW	ASEAN Science and Technology Week
ASW	ASEAN Sub-Committee on Women
ASWGF	ASEAN Sectoral Working Group on Fisheries
ASWGL	ASEAN Sectoral Working Group on Livestock
ASY	ASEAN Sub-Committee on Youth
ASQP	ASEAN Standards and Quality Programme
ATC	ASEAN Traffic Control
ATF	ASEAN Tourism Forum
ATFI	ASEAN Tourism Forum
ATFOA	ASEAN Task Force on AIDS
ATFSSN	ASEAN Task Force on Social Safety Net
ATIC	ASEAN Tourism Information Centre
ATM	ASEAN Transport Ministers
ATRC	ASEAN Telecommunication Regulators' Council
ATS	Amphetamine-Type Stimulants
ATTC	ASEAN Timber Technology Centre
ATTEN	ASEAN Tourism Training and Education Network
AUN	ASEAN University Network
AUN BOT	ASEAN University Network Board of Trustee
AUNILO	ASEAN University Network Inter-Library Online
AUNP	ASEAN-EU University Network Programme
AUNQUANET	ASEAN University Network Quality Assurance Network
AUSAID	Australian Agency for International Development
AVDRC	ASEAN Vegetable Development and Research Center
AVIST	ASEAN Virtual Institute of Science and Technology
AVOC	ASEAN Vegetable Oils Club
AWGASME	ASEAN Working Group on ASEAN Seas and Marine Environment

AWGATE	ASEAN Working Group on Agriculture and Training Extension
AWGCM	ASEAN Working Group on Custom Matters
AWGCME	ASEAN Working Group on Coastal and Marine Environment
AWGEE	ASEAN Working Group on Environmental Economics
AWGEIPAE	ASEAN Working Group on Environmental Information, Public Awareness and Education
AWGEM	ASEAN Working Group on Environment Management
AWGMEA	ASEAN Working Group on Multilateral Environment Agreement
AWGNC	ASEAN Working Group on Nature Conservation
AWGNCB	ASEAN Working Group on Nature Conservation and Biodiversity
AWGTCP	ASEAN Working Group on Technical Cooperation in Pharmaceuticals
AWGTM	ASEAN Working Group on Tax Matters
AWGTP	ASEAN Working Group on Transboundary Pollution
AWP	ASEAN Women's Programme
AWPII	ASEAN Work Programme on HIV/AIDS II
AYDM	ASEAN Youth Day Meeting
BAAIC	Basic Agreement on ASEAN Industrial Complementation
BCJ	Builders-Carpentry and Joineries
BFA	Bilateral Payment Arrangement
BBC	Brand-to-Brand Complementation
BIMP-EAGA	Brunei Darussalam-Indonesia-Malaysia-Philippines East ASEAN Growth Area
BISS	Biodiversity Information Sharing System
BSA	Bilateral Swap Agreements
CAAS	China Academy of Agricultural Sciences
CAMMY	China-ASEAN Ministerial Meeting on Youth
CARAM	Coordination of Action Research on AIDS and Mobility
CARD	Centre for ASEAN Agriculture Research and Development Database
CATC	Civil Aviation Training Centre

CCCA	Coordinating Committee on the Implementation of the CEPT for AFTA
CCEC	Coordinating Committee on Electronic Commerce
CCFAC	Codex Committee on Food Additives and Contaminants
CCFICS	Codex Committee on Food Import and Export
CCFL	Codex Committee on Food Labeling
CCFO	Codex Committee on Fats and Oils
CCGP	Codex Committee on General Principle
CCS	Coordinating Committee on Services
CDC	Cooper Development Center
CDM	Clean Development Mechanism
CEDAW	Convention on the Elimination of All Forms of Discrimination against Woman
CEP	Closer Economic partnership
CEPT	Common Effective Preferential Tariff Scheme
CER	Closer Economic Relations
CERTs	Computer Emergency Response Teams
CGM	Consultative Group Meetings
C&I	Criteria and Indicators
CIDA	Canadian International Development Agency
CITES	Convention on International Trade Endangered Species of Wild Fauna and Flora
CLM	Cambodia, Laos, Myanmar
CLMV	Cambodia, Laos, Myanmar and Vietnam
CLP	Classification, Labeling and Packaging
CMI	Chiang Mai Initiative
CNS/ATM	Communication, Navigation and Surveillance/Air Traffic Management
COCI	Committee on Culture and Information
COE	Certificate of Eligibility
COFAB	Committee on Finance and Banking
COSD	Committee on Social and Development
COST	Committee on Science and Technology
COTAC	Committee on Transportation and Communication
COTT	Committee on Trade and Tourism
CPMS	Cooperative Programme on Marine Science

CRC	Convention on the Right of Children
CRISP	Center for Remote Imaging, Sensing and Processing
CRM	Customs Reforms and Modernisation
CSU	Coordination and Support Unit
CTI	Committee on Trade and Investment
CZERMP	Coastal Zone Environmental and Resources Management Project
DGICM	Directors-General of Immigration and Consular Matters
DIPs	Detailed Implementation Plans
DOTS	Directly-Observed Treatment, Short Course
EAEC	East Asia Economic Caucus
EAEF	EC-ASEAN Energy Facility
EAERR	East Asia / ASEAN Rice Reserve System
EAF	East Asian Forum
EAI	Enterprise for ASEAN Integration
EASG	East Asia Study Group
EATF	E-ASEAN Task Force
EAP-AP	Environmental Assessment Programme for Asia and the Pacific
EAVG	East Asia Vision Group
EAWG	E-ASEAN Working Group
EBU	Europe Broadcasting Union
EC	European Commission
ECAP	ASEAN-EC Patents and Trademarks System
ECCM	Experts Committee on Custom Matters
EC-IIP	European Community International Investment Partner
ECIP	European Community Investment Partner Scheme
ECO	Economic Cooperation Organization
ECOPS	Environmental Cooperation Project Steering Committee
ECU	European Currency Union
EDP	Executive Development Programme
EE	Environmental Education
EE&C-SSN	Energy Efficiency and Conservation-Subsector Network
EG	Expert Group
EGAT	Electricity Generating Authority of Thailand
EGIM	Experts Group Meeting on Immigration Matters

EIB	European Investment Bank
EIP	Environmental Improvement Project
EIPA	European Institute of Public administration Programme
ELTO	English Language Training for Officials
EMC	Electromagnetic Compatibility
EMTC	Energy Management Training Courses
ENRA	Environmental and Natural Resources Accounting
EPG	Eminent Persons Group
EPGG	Energy Policy Governing Group
EPO	European Patent Office
EPSAP	Energy Policy and System Analysis Project
ESA	European Space Agency
ESC	Environmentally Sustainable Cities
ESCAP	UN Economic and Social Commission for Asia and the Pacific
ESSPA	Energy Supply Security Planning in the ASEAN
EU	European Union
EVSL	Experts Group on early Voluntary Sectoral Liberalization
FAO	Food and Agriculture Organization
FANS	Future Air Navigation System
FASC	Federation of ASEAN Shippers Councils
FASA	Federation of ASEAN Shipowners' Association
FASID	Japan Foundation for Advanced Studies on International Development
FCG	Fisheries Consultative Group
FDI	Foreign Direct Investment
FDRS	Fire Danger Rating System
FDS	Feasibility Design Stage
FGRID	Forest Genetic Resource Information Database
FIFSTA	Federation of International Food Science and Technology Associations
FIQC	Fish Inspection and Quality Control
FMD	Foot and Mouth Disease
FOCPF	Future-Oriented Cooperation Projects Fund
FPT	Fish Product Technology

FSDPs	Full Scale Demonstration Projects
FSMP	Fire Suppression Mobilization Plan
GATS	General Agreement on Trade in Services
GATT	General Agreement on Tariff and Trade
GMOs	Genetically Modified Organism
GMP	Good Manufacturing Practices
GRSP	Global Road Safety Partnership
GSP	General System of Preference
HACCP	Hazard Analysis Critical Control Points
HAPUA	Heads of ASEAN Power Utilities/Authorities
HONLEA	Heads of National Drug Law Enforcement Agencies
HPA	Hanoi Plan of Action
HRD	Human Resource Development
HRDM	Human Resources Development and Management
IAECC	India-ASEAN Economic Cooperation Committee
IAPs	Immediate Action Plans
IATEP	Inter-ASEAN Technical Exchange Programme
IBRS	International Business Reply Services
ICAO	International Civil Aviation Organization
ICGFI	International Consultative Group on Food Irradiation
ICLARM	International Centre for Living Aquatic Resources Development
ICMSF	International Commission on Microbiological Specification for Foods
ICP	International Comparison Programme
ICPM	International Committee on Phytosanitary Measures
ICTSD	Information and Communication Technology for Sustainable Development
ICT	Information and Communication Technology
IDCF	IAI Development Cooperation Forum
IDEA	Initiative for Development in East Asia
IDPAS	Institutional Development for ASEAN Secretariat
IEA	International Energy Agency
IFIs	International Financial Institutions
IFF	Intergovernmental Forum on Forests
IILP	Inter-Institutional Linkages Programme

IIP	International Investment Position
ILO	International Labour Organization
ILS	Instrument Landing System
ILSI	International Life Sciences Institute
IMF	International Monetary Fund
IMT-GT	Indonesia-Malaysia-Thailand Growth Triangle
INTA	International Trademark Association
IOM	International Organization for Migration
IP	Intellectual Property
IPD	Information Preparation and Dissemination
IPM	Integrated Pest Management
IPR	Intellectual Property Rights
IRS	Indian Remote Sensing
ISEAS	Institute of Southeast Asian Studies
ISG-CBM	Intersessional Support Group on Confidence-Building Measures
ISM-CTTC	Inter-sessional Meeting on Counter-Terrorism and Transnational Crime
ISRO	Indian Space Research Organization
ISIS	Institute of Strategic and International Studies
ISO	International Standard Organization
ISP	Internet Service Provider
ITB	Internationale Tourisme Bourse
ITS	Intelligent Transport System
ITTO	International Tropical Timber Organization
ITWG	Interim Technical Working Group
IUEP	Integrated Urban Energy Planning
IWRM	Integrated Water Resources Management
JACPP	Japan-ASEAN Cooperation Promotion Programme
JAEP	Japan-ASEAN Exchange Project
JAFTA	Japan-ASEAN Finance Technical Assistance
JAGEF	Japan-ASEAN General Exchange Fund
JATA	Japan Association of Travel Agents
JBIC	Japan Bank for International Cooperation
JCC	Joint Consultative Committee
JCM	Joint Consultative Meeting

JETRO	Japanese External Trade Organisation
JLSAP	Joint Linkages Appraisal Panel
JMC	Joint Management Committee
JPC	Joint Planning Committee
JPC-SC	Joint Planning Committee to the Sub-Committee
JPMC	Joint Planning and Monitoring Committee
JPRC	Joint Planning and Review Committee
JSTC	Joint Science and Technology Committee
KAIST	Korean Advance Institute of Science and Technology
KDI	Korean Development Institute
KIET	Korea Institute for Industrial Economics and Trade
KMA	Korean Metereology Administration
KOICA	Korea International Cooperation Agency
KOTFA	Korean World Travel Fair
KOTRA	Korea Trade Promotion Corporation
KNTC	Korea National Tourism Corporation
KRIBB	Korean Research Institute of Bioscience and Biotechnology
LBI	Legally Binding Instrument
LCR	Living Coastal Resources
LINKS	Legal Information Network System
LTIIR	Land Transport Infrastructure Integration Roadmap
M-ATM	Meeting of the ASEAN Tourism Ministers
MBDS	Mekong Basin Disease Surveilance
MC	Management Committee
MCM	Multinational Cultural Mission
MEAs	Multilateral Environment Agreements
METI	Ministry of Economy, Trade and Industry
MFRD	Marine Fisheries Research Department
MFN	Most Favoured Nation
MITI	Ministry of International Trade and Industry
MLS	Microwave Landing System
MOU	Memorandum of Understanding
MRAs	Mutual Recognition Arrangements
MRLs	Maximum Residue Limits

MT-NIT	Multimodal Transport and New Information Technology
MU	Ministerial Understanding
NACA	Network of Aquaculture Centre in Asia and Pacific
NBRUs	National Biodiversity Reference Units
NCSW	National Council on Social Welfare
NECTEC	National Electronics and Computer Technology Center
NERIC	National Environment Resource Information Centers
NFP	National Forest Programme
NFPWG	National Focal Point Working Group
NGOs	Non-Governmental Organizations
NGUT	Natural Gas Utilization in Transport
NHAPs	National Haze Action Plans
NIIs	National Information Infrastructures
NIIT	National Institute of Information Technology
NRSE	New and Renewable Sources of Energy
NTBs	Non-Tariff Barriers
NTOs	ASEAN National Tourism Organizations
NTTCCs	National Transit Transport Coordinating Committees
NWS	Nuclear Weapon States
ODA	Official Development Assistance
ODS	Ozone Depleting Substances
OECD	Organization for Economic Co-operation Development
OHIM	Office for Harmonization in the Internal Market
OIE	Organisation Internationale des Epizootics
OPCV	Overseas Project Corporation of Victoria
OSHNET	ASEAN Occupational Safety and Health Network
OWP	Overall Working Plan
PAC	Project Advisory Committee
PAC	Project Appraisal Committee
PCA	Post Clearance Audit
PCC	Project Coordinating Committee
PDD	Project Design Document
PEM	Policy Exchange Mechanism
PIDS	Philippine Institute for Development Studies
PITO	Private Investment Trade Opportunities

PIWP	Policy Implementation and Work Programme
PLANTI	Plant Quarantine and Training Institute
PLWHA	People Living with HIV/AIDS
PMC	Post Ministerial Conferences
POATC	Program of Action in Transportation and Communication
POES	Polar Orbiting Environment Satellite
PRA	Pest Risk Analysis
PRESSEA	Promotion of Renewable Energy Sources in Southeast Asia
PROMEEC	Promotion of Energy Efficiency and Conservation
PROSEA	Plant Resources on Southeast Asia
PSC	Project Steering Committee
PTA	Preferential Trading Arrangement
QASAF	Quality Assurance Systems for ASEAN Fruits
QRs	Quantitative Restrictions
RBAAIJV	Revised Basic Agreement on ASEAN Industrial joint Ventures
RCCRF	Regionalization of the Code of Conduct for Responsible Fisheries
RCICM	Regional Training Course on Integrated Coastal Management
RCP	Research Priorities Committee
ROD	Regional Ocean Dynamics
RPS	Regional Partnership Scheme
RTB	Radio Television Brunei
RTD	Research and Technological Development
RTP	Regional Training Programme
SAEI	Southeast Asian Environment Initiative
SAARC	South Asia Association for Regional Cooperation
SCB	Sub-Committee on Biotechnology
SCF	Special Cooperation Fund
SCFST	Sub-Committee on Food Science and Technology
SCIRD	Sub-Committee on Science and Technology Infrastructure and Resources Development
SCMG	Sub-Committee on Meteorology and Geophysics

SCMIT	Sub-Committee on Microelectronics and Information Technology
SCMS	Sub-Committee on Marine Science
SCMST	Sub-Committee on Materials Science and Technology
SCNCER	Sub-Committee on Non-Conventional Energy Research
SCSTA	Sub-Committee on Space Technology Application
SCOT	Sub-Committee on Tourism
SDI	Selective Dissemination of Information
SoE	State of the Environment
SEAFDEC	South East Asia Fisheries Development Centre
SEA HDR	Southeast Asian Human Development Report
SEAMEO	Southeast Asian Ministers on Education Organization
SEANWFZ	Southeast Asia Nuclear Weapons Free Zone
SEOM	Senior Economic Officials Meeting
SMES	Small and Medium-Scale Enterprises
SoER	State of the Environment Report
SFM	Sustainable Forest Management
SHS	Sender-Keeper Management
SKRL	Singapore-Kunming Rail Link
SL	Sensitive List
SLOA	Supplementary Letters of Agreement
SLOM	Senior Labour Officials Meeting
SMCE	Small and Medium-size Cultural Enterprise and Industry
SMEs	Small and Medium Enterprises
SMEWG	SMEs Agencies Working Group
SOM	Senior Officials Meeting
SOM-I	Senior Officials Meeting on Investment
SOMEC	Senior Officials Meeting on Energy Cooperation
SOMHD	Senior Officials Meeting on Health Development
SOMRDPE	Senior Officials Meeting on Rural Development and Poverty Eradication
SOMTC	Senior Officials Meeting on Transnational Crime
SOMTI	Senior Officials Meeting on Trade and Investment
SOMY	Senior Officials Meeting on Youth
SPAE	Strategic Plan of Action and the Environment

SPC	South Pacific Commission
SPF	South Pacific Forum
SPS	Sanitary and Phytosanitary
SRCR	Sub-Regional Climate Review
SRFA	Sub-Regional Firefighting Arrangement
SSN	Social Safety Nets
S&T	Science and Technology
STOM	Senior Transport Officials Meeting
TAC	Treaty of Amity and Cooperation
TAGP	Trans-ASEAN Gas Pipeline Project
TCDC	Technical Cooperation Among Developing Countries
TEDI	Trade Electronic Data Interchange
TEL	Temporary Exclusion List
TELSOM	Telecommunication Senior Officials Meeting
TELMIN	Telecommunication Ministers Meeting
TEMIC	Telecommunications Executive Management Institute
TFGR	Transport Facilitation of Goods Roadmap
TIFA	Trade and Investment Framework Agreement
TIPP	Trade and Investment Promotion Programme
TISI	Thai Industrial Standard Institute
TNC	Trade Negotiating Committee
TNG	Trade Negotiating Group
TOR	Terms of Reference
TPAS	Technology Promotion and Assistance Services
TQMC	Total Quality Management Control
TREATI	Trans-Regional EU-ASEAN Trade Initiative
TRIPs	Trade Related Aspects of Intellectual Property Rights
TROPMED	Tropical Medicine and Public Health
TTCB	Transit Transport Coordinating Board
TWG1	Technical Working Group on Standards and Conformance
TWG2	Technical Working Group on Conformity Assessment
TWG3	Technical Working Group on Testing, Calibration and Laboratory

UAP	Unprocessed Agricultural Products
UNCTAD	United Nations Conference on Trade and Development
UNDCP	United Nations International Drug Control Programme
UNDESA	United Nations Departments for Economic and Social Affairs
UNDP	United Nations Development Programme
UNEP	United Nations Environmental Programme
UNICEF	United Nations International Children Education Fund
UN-ODC	United Nations Office on Drugs and Crime
UNTAET	United Nations Transitional Administration in East Timor
UNSD	United Nations Statistics Division
US-AEP	United States Asian Environmental Partnership
US-EIP	United States Environmental Improvement Programme
USEPA	United States Environmental Protection Agency
USTR	United States Trade Representative
VAC	Visit ASEAN Campaign
VALENTE	ASEAN Energy Database, Valorization of Energy Technology
VAP	Vientiane Action Plan
VAY	Visit ASEAN Millenium Year
WCAIA	Working Committee on ASEAN Investment Area
WEC	West-East Corridor
WGABI	Working Group on Agribusiness
WGASME	Working Group on ASEAN Seas and Marine Environment
WGEIPAE	Working Group on Environmental Information, Public Awareness and Education
WGFDIS	Working Group on Foreign Direct Investment Statistics
WGIPC	Working Group on Intellectual Property Cooperation
WGNC	Working Group on Nature Conservation
WGTEC	Working Group on Trade and Economic
WGTP	Working Group on Transboundary Pollution
WHO	World Health Organization

WIPO	World Intellectual Property Organization
WPPT	WIPO Performances and Phonograms Treaty
WSSD	World Summit on Sustainable Development
WTO	World Trade Organization
WWTTT-CPD	Waste Water Treatment Technology Transfer and Cleaner Production Demonstration
ZOPFAN	Zone of Peace Freedom and Neutrality

Part I

Association of South East Asian Nations (ASEAN): Action Programmes, Priority Sectors and Dispute Settlement

1

INTRODUCTORY OVERVIEW

Introduction

South East Asia is the generally accepted name for a series of island and peninsulas which lie east of India and west of China. South East Asia is blessed with abundant sunshine and plentiful rain. With the exception of North Vietnam and a few mountain locations, virtually all of South Asia falls within the 27-36°C annual temperature range. There are, however, seasonal variations in rainfall and temperature due to changing wind and pressure systems. Warm, humid climatic conditions have given rise to lush tropical rain forests teeming with a wide variety of plant and animal life. Beside the climate, South East Asia nations shares similarities on the archeological background. Archeological evidence for the origins of some prevalent South East Asian decorative motifs may be seen in beautifully ornamented ritual bronze artefacts, such as kettle drums, weapons and bells, which have been uncovered from many sites throughout the regions. The highly stylized designs found on bronze objects from the late Chou period of China (eight-third century BC) also had some influence on South East Asian decorative motifs in terms of asymmetrical layout of design and the merging and modification of motifs to fit in with an overall schema.

This influence is most evident on some textiles from Borneo and Sumatra. This corner of the world is also remarkable for its incredible diversity of ethnic groups, each of which has its own language, customs, mores, and religious belief. South East Asia today has a sprinkling of hunting-gathering Negrito people, such as the Atea of the Philippines, The Semang of Malaysia, and the Orang Kubu of Sumatra. Austroloid people are also thought to have passed through South-East Asia during the early migration period. Traces of these people may be seen in the current racial stock of Timor and Flores. Meanwhile the majority of the present day indigenous population are basically Mongoloid, consisting of various people who migrated from South China and the Tibetan border areas at various times.

The earliest and most far reaching influence which was to permeate South East Asia was that of India. Many local rulers adopted such Indianized ideas as a belief in a god-like king at the head of a hierarchical administration system, an ancestral genealogical pedigree system, the lunar-solar calender, astrology, and various of Hindu ritual worship. Buddhism was brought from India by traders. The basic proportions and much of the iconography for South East Asia religious art come from India cannons of design. Classical Indian art motifs, such as crowned snakes, the Makara water monster, the Kala monster face mask, the garuda bird (the mount of the Hindu God Vishnu), peacocks, the lotus, the 'vase of plenty' and the wishing appear on South East Asia textiles. Local languages have been greatly enriched by the loan from Sanskrit, the ancient and sacred language of India.

Indian epics, such as the Mahabarata and the Ramayana and the Buddhist Jataka Tales, form the basis of classical theatre in South East Asia. The Ramayana is performed as a puppet play in southern Thailand, northern Malaysia and Java, and as a dance drama in Burma, Laos, central Thailand and central Java. Puppet figures from these epics (called wayang) appear on the textiles of Bali and Lombok in Indonesia.

During the early years of Ming Dynasty (1368-1644), China took a more active interest in South East Asia. The influence of China culture can be seen in ceramics. Chinese ceramics have been imitated in brassware by the Maranao people of southern Philippines, while some ceramics motifs have been widely copied on South East Asian textiles. Images of Dragon from stoneware jars may occasionally be seen on warp ikat clothes from Sumba. In Bali and Thailand, the banji, or swastika, motif is a pattern regularly encountered on silk weft ikat. It may also be seen in a supplementary weft on Lao, Shan, and Kachin textiles.

Meanwhile the influence of Muslim to South East Asia may be seen in the soft, loosely woven double ikat-pattern patola cloth, sometimes called cinde. Patola textiles became symbols of wealth and prestige. The royal weft ikat cloth of Thailand and Cambodia is similar with the weft ikat cloths from Inle Lake in Burma and some sarongs, such as the malong andong of southern Philippines. The European influences by the spread of Western hygiene, improved sanitation, and health care have led to a decreased death rate and lead to the increase in population. While education and the spread of Western ideas and technology have been responsible for much material progress, they have contributed to a cleavage between new and traditional ways of life. The influence of the textile motifs can be seen in the use of garden flowers in cloth from Arakan and Amarapura in Burma, Laos, Javanesse Batik and Timor. South East Asian shares some similarities from the ancestors, artefacts up to the influence brought by India, China, Muslim and Europe. However, the South East Asia nations have the same backgrounds. The similarities lead to the unity among the nations.

BASIC BACKGROUND INFORMATION ABOUT ASEAN MEMBER COUNTRIES

(i) Brunei Darussalam

Head of State	:	His Majesty Sultan Haji Hassanal Bolkiah Mu'izzaddin Waddaulah
Capital	:	Bandar Seri Begawan
Land area	:	5,765 sq. km
Population	:	357,800 (2004)
Language	:	Malay, English
Religion	:	Islam
Member of	:	ASEAN, APEC, APT, APDC, Commonwealth, ESCAP, GP 77, GATT/WTO, ICAO, IMO, IMF, WMO, UNDP, WHO, WIPO, WTO-GBT, ASEM, EALAF, UN, OIC, NAM, AASROC, UNESCO, APG, WSIS, IDB, ADB and AMED
Currency	:	B$ (Bruneian Dollar).
GDP	:	US$ 5,4626.6 million (2004) at current market prices
Major Industries	:	Oil and gas, textiles, food and beverages, building materials
Major Exports	:	Oil and gas, ready-made garments
Major Imports	:	Transport equipment and machinery, manufactured goods, food chemicals

(ii) Cambodia

Head of State	:	His Majesty King Norodom Sihamoni
Head of Government	:	Prime Minister Hun Sen
Capital	:	Phnom Penh
Land area	:	181,035 sq. km
Population	:	14,131 thousands (2004)
Language	:	Khmer
Religion	:	Buddhism
Member of	:	ASEAN, CTBTO, ESCAP, FAO, IAEA, IBRD, ICAO, IDA, IFC, IFAD, ILO, IMF, IMO, ITU, LDC, UNO, UNCTAD, UNESCO, UPO, UNIDO, WIPO, WHO
Currency	:	Riel
GDP	:	US$ 4,215 million (2003) at current market prices
Major Industries	:	Textiles and Garments, Beverages, Food Processing, Wood Processing

Major Exports	:	Garments, Textile Product Sawn, Wood Furniture and Rubber
Major Imports	:	Transport equipment and machinery, manufactured goods, food chemicals

(iii) Indonesia

Head of State	:	President Susilo Bambang Yudhoyono
Capital	:	Jakarta
Land area	:	1,890,000 sq.km.
Population	:	215,960 thousands (2004).
Language	:	Bahasa Indonesia
Religion	:	Islam, Christianity, Buddhism, Hinduism
Member of	:	ASEAN, UN, IMF, ESCAP, FAO, ILO, UNESCO, IBRD, IFC, MIGA, IDB, IDA, ADB, WTO, APEC, ASEM, EALAF
Currency	:	Rupiah
GDP	:	US$ 208,625 million (2003) at current market prices
Major Industries	:	Pulp and paper, cement, basic metals and fertilizer, power generation, telecommunication, transportation
Major Exports	:	Textile, electronic goods, footwear, oil & gas, plywood, sawn timber
Major Imports	:	Chemical and pharmaceutical, fertilizer, cotton yarns, textile fabric, machines, motor vehicles

(iv) Laos

Head of State	:	President Choummaly Sayasone
Head of Government	:	Prime Minister Bouasone Bouphavanh
Capital	:	Vientiane
Land area	:	236,800 sq.km
Population	:	5,758 million (2004)
Language	:	Lao
Religion	:	Buddhism
Member of	:	ASEAN, ADB, ESCAP, FAO, IBRD, WHO, IDA, WIPO, IFC, ILO, IMF, UN, NCTAD, UNESCO, UNIDO, UNICEF, WHO, EALAF
Currency	:	Kip
GDP	:	US$ 12,043 thousands (2003) at current market prices
Major Industries	:	Garment industry, wood-based and processing industries, electricity

Major Exports	:	Coffee, electricity, clothing, wood and forest product and Gypsum
Major Imports	:	Industrial machinery, chemicals, iron, electrical machinery and parts, steel, oil, construction material and consumption goods

(v) Malaysia

Head of State	:	DYMM Seri Paduka Baginda Yang Dipertuan Agung Tuanku Syed Sirajuddin Ibni Almarhum Tuanku Syed Putra Jamalullail
Head of Government	:	Prime Minister Abdullah Ahmad Badawi
Capital	:	Kuala Lumpur
Land area	:	330,257 sq.km
Population	:	23,671thousand (2004).
Language	:	Melayu, English, Chinese, Tamil
Religion	:	Islam, Buddhism, Taoism, Hinduism, Christianity
Member of	:	ASEAN, ADB, APEC, ASEM, D-8, EBRD, ECOSOP, ESCAP, FAO, G-15, IAEA, IBRD, ICAO, IDA, IDB, ILO, EALAP
Currency	:	Malaysian Ringgit
GDP	:	US$ 103,737 million (2003) at current market prices
Major Industries	:	Electronic & electrical goods, textiles, clothing & footwear, chemicals, petroleum, wood and metal products and rubber
Major Exports	:	Electronic & electric machinery, petroleum & LNG, textiles, clothing & footwear, palm oil, sawn timber
Major Imports	:	Manufacturing inputs, machinery & transport equipment, metal product

(vi) Myanmar/Burma

Head of State	:	Senior General Than Shwe
Head of Government	:	Prime Minister Lt. Gen. Soe Win
Capital	:	Yangon
Land area	:	676,577 sq.km
Population	:	54,745 thousands (2004)
Language	:	Myanmar
Religion	:	Buddhism, Christianity, Islam
Member of	:	ASEAN, ADB, ESCAP, ACU, FAO, IBRD, IDA, IFC, ILO, IMF, ITU, WTO, UNESCO, UNIDO, UNICEF, EALAF

Currency	:	Myanmar Kyat
GDP	:	US$ 9,605 million (2003) at current market prices
Major Industries	:	Agro-based industries, textiles industries, steel mills
Major Exports	:	Rice, teak, beans & pulses, rubber, coffee, minerals, gems marine products
Major Imports	:	Power tillers, hand tractor, fertilizer, diesel oil, cement, dumper, loader and spare parts, water pumps, hydraulic excavator

(vii) Philippines

Head of State	:	President Gloria Macapagal Arroyo
Capital	:	Manila
Land area	:	76,946 thousand in 2000 (actual); 85,237 thousand in 2005 (projected)
Population	:	82,664 thousands (2004)
Language	:	Filipino, English, Spanish
Religion	:	Christianity (Catholicism, Protestantism, Philippine Independent Church, Iglesia ni Kristo); Islam
Member of	:	APEC, ARF, ACD, ADB, ASEAN, ASEM, CCC, Common Fund for Commodities, CP, ESCAP, FEALAC, FAO, G-24, G-77, IAEA, IBRD, ICAO, ICC, ICFTU, ICRM, IDA, IFAD, IFC, IFRCS, IHO, ILO, IMF, IMO, Interpol, IOC, IOM, ISO, ITU, NAM, OPCW, UN, UNCTAD, UNESCO, UNHCR, UNIDO, UNMIK, UNTAET, UNU, UPU, WCL, WFTU, WHO, WIPO, WMO, World Tourism Organization, World Trade Organization
Currency	:	Peso
GDP	:	US$ 86,123 million (2004) at current market prices
Major Industries	:	Priority sectors : construction materials, electronics, food, giftware and holiday decor, home furnishings, IT & IT-enabled services, marine products, motor vehicle parts and components, organic and natural products, wearables
Major Exports	:	Electronic products; garments; ignition wiring set and other wiring sets used in vehicles, aircrafts, and ships; coconut oil; woodcrafts and furniture; other products manufactured from materials imported on consignment basis; petroleum products; metal components; cathodes and sections of cathodes of refined copper; fresh bananas (per data as of August 2005)

Major Imports	:	Electronic products; mineral fuels, lubricants, and related materials; industrial machinery and equipment; transport equipment; iron and steel; cereal and cereal preparations; textile yarn, fabrics, made-up articles, and related products; telecommunications equipment and electrical machinery; plastics in primary and non-primary forms; organic and inorganic chemicals (per data as of August 2005)

(viii) Singapore

Head of State	:	President S.R. Nathan
Head of Government	:	Prime Minister Lee Hsien Loong
Capital	:	Singapore
Land area	:	697.1 sq. km
Population	:	4.198 million (2004)
Language	:	English, Malay, Mandarin, Tamil
Religion	:	Buddhism, Christianity, Islam, Taoism and Hinduism
Member of	:	ASEAN, ADB, APEC, ARF, COMMONWEALTH, FAO, IAEA, IBRD, IDA, IFC, IMF, IFAD, IMO, ILO, ITU, UNIDO, UPO, WHO, ASEM, EALAF, WTO, WIPO, ICAO, NAM, G77
Currency	:	Singapore Dollar (S$)
GDP	:	US$ 106,818 million (2004) at current market prices
Major Industries	:	Electronics, chemicals, banking and finance, real estate, tourism, trading
Major Exports	:	Petroleum products, industrial machines, radio and television receivers and parts, electronic component and parts, clothing, beverages and tobacco
Major Imports	:	Crude petroleum, iron & steel, industrial machines, electric generators, electronic component and parts

(ix) Thailand

Head of State	:	His Majesty King Bhumibol Adulyadej
Head of Government	:	General Surayud Chulanont
Capital	:	Bangkok
Land area	:	513,254 sq.km
Population	:	64,470 thousands (2003)
Language	:	Thai
Religion	:	Buddhism, Islam
Member of	:	ASEAN, ADB, ASEM, ESCAP, FAO, IBRD, IDA, IFC,

		IMF, ILO, UNCTAD, UNESCO, WHO, WIPO, APEC, EALAF
Currency	:	Baht
GDP	:	US$ 143,303 million (2003) at current market prices
Major Industries	:	Electronics, gems and jewelry, footwear, textiles, clothing, mobiles
Major Exports	:	Textiles, computer and components, integrated circuits and parts, gems and jewelry, footwear
Major Imports	:	Industrial machinery, iron & steel electrical machinery and parts, chassis and body

(x) Viet Nam

Head of State	:	President Nguyen Minh Triet
Head of Government	:	Prime Minister Nguyen Tan Dung
Capital	:	Ha Noi
Land area	:	330,363 sq.km
Population	:	82,222 thousand (2003)
Language	:	Vietnamese
Religion	:	Buddhism, Christianity
Member of	:	ASEAN, IBRD, IDA, IFC, IMF, ASEM, MIGA, UNDP, UNCTAD, GSPT, UNIDO, FAO, IFAD, ICAO, EALAF
Currency	:	Dong
GDP	:	US$ 39,021 million (2003) at current market prices
Major Industries	:	Agriculture, forestry, fishery, industrial construction
Major Exports	:	Crude oil, coal, chromium, tin, cements, woolen carpet, jute carpet, rice cinnamon, marine products
Major Imports	:	Motors, petroleum products, diesel oil, fertilizers

ASEAN: A BRIEF ANALYSIS

Establishment

The Association of Southeast Asian Nations or ASEAN was established on 8 August 1967 in Bangkok by the five original Member Countries, namely, Indonesia, Malaysia, Philippines, Singapore, and Thailand. Brunei Darussalam joined on 8 January 1984, Vietnam on 28 July 1995, Lao PDR and Myanmar on 23 July 1997, and Cambodia on 30 April 1999. The ASEAN region has a population of about 500 million, a total area of 4.5 million square kilometers, a combined gross domestic product of almost US$ 700 billion, and a total trade of about US$ 850 billion.

Objectives

The ASEAN Declaration states that the aims and purposes of the Association are: (1) to accelerate economic growth, social progress and cultural development in the region, and (2) to promote regional peace and stability through abiding respect for justice and the rule of law in the relationship among countries in the region and adherence to the principles of the United Nations Charter. The ASEAN Vision 2020, adopted by the ASEAN Leaders on the 30th Anniversary of ASEAN, agreed on a shared vision of ASEAN as a concert of Southeast Asian nations, outward looking, living in peace, stability and prosperity, bonded together in partnership in dynamic development and in a community of caring societies. In 2003, the ASEAN Leaders resolved that an ASEAN Community shall be established comprising three pillars, namely, ASEAN Security Community, ASEAN Economic Community and ASEAN Socio-Cultural Community.

Fundamental Principles

ASEAN Member Countries have adopted the following fundamental principles in their relations with one another, as contained in the Treaty of Amity and Cooperation in Southeast Asia (TAC):

- mutual respect for the independence, sovereignty, equality, territorial integrity, and national identity of all nations;
- the right of every State to lead its national existence free from external interference, subversion or coercion;
- non-interference in the internal affairs of one another;
- settlement of differences or disputes by peaceful manner;
- renunciation of the threat or use of force; and
- effective cooperation among themselves.

ASEAN Security Community

Through political dialogue and confidence building, no tension has escalated into armed confrontation among ASEAN Member Countries since its establishment more than three decades ago. To build on what has been constructed over the years in the field of political and security cooperation, the ASEAN Leaders have agreed to establish the ASEAN Security Community (ASC). The ASC shall aim to ensure that countries in the region live at peace with one another and with the world in a just, democratic and harmonious environment. The members of the Community pledge to rely exclusively on peaceful processes in the settlement of intra-regional differences and regard their security as fundamentally linked to one another and bound by geographic location, common vision and objectives. It has the following components: political development; shaping and sharing of norms; conflict prevention; conflict resolution; post-conflict peace building; and implementing mechanisms. It will be built on the strong foundation of ASEAN processes, principles, agreements, and structures, which evolved over the years and are contained in the following major political agreements:

- ASEAN Declaration, Bangkok, 8 August 1967;
- Zone of Peace, Freedom and Neutrality Declaration, Kuala Lumpur, 27 November 1971;
- Declaration of ASEAN Concord, Bali, 24 February 1976;
- Treaty of Amity and Cooperation in Southeast Asia, Bali, 24 February 1976;
- ASEAN Declaration on the South China Sea, Manila, 22 July 1992;
- Treaty on the Southeast Asia Nuclear Weapon-Free Zone, Bangkok, 15 December 1997;
- ASEAN Vision 2020, Kuala Lumpur, 15 December 1997; and
- Declaration of ASEAN Concord II, Bali, 7 October 2003.

In recognition of security interdependence in the Asia-Pacific region, ASEAN established the ASEAN Regional Forum (ARF) in 1994. The ARF's agenda aims to evolve in three broad stages, namely, the promotion of confidence building, development of preventive diplomacy and elaboration of approaches to conflicts. The present participants in the ARF include: Australia, Brunei Darussalam, Cambodia, Canada, China, European Union, India, Indonesia, Japan, Democratic Republic of Korea, Republic of Korea (ROK), Lao PDR, Malaysia, Mongolia, Myanmar, New Zealand, Pakistan, Papua New Guinea, the Philippines, the Russian Federation, Singapore, Thailand, the United States, and Viet Nam. The ARF discusses major regional security issues in the region, including the relationship amongst the major powers, non-proliferation, counter-terrorism, transnational crime, South China Sea and the Korean Peninsula, among others.

ASEAN Economy Community

The ASEAN Economic Community shall be the end-goal of economic integration measures as outlined in the ASEAN Vision 2020. Its goal is to create a stable, prosperous and highly competitive ASEAN economic region in which there is a free flow of goods, services, investment and a freer flow of capital, equitable economic development and reduced poverty and socio-economic disparities in year 2020. The ASEAN Economic Community shall establish ASEAN as a single market and production base, turning the diversity that characterises the region into opportunities for business complementation and making the ASEAN a more dynamic and stronger segment of the global supply chain. ASEAN's strategy shall consist of the integration of ASEAN and enhancing ASEAN's economic competitiveness. In moving towards the ASEAN Economic Community, ASEAN has agreed on the following:

- institute new mechanisms and measures to strengthen the implementation of its existing economic initiatives including the ASEAN Free Trade Area

(AFTA), ASEAN Framework Agreement on Services (AFAS) and ASEAN Investment Area (AIA);

- accelerate regional integration in the following priority sectors by 2010: air travel, agro-based products, automotives, e-commerce, electronics, fisheries, healthcare, rubber-based products, textiles and apparels, tourism, and wood-based products;
- facilitate movement of business persons, skilled labour and talents; and
- strengthen the institutional mechanisms of ASEAN, including the improvement of the existing ASEAN Dispute Settlement Mechanism to ensure expeditious and legally-binding resolution of any economic disputes.

Launched in 1992, the ASEAN Free Trade Area (AFTA) is now in place. It aims to promote the region's competitive advantage as a single production unit. The elimination of tariff and non-tariff barriers among Member Countries is expected to promote greater economic efficiency, productivity, and competitiveness. As on 1 January 2005, tariffs on almost 99 percent of the products in the Inclusion List of the ASEAN-6 (Brunei Darussalam, Indonesia, Malaysia, the Philippines, Singapore, and Thailand) have been reduced to no more than 5 percent. More than 60 percent of these products have zero tariffs. The average tariff for ASEAN-6 has been brought down from more than 12 percent when AFTA started to 2 percent today. For the newer Member Countries, namely, Cambodia, Lao PDR, Myanmar, and Viet Nam (CLMV), tariffs on about 81 percent of their Inclusion List have been brought down to within the 0-5 percent range.

Other major integration-related economic activities of ASEAN include the following:

- Roadmap for Financial and Monetary Integration of ASEAN in four areas, namely, capital market development, capital account liberalisation, liberalisation of financial services and currency cooperation;
- trans-ASEAN transportation network consisting of major inter-state highway and railway networks, including the Singapore to Kunming Rail-Link, principal ports, and sea lanes for maritime traffic, inland waterway transport, and major civil aviation links;
- Roadmap for Integration of Air Travel Sector;
- interoperability and interconnectivity of national telecommunications equipment and services, including the ASEAN Telecommunications Regulators Council Sectoral Mutual Recognition Arrangement (ATRC-MRA) on Conformity Assessment for Telecommunications Equipment;
- trans-ASEAN energy networks, which consist of the ASEAN Power Grid and the Trans-ASEAN Gas Pipeline Projects;

- Initiative for ASEAN Integration (IAI) focusing on infrastructure, human resource development, information and communications technology, and regional economic integration primarily in the CLMV countries;
- Visit ASEAN Campaign and the private sector-led ASEAN Hip-Hop Pass to promote intra-ASEAN tourism; and
- Agreement on the ASEAN Food Security Reserve.

ASEAN Socio-Cultural Community

The ASEAN Socio-Cultural Community, in consonance with the goal set by ASEAN Vision 2020, envisages a Southeast Asia bonded together in partnership as a community of caring societies and founded on a common regional identity. The Community shall foster cooperation in social development aimed at raising the standard of living of disadvantaged groups and the rural population, and shall seek the active involvement of all sectors of society, in particular, women, youth, and local communities. ASEAN shall ensure that its work force shall be prepared for, and benefit from, economic integration by investing more resources for basic and higher education, training, science and technology development, job creation, and social protection. ASEAN shall further intensify cooperation in the area of public health, including in the prevention and control of infectious and communicable diseases. The development and enhancement of human resources is a key strategy for employment generation, alleviating poverty and socio-economic disparities, and ensuring economic growth with equity. Among the on-going activities of ASEAN in this area include the following:

- ASEAN Work Programme for Social Welfare, Family, and Population;
- ASEAN Work Programme on HIV/AIDS;
- ASEAN Work Programme on Community-Based Care for the Elderly;
- ASEAN Occupational Safety and Health Network;
- ASEAN Work Programme on Preparing ASEAN Youth for Sustainable Employment and Other Challenges of Globalisation;
- ASEAN University Network (AUN) promoting collaboration among seventeen member universities ASEAN;
- ASEAN Students Exchange Programme, Youth Cultural Forum, and the ASEAN Young Speakers Forum;
- The Annual ASEAN Culture Week, ASEAN Youth Camp and ASEAN Quiz;
- ASEAN Media Exchange Programme; and
- Framework for Environmentally Sustainable Cities (ESC) and ASEAN Agreement on Transboundary Haze Pollution.

External Relations

The ASEAN Vision 2020 affirmed an outward-looking ASEAN playing a pivotal role in the international community and advancing ASEAN's common interests. Building on the Joint Statement on East Asia Cooperation of 1999, cooperation between the Southeast and Northeast Asian countries has accelerated with the holding of an annual summit among the leaders of ASEAN, China, Japan, and the Republic of Korea (ROK) within the ASEAN Plus Three process. ASEAN Plus Three relations continue to expand and deepen in the areas of security dialogue and cooperation, transnational crime, trade and investment, environment, finance and monetary, agriculture and forestry, energy, tourism, health, labour, culture and the arts, science and technology, information and communication technology, social welfare and development, youth, and rural development and poverty eradication. There are now thirteen ministerial-level meetings under the ASEAN Plus Three process. Bilateral trading arrangements have been or are being forged between ASEAN Member Countries and China, Japan, and the ROK. These arrangements will serve as the building blocks of an East Asian Free Trade Area as a long-term goal. ASEAN continues to develop cooperative relations with its Dialogue Partners, namely, Australia, Canada, China, the European Union, India, Japan, the ROK, New Zealand, the Russian Federation, the United States of America, and the United Nations Development Programme. ASEAN also promotes cooperation with Pakistan in some areas of mutual interest.

Consistent with its resolve to enhance cooperation with other developing regions, ASEAN maintains contact with other inter-governmental organisations, namely, the Economic Cooperation Organisation, the Gulf Cooperation Council, the Rio Group, the South Asian Association for Regional Cooperation, the South Pacific Forum, and through the recently established Asian-African Sub-Regional Organisation Conference. Most ASEAN Member Countries also participate actively in the activities of the Asia-Pacific Economic Cooperation (APEC), the Asia-Europe Meeting (ASEM), and the East Asia-Latin America Forum (EALAF).

Structural and Mechanisms

The highest decision-making organ of ASEAN is the Meeting of the ASEAN Heads of State and Government. The ASEAN Summit is convened every year. The ASEAN Ministerial Meeting (Foreign Ministers) is held annually. Ministerial meetings on the following sectors are also held regularly: agriculture and forestry, economics (trade), energy, environment, finance, health, information, investment, labour, law, regional haze, rural development and poverty alleviation, science and technology, social welfare, telecommunications, transnational crime, transportation, tourism, youth. Supporting these ministerial bodies are committees of senior officials, technical working groups and task forces.

To support the conduct of ASEAN's external relations, ASEAN has established committees composed of heads of diplomatic missions in the following capitals: Beijing, Berlin, Brussels, Canberra, Geneva, Islamabad, London, Moscow, New Delhi, New York, Ottawa, Paris, Riyadh, Seoul, Tokyo, Washington D.C. and Wellington.

The Secretary-General of ASEAN is appointed on merit and accorded ministerial status. The Secretary-General of ASEAN, who has a five-year term, is mandated to initiate, advise, coordinate, and implement ASEAN activities. The members of the professional staff of the ASEAN Secretariat are appointed on the principle of open recruitment and region-wide competition.

ASEAN has several specialized bodies and arrangements promoting inter-governmental cooperation in various fields including the following: ASEAN Agricultural Development Planning Centre, ASEAN-EC Management Centre, ASEAN Centre for Energy, ASEAN Earthquake Information Centre, ASEAN Foundation, ASEAN Poultry Research and Training Centre, ASEAN Regional Centre for Biodiversity Conservation, ASEAN Rural Youth Development Centre, ASEAN Specialized Meteorological Centre, ASEAN Timber Technology Centre, ASEAN Tourism Information Centre, and the ASEAN University Network.

In addition, ASEAN promotes dialogue and consultations with professional and business organisations with related aims and purposes, such as the ASEAN-Chambers of Commerce and Industry, ASEAN Business Forum, ASEAN Tourism Association, ASEAN Council on Petroleum, ASEAN Ports Association, Federation of ASEAN Shipowners, ASEAN Confederation of Employers, ASEAN Fisheries Federation, ASEAN Vegetable Oils Club, ASEAN Intellectual Property Association, and the ASEAN-Institutes for Strategic and International Studies. Furthermore, there are 58 Non-Governmental Organizations (NGOs), which have formal affiliations with ASEAN.

OVERVIEW OF FACTS AND FIGURES

ASEAN was established on August 8, 1967, with the signing of the ASEAN Declaration, also known as the Bangkok Declaration, by foreign ministers of Indonesia, Malaysia, the Philippines, Singapore and Thailand. It was later expanded to include Brunei, Vietnam, Laos, Myanmar and Cambodia. Papua New Guinea became its observer in 1995. ASEAN has 10 dialogue partners - Australia, Canada, China, the European Union, India, Japan, Russia, New Zealand, South Korea and the United States.

The ASEAN region spans an area of some 4.5 million square kilometers, where 14 official languages are spoken and about seven religions are adhered to. Its population was estimated at 512 million in 2000. Organization structure of ASEAN comprises Summit meeting (the highest authority of ASEAN bringing together the heads of government of the member countries), Ministerial Meeting, the Standing

Committee, Secretariat, various Committees and Senior Officials' Meeting.

The Bangkok Declaration united the ASEAN members in joint efforts to promote economic cooperation and the welfare of the people in the region. It set out guidelines for ASEAN's activities and defined the aims of the organization. The ASEAN nations come together with three main objectives in mind: to promote the economic, social and cultural development of the region through cooperative programs; to safeguard the political and economic stability of the region against big power rivalry; and to serve as a forum for the resolution of intra-regional differences.

LIST OF ASEAN SUMMITS

Host Country	*ASEAN Summit*	*Date*
Cebu, Philippines	12th ASEAN SUMMIT	10-14 January 2007
Kuala Lumpur, Malaysia	11th ASEAN SUMMIT	12-14 December 2005
Vientiane, Laos	10th ASEAN SUMMIT	29-30 November 2004
Bali, Indonesia	9th ASEAN SUMMIT	6-8 October 2003
Phnom Penh,Cambodia	8th ASEAN SUMMIT	4-5 November 2002
Bandar Seri Begawan, Brunei	7th ASEAN SUMMIT	6-7 November 2001
Hanoi, Vietnam	6th ASEAN SUMMIT	15-16 December 1998
Bangkok, Thailand	5th ASEAN Summit	14-15 December 1995
Singapore	4th ASEAN SUMMIT	27-29 January 1992
Manila, Philippines	3rd ASEAN SUMMIT	14-15 December 1987
Kuala Lumpur	2nd ASEAN SUMMIT	4-5 August 1977
Bali,Indonesia	1st ASEAN SUMMIT	23-24 February 1976

2

12th ASEAN Cebu, Philippines Summit and Beyond

The Philippines aims to steer ASEAN closer to realizing its vision of an ASEAN Community by 2020. In order to achieve this, ASEAN needs to fast track implementation of key programs and projects under the Vientiane Action Program (VAP). Apart from the objective of broadening economic integration of the ten Member Countries of ASEAN, a serious challenge facing ASEAN is how to narrow the development gap among its members to quicken the pace of integration. It is not an easy task since the stages of political, social and economic development in ASEAN vary, such that there are countries that cannot cope with all the requirements of regional integration. Moreover, ASEAN needs to narrow the development gaps not only among ASEAN member countries, but also the gaps within each member country. Support for the development of sub-regional growth areas will facilitate bridging these development gaps.

A Caring and Sharing Community

A Philippine initiative at the 10th ASEAN Summit, the ASEAN Socio-Cultural Community (ASCC) represented ASEAN's goal to raise the living standards of people in the region. Programs, which promote social protection, environmental protection, human resource development and an ASEAN identity, fuel economic growth and contribute to regional stability.

However, the key element is the political will of Member Countries and national efforts aimed at poverty reduction and equitable development, complemented by regional cooperation. Therefore, there is a need to streamline and harmonize national policies with regional objectives. Resources from ASEAN Member Countries should be mobilized to support the programs under the VAP. Finally, national coordination and support from Dialogue Partners and other external partners in institutional capacity building will help accelerate implementation of programs.

Engaging the Civil Society

Over the years, ASEAN has seen the growth of regional networks of non-governmental organizations. One of the most active of these groups is the ASEAN Peoples' Assembly, which is an important partner of ASEAN in moving forward its integration initiatives. At the 12th ASEAN Summit, the Philippines will support the holding of the 5th ASEAN People's Assembly, which coincides with the ASEAN Leaders' Summit.

Objective and Success Criteria

President Arroyo has chosen the theme for the 12th ASEAN Summit, entitled "One Caring and Sharing Community." The theme will reflect the initiatives to be taken by the Philippines in ASEAN community building and common people's participation. Further, we recognize that the strength of ASEAN is its youth who are building ASEAN's bridges to the future.

The overall objective of the Philippine Chairmanship of ASEAN is not only to engage the ASEAN Leaders in exchanging views and resolving issues affecting community building efforts but also to bring ASEAN's activities to the common people in the grassroots level and make them better understand and appreciate ASEAN.

Mission and Vision

The Chairmanship's vision is directed towards ..." a community conscious of its diverse cultures and bounded by a common regional awareness, where people strive for equitable access to opportunities for total human development regardless of gender, race, religion, language, or social and cultural background."

The end goal of the Chairmanship is to help sustain the momentum towards a caring ASEAN where the standard of living of disadvantaged groups are raised and the women and youth are empowered; where the civil society is engaged; and special attention is given to recommendations on the promotion of health, food security and safety, environment protection, and the promotion of common values and norms.

The vision puts the ASEAN people at the center of regional integration with the Governments of Member Countries, Dialogue Partners and other friends of ASEAN providing them the means to fully participate in the process. We also see the need for a strengthened ASEAN Secretariat with an enhanced role to support the realization of our vision.

Mission Statement

The Chairmanship mission is "to steer ASEAN in the implementation of the Vientiane Action Program towards social protection and promotion of the rights of the vulnerable sectors in the community, in order to contribute to poverty alleviation and empowerment through projects implemented with dialogue partners and other supporters."

By the end of the Philippine chairmanship, all outcome documents and decisions by the Leaders and the Ministers should reflect the overall theme of a caring and sharing community, that should result in the following:

- A people-centered approach in ASEAN integration and community building;
- Clearer sense by the ordinary folks including the youth and other vulnerable sectors of the society of the community building efforts by the ASEAN Member Governments;
- Better understanding of the importance of an ASEAN Charter and other initiatives for regional peace and security;
- Stronger sense of regional awareness and common heritage of the region as may be discovered not only in ASEAN capitals but also in the rural areas; and
- Closer cooperation and understanding between ASEAN with dialogue partners.

The date of the 12th Summit of the Association of Southeast Asian Nations (ASEAN) has been moved to Jan. 8-13 next year in Cebu, Marciano Paynor, secretary general of the organizing committee for the ASEAN Summit, announced at a news conference here Sunday. The summit, originally slated for Dec. 10-14, 2006 and was on Dec. 8 postponed to January 2007 because of what the organizing committee called a possible "major weather disturbance." Paynor said the specific date was set by the consensus made by the ASEAN senior officials before they left Cebu. Paynor said as a matter of fact, the ASEAN economic officials meetings have been finished in the past few days, so the 12th summit and its related meetings will start with the ASEAN ministerial meetings in January next year. He also said the registered domestic and international media who were covering the meetings will be acceptable for the January meetings. Cebu Province Governor Gwendolyn Garcia expressed disappointment over the postponement of the summit at the press conference, adding Cebu is ready to well-prepare for the next month summit.

Despite the postponement of the 12th ASEAN Summit, economic ministers of 10 member nations of the Association of Southeast Asian Nations (ASEAN) have signed six economic agreements that would expand further trade and commerce in the region. Four of these agreements were for intra-ASEAN trade, while the others were economic agreements expanding trade with China. The four intra-ASEAN agreements include the ASEAN Framework (Amendment) Agreement for the Integration of Priority Sectors, the ASEAN Sectoral Integration (Amendment) Protocol for the Integration of Priority Sectors, the Protocol to Implement the 5th Package of

Commitments under the ASEAN Framework Agreement on Services (AFAS) and ASEAN MRA (Mutual Recognition Agreement) on Nursing Services. The accords with China include the Agreement on Trade in Services of the Framework Agreement on Comprehensive Economic Cooperation between ASEAN and China, and the Second Protocol to Amend the Framework Agreement on Comprehensive Economic Cooperation between ASEAN and China. Another agreement between ASEAN and China (the Protocol to Amend the Trade in Goods of the Framework Agreement on Comprehensive Economic Cooperation between ASEAN and China) was also completed. But the ASEAN and Chinese economic ministers deferred the signing because the ASEAN leaders wanted to witness its signing ceremony when the Summit is held in Cebu next January. (PNA/Xinhua) On Monday, 4 December 2006, the United Nations General Assembly unanimously granted observer status to ASEAN. The Philippines, as the current chair of ASEAN, had tabled the resolution for ASEAN's observer status on 10 October 2006. The Sixth Committee adopted the resolution before it was sent to the General Assembly. More than 70 countries cosponsored the resolution. The General Assembly also adopted another resolution on "Cooperation between the United Nations and the Association of Southeast Asian Nations" on the same day. The two resolutions mark a strengthening of ASEAN-UN cooperation. ASEAN can now participate in the sessions and work of the General Assembly in the capacity of an observer. The UN and ASEAN will also look to hold more regular summits.

"CHALLENGES AND PROSPECTS FOR THE ASEAN ECONOMIC COMMUNITY"

Remarks by H.E. Ong Keng Yong, Secretary General of ASEAN at the ASEAN Gala Dinner, London, 4 December 2006

H.E. Pengiran Dato Maidin Hashim, Chair of ASEAN London Committee
ASEAN Ambassadors and High Commissioners
Excellencies,
Distinguished Guests,
Ladies and Gentlemen,

Thank you for the generous introduction. I very much appreciate this opportunity to share with you some of my thoughts on the challenges and prospects for the ASEAN Economic Community (or AEC).

Free trade is a significant stimulus to regional production, linkages and competitiveness. ASEAN has made significant progress in that regard since the implementation of the ASEAN Free Trade Area (AFTA) from 1993. The AFTA initiative has been particularly successful in reducing tariffs in the trade in goods.

Currently, some 99.8 per cent of the products in the Inclusion Lists of ASEAN-

6 (Brunei Darussalam, Indonesia, Malaysia, the Philippines, Singapore and Thailand) have been brought down to the tariff range of 0-5 per cent, with about 65 per cent of those products having zero import tariffs. Meanwhile, 91 per cent of the products traded by the CLMV countries (Cambodia, Lao People's Democratic Republic, Myanmar and Viet Nam) under the Common Effective Preferential Tariff package have been moved into their respective Inclusion Lists. About 77 percent of those products are already within the 0-5 per cent tariff band.

However, regional free trade alone is not sufficient to release the full energies and the inherent potential of ASEAN. All of us now have to take a further step forward. Deeper economic integration is necessary for ASEAN to cope effectively with the unprecedented opportunities as well as the unprecedented challenges, on both scale and depth, unleashed by globalisation.

China and India have altered the global economic landscape through huge market openings and greater competition, too. Meanwhile, interlinked supply networks have proliferated all over the world, among many other innovative and more efficient ways in value creation and industrial organization. Last but not least, there are the freer and often instant movements of new ideas, people and resources across national boundaries.

The ASEAN Economic Community

In the midst of two giant economies, ASEAN Leaders made a historic resolution in December 1997 to leverage the region's potential by building an economic community (ASEAN Vision 2020). Henceforth, ASEAN is to be transformed into a stable, prosperous, and highly competitive region with equitable economic development, and reduced poverty and socio-economic disparities.

Notably, that resolution took place in the midst of a severe financial and economic crisis in ASEAN. This underscored once again ASEAN's common perception of the critical importance of greater regional cohesion and complementation in coping with good as well as bad times.

Subsequently, at the Bali Summit in November 2003, ASEAN Leaders declared that the AEC would be the end-goal of regional economic integration (Bali Concord II). This Community shall weld together 10 separate entities as a single market and production base by 2020. The ASEAN Economic Ministers have recently recommended that the target year be sped up to 2015.

Put it simply, there will be a free flow of goods, services, investment and a freer flow of capital in the AEC. This is to be complemented by freer movements of skilled human resources - including regional business persons, professionals, and cultural and artistic talents.

The consequent gains from deeper and broader integration are substantial in

ASEAN. They are estimated by McKinsey and Co to cut as much as one-fifth of production costs of consumer goods in the region.

As such, the AEC building process will empower ASEAN to remain a dynamic and competitive player in the regional and global supply chains. But the same process is also predicated on wide-ranging adjustments and reforms to be carried out by Governments and the business sector, among other stakeholders in the region.

The commitments so far made include, to name just a few, the ASEAN Free Trade Area of 1992; the ASEAN Framework Agreement on Services of 1995; the ASEAN Agreement on Customs and the ASEAN Customs Vision 2020 of 1997; the Framework Agreement on the ASEAN Investment Area and the ASEAN Framework Agreement on Mutual Recognition Agreements, both of 1998; the Initiative for ASEAN Integration of 2000; the ASEAN Framework Agreement for the Integration of Priority Sectors of 2004; and the ASEAN Policy on Standards and Conformance of 2005.

ASEAN has three key strengths in the economic arena. We have abundant natural resources in our region. We have large supplies of professionals and talented people. And, we have the capability to adopt, adapt and advance technology. By leveraging on these strengths the AEC is likely to be realised sooner than later.

ASEAN Charter

A key development complementing the AEC work is the process to establish the ASEAN Charter. A Charter is certainly not a panacea. But at a minimum, it is going to facilitate the transformation of ASEAN into a rules-based regional organization with a legal personality. Provisions in the Charter to establish robust mechanisms for monitoring implementation and ensuring compliance would contribute greatly to ASEAN's effectiveness. Through the Charter, ASEAN will be able to enshrine the values and principles that shaped by our history and experiences in the last 39 years. It will virtually become our new and official birth certificate in the sense that we are re-born as the ASEAN Community. Such a Charter would also serve to make ASEAN a more responsive, dynamic and integrated regional organisation. In short, the Charter will define ASEAN's future.

The ASEAN Eminent Persons Group (EPG) has been working on its recommendation for the drafting of the Charter. In a few days, the EPG's report will be considered by the ASEAN Leaders during the 12th ASEAN Summit in Cebu, the Philippines, from 11-12 December 2006. In that report, the EPG will recommend what should go into an ASEAN Charter. And at the upcoming Summit, a High-Level Task Force is expected to be mandated by the ASEAN Leaders to start drafting an ASEAN Charter, taking into account recommendations of the EPG, among other things.

This achievement would not only become a benchmark for the region to further enhance its cohesiveness and coherence, but also would venture forth a new cooperative spirit for the community building in the region. To be sure, there is a lot more work to do, especially in converging the different levels of ambition. Yet, I am optimistic ASEAN is on the threshold of a quantum leap in collective development and growth.

ASEAN-EU Economic Interaction

Against that backdrop of dynamic changes and developments within ASEAN, the EU has remained, among other roles, an important partner in trade and investment and a major source of technical assistance to ASEAN. The EU's valued roles will continue to be very helpful to AEC building efforts in the coming decade.

As a market, for example, the EU-15 economies took in some US$ 78 billion worth of ASEAN exports in 2005, a steady growth of 5 per cent a year since 2000. The EU was the third largest trading partner, with an average share of 12 per cent of ASEAN trade in the last two years (or just about one percentage point behind Japan and the U.S.A. during 2004-05). Germany, Netherlands, the United Kingdom, and France are the most important EU traders with ASEAN.

Likewise, the EU-15's foreign direct investment (FDI) in ASEAN has been significant, with the largest share of 57 per cent of the FDI hosted by our region in 2000 (totalling US$ 23.5 billion). However, this share fell to 19 per cent of the FDI flows to ASEAN (US$ 38.1 billion) in 2005. Singapore, Indonesia, Malaysia, Viet Nam and Thailand were the main destinations of FDI from the EU.

FDI from the United Kingdom provides a contrast, however. It accounted for 20 per cent (or US$ 2.7 billion) of FDI from the EU-15 in ASEAN in 2000, and 62 per cent (or US$ 4.4 billion) in 2005. Singapore and, to a much lesser extent, Indonesia, Malaysia and Brunei Darussalam were the main hosts of FDI from the United Kingdom.

The sharp upswing in FDI flows into ASEAN, by 62 per cent between 2000 and 2005, is noteworthy. This is an eloquent expression of external market confidence in the prospects for sustained development and stability in our own part of the world.

But there is still much scope for a significant expansion of commercial synergies between ASEAN and the EU, according to the Report of the Vision Group on ASEAN-EU Economic Partnership. Furthermore, such an enlarged relationship will serve a catalyst to the harmonious and broad-based development of the two regions and, more generally, to the growth of world trade and investment in the 21st century. And an ASEAN-EU FTA has been mooted in this context.

In the meantime, however, the deepening integration within ASEAN itself will create numerous additional opportunities for gainful interactions in trade and investment, not just among the regional economies but also among all their external partners as well.

What then is the Remaining Agenda?

On the one hand, it would be a mistake to underestimate the concerted efforts and sacrifices that have been made thus far by all ASEAN stakeholders in sustaining economic cooperation and in AEC building. This applies especially to those in the less developed economies of our region.

Nevertheless, the effective coordination and timely implementation of commitments remain a challenge for attention and management by most Governments and other stakeholders in ASEAN. There is also much room for more systematic and extensive dissemination of information to the public, both at home and abroad, regarding integration initiatives and their (actual or expected) progress and outcomes.

Regular consultations have been held with, and inputs received from, the ASEAN Business Advisory Council and the ASEAN Chamber of Commerce and Industry. However, a perception lingers that the private sector has not been fully and actively involved in the integration and community building processes in ASEAN. There are no easy answers as regards the workable alternatives and options.

On the other hand, it would also be a mistake to under-estimate the remaining tasks to be implemented and the new commitments to be made ahead. ASEAN is not a Customs Union with a common external trade policy, including the same external tariff wall. It is not the single market that the EU has evolved into. We have a large geography and vast seas separating thousands of islands. Communications and infra-structural deficiencies are daily headache for our people.

There are still major barriers to the free movement of resources and inputs in the region at present. Such barriers include large differences in tax rates on (intra- and trans-regional) businesses and investments. On this fiscal matter, ASEAN has yet to embark, for example, on the harmonization and standardization of laws and regulations on business and on competition.

Deeper integration in banking, finance and capital markets is on-going; this can also be an equally challenging process in ASEAN. Meanwhile, significant volatility in Member Countries' rates of exchange and large differences in the rates of interest and inflation would certainly not be conducive to the most optimal allocation of scarce resources. At the same time, however, there is no plan for ASEAN common currency in the next 10-15 years.

There is then an over-arching issue: the development gap in ASEAN. This gap, which is unlikely to be bridged by 2020, can be another barrier to regional integration.

More substantive programmes complementary to or in supplement to the Initiative for ASEAN Integration may be needed. The introduction of a region-wide levy (say, on tourists in or from ASEAN) for funding those programs is an often-cited option for consideration.

Deeper economic integration is an imperative although the symphony of integration is unfinished in ASEAN. All stakeholders must resolve, firmly and soon, to take the next steps toward the AEC. To do less would surely mean a future less rewarding, less prosperous, less secure and less equitable for all the peoples of ASEAN. That is the challenge facing all of us but the challenge can be managed.

ASEAN's resilience has not been derailed by the recent oil price shock and higher interest rates. Economic growth is expected at a respectable rate of about 5.5 per cent in the next few years, according to the Asian Development Bank. All these augur well for the region's own transformation into a vibrant AEC a decade from now

But such dynamism also underpins a meaningful and differentiated role of ASEAN economies in the Pan-Asian region where the world's manufacturer of choice (China) and the world's back office (India) are situated. In particular, ASEAN-China trade has grown substantially and very fast in the recent years. ASEAN now has a free trade agreement on goods with China and with the Republic of Korea, while FTAs with Australia and New Zealand, India and Japan are under negotiation. Thus, ASEAN is not standing alone in our historic efforts at AEC formation. The future looks bright with sustained regional and international collaboration, including from the EU and other partners of ours, in response to the constant emergence of opportunities for inclusive and stable development.

And that is the message I wish to convey to you all tonight. Thank you for your attention.

CEBU RESOLUTION ON SUSTAINABLE DEVELOPMENT

Recalling the Declaration of ASEAN Concord II (Bali Concord II) to establish an ASEAN Community comprising three pillars, namely, political and security cooperation, economic cooperation, and socio-cultural cooperation that are closely intertwined and mutually reinforcing for the purpose of ensuring durable peace, stability and shared prosperity in the region;

Welcoming the implementation of the Vientiane Action Programme (VAP), the medium-term roadmap for the period 2004-2010 which sets out specific programme areas and measures to achieve the goal of establishing the ASEAN Community;

Noting the emphasis of the VAP towards nurturing human, cultural and natural resources of the region for sustained development in a harmonious and people-centred ASEAN through the socio-cultural pillar;

Encouraged by the sustainable development approach of the VAP which stresses that ASEAN's social and environmental agenda is linked inextricably with the economic and security pillars of the ASEAN Community, that social instability can emerge from environmental scarcity or the inequitable use of environmental assets, and that failure to address these critical and persistent issues can further cause both economic and political dislocations;

Mindful of the need to address global environmental issues by all parties based on the principle of common but differentiated responsibility, so that these issues do not cause adverse impact to the prosperity of the region; and

Determined to further enhance environmental cooperation in order to achieve an environmentally sustainable ASEAN Community.

We, the Ministers of ASEAN Member Countries responsible for the environment, do hereby:

Express our satisfaction on the progress of implementation of environmental programmes and measures and related activities in the VAP, and resolve to further enhance regional cooperation;

Reiterate our commitment to address global environmental issues through national and regional cooperation and active participation at international fora, and call upon the global community to continue to work with us to enhance such collaboration;

Launch the Third ASEAN State of the Environment Report 2006 which highlights the environmental conditions of the region, challenges faced and actions being taken to address them, while inviting all parties to foster greater collaboration to address these challenges;

Express our serious concern over the recurring transboundary haze pollution which was aggravated by the extended drier weather condition during El Nino years, and resolve to further enhance preventive, monitoring and mitigation efforts to address land and forest fires;

Commit to continue assisting member countries affected by land and forest fires within the framework of the ASEAN Agreement on Transboundary Haze Pollution, and for this purpose encourage the remaining member countries to quickly ratify the Agreement;

Establish the Sub-regional Ministerial Steering Committee consisting of Ministers from the 5 most affected countries namely, Brunei Darussalam, Indonesia, Malaysia, Singapore and Thailand to oversee the implementation of concrete actions to address land and forest fires and the resulting transboudary haze pollution.

Express our full support and commitment to the effective operations of the recently established ASEAN Centre for Biodiversity, located in the Philippines, to promote biodiversity conservation in the region, and in this respect express our appreciation to the EU for providing financial support to participating member countries for the first three-and-half years of operations of the Centre;

Agree to expedite the respective national process for signing the ASEAN Framework Agreement on access to, and fair and equitable sharing of benefits arising from the utilisation of, biological and genetic resources, in order to sustainably manage the rich biological resources of the region;

Endorse the ASEAN Environmentally Sustainable Cities Award to recognise exemplary national efforts in Member Countries and to promote further efforts towards environmental sustainability in ASEAN cities;

Recognise the importance of strengthening national efforts and regional cooperation for effective environmental law enforcement, to address issues such as illegal trade in wildlife. As for illegal logging, there is a need for effective enforcement of forestry law and other related laws, where appropriate;

Express concern over the impact of climate change on ecosystems, in particular, water resources, which requires mitigation and adaptation measures to minimise the impacts particularly from flood, drought, landslide, and other water-related hazards;

Commit to enhance further cooperation with the People's Republic of China, Japan and the Republic of Korea under the ASEAN Plus Three Framework through regular policy dialogues and implementation of activities of common interest; and

Express our appreciation to dialogue partners, international and regional organisations, and other countries that have collaborated with us in promoting sustainable development initiatives, and call upon these and other prospective partners to further enhance their collaboration.

10TH ASEAN MINISTERIAL MEETING ON THE ENVIRONMENT: JOINT PRESS STATEMENT

10th November, 2006, Cebu, the Philippines

Ministers responsible for environment from the ten ASEAN Member Countries held their formal 10th ASEAN Ministerial Meeting on the Environment in Cebu, the Philippines on 10th November, 2006. The Ministers reviewed regional cooperation on a number of environmental activities in particular those related activities in the Vientiane Action Programme 2006-10. The Ministers welcomed the sustainable development approach of the VAP which stresses that ASEAN's social and environmental agenda is linked inextricably with the economic and security pillars of the ASEAN Community, and resolved to work towards an environmentally sustainable ASEAN Community.

The Ministers adopted the Cebu Resolution on Sustainable Development.

The Ministers launched the Third ASEAN State of the Environment Report 2006 which highlights the environmental conditions of the region, challenges faced and actions being taken to address them. The Ministers expressed the hope that the report would help all parties to better appreciate regional environmental issues and foster greater collaboration.

In the light of the recent haze episode in the region, the Ministers discussed at length the transboundary haze pollution issue. The First Meeting of the Sub-Regional Ministerial Steering Committee (MSC) on Transboundary Haze Pollution held on 9 November 2006 endorsed its Terms of Reference and Indonesia's Plan of Action in Dealing with Transboundary Haze Pollution. Indonesia will chair the MSC for the first two (2) years. The MSC also agreed with Indonesia's proposal that Member Countries of the MSC may, through the Central Government of Indonesia, wish to adopt one or more fire-prone districts/regencies for enhancing capacity to deal with land and forest fires.

The MSC also recognised the urgency and importance of following up on the Regional Workshop in Jakarta on 2 November, 2006 by organising a high-level international conference in December 2006 in Indonesia to generate support and partnership for the implementation of the PoA.

The Ministers expressed their full support and commitment to the effective operations of the recently established ASEAN Centre for Biodiversity, hosted by the Philippines. The Ministers also agreed to expedite the signing of the ASEAN Framework Agreement on access to, and fair and equitable sharing of benefits arising from the utilization of, biological and genetic resources, and to promote further listing of ASEAN Heritage Parks, in order to sustainably manage the rich biological resources of the region.

The Ministers agreed to institute an ASEAN Environmentally Sustainable Cities Award to recognize exemplary national efforts in Member Countries and to promote further efforts towards environmental sustainability in ASEAN cities.

The Ministers also recognized the importance of strengthening national efforts and regional cooperation for effective environmental law enforcement, to address issues such as illegal trade in wildlife. As for illegal logging, there is a need for effective enforcement of forestry law and other related laws, where appropriate.

3

KUALA LUMPUR ASEAN SUMMIT AND ACTION PROGRAMME

Malaysia hosted the 11th ASEAN Summit and Related Summits from 12-14 December 2005. The ASEAN Summit is an annual meeting held on a rotational basis by the country which holds the Chairmanship of the ASEAN Standing Committee. The Related Summits that are to be held around that time are the 9th ASEAN + 3 Summit , 9th ASEAN + China Summit, 9th ASEAN + Japan Summit, 9th ASEAN + Republic of Korea Summit and 4th ASEAN + India Summit. Malaysia also hosted the first ASEAN + Russia Summit. The highlight of these high-level meetings was be the staging of the First East Asia Summit (EAS) on 14th December 2005.

The ASEAN Summit is geared towards strengthening ASEAN as a regional institution that is competent in managing issues of regional and international concern in an effective and productive way. The meetings would provide opportunities to Leaders of ASEAN member countries to evaluate the relations and cooperation within the grouping as well as identifying the most appropriate measures in defining the direction of ASEAN. While Summits of ASEAN and its dialogue partners namely China, Japan, Republic of Korea, India and Russia allows ASEAN to strengthen its cooperation with these nations. The inaugural East Asia Summit is expected to draw ASEAN to closer and substantial relations with China, Japan, Republic of Korea, India, Australia and New Zealand.

Malaysia also hosted two other Summits, namely the Second Brunei Indonesia Malaysia Philippines East ASEAN Growth Areas (BIMP-EAGA) Summit and the First Indonesia Malaysia Thailand Growth Triangle (IMT-GT) Summit on the sidelines of the 11th ASEAN Summit. They were aimed at enhancing sub-regional cooperation. While Cambodia, Laos, Myanmar and Vietnam held their Second CLMV Summit.

To make preparations and lay the groundwork for these top-level meetings, senior officials and Ministers from these countries met in Kuala Lumpur from 6th to 11th December 2005 at various senior officials and ministerial level meetings. ASEAN or the Association of South East Asian Nation has a population of about 500 million, a total area of 4.5 million sq. km. a combined gross domestic product of US$ 737 billion, and a total trade of US$ 720 billion.

The private sector in ASEAN also played an active role during the busy summit period as Kuala Lumpur staged the 2005 ASEAN Business and Investment Summit from Dec. 9 to 11.

The Business and Investment Summit, which is the third in the series, was sponsored by the ASEAN Business Advisory Council.

Besides complementing the 11th ASEAN Summit, its objectives were to foster an exchange of views and perceptions between the private sector and government within ASEAN and East Asia and to facilitate commerce and trade between the communities in this region.

CHAIRMAN'S STATEMENT OF THE FIRST EAST ASIA SUMMIT

Kuala Lumpur, 14 December 2005

1. The First East Asia Summit was held successfully on 14 December 2005 in Kuala Lumpur, Malaysia. The Meeting was chaired by The Honourable Dato Seri Abdullah Ahmad Badawi, Prime Minister of Malaysia, and was attended by Heads of State/Government of ASEAN, Australia, the People's Republic of China, the Republic of India, Japan, the Republic of Korea and New Zealand. Russia was invited as Guest of the Government of Malaysia. Malaysia was privileged to host and chair this historic Summit.

2. We had a productive exchange of views on regional and international political and economic issues as well as on the challenges facing the region and the world.

3. Understanding that the de-nuclearisation of the Korean Peninsula in a peaceful and verifiable manner will greatly contribute to the peace, stability, and prosperity of the Asia Pacific region, we strongly endorsed the Joint Statement adopted at the Fourth Round of the Six-party Talks on September 19, 2005. We also shared the view that the Fifth Round of the Talks should be resumed as soon as possible, as agreed upon, to enable the Parties to the Talks to continue their discussion on ways to faithfully and expeditiously implement the commitments stated in the Joint Statement.

4. We exchanged views on the recent developments in the region, international terrorism, maritime security as well as the need to address the threat of infectious diseases. In this context we adopted the East Asia Summit Declaration on Avian

Influenza Prevention, Control and Response. Leaders acknowledged the ongoing threat that terrorism poses to the region and stressed the continuing need for comprehensive efforts, including at national and regional levels, to combat it.

5. Recognizing the fact that our economies are dependent upon stable fuel supplies and in the light of the uncertainty of global fuel prices, we supported cooperation in the energy field including development of fuel efficient technologies and alternative energy sources.

6. We recognized the increasing inter-linkages and growing inter-dependence among our countries and agreed to deepen integration and cooperation in order to promote the creation of a harmonious and prosperous community of nations.

7. We discussed development issues which include among others, issues such as sustainable development, technology transfer, trade and investment-related issues, challenges to socio-economic development namely poverty, development gap, capacity building and issues related to good governance and promotion of human rights and democracy. We reiterated our commitment for concerted regional and global efforts to respond to these challenges.

8. We reaffirmed our abiding commitment to the objectives of the Doha Development Agenda of the World Trade Organization and the importance of the Hong Kong WTO Ministerial establishing a clear roadmap for completion of the Doha Round in 2006. We reiterated our strong preference that all WTO members must achieve an ambitious and balanced outcome in the Doha Round that is development-orientated and delivers real gains for trade in agriculture, non-agricultural market access and services.

9. We also had an exchange of views on the effort at community building being undertaken in the East Asian region. In this regard we expressed our full support for ASEAN's efforts to realize the ASEAN Community. We also recognized that the East Asian community is a long-term goal that would contribute to the maintenance of peace, security, prosperity and progress in the region and beyond.

10. We had extensive and in-depth discussions on the East Asia Summit and its role in the evolving regional architecture. We agreed that the East Asia Summit with ASEAN as the driving force is an integral part of the overall evolving regional architecture. We also agreed that the East Asian region had already advanced in its efforts to realise an East Asian community through the ASEAN+3 process. In this context we believed that the EAS together with the ASEAN+3 and the ASEAN+1 processes could play a significant role in community building in the region.

11. We reiterated our agreement that the East Asia Summit should remain open and outward looking, with ASEAN as the driving force working in partnership with the other participants of the East Asia Summit. In this context, we welcomed the Russian Federation's expression of interest to participate in the East Asia

Summit and agreed to consider its participation in future East Asia Summits based on the criteria established by ASEAN.

12. We agreed that the EAS would continue to be a leaders'-led Summit for strategic discussions on key issues affecting the region and the evolving regional architecture. We appreciated the informal, retreat style format of our first meeting which enabled us to discuss issues in a frank, spontaneous and free-flowing manner.

13. We also noted that some form of mechanism may be desirable to facilitate follow-up action of the EAS and to coordinate and implement the areas of cooperation we had identified. In this regard we agreed that the officials and the ASEAN Secretariat follow through with the decisions of the EAS.

14. We signed the Kuala Lumpur Declaration on the East Asia Summit outlining its principles and purposes, areas of cooperation and primary modalities.

15. We agreed that the East Asia Summit will be convened annually. In this context we agreed to convene the Second East Asia Summit in Cebu, Philippines on 13 December 2006.

MAIN ACHIEVEMENTS OF ELEVENTH ASEAN SUMMIT

Kuala Lumpur, 12-14 December 2005

- Chairman's Statement of the 11th ASEAN Summit, "One Vision, One Identity, One Community", Kuala Lumpur, 12 December 2005

Press Releases

- Chairman's Statement of the First East Asia Summit, Kuala Lumpur, 14 December 2005
- Chairman's Statement of the First ASEAN-Russian Federation Summit, Kuala Lumpur, 13 December 2005
- Chairman's Statement of the Ninth ASEAN-Republic of Korea Summit, Kuala Lumpur, 13 December 2005
- Chairman's Statement of the Fourth ASEAN-India Summit, Kuala Lumpur, 13 December 2005
- Joint Statement of the Ninth ASEAN-Japan Summit – Deepening and Broadening of ASEAN-Japan Strategic Partnership, Kuala Lumpur, 13 December 2005
- Chairman's Statement of the Ninth ASEAN Plus Three Summit, Kuala Lumpur, 12 December 2005
- Chairman's Statement of the Ninth ASEAN-China Summit, Kuala Lumpur, 12 December 2005
- The Report of the ASEAN-China Eminent Persons' Group

Agreements

- Agreement on Dispute Settlement Mechanism Under the Framework Agreement on Comprehensive Economic Cooperation Among the Governments of the Member Countries of the Association of Southeast Asian Nations and the Republic of Korea, Kuala Lumpur, 13 December
- Framework Agreement on Comprehensive Economic Cooperation Among the Governments of the Member Countries of the Association of Southeast Asian Nations and the Republic of Korea, Kuala Lumpur, 13 December 2005
  - — Annex : Economic Cooperation
- Agreement between the Governments of the Member Countries of the Association of Southeast Asian Nations and the Government of the Russian Federation on Economic and Development Cooperation, Kuala Lumpur, 10 December 2005
- Agreement to Establish and Implement the ASEAN Single Window, Kuala Lumpur, 9 December 2005
- ASEAN Mutual Recognition Arrangement on Engineering Services, Kuala Lumpur, 9 December 2005
- Agreement on the ASEAN Harmonized Electrical and Electronic Equipment (EEE) Regulatory Regime, Kuala Lumpur, 9 December 2005

Declarations

- Kuala Lumpur Declaration on the East Asia Summit, Kuala Lumpur, 14 December 2005
- East Asia Summit Declaration on Avian Influenza Prevention, Control and Response, Kuala Lumpur, 14 December 2005
- Joint Declaration of the Heads of State/Government of the Member Countries of the Association of Southeast Asian Nations and the Head of State of the Russian Federation on Progressive and Comprehensive Partnership, Kuala Lumpur, 13 December 2005
  - — Comprehensive Programme of Action to Promote Cooperation between the Association of Southeast Asian Nations and the Russian Federation 2005-15
- Kuala Lumpur Declaration on the ASEAN Plus Three Summit, Kuala Lumpur, 12 December 2005
- Kuala Lumpur Declaration on the Establishment of the ASEAN Charter, Kuala Lumpur, 12 December 2005
  - — Terms of Reference of the Eminent Persons' Group (EPG) on the ASEAN Charter

— List of Members of the Eminent Person's Group (EPG) on the ASEAN Charter

- Instrument of Accession to the Treaty of Amity and Cooperation in Southeast Asia by Australia, Kuala Lumpur, 10 December 2005
- Instrument of Extension of the Treaty of Amity and Cooperation in Southeast Asia by Australia, Kuala Lumpur, 10 December 2005

AGREEMENT ON DISPUTE SETTLEMENT MECHANISM UNDER THE FRAMEWORK AGREEMENT ON COMPREHENSIVE ECONOMIC COOPERATION AMONG THE GOVERNMENTS OF THE MEMBER COUNTRIES OF THE ASSOCIATION OF SOUTHEAST ASIAN NATIONS AND THE REPUBLIC OF KOREA

Kuala Lumpur, 13 December 2005

The Governments of Brunei Darussalam, the Kingdom of Cambodia, the Republic of Indonesia, the Lao People's Democratic Republic, Malaysia, the Union of Myanmar, the Republic of the Philippines, the Republic of Singapore, the Kingdom of Thailand and the Socialist Republic of Vietnam, Member Countries of the Association of Southeast Asian Nations, and the Republic of Korea;

Recalling the Framework Agreement on Comprehensive Economic Cooperation among the Governments of the Member Countries of the Association of Southeast Asian Nations and the Republic of Korea signed in Kuala Lumpur, Malaysia on the thirteenth day of December 2005; and

Further Recalling Article 5.1 of the Framework Agreement, which provides for the dispute settlement procedures and mechanism for the Framework Agreement and any other Agreement to be concluded thereunder;

Have agreed as follows:

Article 1: Definitions

For the purposes of this Agreement, unless the context otherwise requires:

ASEAN means the Association of Southeast Asian Nations which comprises of Brunei Darussalam, the Kingdom of Cambodia, the Republic of Indonesia, the Lao People's Democratic Republic, Malaysia, the Union of Myanmar, the Republic of the Philippines, the Republic of Singapore, the Kingdom of Thailand and the Socialist Republic of Vietnam;

ASEAN Member Countries means Brunei Darussalam, the Kingdom of Cambodia, the Republic of Indonesia, the Lao People's Democratic Republic, Malaysia, the

Union of Myanmar, the Republic of the Philippines, the Republic of Singapore, the Kingdom of Thailand and the Socialist Republic of Vietnam collectively;

ASEAN Member Country means Brunei Darussalam, the Kingdom of Cambodia, the Republic of Indonesia, the Lao People's Democratic Republic, Malaysia, the Union of Myanmar, the Republic of the Philippines, the Republic of Singapore, the Kingdom of Thailand or the Socialist Republic of Vietnam individually;

Chair means the member of an arbitral panel who serves as the chair of the arbitral panel;

Complaining party means any Party that requests consultations under paragraph 1 of Article 3;

Covered agreements means:

(a) the Framework Agreement;

(b) the Agreement on Trade in Goods under the Framework Agreement;

(c) this Agreement;

(d) any agreement to be concluded among the Parties pursuant to the relevant provisions of the Framework Agreement unless provided otherwise therein;

Days means calendar days, including weekends and holidays;

Framework Agreement means the Framework Agreement on Comprehensive Economic Cooperation among the Governments of the ASEAN Member Countries and the Republic of Korea;

Korea means the Republic of Korea;

Parties means the ASEAN Member Countries and Korea collectively;

Parties to a dispute, or parties to the dispute means both the complaining party and the party complained against;

Party means an ASEAN Member Country or Korea;

Party complained against means any Party to which the request for consultations is made under paragraph 1 of Article 3;

Third party means a Party, other than the parties to a dispute, that delivers a written notice in accordance with Article 7; and

WTO means the World Trade Organisation.

Article 2: Coverage and Application

1. This Agreement shall apply with respect to the avoidance or settlement of all disputes arising between the Parties under the covered agreements. Unless otherwise provided in this Agreement or any other covered agreement, this Agreement shall apply to all disputes between the Parties.

2. The rules and procedures of this Agreement shall apply subject to special or additional rules and procedures on dispute settlement, if any, contained in the other covered agreements. To the extent that there is a conflict between the rules and procedures of this Agreement and such special or additional rules and procedures on dispute settlement contained in a covered agreement, the special or additional rules and procedures shall prevail. In disputes involving rules and procedures under more than one covered agreement, if there is a conflict between special and additional rules and procedures of such covered agreements, the chair of the arbitral panel, in consultation with the parties to the dispute, shall determine the rules and procedures to be followed for that dispute within ten (10) days after a request by any party to the dispute.

3. The provisions of this Agreement may be invoked in respect of measures affecting the operation of any covered agreement taken within the territory of a Party by:

(a) central, regional or local governments and authorities; or

(b) non-governmental bodies in the exercise of powers delegated by central, regional or local governments or authorities.

4. Subject to paragraph 5, nothing in this Agreement shall prejudice any right of the Parties to have recourse to dispute settlement procedures available under any other treaty to which they are parties.

5. Once dispute settlement proceedings have been initiated under this Agreement or under any other treaty to which the parties to a dispute are parties concerning a particular right or obligation of such Parties arising under the covered agreements or that other treaty, the forum selected by the complaining party shall be used to the exclusion of any other for such dispute.

6. For the purposes of paragraphs 4 and 5, the complaining party shall be deemed to have selected a forum when it has requested the establishment of, or referred a dispute to, a dispute settlement panel in accordance with this Agreement or any other treaty to which the parties to a dispute are parties.

Article 3: Consultations

1. A party complained against shall accord due consideration to and afford adequate opportunity for consultations regarding a request for consultations made by a complaining party with respect to any matter affecting the interpretation,

implementation or application of any covered agreement, wherever the complaining party considers that:

(a) a measure of the party complained against is inconsistent with its obligations under the covered agreements; or

(b) the party complained against has otherwise failed to carry out its obligations under the covered agreements, which results in nullification or impairment of any benefits accruing to the complaining party under the covered agreements or impediment of the attainment of any objective of the covered agreements.

2. Any request for consultations shall be submitted in writing, and include the specific measures at issue, and the factual and legal basis (including the provisions of any of the covered agreements alleged to have been breached and any other relevant provision) of the complaint. The complaining party shall send the request to the party complained against and the rest of the Parties. Upon receipt, the party complained against shall promptly acknowledge receipt of such request to the complaining party and the rest of the Parties at the same time.

3. If a request for consultations is made, the party complained against shall reply to the request within seven (7) days after the date of its receipt and shall enter into consultations in good faith within a period of not more than thirty (30) days after the date of receipt of the request, with a view to reaching a mutually satisfactory solution. If the party complained against does not respond within the aforesaid seven (7) days, or does not enter into consultations within the aforesaid thirty (30) days, then the complaining party may proceed directly to request for the establishment of an arbitral panel under Article 5.

4. The parties to a dispute shall make every effort to reach a mutually satisfactory resolution of any matter through consultations under this Article. To this end, the parties to the dispute shall:

(a) provide sufficient information to enable a full examination of how the measure might affect the operation of the covered agreement; and

(b) treat as confidential any information exchanged in the course of consultations which the other party to the dispute has designated as confidential.

5. Consultations shall be confidential and without prejudice to the rights of any Party in any further proceedings under this Agreement or other proceedings before a forum selected by the Parties. The parties to the dispute shall inform the rest of the Parties the outcome of the consultations.

6. In cases of urgency, including those which concern perishable goods, the parties to the dispute shall enter into consultations within a period of no more than ten (10) days after the date of receipt by the party complained against of the request.

If the consultations have failed to settle the dispute within a period of twenty (20) days after the date of receipt by the party complained against of the request, the complaining party may proceed directly to request for the establishment of an arbitral panel under Article 5.

7. In cases of urgency, including those which concern perishable goods, the parties to the dispute and arbitral panels shall make every effort to accelerate the proceedings to the greatest extent possible.

Article 4: Good Offices, Conciliation and Mediation

1. Good offices, conciliation and mediation are procedures that are undertaken voluntarily if the parties to the dispute so agree.

2. Good offices, conciliation or mediation may be requested at any time by any party to a dispute. They may begin at any time and be terminated by any party to a dispute at any time.

3. If the parties to a dispute agree, good offices, conciliation or mediation proceedings may continue before any person or body as may be agreed by the parties to the dispute while the dispute proceeds for resolution before an arbitral panel established under Article 5.

4. Proceedings involving good offices, conciliation and mediation, and in particular, positions taken by the parties to a dispute during these proceedings, shall be confidential, and without prejudice to the rights of any Party in any further proceedings under this Agreement or other proceedings before a forum selected by the Parties.

Article 5: Establishment of Arbitral Panels

1. If the consultations under Article 3 fail to settle a dispute within sixty (60) days after the date of receipt of the request for consultations or within twenty (20) days after such date in cases of urgency including those which concern perishable goods, the complaining party may make a written request to the party complained against to establish an arbitral panel. A copy of this request shall also be communicated to the rest of the Parties.

2. A request for the establishment of an arbitral panel shall give the reasons for the request, including the identification of:

(a) the specific measure at issue; and

(b) the factual and legal basis (including the provisions of any of the covered agreements alleged to have been breached and any other relevant provisions) for the complaint sufficient to present the problem clearly.

3. Upon delivery of the request, an arbitral panel shall be established.

4. Unless otherwise agreed by the parties to the dispute, an arbitral panel shall be established and perform its functions in accordance with the provisions of this Agreement, and the Annex on the Rules and Procedures for the Arbitral Panel Proceedings.

5. Where more than one complaining party requests the establishment of an arbitral panel related to the same matter, a single arbitral panel may, whenever feasible, be established by the parties to the dispute to examine the matter, taking into account their respective rights.

6. Where a single arbitral panel is established under paragraph 5, the arbitral panel shall organise its examination and present its findings to all the parties to the dispute in such manner that the rights which the parties to the dispute would have enjoyed had separate arbitral panels examined the same matter are in no way impaired. If one of the parties to the dispute so requests, the arbitral panel may submit separate reports on the dispute concerned if the timeframe for writing the report so permits. The written submissions by a party to the dispute shall be made available to the other parties to the dispute, and each party to the dispute shall have the right to be present when any of the other parties to the dispute presents its views to the arbitral panel.

7. Where more than one arbitral panel is established to examine the same matter, to the greatest extent possible, the same persons shall be appointed by the parties to the disputes to serve on each of the separate arbitral panels and the timetable for the proceedings of each separate arbitral panel shall be harmonised.

Article 6: Composition of Arbitral Panels

1. Unless otherwise provided in this Agreement or agreed by the parties to the dispute, an arbitral panel shall consist of three (3) members.

2. Each party to the dispute shall appoint one member of the arbitral panel within thirty (30) days after the date of receipt of the request under Article 5. If any party to the dispute fails to appoint a member of the arbitral panel within such period, then the member of the arbitral panel appointed by the other party to the dispute shall act as the sole member of the arbitral panel, notwithstanding paragraph 1.

3. The parties to the dispute shall endeavour to agree on the third member who shall serve as the chair of the arbitral panel within thirty (30) days of the appointment of the second member. If the parties to the dispute are unable to agree on the chair within this period, the chair shall be jointly appointed, by the members of the arbitral panel who have been appointed under paragraph 2, within a further period of thirty (30) days. If the members of the arbitral panel fail to appoint the chair within the aforesaid period, the chair shall be appointed at the request of the members of the arbitral panel by the Director-General of the WTO within thirty (30)

days after the date of receipt of the request. In the event that the Director-General is a national of one of the parties to the dispute, the Deputy Director-General or the officer next in seniority who is not a national of any party to the dispute shall be requested to appoint the chair.

4. The date of establishment of the arbitral panel shall be the date on which the chair is appointed under paragraph 3 or, the 30th day after the date of receipt of the request under Article 5 where only a sole member of the arbitral panel is available.

5. If a member appointed under this Article resigns or becomes unable to act, a successor member shall be appointed in the same manner as prescribed for the appointment of the original member and the successor member shall have all the powers and duties of the original member. The work of the arbitral panel shall be suspended until the successor member is appointed.

6. Any person appointed as a member of an arbitral panel shall have expertise or experience in law, international trade, other matters covered by the covered agreements or the resolution of disputes arising under international trade agreements. A member shall be chosen strictly on the basis of objectivity, reliability, sound judgment and independence and shall conduct himself or herself on the same basis throughout the course of the arbitral panel proceedings. If a party to the dispute believes that a member is in violation of the basis stated above, the parties to the dispute shall consult and if they agree, the member shall be removed and a new member shall be appointed in accordance with this Article. Additionally, the chair shall not be a national of any party to the dispute and shall not have his or her usual place of residence in the territory of, nor be employed by, any party to the dispute nor have dealt with the referred matter in any capacity.

7. Where the original arbitral panel is required for a matter as provided in this Agreement but cannot hear the matter for any reason, a new arbitral panel shall be established in accordance with this Article. The same timeframe which would have applied, had the original arbitral panel heard the matter, shall apply for the newly established arbitral panel.

Article 7: Third Parties

1. Any Party having a substantial interest in a dispute before an arbitral panel and having notified its interest in writing to the parties to such a dispute and the rest of the Parties, shall have an opportunity to make written submissions to the arbitral panel. These submissions shall also be given to the parties to the dispute and may be reflected in the report of the arbitral panel.

2. Third parties shall receive the submissions of the parties to the dispute at the first meeting of the arbitral panel.

3. If a third party considers that a measure that is already the subject of an arbitral panel proceeding nullifies or impairs benefits accruing to it under the covered agreements, such Party may have recourse to normal dispute settlement procedures under this Agreement.

Article 8: Suspension and Termination of Proceedings

1. Where the parties to the dispute agree, the arbitral panel may suspend its work at any time for a period not exceeding twelve (12) months from the date of such agreement. Upon the request of any party to the dispute, the arbitral panel proceeding shall be resumed after such suspension. If the work of the arbitral panel has been suspended for more than twelve (12) months, the authority of the arbitral panel shall lapse unless the parties to the dispute agree otherwise.

2. The parties to the dispute may agree to terminate the proceedings of an arbitral panel at any time before the presentation of the final report to them, in the event that a mutually satisfactory solution to the dispute has been found.

3. Before the arbitral panel makes its decision, it may, at any stage of the proceedings, propose to the parties to the dispute that the dispute be settled amicably.

Article 9: Functions of Arbitral Panels

An arbitral panel shall make an objective assessment of the matter before it, including an examination of the facts of the case and the applicability of and conformity with the relevant covered agreements. Where the arbitral panel concludes that a measure is inconsistent with a provision of any of the covered agreements, it shall recommend that the party complained against bring the measure into conformity with that provision. In addition to its recommendations, the arbitral panel may suggest means by which the party complained against could implement the recommendations. The arbitral panel shall consult regularly with the parties to the dispute and provide them adequate opportunities for the development of a mutually satisfactory resolution. The arbitral panel shall interpret the relevant provisions of the covered agreements in accordance with customary rules of interpretation of public international law. In its findings and recommendations, the arbitral panel cannot add to or diminish the rights and obligations provided in the covered agreements.

Article 10: Proceedings of Arbitral Panels

1. The rules and procedures pertaining to the proceedings before an arbitral panel as set out in the Annex on the Rules and Procedures for the Arbitral Panel Proceedings shall apply unless the parties to the dispute agree otherwise. The arbitral panel may, after consulting the parties to the dispute, adopt additional rules and procedures not inconsistent with the Annex on the Rules and Procedures for the Arbitral Panel Proceedings.

2. In any event the proceedings of the arbitral panel shall be in accordance with the following principles:

(a) a right to at least one hearing before the arbitral panel;
(b) an opportunity for each party to the dispute to provide initial and rebuttal submissions;
(c) a reasonable opportunity for each party to the dispute to submit comments on the interim report presented pursuant to Article 11; and
(d) the protection of confidential information.

3. An arbitral panel shall meet in closed session. The parties to the dispute shall be present at the meetings only when invited by the arbitral panel to appear before it.

Article 11: Interim Report

1. Unless the parties to the dispute otherwise agree, the arbitral panel shall base its report on the relevant provisions of the relevant covered agreement, on the submissions and arguments of the parties to the dispute, and on any information before it, pursuant to Article 13.

2. Unless the parties to the dispute otherwise agree, the arbitral panel shall, within ninety (90) days from the date of its establishment, present to the parties to the dispute an interim report containing:

(a) findings of law and/or fact together with reasons;
(b) its determination as to the interpretation, implementation or application of the relevant covered agreement or whether the measure at issue is inconsistent with obligations of the party complained against under the relevant covered agreement or whether the party complained against has otherwise failed to carry out its obligations under the relevant covered agreement or whether the measure at issue causes nullification or impairment of any benefit accruing to the complaining party under the relevant covered agreement or impediment of the attainment of any objective of the relevant covered agreement, or any other determination requested in the terms of reference; and
(c) where it determines that the measure at issue is inconsistent with the obligations under the relevant covered agreement, its recommendations to bring the measure into conformity with such covered agreement and its suggestion, if any, on means by which the party complained against could implement the recommendations.

3. When the arbitral panel considers that it cannot present its interim report within the period of time referred to in paragraph 2, it shall inform the parties to the dispute in writing of the reasons for the delay together with the estimate of the period within which it will issue its interim report.

4. The parties to the dispute may submit written comments on the interim report within fourteen (14) days of its presentation.

5. In case that such written comments by the parties to the dispute are received as provided for in paragraph 4, the arbitral panel, on its own initiative or at the request of a party to the dispute, may reconsider its report and make any further examination that it considers appropriate.

Article 12: Final Report

1. The arbitral panel shall present a final report to the parties to the dispute, within thirty (30) days of presentation of the interim report.

2. The arbitral panel shall present to the parties to the dispute its final report within 120 days from the date of its establishment. In cases of urgency, including those relating to perishable goods, the arbitral panel shall aim to present its final report to the parties to the dispute within ninety (90) days from the date of its establishment. When the arbitral panel considers that it cannot present its final report within 120 days, or within ninety (90) days in cases of urgency, it shall inform the parties to the dispute in writing of the reasons for the delay together with an estimate of the period within which it will present its report. In no case, however, should the period from the establishment of an arbitral panel to the presentation of the final report to parties to the dispute exceed 180 days or 120 days in the case of urgency, unless the parties to the dispute otherwise agree.

3. The final report of the arbitral panel shall be made publicly available within ten (10) days of its presentation to the parties to the dispute.

Article 13: Information and Technical Advice

1. Upon request of a party to the dispute, or on its own initiative, the arbitral panel may seek information and technical advice from any person or body that it deems appropriate. Any information and technical advice so obtained shall be made available to the parties to the dispute.

2. With respect to factual issues concerning a scientific or other technical matter raised by a party to the dispute, the arbitral panel may request advisory reports in writing from an expert or experts. The arbitral panel may, at the request of a party to the dispute or on its initiative, select, after a consultation with the parties to the dispute, scientific or technical experts who shall assist the arbitral panel throughout its proceedings, but who shall not have the right to vote in respect of any decision to be made by the arbitral panel.

Article 14: Implementation of the Final Report

1. The final report of an arbitral panel shall be binding on the parties to the dispute and shall not be subject to appeal.

2. If, in its final report, the arbitral panel determines that the party complained against has not conformed to its obligations under the relevant covered agreement, or that the party's measure has caused nullification or impairment, the means to implement the recommendations shall be to eliminate the non-conformity, or the nullification or impairment.

3. The parties to the dispute, shall, within twenty (20) days upon presentation of the final report of an arbitral panel agree on:

(a) the means to implement the recommendations of the arbitral panel; and

(b) the reasonable period of time which is necessary to implement the recommendations of the arbitral panel.

4. If the parties to the dispute fail to agree, a party to the dispute may refer the matter to the original arbitral panel. The party complained against shall, within fifteen (15) days after the date of referral of the matter to the arbitral panel, propose the means to implement the recommendations of the original arbitral panel. The arbitral panel shall determine the consistency of the means proposed by the party complained against with the recommendations and/or the reasonable period of time. The arbitral panel shall present its report to the parties to the dispute within thirty (30) days after the date of the referral of the matter to it. No measure can be taken under Article 15 without any determination by the arbitral panel under this paragraph.

5. Where there is disagreement as to the existence or consistency of measures taken with the recommendation of the arbitral panel within the reasonable period of time, such dispute shall be referred to the original arbitral panel. The arbitral panel shall present its report within thirty (30) days after the date of referral of the matter to it.

Article 15: Compensation and the Suspension of Concessions or Benefits

1. Compensation and the suspension of concessions or benefits are temporary measures available in the event that the recommendations are not implemented within a reasonable period of time. However, neither compensation nor the suspension of concessions or benefits is preferred to full implementation of the recommendations to bring a measure into conformity with the covered agreements. Compensation is voluntary and, if granted, shall be consistent with the covered agreements.

2. If the party complained against fails to bring the measure found to be inconsistent with the relevant covered agreement into compliance with the recommendations of the arbitral panel within the reasonable period of time determined pursuant to paragraph 3 of Article 14, the party complained against shall, if so requested, enter into negotiations with the complaining party with a view to

reaching a mutually satisfactory agreement on any necessary compensatory adjustment.

3. If no mutually satisfactory agreement on compensation has been reached within twenty (20) days after the date of receipt of the request of the complaining party to enter into negotiations on compensatory adjustment, the complaining party may at any time thereafter provide a written notice to the party complained against and the rest of the Parties that it intends to suspend the application to the party complained against of concessions or benefits of equivalent effect and may begin suspending concessions or benefits thirty (30) days after the date of receipt of the notice. The notice shall specify the level of concessions or benefits proposed to be suspended and the relevant covered agreement and sector(s) which the concessions or benefits are related to. Within thirty (30) days from the date of receipt of the notice, the party complained against may request the original arbitral panel to rule on whether the benefits which the complaining party proposes to suspend are equivalent to those affected by the measure found to be inconsistent with the relevant covered agreement, and whether the proposed suspension is in accordance with paragraphs 4 and 5. The ruling of the arbitral panel shall be given within forty–five (45) days from the date of receipt of that request. Concessions or benefits shall not be suspended until the arbitral panel has issued its ruling.

4. Any suspension of concessions or benefits shall be restricted to the concessions or benefits granted to the party complained against under the relevant covered agreement, subject to paragraph 5. The party complained against and the rest of the Parties shall be informed of the commencement and details of any such suspension.

5. In considering what concessions or benefits to suspend under paragraph 3:

(a) the complaining party should first seek to suspend concessions or benefits in the same sector or sectors as that affected by the measure or other matter that the arbitral panel has found to be inconsistent with the relevant covered agreement or to have caused nullification or impairment; and

(b) the complaining party may suspend concessions or benefits in other sectors if it considers that it is not practicable or effective to suspend concessions or benefits in the same sector.

6. The suspension of concessions or benefits shall be temporary and shall only be applied until such time as the measure found to be inconsistent with the relevant covered agreement, has been removed, or the party complained against that must implement the arbitral panel's recommendations has done so, or a mutually satisfactory solution is reached.

7. If the party complained against considers that:

(a) the level of concessions or benefits suspended by the complaining party is manifestly excessive; or

(b) it has eliminated the non-conformity, or the nullification or impairment that the arbitral panel has found;

it may request the original arbitral panel to determine the matter. The arbitral panel shall present its determination to the parties to the dispute within thirty (30) days after it reconvenes.

Article 16: Official Language

1. All proceedings pursuant to this Agreement shall be conducted in the English language.

2. Any document submitted for use in any proceedings pursuant to this Agreement shall be in the English language. If any original document is not in the English language, a Party submitting it for use in the proceedings pursuant to this Agreement shall provide an English translation of that document.

Article 17: Expenses

1. Each party to a dispute shall bear the costs of the arbitral panel member, appointed by that party to the dispute, and its own expenses and legal costs.

2. Unless the parties to the dispute otherwise agree, the costs of the chair of the arbitral panel and other expenses associated with the conduct of its proceedings shall be borne in equal parts by the parties to a dispute.

Article 18: Annex

The Annex on the Rules and Procedures for the Arbitral Panel Proceedings and the contents therein shall form an integral part of this Agreement.

Article 19: Amendments

The provisions of this Agreement may be modified through amendments mutually agreed upon in writing by the Parties.

Article 20: Depositary

For the ASEAN Member Countries, this Agreement shall be deposited with the Secretary-General of ASEAN, who shall promptly furnish a certified copy thereof, to each ASEAN Member Country.

Article 21: Entry into Force

1. This Agreement shall enter into force on 1 July 2006, provided that at least one ASEAN Member Country and Korea are among the Signatory Countries that

have by then notified all the other Parties in writing of the completion of their internal procedures. In the event this Agreement does not enter into force on 1 July 2006, it shall enter into force on the first day of the second month following the latter date on which at least one ASEAN Member Country and Korea have notified all the other Parties in writing of the completion of their internal procedures.

2. A Party shall, upon the completion of its internal procedures for the entry into force of this Agreement, notify all the other Parties in writing.

3. Where a Party is unable to complete its internal procedures for the entry into force of this Agreement by the date as set out in paragraph 1, this Agreement shall come into force for that Party upon the date of notification of the completion of its internal procedures.

In witness whereof, the undersigned, being duly authorised thereto, have signed this Agreement on Dispute Settlement Mechanism under the Framework Agreement on Comprehensive Economic Cooperation among the Governments of the Member Countries of the Association of Southeast Asian Nations and the Republic of Korea.

Done at Kuala Lumpur, Malaysia this day of December 2005, in duplicate copies in the English language.

ANNEX: RULES AND PROCEDURES FOR THE ARBITRAL PANEL PROCEEDINGS

Application

1. These Rules are established under Article 10 and shall apply to arbitral panel proceedings under this Agreement unless the parties to the dispute otherwise agree.

2. Any reference made in these Rules to an Article is a reference to the appropriate Article in this Agreement.

Terms of Reference for Arbitral Panels

3. An arbitral panel shall have the following terms of reference unless the parties to the dispute agree otherwise within ten (10) days from the date of the establishment of an arbitral panel:

> "To examine, in the light of the relevant provisions in (name of the covered agreement(s) cited by the parties to the dispute), the matter referred to in the request for the establishment of an arbitral panel pursuant to Article 5, to make findings, determinations, recommendations and suggestions, if any, as provided in Article 11, and to present the written reports referred to in Articles 11 and 12."

4. The parties to the dispute shall promptly deliver the agreed terms of reference to the arbitral panel. The arbitral panel shall address the relevant provisions in the covered agreements cited by the parties to the dispute.

Written Submissions and Other Documents

5. Each party to the dispute shall deliver no less than four copies of its written submissions to the arbitral panel and a copy to the other party to the dispute.

6. A complaining party shall deliver its initial written submission to the party complained against no later than twenty (20) days after the date of the establishment of the arbitral panel. The party complained against shall deliver its written submission to the complaining party no later than twenty (20) days after the date of receipt of the initial written submission of the complaining party.

7. In respect of any request, notice or other document(s) related to the arbitral panel proceeding that is not covered by paragraphs 5 and 6, each party to the dispute may deliver a copy of the document(s) to the other party to the dispute by facsimile, email or other means of electronic transmission.

8. A party to the dispute may at any time correct minor errors of a clerical nature in any request, notice, written submission or other document(s) related to the arbitral panel proceeding by delivering a new document clearly indicating the changes.

Operation of Arbitral Panels

9. The chair of the arbitral panel shall preside at all of its meetings. An arbitral panel may delegate to the chair authority to make administrative and procedural decisions.

10. Except as otherwise provided in these Rules, the arbitral panel may conduct its business by any means, including by telephone, facsimile transmission and computer links.

11. Only members of the arbitral panel may take part in the deliberations of the arbitral panel, but the arbitral panel may, in consultation with the parties to the dispute, retain such number of assistants, interpreters or translators, or designated note takers as may be required for the proceeding and permit them to be present during such deliberations. The members of the arbitral panel and the persons retained by the arbitral panel shall maintain the confidentiality of the arbitral panel proceeding unless such information is already made available to the public.

12. Where a procedural question arises that is not addressed by these Rules, an arbitral panel may adopt an appropriate procedure that is not inconsistent with this Agreement, unless it considers that the procedural question may affect in a

meaningful manner the way in which it examines matters before it, in which case it shall consult with the parties to the dispute.

13. Any time period applicable to the arbitral panel proceeding shall be suspended for a period that begins on the date on which any member of the arbitral panel becomes unable to act and ends on the date on which the successor member is appointed.

14. An arbitral panel may, in consultation with the parties to the dispute, modify any time period applicable in the arbitral panel proceeding and make such other procedural or administrative adjustments as may be required in the proceeding.

15. The venue for the arbitral panel proceedings shall be decided by mutual agreement between the parties to the dispute. If there is no agreement, the venue shall alternate between the capitals of the parties to the dispute with the first session of the arbitral panel proceeding to be held in the capital of the party complained against.

16. All third parties which have notified their interest in the dispute shall be invited in writing to present their views during the first session of the arbitral panel proceeding set aside for that purpose. All such third parties may be present during the entirety of this session.

17. The interim and final report of the arbitral panel shall be drafted without the presence of the parties to the dispute in the light of the information provided and the statements made. Opinions expressed in the report of the arbitral panel by its individual member shall be anonymous.

18. Following the consideration of submissions, arguments and any information before it, the arbitral panel shall present an interim report to the parties to the dispute, including both a descriptive section relating to the facts of the dispute and the arguments of the parties to the dispute and the arbitral panel's findings and conclusions. The arbitral panel shall accord adequate opportunity to the parties to the dispute to review the entirety of its interim report prior to its finalisation and shall include a discussion of any comments by the parties concerned in its final report.

Timetable

19. After consulting the parties to the dispute, the chair of the arbitral panel shall, as soon as practicable and whenever possible within fifteen (15) days after the establishment of the arbitral panel, fix the timetable for the arbitral panel process. In determining the timetable for the arbitral panel process, the arbitral panel shall provide sufficient time for the parties to the dispute to prepare their respective submissions. The arbitral panel should set precise deadlines for written submissions by the parties to the dispute and they shall respect those deadlines.

Decisions of the Arbitral Panel

20. The arbitral panel shall take its decisions by consensus; provided that where the arbitral panel is unable to reach consensus, it may take its decisions by majority vote.

Availability of Information

21. The deliberations of the arbitral panel and the documents submitted to it shall be kept confidential. No party to the dispute shall be precluded from disclosing statements of its own positions to the public. The parties to the dispute shall treat as confidential information submitted by the other party to the dispute to the arbitral panel which that party has designated as confidential. Where a party to the dispute submits a confidential version of its written submissions to the arbitral panel, it shall also, upon request of the other party to the dispute, provide a non-confidential summary of the information contained in its submissions that could be disclosed to the public.

Remuneration and Payment of Expenses

22. The arbitral panel shall keep a record and render a final account of all general expenses incurred in connection with the proceedings, including those paid to their assistants, designated note takers or other individuals that it retains pursuant to paragraph 11.

FRAMEWORK AGREEMENT ON COMPREHENSIVE ECONOMIC COOPERATION AMONG THE GOVERNMENTS OF THE MEMBER COUNTRIES OF THE ASSOCIATION OF SOUTHEAST ASIAN NATIONS AND THE REPUBLIC OF KOREA

Kuala Lumpur, 13 December 2005

The Governments of Brunei Darussalam, the Kingdom of Cambodia, the Republic of Indonesia, the Lao People's Democratic Republic, Malaysia, the Union of Myanmar, the Republic of the Philippines, the Republic of Singapore, the Kingdom of Thailand and the Socialist Republic of Vietnam, Member Countries of the Association of Southeast Asian Nations and the Republic of Korea,

Recalling the decision made at the ASEAN-Korea Summit held on 30 November 2004 at Vientiane, the Lao People's Democratic Republic, by the Joint Declaration on Comprehensive Cooperation Partnership between ASEAN and Korea, to establish an ASEAN-Korea Free Trade Area at an earliest stage with special and differential treatment and additional flexibility for the new ASEAN Member Countries of the Kingdom of Cambodia, the Lao People's Democratic Republic, the Union of Myanmar and the Socialist Republic of Vietnam;

Desiring to adopt a Framework Agreement on Comprehensive Economic Cooperation among them, that will further promote growth and development, increase the living standard of the people throughout the region and provide further dynamic benefits to the region in the long term;

Being confident that the establishment of the ASEAN-Korea Free Trade Area will be a natural extension of their existing relations as well as a stepping stone to elevate their relationship to a higher and more comprehensive level;

Reaffirming the shared belief that the arrangement for the creation of the ASEAN-Korea Free Trade Area should be based on the agreed principles of comprehensiveness in the liberalisation process, meaningful and substantial liberalisation, enhancement of mutual benefits, and consistency with WTO rules and disciplines;

Building on their respective rights and obligations under the Marrakesh Agreement Establishing the World Trade Organisation and the other agreements negotiated thereunder and other multilateral and bilateral instruments of cooperation to which they are parties;

Recognising that the removal of obstacles to trade through the creation of the ASEAN-Korea Free Trade Area will contribute to the harmonious development and expansion of world trade and provide a catalyst to broader international cooperation, in particular within East Asia;

Recognising the importance of capacity building through human resource development to face challenges of globalisation; and

Recognising the different stages of economic development among the ASEAN Member Countries and the need for flexibility to be given to the new ASEAN Member Countries, in particular the need to facilitate their increasing participation in the economic cooperation of the Parties and the expansion of their exports, including, *inter alia*, through the strengthening of their domestic capacity, efficiency and competitiveness,

Have Agreed as follows:

CHAPTER 1: GENERAL PROVISIONS

Article 1.1: Objectives

The objectives of this Framework Agreement are to:

(a) strengthen and enhance economic, trade and investment cooperation among the Parties;

(b) progressively liberalise and promote trade in goods and services as well as create a transparent, liberal and facilitative investment regime;

(c) explore new areas and develop appropriate measures for closer economic cooperation and integration;

(d) facilitate the more effective economic integration of the new ASEAN Member Countries and bridge the development gap among the Parties; and

(e) establish a cooperative framework for further strengthening the economic relations among the Parties.

Article 1.2: Definitions

For the purposes of this Framework Agreement, unless the context otherwise requires:

AEM + Korea means the Economic Ministers of the ASEAN Member Countries and the Minister for Trade of Korea;

ASEAN means the Association of Southeast Asian Nations which comprises of Brunei Darussalam, the Kingdom of Cambodia, the Republic of Indonesia, the Lao People's Democratic Republic, Malaysia, the Union of Myanmar, the Republic of the Philippines, the Republic of Singapore, the Kingdom of Thailand and the Socialist Republic of Vietnam;

ASEAN–Korea FTA means the ASEAN-Korea Free Trade Area established by this Framework Agreement and other relevant agreements stipulated in paragraph 1 of Article 1.4;

ASEAN Member Countries means Brunei Darussalam, the Kingdom of Cambodia, the Republic of Indonesia, the Lao People's Democratic Republic, Malaysia, the Union of Myanmar, the Republic of the Philippines, the Republic of Singapore, the Kingdom of Thailand and the Socialist Republic of Vietnam collectively;

ASEAN Member Country means Brunei Darussalam, the Kingdom of Cambodia, the Republic of Indonesia, the Lao People's Democratic Republic, Malaysia, the Union of Myanmar, the Republic of the Philippines, the Republic of Singapore, the Kingdom of Thailand or the Socialist Republic of Vietnam individually;

Framework Agreement means this Framework Agreement on Comprehensive Economic Cooperation among the Governments of the ASEAN Member Countries and the Republic of Korea;

GATS means the General Agreement on Trade in Services, which is a part of the WTO Agreement;

GATT 1994 means the General Agreement on Tariffs and Trade 1994, including its Notes and Supplementary Provisions, which is a part of the WTO Agreement;

Implementing Committee means the Implementing Committee established under Article 5.3;

Korea means the Republic of Korea;

New ASEAN Member Countries means the Kingdom of Cambodia, the Lao People's Democratic Republic, the Union of Myanmar and the Socialist Republic of Vietnam;

Normal Track means a list of tariff lines of which applied MFN tariff rates shall be gradually reduced and eliminated in accordance with the modality set out in Annex 1 of the Agreement on Trade in Goods under this Framework Agreement;

Parties means the ASEAN Member Countries and Korea collectively;

Party means an ASEAN Member Country or Korea;

WTO means the World Trade Organisation; and

WTO Agreement means the Marrakesh Agreement Establishing the World Trade Organisation, done on 15 April 1994 and the other agreements negotiated thereunder.

Article 1.3: Measures for Comprehensive Economic Partnership

The Parties shall establish, consistent with Article XXIV of GATT 1994 and Article V of GATS, an ASEAN-Korea FTA and strengthen and enhance economic cooperation through the following:

(a) progressive elimination of tariffs and non-tariff barriers in substantially all trade in goods;

(b) progressive liberalisation of trade in services with substantial sectoral coverage;

(c) establishment of an open and competitive investment regime that facilitates and promotes investment among the Parties;

(d) provision of special and differential treatment to the ASEAN Member Countries and additional flexibility to the new ASEAN Member Countries as agreed in the Joint Declaration on Comprehensive Cooperation Partnership between ASEAN and Korea and the core elements attached thereto;

(e) provision of flexibility to the Parties in the ASEAN-Korea FTA negotiations to address their sensitive areas in the goods, services and investment sectors with such flexibility to be negotiated and mutually agreed based on the principle of reciprocity and mutual benefits;

(f) establishment of effective trade and investment facilitation measures;

(g) exploration of the ways and means to expand their economic partnership into new areas and expansion of economic cooperation in areas as may be agreed among the Parties that will complement the deepening of trade and investment link among the Parties; and

(h) establishment of appropriate procedures and mechanisms for the purposes of effective implementation of this Framework Agreement.

Article 1.4: Legal Coverage and Relations to Other Agreements

1. The following agreements shall form part of legal instruments establishing the ASEAN-Korea FTA upon their respective entry into force:

(a) this Framework Agreement (including the Annex on Economic Cooperation);

(b) the Agreement on Trade in Goods under this Framework Agreement as provided for in Article 2.1;

(c) an agreement on trade in services to be concluded in accordance with Article 2.2;

(d) an agreement on investment to be concluded in accordance with Article 2.3;

(e) the Agreement on Dispute Settlement Mechanism under this Framework Agreement as provided for in Article 5.1; and

(f) any other agreements that may be mutually agreed by consensus and concluded by the Parties in the context of the ASEAN-Korea FTA.

2. Except as otherwise provided in this Framework Agreement, this Framework Agreement or any action taken under it shall not affect or nullify the rights and obligations of a Party under the existing agreements to which it is a party.

3. Nothing in this Framework Agreement shall prevent any individual ASEAN Member Country from entering into any bilateral or plurilateral agreement with any other ASEAN Member Countries and/or Korea relating to trade in goods, trade in services, investment, and/or other areas of economic cooperation. The provisions of this Framework Agreement shall not apply to any such bilateral or plurilateral agreement.

CHAPTER 2: LIBERALISATION

Article 2.1: Trade in Goods

1. The Parties shall progressively reduce and eliminate duties and other restrictive regulations of commerce [except, where necessary, those permitted under Article XXIV(8)(b) of GATT 1994] on substantially all trade in goods among the Parties, in accordance with the provisions, schedules and programme for the Normal Track in the Agreement on Trade in Goods under this Framework Agreement.

2. The Agreement on Trade in Goods under this Framework Agreement shall include, but not limited to:

(a) detailed rules governing the progressive tariff reduction and/or elimination programme as well as other related matters;
(b) rules of origin;
(c) modification of commitments;
(d) non-tariff measures, sanitary and phytosanitary measures, and technical barriers to trade;
(e) safeguards measures; and
(f) WTO disciplines and reduction and elimination of non-tariff barriers.

Article 2.2: Trade in Services

1. The Parties shall progressively liberalise trade in services among the Parties with substantial sectoral coverage in conformity with Article V of GATS.

2. For this purpose, the Parties shall enter into negotiations on the progressive liberalisation of trade in services. Such liberalisation shall be directed to:

(a) provision for the absence or elimination of substantially all discrimination among the Parties only in the sectors covered under paragraph 1, through:
  (i) elimination of existing discriminatory measures; and/or
  (ii) prohibition of new or more discriminatory measures with respect to trade in services among the Parties;

either at the entry into force of the agreement referred to in paragraph 3 or on the basis of an agreed time-frame, except for measures permitted under Articles XI, XII, XIV, XIVbis of GATS:

(b) expansion in the depth and scope of liberalisation of trade in services beyond those undertaken by the Parties under GATS; and
(c) enhanced cooperation in services among the Parties in order to improve efficiency and competitiveness, as well as to diversify the supply and distribution of services of the respective service suppliers of the Parties.

3. The Parties shall begin negotiations on an agreement on trade in services at the beginning of 2006 with a goal of concluding the negotiations not later than 31 December 2006.

Article 2.3: Investment

1. The Parties shall create a liberal, facilitative, transparent and competitive investment regime with business-friendly environment.

2. For this purpose, the Parties shall enter into negotiations on the liberalisation of investment regime. Such negotiations shall be directed to:

(a) progressive liberalisation of the investment regime;

(b) strengthening of cooperation in investment, facilitation of investment and improvement of transparency of investment rules and regulations; and

(c) provision of the protection under the investment régime.

3. The Parties shall begin negotiations on an agreement on investment at the beginning of 2006 with a goal of concluding the negotiations not later than 31 December 2006.

Article 2.4: Most-Favoured Nation Treatment

Korea shall accord to all the ASEAN Member Countries which are not WTO members the Most-Favoured Nation Treatment consistent with the WTO rules and disciplines upon the entry into force of this Framework Agreement.

CHAPTER 3: ECONOMIC COOPERATION

Article 3.1: Scope and Implementation of Cooperation

1. The Parties, on the basis of mutual benefits, shall explore and undertake cooperation projects in the following areas:

(a) customs procedures;

(b) trade and investment promotion;

(c) small and medium enterprises;

(d) human resource management and development;

(e) tourism;

(f) science and technology;

(g) financial services;

(h) information and communication technology;

(i) agriculture, fisheries, livestock, plantation commodities and forestry;

(j) intellectual property;

(k) environmental industry;

(l) broadcasting;

(m) construction technology;

(n) standards and conformity assessment and sanitary and phytosanitary measures;

(o) mining;

(p) energy;

(q) natural resources;

(r) shipbuilding and maritime transport; and

(s) film.

2. The Parties shall undertake economic cooperation projects at mutually agreed time periods, when feasible. These projects shall be monitored by the Implementing Committee for their effective implementation.

3. Details of such cooperation are specified in the Annex on Economic Cooperation.

Article 3.2: Capacity Building Programmes and Technical Assistance

1. The Parties, recognising that capacity building programmes and technical assistance are important, particularly for the new ASEAN Member Countries, in order to expand their trade and investment with Korea, shall implement such programmes on a mutually agreed basis.

2 The Parties shall strengthen cooperation and support for the realisation of ASEAN integration objectives by implementing projects furthering the Bali Concord II, the Initiative for ASEAN Integration (IAI), as well as the Vientiane Action Programme (VAP), including providing technical assistance and capacity building for the new ASEAN Member Countries based on the experiences and expertise of Korea in development.

3. The Parties shall strengthen ASEAN's integration efforts in narrowing the development gaps among the ASEAN Member Countries and between the ASEAN Member Countries and Korea by enhancing regional and sub-regional development.

4. The Parties, recognising the development gaps among the ASEAN Member Countries and between the ASEAN Member Countries and Korea, shall enhance regional and sub-regional development, through cooperation initiatives including:

(a) the Mekong Sub-region;

(b) the Ayeawady-Chao Phraya-Mekong Economic Cooperation Strategy (ACMECS);

(c) the Brunei Darussalam-Indonesia-Malaysia-Philippines East ASEAN Growth Area (BIMP-EAGA);

(d) the growth triangles such as the Indonesia-Malaysia-Thailand (IMT-GT) and the Indonesia-Malaysia-Singapore (IMS-GT);

(e) the Greater Mekong Sub-Region (GMS) programme;

(f) the Second East-West Economic Corridor;

(g) the ASEAN Mekong Basin Development Corporation (AMBDC);

(h) the Singapore-Kunming Rail Link (SKRL) project; and

(i) sharing experiences with the Mekong River Commission (MRC) in formulating and implementing priority programmes in the Mekong River Basin.

CHAPTER 4: OTHER AREAS

Article 4.1: Expansion of Economic Partnership into New Areas

With the aim of achieving the comprehensive ASEAN-Korea FTA, the Parties shall explore ways and means to expand their economic partnership into new areas where the Parties have mutual interests, as may be agreed by the Parties.

CHAPTER 5: FINAL PROVISIONS

Article 5.1: Dispute Settlement

1. Any dispute concerning the interpretation, implementation or application of this Framework Agreement shall be resolved through the procedures and mechanism as set out in the Agreement on Dispute Settlement Mechanism under this Framework Agreement.

2. Notwithstanding paragraph 1, any disputes arising from paragraph 3 of Article 2.2 (Trade in Services), paragraph 3 of Article 2.3 (Investment), Chapters 3 (Economic Cooperation) and 4 (Other Areas), and the Annex on Economic Cooperation shall not be subject to the Agreement on Dispute Settlement Mechanism under this Framework Agreement.

Article 5.2: Institutional Arrangements for the Negotiations

1. There shall be established an ASEAN-Korea Trade Negotiating Committee to carry out negotiations set out in this Framework Agreement.

2. The ASEAN-Korea Trade Negotiating Committee may establish any working group as may be necessary to assist it in undertaking negotiations on specific areas in the ASEAN-Korea FTA.

3. Commencing immediately at the beginning of the negotiations envisaged in this Framework Agreement and continuing until the formal completion of such negotiations by 31 December 2006, the Parties shall endeavour not to take any trade restrictive or distorting measures in such a manner as to affect negatively the negotiating position of any other Party.

Article 5.3: Implementation of the Framework Agreement

1. The AEM + Korea shall have the ultimate authority concerning all matters relating to the implementation of this Framework Agreement and any other agreements concluded or to be concluded in accordance with this Framework Agreement. An Implementing Committee, which is hereby established to be composed of the senior economic officials of the Parties or their designees, shall convene as appropriate to discharge such functions as provided for in paragraph 2 under the supervision and guidance of the AEM + Korea.

2. The Parties, through the Implementing Committee, shall:

(a) coordinate, supervise and oversee the implementation and appropriate application of the provisions of this Framework Agreement and any other agreements concluded or to be concluded in accordance with this Framework Agreement;

(b) review the implementation of this Framework Agreement and any other agreements concluded or to be concluded in accordance with this Framework Agreement;

(c) supervise the work of the committees and working groups established under this Framework Agreement and any other agreements concluded or to be concluded in accordance with this Framework Agreement; and

(d) consider any other matter that may affect the operation of this Framework Agreement and any other agreements concluded or to be concluded in accordance with this Framework Agreement, or that is entrusted to the Implementing Committee by the Parties.

3. In the fulfilment of its functions, the Implementing Committee may:

(a) establish and delegate responsibilities to ad hoc or standing committees, working groups or expert groups and assign them with tasks on specific matters; and

(b) take such other action in the exercise of its functions, as the Parties may agree.

4. The Implementing Committee shall keep the AEM + Korea informed of its activities on a regular basis.

5. The Implementing Committee shall establish its rules and procedures, which shall be approved by the AEM + Korea.

6. The Implementing Committee shall convene within one year of the date of entry into force of this Framework Agreement and then annually or otherwise as appropriate.

Article 5.4: Secretariat and Contact Points

1. The ASEAN Secretariat for the ASEAN Member Countries and the Ministry of Foreign Affairs and Trade of Korea for Korea shall jointly provide the necessary secretariat support for the purposes of this Framework Agreement and any other agreements concluded or to be concluded in accordance with this Framework Agreement. The ASEAN Secretariat and the Ministry of Foreign Affairs and Trade of Korea shall monitor and report to the Implementing Committee on the implementation of this Framework Agreement and any other agreements concluded or to be concluded in accordance with this Framework Agreement.

2. All official communications or notifications among the Parties for the purposes of the implementation of this Framework Agreement and any other agreements concluded or to be concluded in accordance with this Framework Agreement shall be made in the English language and through the ASEAN Secretariat and the Ministry of Foreign Affairs and Trade of Korea as appropriate.

3. The Parties shall designate their respective contact point to facilitate all other communications with one another on any matter covered by this Framework Agreement and any other agreements concluded or to be concluded in accordance with this Framework Agreement. At the request of a Party, the contact point of the requested Party shall identify the office or official responsible for the matter and assist in facilitating communications with the requesting Party.

Article 5.5: Annexes and Future Legal Instruments

1. The Annex on Economic Cooperation shall form an integral part of this Framework Agreement.

2. The Parties may adopt legal instruments in the future pursuant to the provisions of this Framework Agreement. Upon their respective entry into force, such instruments shall form part of this Framework Agreement.

Article 5.6: Amendments

The provisions of this Framework Agreement may be modified through amendments mutually agreed upon in writing by the Parties.

Article 5.7: Depositary

For the ASEAN Member Countries, this Framework Agreement shall be deposited with the Secretary-General of ASEAN, who shall promptly furnish a certified copy thereof to each ASEAN Member Country.

Article 5.8: Entry into Force

1. This Framework Agreement shall enter into force on 1 July 2006, provided that at least one ASEAN Member Country and Korea are among the Signatory Countries that have by then notified all the other Parties in writing of the completion of their internal procedures. In the event this Framework Agreement does not enter into force on 1 July 2006, it shall enter into force on the first day of the second month following the latter date on which at least one ASEAN Member Country and Korea have notified all the other Parties in writing of the completion of their internal procedures.

2. A Party shall, upon the completion of its internal procedures for the entry into force of this Framework Agreement, notify all the other Parties in writing.

3. Where a Party is unable to complete its internal procedures for the entry into

force of this Framework Agreement by the date as set out in paragraph 1, this Framework Agreement shall come into force for that Party upon the date of notification of the completion of its internal procedures.

In witness whereof, the undersigned, being duly authorised thereto, have signed this Framework Agreement on Comprehensive Economic Cooperation among the Governments of the Member Countries of the Association of Southeast Asian Nations and the Republic of Korea.

Done at Kuala Lumpur, Malaysia this Thirteenth day of December 2005, in duplicate copies in the English language.

THE GOVERNMENTS OF BRUNEI DARUSSALAM, THE KINGDOM OF CAMBODIA, THE REPUBLIC OF INDONESIA, THE LAO PEOPLE'S DEMOCRATIC REPUBLIC, MALAYSIA, THE UNION OF MYANMAR, THE REPUBLIC OF THE PHILIPPINES, THE REPUBLIC OF SINGAPORE, THE KINGDOM OF THAILAND AND THE SOCIALIST REPUBLIC OF VIETNAM, MEMBER COUNTRIES OF THE ASSOCIATION OF SOUTHEAST ASIAN NATIONS AND THE REPUBLIC OF KOREA

Recalling the decision made at the ASEAN-Korea Summit held on 30 November 2004 at Vientiane, the Lao People's Democratic Republic, by the Joint Declaration on Comprehensive Cooperation Partnership between ASEAN and Korea, to establish an ASEAN-Korea Free Trade Area at an earliest stage with special and differential treatment and additional flexibility for the new ASEAN Member Countries of the Kingdom of Cambodia, the Lao People's Democratic Republic, the Union of Myanmar and the Socialist Republic of Vietnam;

Desiring to adopt a Framework Agreement on Comprehensive Economic Cooperation among them, that will further promote growth and development, increase the living standard of the people throughout the region and provide further dynamic benefits to the region in the long-term;

Being confident that the establishment of the ASEAN-Korea Free Trade Area will be a natural extension of their existing relations as well as a stepping stone to elevate their relationship to a higher and more comprehensive level;

Reaffirming the shared belief that the arrangement for the creation of the ASEAN-Korea Free Trade Area should be based on the agreed principles of comprehensiveness in the liberalisation process, meaningful and substantial liberalisation, enhancement of mutual benefits, and consistency with WTO rules and disciplines;

Building on their respective rights and obligations under the Marrakesh Agreement Establishing the World Trade Organisation and the other agreements negotiated thereunder and other multilateral and bilateral instruments of cooperation to which they are parties;

Recognising that the removal of obstacles to trade through the creation of the ASEAN-Korea Free Trade Area will contribute to the harmonious development and expansion of world trade and provide a catalyst to broader international cooperation, in particular within East Asia;

Recognising the importance of capacity building through human resource development to face challenges of globalisation; and

Recognising the different stages of economic development among the ASEAN Member Countries and the need for flexibility to be given to the new ASEAN Member Countries, in particular the need to facilitate their increasing participation in the economic cooperation of the Parties and the expansion of their exports, including, *inter alia*, through the strengthening of their domestic capacity, efficiency and competitiveness,

Have agreed as follows:

CHAPTER 1: GENERAL PROVISIONS

Article 1.1: Objectives

The objectives of this Framework Agreement are to:

(a) strengthen and enhance economic, trade and investment cooperation among the Parties;

(b) progressively liberalise and promote trade in goods and services as well as create a transparent, liberal and facilitative investment regime;

(c) explore new areas and develop appropriate measures for closer economic cooperation and integration;

(d) facilitate the more effective economic integration of the new ASEAN Member Countries and bridge the development gap among the Parties; and

(e) establish a cooperative framework for further strengthening the economic relations among the Parties.

Article 1.2: Definitions

For the purposes of this Framework Agreement, unless the context otherwise requires:

AEM + Korea means the Economic Ministers of the ASEAN Member Countries and the Minister for Trade of Korea;

ASEAN means the Association of Southeast Asian Nations which comprises of Brunei Darussalam, the Kingdom of Cambodia, the Republic of Indonesia, the Lao People's Democratic Republic, Malaysia, the Union of Myanmar, the Republic of the Philippines, the Republic of Singapore, the Kingdom of Thailand and the Socialist Republic of Vietnam;

ASEAN–Korea FTA means the ASEAN-Korea Free Trade Area established by this Framework Agreement and other relevant agreements stipulated in paragraph 1 of Article 1.4;

ASEAN Member Countries means Brunei Darussalam, the Kingdom of Cambodia, the Republic of Indonesia, the Lao People's Democratic Republic, Malaysia, the Union of Myanmar, the Republic of the Philippines, the Republic of Singapore, the Kingdom of Thailand and the Socialist Republic of Vietnam collectively;

ASEAN Member Country means Brunei Darussalam, the Kingdom of Cambodia, the Republic of Indonesia, the Lao People's Democratic Republic, Malaysia, the Union of Myanmar, the Republic of the Philippines, the Republic of Singapore, the Kingdom of Thailand or the Socialist Republic of Vietnam individually;

Framework Agreement means this Framework Agreement on Comprehensive Economic Cooperation among the Governments of the ASEAN Member Countries and the Republic of Korea;

GATS means the General Agreement on Trade in Services, which is a part of the WTO Agreement;

GATT 1994 means the General Agreement on Tariffs and Trade 1994, including its Notes and Supplementary Provisions, which is a part of the WTO Agreement;

Implementing Committee means the Implementing Committee established under Article 5.3;

Korea means the Republic of Korea;

New ASEAN Member Countries means the Kingdom of Cambodia, the Lao People's Democratic Republic, the Union of Myanmar and the Socialist Republic of Vietnam;

Normal Track means a list of tariff lines of which applied MFN tariff rates shall be gradually reduced and eliminated in accordance with the modality set out in Annex 1 of the Agreement on Trade in Goods under this Framework Agreement;

Parties means the ASEAN Member Countries and Korea collectively;

Party means an ASEAN Member Country or Korea;

WTO means the World Trade Organisation; and

WTO Agreement means the Marrakesh Agreement Establishing the World Trade Organisation, done on 15 April 1994 and the other agreements negotiated thereunder.

Article 1.3: Measures for Comprehensive Economic Partnership

The Parties shall establish, consistent with Article XXIV of GATT 1994 and Article V of GATS, an ASEAN-Korea FTA and strengthen and enhance economic cooperation through the following:

(a) progressive elimination of tariffs and non-tariff barriers in substantially all trade in goods;

(b) progressive liberalisation of trade in services with substantial sectoral coverage;

(c) establishment of an open and competitive investment regime that facilitates and promotes investment among the Parties;

(d) provision of special and differential treatment to the ASEAN Member Countries and additional flexibility to the new ASEAN Member Countries as agreed in the Joint Declaration on Comprehensive Cooperation Partnership between ASEAN and Korea and the core elements attached thereto;

(e) provision of flexibility to the Parties in the ASEAN-Korea FTA negotiations to address their sensitive areas in the goods, services and investment sectors with such flexibility to be negotiated and mutually agreed based on the principle of reciprocity and mutual benefits;

(f) establishment of effective trade and investment facilitation measures;

(g) exploration of the ways and means to expand their economic partnership into new areas and expansion of economic cooperation in areas as may be agreed among the Parties that will complement the deepening of trade and investment link among the Parties; and

(h) establishment of appropriate procedures and mechanisms for the purposes of effective implementation of this Framework Agreement.

Article 1.4: Legal Coverage and Relations to Other Agreements

1. The following agreements shall form part of legal instruments establishing the ASEAN-Korea FTA upon their respective entry into force:

(a) this Framework Agreement (including the Annex on Economic Cooperation);

(b) the Agreement on Trade in Goods under this Framework Agreement as provided for in Article 2.1;

(c) an agreement on trade in services to be concluded in accordance with Article 2.2;

(d) an agreement on investment to be concluded in accordance with Article 2.3;

(e) the Agreement on Dispute Settlement Mechanism under this Framework Agreement as provided for in Article 5.1; and

(f) any other agreements that may be mutually agreed by consensus and concluded by the Parties in the context of the ASEAN-Korea FTA.

2. Except as otherwise provided in this Framework Agreement, this Framework Agreement or any action taken under it shall not affect or nullify the rights and obligations of a Party under the existing agreements to which it is a party.

3. Nothing in this Framework Agreement shall prevent any individual ASEAN Member Country from entering into any bilateral or plurilateral agreement with any other ASEAN Member Countries and/or Korea relating to trade in goods, trade in services, investment, and/or other areas of economic cooperation. The provisions of this Framework Agreement shall not apply to any such bilateral or plurilateral agreement.

CHAPTER 2: LIBERALISATION

Article 2.1: Trade in Goods

1. The Parties shall progressively reduce and eliminate duties and other restrictive regulations of commerce [except, where necessary, those permitted under Article XXIV(8)(b) of GATT 1994] on substantially all trade in goods among the Parties, in accordance with the provisions, schedules and programme for the Normal Track in the Agreement on Trade in Goods under this Framework Agreement.

2. The Agreement on Trade in Goods under this Framework Agreement shall include, but not limited to:

(a) detailed rules governing the progressive tariff reduction and/or elimination programme as well as other related matters;

(b) rules of origin;

(c) modification of commitments;

(d) non-tariff measures, sanitary and phytosanitary measures, and technical barriers to trade;

(e) safeguards measures; and

(f) WTO disciplines and reduction and elimination of non-tariff barriers.

Article 2.2: Trade in Services

1. The Parties shall progressively liberalise trade in services among the Parties with substantial sectoral coverage in conformity with Article V of GATS.

2. For this purpose, the Parties shall enter into negotiations on the progressive liberalisation of trade in services. Such liberalisation shall be directed to:

(a) provision for the absence or elimination of substantially all discrimination among the Parties only in the sectors covered under paragraph 1, through:
  (i) elimination of existing discriminatory measures; and/or
  (ii) prohibition of new or more discriminatory measures with respect to trade in services among the Parties,

either at the entry into force of the agreement referred to in paragraph 3 or on the basis of an agreed time-frame, except for measures permitted under Articles XI, XII, XIV, XIVbis of GATS;

(b) expansion in the depth and scope of liberalisation of trade in services beyond those undertaken by the Parties under GATS; and

(c) enhanced cooperation in services among the Parties in order to improve efficiency and competitiveness, as well as to diversify the supply and distribution of services of the respective service suppliers of the Parties.

3. The Parties shall begin negotiations on an agreement on trade in services at the beginning of 2006 with a goal of concluding the negotiations not later than 31 December 2006.

Article 2.3: Investment

1. The Parties shall create a liberal, facilitative, transparent and competitive investment regime with business-friendly environment.

2. For this purpose, the Parties shall enter into negotiations on the liberalisation of investment regime. Such negotiations shall be directed to:

(a) progressive liberalisation of the investment regime;

(b) strengthening of cooperation in investment, facilitation of investment and improvement of transparency of investment rules and regulations; and

(c) provision of the protection under the investment regime.

3. The Parties shall begin negotiations on an agreement on investment at the beginning of 2006 with a goal of concluding the negotiations not later than 31 December 2006.

Article 2.4: Most-Favoured Nation Treatment

Korea shall accord to all the ASEAN Member Countries which are not WTO members the Most-Favoured Nation Treatment consistent with the WTO rules and disciplines upon the entry into force of this Framework Agreement.

CHAPTER 3: ECONOMIC COOPERATION

Article 3.1: Scope and Implementation of Cooperation

1. The Parties, on the basis of mutual benefits, shall explore and undertake cooperation projects in the following areas:

(a) customs procedures;
(b) trade and investment promotion;
(c) small and medium enterprises;
(d) human resource management and development;
(e) tourism;
(f) science and technology;
(g) financial services;
(h) information and communication technology;
(i) agriculture, fisheries, livestock, plantation commodities and forestry;
(j) intellectual property;
(k) environmental industry;
(l) broadcasting;
(m) construction technology;
(n) standards and conformity assessment and sanitary and phytosanitary measures;
(o) mining;
(p) energy;
(q) natural resources;
(r) shipbuilding and maritime transport; and
(s) film.

2. The Parties shall undertake economic cooperation projects at mutually agreed time periods, when feasible. These projects shall be monitored by the Implementing Committee for their effective implementation.

3. Details of such cooperation are specified in the Annex on Economic Cooperation.

Article 3.2: Capacity Building Programmes and Technical Assistance

1. The Parties, recognising that capacity building programmes and technical assistance are important, particularly for the new ASEAN Member Countries, in

order to expand their trade and investment with Korea, shall implement such programmes on a mutually agreed basis.

2. The Parties shall strengthen cooperation and support for the realisation of ASEAN integration objectives by implementing projects furthering the Bali Concord II, the Initiative for ASEAN Integration (IAI), as well as the Vientiane Action Programme (VAP), including providing technical assistance and capacity building for the new ASEAN Member Countries based on the experiences and expertise of Korea in development.

3. The Parties shall strengthen ASEAN's integration efforts in narrowing the development gaps among the ASEAN Member Countries and between the ASEAN Member Countries and Korea by enhancing regional and sub-regional development.

4. The Parties, recognising the development gaps among the ASEAN Member Countries and between the ASEAN Member Countries and Korea, shall enhance regional and sub-regional development, through cooperation initiatives including:

(a) the Mekong Sub-region;
(b) the Ayeawady-Chao Phraya-Mekong Economic Cooperation Strategy (ACMECS);
(c) the Brunei Darussalam-Indonesia-Malaysia-Philippines East ASEAN Growth Area (BIMP-EAGA);
(d) the growth triangles such as the Indonesia-Malaysia-Thailand (IMT-GT) and the Indonesia-Malaysia-Singapore (IMS-GT);
(e) the Greater Mekong Sub-Region (GMS) programme;
(f) the Second East-West Economic Corridor;
(g) the ASEAN Mekong Basin Development Corporation (AMBDC);
(h) the Singapore-Kunming Rail Link (SKRL) project; and
(i) sharing experiences with the Mekong River Commission (MRC) in formulating and implementing priority programmes in the Mekong River Basin.

CHAPTER 4: OTHER AREAS

Article 4.1: Expansion of Economic Partnership into New Areas

With the aim of achieving the comprehensive ASEAN-Korea FTA, the Parties shall explore ways and means to expand their economic partnership into new areas where the Parties have mutual interests, as may be agreed by the Parties.

CHAPTER 5: FINAL PROVISIONS

Article 5.1: Dispute Settlement

1. Any dispute concerning the interpretation, implementation or application of

this Framework Agreement shall be resolved through the procedures and mechanism as set out in the Agreement on Dispute Settlement Mechanism under this Framework Agreement.

2. Notwithstanding paragraph 1, any disputes arising from paragraph 3 of Article 2.2 (Trade in Services), paragraph 3 of Article 2.3 (Investment), Chapters 3 (Economic Cooperation) and 4 (Other Areas), and the Annex on Economic Cooperation shall not be subject to the Agreement on Dispute Settlement Mechanism under this Framework Agreement.

Article 5.2: Institutional Arrangements for the Negotiations

1. There shall be established an ASEAN-Korea Trade Negotiating Committee to carry out negotiations set out in this Framework Agreement.

2. The ASEAN-Korea Trade Negotiating Committee may establish any working group as may be necessary to assist it in undertaking negotiations on specific areas in the ASEAN-Korea FTA.

3. Commencing immediately at the beginning of the negotiations envisaged in this Framework Agreement and continuing until the formal completion of such negotiations by 31 December 2006, the Parties shall endeavour not to take any trade restrictive or distorting measures in such a manner as to affect negatively the negotiating position of any other Party.

Article 5.3: Implementation of the Framework Agreement

1. The AEM + Korea shall have the ultimate authority concerning all matters relating to the implementation of this Framework Agreement and any other agreements concluded or to be concluded in accordance with this Framework Agreement. An Implementing Committee, which is hereby established to be composed of the senior economic officials of the Parties or their designees, shall convene as appropriate to discharge such functions as provided for in paragraph 2 under the supervision and guidance of the AEM + Korea.

2. The Parties, through the Implementing Committee, shall:

(a) coordinate, supervise and oversee the implementation and appropriate application of the provisions of this Framework Agreement and any other agreements concluded or to be concluded in accordance with this Framework Agreement;

(b) review the implementation of this Framework Agreement and any other agreements concluded or to be concluded in accordance with this Framework Agreement;

(c) supervise the work of the committees and working groups established under this Framework Agreement and any other agreements concluded or to be concluded in accordance with this Framework Agreement; and

(d) consider any other matter that may affect the operation of this Framework Agreement and any other agreements concluded or to be concluded in accordance with this Framework Agreement, or that is entrusted to the Implementing Committee by the Parties.

3. In the fulfilment of its functions, the Implementing Committee may:

(a) establish and delegate responsibilities to ad hoc or standing committees, working groups or expert groups and assign them with tasks on specific matters; and

(b) take such other action in the exercise of its functions, as the Parties may agree.

4. The Implementing Committee shall keep the AEM + Korea informed of its activities on a regular basis.

5. The Implementing Committee shall establish its rules and procedures, which shall be approved by the AEM + Korea.

6. The Implementing Committee shall convene within one year of the date of entry into force of this Framework Agreement and then annually or otherwise as appropriate.

Article 5.4: Secretariat and Contact Points

1. The ASEAN Secretariat for the ASEAN Member Countries and the Ministry of Foreign Affairs and Trade of Korea for Korea shall jointly provide the necessary secretariat support for the purposes of this Framework Agreement and any other agreements concluded or to be concluded in accordance with this Framework Agreement. The ASEAN Secretariat and the Ministry of Foreign Affairs and Trade of Korea shall monitor and report to the Implementing Committee on the implementation of this Framework Agreement and any other agreements concluded or to be concluded in accordance with this Framework Agreement.

2. All official communications or notifications among the Parties for the purposes of the implementation of this Framework Agreement and any other agreements concluded or to be concluded in accordance with this Framework Agreement shall be made in the English language and through the ASEAN Secretariat and the Ministry of Foreign Affairs and Trade of Korea as appropriate.

3. The Parties shall designate their respective contact point to facilitate all other communications with one another on any matter covered by this Framework Agreement and any other agreements concluded or to be concluded in accordance with this Framework Agreement. At the request of a Party, the contact point of the requested Party shall identify the office or official responsible for the matter and assist in facilitating communications with the requesting Party.

Article 5.5: Annexes and Future Legal Instruments

1. The Annex on Economic Cooperation shall form an integral part of this Framework Agreement.

2. The Parties may adopt legal instruments in the future pursuant to the provisions of this Framework Agreement. Upon their respective entry into force, such instruments shall form part of this Framework Agreement.

Article 5.6: Amendments

The provisions of this Framework Agreement may be modified through amendments mutually agreed upon in writing by the Parties.

Article 5.7: Depositary

For the ASEAN Member Countries, this Framework Agreement shall be deposited with the Secretary-General of ASEAN, who shall promptly furnish a certified copy thereof to each ASEAN Member Country.

Article 5.8: Entry into Force

1. This Framework Agreement shall enter into force on 1 July 2006, provided that at least one ASEAN Member Country and Korea are among the Signatory Countries that have by then notified all the other Parties in writing of the completion of their internal procedures. In the event this Framework Agreement does not enter into force on 1 July 2006, it shall enter into force on the first day of the second month following the latter date on which at least one ASEAN Member Country and Korea have notified all the other Parties in writing of the completion of their internal procedures.

2. A Party shall, upon the completion of its internal procedures for the entry into force of this Framework Agreement, notify all the other Parties in writing.

3. Where a Party is unable to complete its internal procedures for the entry into force of this Framework Agreement by the date as set out in paragraph 1, this Framework Agreement shall come into force for that Party upon the date of notification of the completion of its internal procedures.

In witness whereof, the undersigned, being duly authorised thereto, have signed this Framework Agreement on Comprehensive Economic Cooperation among the Governments of the Member Countries of the Association of Southeast Asian Nations and the Republic of Korea.

Done at Kuala Lumpur, Malaysia this Thirteenth day of December 2005, in duplicate copies in the English language.

AGREEMENT BETWEEN THE GOVERNMENTS OF THE MEMBER COUNTRIES OF THE ASSOCIATION OF SOUTHEAST ASIAN NATIONS AND THE GOVERNMENT OF THE RUSSIAN FEDERATION ON ECONOMIC AND DEVELOPMENT COOPERATION

Kuala Lumpur, 10 December 2005

Agreement between the Governments of the Member Countries of the Association of Southeast Asian Nations and the Government of the Russian Federation on Economic and Development Cooperation, Kuala Lumpur, 10 December 2005;

The Governments of Brunei Darussalam, the Kingdom of Cambodia, the Republic of Indonesia, the Lao People's Democratic Republic, Malaysia, the Union of Myanmar, the Republic of the Philippines, the Republic of Singapore, the Kingdom of Thailand and the Socialist Republic of Viet Nam, the Member Countries of the Association of Southeast Asian Nations (ASEAN), on the one part, and the Government of the Russian Federation, on the other part (collectively referred to as "the Parties", and each individual Government of a Member Country of ASEAN or the Government of the Russian Federation as "Each Party");

Acknowledging the need to further strengthen friendly relations between the Member Countries of ASEAN and the Russian Federation;

Confident that the Agreement shall contribute to establishing a favourable climate for the development of multifaceted cooperation between the Parties;

Cognisant of the need to improve the conditions which have positive influences on economic, trade and investment activities and which also impact upon socio-economic, scientific, technological and cultural development;

Recognising that ASEAN comprises developing countries which aim to enhance their self-reliance, economic resilience as well as social well-being of its peoples;

Recognising also the different stages of economic development among the Member Countries of ASEAN and the need to facilitate the effective participation of the newer Member Countries of ASEAN, namely the Kingdom of Cambodia, the Lao People's Democratic Republic, the Union of Myanmar and the Socialist Republic of Viet Nam in regional trade and economic integration;

Affirming the commitment to the Dialogue Partnership between the Parties as established in 1996;

Have agreed as follows:

Article 1: Principles and Aims of Economic and Development Cooperation

1. Cooperation between the Parties shall be based on principles of equality of rights, mutual respect and benefit, common understanding, goodwill, friendly assistance and support, taking into account the potentials of the Parties and willingness to achieve practical results.

2. With a view to strengthening their relationship, the Parties, subject to their respective national legislation, shall undertake to hold a comprehensive dialogue and promote further cooperation between them in all sectors of mutual interest. Their efforts will, in particular, be aimed at:

(a) developing a favourable environment for the promotion and development of trade and investment between ASEAN and the Russian Federation in mutually beneficial ways;

(b) encouraging cooperation in the areas of mutual interest related to trade in goods and services as well as investment including industry, technical regulations, standards and procedures of conformity assessment, intellectual property and e-commerce in order to facilitate trade and investment flows;

(c) developing cooperation in all other sectors of mutual interest including small and medium enterprises, science and technology, energy, minerals, transport, finance, agriculture, technical cooperation, tourism, information and communication technologies, environment protection and management for the purpose of, *inter alia*, sustainable development and disaster management;

(d) raising the Russian Federation's role and creating a positive profile in Southeast Asia, and concurrently raising ASEAN's role and creating a positive profile in the Russian Federation;

(e) promoting participation of the business sectors in relevant areas of cooperation that have been mutually identified, which include socio-economic capacity building, personnel exchanges and technology transfer;

(f) supporting ASEAN regional integration including, *inter alia*, the Initiative for ASEAN Integration (IAI) launched in 2000 and providing special and differential treatment for the newer Member Countries of ASEAN, namely the Kingdom of Cambodia, Lao People's Democratic Republic, the Union of Myanmar and the Socialist Republic of Viet Nam by the Russian Federation in order to facilitate their effective participation under this Agreement.

Article 2: Economic Cooperation

1. The Parties shall, subject to relevant international law and their respective national legislation, cooperate in promoting trade, economic and investment activities by governmental bodies and other relevant entities. Concrete programmes may be

developed, in particular through the exchange of visits of businessmen and investors of the Member Countries of ASEAN and the Russian Federation with a view to promote partnership among them.

2. In this regard, the Parties shall, as appropriate, encourage and facilitate, *inter alia*:

(a) exchange of information on any problems that may arise with regard to their trade and investment for the purpose of seeking mutually satisfactory solutions to these problems including information relevant to economic cooperation, in particular information exchange on macro-economic indices and socio-economic development strategies, tariff regulation, sanitary and phytosanitary measures, technical regulations, standards and conformity assessment procedures and other non-tariff measures to facilitate trade and effective implementation of investment policy;

(b) joint studies on economic issues of mutual interest;

(c) contacts between governmental bodies and other relevant entities;

(d) trade and investment promotion activities including the organisation of relevant seminars, conferences, trade and investment fairs and business meetings;

(e) participation of governmental bodies and other relevant entities of the Member Countries of ASEAN and the Russian Federation in international and national exhibitions, shows, fairs and other promotion and information activities held in ASEAN and the Russian Federation.

3. The Parties shall develop and further enhance cooperation in the spheres of mutual interest in accordance with relevant international law and their national legislation.

Article 3: Other Areas of Cooperation

Subject to the terms of this Agreement and their respective national legislation, the Parties shall also endeavour to foster closer cooperation and interaction in areas of mutual interest including the following:

I. Small and Medium Enterprises

Recognising the important role of small and medium enterprises in maintaining the dynamism of their respective national economies, the Parties shall develop close cooperation between small and medium enterprises of the Member Countries of ASEAN and the Russian Federation. The Parties shall share their best practices and experiences aimed at developing cooperation between their small and medium enterprises in the field of technology, human resources and skills, financing and information.

II. Science and Technology

1. In accordance with their mutual interest and the aims of their policies on science and technology, the Parties shall undertake to develop and broaden cooperation in science and technology. To this end the Parties shall undertake to promote in particular:

(a) exchange of information and know-how in the field of science and technology;

(b) dialogue about the elaboration and implementation of the respective research and technological development policies;

(c) strengthening of cooperation in science and technology in sectors of common interest, such as biotechnology, micro-electronics, meteorology and geophysics, nanotechnology, new materials, space technology applications, geo-informatics and energy technology and energy efficiency.

2. The cooperation activities of the Parties shall include joint research in fields of mutual interest, the establishment of direct ties between scientific organisations, the transfer of technology on the basis of mutual benefit and jointly organising conferences, symposia, seminars and working meetings.

III. Energy

The Parties shall promote joint studies and research, as well as contacts between the appropriate bodies responsible for developing energy policies of the Parties with a view to, inter alia, promoting efficient energy use and the wide utilisation, where possible, of renewable and alternative energy sources (solar, wind, sea tides and waves, hydro, geothermal waters, biomass and others). Where relevant, the Parties shall explore the possibility of assisting each other in training experts in areas of particular interest in the field of energy.

IV. Mineral Resources Utilisation

The Parties shall encourage cooperation in research, innovation and application of emerging and advanced technologies in mining and geosciences including environment management, mine rehabilitation and the efficient mining, processing and recycling of minerals.

V. Transport

The Parties shall endeavour to develop cooperation in the transport sector with a view to improving the movement of goods and passengers, promoting safety, maintaining internationally accepted operating standards, and increasing the efficiency of their transport systems. In this regard, the Parties shall endeavour to:

(a) promote exchange of information on their respective transport policies and practices, especially regarding urban transport, maritime transport,

transport logistics and the interconnection and inter-operability of multimodal transport networks, as well as the management of railways, ports and airports; and

(b) explore possibilities for joint cooperation in the identification and selection of routes linking the two regions and the development of transport infrastructure and networks, as well as transport-related activities.

VI. Information and Communication Technologies

Recognising the important role of information and communication technologies for socio-economic development, the Parties shall endeavour to promote cooperation in this sphere in such areas as e-government, tele-medicine, distance education, cyber security, satellite communication and other mutually agreed areas.

VII. Human Resources Development Cooperation

The Parties shall cooperate to realise concrete activities and programmes through, *inter alia*, human resources development and capacity building by means of sharing best practices, training programmes, seminars and exchange programmes.

VIII. Environmental Management and Protection

Recognising the importance of environmental protection and efficient management of natural resources for their respective sustainable socio-economic development, the Parties shall endeavour, where appropriate, to strengthen cooperation in the field of environmental management and protection in the following priority areas:

(a) transboundary environmental pollution abatement;

(b) conservation of biological diversity and objects of natural heritage and the setting up of networks of nature reserve protected areas;

(c) coastal and marine environmental protection and efficient management of marine resources;

(d) broad application of advanced environmentally sound technologies and strategies of environment-friendly production and consumption of products;

(e) sustainable water resources management;

(f) sustainable forest management including conservation of forest resources and combating forest fires;

(g) combating the illicit felling of trees and trade of illegally procured timber;

(h) implementation of measures to stabilise the climatic system and adaptation of population and economy to the negative consequences of climate change;

(i) environmental education and awareness.

IX. Tourism

Cognisant that tourism is important in strengthening mutual understanding, expressing goodwill and developing relations among peoples, the Parties shall enhance and promote cooperation in the field of tourism. Their efforts, *inter alia*, shall be aimed at:

(a) encouraging tourism authorities to establish contacts and facilitate cooperation within the tourism sector;

(b) encouraging tourism authorities to strengthen cooperation on tourism advertisement and promotion aimed at further promoting tourism between the Member Countries of ASEAN and the Russian Federation;

(c) endeavouring to simplify visa and other formalities for travelers who are the citizens of the Member Countries of ASEAN and the Russian Federation;

(d) encouraging participation of Each Party in international and national tourism fairs and exhibitions held in the Member Countries of ASEAN and the Russian Federation;

(e) creating favourable transport conditions for the development of tourism.

X. Sports

The Parties shall facilitate cooperation in the field of sports between sports organisations and federations, as well as sports-related societies and clubs. Specific areas of cooperation and activities shall be identified between governmental bodies and relevant entities of the Parties.

XI. Culture

The Parties shall actively promote greater awareness, understanding and appreciation of each other's arts and culture through artistic collaboration, joint research and study, training and education, exchange of information, and people-to-people exchange and contacts. Specific areas of cooperation and activities shall be identified between governmental bodies and relevant entities of the Parties.

Article 4: Protection of Intellectual Property Rights

In accordance with the international treaties which they are party to and also with their respective national legislation, the Parties shall ensure effective protection of intellectual property rights obtained as the result of their cooperation within the framework of this Agreement.

Article 5: Cooperation Mechanism

1. The Parties shall entrust the ASEAN-Russian Federation Joint Cooperation Committee (ARJCC) to oversee the implementation of this Agreement and the realisation of its principles and aims.

2. Upon entry of this Agreement into force, the ARJCC shall discuss and approve the Terms of Reference of the ARJCC.

Article 6: Funding

1. The Parties shall set up the ASEAN-Russian Federation Dialogue Partnership Financial Fund (DPFF). The amount of contributions by the Russian Federation to this Fund shall be determined by the Government of the Russian Federation.

2. The ARJCC shall elaborate and approve the Terms of Reference of the DPFF.

Article 7: Other Agreements

1. This Agreement and any action taken thereunder shall in no way affect the powers of the Parties to undertake activities, whether bilaterally or multilaterally amongst themselves in the field of economic cooperation or any other fields, and conclude, where appropriate, new economic cooperation agreements or other agreements.

2. This Agreement and any action taken thereunder shall not affect the rights and obligations of the Parties under any existing agreements to which they are party to.

Article 8: Confidentiality

1. Each Party shall not disclose or distribute any confidential information, documents or data received pursuant to the implementation of this Agreement to any third party except with the prior consent in writing of Each Party from whom such information, documents or data were received.

2. Such disclosure or distribution shall be subject to such conditions and restrictions as may be imposed by Each Party consenting to the disclosure or distribution.

3. In the event of the termination of this Agreement, the provisions of this Article shall continue to apply to the confidential information, documents and data received pursuant to the implementation of this Agreement unless the Parties agree otherwise.

Article 9: Amendments to the Agreement

Any amendments to this Agreement shall be mutually agreed upon by the Parties in writing.

Article 10: Settlement of Disputes

In case of any dispute between the Parties related to the interpretation and/or implementation of this Agreement, the Parties shall endeavour to settle such dispute through consultation and negotiation.

Article 11: Entry into Force, Duration and Termination

1. This Agreement shall enter into force upon the expiry of thirty (30) days from the date on which all the Parties have notified the Secretary-General of ASEAN in writing that they have completed their internal procedures necessary for its entry into force.

2. The Secretary-General of ASEAN shall inform all the Parties of any deposited notification as well as the date of entry into force of this Agreement.

3. This Agreement shall remain in force for an initial period of five (5) years and shall be automatically extended for successive periods of five (5) years unless the Secretary-General of ASEAN receives the notice of intention to terminate the Agreement from either the Governments of all the Member Countries of ASEAN or the Government of the Russian Federation not later than six months before the expiry of the current period.

4. Termination of this Agreement shall not affect any rights and obligation arising from or based on this Agreement before or up to the date of termination including the implementation of on-going activities or programmes which have been agreed upon prior to the termination of this Agreement unless the Parties agree otherwise.

In witness whereof the undersigned, being duly authorised thereto by their respective Governments have signed this Agreement.

Done at Kuala Lumpur, Malaysia, on the Tenth Day of December in the Year Two Thousand and Five in two originals, one in English and one in Russian, both texts being equally authentic.

In the event of any divergence in interpretation between the two texts, the English text shall be used.

AGREEMENT TO ESTABLISH AND IMPLEMENT THE ASEAN SINGLE WINDOW

Kuala Lumpur, 9 December 2005

The Governments of Brunei Darussalam, the Kingdom of Cambodia, the Republic of Indonesia, the Lao People's Democratic Republic (hereinafter referred to as "Lao PDR"), Malaysia, the Union of Myanmar, the Republic of the Philippines, the Republic of Singapore, the Kingdom of Thailand and the Socialist Republic of Viet Nam, Member Countries of the Association of South East Asian Nations (hereinafter collectively referred to as "ASEAN" or "Member Countries" or individually as "Member Country"):

Recalling the Declaration of ASEAN Concord II (Bali Concord II) of October 7

2003, pursuant to which ASEAN is working towards the realisation of an ASEAN Economic Community by 2020;

Recalling that in moving towards the ASEAN Economic Community, ASEAN shall, *inter alia,* institute new mechanisms and measures to strengthen the implementation of its existing economic initiatives including the ASEAN Free Trade Area (AFTA);

Recognising that the ASEAN Cooperation in Customs supports the implementation of AFTA, and the establishment of the ASEAN Economic Community through its trade facilitation measures;

Recalling the decision of the Leaders for ASEAN to adopt the Single Window approach including the electronic processing of trade documents at national and regional level as one of the mechanisms to realise the ASEAN Economic Community;

Recalling Article 8(f) of the ASEAN Framework Agreement for the Integration of Priority Sectors, that Member Countries shall develop the Single Window approach, including the electronic processing of trade documents at national and regional level by 31 December 2005;

Recalling that ASEAN Customs Administrations are ultimate decision-makers for release and clearance of cargo at import and export points on the basis of communicated information from agencies of Member Countries;

Recalling the leading role by ASEAN Customs Administrations in the international supply chain, and in trade facilitation initiatives;

Noting international best practices and provisions of GATT 1994 and the International Convention on the Simplification and Harmonization of Customs Procedures as well as other internationally accepted legal instruments for trade facilitation as reference;

Agreeing that an effective and efficient arrangement to expedite customs release and clearance will promote trade facilitation, achieve better economic efficiency and effectiveness of ASEAN economies and further the establishment of the ASEAN Economic Community by the year 2020;

Mindful of the different levels of economic development and diverse cultural backgrounds of Member Countries;

Mindful of different systems and documentation requirements for clearance of goods in use in Member Countries; and

Desiring to establish the legal framework for the establishment and the implementation of the ASEAN Single Window in Member Countries,

Have Agreed as Follows:

PART I: GENERAL PROVISIONS

Article 1: Definition of the ASEAN Single Window and the National Single Window

1. The ASEAN Single Window is the environment where National Single Windows of Member Countries operate and integrate.

2. The National Single Window is a system which enables:

(a) a single submission of data and information;

(b) a single and synchronous processing of data and information; and

(c) a single decision-making for customs release and clearance. A single decision-making shall be uniformly interpreted as a single point of decision for the release of cargoes by the Customs on the basis of decisions, if required, taken by line ministries and agencies and communicated in a timely manner to the Customs.

Article 2: General Definitions

For the purposes of this Agreement:

1. "Customs Administration" means the government agency which is responsible for the administration of Customs law and related national legislation.

2. "Lead agency" means the government agency appointed by Member Countries to take the leading role in the establishment and the implementation of the ASEAN Single Window.

3. "Line ministries and agencies" means government agencies which are responsible for the administration and enforcement of trade laws and regulations as relevant to the release and clearance of cargo.

PART II: OBJECTIVES AND PRINCIPLES

Article 3: Objectives

The objectives of this Agreement to Establish and Implement the ASEAN Single Window (hereinafter referred to as "this Agreement") are:

(a) To provide a legal framework to establish and implement the ASEAN Single Window;

(b) To ensure the implementation of regional commitments by ASEAN to establish and implement the ASEAN Single Window;

(c) To strengthen the coordination and partnership among ASEAN Customs

Administrations and relevant line ministries and agencies, and economic operators (importers, exporters, transport operators, express industries, customs brokers, forwarders, commercial banking entities and financial institutions, insurers, and those relevant to the international supply chain) to effectively and efficiently implement the ASEAN Single Window.

Article 4: Principles of the implementation of the ASEAN Single Window

Member Countries shall ensure that transactions, processes and decisions under their National Single Windows and the ASEAN Single Window are performed, carried out or made in a manner complying with the principles of:

1. consistency;
2. simplicity;
3. transparency; and
4. efficiency.

PART III: DEVELOPMENT OF THE ASEAN SINGLE WINDOW

Article 5: Obligations of Member Countries

1. Member Countries shall develop and implement their National Single Windows in a timely manner for the establishment of the ASEAN Single Window. Brunei Darussalam, Indonesia, Malaysia, Philippines, Thailand and Singapore shall operationalise their National Single Windows by 2008, at the latest. Cambodia, Lao PDR, Myanmar, and Viet Nam shall operationalise their National Single Windows no later than 2012.

2. Member Countries shall ensure that their line ministries and agencies co-operate with, and provide necessary information to their Lead agency in accordance with their national laws in the development and implementation of their National Single Windows.

3. Member Countries shall make use of information and communication technology that are in line with relevant internationally accepted standards in the development and implementation of their National Single Windows.

4. Member Countries shall work in partnership with industries and businesses to support the establishment of their National Single Windows.

Article 6: Technical Matters of the ASEAN Single Window

Member Countries shall, by means of a Protocol to be agreed upon, adopt relevant internationally accepted standards, procedures, documents, technical details and formalities for the effective implementation of the ASEAN Single Window.

PART IV: IMPLEMENTATION

Article 7: Monitoring Mechanisms

1. The Ministers responsible for ASEAN economic integration, with the assistance of the Senior Economic Officials Meeting (SEOM) and the ASEAN Directors-General of Customs, shall regularly oversee, monitor, coordinate and review the implementation of this Agreement.

2. The ASEAN Secretariat shall:

(a) provide support to the Ministers, the SEOM, the ASEAN Directors-General of Customs and relevant ASEAN bodies for overseeing, monitoring, coordinating and reviewing the implementation of this Agreement; and

(b) regularly report to the SEOM and the ASEAN Directors-General of Customs and Leaders of agencies of regional economic integration on the progress in the implementation of this Agreement.

PART V: OTHER PROVISIONS

Article 8: Dispute Settlement

The provisions of the ASEAN Protocol on Enhanced Dispute Settlement Mechanism, done at Vientiane, Lao PDR on the 29th day of November 2004, shall apply to disputes arising under this Agreement.

Article 9: Further Measures

The Ministers responsible for ASEAN economic integration shall meet whenever necessary to review this Agreement for the purpose of considering further measures to improve the development and/or implementation of the ASEAN Single Window.

Article 10: Final Provisions

1. The provisions of this Agreement may be modified through amendments to be mutually agreed upon in writing by all Member Countries.

2. This Agreement shall be deposited with the Secretary-General of ASEAN, who shall promptly furnish a certified copy thereof to each Member Country.

Article 11: Entry into Force

1. This Agreement shall enter into force upon signing.

2. Each Member Country shall, upon the completion of its national procedures of ratification of this Agreement, notify the ASEAN Secretariat in writing.

In witness whereof, the undersigned, being duly authorised thereto by their respective Governments, have signed this Agreement to Establish and Implement the ASEAN Single Window.

Done at Kuala Lumpur, Malaysia, on this Ninth Day of December in the Year Two Thousand and Five, in a single copy in the English language.

THE GOVERNMENTS OF BRUNEI DARUSSALAM, THE KINGDOM OF CAMBODIA, THE REPUBLIC OF INDONESIA, THE LAO PEOPLE'S DEMOCRATIC REPUBLIC (HEREINAFTER REFERRED TO AS "LAO PDR"), MALAYSIA, THE UNION OF MYANMAR, THE REPUBLIC OF THE PHILIPPINES, THE REPUBLIC OF SINGAPORE, THE KINGDOM OF THAILAND AND THE SOCIALIST REPUBLIC OF VIET NAM, MEMBER COUNTRIES OF THE ASSOCIATION OF SOUTH EAST ASIAN NATIONS (HEREINAFTER COLLECTIVELY REFERRED TO AS "ASEAN" OR "MEMBER COUNTRIES" OR INDIVIDUALLY AS "MEMBER COUNTRY"):

Recalling the Declaration of ASEAN Concord II (Bali Concord II) of October 7 2003, pursuant to which ASEAN is working towards the realisation of an ASEAN Economic Community by 2020;

Recalling that in moving towards the ASEAN Economic Community, ASEAN shall, inter alia, institute new mechanisms and measures to strengthen the implementation of its existing economic initiatives including the ASEAN Free Trade Area (AFTA);

Recognising that the ASEAN Cooperation in Customs supports the implementation of AFTA, and the establishment of the ASEAN Economic Community through its trade facilitation measures;

Recalling the decision of the Leaders for ASEAN to adopt the Single Window approach including the electronic processing of trade documents at national and regional level as one of the mechanisms to realise the ASEAN Economic Community;

Recalling Article 8(f) of the ASEAN Framework Agreement for the Integration of Priority Sectors, that Member Countries shall develop the Single Window approach, including the electronic processing of trade documents at national and regional level by 31 December 2005;

Recalling that ASEAN Customs Administrations are ultimate decision-makers for release and clearance of cargo at import and export points on the basis of communicated information from agencies of Member Countries;

Recalling the leading role by ASEAN Customs Administrations in the international supply chain, and in trade facilitation initiatives;

Noting international best practices and provisions of GATT 1994 and the International Convention on the Simplification and Harmonization of Customs Procedures as well as other internationally accepted legal instruments for trade facilitation as reference;

Agreeing that an effective and efficient arrangement to expedite customs release and clearance will promote trade facilitation, achieve better economic efficiency and effectiveness of ASEAN economies and further the establishment of the ASEAN Economic Community by the year 2020;

Mindful of the different levels of economic development and diverse cultural backgrounds of Member Countries;

Mindful of different systems and documentation requirements for clearance of goods in use in Member Countries; and

Desiring to establish the legal framework for the establishment and the implementation of the ASEAN Single Window in Member Countries,

Have agreed as follows:

PART I: GENERAL PROVISIONS

Article 1: Definition of the ASEAN Single Window and the National Single Window

1. The ASEAN Single Window is the environment where National Single Windows of Member Countries operate and integrate.

2. The National Single Window is a system which enables:

(a) a single submission of data and information;

(b) a single and synchronous processing of data and information; and

(c) a single decision-making for customs release and clearance. A single decision-making shall be uniformly interpreted as a single point of decision for the release of cargoes by the Customs on the basis of decisions, if required, taken by line ministries and agencies and communicated in a timely manner to the Customs.

Article 2: General Definitions

For the purposes of this Agreement:

1. "Customs Administration" means the government agency which is responsible for the administration of Customs law and related national legislation.

2. "Lead agency" means the government agency appointed by Member Countries to take the leading role in the establishment and the implementation of the ASEAN Single Window.

3. "Line ministries and agencies" means government agencies which are responsible for the administration and enforcement of trade laws and regulations as relevant to the release and clearance of cargo.

PART II: OBJECTIVES AND PRINCIPLES

Article 3: Objectives

The objectives of this Agreement to Establish and Implement the ASEAN Single Window (hereinafter referred to as "this Agreement") are:

(a) To provide a legal framework to establish and implement the ASEAN Single Window;

(b) To ensure the implementation of regional commitments by ASEAN to establish and implement the ASEAN Single Window;

(c) To strengthen the coordination and partnership among ASEAN Customs Administrations and relevant line ministries and agencies, and economic operators (importers, exporters, transport operators, express industries, customs brokers, forwarders, commercial banking entities and financial institutions, insurers, and those relevant to the international supply chain) to effectively and efficiently implement the ASEAN Single Window.

Article 4: Principles of the implementation of the ASEAN Single Window

Member Countries shall ensure that transactions, processes and decisions under their National Single Windows and the ASEAN Single Window are performed, carried out or made in a manner complying with the principles of:

1. consistency;
2. simplicity;
3. transparency; and
4. efficiency.

PART III: DEVELOPMENT OF THE ASEAN SINGLE WINDOW

Article 5: Obligations of Member Countries

1. Member Countries shall develop and implement their National Single Windows in a timely manner for the establishment of the ASEAN Single Window. Brunei Darussalam, Indonesia, Malaysia, Philippines, Thailand and Singapore shall operationalise their National Single Windows by 2008, at the latest. Cambodia, Lao PDR, Myanmar, and Viet Nam shall operationalise their National Single Windows no later than 2012.

2. Member Countries shall ensure that their line ministries and agencies co-operate with, and provide necessary information to their Lead agency in accordance with their national laws in the development and implementation of their National Single Windows.

3. Member Countries shall make use of information and communication technology that are in line with relevant internationally accepted standards in the development and implementation of their National Single Windows.

4. Member Countries shall work in partnership with industries and businesses to support the establishment of their National Single Windows.

Article 6: Technical Matters of the ASEAN Single Window

Member Countries shall, by means of a Protocol to be agreed upon, adopt relevant internationally accepted standards, procedures, documents, technical details and formalities for the effective implementation of the ASEAN Single Window.

PART IV: IMPLEMENTATION

Article 7: Monitoring Mechanisms

1. The Ministers responsible for ASEAN economic integration, with the assistance of the Senior Economic Officials Meeting (SEOM) and the ASEAN Directors-General of Customs, shall regularly oversee, monitor, coordinate and review the implementation of this Agreement.

2. The ASEAN Secretariat shall:

(a) provide support to the Ministers, the SEOM, the ASEAN Directors-General of Customs and relevant ASEAN bodies for overseeing, monitoring, coordinating and reviewing the implementation of this Agreement; and

(b regularly report to the SEOM and the ASEAN Directors-General of Customs and Leaders of agencies of regional economic integration on the progress in the implementation of this Agreement.

PART V: OTHER PROVISIONS

Article 8: Dispute Settlement

The provisions of the ASEAN Protocol on Enhanced Dispute Settlement Mechanism, done at Vientiane, Lao PDR on the 29th day of November 2004, shall apply to disputes arising under this Agreement.

Article 9: Further Measures

The Ministers responsible for ASEAN economic integration shall meet whenever necessary to review this Agreement for the purpose of considering further measures to improve the development and/or implementation of the ASEAN Single Window.

Article 10: Final Provisions

1. The provisions of this Agreement may be modified through amendments to be mutually agreed upon in writing by all Member Countries.

2. This Agreement shall be deposited with the Secretary-General of ASEAN, who shall promptly furnish a certified copy thereof to each Member Country.

Article 11: Entry into Force

1. This Agreement shall enter into force upon signing.

2. Each Member Country shall, upon the completion of its national procedures of ratification of this Agreement, notify the ASEAN Secretariat in writing.

In witness whereof, the undersigned, being duly authorised thereto by their respective Governments, have signed this Agreement to Establish and Implement the ASEAN Single Window.

Done at Kuala Lumpur, Malaysia, on this Ninth Day of December in the Year Two Thousand and Five, in a single copy in the English language.

ASEAN MUTUAL RECOGNITION ARRANGEMENT ON ENGINEERING SERVICES

Kuala Lumpur, 9 December 2005

The Governments of Brunei Darussalam, the Kingdom of Cambodia, the Republic of Indonesia, Lao People's Democratic Republic, Malaysia, the Union of Myanmar, the Republic of the Philippines, the Republic of Singapore, the Kingdom of Thailand, and the Socialist Republic of Viet Nam, Member Countries of the Association of South East Asian Nations (hereinafter collectively referred to as "ASEAN" or "ASEAN Member Countries" or singularly as "ASEAN Member Country");

Recognising the objectives of the ASEAN Framework Agreement on Services (hereinafter referred to as "AFAS"), which are to enhance cooperation in services amongst ASEAN Member Countries in order to improve the efficiency and competitiveness, diversify production capacity and supply and distribution of services of their services suppliers within and outside ASEAN; to eliminate substantially restrictions to trade in services amongst ASEAN Member Countries; and to liberalise trade in services by expanding the depth and scope of liberalisation beyond those undertaken by ASEAN Member Countries under the General Agreement on Trade in Services (hereinafter referred to as "GATS") with the aim to realising free trade in services;

Noting that Article V of AFAS provides that ASEAN Member Countries may recognise the education or experience obtained, requirements met, and license or certification granted in other ASEAN Member Countries, for the purpose of licensing or certification of service suppliers;

Noting the decision of the Bali Concord II adopted at the Ninth ASEAN Summit held in 2003 calling for completion of Mutual Recognition Arrangements (hereinafter referred to as "MRAs" or singularly as "MRA") for qualifications in major professional services by 2008 to facilitate free movement of professionals/skilled labour/talents in ASEAN; and

Desiring to provide a generic model MRA for Engineering Services in strengthening professional capabilities by promoting the flow of relevant information and exchanging expertise, experiences and best practices suited to specific needs of ASEAN Member Countries;

Have agreed on this ASEAN Mutual Recognition Arrangement on Engineering Services (hereinafter referred to as "this Arrangement") as follows:

Article 1: Objectives

The objectives of this Arrangement are:

1.1 To facilitate mobility of engineering services professionals; and

1.2 To exchange information in order to promote adoption of best practices on standards and qualifications.

Article 2: Definitions

In this Arrangement, unless the context otherwise requires:

2.1 Accreditation refers to quality assurance of graduate engineers by national professional bodies.

2.2 Assessment or Evaluation refers to particular processes for reporting or comparison of achievement against criteria, standards, or a benchmark.

2.3 Benchmark refers to an agreed level by which others can be measured.

2.4 Certification refers to the issuance of a certificate or license to those who have met specified requirements for registration.

2.5 Country of Origin refers to the country where the Professional Engineer has an existing license to practise engineering.

2.6 Criteria or Standards refers to a specification of qualities required to be met.

2.7 Engineering Services refers to the activities covered under Central Product Classification (hereinafter referred to as "CPC") Code 8672 of the Provisional CPC of the United Nations.

2.8 Graduate Engineer refers to a natural person who holds the nationality of an ASEAN Member Country and has satisfactorily completed a higher education engineering program that is assessed as meeting required criteria in a discipline of engineering determined by a recognised professional engineering body or state authority.

2.9 Host Country refers to the country where the ASEAN Chartered Professional Engineer (ACPE) applies to work, not in independent practice, but in collaboration with the local Professional Engineer, where appropriate, to practise Engineering.

2.10 Professional Engineer (also known as Practitioner) refers to a natural person who holds the nationality of an ASEAN Member Country and is assessed by a Professional Regulatory Authority (PRA) of any participating ASEAN Member Country as being technically, morally, and legally qualified to undertake independent professional engineering practice and is registered and licensed for such practice by the Authority. ASEAN Member Countries may have different nomenclatures and requirements for this term.

2.11 Professional Regulatory Authority (PRA) refers to the designated government body or its authorised agency in charge of regulating the practice of engineering services as listed in APPENDIX I. Any amendment to this list can be made administratively by the ASEAN Member Country concerned and notified by the Secretary-General of ASEAN to all ASEAN Member Countries. ASEAN Member Countries may have different nomenclatures for this term.

2.12 Recognition refers to acceptance by an authority of demonstration of compliance with requirements.

2.13 Registered Foreign Professional Engineer (RFPE) refers to an ASEAN Chartered Professional Engineer (ACPE) who has successfully applied to and is authorised by the Professional Regulatory Authority (PRA) of a Host Country to work, not in independent practice, but in collaboration with one or more Professional Engineer of the Host Country.

2.14 Registration refers to the process of placing on a Register those who meet specified requirements within a jurisdiction.

2.15 Words in the singular include the plural.

Article 3: Recognition, Qualifications, and Eligibility

3.1 Qualifications to Become an ASEAN Chartered Professional Engineer (ACPE)

A Professional Engineer who possesses the following qualifications:

3.1.1 Completed an accredited engineering degree recognised by the professional engineering accreditation body whether in the Country of Origin or Host Country or assessed and recognised as having the equivalent of such a degree;

3.1.2 Possess a current and valid professional registration or licensing certificate to practice engineering in the Country of Origin issued either by the Professional Regulatory Authority (PRA) of the ASEAN Member Countries and in accordance with its policy on registration/licensing/certification of the practice of engineering or the Monitoring Committee pursuant to Article 4.2.2 and item 1.2 of Appendix II of this Arrangement;

3.1.3 Acquired practical and diversified experience of not less than seven (7) years after graduation, at least two (2) years of which shall be in responsible charge of significant engineering work as stipulated in Appendix IV, D - Example IV;

3.1.4 In compliance with Continuing Professional Development (CPD) policy of the Country of Origin at a satisfactory level; and

3.1.5 Obtained certification from the Professional Regulatory Authority (PRA) of the Country of Origin with no record of serious violation on technical, professional or ethical standards, local and international, for the practice of engineering is eligible to apply to the ASEAN Chartered Professional Engineer Coordinating Committee (ACPECC) to be registered as an ASEAN Chartered Professional Engineer (ACPE) under the ASEAN Chartered Professional Engineers Register (ACPER).

3.2 ASEAN Chartered Professional Engineer (ACPE)

A Professional Engineer who possesses the above qualifications and complies with the Guidelines on Criteria and Procedures as per Appendix II and satisfies the Assessment Statement as per Appendix III, may, upon acceptance and payment of fees, be emplaced on the ASEAN Chartered Professional Engineers Register (ACPER) and accorded the title of ASEAN Chartered Professional Engineer (ACPE). An ASEAN Chartered Professional Engineer (ACPE) shall practise engineering only in the specific discipline or disciplines in which he/she has been adjudged to be competent under this Arrangement.

3.3 Eligibility of an ASEAN Chartered Professional Engineer (ACPE) to Practise in a Host Country

3.3.1 An ASEAN Chartered Professional Engineer (ACPE) shall be eligible to apply to the Professional Regulatory Authority (PRA) of a Host Country to be registered as a Registered Foreign Professional Engineer (RFPE). The applicant shall submit with his application a sworn undertaking to:

(a) be bound by local and international codes of professional conduct in accordance with the policy on ethics and conduct established and enforced by the Country of Origin;

(b) be bound by prevailing laws and regulations of the Host Country; and

(c) work in collaboration with local Professional Engineers in the Host Country subject to domestic laws and regulations of the Host Country governing the practice of engineering thereto.

3.3.2 Upon approval, the successful ASEAN Chartered Professional Engineer (ACPE) applicant shall, subject to domestic laws and regulations and where applicable, not making submissions to statutory authorities of the Host Country, be permitted to work as a Registered Foreign Professional Engineer (RFPE), not in independent practice, but in collaboration with designated Professional Engineers in the Host Country, within such area of his own competency as may be recognised and approved by the Professional Regulatory Authority (PRA) of the Host Country.

Article 4

Professional Regulatory Authority, Monitoring Committee and ASEAN Chartered Professional Engineer Coordinating Committee

4.1 Professional Regulatory Authority (PRA)

The Professional Regulatory Authority (PRA) of each participating ASEAN Member Country shall be responsible for the following:

4.1.1 Consider applications from and authorise the ASEAN Chartered Professional Engineers (ACPEs) to work as Registered Foreign Professional Engineers (RFPEs), not in independent practice, but in collaboration with designated local Professional Engineers in the Host Country subject to the domestic laws and regulations and where applicable, not making submissions to statutory authorities of the Host Country as provided for by this Arrangement;

4.1.2 Monitor and assess the professional practice of the Registered Foreign Professional Engineers (RFPEs) and to ensure compliance with this Arrangement;

4.1.3 Report to relevant local and international bodies developments in the implementation of this Arrangement;

4.1.4 Maintain high standards of professional and ethical practice in engineering;

4.1.5 Notify the ASEAN Chartered Professional Engineer Coordinating Committee (ACPECC) Secretariat (set up under Article 4.3.5) promptly in writing when a Registered Foreign Professional Engineer (RFPE) has contravened this Arrangement, or when a Professional Engineer who is also an ASEAN Chartered Professional Engineer (ACPE) is no longer qualified to undertake independent professional engineering practice in the Country of Origin, has not complied with Continuing Professional Development (CPD) policy of the Country of Origin at a satisfactory level, or has seriously violated technical, professional or ethical standards either in the Country of Origin or in the Host Country whereby such violations have led to deregistration or suspension from practice;

4.1.6 Prepare rules and regulations to enable the implementation of this Arrangement; and

4.1.7 Exchange information regarding laws, practices and prevailing developments in the practice of engineering within the region with the view to harmonisation in accordance with regional and/or international standards.

4.2 Monitoring Committee (MC)

4.2.1 A Monitoring Committee (MC) shall be established in and by each participating ASEAN Member Country to develop, process and maintain an ASEAN Chartered Professional Engineers Register (ACPER) in the Country of Origin.

4.2.2 The Monitoring Committee (MC) shall be recognised as competent by, and may exercise some functions on behalf of, the authorities responsible for the registration and licensing of professional engineers in the country concerned.

4.2.3 The Monitoring Committee (MC) shall also be recognised as an authorised body and shall be able to certify the qualification and experience of individual professional engineers directly or by reference to other competent bodies.

4.2.4 The specific responsibilities of the Monitoring Committee (MC) for the development and maintenance of the ASEAN Chartered Professional Engineers Register (ACPER) are given in the ensuing Articles 4.2.5 and 4.2.6 below and in Appendices II, III and IV to this Arrangement.

4.2.5 The Monitoring Committee (MC) of each participating ASEAN Member Countries seeking authorisation to initiate a Register for the purpose of the ASEAN Chartered Professional Engineers Register (ACPER) shall prepare a statement setting out the criteria and procedures for assessing compliance with the qualifications set out at Article 3.1 for Professional Engineer applicants. The statement shall be reviewed by the ASEAN Chartered Professional Engineer Coordinating Committee (ACPECC). Guidelines on criteria and procedures and examples are set out in Appendices II, III and IV.

4.2.6 Each authorised Monitoring Committee (MC) shall further undertake to:

4.2.6.1 Ensure that all practitioners registered as ASEAN Chartered Professional Engineers (ACPEs) by the ASEAN Chartered Professional Engineer Coordinating Committee (ACPECC) Secretariat comply fully with the requirements specified in this Arrangement, and that a substantial majority of these practitioners have demonstrated their compliance through the primary procedures and criteria as shown in Appendices II, III and IV;

4.2.6.2 Ensure that practitioners applying for registration as ASEAN Chartered Professional Engineers (ACPEs) are required to provide evidence that they have complied with the Continuing Professional Development (CPD) of the Country of Origin at a satisfactory level;

4.2.6.3 Ensure that practitioners registered by the ASEAN Chartered Professional Engineer Coordinating Committee (ACPECC) Secretariat as ASEAN Chartered Professional Engineers (ACPEs) apply from time to time for renewal of their registration, and in so doing, provide evidence that they have complied with the Continuing Professional Development policy of the Country of Origin at a satisfactory level;

4.2.6.4 Ensure the implementation and execution of the changes agreed under Article 6.3 as directed by the ASEAN Chartered Professional Engineer Coordinating Committee (ACPECC); and

4.2.6.5 Where Article 4.1.5 is applicable, withdraw and deregister the said ASEAN Chartered Professional Engineer (ACPE) from the ASEAN Chartered Professional Engineers Register (ACPER).

4.3 ASEAN Chartered Professional Engineer Coordinating Committee (ACPECC)

4.3.1 The ASEAN Chartered Professional Engineer Coordinating Committee (ACPECC) shall be established and shall have the authority to confer and withdraw the title of ASEAN Chartered Professional Engineer (ACPE). This authority may be delegated in writing from time to time by the ASEAN Chartered Professional Engineer Coordinating Committee (ACPECC) to the authorised Monitoring Committee (MC) in each participating ASEAN Member Country. Members of the ASEAN Chartered Professional Engineer Coordinating Committee (ACPECC) shall comprise of one appointed representative from each Monitoring Committee (MC) of the participating ASEAN Member Countries.

4.3.2 The functions of the ASEAN Chartered Professional Engineer Coordinating Committee (ACPECC) shall include:

4.3.2.1 Facilitating the development and maintenance of authoritative and reliable Registers of ASEAN Chartered Professional Engineers (ACPER);

4.3.2.2 Promoting the acceptance of ASEAN Chartered Professional Engineers (ACPEs) in each participating ASEAN Member Country as possessing general technical and professional competence that is substantially equivalent to that of professional engineers registered or licensed in the Country of Origin;

4.3.2.3 Developing, monitoring, maintaining and promoting mutually acceptable standards and criteria for facilitating practice by ASEAN Chartered Professional Engineers (ACPEs) throughout the participating ASEAN Member Country;

4.3.2.4 Seeking to gain a greater understanding of existing barriers to such practice and to develop and promote strategies to help governments and licensing authorities reduce those barriers and manage their processes in an effective and non-discriminatory manner;

4.3.2.5 Through the mechanisms available within ASEAN, encouraging the relevant governments and licensing authorities to adopt and implement streamlined procedures for granting rights to practice to ASEAN Chartered Professional Engineers (ACPEs);

4.3.2.6 Identifying and encouraging the implementation of best practice for the preparation and assessment of engineers intending to practise at the professional level; and

4.3.2.7 Continuing mutual monitoring and information exchange by whatever means that are considered most appropriate, including but not limited to:

(a) regular communication and sharing of information concerning assessment procedures, criteria, systems, manuals, publications and lists of recognised practitioners;

(b) informing all Professional Regulatory Authorities (PRAs) when it has been notified that an ASEAN Chartered Professional Engineer (ACPE) is no longer qualified to undertake independent professional engineering practice in the Country of Origin, has not complied with the Continuing Professional Development (CPD) policy of the Country of Origin at a satisfactory level, or has seriously violated technical, professional or ethical standards either in the Country of Origin or the Host Country, whereby such violations have led to deregistration or suspension from practice or withdrawal from the ASEAN Chartered Professional Engineers Register (ACPER);

(c) verifying the operation of the procedures of participating ASEAN Member Countries; and

(d) observing the open meetings of any Professional Regulatory Authorities (PRAs) and / or commissions responsible for implementing key aspects of these procedures and relevant open meetings of the governing bodies of the participating ASEAN Member Countries.

4.3.3 The ASEAN Chartered Professional Engineer Coordinating Committee (ACPECC) may, whenever it deems appropriate, invite the non-participating ASEAN Member Countries to attend as observers to its meetings.

4.3.4 The ASEAN Chartered Professional Engineer Coordinating Committee (ACPECC) shall report its progress of work to ASEAN Coordinating Committee on Services (CCS).

4.3.5 The administration of the ASEAN Chartered Professional Engineer Coordinating Committee (ACPECC) shall be facilitated by a Secretariat. The establishment and funding of the Secretariat shall be decided by the ASEAN Chartered Professional Engineer Coordinating Committee (ACPECC).

4.3.6 General Meetings of the ASEAN Chartered Professional Engineer Coordinating Committee (ACPECC) shall be held at least once in each two year period to deal with applications by Monitoring Committees seeking authorisation to initiate Registers and/or authorisation to review the Guidelines on Criteria and Procedures (Appendix II), Assessment Statement (Appendix III), Appendix IV and other related guidelines, procedures and documentation, and recommend any amendments to all the Professional Regulatory Authorities (PRAs).

Article 5: Mutual Exemption

5.1. The participating ASEAN Member Countries recognise that any arrangement, which would confer exemption from further assessment by the Professional Regulatory Authority (PRA) that control the right to practise in each country, could be concluded only with the involvement and consent of the Professional Regulatory Authority (PRA) and the relevant government agencies;

5.2 The participating ASEAN Member Countries note that licensing or registering authorities have statutory responsibility for protecting the health, safety, environment, and welfare of the community within their jurisdictions, and may require Professional Engineers seeking the right to independent practice to submit themselves to some form of supplemental assessment;

5.3 The participating ASEAN Member Countries consider that the objectives of such assessment should be to provide the relevant authorities with a sufficient degree of confidence that the Professional Engineers concerned:

5.3.1 Understand the general principles behind applicable codes of practice and laws;

5.3.2 Have demonstrated a capacity to apply such principles safely and efficiently; and

5.3.3 Are familiar with other special requirements operating within the Host Country.

Article 6: Amendments

6.1 Any ASEAN Member Country may request in writing any amendment to all or any part of this Arrangement.

6.2 Unless otherwise provided by this Arrangement, the provisions of this Arrangement may only be modified through amendments mutually agreed upon in writing by the Governments of all ASEAN Member Countries. Any such amendment agreed to shall be reduced in writing and shall form part of this Arrangement and shall come into force on such date as may be determined by all the ASEAN Member Countries.

6.3 Notwithstanding Article 6.2 above, the provisions in Appendices II, III and IV and other related guidelines, procedures and documentation may be modified through amendments mutually agreed upon in writing by all the Professional Regulatory Authorities of the participating ASEAN Member Countries, provided that the amendments shall not contradict or modify any of the provisions in the main text of this Arrangement. All approved changes shall be implemented by the ASEAN Chartered Professional Engineer Coordinating Committee (ACPECC).

6.4 Any amendment agreed to under Article 6.3 shall be reduced in writing and shall form part of this Arrangement and shall come into force on such date as may be determined by the participating ASEAN Member Countries.

6.5 Any amendment shall not prejudice the rights and obligations arising from or based on this Arrangement prior or up to the date of such amendment.

6.6 In the event that any provision in Articles 1 to 8 is inconsistent with any provision in Appendices II to IV, the provision in Articles 1 to 8 shall take precedence.

Article 7: Dispute Settlement

The provisions of the ASEAN Protocol on Enhanced Dispute Settlement Mechanism, done at Vientiane, Lao PDR on the 29 November 2004, shall apply to disputes concerning the interpretation, implementation, and/or application of any of the provisions under this Arrangement.

Article 8: Final Provisions

8.1 The terms and definitions and other provisions of the GATS and AFAS shall be referred to and shall apply to matters arising under this Arrangement for which no specific provision has been made herein.

8.2 This Arrangement shall enter into force on the date of signature by all ASEAN Member Countries.

8.3 After this Arrangement enters into force pursuant to Article 8.2, any ASEAN Member Country which wishes to participate in this Arrangement (referred to in this Arrangement as a "participating ASEAN Member Country") shall notify the ASEAN Secretary-General in writing of its effective date of participation, and the ASEAN Secretary-General shall thereafter notify the rest of the ASEAN Member Countries of the same.

8.4 Any participating ASEAN Member Country wishing to cease participation in this Arrangement shall notify the ASEAN Secretary-General in writing at least twelve months prior to the date of its effective date of non-participation, and the ASEAN Secretary-General shall thereafter notify the rest of the ASEAN Member Countries of the same.

8.5 This Arrangement shall be deposited with the ASEAN Secretary-General, who shall promptly furnish a certified copy thereof to each ASEAN Member Country.

In witness whereof, the undersigned, being duly authorised thereto by their respective governments, have signed this ASEAN Mutual Recognition Arrangement on Engineering Services.

Done at Kuala Lumpur, Malaysia, this Ninth Day of December in the Year Two Thousand and Five, in a single copy in the English Language.

AGREEMENT ON THE ASEAN HARMONIZED ELECTRICAL AND ELECTRONIC EQUIPMENT (EEE) REGULATORY REGIME

Kuala Lumpur, 9 December 2005

The Governments of Brunei Darussalam, the Kingdom of Cambodia, the Republic of Indonesia, the Lao People's Democratic Republic, Malaysia, the Union of Myanmar, the Republic of the Philippines, the Republic of Singapore, the Kingdom of Thailand and the Socialist Republic of Vietnam, Member Countries of the Association of Southeast Asian Nations (hereinafter collectively referred to as "ASEAN" and individually as "a Member Country");

Mindful that in 1992 the ASEAN Heads of Government declared that an ASEAN Free trade Area shall be established in the region and that in 1998 they agreed to accelerate its implementation to the year 2002;

Noting the Agreement on the Common Effective Preferential Tariff (CEPT) Scheme for the ASEAN Free Trade Area (AFTA) signed on 28 January 1992 and the Protocol to amend the above Agreement signed on 15 December 1995, which provide for cooperation to supplement and complement the liberalization of trade including, among others, the harmonization of standards, reciprocal recognition of test reports and certification of products;

Mindful that the Declaration of ASEAN Concord II (Bali Concord II) adopted by the ASEAN Heads of Government during the 9th ASEAN Summit in Bali, Indonesia on 7 October 2003, commits ASEAN to deepen and broaden its internal economic integration and linkages, with the participation of the private sector, so as to realize an ASEAN Economic Community;

Mindful that the ASEAN Economic Community shall be the end-goal of ASEAN economic integration as outlined in the ASEAN Vision 2020 and that the ASEAN Economic Community will result in ASEAN becoming a single market and production base, turning the diversity that characterizes the region into opportunities for business complementation and making ASEAN a more dynamic and stronger segment of the global supply chain and the world economy;

Reiterating their commitment to the Agreement on Technical Barriers to Trade (TBT) of the World Trade Organization (WTO), which encourages Contracting Parties to enter into negotiations for the conclusion of agreement for the mutual recognition of results of each other's conformity assessment and mandates, among others, the elimination of unnecessary obstacles to trade, including those relating to technical regulations;

Recalling that the ASEAN Framework Agreement on Mutual Recognition Arrangements was signed on 16 December 1998 and the ASEAN Sectoral Mutual Recognition Arrangement for Electrical and Electronic Equipment was signed on 5 April 2002 to facilitate the elimination of technical barriers to trade and to enhance trade in ASEAN;

Having regard to the ASEAN Framework Agreement for the Integration of Priority Sectors; the ASEAN Sectoral Integration Protocol for Electronics and Roadmap for Electronics Integration signed on 29 November 2004 in Vientiane, Lao PDR;

Having regard to the ASEAN Policy Guideline on Standards and Conformance endorsed by ASEAN Economic Ministers on 28 September 2005 in Vientiane, Lao PDR;

Desiring to formulate an agreement to deepen and broaden cooperation in the electrical and electronic sectors so as to contribute to the realization of the ASEAN Economic Community.

Have agreed as follows:

Article 1: Objectives

The objectives of the Agreement on the ASEAN Harmonized Electrical and Electronic Equipment Regulatory Regime (hereinafter referred as "the Agreement") are:

(a) To enhance cooperation amongst Member Countries in ensuring the protection of human health and safety and property and the preservation of the environment insofar as they are affected by trade of electrical and electronic equipment in ASEAN;

(b) To eliminate restrictions to trade of electrical and electronic equipment through harmonization of technical requirements and registration; and

(c) To facilitate the negotiations for Mutual Recognition Agreements on Conformity Assessment between ASEAN and other countries or group of countries (blocs.)

Article 2: Definition and Scope of Electrical and Electronic Equipment (EEE)

1. This Agreement applies to all instances where a Member Country carries out regulatory action in respect of Electrical and Electronic Equipment (EEE).

2. For the purpose of this Agreement, EEE means all new electrical and electronic equipment that are intended to be either directly connected or plugged-in to the low voltage power supply or is battery powered, but does not include any equipment covered by the ASEAN Sectoral Arrangement on Conformity Assessment of Telecommunication Equipment and does not apply to medical equipment.

Article 3: Documens for EEE

The following Appendices are an integral part of this Agreement:

(i) Terminology (Appendix A).

(ii) ASEAN Essential Requirements for EEE (Appendix B).

(iii) ASEAN Harmonized Conformity Assessment Procedures for EEE (Appendix C).

(iv) Technical Files (Appendix D).

Article 4: Implementation

A. Member Countries with existing EEE Regulatory Regime

1. This Agreement requires Member Country with an existing EEE regulatory regime to undertake all necessary measures to fully implement this Agreement including all the Appendices listed in Article 3 not later than 31st December 2010, including:

(a) Enacting any necessary laws and/or technical regulations and administrative provisions; and

(b) Developing any necessary technical infrastructure in place to implement this Agreement including effective market surveillance systems and/or relevant product liability requirements.

2. Member Country shall submit to the Joint Sectoral Committee for Electrical and Electronic Equipment (hereinafter called "JSC EEE") through the ASEAN Secretariat, the draft text of the new laws and/or technical regulations and administrative provisions constituting their EEE regulatory regime for comments by the JSC EEE within 6 (six) months prior to the entry into force of the new laws and/or technical regulations and administrative provisions. Member Countries shall also allow at least 6 (six) months interval between the publication of the new laws and/or technical regulations and administrative provisions and their entry into force in order to allow time for producers in exporting Member Countries to adapt their products or methods of production to the new requirements.

B. Member Countries without EEE Regulatory Regime

3. This Agreement does not oblige Member Countries that do not have an EEE regulatory regime to develop one.

4. Where a Member Country decides to develop an EEE regulatory regime, it shall comply with this Agreement including all Appendices listed in Article 3. In such cases, it shall submit to the JSC EEE, through the ASEAN Secretariat, the draft text of the laws, technical regulations and administrative provisions constituting its EEE regulatory regime for comments by the JSC EEE within 6 (six) months prior to the entry into force of the new regulatory regime. Member Countries shall also allow an interval of at least 6 (six) months between the publication of the new regulatory regime and its entry into force in order to allow time for producers in exporting Member Countries to adapt their products or methods of production to the new requirements.

Article 5: Other Matters Pertaining to Implementation

1. Member Countries shall undertake all necessary measures to ensure that only EEE which comply with the Appendix B (ASEAN Essential Requirements) and are registered with the relevant Regulatory Authority and if required, bear the relevant Conformity Mark and/or registration mark may be allowed to be placed in the ASEAN regulated market.

2. The supplier responsible for placing the EEE in the market shall ensure that their products comply with Appendix B (ASEAN Essential Requirements), are registered with the relevant Regulatory Authority in Member Countries and if required, bear the relevant Conformity Mark and/or registration mark.

3. The ASEAN Conformity Mark when introduced may be affixed on the EEE to demonstrate that it complies with Appendix B (ASEAN Essential Requirements).

Article 6: Compliance with Essential Requirements

1. An EEE placed in the market or put into service must comply with Appendix B (ASEAN Essential Requirements). Member Countries shall provide that non compliance with Appendix B shall amount to non- compliance with the relevant Member Countries' laws, and/or technical regulations and administrative provisions.

2. The JSC EEE shall identify and reach consensus on the list of the relevant international standards to be used to demonstrate the compliance of an EEE to the ASEAN Essential Requirements as stated in Appendix B (ASEAN Essential Requirements). In the absence of international standards, relevant regional or national standards shall be used in that respective order. If necessary, the JSC EEE may supplement the listed standards with mutually agreed harmonized regulatory requirements. If different editions of international standards are being used in ASEAN Member Countries, or more than one standard can be applied for a specific EEE, the JSC EEE may consider listing more than one standard for such an EEE. The ASEAN Secretariat shall maintain the list of relevant standards and harmonized regulatory requirements.

3. For the purpose of mutual acceptance of the test reports and / or certifications to facilitate intra ASEAN trade, the Conformity Assessment Bodies (CABs) listed by the JSC EE MRA (to be replaced by the JSC EEE as provided for in Article 12 (4) of this Agreement) shall attest an EEE for compliance in accordance with the listed standards and harmonized regulatory requirements as mentioned in paragraph 2 above.

Article 7: Registration Procedure

The Regulatory Authority of participating Member Countries shall complete the registration not later than five working days or seven calendar days, whichever is longer, after the submission of the Certificate of Conformity (CoC) and compliance with administrative requirements by the supplier if applicable, so as to avoid unnecessary burdens once a regulated EEE has complied with the Appendix B (ASEAN Essential Requirements).

Article 8: Technical Files

1. The supplier responsible for placing the EEE in the market shall in accordance with Appendix D provide and keep the technical files readily accessible to the Regulatory Authority of the Member Country concerned.

2. The supplier shall keep the technical files of the EEE for not less than 10 years after the last EEE has left the production line.

3. The Listed CABs in each Member Country shall also keep the technical file of a regulated EEE which is tested and certified by them in compliance with Appendix B (ASEAN Essential Requirements) for not less than 6 years after the expiry date of the Certificate of Conformity (CoC).

Article 9: Rights of Regulatory Authority

1. Nothing in this Agreement shall prevent the Regulatory Authority in a Member Country from taking all appropriate and immediate measures within its territory whenever it ascertains that the registered EEE may represent a hazard to human health, safety, environment and property or otherwise fail to satisfy the requirements of this Agreement.

2. The Regulatory Authority of the Member Country concerned shall immediately inform the relevant Regulatory Authorities in other Member Countries and the ASEAN Secretariat, of any such measure(s), indicating the reasons for its decision in any of the following circumstances:

(a) Failure to satisfy the Appendix B (ASEAN Essential Requirements);

(b) Incorrect application of the listed standards;

(c) Shortcomings in the listed standards; and

(d) Occurrence of accidents involving the registered EEE.

Article 10: Other Areas of Cooperation

Member Countries shall strengthen and enhance existing cooperation efforts in EEE and cooperate in areas that are not covered by existing cooperation arrangements, which may include but are not limited to the following:

(a) Establishing or improving EEE related infrastructural facilities; and

(b) Encouraging and promoting cooperation pertaining to:

(i) Marking and product registration of EEE;

(ii) Testing and certification of EEE and accreditation and designation of CABs; and

(iii) The sharing of safety alert of EEE as appropriate.

Article 11: Dispute Settlement

Any dispute between Member Countries regarding the interpretation or implementation of this Agreement including its Appendices shall be settled amicably by consultations between the disputing Member Countries. The JSC EEE may, as appropriate, and if the disputing Member Countries agree, assist in such consultations. If the dispute cannot be so resolved, it shall be resolved according to the Protocol on Enhanced ASEAN Dispute Settlement Mechanism signed on 29 November 2004 in Vientiane, Lao PDR.

Article 12: Institutional Arrangements

1. The JSC EEE shall be responsible for the effective functioning of this Agreement, which may include, but is not limited to, coordinating, reviewing and monitoring the implementation of this Agreement, including its Appendices.

2. The JSC EEE, in the performance of its functions, shall make its decisions and adopt its own rules and procedures by consensus only.

3. The JSC EEE may establish or consult any body or bodies for the purpose of receiving advice on any matter of a scientific or technical nature in the field of EEE.

4. The JSC EEE will also take over the role of the JSC EE MRA in the listing, suspension, removal and verification of Testing Laboratories and/or Certification Bodies in accordance with this Agreement and the ASEAN Sectoral Mutual Recognition Arrangement for Electrical and Electronic Equipment.

5. The ASEAN Consultative Committee for Standards and Quality (ACCSQ) and the ASEAN Secretariat shall provide support to the JSC EEE in coordinating and monitoring the implementation of this Agreement including its Appendices and shall assist the JSC EEE in all matters relating thereto.

Article 13: Final Provisions

1. This Agreement shall enter into force on the deposit of the instruments of the ratification or acceptance by all signatory Governments with the Secretary General of ASEAN.

2. The provisions of this Agreement may be amended by written agreement of all Member Countries. All amendments shall enter into force on the date of such agreement.

3. This Agreement shall be deposited with the Secretary-General of ASEAN, who shall promptly furnish a certified copy thereof to each Member Country.

In witness whereof, the undersigned, being duly authorized by their respective Governments, have signed this Agreement on the ASEAN Harmonized EEE Regulatory Regime.

Done at Kuala Lumpur, Malaysia, this Ninth Day of December in the Year Two Thousand and Five, in a single copy in the English language.

4

Vietiane ASEAN Summit and Action Programme

CHAIRMAN'S STATEMENT OF THE 10TH ASEAN SUMMIT

Vientiane, 29 November 2004

1. ASEAN Leaders today held a very productive meeting under the Theme "Advancing a Secure and Dynamic ASEAN Family through Greater Solidarity, Economic Integration and Social Progress".

2. We took note of the convening of this Summit at a time when our region is being confronted with fundamental changes in the regional and international scene such as the recent terrorist attacks, the hike in oil prices, the spread of avian flu, etc. In responding to those challenges, we stressed the importance of a higher degree of coherence of efforts to achieve the objectives of ASEAN Vision 2020.

3. During the ASEAN Summit, we discussed issues of common concern to all members, including political and economic developments, in particular the latest developments on terrorism, the Korean Peninsular, the situation in Iraq and the Middle East.

Vientiane Action Programme (VAP): A Vehicle to Building an ASEAN Community Through Realizing Comprehensive Integration

4. We adopted the ASEAN Security Community Plan of Action and the ASEAN Socio-Cultural Community Plan of Action to implement the Declaration of ASEAN Concord II to realize the establishment of the ASEAN Community comprising three pillars, namely the ASEAN Security Community (ASC), ASEAN Economic Community (AEC) and Socio-Cultural Community (ASCC) that are closely intertwined and mutually reinforcing for the purpose of ensuring durable peace, stability and shared prosperity in the region and beyond. In this connection, we reaffirmed our commitment to achieving an ASEAN Community through initiatives and approaches to accelerate economic integration.

5. In furtherance of, and intensifying, our cooperation in the fight against transnational crimes, we also adopted the ASEAN Declaration against Trafficking in Persons, Particularly Women and Children.

6. We noted the Assessment Report on the Implementation of the Ha Noi Plan of Action (HPA) and agreed that the successful implementation of the HPA has significantly contributed to the realization of the end-goal of the ASEAN Vision 2020 and the Declaration of the ASEAN Concord II leading to the establishment of the ASEAN Community in 2020.

7. At the 10th ASEAN Summit, we signed the Vientiane Action Programme, a six-year plan, which is the successor of the HPA to realize the end goal of the ASEAN Vision and the Declaration of ASEAN Concord II. The VAP focuses on deepening regional integration and narrowing the development gap within ASEAN, particularly the least developed Member Countries. We agreed to establish an ASEAN Development Fund (ADF) to support the implementation of the VAP and future action programmes. In this connection, we called on our Dialogue Partners, other countries and regional and international organizations to support the implementation of the VAP.

8. To further deepen regional economic integration, we also signed the ASEAN Framework Agreement for the Integration of Priority Sectors and we tasked the Ministers responsible for ASEAN Economic Integration to continue coordination and monitoring of the implementation of all measures specified in the Road Maps to ensure the successful integration of the priority economic sectors within the time frame.

9. We noted with satisfaction that our respective economies have recovered with good prospect for further economic growth for the remaining year and in 2005.

Bridging the Development Gap

10. Bridging the development gap is extremely important for regional economic integration and is a crucial part of confidence-building efforts to assist members to cope with challenges. In this regard, we noted progress made in the implementation of the Initiative for ASEAN Integration (IAI) and Road Map for Integration of ASEAN (RIA). We welcomed Singapore's additional contribution of US$ 28.9 million (US$ 17.6 million) to support the implementation of the IAI as an important symbol of its commitment to foster closer economic integration and enhance ASEAN's competitiveness as a region. Our top priorities include developing human resources, infrastructure, information technology, and energy with the support and cooperation of the private sector, our Dialogue Partners, other countries, and regional and international financial institutions.

11. We reaffirmed the importance of sub-regional growth areas in ASEAN

development and integration process such as the Mekong Basin Development Cooperation and the BIMP-EAGA. We discussed ways and means to accelerate the pace of development of these growth areas in ASEAN. We welcomed the contribution of other sub-regional development frameworks in the region such as the GMS, and ACMECS to help close the development gap within ASEAN. These frameworks should serve as building blocks for East Asia and Asia-wide cooperation. We also welcomed the Asia Cooperation Dialogue (ACD) and Asian Bond Market Development.

CLMV Summit

12. We listened with interest to the outcome of the CLMV Summit and we supported the Vientiane Declaration on Enhancing Economic Cooperation and Integration among Cambodia, Laos, Myanmar and Viet Nam to convey, as a message, of our strong political will and determination of the Leaders of CLMV countries to accelerate the narrowing of their development gaps and ASEAN's economic integration.

Regional and International Political and Economic Issues

13. We discussed a wide range of issues related to ASEAN political and security cooperation.

14. We reaffirmed the importance of the Treaty of Amity and Cooperation in Southeast Asia as a code of conduct governing relations between countries in the region for the promotion of peace and stability in the region. We warmly welcomed the accession of the Republic of Korea and the Russian Federation to the TAC and encouraged other non-Southeast Asian countries to accede to the Treaty. We also welcomed the steps being taken by ASEAN and China to implement the Declaration on Conduct of Parties in the South China Sea.

15. We underlined the importance of strengthening relations and cooperation with other regions such as with Latin America and Europe through FEALAC and ASEM respectively. In this regard, we strongly supported Indonesia's initiative to build a bridge of cooperation between Asia and Africa through the convening of the Asia-Africa Summit on 21-22 April 2005 in Jakarta and the observance of Golden Jubilee of the 1955 Asia-Africa Conference on 23 April 2005 in Bandung, Indonesia.

16. We condemned in the strongest terms the recent terrorist acts and reaffirmed our determination to work together to mitigate the adverse impact of such attacks on ASEAN countries and urged the international community to assist us in this effort.

17. We reaffirmed our commitment to a peaceful and comprehensive solution to the nuclear issue on the Korean Peninsular. In this connection, we noted with

encouragement the achievement by the three rounds of the Six-Party Talks. We shared the view that the Six-Party Talks should be reconvened at the earliest possibility to bring about the common goal of denuclearisation on the Korean Peninsular.

18. We noted that current developments in Iraq and the Middle East remained causes of great concern. With regard to the post-war Iraq, we reaffirmed our position that the United Nations must continue to play a central role in the reconstruction and rehabilitation of Iraq taking the responsibility for the maintenance of international peace and security.

19. While discussing current economic developments in the region and in the world, we expressed our determination to work together to minimize the adverse impact on our economies brought about by the hike in oil prices and avian flu. In this connection, we supported energy cooperation, in particular, in alternative energy, such as bio-fuels, and hydroelectric power, and the establishment of the Outbreak Response Teams.

Strengthening Cooperation with Dialogue Partners

20. We noted the progress made in the political and economic cooperation with our Dialogue Partners. In this regard, we expressed satisfaction with the overall progress of the ASEAN+3 cooperation. We reaffirmed our determination to continue to drive the ASEAN+3 cooperation and to work closely with China, Japan and the Republic of Korea in promoting East Asia cooperation.

21. We discussed the convening of an East Asia Summit (EAS). We agreed to hold the first EAS in Malaysia in 2005 and in this connection, tasked our Foreign Ministers to work out the details concerning its modality and participation.

22. We expressed our satisfaction with the deepening of ASEAN-India cooperation. We welcomed the enhancement of AFTA-CER linkages, which will lay the firm foundation for future cooperation. We were also pleased to upgrade the relations between ASEAN and the Russian Federation and looked forward to the ASEAN-Russia Summit in Malaysia next year.

Institutional Strengthening of ASEAN

23. We directed our Ministers, Senior Officials and the ASEAN Secretariat to continue the work of developing an ASEAN Charter and to review ASEAN's mechanism, including the frequency of ASEAN's meetings at all levels, with a view to rationalize them and make them more effective. We also agreed to further strengthen the ASEAN Secretariat, particularly in undertaking policy analysis and providing recommendations to ASEAN Member Countries in carrying out ASEAN cooperation. We agreed to consider the findings and recommendations of our Ministers and Officials on this matter at our next meeting.

Other Matters

24. We reaffirmed our commitment to the United Nations. We further underlined the importance of reform of the United Nations and the enhanced role of ASEAN and ASEAN Member States within the United Nations system. In this connection, we endorsed the candidature of H.E. Dr. Surakiart Sathirathai, Minister of Foreign Affairs of Thailand, for the post of United Nations Secretary-General and underscored the importance of Indonesia's intention to seek permanent membership in the United Nations Security Council.

25. In order to strengthen the cooperation between ASEAN and the United Nations we decided to convene the second ASEAN-UN Summit in New York during the 60th session of the UN General Assembly. In this regard, we tasked our Foreign Ministers to make the necessary preparations to ensure the success of the said Summit.

26. We expressed our appreciation to the ASEAN Business Advisory Council (ABAC) and agreed to continue our support for its role as an important component to the overall strategy of increasing the private sector's engagement in ASEAN economic policy deliberations. We once again underlined the need for closer coordination between the private sector and relevant government agencies in the implementation of ABAC's recommendations.

VIENTIANE ACTION PROGRAMME (VAP 2004-2010)

I. PREAMBLE

Theme: Towards Shared Prosperity and Destiny in an Integrated, Peaceful and Caring ASEAN Community

We, the Heads of State and Government of the Association of Southeast Asian Nations (hereinafter referred to as "ASEAN"), gathered here in Vientiane, Laos, on 29 November 2004 for the Tenth ASEAN Summit; NOTING that ASEAN Vision 2020 envisions ASEAN as a concert of Southeast Asian Nations, outward-looking, living in peace, stability and prosperity, bonded together in partnership in dynamic development and in a community of caring societies;

Noting further that the Hanoi Plan of Action (HPA), the first in a series of action plans or programmes leading to the end-goal of ASEAN Vision 2020, ends in 2004 and that a successor action plan or programme is needed to guide further progress towards ASEAN Vision 2020;

Recalling the Declaration of ASEAN Concord II, which elaborates on the themes of ASEAN Vision 2020 by setting concrete milestones to reach the goals of a broad and comprehensive ASEAN Community, founded on the three pillars of political and security cooperation, economic integration, and socio-cultural cooperation, to form the ASEAN Security Community, the ASEAN Economic Community and the ASEAN Socio-Cultural Community by 2020;

Acknowledging that the global and regional economic environment has changed and is continuously challenged by new developments which have an impact on the trade and investment flows, and the economic competitiveness of ASEAN, and that ASEAN now has to work within a new strategic context;

Recognising that deepening and broadening the integration of ASEAN must be accompanied by technical and development cooperation to address the development gap among the Member Countries so that the benefits of ASEAN integration are shared and which will enable all ASEAN Member Countries to move forward in a unified and cohesive manner;

Reiterating our commitment to strengthen efforts to narrow the development gap in ASEAN by building upon existing initiatives such as the Initiative for ASEAN Integration (IAI), the Roadmap for the Integration of ASEAN (RIA), the Ha Noi Declaration on Narrowing Development Gap for Closer ASEAN Integration of 23 July 2001 and the Vientiane Declaration on Enhancing Economic Cooperation and Integration among Cambodia, Lao PDR, Myanmar and Viet Nam of 28 November 2004;

Do Hereby Declare That

1. We agree to pursue the comprehensive integration of ASEAN towards the realisation of an open, dynamic and resilient ASEAN Community by 2020 as envisioned in the Declaration of ASEAN Concord II and its annexes in the form of the action plans of the ASEAN Security Community (ASC), the ASEAN Socio-Cultural Community (ASCC) and the Recommendations of the High-Level Task Force on ASEAN Economic Integration;

2. We shall address, by various ways and means, the development issues and special needs of the less developed ASEAN Member Countries and sub-regional areas of ASEAN, including the implementation of the concept of "Prosper Thy Neighbour" by instituting programmes to narrow the development gap, reducing socio-economic disparities and eradicating poverty within ASEAN, and by doing so, move forward in a unifying and cohesive manner to prosper ASEAN. We also recognise the contributions of sub-regional arrangements such as, the Brunei, Indonesia, Malaysia, Philippines' East ASEAN Growth Area (BIMP-EAGA), Indonesia, Malaysia, Thailand-Growth Triangle (IMT-GT), Indonesia, Malaysia, Singapore-Growth Triangle (IMS-GT), ASEAN Mekong Basin Development Cooperation (AMBDC), Greater Mekong Sub-region (GMS) and the Ayeyawady-Chao Phraya-Mekong Economic Cooperation Strategy (ACMECS) to reducing the development gap within the region;

3. We shall strengthen further ASEAN's institutional framework both in terms of its structure and process to ensure that it is responsive to the challenges and needs of moving towards an ASEAN Community, including in terms of coordination and efficiency as well as in strengthening its ability to shape events in Southeast Asia and beyond;

4. We shall adopt greater outward-looking external relation strategies with our Dialogue Partners and friends in building a peaceful, secure and prosperous ASEAN, strengthening our economic linkages and deepening our socio-cultural cooperation with East Asia and beyond;

5. We recognise the need to strengthen ASEAN and shall work towards the development of an ASEAN Charter;

6. We shall, first and foremost, work closely between and among ourselves to generate our own indigenous resources as well as reach out to our Dialogue Partners and all others who wish to engage ASEAN on the basis of equality, non-discrimination and mutual benefit, to build bridges between the public sector and all other sectors of society within and outside ASEAN in order to facilitate a synergy of experience, expertise and resources available thereof for the attainment of the ASEAN Community;

7. We shall promote an ASEAN cultural heritage as a creative expression of the ASEAN spirit, and as a basis for an enduring bond of an ASEAN regional identity, since it originates from common ties throughout history and a shared aspiration for peace and prosperity;

8. We hereby endorse the Vientiane Action Programme (VAP), the successor to the HPA, to be implemented for the period 2004-2010, as an instrument to unify and cross-link the strategies and goals of the three pillars of the ASEAN Community and as an integral part of the action plans and programmes building up to the realisation of the goals of ASEAN Vision 2020;

9. As the process leading to the establishment of the ASEAN Community is continuously evolving, the VAP should therefore be perceived as an evolving document. Therefore, the lists of activities that are envisaged as being implementable in the period of 2004-2010, as contained in the various annexes to the VAP, are non-exhaustive; and

10. We commit ourselves, therefore, to implement the VAP paying attention to its two dimensions, the first being the broader integration of the ten Member Countries into one cohesive ASEAN Community, and the second being the identification of new strategies for narrowing the development gap to quicken the pace of integration, and working closely among ourselves, with our Dialogue Partners and others, to mobilise political will and generate the required resources for the effective implementation of the VAP.

II. GOALS AND STRATEGIES TOWARDS REALISING THE ASEAN COMMUNITY

1. ASEAN Security Community

Theme: Enhancing Peace, Stability, Democracy and Prosperity in the Region Through Comprehensive Political and Security Cooperation Strategic Thrusts

The ASEAN Security Community (ASC) embodies ASEAN's aspirations to achieve peace, stability, democracy and prosperity in the region where ASEAN Member Countries live at peace with one another and with the world at large in a just, democratic and harmonious environment. The ASC subscribes to the principle of comprehensive security, which acknowledges the strong interdependencies of the political, economic and social life of the region.

Thus, it views political and social stability, economic prosperity, and equitable development as strong foundations for the ASEAN Community, and will accordingly pursue programmes that will build on these foundations. On the external relations front, the ASC shall contribute to further promote peace and security in the Asia Pacific region, strengthen ASEAN's role as the driving force of the ASEAN Regional Forum (ARF), and continue to enhance ASEAN's engagement with Dialogue Partners and friends. Consistent with the ASC Plan of Action, the VAP for the ASC shall be pursued along five strategic thrusts, namely, political development, shaping and sharing of norms, conflict prevention, conflict resolution, and post-conflict peace-building, the implementation of which shall focus on actions that are conceivably achievable by 2010.

1.1 Political Development

In support of our commitment to enhance a political environment in which ASEAN Member Countries have strong adherence to peaceful ways of settling intra-regional differences and regard their individual security as fundamentally linked together and bound by geographic location, common vision and shared values, the strategies for political development are:

(i) Promote understanding and appreciation of political systems, culture and history of member countries through increasing people-to-people contacts and track-two activities;

(ii) Promote human rights and obligations;

(iii) Lay the groundwork to establish an institutional framework to facilitate the free flow of information among ASEAN Member Countries;

(iv) Establish programmes for mutual support and assistance among ASEAN member countries in the development of a strategy for strengthening the rule of law, judiciary systems and legal infrastructure, effective and efficient civil services, and good governance in public and private sectors;

(v) Increase the participation of non-governmental organisations such as the ASEAN Inter-Parliamentary Organisation (AIPO), the ASEAN People's Assembly (APA), the ASEAN Business Advisory Council (ABAC), the ASEAN Institute for Strategic and International Studies (ISIS) and the academia, especially the ASEAN University Network (AUN), in moving forward ASEAN political development initiatives, and strengthen the role of the ASEAN Foundation; and

(vi) Prevent and combat corruption.

1.2 *Shaping and Sharing of Norms*

In order to contribute to building collective responsibilities and forming a standard or common adherence to norms of good conduct in a democratic, tolerant, participatory and open community, as a means to consolidating and strengthening ASEAN's solidarity, cohesiveness and harmony (the "we feeling"), the strategies for shaping and sharing of norms include:

(i) Initiate the preparatory activities to develop an ASEAN Charter;

(ii) Encourage accession to the Treaty of Amity and Cooperation (TAC) by non-ASEAN countries;

(iii) Ensure the full implementation of the Declaration on the Conduct of Parties in the South China Sea (DOC) and work towards the adoption of a regional code of conduct in the South China Sea;

(iv) Work towards resolving outstanding issues to ensure signing of the Nuclear Weapon States to the Protocols to the Southeast Asia Nuclear Weapon Free Zone (SEANWFZ) treaty; and

(v) Work towards concluding an ASEAN Mutual Legal Assistance Agreement and an ASEAN convention on counter terrorism, and the establishment of an ASEAN extradition treaty as envisaged by the 1976 Declaration of ASEAN Concord.

1.3 *Conflict Prevention*

Guided by the principle articulated in the TAC, ASEAN's key code of conduct governing relations between states and a key diplomatic instrument for the promotion of peace and stability in the region, the strategies for conflict prevention are:

(i) Strengthen confidence-building measures through increased opportunities for exchanges and interactions among military officials, and between military officials and civilian personnel, and promote the voluntary exchange of observers at military exercises;

(ii) Promote greater transparency and understanding of defence policies and threat perceptions through the publication and exchange of security outlook or defence white papers among ASEAN Member Countries, and voluntary briefings on political and security developments in the region;

(iii) Develop an ASEAN early warning system based on existing mechanism to prevent occurrence/escalation of conflicts;

(iv) Strengthen the ARF process;

(v) Combat transnational crimes and other transboundary problems through regional cooperation activities;

(vi) Establish an ASEAN Arms Register to be administered by the ASEAN Secretariat, in line with a similar activity being conducted in the ARF; and

(vii) Promote ASEAN maritime security cooperation.

1.4 Conflict Resolution

In support of the collective interests of all Member Countries for comprehensive solutions to conflicts and establishing durable peace and security, and while continuing to use national, bilateral and international mechanisms for dispute settlement, the strategies for conflict resolution shall focus on exploring innovations and modalities such as:

(i) Utilise existing and planned national peace-keeping centres in some ASEAN Member countries to establish regional arrangements for the maintenance of peace and stability;

(ii) Build upon the existing modes of pacific settlement of disputes to strengthen them with additional mechanisms as needed; and

(iii) Undertake joint conflict management and resolution research studies and exchanges among ASEAN centres of excellence on peace.

1.5 Post-Conflict Peace-Building

Creating the conditions necessary for sustainable peace and preventing the resurgence of conflict requires certain types of multidisciplinary expertise and institutions. Thus, the strategies for post-conflict peace-building are:

(i) Strengthen humanitarian assistance by providing safe havens in conflict areas;

(ii) Implement human resources development and capacity building programmes in areas undergoing post-conflict resolution and rehabilitation;

(iii) Work towards the establishment of an ASEAN [humanitarian crisis management/assistance] centre;

(iv) Reduce inter-communal tensions through educational exchanges and curriculum reform; and

(v) Increase cooperation in reconciliation and promotion of a culture of peace.

2. ASEAN Economic Community

Theme: Enhancing Competitiveness for Economic Growth and Development Through Closer Economic Integration

Strategic Thrusts

The ASEAN Economic Community (AEC) embodies the realisation of ASEAN's aspiration of a stable, prosperous and highly competitive region, functioning as a single market and production base by 2020, in which there is a free flow of goods, services and skilled labour, and a freer flow of capital, along with equitable economic development and reduced poverty and socioeconomic disparities within and across its Member Countries. The overall strategy for realising the AEC involves deepening and broadening economic integration in the product and factor markets, and accelerating the integration process towards a single market and production base. The VAP will:

(a) Intensify current economic cooperation initiatives and measures targeted for completion on or before 2010 and implement new ones to accelerate integration in the eleven priority sectors, as recommended by the High Level Task Force (HLTF) on ASEAN Economic Integration, which is attached to the Bali Concord II;

(b) Remove, to the extent feasible and agreeable to all Member Countries, barriers to the free flow of goods, services and skilled labour, and freer flow of capital by 2010; and

(c) Develop and implement other measures to put in place *all* the essential elements or conditions for ASEAN to function as a single market and production base initially for the priority sectors by 2010. These measures include enhancing the attractiveness of ASEAN as an investment destination; accelerating the liberalisation of trade in goods; improving trade and business facilitation; reducing trade transaction costs; promoting regional trade in services; upgrading competitiveness of ASEAN SMEs, strengthening the ASEAN Dispute Settlement System; and such other integration support measures as may be required. Implementation of the VAP will be on basis of current and new initiatives.

2.1 Initial Eleven Priority Sectors for Integration

Acceleration of economic integration towards a single market and production base will begin with eleven sectors, selected on the basis of comparative advantage in natural resource endowments, labour skills and cost competitiveness, and value-added contribution to ASEAN's economy. These sectors are expected to demonstrate that integration enhances competitiveness and thereby ASEAN's attractiveness as an investment destination. As the institutional capacity of ASEAN for economic integration is built through experience, more sectors will be included in the accelerated integration programme. The following priority sectors have been identified to be fully integrated by 2010:

(i) Agro-Based Products
(ii) Automotive
(iii) Electronics
(iv) Fisheries
(v) Rubber-Based Products
(vi) Textiles and Apparels
(vii) Wood-Based Products
(viii) Air Travel
(ix) e-ASEAN (ICT)
(x) Healthcare
(xi) Tourism.

The proposed approaches to integrate these priority sectors are premised on combining the economic strengths of ASEAN Member Countries for regional advantage; facilitating and promoting intra-ASEAN investments; improving the conditions to attract and retain manufacturing and other economic activities within the region; promotion of intra-industry trade and outsourcing within ASEAN; and promoting the development of "Made in ASEAN" products and services. A roadmap will serve as the basis for economic integration of each of the priority sectors, with active involvement of the private sector. The roadmaps in the form of Framework Agreement and Protocols for each of the priority sectors will contain detailed and specific measures to be implemented from 2005 to 2010.

2.2 *ASEAN Investment Area*

A free and open investment regime in ASEAN is the key to enhancing ASEAN's competitiveness as a single production base. Sustained inflows of investments will maintain the dynamic development of regional production and distribution networks. Implementation of the ASEAN Investment Area (AIA) launched in 1998, will be intensified, as follows:

2.2.1 *Investment Liberalisation*

Enhance the coverage of the AIA Agreement with a view towards establishment of ASEAN as a competitive investment area; collapse the different end dates for the liberalisation process; open up all industries for investment; agree on a timetable for phasing out the sensitive lists; and grant national treatment to both ASEAN and non-ASEAN investors.

2.2.2 *Investment Facilitation*

Improve the investment environment both unilaterally and regionally, comparing the competitiveness and ease of investing in ASEAN *vis-a-vis* other regions, identify clusters of impediments to be eliminated or reduced that hinder FDI, undertake continuous evaluations of the investment policy framework by benchmarking its relevance against emerging global and regional FDI trends, and strengthen ASEAN institutional capacity on all investment-related measures.

2.2.3 *Investment Promotion*

Adopt a strategic promotion and outreach programme, focussing on high potential countries and regions such as, China, India, Japan, Korea, the US and the EU. These strategies would be carried out by fully implementing the ASEAN Strategic Investment Action Plan (SIAP) for 2004-2008 and the subsequent SIAP 2 from 2008 onwards.

2.3 *Trade in Goods*

Free flow of goods is a minimum necessary condition for the AEC to function as a single market and production base. Tariff and non-tariff barriers to the flow of goods in the product market will be gradually removed at a pace comfortable to Member Countries, as follows:

2.3.1 *Tariffs*

Eliminate tariffs for products by 2010 for ASEAN-6 and 2015 for CLMV.

2.3.2 *Non-Tariff Barriers*

Ensure full transparency of Non-Tariff Measures (NTMs) through the maintenance of the database of ASEAN NTMs; set clear criteria to identify NTMs that are barriers to trade for elimination; set a clear and definitive work programme and schedule for removal of Non-Tariff Barriers (NTBs); and adopt and ensure compliance with the World Trade Organisation (WTO) Agreements on Technical Barriers to Trade, Sanitary and Phyto-Sanitary and Import Licensing Procedures, along with implementation guidelines deemed appropriate for ASEAN.

2.3.3 *ASEAN Integration System of Preference (AISP)*

Improve the AISP for the benefits of CLMV and hasten their integration into ASEAN.

2.3.4 *Trade in Minerals*

Enhance trade and investment in the minerals sector.

2.3.5 *Trade Facilitation*

2.3.5.1 *Customs:* Integrate customs structures in ASEAN for a harmonised customs environment by the adoption of the WTO agreement on customs valuation, customs-related agreements under the WTO, World Customs Organisation (WCO), UN bodies and international organisations, and set up the service commitment charter for trade facilitation. The strategy would also include the development of the Single Window approach to modernise customs procedures and practices and improve customs control and compliance in cooperation with line ministries and business through the implementation of defined programmes of the 2005-10 ASEAN Strategic Plan of Customs Development.

2.3.5.2 *Rules of Origin:* Continuously strengthen the Common Effective Preferential Tariff (CEPT) Scheme Rules of Origin (ROO) upon commencement of the VAP by 1 January 2005 by making it more transparent, predictable and standardised taking into account the best practices of other Regional Trading Arrangements (RTAs), including the WTO ROO, and adopting substantial transformation as alternative criteria for conferring origin status.

2.3.5.3 *Standards and Conformance:* Focus on sectors with significant potential for trade, including acceleration of implementation of the framework agreement on Mutual Recognition Arrangements (MRAs) and establishment of specific targets for harmonisation of standards and technical regulations. Where possible, ASEAN technical regulations, based as appropriate on existing international performance criteria, will be developed for national application.

2.3.6 *Intellectual Property (IP)*

Move intellectual property development and cooperation in ASEAN to a higher plane to achieve a culture of learning, innovation and creativity through:

(a) Drawing on the diverse strength of ASEAN Member Countries in creativity and innovation;

(b) Development of a regional identity and profile in IP harmonisation, generation, commercialisation, protection, enforcement and awareness; and

(c) Optimising the benefit to businesses from Intellectual Property Rights (IPR) by encouraging cross-border collaboration and networking for the widening and deepening of ASEAN's science and technology base and research and development activities, and commercialisation of their results and outputs.

These strategies would be carried out through the full implementation of the ASEAN IPR Action Plan for 2004-10.

2.3.7 *Industrial Cooperation and Enterprise Development*

2.3.7.1 *Industrial Cooperation:* Enhance inter- and intra-industry linkages in ASEAN and promote suitable outsourcing, including the identification of strengths and weaknesses inherent to each ASEAN Member Country in order to foster industrial complementation within the region.

2.3.7.2 *Small and Medium Enterprises (SME):* Nurture the growth and accelerate the transformation and integration of SMEs into regional and international production networks to be competitive and dynamic suppliers of the regional and global markets, building on the comparative and agglomeration advantages of Member Countries; promote a culture of entrepreneurship, innovation and networking; facilitate SMEs' access to information, markets, human resource and business development services, credit and finance, and modern technologies; improve public-private sector synergies in fostering SME support and linkages; facilitate networking between ASEAN SMEs for joint ventures; and facilitate the transformation of ASEAN SMEs into ASEAN MNCs. The strategies would be carried out through the full implementation of the ASEAN SME Action Plan for 2004-10.

2.4 *Trade in Services*

Free flow of non-factor services such as in finance, transportation and information and communications technologies (ICT) are critical inputs to production and trade of goods. Trade in services will be liberalised at a pace comfortable to all Member Countries to enable the AEC to function as a single production base. High quality service industries in the region will be promoted to allow ASEAN to position itself as a global outsourcing hub.

2.4.1 *Services Liberalisation*

Accelerate regional integration towards creating a single market in services through progressive liberalisation earlier than 2020; subsequent rounds of negotiations be launched with clear targets and parameters, and the use of the ASEAN minus-X formula. This is aimed at enhancing ASEAN's competitiveness in the area of services and as a hub for outsourcing activities. Undertake facilitation and cooperation activities on an on-going basis to further enhance Member Countries' understanding of the services sector, the cost and benefits of liberalisation of trade in services, capacity building and to facilitate movement of business persons, experts, professionals, skilled labour and talents.

2.4.2 *Tourism*

To facilitate travel into and within ASEAN: (a) substantially reduce restrictions to trade in tourism and travel services; (b) enhance the development and promotion of ASEAN as a single tourism destination; (c) strengthen cooperation to develop, upgrade and expand tourism and travel facilities and services; and (d) create favourable conditions for the public and private sector to engage more deeply in tourism development, intra-ASEAN travel and investment in tourism services and facilities.

2.5 *Finance Cooperation*

Promote economic growth and financial stability in the region through strengthening surveillance mechanisms, enhancing domestic financial systems and facilitating the development and orderly integration of financial markets as part of the Roadmap for Financial and Monetary Integration of ASEAN.

2.6 *Transport*

Gear up ASEAN transport as a critical logistics and services support sector through the implementation of the ASEAN Transport Action Plan for 2005-10, focusing on cooperation activities towards facilitating seamless movement of peoples and goods; enhancing integration and efficiency of multimodal transport infrastructures, facilities and services; accelerating open sky arrangements; and advancing liberalisation in air and maritime transport services.

2.7 *Telecommunications and IT*

Leverage on information and communications technology (ICT), via public-private sector partnerships and strong external linkages, to build a connected, vibrant and secure ASEAN Community by:

- Striving for universal access to ICT infrastructure and services;
- Encouraging the development of a pervasive, inter-connected and secure ASEAN information infrastructure;
- Strengthening the cooperation and assistance on regulatory policy and strategy issues;
- Creating digital opportunities through e-government, e-commerce and e-society initiatives;
- Enhancing the competitiveness and dynamism of the ASEAN ICT sector by promoting and facilitating trade and investment in ICT services; and
- Developing highly skilled ICT human resources.

2.8 *Science and Technology (S&T)*

Foster science and technology (S&T) as a key factor in sustaining economic growth, enhancing community well-being and promoting integration in ASEAN, through human resource, research and technology development and provision of technical services to meet the needs of economic integration; apply S&T tools and methodologies to enhance economic and industrial planning; and formulate a systematic approach in the implementation of the ASEAN-help-ASEAN programmes to address the S&T needs and strengthen the S&T infrastructure of less developed Member Countries. Furthermore, S&T will be used as major tool for ASEAN to move forward in a unified and cohesive manner.

2.9 *Energy*

Pursue sustainable energy development through the implementation of the ASEAN Plan of Action for Energy Cooperation for 2004-2009, based primarily on individual sectoral plans of action and roadmaps, including but not limited to the ASEAN Power Grid, the Trans-ASEAN Gas Pipeline (TAGP), Coal, Energy Efficiency and Conservation, Renewable Energy, and Regional Energy Policy and Planning, focusing on cooperation activities, including with the ASEAN Dialogue Partners, to enhance the integration of the regional energy infrastructures, promote energy security, create responsive policies to progressively enhance market reforms and liberalisation, as well as preserve the sustainability of environment.

2.10 *Food, Agriculture and Forestry Sectors*

Enhance the competitiveness of the food agriculture and forestry sectors through developing appropriate technologies to increase productivity and by promoting inter- and extra-ASEAN trade and greater private sector investment in the food, agriculture and forestry sectors.

2.11 *Institutional Strengthening*

2.11.1 *Dispute Settlement Mechanism*

Establish an effective system to ensure proper implementation of all economic agreements and expeditious resolution of any disputes through appropriate advisory, consultative, and adjudicatory mechanisms. The feasibility of establishing a common legal framework for the incorporation or registration of ASEAN companies to assist in dispute settlement would also be explored.

2.11.2 *Statistics*

Provide the necessary statistical support for ASEAN initiatives, planning and policy making through improved quality and availability of important statistics, adoption of international good practices, promotion of greater awareness of statistics, enhanced networking and close partnership between users in policy areas and statistical systems, and wider dissemination of ASEAN statistics through the annual publication of the ASEAN Statistical Yearbook and a continuous expansion of statistical coverage on Member Countries and the ASEAN Secretariat's Websites.

2.12 *Economic Relations with Dialogue Partners*

The economic growth of the ASEAN region in past decades has been largely driven by FDI flows and exports. While exports have stabilised and are again beginning to expand, ASEAN has experienced a sustained decline in FDI flows since the 1997-1998 economic and monetary crisis. Since internal measures, aimed at creating a single ASEAN market and production base, may not be sufficient to attract the volume of investment required to sustain economic growth, efforts will be made to strengthen external economic relations and the terms of trade with major Dialogue Partners through the establishment of Free Trade Areas (FTAs) and Closer Economic Partnerships (CEPs).

The strategy for ASEAN external economic cooperation will involve strengthening linkages and promoting the coherence of agreements with major trading partners such as China, Japan, Korea, the US, Australia, New Zealand, the EU and emerging economies such as India. The promotion of the coherence of agreements might include increasing coordination of extra- ASEAN economic agreements and the closer alignment of MFN tariffs.

3. ASEAN Socio-Cultural Community

Theme: Nurturing Human, Cultural and Natural Resources for Sustained Development in a Harmonious and People-Centred ASEAN

Strategic Thrusts

The ASEAN Socio-Cultural Community (ASCC) represents ASEAN's aspirations to lift the quality of life of its peoples, sustainably use natural resources and strengthen its cultural identity towards a people-centred ASEAN. The roadmap for the Community focuses on four strategic thrusts to support other ASEAN Community goals: strong and functional systems of social protection that address poverty, equity and health impacts of economic growth; promoting environmental sustainability and sustainable natural resource management that meets current and future needs; social governance that manages impacts of economic integration; and the preservation and promotion of the region's cultural heritage and cultural identity.

Since economic growth could be threatened by social inequities that could in turn undermine political stability, the ASEAN socio-cultural action programme is linked inextricably with the economic and security pillars of the ASEAN Community.

The establishment of the ASCC stems from the premise that economic integration and security alone will not be sufficient to realise the vision of an ASEAN Community. The human, natural and cultural resources of ASEAN provide the means for economic growth. The sustainable development and conservation of these resources allows for the region to prosper now and into the future, thereby enabling people to uplift their living standards and have a decent and healthy lifestyle. Measures taken to promote social protection, cultural identity, the conservation of natural resources and the protection of the environment fuel economic growth and sustain life.

3.1 Building a Community of Caring Societies

The hallmark of a strong and resilient community of caring societies is its commitment and capability to address the core issues of poverty, equity and health. National initiatives will fundamentally drive the manner and extent to which these issues are addressed. However, the Member Countries can gain significant leveraging of political commitment and goals at the national level through regional advocacy. The regional interventions that will complement the national actions include:

(i) Raising the standard of living of marginalised, disadvantaged groups by strengthening the capacity of officials in rural development and poverty alleviation administrations and promoting approaches that engage these groups in society;

(ii) Facilitating universal access to education and promoting high standards through networking and institutional collaborations.

(iii) Reducing the social risks faced by children, women, elderly and persons with disabilities, by supporting programmes consistent with international conventions and promoting services such as aged care, health care and education;

(iv) Increasing the effective participation of family, civil society and the private sector in tackling poverty and social welfare issues through the establishment of networking and exchange programmes, and promoting the professions involved in poverty and social welfare issues;

(v) Increasing the participation of women and youth in the productive workforce through skills training and increasing access to microfinance and information systems;

(vi) Addressing health development concerns;

(viii) Preventing the spread and reducing the harm of HIV/AIDS and other infectious diseases;

(viii) Enhancing food security, in particular the establishment of food security information systems;

(ix) Ensuring a region of disaster-resilient nations by minimising the adverse effects of disasters in pursuit of safer communities and sustainable development.

(x) Ensuring a Drug Free ASEAN by 2015 through prevention, treatment and community-based control of drug abuse, including the promotion of alternative development, as well as the elimination of drug trafficking; and

(xi) Promoting science and technology in ASEAN to improve regional human resources by developing science and technology culture and increasing usage of applied science and technology in socio-economic activities.

3.2 *Managing the Social Impact of Economic Integration*

Domestic policy adjustments and emerging regional production arrangements from economic integration will have a profound social impact that will be felt mostly in the labour market. Consequently there is a need to:

(i) Enhance human resource development through the networking of skills training institutions, and the development of regional assessment and training programmes;

(ii) Strengthen the capacity of governments to monitor labour markets and monitor human resource indicators; and

(iii) Promote social protection and social risk management systems. The inclusion of health services as one of the eleven priority sectors for vertical integration will require strategies to address the impact of liberalisation in the health sector. In addition, the development of mutual recognition arrangements shall facilitate labour mobility in the region and will support the realisation of the AEC.

3.3 *Promoting Environmental Sustainability*

The ASCC promotes a clean and green ASEAN with fully established mechanisms for sustainable development to ensure the protection of the region's environment, the sustainability of its natural resources and the high quality of life of its people. The medium-term strategies and milestones in pursuit of this goal are:

Environmental Management

(i) Effectively address global environmental issues without impinging on competitiveness, or social and economic development based on the principle of common but differentiated responsibility;

(ii) Prevent transboundary haze pollution as a result of land and/or forest fires through concerted national efforts and intensified regional action and international cooperation, pursued in the context of sustainable development and in accordance with the provisions of the ASEAN Agreement on Transboundary Haze Pollution;

(iii) Establish a clean and green ASEAN, rich in cultural traditions (where the values and practices of the people are in accord with the rhythm and harmony of nature), with citizens who are environmentally literate, imbued with the environmental ethic, and willing and capable to ensure the sustainable development of the region through environmental education and public participation efforts;

(iv) Aim for zero waste and minimal impact on the environment, and promote business opportunities in environmental goods and services, through relevant environmentally sound technologies;

(v) Ensure cities/urban areas in ASEAN are environmentally sustainable, while meeting the social and economic needs of the people; and

(vi) Strive for harmonisation of environmental policies, legislation, regulations, standards and databases, taking into account the national circumstances of Member Countries, to support the integration of the environmental, social and economic goals of the region.

Natural Resource Management

(i) Ensure ASEAN's coastal and marine environment are sustainably managed, representative ecosystems, pristine areas and species are protected; economic activities are sustainably managed, and public awareness of the coastal and marine environment instilled;

(ii) Ensure ASEAN's rich biological diversity is conserved, and sustainably managed, and the benefits arising from these biological and genetic resources are fairly and equitably shared toward enhancing social, economic and environmental well-being;

(iii) Promote sustainability of water resources to ensure sufficient water quantity of acceptable quality to meet the needs of the people of ASEAN in terms of health, food security, the economy and the environment, taking into consideration the strong linkage between water, health and poverty;

(iv) Ensure sustainable management of land-based resources while enhancing optimum agricultural production;

(v) Promote the sustainable management of forest resources and critical ecosystems through the eradication of unsustainable practices as well as strengthening the preservation and management of the ASEAN Heritage Parks; and

(vi) Promote environmentally sound and socially responsible mineral development practices in the sustainable management and optimum utilisation of mineral resources.

3.4 *Promoting an ASEAN Identity*

Amidst the diversity of their historical experience and cultural heritage, common threads of historical ties, habitation of a geographical area and aspirations for peace and prosperity weave the ASEAN nations together and form the foundations of an ASEAN identity. The strategies to foster ASEAN awareness and build an ASEAN identity are:

(i) Mainstream the promotion of ASEAN awareness and regional identity in national communications plans and educational curricula, people-topeople contact including through arts, tourism and sports, especially among the youth, and the promotion of ASEAN languages learning through scholarships and exchanges of linguists;

(ii) Preserve and promote ASEAN cultural heritage through the promotion of exchanges, meetings of experts and the implementation of the ASEAN Declaration on Cultural Heritage;

(iii) Encourage dialogue amongst Member Countries to promote a deeper understanding of the regions' civilisation, cultures and religions; and

(iv) Further promote ASEAN's standing in the international community through the proactive engagement of ASEAN in international issues and strengthening communication mechanisms.

4. Goals and Strategies for Narrowing The Development Gap

Theme: Progressing Together Through Cooperation in Development

We have explicitly and repeatedly declared the need to narrow the development gap if ASEAN Member Countries are to move forward in a unified manner to realise Vision 2020. This need was first recognised and officially announced in the Hanoi Declaration on Narrowing Development Gap for Closer ASEAN Integration of 2001. It was reaffirmed in the Bali Concord II of 2003. The development gap is often manifested by disparity in per capita GDP (income). It can also be manifested by disparities in other dimensions of human development, such as life expectancy and the literacy rate. The gap can also be measured by disparity in poverty incidence. The gap must be narrowed as an end in itself, if the principle that development is a fundamental human right is to be followed. It must also be narrowed, as a necessary condition for realising the end goal of economic integration: one community of ten nations functioning as a single market and production base. Indeed, efforts to narrow the development gap would be self-reinforcing. They would help remove the biggest constraint to the formation of the AEC, which in turn would help narrow that gap.

4.1 Goal

The practical goal of the VAP for narrowing the development gap is to reduce the large disparities in terms of per capita GDP as well as other human development dimensions. The development gap exists between the ASEAN- 6 and the CLMV countries, and within the ASEAN-6 countries, where some isolated pockets of underdevelopment persist. To realise this goal, ASEAN Member Countries will determine and agree, at an appropriate forum the extent to which the gap could be realistically narrowed through the VAP by 2010 and its successor programmes or plans of action by 2015 and by 2020. By sharing experiences on how they have planned and implemented their development policies, strategies and programmes, Member Countries can draw lessons from one another and apply these to their own development strategies.

4.2 *Strategy*

To achieve the goal, technical and development cooperation among ASEAN Member Countries and with Dialogue Partners will be intensified as the main strategy to help less developed Member Countries accelerate the process of economic integration, but in a way that leads to equitable and inclusive development. A key element is to ensure that regional cooperation supplements rather than supplants national efforts. The Initiative for ASEAN Integration (IAI), ASEAN's main instrument for narrowing the development gap, will be strengthened to address development needs of the CLMV and other sub-regional areas.

This will include broadening and deepening the scope of the IAI CLMV Work Plan as well as developing innovative modalities for resource mobilisation. For the other sub-regional areas, it will involve strengthening the framework for sub-regional cooperation within ASEAN's covering policy, coordination mechanisms and work programme. Addressing both the benefit and cost of economic integration is another important feature of the strategy.

To help narrow the development gap, it will seek to ensure that the benefit of economic integration is maximised and equitably distributed across and within Member Countries. It will also seek to ensure that the cost of integration in terms of economic dislocation and disruption arising from market adjustments is minimised and the burden is equitably shared across and within Member Countries. Intensification of regional cooperation to prevent or mitigate the social costs of integration would also contribute directly towards the realisation of the two other pillars of the ASEAN Community.

The programme for narrowing the development gap will include specific regional cooperation activities aimed at assisting less developed Member Countries in removing tariff, non-tariff and physical barriers to the free flow of goods and services in the product and factor market. The programme will also include activities that supplement national efforts directly aimed at poverty reduction and the promotion of equitable and inclusive development.

5. Implementation Mechanisms

The attainment of the Bali Concord II goals does not simply mean strengthening existing cooperation activities among the ASEAN Member Countries. Deepening integration, especially in the economic sphere, will also require the Member Countries to intensify dialogue, make binding commitments, identify appropriate implementing timetables and mechanisms, extend national and regional capacities and competences, and develop institutional frameworks, responses and human resources in a range of areas that extend far beyond the existing scope of ASEAN integration.

Three major issues have to be addressed. First, resource mobilisation to support the various programmes and projects required to attain the targets; second, strengthening existing institutions and, as necessary, the establishment of appropriate institutional arrangements to facilitate coordination among the various implementing bodies and with external partners; and third, developing a monitoring and evaluation framework to track progress with regard to the attainment of integration objectives, and to assess the outcomes of programmes and projects directed towards them. There are potentially five levels of cooperation among the ASEAN Member Countries in moving towards the ASEAN Community. The levels are:

(i) Confidence-building, an initial step characterised by understanding common problems, exploring common interests and identifying mutual gains of cooperating on a regional basis;

(ii) Harmonisation, which aims to achieve compatible national approaches by ASEAN Member Countries;

(iii) Special assistance, which focuses on capacity building to bridge development gaps across Member Countries, in particular, for less developed countries;

(iv) Joint efforts, which are about developing regional approaches and regional institutions; and

(v) Regional integration and expansion, where regional institutions can act in unison to further the ASEAN cause on behalf of Member Countries to attain the intended goals and objectives.

Within each level, there are three types of development cooperation interventions that may be carried out. These three types of interventions are the formulation of regional policy initiatives, the development of regional implementation mechanisms and human capacity building. Accordingly, the implementation and coordination mechanisms for the VAP, the resource mobilisation strategy and the success measures to be used for monitoring and evaluating a project under the VAP should be fine-tuned to fit the level of cooperation and the type of development intervention.

5.1 *Resource Mobilisation*

ASEAN is entering a resource-intensive period in its progress towards the ASEAN Community. The period covered by the HPA saw the implementation of many activities intended to lay the groundwork for the more substantive measures to deepen integration that would be undertaken during the period of the VAP. Thus, it is anticipated that the VAP would essentially need more resources than the HPA. With respect to the five levels of cooperation described above, the VAP operates mainly at the first three levels, and shall also aim toward strategies involving action at the fourth level.

There are three broad sources of funding for the implementation of the VAP. These are direct contributions from all or some Member Countries towards specific activities; ASEAN pooled resources, and external funding. ASEAN will adopt a mix of these approaches towards resource mobilisation, so that internal ASEAN resources and external funding complement each other. Member Country contributions will be enhanced to form a predictable and reliable resource to facilitate implementation of the VAP. While Member Countries will continue making "in-kind" contributions to ASEAN activities and directly finance the implementation of activities at the national level, ASEAN will ensure the availability of a common pool of financial resources by establishing an ASEAN Development Fund, to be made up from contributions of Member Countries, based on a mutually acceptable scheme.

The ASEAN Development Fund shall serve as ASEAN's common pool of financial resources to support the implementation of the VAP through the following roles:

(a) For complex projects of relatively large scale, the Fund will provide seed funding for some initial activities such as feasibility studies, meetings with donor institutions, project design development, etc., leading towards obtaining major funding to implement the full project, from a Dialogue Partner or donor institution; and

(a) The fund can fully support small scale projects of a confidential or strategic nature.

Another important strategy to promote the commitment of national funding to regional programmes is to mainstream the ASEAN agenda into national development programmes. In this way, the allocation of national funds to implement regional initiatives could be more easily secured. Contributions from Dialogue Partners and other donor institutions will remain an important funding source for ASEAN, especially for funds intended to support very specific programmes and activities. Another possible source of complementary funding for ASEAN activities is the private sector. ASEAN will embark on a fund-raising programme to encourage and generate private sector support for ASEAN activities, especially those that would result in direct benefits to business and industry. Resource mobilisation from both internal and external sources to support the VAP could be undertaken through, among others, the convening of an ASEAN development cooperation forum.

5.2 *Institutional Arrangements*

The VAP has been designed along thematic lines to minimise the risk of fragmentation that may arise from a sectoral approach. Thus, there may be projects that have to be implemented jointly by two or more ASEAN bodies, or multi-component programmes where different ASEAN bodies are responsible for individual components. In such cases, the current mechanisms for closer coordination of inputs in project design and efficiency in joint management and implementation of projects need to be strengthened to ensure better coherence, complementation, efficiency, flexibility, transparency and accountability, without unduly creating additional complexity to the overall ASEAN cooperation structure. The ASEAN Secretariat will facilitate the consultation process among ASEAN bodies and seek the most efficient modality in setting up the appropriate institutional arrangement at the programme/project level. Approaches and mechanisms to closely involve other ASEAN stakeholders, including the private sector and civil society, must also be addressed.

5.3 Monitoring and Evaluation

The VAP needs to have a mechanism for monitoring and evaluation to ensure that targets are achieved, timely corrective measures are undertaken if needed, and that initiatives and activities remain consistent with the stated goals of the VAP and are responsive to emerging issues and priorities. The monitoring and evaluation mechanism should also fulfil the principles of transparency and accountability. For this purpose a monitoring and evaluation framework for the VAP has been developed, using a VAP scorecard as a basic tool. The scorecard offers the possibility of both quantitative ratings at the project level as well as qualitative assessment of impact at higher levels, and allows aggregation across diverse elements, sectors and countries to form an overall picture of VAP performance. Thus, the monitoring and evaluation process will be undertaken at two levels:

- At the micro-level, with a monitoring and evaluation plan built into each project; and
- At the macro-level, with a consolidated assessment mechanism introduced to help ensure that the overall VAP is on track in achieving its agreed objectives.

At the micro-level, different projects will have their own set of success indicators, depending on their stated objectives. At the macro-level, to permit aggregation, a generic set of criteria will be used.

The generic criteria include:

Appropriateness/Relevance

Conformity with VAP priorities
Sectoral need
Contribution to Millennium Development Goals

Quality of Design

Objectives
Programme logic
Performance indicators
Risks

Effectiveness

Achievement of planned processes and results
Outputs delivered
Outcomes achieved

Efficiency

Level of resources needed to achieve outputs and targets

Impact

Contribution to VAP goals
Avoidance of negative consequences

Sustainability

Retention of knowledge gained (knowledge management)
Risk management plan in place
On-going resources available
Political will to sustain momentum
Continuity of flow of benefits

The baseline situation at the beginning of the implementation of the VAP must be established to have a reference or benchmark for the periodic monitoring and evaluation exercises to be undertaken. One important issue to be addressed is defining which stakeholder perspectives would form part of the scorecard assessment. It is suggested that, to obtain a balanced view, the widest range of stakeholder views be obtained, i.e., the beneficiaries, the implementing bodies, the programme managers and the sponsoring ASEAN bodies should all be invited to participate in the assessment. Whenever possible, over the longer term, the review should take in relevant inputs from Dialogue Partners or their specialist agencies with interest in the project. The information gathered from the views of external evaluators would be useful in the development of new cooperation programmes and formulation of new projects with Dialogue Partners. Progress in the implementation of the VAP shall be reported annually by the Secretary-General to the ASEAN Summit through the ASEAN Ministerial Meeting (AMM) after consideration by the ASEAN Standing Committee. Formal reviews shall be undertaken by the ASEAN Secretariat every two years. Any recommendations for revisions or updating the VAP arising from the formal review shall likewise be submitted to the Summit so that guidance for the relevant sectoral bodies can be issued accordingly. A final review will be conducted in 2010 and reported to the Summit. This review will guide the preparation of the next action programme for the medium-term period of 2010-1015. We charge our Ministers and Senior Officials to begin the implementation of the VAP.

Done at Vientiane, Lao PDR, on the Twenty Ninth Day of November, Two Thousand and Four.

5

ASEAN+3 and Community Plans of Action: Socio-Culture and Security

CHAIRMAN'S STATEMENT OF THE 8TH ASEAN+3 SUMMIT

Vientiane, 29 November 2004

"Strengthening ASEAN + 3 Cooperation"

1. The ASEAN+3 Summit was held successfully on 29 November 2004 in Vientiane. The Meeting was chaired by H.E. Mr. Bounnhang Vorachith, Prime Minister of the Lao People's Democratic Republic (Lao PDR), and was attended by Heads of State/Government of ASEAN, China, Japan and the Republic of Korea. It was the first time that the Lao PDR was privileged of hosting and chairing this important Summit.
2. We welcomed President of Indonesia, H.E. Dr. Susilo Bambang Yudhoyono; Prime Minister of Malaysia, H.E. Dato' Abdullah Bin Haji Ahmad Badawi; Prime Minister of the Union of Myanmar, H.E. Mr. Lieutenant General Soe Win, and Prime Minister of Singapore, H.E. Mr. Lee Hsien Loong who participated in the ASEAN+3 Summit for the first time. We also welcomed and congratulated H.E. Gloria Macapagal-Arroyo on her re-election as President of the Philippines.
3. We exchanged views on regional and international political and security, and economic issues. We also discussed ways and mechanisms to strengthen the ASEAN+3 cooperation and its future direction. The ASEAN+3 Leaders shared their concerns on the challenges facing the region and the world such as terrorism, recent developments in Iraq, Middle East, and current situation in the Korean Peninsular, as well as the avian flu outbreak and other challenges to socio-economic development

such as poverty, development gap, etc. We reiterated our determination to further make concerted efforts to fight terrorism in East Asia and our commitment to support global efforts to combat international terrorism.

4. We reaffirmed our commitment to a peaceful and comprehensive solution to the nuclear issue on the Korean Peninsular and the necessity to engage into dialogue to promote mutual confidence and common approach. In this connection, we noted with encouragement the achievement by the three rounds of the Six-Party Talks, and we shared the view that the Six-Party Talks should be reconvened at the earliest possibility to bring about the common goal of denuclearisation of the Korean Peninsular.
5. We welcomed the accession of the Republic of Korea and the Russian Federation to the Treaty of Amity and Cooperation in Southeast Asia, and encouraged other non-Southeast Asian countries to accede to the Treaty. We shared the view that efforts should be pursued to enhance the role of the Treaty as a code of conduct for the inter-state relations in the region.
6. Taking into account the current high oil price, we supported energy cooperation, in particular, in alternative energy, such as bio-fuels, and hydroelectric power. We welcomed the outcomes of the 1st ASEAN+3 Energy Ministers Meeting in the Philippines in June 2004.
7. We noted with satisfaction the steady progress in ASEAN+3 cooperation and encouraged a speedy implementation of the short and long term measures of the East Asia Study Group (EASG), which we adopted in 2002, aiming to broadening and deepening East Asia cooperation. We also noted the expanding and deepening of ASEAN+3 sectoral cooperation, especially in the monetary and financial and economic sectors. In this regard, we welcomed the setting up of the ASEAN+3 Unit in the ASEAN Secretariat last year. We expressed the need to strengthen the ASEAN+3 Unit in coordination and implementation of the cooperation and welcomed the Plus Three countries assistance to the Unit.
8. We recognised the need to develop the Asian Bond Market, and to combat emerging diseases through new mechanisms, such as the establishment of "Outbreak Response Teams".
9. We exchanged views on the establishment of an East Asia Free Trade Area (EAFTA) and welcomed the decision by the ASEAN+3 Economic Ministers to set-up an expert group to conduct a feasibility study on EAFTA.
10. The Leaders of the Plus Three countries supported ASEAN Leaders' decision to convene the first East Asia Summit (EAS) in Malaysia in 2005. The ASEAN+3 Leaders supported Japan's proposal to host an

ASEAN+3 Foreign Ministers Meeting in Kyoto in May 2005 to discuss the concept and modalities of an EAS.

11. We agreed that the establishment of an East Asian Community is a long-term objective. We reaffirmed the role of ASEAN+3 process as the main vehicle for the eventual establishment of an East Asian Community. China, Japan, and the Republic of Korea reiterated their support for ASEAN's role as the major driving force in East Asia cooperation. In addition, to mark the 10th Anniversary of the ASEAN+3 cooperation in 2007, we agreed to consider the idea of issuing the 2nd Joint Statement on East Asia cooperation as well as a work plan to consolidate the existing and future cooperation.
12. The Leaders of China, Japan and the Republic of Korea welcomed the adoption of the Vientiane Action Programme (VAP) and expressed their support to ASEAN in implementing activities and projects in support of the VAP. They agreed to strengthen their efforts in assisting ASEAN to narrow the development gaps within ASEAN, and between ASEAN and the Plus Three countries.
13. The Leaders of China, Japan and the Republic of Korea also welcomed the CLMV and the CLV Summits and expressed their support to the implementation of the Vientiane Declaration on Enhancing Economic Cooperation and Integration among Cambodia, Laos, Myanmar and Viet Nam; and the Vientiane Declaration on the Establishment of the Cambodia-Laos-Viet Nam Development Triangle.
14. The ASEAN Leaders acknowledged with appreciation China, Japan, and the Republic of Korea for their assistance in implementing projects under the IAI Work Plan. They also expressed appreciation to China, Japan and the Republic of Korea for their support to Cambodia, Laos and Myanmar to participate in the Asia-Europe Meeting.

ASEAN SOCIO-CULTURAL COMMUNITY (ASCC) PLAN OF ACTION

Specific Measures

I. Building a Community of Caring Societies

(a) Implement an "MDG Plus" initiative to accelerate poverty reduction in ASEAN;

(b) Facilitate universal access to education for vulnerable groups (youth, women, persons with disabilities) to obtain the skills and knowledge necessary for gainful employment and meaningful participation in society;

(c) Strengthen educational networks and institutional collaboration to improve standards of, and access to, education;

(d) Ensure a better future for children by safeguarding their rights, ensuring their survival and development, and protecting them from abuse, neglect and violence;

(e) Create enabling environments to prepare the youth for their future role as ASEAN citizens equipped with the necessary skills in leadership, entrepreneurship, and technical and vocational abilities;

(f) Promote the equitable and effective participation of women in all fields both as agents and beneficiaries of development;

(g) Promote community-based support systems for the elderly to supplement the role of families as primary caregiver and to build the capacity of health care professionals to address the needs of the elderly;

(h) Ensure access of persons with disabilities to opportunities and protection against all forms of discrimination;

(i) Strengthen social welfare mechanisms to make them more responsive to emerging social issues resulting from globalisation as well as demographic shifts;

(j) Strengthen regional mechanisms and networks for combating human trafficking;

(k) Ensure a healthy ASEAN Community living in harmony and safe environments;

(l) Promote an enabling environment for the prevention of HIV/AIDS and for the comprehensive treatment, care and support for people living with HIV/AIDS in ASEAN;

(m) Enhance the effectiveness of regional surveillance, preparedness, early warning, and response to emerging and resurging infectious diseases;

(m) Ensure access to safe, quality and affordable medicines by building ASEAN capacity and competitiveness in pharmaceuticals as well as traditional medicines/complementary and alternative medicines;

(o) Promote an enabling environment that allows ASEAN citizens to make healthy lifestyle choices accessible, affordable and sustainable and consistent with their views, beliefs, and culture in supportive environments;

(p) Strengthen food security by enhancing stability in food production and supply and protect the region against fluctuations in production of basic commodities;

(q) Strengthen food safety systems to ensure the protection of consumers' health by increasing the level of credibility and competency of regulatory authorities, and enhancing industry and consumer awareness and participation in food safety;

(r) Promote activities related to community-based drug prevention aimed at families, schools and youth through publications, campaigns and training;

(s) Strengthen cooperation with the private sector, in creating a science and technology community in the region;

(t) Promote applied science and technology in socio-economic activities to improve social well-being; and

(u) Establish efficient and well-functioning regional mechanisms for disaster prevention and management, including a coordinated response action plan in ASEAN and a network of training institutes.

II. Managing the Social Impact of Economic Integration

(a) Support the efforts of the ASEAN Economic Community to facilitate the movement of professional and skilled persons, including mutual skills recognition arrangements for qualification in professional services to realise regional economic integration in ASEAN;

(b) Develop a well-prepared labour force in ASEAN that would benefit from and cope with the challenges of regional economic integration;

(c) Establish a technologically competitive ASEAN, competent in strategic and enabling technologies, with an adequate pool of technically trained manpower, strong networks of scientific and technical institutions and centres of excellence;

(d) Strengthen systems of social protection at the national level and work towards adoption of appropriate measures at the regional level to provide a minimum uniform coverage for skilled workers in the region;

(e) Promote sound industrial relations, industrial harmony, high productivity and social practice through tripartite cooperation;

(f) Secure the benefits of trade liberalisation in healthcare services in terms of increased availability and better accessibility to quality and affordable health-related products and services;

(g) Enhance the competitiveness of ASEAN health and related industries;

(h) Strengthen regional training on management of innovation and technology, and establish a mechanism for its regional certification and accreditation; and

(i) Consider the establishment of centres for training and research to support the development of human resources and institutional capacity in regional as well as international cooperation.

III. Enhancing Environmental Sustainability

(a) Effectively address global environmental concerns by building national capacities to address issues and commitments to multilateral environmental agreements through awareness-raising and informed policy choices;

(b) Effectively manage transboundary haze pollution resulting from land

and/or forest fires through concerted national efforts and intensified regional action and international cooperation in accordance with the provisions of the ASEAN Agreement on Transboundary Haze Pollution (the Haze Agreement), including the operationalisation of the ASEAN Centre for Transboundary Haze Pollution Control and the ASEAN Haze Fund;

(c) Promote the sustainable use of ASEAN's coastal and marine environment through the implementation of the ASEAN criteria for marine waters, and marine heritage and protected areas;

(d) Ensure the conservation of ASEAN's rich biological diversity through the implementation of the ASEAN Framework Agreement on Access to, and Equitable Sharing of Genetic and Biological Resources (expected to be concluded in 2004);

(e) Promote the sustainable management of forest resources, which include protection of forests in an ecologically sound and integrated manner by developing and adopting common criteria for sustainable forest management in ASEAN, and eradicating unsustainable practices and related activities;

(f) Promote the preservation of ASEAN Heritage Parks through coordinated systems of management;

(g) Promote sustainability of water resources to ensure sufficient water quantity of acceptable quality to meet the needs of ASEAN in terms of health, food security and environmental sustainability through among others, the promotion of integrated river basin management and awareness promotion;

(h) Promote environmental education through formal and non-formal education systems, capacity building and networking;

(i) Promote environmentally-sound technologies in active partnership with the business sector through innovative financial mechanisms and labelling schemes;

(j) Promote quality living standards in ASEAN cities/urban areas by achieving standards for environmental pollution reduction, including ensuring good ambient air and water quality, and minimum solid waste disposal;

(k) Establish parameters for harmonising environmental policies, legislation, regulations, standards and databases, and preparing regular state of the environment reports; and

(l) Pursue joint research in developing alternative fuels in order to prevent environmental devastation and resource exhaustion.

IV. Strengthening the Foundations of Regional Social Cohesion

(a) Promote ASEAN awareness with the ultimate goal of fostering an ASEAN regional identity by promoting interactions and exchanges among artists, writers, media practitioners, scholars, students, cultural entrepreneurs, professionals, experts in culture and sports and others;

(b) Promote people-to-people contact, especially among the youth through youth volunteer programmes and youth camps;

(c) Promote ASEAN languages learning through scholarships and exchange of linguists;

(d) Coordinate efforts for the documentation, preservation and safeguarding of national and regional treasures and other properties, antiquities, and works of historic, archaeological, anthropological and scientific significance;

(e) Enhance ASEAN cooperation in culture and information to formulate and implement effective and efficient programmes in a concerted manner in order to promote the rich and vast cultures of ASEAN;

(f) Promote confidence-building at the national and regional levels by promoting the learning of core values, customs and traditions and integrating multiple perspectives on civilisations through regular dialogue mechanisms; and

(g) Promote an image of unity, stability and dynamism of ASEAN by strengthening contacts with mass media, the international fora and other channels of communication.

ASEAN SECURITY COMMUNITY PLAN OF ACTION

Introduction

Leaders at the Ninth ASEAN Summit in Bali adopted the Declaration of ASEAN Concord II (Bali Concord II), which stipulated the establishment of an ASEAN Community resting on three pillars: an ASEAN Security Community, an ASEAN Economic Community and an ASEAN Socio-Cultural Community. These three pillars shall be developed and implemented in a parallel and balanced manner. Recognising the strong interconnections among political, economic and social realities, the ASEAN Security Community acknowledges the principle of comprehensive security, and commits to address the broad political, economic, social and cultural aspects of building an ASEAN Community.

It is also acknowledged that political and social stability, economic prosperity, narrowed development gap, poverty alleviation and reduction of social disparity would constitute strong foundation for a sustained ASC given its subscription to the principle of comprehensive security. The realisation of an ASEAN Security Community would ensure that countries in the region live at peace with one another and with the world at large in a just, democratic and harmonious environment. The ASC would be based on shared norms and rules of good conduct in inter-state relations; effective conflict prevention and resolution mechanisms; and post-conflict peace building activities.

The ASC promotes an ASEAN-wide political and security cooperation in consonance with the ASEAN Vision 2020 rather than a defence pact, military alliance or a joint foreign policy. The ASC Plan of Action is mutually-reinforcing with bilateral cooperation between ASEAN Member Countries while recognising the sovereign rights of the Member Countries to pursue their individual foreign policies and defence arrangements.

In addressing future security challenges, ASEAN Member Countries share the responsibility for strengthening peace, stability and security of the region free from foreign military interference in any form or manifestation. The ASC shall contribute to the further promotion of peace and security in the wider Asia Pacific region. In this regard, the ASC is open and outward looking, engaging ASEAN's friends and Dialogue Partners to promote peace and stability in the region.

The ASC will reflect ASEAN's determination to move forward the stages of ASEAN Regional Forum (ARF) at a pace comfortable to all. In this regard, the ASC will strengthen ASEAN's role as the driving force in the ARF. Since its inception in 1967, ASEAN has developed confidence and maturity to address issues of common concern as one ASEAN family. The ASC process shall therefore be progressive.

This process shall be guided by well-established principles of non-interference, consensus-based decision-making, national and regional resilience, respect for the national sovereignty, the renunciation of the threat or the use of force, and peaceful settlement of differences and disputes which have served as the foundation of ASEAN cooperation. ASEAN shall strengthen existing initiatives, launch new ones and set appropriate implementation frameworks.

The ASC upholds the existing ASEAN political instruments such as the Declaration on ZOPFAN, the TAC and the SEANWFZ Treaty, which shall play a pivotal role in the area of confidence building measures, preventive diplomacy and the approaches to conflict resolution. It shall abide by the UN Charter and other principles of international law. ASEAN shall explore innovative ways to implement the Plan of Action which comprises six components, but not limited to, as follows: political development, shaping and sharing of norms, conflict prevention, conflict resolution, post-conflict peace building, and implementing mechanisms. A list of areas of activities, which is non-exhaustive, is provided to ensure a coordinated process of cooperation towards an ASEAN Security Community.

I. Political Development

One of the main objectives of the ASEAN Security Community as envisaged in the Bali Concord II is to bring ASEAN's political and security cooperation to a higher plane. In working towards this objective, ASEAN Member Countries shall promote political development in support of ASEAN Leaders' shared vision and common values to achieve peace, stability, democracy and prosperity in the region. This is the highest political commitment that would serve as the basis for ASEAN political cooperation.

In order to better respond to the new dynamics within the respective ASEAN Member Countries, ASEAN shall nurture such common socio-political values and principles. In this context, ASEAN Member Countries shall not condone unconstitutional and undemocratic changes of government or the use of their territory for any actions undermining peace, security and stability of other ASEAN Member Countries. A conducive political environment will ensure continued peace, security and stability in the region, in which member countries shall rely exclusively on peaceful processes in settling intra-regional differences and disputes and consider their individual security as fundamentally linked together and bound by geographic location, common vision and objectives.

II. Shaping and Sharing of Norms

Shaping and sharing of norms aim at achieving a standard of common adherence to norms of good conduct among members of the ASEAN Community; consolidating and strengthening ASEAN's solidarity, cohesiveness and harmony (the "we feeling"); and contributing to the building of a democratic, tolerant, participatory and transparent community in Southeast Asia. These norms setting activities shall adhere to the following fundamental principles:

1. Non-alignment;
2. Fostering of peace-oriented attitudes of ASEAN Member Countries;
3. Conflict resolution through non-violent means;
4. Renunciation of nuclear weapons and other weapons of mass destruction and avoidance of arms race in Southeast Asia; and
5. Renunciation of the threat or the use of force.

ASEAN Member Countries shall therefore engage in such activities as strengthening the ASEAN Declaration of 1967, the ZOPFAN, the TAC and the SEANWFZ regimes, developing regional legal frameworks, and establishing a Code of Conduct in the South China Sea.

III. Conflict Prevention

Based on the principles contained in the TAC, which is the key code of conduct governing relations between states and diplomatic instrument for the promotion of peace, security and stability in the region, the objectives of conflict prevention shall be:

1. To strengthen confidence and trust within the Community;
2. To mitigate tensions and prevent disputes from arising between or among member countries as well as between member countries and non-ASEAN countries; and
3. To prevent the escalation of existing disputes.

ASEAN Member Countries shall enhance security cooperation by strengthening confidence building measures; carrying out preventive diplomacy; resolving outstanding regional issues; as well as enhancing cooperation on non-traditional security issues.

IV. Conflict Resolution

It is essential that any disputes and conflicts involving ASEAN Member Countries be resolved in a peaceful way and in the spirit of promoting peace, security and stability in the region. While continuing to use national, bilateral and international mechanisms, ASEAN Member Countries shall endeavour to use the existing regional dispute settlement mechanisms and processes in the political and security areas and work towards innovative modalities including arrangements to maintain regional peace and security so as to better serve theirs as well as collective interests of all members for peace and security.

V. Post-conflict Peace Building

Post-conflict peace building seeks to create the conditions necessary for a sustainable peace in conflict-torn areas and to prevent the resurgence of conflict. It is a process involving broad-based inter-agency cooperation and coordination across a wide range of issues. ASEAN activities related to post-conflict peace building shall include the establishment of appropriate mechanisms and mobilisation of resources. As an ASEAN family, members should assist each other in post-conflict peace building efforts, such as humanitarian relief assistance, reconstruction and rehabilitation.

VI. Implementing Mechanisms

To ensure the effective implementation of this Plan of Action, the following measures will be undertaken:

1. The AMM shall take necessary follow-up measures to implement this Plan of Action including consultation and coordination with other relevant ASEAN ministerial bodies; to set-up *ad-hoc* groups as appropriate; and to report annually the progress of implementation to the ASEAN Summit; as well as to introduce new measures and activities to strengthen the ASEAN Security Community as appropriate;
2. The AMM shall undertake overall review of progress of this Plan of Action. The AMM shall inscribe permanently an agenda item entitled

"Implementation of the ASC Plan of Action" in the agenda of its meetings; and

3. The Secretary-General of ASEAN shall assist the ASEAN Chair in monitoring and reviewing the progress of implementation of this Plan of Action.

VII. Areas of Activities

To realise the ASEAN Security Community by 2020, ASEAN shall endeavour to work towards the implementation of the areas of activities in the following Annex. It is acknowledged that some of these activities are already ongoing and at various stages of implementation. Additional activities could also be implemented in the future. ASEAN will make every effort to promptly carry out activities which gain consensus support.

ASEAN SECURITY COMMUNITY PLAN OF ACTION

Activities

I. Political Development

1. Promotion of a just, democratic and harmonious environment :
   - (a) Strengthening democratic institutions and popular participation;
   - (b) Promoting understanding and appreciation of political system, culture and history of ASEAN Member Countries;
   - (c) Strengthening the rule of law and judiciary systems, legal infrastructure and capacity building;
   - (d) Promoting free flow of information among and within ASEAN Member Countries;
   - (e) Enhancing good governance in public and private sectors;
   - (f) Strengthening effective and efficient civil services; and
   - (g) Preventing and combating corruption.
2. Promotion of human rights and obligations:
   - (a) Establishing a network among existing human rights mechanisms;
   - (b) Protecting vulnerable groups including women, children, people with disabilities, and migrant workers; and
   - (c) Promoting education and public awareness on human rights.
3. Promotion of people-to-people contacts:
   - (a) Encouraging the role of ASEAN Inter-Parliamentary Organisation (AIPO) in political and security cooperation;
   - (b) Promoting public participation and the contribution of the ASEAN People's Assembly (APA) to the ASEAN community building;
   - (c) Strengthening the role of the ASEAN Foundation;

(d) Encouraging the contribution of ASEAN-ISIS to political development;

(e) Strengthening the role of the ASEAN Business Advisory Council (ABAC); and

(f) Supporting the activities of the ASEAN University Network.

II. Shaping and Sharing of Norms

1. Strengthening the TAC regime:
   (a) Accession to the TAC by non-ASEAN countries; and
   (b) Periodic assessment of the implementation of the TAC and exploration of ways and means for its effective implementation.
2. Working towards development of an ASEAN Charter which will *inter alia* reaffirm ASEAN's goals and principles in inter-state relations, in particular the collective responsibilities of all ASEAN Member Countries in ensuring non-aggression and respect for each other's sovereignty and territorial integrity; the promotion and protection of human rights; the maintenance of political stability, regional peace and economic progress; and the establishment of effective and efficient institutional framework for ASEAN.
3. Resolving all outstanding issues to ensure early signing of the Nuclear Weapon States to the Protocol to the SEANWFZ Treaty.
4. ASEAN Treaty on Mutual Legal Assistance (MLA) Agreement:
   (a) Compilation of existing bilateral MLA Agreements among ASEAN Member Countries and between ASEAN and other countries;
   (b) Identification of issues relating to the establishment of an ASEAN MLA Agreement; and
   (c) Conclusion of ASEAN MLA Agreement.
5. ASEAN Extradition Treaty as envisaged by the 1976 Declaration of ASEAN Concord:
   (a) Identification of ASEAN political decisions to establish Extradition Treaty and bilateral Extradition Treaties between ASEAN Member Countries; and
   (b) Establishment of a working group on ASEAN Extradition Treaty under the purview of ASEAN Senior Law Officials Meeting (ASLOM).
6. Ensuring the implementation of the Declaration on the Conduct of Parties in the South China Sea (DOC) through, *inter alia*:
   (a) Establishing an ASEAN–China Working Group on the Implementation of the DOC;

(b) Establishing a review mechanism on the implementation of the DOC; and

(c) Working towards the adoption of the Code of Conduct in South China Sea (COC).

7. ASEAN Convention on Counter Terrorism:

(a) Identification and analysis or assessment of documents and relevant instruments related to counter terrorism;

(b) Working towards accession to and ratification of the relevant UN conventions on counter terrorism; and

(c) Preparation, negotiation and conclusion of an ASEAN convention on counter terrorism.

III. Conflict Prevention

1. Strengthening Confidence Building Measures:

(a) Organising and conducting regional military exchanges among high-ranking officials, military academies, and staff colleges of ASEAN Member Countries, apart from increasing bilateral visits and exchanges;

(b) Periodic publication of strategic assessments on the security environment, defence policies, and other security issues, such as Defence White Papers and equivalent documents;

(c) Working towards convening of an annual ASEAN Defence Ministers Meeting (ADMM);

(d) Promoting exchange of observers at military exercises;

(e) Establishment of an ASEAN Arms Register to be administered by the ASEAN Secretariat, in line with a similar activity being conducted in the ARF;

(f) Utilising military and civilian personnel in disaster relief operation;

(g) Promotion of civil-military relations; and

(h) Exploring joint development and sharing of resources.

2. Strengthening Preventive Measures:

(a) Publishing an ASEAN Members Annual Security Outlook;

(b) Voluntary briefing by ASEAN Member Countries on national security issues; and

(c) Developing an ASEAN early warning system based on existing mechanisms to prevent occurrence/escalation of conflicts.

3. Strengthening the ARF process in support of the ASEAN Security Community:

(a) ARF Unit within the ASEAN Secretariat;

(b) Enhanced role of the ARF Chair;

(c) Strengthening ASEAN's role in addressing the four overlapping issues of CBMs and Preventive Diplomacy (Enhanced role of the ARF Chair, Annual Security Outlook, Register of Experts/Eminent Persons, Voluntary Briefing on Regional Issues); and

(d) Moving the ARF to the preventive diplomacy stage and beyond (implementation of the Concept Paper on Preventive Diplomacy, establishment of an Intersessional Support Group on Preventive Diplomacy).

4. Enhancing cooperation on non-traditional security issues:

(a) Combating transnational crimes and other trans-boundary problems, including money laundering, illegal migration, smuggling and illegal trade of natural resources, trafficking in persons, drugs and precursors, as well as communicable diseases;

(b) Promoting ASEAN maritime security cooperation;

(c) Strengthening law enforcement cooperation; and

(d) Promoting cooperation on environmental issues including haze, pollution and floods.

5. Strengthening efforts in maintaining respect for territorial integrity, sovereignty and unity of member countries as stipulated in the Declaration on Principles of International Law Concerning Friendly Relations and Cooperation among States in Accordance with the Charter of the United Nations:

(a) Strengthening cooperation on the state's obligation not to intervene in the affairs of other neighbouring states, including refraining from the use of military, political, economic or other form of coercion aimed against the political independence or territorial integrity of other neighbouring states;

(b) Enhancing cooperation among ASEAN Member Countries to prevent the organisation, instigation, assistance and participation in terrorist acts in other neighbouring ASEAN Member Countries;

(c) Preventing the use of territory of any ASEAN Member Country as base for any activities against security and stability of neighbouring ASEAN Member Countries; and

(d) Strengthening cooperation to address subversive and insurgency activities aimed at neighbouring ASEAN Member Countries.

6. Strengthening cooperation to address threats and challenges posed by separatism.

IV. Conflict Resolution

1. Strengthening Dispute Settlement Mechanisms:
   (a) The use of existing modes of pacific settlement of disputes such as negotiations and consultations, good offices, conciliation and mediation by all ASEAN Member Countries, or use of the High Council of the TAC as a preferred option; and
   (b) If the High Council so requires, it may establish on an ad hoc basis an Experts Advisory Committee (EAC) or an Eminent Persons Group (EPG), which may extend assistance to the High Council to provide advice or counsel on the settlement of disputes upon request, in accordance with the Rules of Procedure of the High Council of TAC.
2. Developing regional cooperation for maintenance of peace and stability:
   (a) Promoting technical cooperation with the UN and relevant regional organisations in order to benefit from their expertise and experiences;
   (b) Establishing/assigning national focal points for regional cooperation for maintenance of peace and stability;
   (c) Utilisation of national peace keeping centres which currently exist, or are being planned, in some ASEAN Member Countries to establish regional arrangement for the maintenance of peace and stability; and
   (d) Establishing a network among existing ASEAN Member Countries' peace keeping centres to conduct joint planning, training, and sharing of experiences, with a view to establishing an ASEAN arrangement for the maintenance of peace and stability.
3. Developing Supporting Initiatives:
   (a) Promoting exchange and cooperation among ASEAN centres of excellence on peace, and conflict management and resolution studies; and
   (b) Considering the establishment of an ASEAN Institute for Peace and Reconciliation.

V. Post-conflict Peace Building

1. Strengthening ASEAN humanitarian assistance:
   (a) Providing safe havens in conflict areas;
   (b) Ensuring the delivery of basic services or assistance to victims of conflict;
   (c) Orderly repatriation of refugees/displaced persons and resettlement of internally displaced persons;

(d) Ensuring safety of humanitarian relief assistance workers;

(e) Promoting the role of humanitarian relief assistance organisations;

(f) Considering the establishment of an ASEAN Humanitarian Assistance Centre; and

(g) Intensifying cooperation with the United Nations and other organisations/donor countries.

2. Developing cooperation in post-conflict reconstruction and rehabilitation in affected areas by:

   (a) Undertaking human resources development and capacity building;

   (b) Assisting in institutional building and promoting popular participation;

   (c) Reducing inter-communal tensions through educational exchanges and curriculum reform; and

   (d) Increasing cooperation in reconciliation and promotion of a culture of peace.

3. Establishing a mechanism to mobilise necessary resources to facilitate post-conflict peace building (e.g. a Stability Fund), including through cooperation with donor countries and international institutions.

6

Priority Sectors' Integration

The ASEAN Leaders agreed to accelerate the integration of 11 priority sector under the Framework Agreement for the Integration of Priority Sectors and 11 ASEAN Sectoral Integration Protocols reaffirming ASEAN's commitment to fast track the integration towards the ASEAN Economic Community (AEC) that ASEAN Leaders agreed to establish by 2020. The AEC is envisaged as a single market and production base with free flow of goods, services, investment, skilled labor and freer flow of capital. The 11 priority sectors are electronics, e-ASEAN, healthcare, wood-based products, automotives, rubber-based products, textiles and apparels, agro-based products, fisheries, air travel and tourism.

These sectors were selected on the basis of comparative advantage in natural resource endowments, labour skills and cost competitiveness, and value-added contribution to ASEAN's economy. These selected sectors accounted for more than 50% of intra-ASEAN trade in 2003. In value terms, the priority sectors contributed US$ 48.4 billion and US$ 43.4 billion of intra-ASEAN exports and imports, respectively, in 2003. Attached to each protocol is a roadmap to serve as the basis for economic integration of each of the priority sectors. These roadmaps were prepared with active involvement of the private sector. The roadmaps aim to:

(i) enhance the competitiveness of ASEAN;

(ii) strengthen regional integration efforts through liberalization, facilitation and promotion measures; and

(iii) promote private sector participation.

The roadmap includes specific measures that are of direct relevance to each sector, as well as common measures that cut across all priority integration sectors to be implemented with timelines from now on to the year 2010. According to the roadmaps, import duties for products under the priority sectors will be fully eliminated by 2007 for ASEAN-6 and 2012 for the new members of ASEAN or 3 years earlier than the original target under the ASEAN Free Trade Area (AFTA). Approximately 4,000 tariff lines or about 40% of total tariff lines in ASEAN are included in the fast track integration. Apart from tariff elimination, the roadmaps will also focus on trade and investment facilitation measures. Among others, the ASEAN Single Window will be developed, including the electronic processing of trade documents at national and regional levels.

Product standards and technical regulations will be harmonized, mutual recognition of test reports and certification will be concluded to reduce the transaction costs of doing business in ASEAN. ASEAN nationals traveling within ASEAN will be exempted from visa. Movement of business people, experts, professionals and talents will be facilitated.

It is expected that implementing the measures in the roadmaps will not only accelerate the integration of ASEAN but also serve as a showcase for more sectors to be included in the accelerated integration programme. This initial exercise is critical in paving the way for the deeper economic integration of ASEAN and to achieve the objective of the ASEAN Economic Community by 2020 or earlier. It is also critical in preparing ASEAN in the light of the various free trade area negotiations being pursued with China, India, Japan, Australia and New Zealand and Republic of Korea.

ASEAN FRAMEWORK AGREEMENT FOR THE INTEGRATION OF PRIORITY SECTORS: VIENTIANE, 29TH NOVEMBER 2004

We, the Heads of Government/State of Brunei Darussalam, the Kingdom of Cambodia, the Republic of Indonesia, the Lao People's Democratic Republic (hereinafter referred to as "Lao PDR"), Malaysia, the Union of Myanmar, the Republic of the Philippines, the Republic of Singapore, the Kingdom of Thailand and the Socialist Republic of Viet Nam, Member States of the Association of South East Asian Nations (hereinafter collectively referred to as "ASEAN" or "Member States" or singularly as "Member State");

Recalling the Declaration of ASEAN Concord II (Bali Concord II) adopted during the 9th ASEAN Summit in Bali, Indonesia on 7 October 2003, pursuant to which ASEAN is committed to deepen and broaden its internal economic integration and linkages, with the participation of the private sector, to realise an ASEAN Economic Community;

Reaffirming that the ASEAN Economic Community shall be the end-goal of ASEAN economic integration as outlined in the ASEAN Vision 2020;

Reiterating that the ASEAN Economic Community will result in ASEAN becoming a single market and production base, turning the diversity that characterises the region into opportunities and business complementation to make ASEAN a more dynamic and stronger segment of the global supply chain and the world economy;

Desiring to combine the economic strengths of Member States in key strategic sectors for regional cohesiveness and enhanced global competitiveness by accelerating the integration of the eleven priority sectors in the Bali Concord II and such other sectors as may be agreed upon as necessary,

Have agreed as follows:

PART I: OBJECTIVE, DEFINITION AND APPLICATION

Article 1: Objective

The objective of this ASEAN Framework Agreement for the Integration of Priority Sectors (hereinafter referred to as the "Framework Agreement") is to identify measures to be implemented, with clear timelines, in a mutually beneficial manner, by Member States in respect of the priority sectors identified in paragraph 1 of Article 2 of this Framework Agreement so as to enable the progressive, expeditious and systematic integration of these sectors in ASEAN.

Article 2: Definition

For the purposes of this Framework Agreement:

1. "priority sectors" means:

   (a) the 11 sectors listed below:

      (i) agro-based products;
      (ii) air travel;
      (iii) automotives;
      (iv) e-ASEAN;
      (v) electronics;
      (vi) fisheries;
      (vii) healthcare;
      (viii) rubber-based products;
      (ix) textiles and apparels;
      (x) tourism;
      (xi) wood-based products; and

   (b) such other sectors as may be identified by the Ministers responsible for ASEAN economic integration under Articles 19 and 20 of this Framework Agreement.

   (c) Air travel shall be deemed to refer to air transport.

2. "ASEAN Sectoral Integration Protocol" means the individual integration protocol for each priority sector which identifies the common and specific measures for each priority sector.
3. "ASEAN-6" means Brunei Darussalam, Indonesia, Malaysia, the Philippines, Singapore and Thailand.
4. "CLMV" means Cambodia, Lao PDR, Myanmar, and Viet Nam.

Article 3: Applicability to the ASEAN Sectoral Integration Protocols

The provisions of this Framework Agreement shall apply to each priority sector and be deemed to be included in each ASEAN Sectoral Integration Protocol unless provided otherwise therein.

PART II: LIBERALISATION

Article 4: Trade in Goods

1. Member States shall eliminate all Common Effective Preferential Tariff for the ASEAN Free Trade Area (CEPT-AFTA) tariffs in relation to products (other than those in the sensitive, highly sensitive and general exception lists) covered by the individual ASEAN Sectoral Integration Protocols, except those listed in accompanying negative lists to the Protocols, which in total for each Member State shall not exceed 15% of the total product list appearing as Annex XII to this Framework Agreement, by:
   (a) 1 January 2007 for ASEAN-6; and
   (b) 1 January 2012 for CLMV.
2. Member States shall implement the following actions in relation to non-tariff measures (hereinafter referred to as "NTMs") to ensure transparency, in accordance with the timelines indicated:
   (a) establish the database of ASEAN NTMs by 30 June 2004;
   (b) establish criteria to identify NTMs that are barriers to trade by 30 June 2005; and
   (c) establish a definitive work programme for the removal of NTMs that are barriers to trade by 31 December 2005.
3. Member States shall adopt the WTO Agreement on Import Licensing Procedures and develop common implementation guidelines appropriate for ASEAN for this purpose by 31 December 2004.
4. Member States shall endeavour to expand the coverage of the ASEAN Integration System of Preferences (AISP) Scheme by including products in the priority sectors.

Article 5: Trade in Services

Member States shall integrate trade in services by:

(a) setting clear targets and schedules for progressive liberalisation for each round of negotiations towards achieving freer flow of trade in services earlier than 2020;

(b) accelerating the service liberalisation for the priority sectors by 2010;

(c) accelerating the development of Mutual Recognition Arrangements (hereinafter referred to as "MRAs") by 1 January 2008;

(d) applying the ASEAN-X formula; and

(e) promoting joint ventures and cooperation, including third country markets.

Article 6: Investment

Member States shall undertake the following measures:

(a) Accelerate the opening up of sectors currently in the Sensitive List (hereinafter referred to as "SL") by transferring these sectors into the Temporary Exclusion List (hereinafter referred to as "TEL") under the Framework Agreement on the ASEAN Investment Area (AIA), using the ASEAN-X formula, beginning 2004.

(b) Reduce restrictive investment measures in the SL beginning 2004 and complete the progressive elimination of restrictive investment measures in the TEL by 31 December 2010 for ASEAN-6, 2013 for Viet Nam and 2015 for Cambodia, Lao PDR and Myanmar.

(c) Identify programmes and activities to promote investments in ASEAN by 31 December 2005.

(d) Promote manufacturing processes in ASEAN to take advantage of their comparative strengths through:

    (i) the establishment of a network of ASEAN free trade zones to facilitate outsourcing activities beginning 2005; and

    (ii) undertaking more efficient joint ASEAN facilitation and promotion measures to promote foreign direct investments on an ongoing basis.

(e) Promote and facilitate joint/cross border investments in manufacturing activities, on an ongoing basis, through:

    (i) special incentives, where appropriate, to be given by CLMV for investments from ASEAN; and

    (ii) special measures, where appropriate, to be given by ASEAN-6 to promote and facilitate relocation of investment to CLMV especially for labour intensive manufacturing activities.

PART III: TRADE AND INVESTMENT FACILITATION

Article 7: Rules of Origin

Member States shall, by 31 December 2004, improve the CEPT Rules of Origin by:

(a) making them more transparent, predictable and standardised, taking into account the best practices of other Regional Trade Agreements, including the rules of origin of the WTO; and

(b) adopting substantial transformation as an alternative criteria for conferring origin status.

Article 8: Customs Procedures

Member States shall implement the following measures, in accordance with the timelines indicated, so as to expedite customs clearance and simplify customs procedures:

(a) Extend the application of the ASEAN Harmonised Tariff Nomenclature (AHTN) for extra-ASEAN trade on an on-going basis.

(b) Simplify, improve and harmonise customs declaration forms by 31 December 2005.

(c) Ensure full implementation of the Green Lane System for CEPT products or similar system at entry points of all Member States by 31 December 2004.

(d) Develop common implementation guidelines, by 31 December 2004, to fulfil the obligations of the WTO Agreement on Customs Valuation.

(e) Each ASEAN customs authority to adopt a service commitment (client charter) by 31 December 2004; and

(f) Develop the Single Window approach, including the electronic processing of trade documents at national and regional level by 31 December 2005.

Article 9: Standards and Conformance

Member States shall take the following steps to accelerate the development of MRAs and harmonise product standards and technical regulations:

(a) Accelerate the implementation and where appropriate the development of sectoral MRAs for priority sectors beginning 1 January 2005.

(b) Encourage domestic regulators to recognise test reports issued by testing laboratories which are accredited by national accreditation bodies in ASEAN that are signatories to International Laboratory Accreditation Cooperation (ILAC) and Asia-Pacific Laboratory Accreditation Cooperation (APLAC) MRAs.

(c) Set, by 31 December 2005, clear targets and schedules for harmonisation of standards in the priority sectors wherever required. Where international standards are not available and when requested by industry, align national standards among Member States.

(d) Harmonise and/or develop technical regulations as appropriate, for national application by 31 December 2010.

(e) Ensure compliance with the requirements of the WTO Agreements on Technical Barriers to Trade and the Application of Sanitary and Phyto-Sanitary Measures.

(f) Explore the development of ASEAN policy on standards and conformance to further facilitate the realisation of the ASEAN Economic Community, beginning 2005.

Article 10: Logistics Services

Expedite the development of integrated transport logistics services within ASEAN through:

(a) Promotion of efficient door-to-door cargo transport and cross-border transport facilitation through the expeditious implementation of the ASEAN Framework Agreement on the Facilitation of Goods in Transit, and the ASEAN Framework Agreement on Multimodal Transport;

(b) Improvement of land transport network infrastructures and services to achieve better inter-connectivity, inter-operability and inter-modality with the national, regional and international maritime and air transport gateways.

(c) Strengthening intra-ASEAN maritime and shipping transport services; and

(d) Establishment of enabling and conducive policy environment for increased private sector involvement and/or public-private partnerships in the development of transport infrastructure and the provision and operation of transport logistics facilities and services.

Article 11: Facilitation of Travel in ASEAN

Member States shall:

(a) harmonise procedures for the issuance of visas to international travelers in ASEAN by 31 December 2004; and

(b) provide visa exemption for intra-ASEAN travel by ASEAN nationals by 2005.

Article 12: Movement of Business Persons, Experts, Professionals, Skilled Labour and Talents

Member States shall, taking into account their respective domestic laws and regulations:

(a) develop an ASEAN agreement to facilitate the movement of business persons, including the adoption of an ASEAN Travel Card, by 31 December 2005;
(b) develop an ASEAN agreement to facilitate the movement of experts, professionals, skilled labour and talents by 31 December 2005; and
(c) accelerate completion of MRAs to facilitate free movement of experts, professionals, skilled labour and talents in ASEAN by 31 December 2008.

PART IV: PROMOTION AND MONITORING

Article 13: Trade and Investment Promotion

Member States shall, beginning 2005 and on an ongoing basis, work in close cooperation with the ASEAN Business Advisory Council (ASEAN-BAC), the ASEAN Chambers of Commerce and Industry (ASEAN-CCI), and relevant industry clubs/associations to:

(a) intensify joint intra-ASEAN and extra-ASEAN trade promotion efforts;
(b) organise regular private sector driven ASEAN selling and buying missions;
(c) assist CLMV in organising promotional activities; and
(d) undertake more effective joint ASEAN facilitation and promotion measures and develop new sources of inward foreign direct investment, particularly from potential countries such as the People's Republic of China, India and the Republic of Korea.

Article 14: ASEAN Trade and Investment Statistics

Member States shall establish an effective system to monitor ASEAN trade and investments through:

(a) provision of updates to the ASEAN Secretariat of the latest trade (goods and services) and investment statistics; and
(b) preparation of consolidated industry profiles, by the respective associations, which, *inter alia*, cover information such as production capacity and product range.

PART V: OTHER AREAS FOR INTEGRATION

Article 15: Intellectual Property Rights

Member States shall expand the scope of ASEAN intellectual property rights cooperation beyond trademarks and patents to include cooperation in copyrights information exchange and enforcement by 31 December 2004.

Article 16: Industrial Complementation

Member States shall promote complementation among ASEAN manufacturers, as applicable, through:

(a) identification and development of specialisation of production processes, research and development (R&D), and testing facilities based on comparative advantage of individual Member State; and

(b) development of guidelines on promoting outsourcing arrangements among Member States, as applicable.

Article 17: Human Resource Development

Member States shall cooperate to develop and upgrade skills and capacity building through joint training and workshops.

PART VI: GENERAL PROVISIONS

Article 18: General Exceptions

Nothing in this Framework Agreement shall prevent any Member State from taking actions and adopting measures which it considers necessary for the protection of its national security, the protection of public morals, the protection of human, animal or plant life and health, and the protection of articles of artistic, historic and archaeological value.

Article 19: Institutional Arrangement

1. The Ministers responsible for ASEAN Economic Integration, with the assistance of the Senior Economic Officials (SEOM), shall oversee, monitor and/or coordinate the implementation of this Framework Agreement.
2. The ASEAN Secretariat shall:
   (a) provide support to the Ministers and the SEOM for supervising, coordinating and reviewing the implementation of this Framework Agreement; and
   (b) monitor and regularly report to the SEOM on the progress in the implementation of this Framework Agreement.
3. Member States shall cooperate with the ASEAN Secretariat in the performance of its duties.

Article 20: Review

The Ministers responsible for ASEAN Economic Integration shall meet as and when necessary to review this Framework Agreement for the purpose of considering further measures and/or other sectors for priority integration or any other relevant matters as may be agreed.

Article 21: Sectoral Integration Protocols and Annexes

The ASEAN Sectoral Integration Protocols attached to this Framework Agreement as Annexes (I) to (XI) and the total product list attached as Annex (XII) shall form an integral part of this Framework Agreement.

Article 22: Consultations

Member States shall accord adequate opportunity for consultations regarding any representations made by another Member State with respect to any matter that would affect the implementation of this Framework Agreement.

Article 23: Dispute Settlement

The provisions of the ASEAN Protocol on Enhanced Dispute Settlement Mechanism, done at Vientiane, Lao PDR on the 29th day of November 2004, shall apply to disputes arising under this Framework Agreement.

Article 24: Relation to other Agreements

1. Except as provided in paragraph 2 hereof, this Framework Agreement or any action taken under it shall not affect or nullify the rights and obligations of a Member State under existing agreements or international conventions to which it is also a party.

2. The provisions in this Framework Agreement shall prevail over the rights and obligations in other relevant ASEAN agreements to the extent that the same subject matter is governed by this Framework Agreement.

Article 25: Final Provisions

1. The provisions of this Framework Agreement may be modified through amendments mutually agreed upon in writing by all Member States.

2. This Framework Agreement shall be deposited with the Secretary-General of ASEAN, who shall furnish a certified copy to each Member State.

Article 26: Entry into Force

1. This Framework Agreement shall enter into force on 31 August 2005. Notwithstanding the specified date of entry into force, Member States undertake to carry out the obligations which arise prior to the date of entry into force of this Framework Agreement in accordance with the timelines indicated herein and the Roadmaps attached to the ASEAN Sectoral Integration Protocols as Appendices.

2. Member States undertake to complete their internal procedures of ratification for the entry into force of this Framework Agreement.

3. Each Member State shall upon the completion of its internal procedures of ratification of this Framework Agreement notify the ASEAN Secretariat in writing.

In witness whereof, We have signed this ASEAN Framework Agreement for the Integration of Priority Sectors.

Done at Vientiane, Lao PDR this 29th day of November 2004, in single copy, in the English Language.

7

DECLARATION AGAINST TRAFFICKING

ASEAN DECLARATION AGAINST TRAFFICKING IN PERSONS PARTICULARLY WOMEN AND CHILDREN

We, the Heads of States/Governments of Brunei Darussalam, the Kingdom of Cambodia, the Republic of Indonesia, the Lao People's Democratic Republic, Malaysia, the Union of Myanmar, the Republic of the Philippines, the Republic of Singapore, the Kingdom of Thailand, the Socialist Republic of Viet Nam, members of the Association of the Southeast Asian Nations, hereinafter referred to as ASEAN,

Reaffirming the Ha Noi Declaration of 1998 and the Ha Noi Plan of Action, which, among others, committed to intensify individual and collective efforts to address transnational crimes, including the trafficking in persons;

Expressing the urgent need for a comprehensive regional approach to prevent and to combat trafficking in persons, particularly women and children;

Acknowledging that social, economic and other factors that cause people to migrate also make them vulnerable to trafficking in persons;

Recognizing that the immorality and inhumanity of this common concern elicits the need to strengthen legislative, law enforcement and judicial responses to ensure deterrent action is taken against persons involved in individual or syndicated activities of trafficking in persons, particularly women and children;

Appreciating that a successful campaign against the scourge of trafficking in persons, particularly women and children, requires continuing dialogue, exchange of information and cooperation among ASEAN;

Reaffirming's unwavering desire to embrace the spirit behind the United Nations Convention against Transnational Organized Crime and its relevant protocols as it reflects the commitment of the Member States of the United Nations to prevent and combat transnational organized crime;

Reaffirming through this Declaration a commitment to human development and security, and the improvement of the quality of life of the peoples of ASEAN;

Hereby Declare, to the extent permitted by their respective domestic laws and policies, to undertake concerted efforts to effectively address an emerging regional problem, namely, the trafficking in persons, particularly women and children, through the following measures:

1. To establish a regional focal network to prevent and combat trafficking in persons, particularly women and children, in the ASEAN region;
2. To adopt measures to protect the integrity of their respective passports, official travel documents, identity and other official travel documents from fraud;
3. To undertake regular exchange of views, information sharing on relevant migratory flows, trends and pattern, strengthening of border controls and monitoring mechanisms, and the enactment of applicable and necessary legislations;
4. To intensify cooperation among our respective immigration and other laws enforcement authorities;
5. To distinguish victims of trafficking in persons from the perpetrators, and identify the countries of origin and nationalities of such victims and thereafter ensure that such victims are treated humanely and provided with such essential medical and other forms of assistance deemed appropriate by the respective receiving/recipient country, including prompt repatriation to their respective countries of origin;
6. To undertake actions to respect and safeguard the dignity and human rights of genuine victims of trafficking in persons;
7. To undertake coercive actions/measures against individual and/or syndicate engaged in trafficking in persons and shall offer one another the widest possible assistance to punish such activities; and
8. To take measures to strengthen regional and international cooperation to prevent and combat trafficking in persons.

All Member Countries reaffirm their commitment to accomplish the elements of this Declaration through maximum efforts by such appropriate instruments as may be necessary and consistent with their respective national laws and policies.

Adopted by the Heads of State/Government of ASEAN Member Countries on this Twenty-ninth Day of November 2004 in Vientiane, Lao People's Democratic Republic.

8

Conflict Resolution Mechanism

ASEAN PROTOCOL ON ENHANCED DISPUTE SETTLEMENT MECHANISM

The Governments of Brunei Darussalam, the Kingdom of Cambodia, the Republic of Indonesia, the Lao People's Democratic Republic, Malaysia, the Union of Myanmar, the Republic of the Philippines, the Republic of Singapore, the Kingdom of Thailand and the Socialist Republic of Viet Nam, Member States of the Association of South East Asian Nations (hereinafter collectively referred to as "ASEAN" or "Member States" or singularly as "Member State");

Recalling the Framework Agreement on Enhancing ASEAN Economic Cooperation signed in Singapore on 28 January 1992, as amended by the Protocol to Amend the Framework Agreement on Enhancing ASEAN Economic Cooperation signed in Bangkok on 15 December 1995 (the "Agreement") and the Protocol on Dispute Settlement Mechanism signed in Manila on 20 November 1996 (the "1996 Protocol on DSM");

Further Eecalling that the 9th ASEAN Summit held in Bali on 7-8 October 2003, had decided on institutional strengthening of ASEAN, including the improvement of the ASEAN Dispute Settlement Mechanism, as reflected in the Bali Concord II;

Desiring to replace the 1996 Protocol on DSM with the ASEAN Protocol on Enhanced Dispute Settlement Mechanism (hereinafter referred to as "Protocol");

Have agred as follows:

Article 1: Coverage and Application

1. The rules and procedures of this Protocol shall apply to disputes brought pursuant to the consultation and dispute settlement provisions of the Agreement as well as the agreements listed in Appendix I and future ASEAN economic agreements (the "covered agreements").

2. The rules and procedures of this Protocol shall apply subject to such special or additional rules and procedures on dispute settlement contained in the covered agreements. To the extent that there is a difference between the rules and procedures of this Protocol and the special or additional rules and procedures in the covered agreements, the special or additional rules and procedures shall prevail.

3. The provisions of this Protocol are without prejudice to the rights of Member States to seek recourse to other fora for the settlement of disputes involving other Member States. A Member State involved in a dispute can resort to other fora at any stage before a party has made a request to the Senior Economic Officials Meeting ("SEOM") to establish a panel pursuant to paragraph 1 Article 5 of this Protocol.

Article 2: Administration

1. The SEOM shall administer this Protocol and, except as otherwise provided in a covered agreement, the consultation and dispute settlement provisions of the covered agreements. Accordingly, the SEOM shall have the authority to establish panels, adopt panel and Appellate Body reports, maintain surveillance of implementation of findings and recommendations of panel and Appellate Body reports adopted by the SEOM and authorise suspension of concessions and other obligations under the covered agreements.

2. The SEOM and other relevant ASEAN bodies shall be notified of mutually agreed solutions to matters formally raised under the consultation and dispute settlement provisions of the covered agreements.

Article 3: Consultations

1. Member States shall accord adequate opportunity for consultations regarding any representations made by other Member States with respect to any matter affecting the implementation, interpretation or application of the Agreement or any covered agreement. Any differences shall, as far as possible, be settled amicably between the Member States.

2. Member States which consider that any benefit accruing to them directly or indirectly, under the Agreement or any covered agreement is being nullified or impaired, or that the attainment of any objective of the Agreement or any covered agreement is being impeded as a result of failure of another Member State to carry out its obligations under the Agreement or any covered agreement, or the existence of any other situation may, with a view to achieving satisfactory settlement of the matter, make representations or proposals to the other Member State concerned, which shall give due consideration to the representations or proposals made to it.

3. All such requests for consultations shall be notified to the SEOM. Any

request for consultations shall be submitted in writing and shall give the reason for the request including identification of the measures at issue and an indication of the legal basis for the complaint.

4. If a request for consultations is made, the Member State to which the request is made shall reply to the request within ten (10) days after the date of its receipt and shall enter into consultations within a period of thirty (30) days after the date of receipt of the request, with a view to reaching a mutually satisfactory solution.

5. In cases of urgency, including those which concern perishable goods, the parties to the dispute, panels and the Appellate Body shall make every effort to accelerate the proceedings to the greatest extent possible.

Article 4: Good Offices, Conciliation or Mediation

1. Member States which are parties to a dispute may at any time agree to good offices, conciliation or mediation. They may begin at any time and be terminated at any time. Once procedures for good offices, conciliation or mediation are terminated, a complaining party may then proceed with a request to the SEOM for the establishment of a panel.

2. If the parties to a dispute agree, procedures for good offices, conciliation or mediation may continue while the panel process proceeds.

3. The Secretary-General of ASEAN may, acting in an ex officio capacity, offer good offices, conciliation or mediation with the view to assisting Member States to settle a dispute.

Article 5: Establishment of Panels

1. If the Member State to which the request for consultations is made does not reply within ten (10) days after the date of receipt of the request, or does not enter into consultations within a period of thirty (30) days after the date of receipt of the request, or the consultations fail to settle a dispute within sixty (60) days after the date of receipt of the request, the matter shall be raised to the SEOM if the complaining party wishes to request for a panel. The panel shall be established by the SEOM, unless the SEOM decides by consensus not to establish a panel.

2. A panel shall be established at the meeting of the SEOM held immediately after the receipt of the request for a panel and accordingly the request shall be placed on the agenda of the SEOM at that meeting. In the event that no the SEOM meeting is scheduled or planned within forty five (45) days of receipt of the request, the establishment of the panel or the decision not to establish it shall be done or taken, as the case may be, by circulation. A non-reply shall be considered as agreement to the request for the establishment of a panel. The issue of the establishment of the panel shall be settled within the forty-five (45) day-period, irrespective of whether it is settled at the SEOM or by circulation.

3. The request for the establishment of a panel shall be made in writing. It shall indicate whether consultations were held, identify the specific measures at issue and provide a brief summary of the legal basis of the complaint sufficient to present the problem clearly. In case the complainant requests the establishment of a panel with other than standard terms of reference, the written request shall include the proposed text of the special terms of reference.

Article 6: Terms of Reference of Panels

1. Panels shall have the following terms of reference unless the parties to the dispute agree otherwise prior to the establishment of a panel:

> "To examine in the light of the relevant provisions in (name of the covered agreement(s) cited by the parties to the dispute), the matter referred to the SEOM by (name of party) in (document) .. and to make such findings as will assist the SEOM in the adoption of the panel report or in making its decision not to adopt the report."

2. Panels shall address the relevant provisions in any covered agreement or agreements cited by the parties to the dispute.

3. In establishing a panel, the SEOM may authorise its Chairman to draw up the terms of reference of the panel in consultation with the parties to the dispute, notwithstanding the provisions in paragraph 1 hereof. The terms of reference thus drawn up shall be circulated to all Member States. If other than standard terms of reference are agreed upon, any Member State may raise any point relating thereto with the SEOM at the time of establishment of a panel.

Article 7: Function of Panel

The function of the panel is to make an objective assessment of the dispute before it, (including an examination of the facts of the case and the applicability of and conformity with the sections of the Agreement or any covered agreements) and its findings and recommendations in relation to the case.

Article 8: Panel Procedures, Deliberations and Findings

1. A panel shall, apart from the matters covered in Appendix II regulate its own procedures in relation to the rights of parties to be heard and its deliberations.

2. A panel shall submit its findings and recommendations to the SEOM in the form of a written report within sixty (60) days of its establishment. In exceptional cases, the panel may take an additional ten (10) days to submit its findings and recommendations to the SEOM.

3. Before submitting its findings and recommendations to the SEOM, the panel shall accord adequate opportunity to the parties to the dispute to review the report.

4. A panel shall have the right to seek information and technical advice from any individual or body which it deems appropriate. A Member State shall respond promptly and fully to any request by a panel for such information as the panel considers necessary and appropriate.

5. Panel deliberations shall be confidential. The reports of panels shall be drafted without the presence of the parties to the dispute in the light of the information provided and the statements made.

Article 9: Treatment of Panel Report

1. The SEOM shall adopt the panel report within thirty (30) days of its submission by the panel unless a party to the dispute formally notifies the SEOM of its decision to appeal or the SEOM decides by consensus not to adopt the report. If a party has notified its decision to appeal, the report by the panel shall not be considered for adoption by the SEOM until after the completion of the appeal. SEOM representatives from Member States which are parties to a dispute can be present during the deliberations of the SEOM.

2. In the event that no meeting of the SEOM is scheduled or planned to enable adoption or non-adoption of the panel report, as the case may be, within the thirty (30) day period in paragraph 1 hereof, the adoption shall be done by circulation. A non-reply shall be considered as acceptance of the decision and/or recommendation in the panel report. The adoption or non-adoption shall be completed within the thirty (30) day period in paragraph 1 hereof, notwithstanding the resort to a circulation process.

Article 10: Procedures for Multiple Complainants

1. Where more than one Member State requests the establishment of a panel related to the same matter, a single panel may be established to examine these complaints taking into account the rights of all Member States concerned. A single panel should be established to examine such complaints whenever feasible.

2. The single panel shall organize its examination and present its findings and recommendations to the SEOM in such a manner that the rights which the parties to the dispute would have enjoyed had separate panels examined the complaints are in no way impaired. If one of the parties to the dispute so requests, the panel shall submit separate reports on the dispute concerned. The written submissions by each of the complainants shall be made available to the other complainants, and each complainant shall have the right to be present when any one of the other complainants presents its views to the panel.

3. If more than one panel is established to examine the complaints related to the same matter, to the greatest extent possible, the same persons shall serve as panelists on each of the separate panels and the timetable for the panel process in such disputes shall be harmonized.

Article 11: Third Parties

1. The interests of the parties to a dispute and those of other Member States under a covered agreement at issue in the dispute shall be fully taken into account during the panel process.

2. Any Member State having a substantial interest in a matter before a panel and having notified its interest to the SEOM (referred to in this Protocol as a "third party") shall have an opportunity to be heard by the panel and to make written submissions to the panel. These submissions shall also be given to the parties to the dispute and shall be reflected in the panel report.

3. Third parties shall receive the submissions of the parties to the dispute to the first substantive meeting of the panel.

4. If a third party considers that a measure already the subject of a panel proceeding nullifies or impairs benefits accruing to it under any covered agreement, that Member State may have recourse to normal dispute settlement procedures under this Protocol. Such a dispute shall be referred to the original panel wherever possible.

Article 12: Appellate Review

1. An Appellate Body shall be established by the ASEAN Economic Ministers ("AEM"). The Appellate Body shall hear appeals from panel cases. It shall be composed of seven (7) persons, three (3) of whom shall serve on any one case. Persons serving on the Appellate Body shall serve on cases in rotation. Such rotation shall be determined in the working procedures of the Appellate Body.

2. The AEM shall appoint persons to serve on the Appellate Body for a four-year term, and each person may be reappointed once. A person appointed to replace a person whose term of office has not expired shall hold office for the remainder of the predecessor's term.

3. The Appellate Body shall comprise of persons of recognised authority, irrespective of nationality, with demonstrated expertise in law, international trade and the subject matter of the covered agreements generally. They shall be unaffiliated with any government. All persons serving on the Appellate Body shall be available at all times and on short notice, and shall stay abreast of dispute settlement activities and other relevant activities of ASEAN. They shall not participate in the consideration of any disputes that would create a direct or indirect conflict of interest.

4. Only parties to the dispute, not third parties, may appeal a panel report. Third parties, which have notified the SEOM of a substantial interest in the matter pursuant to paragraph 2 of Article 11 may make written submissions to, and be given an opportunity to be heard by the Appellate Body.

5. As a general rule, the proceedings of the Appellate Body shall not exceed sixty (60) days from the date a party to the dispute formally notifies its decision to appeal to the date the Appellate Body circulates its report. In fixing its timetable the Appellate Body shall take into account the provisions of paragraph 5 of Article 3. When the Appellate Body considers that it cannot provide its report within sixty (60) days, it shall inform the SEOM in writing of the reasons for the delay together with an estimate of the period within which it will submit its report. In no case shall the proceedings exceed ninety (90) days.

6. An appeal shall be limited to issues of law covered in the panel report and legal interpretations developed by the panel.

7. The Appellate Body shall be provided with the appropriate administrative and legal support as it requires.

8. Working procedures of the Appellate Body shall be drawn up by the SEOM. Any amendments thereto, shall be drawn up from time to time as necessary by the Appellate Body in consultation with the SEOM and the Secretary-General of ASEAN, and communicated to the Member States for their information.

9. The proceedings of the Appellate Body shall be confidential. The reports of the Appellate Body shall be drafted without the presence of the parties to the dispute and in the light of the information provided and the statements made.

10. Opinions expressed in the Appellate Body report by the individuals serving on the Appellate Body shall be anonymous.

11. The Appellate Body shall address each of the issues raised in accordance with paragraph 6 hereof during the appellate proceeding.

12. The Appellate Body may uphold, modify or reverse the legal findings and conclusions of the panel.

13. An Appellate Body report shall be adopted by the SEOM and unconditionally accepted by the parties to the dispute unless the SEOM decides by consensus not to adopt the Appellate Body report within thirty (30) days following its circulation to the Member States. In the event that no meeting of the SEOM is scheduled or planned to enable adoption or non-adoption of the report, as the case may be, within the thirty (30) day period, adoption shall be done by circulation. A non-reply within the said thirty (30) day period shall be considered as an acceptance of the Appellate Body report. This adoption procedure is without prejudice to the rights of Member States to express their views on an Appellate Body report. The adoption process shall be completed within the thirty (30) day period irrespective of whether it is settled at the SEOM or by circulation.

Article 13: Communications with the Panel or Appellate Body

1. There shall be no ex parte communications with the panel or Appellate Body concerning matters under consideration by the panel or the Appellate Body.

2. Written submissions to the panel or the Appellate Body shall be treated as confidential, but it shall be made available to the parties to the dispute. Nothing in this Protocol shall preclude a party to a dispute from disclosing statement of its own positions to the public. Member States shall treat as confidential information submitted by another Member State to the panel or the Appellate Body which that Member State has designated as confidential. A party to a dispute shall also, upon request of a Member State, provide a non-confidential summary of the information contained in its written submissions that could be disclosed to the public.

Article 14: Panel and Appellate Body Recommendations

1. Where a panel or the Appellate Body concludes that a measure is inconsistent with a covered agreement, it shall recommend that the Member State concerned bring the measure into conformity with that agreement. In addition to its recommendations, a panel or the Appellate Body may suggest ways in which the Member State concerned could implement the recommendations.

2. In their findings and recommendations, a panel and the Appellate Body cannot add to or diminish the rights and obligations provided in the covered agreements.

3. The panels and the Appellate Body shall also deal with the issue of expenses to be borne by the parties to the dispute, including third parties, to replenish the ASEAN Dispute Settlement Mechanism ("DSM") Fund as part of their findings and recommendations. The panels and the Appellate Body may apportion the expenses in the manner appropriate to the particular case.

Article 15: Surveillance of Implementation of Findings and Recommendations

1. Since prompt compliance with the findings and recommendations of panel and Appellate Body reports adopted by the SEOM is essential in order to ensure effective resolution of disputes, parties to the dispute who are required to do so shall comply with the findings and recommendations of panel reports adopted by the SEOM within sixty (60) days from the SEOM's adoption of the same, or in the event of an appeal sixty (60) days from the SEOM's adoption of the findings and recommendations of the Appellate Body reports, unless the parties to the dispute agree on a longer time period.

2. When a party to the dispute requests for a longer time period for compliance, the other party shall take into account the circumstances of the particular case and accord favourable consideration to the complexity of the actions required to comply with the findings and recommendations of panel and Appellate Body reports adopted by the SEOM. The request for a longer period of time shall not be unreasonably denied. Where it is necessary to pass national legislation to comply with the findings and recommendations of panel and Appellate Body reports, a longer period appropriate for that purpose shall be allowed.

3. The decision of the parties on the extension of time shall be made within fourteen (14) days from the SEOM's adoption of the findings and recommendations of the panel report, or in the event of an appeal fourteen (14) days from the SEOM's adoption of the findings and recommendations of the Appellate Body's reports.

4. Any party required to comply with the findings and recommendations shall provide the SEOM with a status report in writing of their progress in the implementation of the findings and recommendations of panel and Appellate Body reports adopted by the SEOM.

5. Where there is disagreement as to the existence or consistency with a covered agreement of measures taken to comply with the findings and recommendations of panel and Appellate Body reports adopted by the SEOM such dispute shall be decided through recourse to these dispute settlement procedures, including wherever possible resort to the original panel. The panel shall circulate its report within sixty (60) days, after the date of referral of the matter to it. When the panel considers that it cannot provide its report within this time frame, it shall inform the SEOM in writing of the reasons for the delay together with an indication of the period within which it will submit its report. In no case shall the proceedings for this purpose and the submission of the report exceed ninety (90) days after the date of reference of the matter to the panel.

6. The SEOM shall keep under surveillance the implementation of the findings and recommendations of panel and Appellate Body reports adopted by it. The issue of implementation of the findings and recommendations of panel and Appellate Body reports adopted by the SEOM may be raised at the SEOM by any Member State at any time following their adoption. Unless the SEOM decides otherwise, the issue of implementation of the findings and recommendations of panel and Appellate Body reports adopted by the SEOM shall be placed on the agenda of the SEOM meeting and shall remain on the SEOM's agenda until the issue is resolved. At least ten (10) days prior to each such the SEOM meeting, the party concerned shall provide the SEOM with a status report in writing of its progress in the implementation of the findings and recommendations of panel and Appellate Body reports adopted by the SEOM.

Article 16: Compensation and the Suspension of Concessions

1. Compensation and the suspension of concessions or other obligations are temporary measures available in the event that the findings and recommendations of panel and Appellate Body reports adopted by the SEOM are not implemented within the period of sixty (60) days or the longer time period as agreed upon by the parties to the dispute as referred to in Article 15. However, neither compensation nor the suspension of concessions or other obligations is preferred to full implementation of a recommendation to bring a measure into conformity with the covered agreements. Compensation is voluntary and, if granted, shall be consistent with the covered agreements.

2. If the Member State concerned fails to bring the measure found to be inconsistent with a covered agreement into compliance therewith or otherwise comply with the findings and recommendations of panel and Appellate Body reports adopted by the SEOM within the period of sixty (60) days or the longer time period as agreed upon by the parties to the dispute as referred to in Article 15, such Member State shall, if so requested, and no later than the expiry of the period of sixty (60) days or the longer time period referred to in Article 15, enter into negotiations with any party having invoked the dispute settlement procedures, with a view to developing mutually acceptable compensation. If no satisfactory compensation has been agreed within twenty (20) days after the date of expiry of the period of sixty (60) days or the longer time period as agreed upon by the parties to the dispute as referred to in Article 15, any party having invoked the dispute settlement procedures may request authorization from the SEOM to suspend the application to the Member State concerned of concessions or other obligations under the covered agreements.

3. In considering what concessions or other obligations to suspend, the complaining party shall apply the following principles and procedures:

(a) the general principle is that the complaining party should first seek to suspend concessions or other obligations with respect to the same sector(s) as that in which the panel or Appellate Body has found a violation or other nullification or impairment;

(b) if that party considers that it is not practicable or effective to suspend concessions or other obligations with respect to the same sector(s), it may seek to suspend concessions or other obligations in other sector(s) under the same agreement;

(c) if that party considers that it is not practicable or effective to suspend concessions or other obligations with respect to other sector(s) under the same agreement, and that the circumstances are serious enough, it may seek to suspend concessions or other obligations under another covered agreement;

(d) in applying the above principles, that party shall take into account:
  (i) the trade in the sector or under the agreement under which the panel or Appellate Body has found a violation or other nullification or impairment, and the importance of such trade to that party;
  (ii) the broader economic elements related to the nullification or impairment and the broader economic consequences of the suspension of concessions or other obligations;

(e) for purposes of this paragraph, "sector" means:
  (i) with respect to goods, all goods;
  (ii) with respect to services, a principal sector as identified in the current schedules of commitments under the ASEAN Framework Agreement on Services (AFAS).

(f) for purposes of this paragraph, "agreement" means:
  (i) with respect to goods, the agreements in relation to goods listed in Appendix I to this Protocol;
  (ii) with respect to services, the ASEAN Framework Agreement of Services and subsequent protocols; and
  (iii) any other covered agreement as defined in Article 1 of this Protocol.

4. The level of the suspension of concessions or other obligations authorized by the SEOM shall be equivalent to the level of the nullification or impairment.

5. The SEOM shall not authorise suspension of concessions or other obligations if a covered agreement prohibits such suspension.

6. When the situation described in paragraph 2 hereof occurs, the SEOM, upon request, shall grant authorization to suspend concessions or other obligations within thirty (30) days of the expiry of the sixty (60) day-period or the expiry of the longer period agreed upon by the parties to the dispute, as the case may be, referred to in Article 15, unless the SEOM decides by consensus to reject the request. In the event that no meeting of the SEOM is scheduled or planned to enable authorisation to suspend concessions or other obligations within the thirty (30) day period, the authorisation shall be done by circulation. A non-reply within the said thirty (30) day period shall be considered as an acceptance of the authorisation. The authorisation process shall be completed within the thirty (30) day period irrespective of whether it is settled at the SEOM or by circulation.

7. However, if the Member State concerned objects to the level of suspension proposed, or claims that the principles and procedures set forth in paragraph 3 have not been followed where a complaining party has requested authorisation to suspend concessions or other obligations pursuant to paragraph 3(b) or (c), the matter shall be referred to arbitration. Such arbitration shall be carried out by the

original panel, if members are available, or by an arbitration appointed by the Secretary-General of ASEAN and shall be completed within sixty (60) days after the date of expiry of the sixty (60) day period or the expiry of the longer period agreed upon by the parties to the dispute, as the case may be, referred to in Article 15. Concessions or other obligations shall not be suspended during the course of the arbitration.

8. The arbitrator acting pursuant to paragraph 7 hereof shall not examine the nature of the concessions or other obligations to be suspended but shall determine whether the level of such suspension is equivalent to the level of nullification or impairment. The arbitrator may also determine if the proposed suspension of concessions or other obligations is allowed under the covered agreement. However, if the matter referred to arbitration includes a claim that the principles and procedures set forth in paragraph 3 hereof have not been followed, the arbitrator shall examine that claim. In the event the arbitrator determines that those principles and procedures have not been followed, the complaining party shall apply them consistent with paragraph 3 hereof. The parties shall accept the arbitrator's decision as final and the parties concerned shall not seek a second arbitration. The SEOM shall be informed promptly of the decision of the arbitrator and shall, upon request, grant authorisation to suspend concessions or other obligations where the request is consistent with the decision of the arbitrator, unless the SEOM decides by consensus to reject the request.

9. The suspension of concessions or other obligations shall be temporary and shall only be applied until such time as the measure found to be inconsistent with a covered agreement has been removed, or the Member State that must implement recommendations and findings of the panel and Appellate Body reports adopted by the SEOM provides a solution to the nullification or impairment of benefits, or a mutually satisfactory solution is reached. In accordance with paragraph 6 of Article 15, the SEOM shall continue to keep under surveillance the implementation of adopted recommendations and findings of the panel and Appellate Body reports adopted by the SEOM, including those cases where compensation has been provided or concessions or other obligations have been suspended but the recommendations to bring a measure into conformity with the covered agreements have not been implemented.

10. The dispute settlement provisions of the covered agreements may be invoked in respect of measures affecting their observance taken by regional or local governments or authorities within the territory of a Member State. When the SEOM has ruled that a provision of a covered agreement has not been observed, the responsible Member State shall take such reasonable measures as may be available to it to ensure its observance. The provisions of the covered agreements and this Protocol relating to

compensation and suspension of concessions or other obligations shall apply in cases where it has not been possible to secure such observance.

Article 17: ASEAN DSM Fund

1. There shall be established an ASEAN DSM Fund (hereinafter referred to as 'the Fund') for the purposes of this Protocol. The Fund shall be a revolving fund, separate from ASEAN Secretariat's regular budget. The initial sum for the Fund shall be contributed equally by all the Member States. Any drawdown from the Fund shall be replenished by the parties to the dispute in line with the provision of paragraph 3 of Article 14. The ASEAN Secretariat shall be responsible for administering the Fund.

2. The Fund shall be used to meet the expenses of the panels, the Appellate Body and any related administration costs of the ASEAN Secretariat. All other expenses, including legal representation, incurred by any party to a dispute shall be borne by that party.

3. The subsistence allowances and other expenses of the panels and the Appellate Body shall be in accordance with the criteria approved by the AEM on the recommendations of the ASEAN Budget Committee.

Article 18: Maximum Time-Frame

The total period for the disposal of disputes under this Protocol until the stage contemplated under paragraph 7 of Article 16, shall not exceed 445 days, unless the longer time period under Article 15 applies.

Article 19: Responsibilities of the Secretariat

1. The ASEAN Secretariat shall have the responsibility of assisting the panels and the Appellate Body, especially on the legal, historical and the procedural aspects of the matters dealt with, and of providing secretarial and technical support.

2. The ASEAN Secretariat shall assist the SEOM to monitor and maintain surveillance of the implementation of the findings and recommendations of the panel and Appellate Body reports adopted by it.

3. The ASEAN Secretariat shall be the focal point to receive all documentations in relation to disputes and shall deal with them as appropriate.

4. The ASEAN Secretariat in consultation with the SEOM shall administratively update the list of covered agreements in Appendix I, as may be required from time to time. The Secretariat shall inform Member States as and when the changes have been made.

Article 20: Venue for Proceedings

1. The venue for proceedings of the panels and the Appellate Body shall be the ASEAN Secretariat.

2. Notwithstanding the provisions of paragraph 1 above, panel and Appellate Body proceedings, apart from substantive meetings, may be held at any venue which the panels and the Appellate Body consider appropriate in consultation with the parties to the dispute, having regard to the convenience and cost effectiveness of such venue.

Article 21: Final Provisions

1. This Protocol shall enter into force upon signing.

2. This Protocol shall replace the 1996 Protocol on DSM and shall not apply to any dispute which has arisen before its entry into force. Such dispute shall continue to be governed by the 1996 Protocol on DSM.

3. The provisions of this Protocol may be modified through amendments mutually agreed upon in writing by all Member States.

4. This Protocol shall be deposited with the Secretary-General of ASEAN, who shall promptly furnish a certified copy thereof, to each ASEAN Member State.

In Witness whereof, the undersigned, being duly authorised thereto by their respective Governments, have signed the ASEAN Protocol on Enhanced Dispute Settlement Mechanism.

Done at Vientiane, Lao PDR on 29 November 2004, in a single copy in the English language.

Part II

ASEAN and Prominent World Countries: Partnership and Relationship

9

General Analysis of South-East Asia's Status and Interaction

South East Asia, a geographical bridge between Indian and Pacific ocean lies astride the vital sea lanes on which China, Japan and the US depend for their trade and commercial links with West Asia and the east coast of Africa. About 50000 vessels use the 500 nautical mile Malacca straits every year. Considered a repository of large quantities of raw materials including oil and natural gas, its strategic potential is obvious. It is therefore not surprising that every major power tries to garner as much influence as possible over the region. The region, with its complexity in ethnicity, languages, religion and different levels of economic development presents a complex mosaic of security problems. A study of the region's relations with the major powers could be divided into three periods,

1. Post colonial and Cold war
2. Post cold war
3. Post Sept. 11, 2001.

During the colonial period, independence and student movements as well as other groups, like the communist movements had some convergence of interests despite the ethnic or national divides in the region. The convergence did not however translate into much during the colonial period, leaving the countries of the region governed on different principles of the concerned colonizers. The failure of the attempted coup in Indonesia, and establishment of Suharto's New Order government in 1965 helped in removing the sub-regional strains produced by his predecessor's policies including efforts to crush the newly formed Malaysia. ASEAN, established in this climate in 1967 helped in gradually building a sense of common interest and regional association among its members. AFTA, the ASEAN Free Trade Agreement created in 1992 by the parent body has become a key institution in Southeast Asia succeeding in developing a sense of community among its very disparate members, and paving the way for closer economic cooperation. The annual post-Ministerial consultations held after ASEAN's meetings provided a venue for the ASEAN member governments, to meet, at foreign Minister level, with their counterparts and discuss matters of mutual and regional interests.

These counterparts, termed "dialogue partners", include USA, Russia, Australia, Canada, the European Union, India, China, Japan and New Zealand. Discussions on regional security were further developed leading to the creation of the ASEAN Regional Forum (ARF) which includes ASEAN and its dialogue partners. A significant aspect of the economic policies of the region since the ending of the cold war and collapse of the Soviet Union, has been the total change over to market economics, albeit with more governmental political control than in the West. There is virtual unanimity among these countries about the commitment to economic development based on relatively open markets, private ownership and competition.

Simultaneously there has been unprecedented economic growth stymied to some extent by the economic meltdown in 1997. Many believe that Southeast Asia will develop in this century as a major centre of economic power and influence. The region became a battle ground of the cold war with many a proxy battle. The 30 year Vietnam War was one of those tragic battles based on Eisenhower's so called "domino" theory. Again the Soviet invasion of Afghanistan and Vietnam's invasion of Cambodia brought back the cold war to the region. Historically the region's security problems were communist insurgencies, ethnic separatist movements, religious and racial issues. Thailand, Malaysia and Singapore have neutralized communist insurgencies by the mid 80s.The Thai Muslim groups have also petered out.

In Philippines communist and Muslim insurgencies (Moro Islamic Liberation Front) in the south continue to pose significant problems. In Burma the key issue of autonomy for different ethnic groups like Kachin and Karens remains unresolved. In Indonesia Independence of East Timor has been resolved though the problem of Aceh is still festering. After World War II most of these countries followed international policies which were in greater accord with those of the west, more particularly the U.S. Most of them developed an intense anti-communist attitude and relied on US military presence in the region for security against onslaught of communism.

With the end of World War II and subsequent beginning of cold war, the western countries brought the countries of this region into various defence and security arrangements like the five power defence arrangements which included Malaysia, Singapore, Brunei UK, Australia and New Zealand. Bilateral security pacts between the U.S and Philippines and U.S. and Thailand, gave the U.S., bases in these countries. ANZUS signed in 1951 between Australia, New Zealand and the US was another piece of alliance system augmenting the US presence in the region and was the direct result of the assessment by Australia and NZ that it is the US and not UK which can guarantee their security. Vietnam had signed a treaty of friendship with the USSR, apprehending security threats from China.

After the Vietnam War a kind of regional balance existed between Soviet supported communist Indo China and anti communist ASEAN whose security was underwritten by the U.S. Vietnam's invasion of Kampuchea however created consternation among the ASEAN countries and brought these, China and the U.S. together in a common cause. After the cold war the interests of the major powers in the region have been much less conflicting and have contributed to regional stability. Economic issues took the forefront in developments in this region which saw a remarkable forward movement. The US withdrawal from its bases in the Philippines and withdrawal of the Soviet Union from Camranh Bay in Vietnam brought the security issues again to the fore, particularly in view of the aggressive behaviour of China with regard to Paracels and Spratlys group of islands in South China Sea.

ASEAN tried to deal with the new security situation by forming ASEAN regional Forum (ARF) in 1994 at the multi lateral level and the council on security cooperation in the Asia pacific (CSCAP) at the unofficial level. China was included in the ARF as part of the new policy of "constructive engagement" instead of confrontation. Through the 1976 Treaty of Amity and Cooperation, ASEAN members had already pledged among themselves to resolve intra-ASEAN disputes peacefully (or postpone their resolution). The idea behind the concept of a larger security order was that the commitment to peaceful resolution of disputes could be extended to other states. While ASEAN would not expect outsiders to come automatically to members' aid in times of crisis, outside countries could be asked to renounce the use of force in settling any conflicts with the Association's members.

The unstated object of these concerns was evidently China—the only non regional state with territorial claims in Southeast Asia. The The U.S., Japan and China had to be persuaded to see that such security multilateralism was in their interests. The first Bush administration opposed the idea, fearing that a multilateral security body would somehow weaken traditional bilateral U.S. ties in the region.The Clinton administration saw multilateral diplomacy as a useful tool to make the allies share the security costs. Clinton did not think that a Pacific security forum would harm the traditional U.S. alliances. Japan viewed ARF as giving it a role in regional security affairs independent of the United States.

China was however suspicious of any institutionalized multilateral security arrangements and preferred bilateral dealings. Although the 1995 ARF meeting discussed the Spratlys issue with the Chinese making some vague promises about future ministerial discussions, China continued to insist on bilateral discussions with other claimants on the issue of Spratlys and refused to accept third-party mediation. It made acknowledgement of its sovereignty a precondition for considering joint development activities. The continued hard line coupled with

Beijing's growing naval activities in South China Sea forms the basis of the perceived "China Threat" in the region.

The council for security cooperation in Asia Pacific (CSCAP) had been established in June 1993 as a track II or non governmental forum to deal with security issues. Australia, Canada, Japan, South Korea and the U.S. in addition to ASEAN countries became founding members. India is also a member. It is a process parallel to the ARF and deals with security issues. With the growing economic foundations of these countries security has become an important agenda point in ASEAN foreign ministers meetings. Main hurdles in a smooth security environment include the bilateral disputes between the countries in the region like the unresolved territorial disputes and spill over of internal conflicts of one country into the neighbour. Politico security issues like US military presence in the region, perceived potential threats from China, larger role for Japanese in regional security, security of maritime routes, etc. exist. Chinese awarding of a contract to a U.S firm for drilling rights in disputed area, its occupation of Mischief reef claimed by Philippines, building of a runway on one of the Paracel islands which can accommodate both fighter and transport aircraft are all disturbing developments for the countries of the region. Notwithstanding China's bellicose attitude, the South East Asian states prefer to deal with China as an important power with whom they should have constructive engagement. They have been careful to avoid provocative rhetoric against China. The strains between the U.S. and China, over Taiwan and the U.S. attitude of domination have led to apprehension among these countries that the region may witness heightened tension and instability.

ASEAN states however have also successfully used the fears and ambitions of the major external powers to counter-balance each of them, without greatly sacrificing their independence. The relations between South East Asia and the individual big powers could now be discussed in some detail.

ASEAN Relationship with China

From early on China realized the need for improving relations with these states and as a preliminary step, offered in the Afro Asian Conference Bandung (1955), to sign the dual nationality treaty with those states with Chinese minorities, provided they recognized Taiwan as inalienable part of mainland China. With the exception of Indonesia, which has a sizeable Chinese minority, other states which followed pro-western and anti-communist policies did not respond favourably to this offer? China itself had not been recognised at that time by most of these states. Indonesia and the former Burma recognised China and the former signed the dual nationality treaty. The communist inspired coup in 1965, thought to have been orchestrated by China led to Indonesia breaking off diplomatic relations with China in 1967 and repudiating the treaty in 1969. ASEAN itself was not initially recognized by China. Among others, the reasons were the Vietnam War in which these nations sided with the U.S. and their continued recognition of Taiwan. The Sino-Soviet split in 1966 and the armed clashes between the two at Ussuri river in 1960, saw the start of realignments in the triangular relationship between the U.S., U.S.S.R. and China. With the U.S. ending the Vietnam war, recognizing PRC and accepting that "there is but one China and Taiwan is a part of China" South East Asian Countries had now to rethink their strategy towards China with the clear message that there could be no more containment of China but only accommodation. Normalisation of ASEAN China relations naturally followed. Malaysia was the first to establish diplomatic relations (May 1974), Thailand (July 1975), Philippines (June 1975), Indonesia (August 1990), Singapore (October 1990). The delay by the Indonesians is due to the painful memories of the1965 coup. With the majority of population (75%) being Chinese, Singapore decided to wait for all others to establish diplomatic relations first. The greatest success for China in these developments was acceptance by all these countries that Taiwan is part of the PRC. Deng Xiao Peng's rise to power towards the end of the 70s and his emphasis on economic development and modernization saw some fundamental changes in the foreign policy of PRC. China needed help of the ASEAN countries in its modernization, particularly the Chinese community which controlled the economy in many of these countries.

Sino ASEAN relations therefore saw an upswing. The Third Indo-China war from December 1978, following Vietnamese invasion of Kampuchea further strengthened the growing relations between China and the ASEAN states as the stand of both coincided. China aided the Khmer Rouge through Thailand as it has no direct border with Kampuchea. Collapse of the Soviet Union and China's normalisation of relations with the successor state Russia, U.S. withdrawal of its military from the region with the dismantling of Clark and Subic Bay bases in Philippines, withdrawal of Soviet forces from Camranh Bay in Vietnam and establishment of diplomatic relations with Indonesia were developments which gave greater opportunities to China for increased interactions with South east Asia. Simultaneously the new security situation also led to assertive policies by China. It carried out a show of force in Taiwan straits by holding military exercises involving medium range M9 missiles in July 1995 followed by another round in March 1996. These tests evoked serious concern among the ASEAN countries. Indonesia promptly entered into military cooperation agreement with Australia in Dec. 1995. Another area of assertiveness by China was the South China Sea. It involves conflicting claims by at least six countries. Chinese internal documents gave the *raison d'etre* for China's stand on the South China sea. They said that the regions holds reserves of resources worth US $ 1 trillion which includes oil, natural gas, fish and modules of minerals like Manganese phosphorous etc. A Chinese survey in the region in 1989 announced that the south china sea floor contained 25 billion cm of natural gas, 370000 tons of phosphorous, 105 billion barrels of oil etc. They saw these as the main fall back position for "lebensraum" for the Chinese people in the coming century.

China sees the geographical location of the south China sea between Indian and Pacific ocean as strategically vital. The importance of South China sea has been admirably expounded by Li Hua Qing, a PLA Navy commander and the most articulate proponent of China's push into the south China sea and securing it for economic exploitation. In an interview in 1984 Li said that one of the PLA-N 's main goals was to assert China's sovereignty over its rich maritime resources including its off shore petroleum deposits, its manganese modules and its fish. Liu noted that China had a large and increasing population whose diet would require the protein supplied by fish. He also called for modernizing the navy. Since the late 1980s Chinese naval planners had called for changing from a coastal defence strategy to an offshore defence strategy extending the defence perimeter to between 200 nms and 400 nms from the coast, and even more in the case of the south China sea islands. China's actions in South China Sea had caused considerable disquiet among the nations of the region. It used force in 1974 to recapture some of the islands in the Paracel group till then occupied by the former South Vietnam. In a major naval encounter with unified Vietnam in March 1988, it destroyed several Vietnamese ships and occupied six islands of Spratly group. It decided to give legitimacy to its action by passing a law in National People's Congress (NPC) in Feb. 1992 declaring the entire archipelago of Paracel and Spratly group of islands as Chinese territory. It is interesting to note here that China, in a strict legal sense, is not eligible to be considered as an archipelagic state under the 1982 Law of the Sea convention with respect to Paracel islands though in May 1996 China laid claim under archipelagic principles.

ASEAN tried to defuse the situation by coming out with a Spratly declaration in its July 1992 ministerial meeting emphasizing restraint and calling for joint development without affecting the sovereignty claims. China agreed to explore possibilities of joint exploration of South China sea resources without giving up its claims. Alongside these apparently conciliatory gestures came the Chinese occupation of Mischief Reef 250 km off the Phillipine island of Palawan in Feb. 1995.

Chinese frigates confronted Philippine naval vessels, arrested Filipino fishermen, built structures on the island and left troops in place to guard what was expected to be a Chinese naval facility. China however claimed that the structures are for fishermen. Philippines promptly signed a military cooperation agreement with UK on 3rd Jan. 1996 thus reassuring itself of extra regional support from the U.K. By the early 1990s China had pushed into Spratly islands and built up a relatively strong base there. These are a group of 230 islands and atolls and falls far south of mainland China and nearer to many South east Asian countries.

Only seven islands are more than 1 sq. km. in area and stay above water during high tide. The largest island - Thity, 625 square miles in area, is controlled by the Philippines. Vietnam controls the largest number of Spratly islands. The southern most end point of Spratly stretches 1800 nautical miles from undisputed territory of Hainan island of China, and 400 nautical miles from southern most tip of China's paracels. Chinese moves in the south China sea started in 1970 with survey operations in the Amphirite group done by navigational offices of PLA-Navy. Meteorological station was set-up in Woody island. The western cluster of Paracels, the crescent group, was taken from the South Vietnamese in 1974. Construction of military infrastructure in the Amphitrite group began in 1971. A harbour was made with 350 meter reinforced concrete wharf for mid-sized ships in woody island. The seizing of the island from south Vietnamese was also attributed to the fear that North Vietnamese may give bases there to the Soviet Union to complete the encirclement of China. Survey operations continued from 1975 to 78. PLA Navy activity in south china sea increased with completing of surveys and knowing the area better. PLA marine corps was established in Hainan island in Dec 1979 with south China sea as main area of operations. Administrative controls were increased in the islands, airstrips built (woody island)and air service to Hainan established. The Paracels served as a stepping stone to China's advance in the spratlys. In August 1988 China completed construction of a permanently occupied observation station at "Fiery Cross" following the UNESCO request in March 87 in the context of a comprehensive global oceanic survey to establish an oceanic observation station in the Spratlys, - a god sent justification for its actions in south China sea.

In 1990, China had offered to discuss joint development of the islands. According to the offer, claims of sovereignty would be put aside without prejudice while littoral countries worked together for mutual economic benefit to exploit sea bed and marine resources. Vietnam, China and the Philippines would withdraw their military forces from the islands. This applied only to Spratlys while Paracels - a group of 15 islands and less than 150 nms from China's Hanin island and about 240 nms from Da Nang the Vietnamese port - remained firmly under the control of China. China opposed establishment of an international organization in the region to settle disputes but wanted the countries concerned to settle it bilaterally. It signed a series of bilateral agreements renouncing the use of military power in settling the claims in the Spratly group.This was part of its dual policy of finding acceptability among neighbours without compromising on its claims. Its desire to strengthen its relations with these countries was also evident when it played a proactive role by making a contribution of 4 billion dollars in the initiatives by the IMF and did not devalue its renminbi though suffering trade losses due to it, during the economic crisis in the region in 1997.

However China continued its activities to consolidate its control. China's position is clear. The Spratlys are within Chinese territory and other countries are definitely not allowed to invade and occupy them. The 1992 law on territorial waters passed by the National People's Congress laid out number of regulations regarding use of and transit near these islands and their surrounding waters. It gave oil concession to Crestone, a U.S. company to explore oil in 9700 sq miles of vanguard bank area of the western Spratlys. The company was given assurance that China would use all necessary military force to protect company's operations. China's transition from continental power into maritime state followed normalization of its relations with the U.S. which encouraged moves to bring China more deeply into world economy. It has been argued by some analysts that while there is no evidence that considerations of broad influence in Southeast Asia have motivated China's behaviour, it is in this area that the long-term consequences of its policies might be felt. The shift was also related to Soviet naval power build up in Asia and Chinese concern on expansion of Japan's naval capabilities. Japan's power essentially comes from the fact that the present international situation places emphasis on the economic component of national power, which, in the pacific region makes Japan particularly powerful.

China also sees the possible resurgence of Russian nationalism leading to Russian naval threat. A seminar in Beijing in 1994 also saw naval threat from India. With a move towards the Bay of Bengal and into the Indian ocean, even without attempts to annex territory, China has shifted the zone of potential conflict from east of straits of Malacca in the south pacific and south China sea to the Indian ocean. China is trying to open up an alternative route to the Indian ocean through Myanmar. It is working on road and rail construction in Myanmar and has established navigation facilities in Myanmar controlled islands in the Bay of Bengal. Panelists in a 1994 seminar in Beijing pointed out the importance of a transport route from Yunnan to Rangoon in the event of a blockade of sea lanes. China is helping Myanmar in expanding the latter's naval facilities on Great Coco island, the site of a major signals intelligence facility near India's strategically important Andaman and Nicobar islands.

The Chinese naval vessels are now equipped with surface to surface missiles (SSMs). They have reverse engineered French Exocet missiles and equipped both submarines and surface combatants to fire them. The destroyers are equipped with Crotale surface to Air missiles or Chinese made SAMs. Where there is no integration of the missile with the ship, shoulder fired SAMs have been provided. Chinese electronic counter measures have also improved with jamming devices and chaff launchers. The draw back in all this is the problem of absorption of technology due to poor education of the Chinese sailors. Though the Chinese naval forces is marginally larger than all south east Asian naval assets put together Malaysia, Indonesia and Singapore possess better technologies and combined, would present a credible challenge to a PRC naval task force.

China's reasonably good amphibious operation capability cannot extend more than 500 km. since sufficient air power to support it is not available. Japanese see the Chinese naval build up as a natural and good balance against Russia. Lee Kuan Yew, the former strong P.M. of Singapore sees a dramatic build up in Chinese naval capability in the next ten years or so but considers US seventh fleet as a good counter balance. PM Goh Chok Tong of Singapore voiced the anxieties of ASEAN when he commented on China's " rising power and military ambitions creating anxiety." Other security related developments quickly followed. The Dec 1995 ASEAN summit declared South East Asia as Nuclear weapon Free Zone. Efforts were made to draw China into Mekong River Project to constrain China in security terms. The US returned to the region by revitalising the US Japan security relationship in the Clinton – Hashimoto Joint communiqué in April 1996. Somewhat concerned with this development China sought to placate ASEAN by signing UN convention on Law of Sea (UNCLOS) in May 1995 indicating that it would be willing to discuss the difference over south china sea with other countries in the region based on UNCLOS 1982. This negates the Law of Territorial waters passed by NPC in 1992 declaring the entire south china sea as its national waters. The Chinese threat has to some extent been mitigated by drawing it into multilateral forums like ASEAN Regional Forum (ARF), Asia Pacific Economic Cooperation (APEC) and making it a dialogue partner of ASEAN.

China has since been ready to talk on number of issues including south china sea which it had refused in the past. ASEAN would also not miss the opportunity to engage economically with China which is expected to be world's largest economy by 2020. While China had historically considered SEA as its soft underbelly, its relations with these countries have improved dramatically in the last couple of decades. Both Government to Government and People to People contacts have increased, SEA has become the favourite destination of Chinese tourists. One of the main aims of the ARF would be to undertake, particularly with China, Confidence Building Measures (CBMs) and engage in Preventive Diplomacy and finally move towards conflict resolution. China has made it explicitly clear in meetings with the ASEAN states that it believes that "countries from outside the region" should not be allowed to conduct joint military exercises with ASEAN states. This has not prevented the members from both continuing and expanding upon the regular bilateral and multilateral military exercises with the US Pacific Command:

The annual US-Thai Cobra Gold Exercises now include Singapore and Malaysia. Indonesia, Malaysia, and the US are also reported to have carried out joint military exercises throughout the late 1990s. China has also made it clear that it is not pleased by ASEAN's engagement of India. Nevertheless, ASEAN diplomats have encouraged India to resolve its internal political and economic issues so that it can apply more energy towards being active in the region. In the economic arena, the ASEAN states have been in discussions, both individually and collectively, on establishing Free Trade Agreement (FTA) with Japan, as well as China. Japan's recent push for an FTA with the ASEAN states is seen as a response to China's own work in this area. Like elsewhere in the world, the security questions continue to be influenced by economic issues. China's trade with Southeast Asia has shown phenomenal growth from mid-80s. China's steady ascent as an economic and regional military power would be one of the main factor of uncertainty in considering the security and stability of Southeast Asia. There are two views on the "China Threat" for the region. One is that by embracing market economy and integrating with global economy any inclination of China to establish its claims in the region by military means would be constrained by the negative economic consequences. At the eighth summit in Nov. 2002, ASEAN and China also agreed to establish the ASEAN-China Free Trade Agreement, which will cover a market of 1.7 billion consumers with a combined gross domestic product of US$ 1.5 trillion to US$ 2 trillion and annual two-way trade of US$ 1.2 trillion.

It is interesting to see that by the end of the last century China has established more than 500 joint ventures with the countries in the region involving investment more than 900 million dollars. The southeast Asian countries had established more than 13000 projects in China and invested 10 billion dollars. China and the six original ASEAN states - Brunei, Indonesia, Malaysia, the Philippines, Singapore and Thailand - are to be in the free-trade area by 2010. The less developed members Cambodia, Laos, Myanmar and Vietnam would follow by 2015. Other agreements signed were cooperation in such areas as drug trafficking, agricultural cooperation and a landmark declaration on territorial disputes in the South China Sea. The declaration on south China sea stresses a desire to prevent further tensions due to territorial disputes over the resource-rich Spratly Islands, Chinese Deputy Foreign Minister Wang Yi said after the signing that China and ASEAN are seeking "common security" in their ties "with a new concept and a modality of security that is a clean break from Cold War models of security". The other point of view on the Chinese threat is that China, through military modernization and acquisition of high technology weapons would not be averse to using military means to achieve regional goals such as control over south China sea and retaking of Taiwan.

ASEAN Relathionship with Russia

The collapse of the former Soviet Union removed largely the political influence of the successor state Russia. External isolation arising from political, economic and military weakness became evident after collapse of the Soviet Union. In addition to the serious economic woes, entrenched feudalism and lawlessness by gangster groups kept Russia preoccupied with its domestic problems and denied it the opportunity to play a meaningful role in Asia Pacific affairs. Russia, like China, however is concerned about the negative impact of US dominance on Asia Pacific's international relations and foreign policy. Russia yet remains a major military and nuclear power with vast resources (gas and energy supplies) for exploitation and development in Russian Far east, which is vital for Asia Pacific region with its fast growing economy. It has a role to play in easing tensions in the Korean peninsula. Reforms in Russia has brought in a more positive political attitude towards Russia. Sino Russian rapprochement and improvement of Russian ASEAN relations are visible positive developments. Russia is also aware of the vast potential in trade expansion and economic cooperation with the East Asian countries.

The former Soviet Union's exports were of the order of 10 billion dollars or 10% of its exports at the end of cold war and imports were 10.3 billion dollars or 8% of its imports. Russia sees the need for the gradual integration of its economy with the well formed economic structure of East Asia. On its part ASEAN does not see a Russian threat to the region. ASEAN would stand to benefit politically and economically by integrating Russian power into Asian balance of power comprising major actors like China, Japan, India and the US. In the next 10 years or so Russia can be expected to rebuild itself as a major world power with a capacity to project its power in the Asia pacific region.

The relevance of Russian power to South East Asia would be largely economic in terms of economic interaction between South East Asia and the Russian Far East. Russian interest would be to focus on economic cooperation as a strategy to influence regional balance of power in favour of Russia's long-term political and security interests. There is also a view that Moscow would not be too perturbed by present US predominant military influence in the region, given its own weakness at present to act as a counter weight to China's domination of the region.

ASEAN Relathionship with U.S.A.

The fear of remilitarized Japan and Chinese strategic aims in the region caused considerable concern about the reduction of US military presence in the region. Singapore signed an MOU offering access to certain facilities for the US navy, basically to relocate US navy's 7th fleet logistical command from Subic bay to Singapore. Malaysia was equally willing to offer base facilities to the US military. Even Jakarta has done so. Surabaya, PT PAL entered into an agreement to service US warships. Thailand and Brunei have also offered their facilities. Thus almost all of them are urging continued presence of the US in the region. The US has been a strong supporter of multilateral arrangements in the region. The US has also often indicated that reduction of the military presence in the region consequent to the disappearance of the "Soviet threat" does not mean reduced commitment of the US to the region. A National security strategy paper acknowledged the growing importance of the region to the U.S. Winston Lord the U.S. Asst. Secy. of State said in June 1994 before the senate committee on foreign affairs that Asia being the most lucrative terrain for American jobs and exports is the key to the economic health of the US.

The Asia pacific has acquired more than 70 billion dollars in U.S. direct investment. Developing multilateral forums for security consultations, while maintaining solid foundations of its alliances was one among ten goals of the US policy in Asia. In the past the U.S. preferred to operate bilaterally with its Asian allies. Five of America's seven bilateral security treaties are in Asia. The US has shown its willingness to entertain multilateral solutions to the security situation in Asia. There has also been a new formulation in the U.S. Policy for the region called "cooperative vigilance". This involves "mobile and flexible" arrangements instead of fixed bases with greater access at a time on need basis and stationing of fewer forces on permanent basis. While US political leadership in the region would dwindle and could be largely replaced by Japan due to its economic influence, it would still be a leader who cannot be ignored largely due to the concerns of the regional countries over rising power of Japan and strategic ambitions of China. While US is moving towards a new concept of power projection based on multilateral consultations, China is going ahead with building a strong blue water navy and power projection to go along with the opening to the outside world and emphasis on sea trade. During the Clinton administration, the United States had basically completed its military deployment in Asia by elevating military cooperative relations with the peripheral states around China. it had however explicitly adhered to the "one China" principle.

With coming to power of Bush (Jr.) the situation greatly changed. The words and actions of the administration after September 11 are very different with a strong tilt towards Taiwan such as declaring the intention to protect Taiwan by force, improving the scale and level of arms sales to Taiwan, allowing its defense minister to visit the United States and meet senior functionaries. Bush included China as one of the allies in the "axis of evil" countries. The new Nuclear Posture Review listed China as one of the countries that could be struck by nuclear weapons in an emergency. The National Security Strategy of the United States issued on Sept. 20, 2001 a comprehensive document laying out America's foreign and security policy in the wake of last September's terrorist attack - welcomed the emergence of a strong, peaceful, and prosperous China, but warns China against pursuing "advanced military capabilities that can threaten its neighbours in the Asia-Pacific region". The abolition of the ABM Treaty and the establishment of NMD and TMD systems will raise America's strategic deterrence against China and weaken latter's strategic deterrence against the United States. During a five nation tour of Asia towards end July 2001 Colin Powell unveiled a controversial plan to forge closer US military ties with Japan, Australia and South Korea—a move that China immediately attacked as a NATO-like alliance aimed at itself.

The proposal for a four-power defence forum, which was announced in Canberra following Australian ministerial talks with Powell and US Defence Secretary Donald Rumsfeld, has been as usual dressed up in diplomatese as "tentative" and "in the early stage". The purpose of such a proposal seems to be to bring its major allies in the region into line in preparation for any future confrontation with China. All these developments are likely to be interpreted by

China as the widening of the Sino-US strategic imbalance, the deterioration of China's national-security environment and a challenge posed to China. It may well switch back to conservative politics and be forced to become an actual "strategic rival" of the United States in East Asia. One could then witness the return of cold war with China replacing the former Soviet Union as the U.S. rival. The right wing in the Bush administration made a concerted push to place a far higher priority on US engagement in South East Asia, where, it was argued, Washington had crucial strategic and economic interests. It saw a security "threat" from China and advocated military engagement with the region. A Council on Foreign Relations task force report outlined the extent of US interests in the region. It pointed out that the region with nearly 525 million people and a $700 billion GNP, and being the fifth largest trading partner of the U.S, cannot remain an "afterthought" in US policy. It then recorded the investments of US-based firms, second only to Japanese companies, with most of the top Fortune 500 multinational corporations with significant interests in South East Asia. With the exception of Indonesia, US direct investment is beginning to grow again after the Asian financial crisis. It noted the oil and gas reserves and production levels in Indonesia and Brunei. Indonesia, the only Asian member of OPEC, accounts for 20 percent of the world's liquefied natural gas (LNG) exports, and its reserves are still not fully known. New oil and gas fields are being discovered there, in Malaysia, in Vietnam and in the Philippines. Repeating by now the well known geopolitical importance of the region with some of word's most critical sea-lanes the task force report pointed out that any disruption or dislocation of energy supplies would have an immediate and devastating impact on the economies of East Asia and would have significant secondary effects on the US economy, as well.

It recommended strengthening of the US military presence for the purpose of maintaining regional security through the prevention of intraregional conflict and domination by an outside power or coalition and emphasized "joint and combined military training exercises" as well as "individual and small group exchanges and training". A RAND report in 2000 explicitly drew attention to the danger posed by China to prevent US predominance in South East Asia and advocated what it termed "a hedging strategy" to strengthen the US military presence and access to facilities in the region. No explanation was offered as to why an economically weaker China, heavily dependent on foreign investment and export markets, particularly American, and lacking in sophisticated naval and air power would present any challenge to the US. As in North East Asia where the US maintains tens of thousands of troops along with naval and air support, the "Chinese threat" is a convenient pretext for maintaining and strengthening Washington's military position in South East Asia. The report adds that economic growth in the Asia-Pacific region, which is important to the economic security and well-being of the United States and other powers, depends on preserving American presence and influence in the region and unrestricted access to sea lanes. The RAND study advocated "a robust security assistance programme to allies in the region, particularly the Philippines".

It called for the provision of "urgently needed air defence and naval patrol assets to the Philippines . . . to reestablish deterrence *vis-à-vis* China" and advocated the restoration of "full military-to-military ties with Indonesia with resumption of transfer of military equipment and spare parts to prevent further deterioration of Indonesian defense capabilities. In view of the current weaknesses in regional security arrangements, especially considering the China factor, the U.S. is unlikely to give up its political, economic and security presence in the region. Japan is one of the countries which would actively work for the continuance, if not enhancing of this presence. China on its part, while wanting to improve its economic ties to the U.S., will at the same time strengthen its links to Russia as a counter weight to the growing U.S. pressure against it, particularly on the Taiwan issue. Amidst all this the U.S.-led war against Iraq has brought in some uncertainties in the region. The fear of a backlash by Islamic militants has increased the economic uncertainties.

A local leader of the fundamentalist Islamic party PAS in Malaysia was quoted as having said that though they do not like Saddam Hussein, the U.S. invasion of Iraq is a crusade against Islam. The economic uncertainties are further overshadowed by the possibility of a backlash within the country by the militant Muslim factions. Malaysian government is trying to persuade the fundamentalist opposition party PAS to have a common stand on Iraq. Singapore with an all time high unemployment figures and the fear of retaliation from Islamic fundamentalists because of its pro-US stance is nervous. Thailand has tightened security along its border with Malaysia, fearing incursions from Malaysia into Thailand's Muslim-majority southern district to strengthen militancy. The Pro-American Philippine Government (as well as the Thai Government) expelled two Iraqi diplomats in the last week of March on charges of spying, which was not to the liking of some of its neighbors.

Indonesia, in spite of its oil, has a falling FDI, a deteriorating law-and-order situation and the image of sheltering terrorists. The image of a liberal Islamic country was seriously damaged by the bombing of a nightclub in Bali. Governments are worried about a possible swing to the right and ASEAN official sources have been quoted by the press as saying that the number of arrests of suspected militants in the region has exceeded 20,000, essentially to prevent militant violence. All the ASEAN countries are preparing themselves mentally for bad days ahead and losing hope of increased foreign direct investment (FDI) and bilateral aid. With all this, the ASEAN foreign ministers could not find a unified position on Iraq at their two-day retreat in Kota Kinabalu, Malaysia in March 2003. With the exception of South Korea, Japan, the Philippines and Singapore, four countries who depend upon US military for their national security, leaders of other countries in East Asia have, in principle, opposed the US war in Iraq. Even in Philippines, middle-class Filipinos including house wives have come out in force to protest against the war, largely at the encouragement of Catholic Church leaders.

As a Malaysian official put it "If the Iraq war continues for a month, some of us will be in the deep sea and others [ASEAN countries] on rocking boats." The war also is bringing back the "ugly American " image of the U.S. A Hotel owner in a Thailand tourist resort banned American tourists. Vietnamese media criticized U.S. for its action. The muslims in various countries of the region labeled the war as an unjust war against Islam. In South Korea recent newspaper surveys put the opposition to the war as high as 80 percent, showing the changing perceptions in a country that hosts 37,000 US troops and is one of the staunchest supporters of the U.S. In Muslim majority Malaysia the war has led to widespread resentment. The Malaysian parliament passed a unanimous motion protesting against the "US-led invasion" of Iraq. People were reported to be holding the view that the war is being waged by a superpower armed to the teeth against a country that has gone through almost a decade of economic sanctions, with their military defenses reduced to a minimum. Prime Minister Mahathir termed it as a return to the stone age.

The President of another Muslim majority country Indonesia, Megawati, said that her country would not support any US-backed initiatives for war. She deplored the invasion as "an act of aggression," which is in contravention of international law and called for United Nations action for peaceful disarmament of Iraq. The country witnessed a sudden emergence of anti Americanism with anti-war protests and anti-American rhetoric by students as well as by Muslim-dominated political and religious groups in Indonesia. In Philippines middle-class Filipinos, especially house wives, protested against the war, largely with the encouragement of Catholic Church leaders. Archbishop Cardinal Sin termed the war illegal under the United Nations Charter and immoral under the Christian principles.The Government itself, in view of its dependence on the U.S. for its security. was muted in its reaction. So was the reaction of Singapore. China firmly opposed the war and called for the immediate cessation of hostility. This is in contrast to its almost neutral stance during Operation Desert Storm in 1991. China then abstained from exercising its right of veto to block the military campaign. China at that time required the goodwill of the United States to overcome the international opprobrium over the brutal crackdown on student activists in Tiananmen Square in 1989.

Much has been made of Washington's growing security presence in Southeast Asia in the aftermath of September 11. The administration of George W. Bush, however, was likely to have pursued a greater regional role even without the war on terrorism. During visits to the region in the spring of 2001, administration officials complained that China had "eaten our lunch" diplomatically. Even if the threat of terrorism in the region were to subside, Washington would still seek a more active role in the region, finding ways to reinvigorate relationships with individual ASEAN states. There is however no doubt that the war against terrorism started post Sept. 11, 2001, has seen a more assertive presence and activity of the US in the region. Discovery of Al Qaeda cells in Indonesia and terrorist activities like the bomb explosion in Bali (Indonesia), arrest of Al Qaeda members in Malaysia, the Philippines, Indonesia and Singapore and Islamic terrorist activities in the Philippines have hastened the cooperation of the regional countries with the US in the war against terrorism. Since the mid-1990s, a number of dramatic terrorist attacks have been planned in the region, including attacks on the Pope, President Bill Clinton, and commercial jets. These plans went awry purely by accident. All these factors have made the region the second front in war against terrorism. Southeast Asia is however unlikely to become the second centre of Islamic fundamentalist terrorism as the profound ethnic and religious diversity (including in the practice of Islam) that characterizes the area militates against the establishment of a fundamentalist hegemony by any one group. Terrorist activities can also affect the foreign investments. These have already come down drastically after the 1997 financial crisis. It was US$ 10 billion in 2000, a 37 percent decline from the $16 billion in 1999. The figure was $27 billion in 1997 and $19 billion in 1998, the year the worst effects of the financial crisis were felt. Incidents like the Bali bombing where 200 people lost their lives could in fact make China an even more attractive investment site than other ASEAN countries. These hard realities made the ARF in its meeting in Aug. 2002 pledge to fight international terrorism. The ARF Statement on Measures Against Terrorist Financing lays out specific steps that the members will take to fight the terrorist threat. This includes :

- freezing terrorist assets;
- implementation of international standards;
- international cooperation on the exchange of information and outreach;
- technical assistance; and
- compliance and reporting.

During the negotiations among Association of Southeast Asian Nations (ASEAN) member states that preceded the US-ASEAN Joint Declaration for Cooperation to Combat International Terrorism. Indonesia and Vietnam were both reluctant to sign any agreement that might legitimize foreign intervention on their soil. Their concerns were addressed by recognizing in the agreement "the principles of sovereign equality, territorial integrity and non-intervention in the domestic affairs of other states", the guiding principles of ASEAN diplomacy. Opening a "second front," in the war against terrorism, the Bush administration has rapidly increased military and economic support for the Philippines. President Bush recently announced a grant of $78 million in new military aid, including $20 million to purchase U.S. weapons and services and $21 million worth of secondhand arms. In January 2002, the U.S. sent nearly 1,300 U.S. advisers and support personnel to participate in as a six-month training mission to bolster the counter-terrorism capabilities of Philippine forces. They were deployed in the south of the archipelago to assist in hostage rescue and counter-insurgency operations. The mission was credited with killing or capturing some Abu Sayyaf members. The move was widely heralded as the opening of a second front in Washington's war on terrorism.

More recently, in February 2003, the United States sent about 3,000 troops to engage in a major combat offensive in the southern Philippines aimed at wiping out the militant Muslim group of Abu Sayyaf. The deployment followed hard on the heels of the arrests of dozens of alleged Al Qaeda operatives in Singapore, Malaysia, and the Philippines. With the Taliban in Afghanistan having been routed, Southeast Asia - home to radical Islamist groups such as the Jemaah Islamiah (JI), Abu Sayyaf group, and the Kumpulan Mujahideen Malaysia (KMM) - was starting to seem like the new home base for the terrorist movement that had brought down the World Trade Center. An official in the region was quoted as calling Al Qaeda the McDonald's of terrorism, "with Osama bin Laden sending his representatives to Southeast Asia looking for potential franchisees. Al Qaeda provided the plans for terrorist operations, and the local operators" were sent to Afghanistan for training by Al Qaeda in explosives and weapons. September 11 and its aftermath have already transformed U.S. relations with many Southeast Asian nations. The strained relations with Muslim-majority Malaysia have seen considerable improvement. Prime Minister Mahathir bin Mohamad has come in for considerable praise by the U.S. for supporting the U.S. war on terrorism. Indonesia, on the other hand received initially some brickbats for failing to be similarly cooperative and crack down on its own extremists. There has however been some toning down of the criticism in recent months, The Philippines has come in for considerable attention from the U.S. in latter's war against terrorism. Philippines had not occupied such a prominent place in U.S. foreign policy since the end of the Cold War.

Thus Al Qaeda led terrorism has seen once again the prominent hand of the U.S. in the regional affairs of South East Asia. September 11, 2001 also presented the Bush administration the opportunity to give effect to the proposals drawn up by think tanks such as RAND and the Council on Foreign Affairs taskforce. The "global war on terrorism" was a good pretext to overcome local opposition to an enhanced US military presence in South East Asia. Under strong pressure from Washington, one national leader after another was compelled to offer support, including the use of staging facilities and military bases and the granting of over flight rights for US forces bound for Afghanistan. Philippine President Gloria Arroyo has been in the forefront but all the other governments, including that of Indonesia which has been repeatedly chided for insufficient cooperation, have cooperated in varying degrees. Senior Policy Analyst Angel Rabasa, one of the authors of the 2000 Rand study, appeared before the Congressional Subcommittee on East Asia and the Pacific last December to argue that China's emergence as a major regional power required "a robust security assistance. . . especially to the Philippines" where the US should provide "urgently needed air defence and naval patrol assets . . . to reestablish deterrence *vis-à-vis* China." Heritage foundation has argued that Washington must always keep open the option of direct military intervention if there is a clear and immediate threat to US citizens or property that local security forces in Southeast Asia cannot handle.

ASEAN Relationship with Japan

Japan which already has a large economic role in the region appears to be ready to play a greater role in political and security issues. Under pressure from the U.S. during the tenure of Reagan as President, it agreed to share the security responsibility of the US by partially financing US defence efforts. In 1981 it announced a national security policy to include territorial, air and sea lane defences up to 1000 miles. Later it expressed its desire to double its defence expenditure. In 1987 it abandoned the policy of restricting defence expenditure to 1% of its GNP. Given its GNP even the 1% of GNP expenditure in absolute terms was huge and the country became the biggest defence spender after the US and the USSR in late 80s. By the end of the last century it was spending more than 30 billion dollars. Japan's military capability has tremendously increased and as one analyst put it the SDF of Japan is no mean animal in its array of equipment. level of military technology and other issues. At present the Japanese constitution provides only for self-defence forces with minimum necessary force for self defence. But the minimum necessary has been interpreted differently at different times by the extant Japanese government taking into account the prevailing international situation, the standards of military technology, etc. While trying to spread its influence in Indo China, it has targeted the SEA countries as possible partners in economic growth and development. It would not be averse to playing a security role in protecting its economic interests. It is the largest foreign investor in the region and largest trading partner in this Asian grouping. Its redeployment of production facilities in these countries following upward movement of its currency yen called for heavy financial investment in the region. Japan has become the core of a production structure in which ASEAN economies are integrated. Japan has followed a policy of strategic control of the region's market with hundreds and millions of consumers. It also tries to restrict defence expenditure in other regions by using aid as a lever. In 1994 Japan approved the UN peace keeping operations cooperation law that would allow 2000 SDF personnel to be deployed abroad for logistical support to UN operations. Thus Japan could be expected to play a proactive role in this region which is vital for it both from economic and strategic point of view. It is not inconceivable that its defence forces may plan for a future contingency when its strategic interests may be affected.

Thus, the dynamic multilateral diplomacy, economic growth, social change and military modernization portends possibilities of stable prosperity but problems still remain threatening times of tensions in the region. To sum up, the major security threat perception of the regional countries concerns only China. They would prefer to deal with this in two simultaneous tracks. One, by increasing economic interactions, engaging in dialogues and drawing China as much as possible into multilateral discussions. Simultaneously they would prefer the U.S. to return to the region to provide for any eventuality. They would also not be averse to, if not actively encourage, the presence of other powers like India in the region as a counter balance against China. None of them are however seeking to confront China militarily either individually or as a group. The current unhappiness in the region over U.S.'s invasion of Iraq would not, in the long-term, affect the region's desire for return of the U.S. to the region to keep peace and security.

Revisiting Southeast Asia after the Cold War

The pattern of inter-state relations and the policies of major powers towards Southeast Asia have undergone several twists and turns since the end of the Second World War. In the initial years, the international politics was naturally affected by the manner in which the process of decolonisation was completed. The circumstances in which the departing colonial authorities transferred sovereignty, whether or not they were sympathetic to nationalist aspirations, shaped the world view and consequently the foreign policies of the newly independent countries. The onset of the Cold War and the attempts made by Moscow and Washington to incorporate the region within their strategic framework, cast their long shadow on Southeast Asia. During the First Indo-China Conflict, spanning from 1945 to 1954, there was the inevitable confrontation between the forces of French imperialism and the resurgent nationalist aspirations of the Indo-Chinese peoples. The ideological conflict and Washington's refusal to reconcile itself to realities in Indo-China led to the Second Indo-China War (1959-1975), which began first with US intervention in Vietnam and later on Laos and Cambodia. It was rationalised as an attempt to defend the "free world" against "monolithic communism"; however, it gradually turned out to be a bitter conflict between United States and its allies and the radical nationalist forces in Indo-China, supported for their own selfish reasons, by China and Soviet Union. The onset of the Sino-Soviet and Sino-Vietnamese conflicts made the situation in Southeast Asia more complex. After 1975, the hitherto concealed antagonisms among the three communist states - Soviet Union, China and Vietnam - burst into the open, leading to Vietnamese intervention in Cambodia, Chinas "punitive expedition" against Vietnam, confrontation between ASEAN (supported by both United States and China) and Vietnam - all major strands of the Third Indo-China Conflict. Caught between the Tiger and the Crocodile, the people of Cambodia underwent enormous suffering.

As the *New York Times*, in an editorial some years ago, wrote, "If the Heavens could weep over a peoples suffering, Cambodia would never know any drought". With the end of the Cold War, like other parts of the world, Southeast Asia has also entered a period of transition. The guns, at last, are silenced in Cambodia and the war weary people are provided an opportunity to enjoy the benefits of peace.

The UN role in Cambodia, under extremely difficult circumstances, the successful conduct of a general election and the political marginalisation of the Khmer Rouge are portends of the seminal changes on the anvil. The new opportunities of co-operation among hitherto adversaries, the dynamics of continuity and change and the attempts made by the Southeast Asian governments to acquire the necessary flexibility and responsiveness to meet the challenges of the new situation make Southeast Asia an interesting laboratory of international politics. The collapse of the Berlin Wall brought the era of ideological conflict to an end; however, it has not resulted in, as Francis Fukuyama claims in his famous 1989 article The End of History. It is no doubt true that containment of communism has ceased to be the dominating force in international relations, because the communist world itself has been shattered in many parts of the world, and the communists themselves are discarding many tenets of orthodox Marxism-Leninism. The removal of centralised rule and party dictatorship have released ethnic antagonisms which are deeply rooted in historical memories. What is more, socialist planning, as an instrument of eradicating poverty and ushering in a classless society, is under critical re-evaluation. China and Vietnam, the two major outposts of communism in Asia, have today recognised the value of market economy and private ownership. This fact was most tellingly illustrated by Vietnamese Foreign Minister Nguyen Co Thach who told the Australian Foreign Minister Gareth Evans that his favourite bed time reading was Samuelson's *Economics*. The continued pre-eminence of the United States, more so after the Gulf War, coupled with the disintegration of the Soviet Union, should not make us conclude that the world is becoming uni-polar.

A more deeper analysis of the cross-currents impinging upon Southeast Asia reveals that there will be increasing strategic fluidity in the region. As Earl C. Ravenal wrote in an article in *Foreign Policy* a couple of years ago, the US experience with the Vietnamese quagmire and the Russian misadventure in Afghanistan throw up interesting conclusions: "The shifting and unsound basis of political allegiance; the transcience of any gains, political or military; the exemplary ingratitude of clients; the grossly unfavourable cost benefit ratio of intervention; the bottomless pit of economic aid; and finally the rise of self-sufficient and powerful regional hegemonic powers, suspicious and resentful of extra-regional penetration." The United States is unlikely to maintain its military presence in the region in a big way. The member states of ASEAN do want a continued American security presence, but the absence of a Soviet threat, the decline in American economic strength and the downgrading of Southeast Asia as a region of pre-eminent strategic importance - all these facts are leading to the end of an important chapter in American history. The closure of the Subic Bay in November 1992, on the insistence of Manila, marks the end of high profile American military presence in Southeast Asia. Sheldon Simon rightly points out, "Faced with a massive balance of payments deficit and a declining dollar, the United States foresees a lengthy period of no growth defence budgets and a continued low priority for Southeast Asia as a region for naval and air deployments". However, it will have vital economic stakes, including the maintenance of maritime passage through the region.

As far as Moscow is concerned, preoccupied as it will be with domestic turmoil and fashioning a new set of relations with United States and Europe, Southeast Asia will be a low priority area in the 1990's. Bordering on Myanmar, Laos and Vietnam, China's foreign policy will be watched with keen interest in all Southeast Asian capitals. Beijing is conscious of the growing importance of economic strength and technological capabilities in international relations; naturally it has lent its support to the process of detente and is keen to avoid tensions which may undermine its economic development. However, the brutal suppression of pro-democracy movement in June 1990 is an illustration that China's ruling elites will be prepared to go to any extent in order to cling on to power. While there was understandable criticism in the United States, the ASEAN countries were less inclined than the West to allow the Tiananmen incident to disrupt their relations with China. The present Chinese policy of maintaining an influential position is a prelude for an era of enhanced political and security role in Southeast Asia. Diplomatic relationship with Indonesia has been restored and negotiations are under way to improve relations with Vietnam. However, there are severe limitations to China's playing a major role in Southeast Asia. China's growing blue water naval capability in the South China Sea; Beijing's support to the tyrannical regime in Myanmar and growing security stakes in that country; the conflicting claims over Spratlys and Paracels - all these are likely flashpoints in China's relations with Southeast Asian countries. What is more, the Sino-Vietnamese conflict in March 1988 near Spratlys is a grim warning that China would take advantage of the vulnerability of its southern neighhbours and could even resort to force to buttress its territorial claims. Beijing also has entered into a contract with an American company, Crestone, to conduct oil exploration near Spratlys, which Hanoi considers as part of its continental shelf.

The question of Japan's security capabilities will be another dimension in Southeast Asia's security scenario. Japan is the world's second largest economic power, with the prospect of overtaking the United States soon. From a strategic angle, the Soviet threat that drew Japan in a security partnership with the United States is gone. The US-Japan relations, both economic and political, are going to enter into a troubled era. So long as the convergence of interests remained, Japan was not suspect in the eyes of the regional actors. A positive aspect of this policy is Tokyo's contribution to the UN Forces for maintenance of peace and security in Cambodia. But there are signals to the contrary also. It is necessary to remind ourselves that in absolute terms, Japan's defence budget of US Dollars 30.09 billion is four times more than the defence budgets of member states of ASEAN put together. Any aggressive posture by Japan, in addition to its status as an economic colossus, will naturally create resentment in Southeast Asia and revive memories of Japanese Occupation during the Second World War.

This concern about a possible security challenge by Japan is also shared by Beijing. How has Southeast Asia responded to the new challenges and continuing strategic fluidity in the region? It is a strange paradox, but true, that the onset of peace has triggered an "arms race" in the region. Except for Vietnam, which has made substantial reductions in defence allocation, there is an upswing in all ASEAN countries. In a recent article in the *Asian Defence Journal*, Amitav Acharya provides a detailed analysis. The increase in defence budget in Thailand in 1992 was 13.5 percent over 1991, 30.8 percent over 1990 and 55.0 percent over 1989. Singapore's 1992 defence budget represents an 11.6 percent increase over 1991, 20.3 percent over 1990 and 40.9 percent over 1989. Malaysia's defence expenditure in 1992 increased by 21.8 percent over 1991, while for Indonesia, the 1992 defence budget is 14.1 percent over the previous year. The defence budget of the Philippines for 1992 is 42.9 percent higher than 1989. How does one explain the military build up in ASEAN countries? The official explanation is the necessity to expand, update and modernise defence capabilities. This reasoning is undoubtedly true. But what is left unstated is the fact of uncertainty about the future and the necessity to cope with threats from both within and outside the region. While ASEAN, over the years, have emerged as a viable regional organisation and the Vietnamese occupation of Cambodia provided the rallying point, there are unresolved disputes among Southeast Asian countries. As Amitav Acharya points out, "Such rivalries include long standing territorial disputes, such as the Philippines claim to Sabah, or the Horsburg Lighthouse between Singapore and Malaysia, or the Sipidan and Ligitan islands between Indonesia and Malaysia.

There can be no question that some bilateral relationships within ASEAN remain tenuous, with Singapore-Malaysia relations being the most vulnerable to mutual suspicions and periodic crises." How will Southeast Asian countries respond to the challenges of the 1990's? An optimistic scenario will be Vietnam normalising relations with the United States and getting the much needed economic assistance for the rehabilitation of its war ravaged economy. Cambodia, Laos, Vietnam and Myanmar would become members of ASEAN and an era of co-operative co-existence could begin in Southeast Asia. Although ASEAN is far away from emerging as a security organisation, the member states have bilateral security agreements, provision of training facilities, joint military exercises and exchange of intelligence. Given good will and understanding, even the arms race, referred to earlier, could become a common shield against external intervention.

A more realistic assessment will be that Southeast Asia will witness considerable strategic fluidity in the 1990's. With the settlement of the Cambodian conflict, the core focus of ASEAN unity and the major rallying point of ASEAN capitals have been swept off the ground. In other words, ASEAN may no longer be the primary pillar in the foreign policies of these countries. In the past, despite the facade of unity, even purely local events have created frictions among ASEAN countries. The visit of Israeli President to Singapore, Kuala Lumpur's decision to send the Boston Symphony Orchestra home, Thai criticism of Singapore's treatment of illegal immigrants, Singapore's decision to provide 'facilities' to the United States, the capture of Thai trawlers fishing illegally in Malaysian waters, the presence of a large number of Indonesian illegal immigrants in Malaysia, Jakarta's lukewarm response to Kuala Lumpur's recent major foreign policy initiatives - all these have created differences. It is also likely that Vietnam and Indonesia, given their size, population, historical memories and desire to play a major role, may chart out their own foreign policies and may find convergence of interests, especially against the machinations of Beijing. Coming together of Vietnam and Indonesia would be a positive factor in strengthening the forces of peace and security in the region. It is unfortunate, but true, that India has neglected Southeast Asia for long. Since Southeast Asia, next only to South Asia, is going to be a region of "primary strategic interest" to India, New Delhi must try to develop a perception and understanding of the common security interests that we share with Southeast Asian countries. Given our national heritage, commitment to the sovereignty of states and peaceful co-existence of nations, our inputs must strengthen those forces which would advocate and pursue the objectives of Zone of Peace, Freedom and Neutrality in Southeast Asia.

Terrorism and South-East Asia: Contemporary Scenario

Efforts to combat terrorism through UN resolutions and action have been going on for the last several years. To enable meaningful action, it is necessary for the international community to agree on a firm and specific definition of the term 'terrorism'. None of the several academic definitions of this term, currently under discussion, commands universal acceptance. Terrorism is a concept that concerns both its cause and consequences. Its consequences attract condemnation that has to be general based on a broadly accepted definition of this term. Certain operational definitions have received majority acceptance without any particular definition able to claim universal acceptance. The acceptable and generally accepted operational definition includes substantive damage to individuals and/or state security forces, or public buildings, installations and other facilities. The issue concerns a society under attack, capable of anticipating mostly the instruments and means of destruction that may be employed by a terrorist. The world has witnessed several dramatic ways of inflicting damage or causing mayhem and destruction, and attracting huge worldwide publicity (e.g. hijacking, hostage taking, use of explosives with or without the desire of involving suicidal attack and narcotics-related terror). In all these aspects covering the deed, as also the attempt, it is difficult to focus on the primary objective of the terrorist. Often the intention is to coerce a state to do a specific something, or to desist from doing a specific something, making the line between terrorism and organised crime indistinguishably thin. One difference between the criminal's coercion, and the act of terrorists is politics.

The terrorist's purpose is always political, and more often than not, propaganda motivated - the desire to keep alive an issue or a dispute or an ideological principle. Acts of terror are seen, and analysed, either in terms of their consequences, or their causes. Consequences are invariably horrendous, as the targets are almost always ordinary citizens and. therefore, the world at large finds it simple enough to condemn such attempts/acts unequivocally, and with moral clarity and certitude. Sovereign states have to deal with each incident of terrorism almost instantaneously for the sake of reassuring their people that such crimes against the people shall not go unpunished, and that their recurrence must be prevented. Those focussing on causes of terrorism, try to discover and analyse motivations, roots, occasionally even the justification for such attempts or acts. In general, causes of terrorism are : disaffection, alienation, poverty, lack of social justice, lack of liberty, lack of respect for the individuals and their rights. Often, however, terrorism is a response to a specific and broader crisis or complaint about injustice, as seen in the Palestinian case. Against this background, and when one is analysing the causes of terrorism in the ASEAN region, one is surprised that it can co-exist with the palpable reality of the remarkable economic success of ASEAN states in the last two decades, which has made them enormously productive and affluent. Their economic growth results from the expansion of their foreign trade. It is not usual or normal for the people of a region or country with booming profitable trade and production of wealth to spare time or pay attention towards terrorism and violence. Pursuing this line of reasoning, one sees clearly that ASEAN as an organisation has shown both tolerance and wisdom in the conduct of its regional politics.

Their thinking and planning have been based on the primary importance being attached to the requirements of economic growth, development and success of the people and countries of their region. This has made it possible for this region to submerge a host of minor or petty *inter-se* differences and prejudices. Member-states of ASEAN have generally refused to exaggerate state-to-state relations their *inter-se* irritants. Thus, unlike in other regions and sub-regions of Asia, a number of their traditional and classic *inter-se* differences have got eroded, sometimes even eliminated. ASEAN has been remarkable in its ability to strengthen their unity as an instrument assisting their pursuit of prosperity. The region has deliberately and consciously viewed with tolerance even those issues which could have become potentially nasty, more particularly in the areas of religion and culture. This has helped within the region build a broad mutual acceptance, and an atmosphere of concern and consideration within the region. Manifestations of intolerance and rigidity espoused by certain hardliners amongst them, using Islam as an element, in this region, have not found the region sympathising with them. And the region, on the whole, has remained balanced and moderate, and the entire membership continues to make every effort to maintain tolerance. The US-led international coalition against terrorism promises to be involved in a multi-faceted struggle against all terrorist groups globally.

It will gradually attend also to those states which try to confront with violence and frighten much larger populations, within which some groups may agree to support and shelter terrorists. Anglo-Saxon nations, and several members of the NATO do not see this as a war against Islam or Muslim populations. They do note, however, as do numerous Islamic scholars and intellectuals that the ideology of radical Islamism is fundamentally religious, and has profited in the last two decades from socio-economic discontent, and the failures of certain Muslim states to move towards democracy and productivity. Radical Islamic groups have deliberately gained support and prestige by providing aid to the poor and dispossessed. However, this has not happened in all, or even a majority of countries, in each region. Manifestations and ripples produced by Islam in the ASEAN region have been comparatively mild, and even when some people have been excited, nothing really sizzling has happened. In recent years, however, the problems of the Moros in the Philippines, and other splinter organisations that have waxed and waned there, have become insistent and obtrusive. Moros is a word derived from the old word "Moor" which in earlier centuries was used by the Europeans as a synonym for Muslims. On Easter Sunday in April 2000 a nebulous Islamic armed group called Abu Sayyaf, which had been active since 1999 on the island of Jolo in the Sulu Province of the Philippines, took 21 foreign tourists and several Malaysians hostage. This was attempted successfully in the diving resort of Sipadan in the Malaysian State of Sabah. It was ironic that this attack took place on Malaysian territory, as the Moro National Liberation Front (MNLF) had been enjoying a certain amount of clandestine backing from Malaysia. Indeed. Malaysia had long been known for providing clandestine support to the Independence Movement in Southern Philippines, but it had always acted with caution and great discretion. The Moro National Liberation Front had often used the Malaysian State of Sabah as the training ground and refuge for their Muslim fighters. By making this attack, the Abu Sayyaf mercenaries and fundamentalists signalled to the Malaysian Government that terrorism and criminality can often be insensitive enough to bite the hand of its own protectors.

Over the years several organisations came up with roughly the same objective, i.e. to get the Moros (or the Muslim filipinos) to secede from that country, and achieve a separate identity', perhaps also independent sovereignty These were the MNLF, the MIM (Muslim Independence Movement), the BMLO (the Bangsa Moro Liberation Organisation), the MILF (the Moro Islamic Liberation Front), the NPA (the New People's Army which was a Communist Guerilla outfit which resurrected itself later partly as an Islamic organisation). Between 1970s and the year 2000 all or some of these organisations received backing, support and sympathy from Tun Mustafa Harun of Sabah State of Malaysia, and his Successor Chief Minister of Sabah, Harris Salleh. Over the years a number of notorious separatist Muslim leaders also emerged, e.g. Nur Misuari, Rashid Lucman, Hashim Salamat, Dimas Pindato. During these years, money and weapons started trickling into the Moro National Liberation Front and some of other organisations from Saudi Arabia, Libya, Sudan, Pakistan, Iraq and Syria. Unfortunately, Malaysia chose to be a middleman between the multiplicity of Muslim leaders and these several Muslim organisations of this region on the one hand, and the Islamic contributing countries of the Middle-East and from other regions, e.g. Sudan and Pakistan.

As a result of the negotiations of the Moro leaders with President Marcos of the Philippines and his successor President Corazon Aquino, the Autonomous Region of Muslim Mindanoa was constituted. This was a difficult one, but it did materialise. There were lots of differences on certain basic aspects amongst the Muslim leaders and organisations, and as a result of this the original objective of full independence for the Moros was given up gradually, and the concept of Autonomy for the region became acceptable. Emergence of the Abu Sayyaf group between 1991 and 1995 was indeed a major and radical event, as its founder Abdur Rajak Jan Jalani brought in the slogan of *Jehad* against the Government as also the Christians of Mindanoa. The formal name of the organisation of Abu Sayyaf became Al Harkatul Islamia. Jan Jalani had his early training in Lumut in Malaysia, and later training in Palestine and Libya. Abu Sayyaf group did have some shady dealings with Saudi Arabia as also with Al Qaeda.

They kept declaring that the fight of Abu Sayyaf is "a continuation of the Crusades and the Moro Wars against Catholics and Europeans". Luckily for the Philippines and for Malaysia, after certain gruesome and bloody massacres against Christians in the Philippines - incidents which came to be known as the Jabidah massacre, the manili massacre and the IPIL massacre - Abu Sayyaf strayed from their so-called purely Islamic and ideological ideology and got involved with the bombing of Churches, attacks on missionaries and Church dignitaries, kidnapping of rich Christian businessmen, all for ransom. In other words, they did not show adequate stamina or moral strength to remain ideologically motivated, but turned into greedy mercenaries and criminally motivated extortionists. In due course, some of the veterans of violence in this region sought and received assistance for their training and finances from countries such as Pakistan, Afghanistan, Sudan, Syria, Egypt and Saudi Arabia. There is a documentary evidence to show that kidnapping of foreigners, bombing of foreign aeroplanes, murder of missionaries, etc., were started, in this region, because terrorist groups in Pakistan and

Afghanistan saw a major opportunity of making the Philippines the clandestine headquarters for a global, Islamic fundamentalist armed struggle to be waged worldwide.

Their logic was that the Philippines was a soft society with a feeble and soft army and police force, riddled with corruption and. therefore, easily capable of being made a conduit for funds and money laundering. Muslim radicals from certain West Asian and South Asian countries like Pakistan. Afghanistan, Egypt and Yemen, etc., were gradually being infiltrated into the Philippines under the guise of teachers, academics and Muslim NGO activists. The Philippines was obviously a convenient country because it was politically free, entry into the country was easy and unhindered, and it was well located for impacting the potential of Muslim fundamentalism and terrorism in Aceh in Indonesia, and certain regions of Malaysia, e.g. Sabah where fundamentalist militant movements already existed. One such well-known movement in Malaysia was Al Ma'unah. The negotiations for the release of the hostages who had been taken on Easter Sunday. 2000 dragged on for months together. As the negotiations dragged on, apart from the Philippines (which in the meanwhile had started using harsh military methods for the release of the hostages), the Government agencies (mostly the secret services) belonging to Germany, Libya, Malaysia and an African-American individual (Mr. Carl Shilling), got conspicuously involved with the process. This resulted in various heavy payments in US dollars being demanded by and provided to the Abu Sayyaf group.

The availability of this sudden wealth made the Abu Sayyaf group to get fractured within itself and lose its single mindedness. Also, they developed the practice of expanding their extortionist activities even while negotiations and other efforts for the release of hostages were in progress. In due course, most hostages, with just a few exceptions, got released. Libya played a prominent and successful role in the process, and was able with some justification, to claim the largest amount of credit for its straightforward, honest, and somewhat understated role. This enabled Libya once again to become marginally acceptable to "respectable countries". The result was that European businessmen started frequenting that country once again. The Philippines Government came out of the affair fairly well, even though still rated as an inefficient and a somewhat corrupt regime. The blame got attached personally to President Estrada, whereas the Kudos attached itself to the Philippines Armed Forces. Nur Musuari lost his standing as a credible Islamic leader because he proved both inefficient in negotiation and corrupt. By now he has been jailed. Malaysia seems to have learnt its lesson as a backer of terrorism, and has already denounced Abu Sayyaf decisively. It has found it necessary to treat Nur Musuari without any indulgence and often quite harshly, something which he perhaps deserved. Indonesia remained generally indifferent towards all these developments, and this seems to have paid-off, insofar as the reputation and standing of Indonesia are concerned.

Indonesian Struggle Against Terrorism

Finally, the September 11 attacks on the United States and its global campaign against terrorism has put Indonesia on the focus allegedly for being a hotbed of terrorist networks. The Ball blast brought into sharp focus the dilemma of the then Indonesian government under Megawati Sukarnoputri in facing the growth of radical Islam and the threat of terrorism within the country. Megawati had for many months ignored calls from neighbours and in particular from Singapore, which foiled several planned attacks in 2002 and whose senior minister Lee Kuan Yew openly called Indonesia a safe haven for the terrorists in the region, to tackle the terrorist network in her country. Confronted by an unprecedented challenge of the tragedy of Bali, the mounting international pressure and an almost irresistible obligation to track down any possible suspects, the Indonesian government pledged after the Bali blast to press ahead with tough new anti-terror laws and formed an international investigative team to hunt for the culprits. With international help and a more active role by its police forces Indonesia has been able to arrest most of the people who were involved in the Bali blast, and was prosecuting its fight against terrorism with renewed vigor.

The dilemma and hesitation on the part of Megawati's government in the past in moving firmly against the radical Islamic groups was not due to any conviction that terrorist networks did not exist in Indonesia, but essentially because of two main factors: first, her own sense of insecurity emanating from the nature of her coalition government and the fear that rapid move against the radical Islamic groups and particularly detention of Abu Bakar Ba'asyir, who is suspected to be the leader of *Jemaah Islamiyah*, a radical Islamic group operating in Malaysia and Indonesia, allegedly linked to Al Qaeda attempting to carve out an Islamic state, and has a popular following in the country including in her own cabinet, would trigger a Muslim backlash, bring instability in one of the most volatile nations in the region and were to bring down her government; second, the declining state capability in the allocation of resources, maintenance of law and order and weakness of the state apparatus in dealing with such emerging threats. Megawati has not forgotten the fact that despite her party polling the largest number of votes, she could not become the president of the country in the first place because of the opposition of the Islamic groups, who ganged up against her and promoted a minority party leader, Abdurrahman Wahid to be the head of the state.

Since then she had taken extreme care to maintain close liaison with the leading Islamic figures, brought Islamic parties into her government and pursued a policy of appeasement towards radical groups like the Laskyar Jihad, Front Pembela Islam (FPI-Front for the Defence of Islam) and Majelis Mujaheedeen Indonesia (MMI-Indonesian Mujaheedeen Council) of which Ba'asyir is the acknowledged leader. In the world's most populous Muslim country while the majority are still quite moderate, yet in recent years radical Islam of Wahabi and

Salafi variant inspired and promoted by Saudi Arabia has a significant following in Indonesia rocked by religious tensions and ethnic separatism. It is no accident that the leaders of all the three radical Muslim groups mentioned above are of Arabic descent. United States' war against Iraq has somewhat united the moderate and the radical groups in their opposition against the West, making things even more difficult for Megawati to act firmly against these groups, for she was afraid of being accused as a puppet of the United States by radical figures.

The declining state capability was also an important factor casting doubts on the government's ability to deal with the threat of terrorism. The myth of the Indonesian army as invincible is already gone after the fall of Soeharto and the revelation of its past abuses. The police, which are supposed to look after internal security is now separated from the armed forces since 2000, but it is poorly trained and ill-equipped to handle many-sided social tensions that Indonesia now confronts. A lack of professionalism is a major obstacle as well. This is a chronic problem of the police and the military. The police do not have necessary equipments, like computers and proper communications equipment; in some cases not even phones. Obviously they cannot compete with a sophisticated terrorist network. Analysts are unanimous on their opinion that the reasons why terrorism has been able to take root in the world's most populous Muslim nation run the gamut from a lack of political will and effective leadership to bureaucratic obstacles and an underpaid, poorly trained security force that has left the country with porous borders and lax law enforcement. Both the armed forces and the police are wrecked by corruption and indiscipline.

The lack of empowering legislation to provide a legal and political cover was also an enduring problem for security agencies, which under former President Soeharto's 1965-1998 rules did not need to bother with such niceties. In a new democratic environment, police have had to rely on a criminal code, with its onerous rules of evidence, to tackle terror suspects. The more decisive action to deal with the threat of terrorism in the country was possible with the two new preventive decrees that were rushed through parliament within a week after the Ball incident - a stark contrast to the slower days before Bali. The anti-terrorism regulations authorize the death sentence for some terrorist acts, up to six month's detention without trial and the use of intelligence information as *prima facie* evidence once a court has approved it. These decrees are tamer than the Internal Security Act (ISA) used in Singapore and Malaysia but are nonetheless a watershed. Until Bali, Indonesian politicians of all stripes, who feared that these might be misused to establish another Soeharto-like grip to curtail political freedom, vigorously opposed these.

Now even many Muslim social and political leaders, like the heads of *Nahdlatul Ulama* and *Muhammadiyah*, have supported the regulations. The Bali bombings have made a backlash by militants against government's tough measures against the radical groups less likely. In the past few months, the government has quietly placed a restraining hand on some of Indonesia's more violent Muslim groups. *Jafar Umar Thalib*, leader of the Laskyar Jihad Islamic militia, is facing trial for inciting unrest between Muslims and Christians on the island of Ambon. And members of the Islamic Defenders Front, including their leader, were recently taken into custody for damaging public property in raids on nightclubs and other entertainment centres. Laskyar Jihad militants left Ambon two days after the Bali attacks, ostensibly on the ground that their funds had run out, are for the time being lying low. The prosecution of the case against Abu Bakar Ba'asyir is also progressing satisfactorily with new arrests of another 12 members of the JI by the Indonesian police. Some arrests of the culprits of the Marriot and Australian Embassy bombings have also been arrested in recent days. Even then neither the international community, nor its neighbours have yet any confidence in Indonesia to deal with terrorism with firmness and strong determination.

Terrorism resulting in the violence against innocent people, whose worst manifestation in the case of Indonesia was in the Bali bombing, which took more than 200 lives and caused incalculable economic damage to the Balinese in particular and the country as a whole, has now emerged as a formidable threat to the stability of the state and security of the people. The resulting loss of confidence in Indonesia among the foreign investors and the declining security for the foreigners in the country has further complicated its attempt at economic recovery and political stability, and thereby undermining Indonesia's stock in the eyes of its neighbours. Even before Indonesia could recover from the Bali shock by a fairly successful campaign against its suspected perpetrators and bringing them to book, it received a further blow to its attempt to regain political and economic stability by the Jakarta bombing of the J.W. Marriott hotel on the afternoon of 6 August. The Rupiah plunged again, though not so significantly as was the case in the past, eroding further the confidence of the investors. The latest terrorist attack was on the Australian Embassy a few months back, which again killed only Indonesians, creating further setback to establish the country's credibility to the foreign investors, as well as to the international community. The loss of Indonesia's preeminent position in the region has affected ASEAN's own stock in the eyes of the world. What has gone wrong with Indonesia and can it recover from the current malaise? What implications Indonesian instability has for Southeast Asia? To get an answer to these questions we have to diagnose the Indonesian illness first and then its impact on the region.

Indonesian Crises

Democratic transition in any country is always fraught with stress, strains and uncertainties, and can never be expected to be smooth and orderly. In the case of Indonesia, it has been even more disorderly and messy because it is taking place in the midst of a severe economic crisis when the bottom seemed to have been knocked out of the whole economic and political structure resulting in the decline of state capability in the allocation of resources and maintenance of order. The breakdown of Soeharto's authoritarian control and the resultant weak capacity of the government gave rise to the assertion of religious and ethnic identities as well as regional separatism. The invincibility of the country's armed forces, recently renamed as the TNI, in retaining control over the social and political forces has now proved to be a myth. While in the past it was able to instill a sense of fear, a powerful stimulus to political passivity, among the people, its capacity to control social violence in the post-Soeharto era has proved to be inadequate. Authoritarian political institutions that broke down under the pressure of economic collapse and social turmoil has been replaced now with institutions that are either very weak to establish order and legitimacy, or like the newly assertive parliament whose members by and large are viewed by the people as self-aggrandizing and unrepresentative of popular aspirations and their democratic impulses. Some members are also carry-over from the old regime of Soeharto, and have joined the bandwagon of democracy by wearing a new colour.

Indonesia's 'top-down democracy' has gone into disrepute with the fall of Soeharto, but the development of a 'bottom-up democracy' is yet to begin and faces an uphill task for it to take root in an uninitiated soil. The downfall of Soeharto in May 1998 was celebrated as heralding the birth of a 'new Indonesia', and a 'second independence' from the oppressive rule of their own ruler and its worst manifestations in the form of "cronyism, corruption and collusion" (KKN). The change brought rising expectations and hope that it would usher Indonesia towards democracy, good governance, transparency and accountability of its new leaders. Now after 6 years after the changeover the rising expectations continue, but the hope for democracy and good governance is dimming as the people witness the greed, hypocrisy, hunger for power, horse-trading, corruption of the new power elites and the slide of the country towards further political, economic, ethnic and religious turmoil halting the movement towards demilitarizing its society and establishing democracy in the country. The absence of democratic tradition in the country, a weak civil society without experience in social and political mobilization as well as in party building and a continuing culture of corruption in the judiciary and bureaucracy together with a static economy and heavy debt are making the transition a challenging and difficult one. From a fulcrum and an accepted leader in Southeast Asia, Indonesia has been reduced to a sick and problem state in the region, causing concern that its instability might spill into the region and pose a threat to regional stability. While the rest of the region has somehow recovered from the great Asian economic crisis, Indonesia, the largest country in Southeast Asia, is still under economic and political turmoil causing serious concern about the very survival of the country.

Indonesia does not have a tradition of democratic political culture and movements. Even if it tried to practice parliamentary democracy in the early years of independence, the political parties were highly faction-ridden and were based on personalities rather than on organized grassroots support. Political changes in the past had never been the product of any sustained, disciplined and organized political movements with grassroots support, but always had been the result of sudden and short bursts of movements arising from economic crisis and heightened political tension. Such changes can bring anarchy unless channeled and regulated by a responsible and accountable leadership. To consolidate such changes along democratic lines, there is a need for organized collective action based on political party building and routinized patterns of elite recruitment-essential conditions for grassroots democracy. Democratization also requires an acceptance and a commitment to respect pluralism reflecting the diversity of religious affinity, provincial identity, as well as linguistic and ethnic origin. Political parties that have been formed in the post-Soeharto era have not been able to overcome the shortcomings of the old party system characterized by narrow sectarian interests and lack of organizational capacity. They still rely for the societal support on their leaders rather than on collective action based on party building, elite recruitment and constructive programme and action at the grassroots level.

Political System of Indonesia

Republic of Indonesia was born on 17th August 1945 and the Dutch colonial masters left on 27th December 1949. After getting independence, Indonesia tried to be assertive in the politics of the region in particular and Third World in general. President Sukarno was vocal against the western world and opposed the US policy of containment. He endeavoured to nurture a system, which could prove ideal and indigenous by Asian standards. Thus, the word *Pancasila*, also pronounced as *Panchaseela*, was popularised for the political system. *Panchaseela* became the ideological and philosophical foundation of the Republic and its ideals were incorporated in the Constitution declared on 18th August 1945. *Panchaseela* is a Sanskrit word, which was also considered as the philosophical foundation of Indian Foreign Policy, but for India this word was incorporated in the document much later. Indonesia wanted to incorporate the ideals of *Panchaseela*, both in foreign policy and domestic matters since its inception. The Constitution of 1945 explained five principles of *Panchaseela*, which are as follows: (i) Belief in the one and only God; (ii) A just and civilised humanity; (iii) Unity of Indonesia; (iv) Democracy guided by the inner wisdom of deliberations of the representatives; and (v) Social justice.

The Articles of the 1945 Constitution enumerated the ideals and goals for which the nation was born. The founding fathers were inspired by the urge for unity, common goals and democracy built upon the age old Indonesian concepts of GotongRoyong (mutual assistance), deliberations of representatives (Musya Warah) and consensus (Mufakat). Preceded by a preamble including Panchaseela, the Constitution had 37 Articles defining the role of the Chief Executive (President),

Legislature (MPR and DPR) and the Judiciary. The founding fathers envisaged the foundation of a unitary state with sovereignty vested in the legislature. However, subsequent developments favoured the adoption of a presidential system in which the President was very powerful. The President was projected as primus interpares, and his council of ministers always looked to him for guidance and support. Both Sukarno and Suharto believed in the personality cult and strengthened the powers of the President enormously. The sovereignty of the people was symbolised by Madjelis Permmjawaratan Rakjat (MPR), also known as people's consultative assembly. The number of members and the role of MPR have been changing.

According to Law 16 of 1969, MPR was consisted of the members of the Dewan Perwdkilan Rakjat (DPR) augmented with the representatives of the regions, political and *Karja* (functional) groups. The total number of appointed members to MPR was fixed at one-third of the total number of MPR members, and the number of MPR members was to be twice the total number of the members in DPR. Accordingly, the strength of the MPR had been fixed at 1000 out of which 425 were elected, 75 appointed by the armed forces and the remaining 500 were government appointees. MPR met every five years to elect and re-elect President and the latter was legally accountable to this House. The legislative powers are in fact vested in the DPR, also known as the House of People's Representatives. According to 1969 act, the strength of DPR had been fixed at 460 members, of which 360 were elected and 100 nominated.

However, this figure was increased in 1975 to 500 of which 400 were elected and 100 were appointed members. Members of the DPR pledged that they would always uphold the message of the people's suffering, that they would adhere to and defend *Panchaseela* as the basis and ideology of the state, the 1945 Constitution and all existing laws and regulations in force in the Republic of Indonesia, that they would endeavour to the best of their ability to promote the welfare of the Indonesian people and be loyal to the country, nation and the state of Indonesia. They, however, proved a rubber stamp during 1965-99, but they are emerging as important institution for rule making ever since Abdurrahman Wahid came into power.

The most striking feature of Indonesian politics is that it has not declared any state religion. Although the Muslims are in overwhelming majority and most of its neighbouring states have declared their state religion in order to maintain their national unity, Indonesia has abstained from doing so. Malaysia and Brunei, the two immediate neighbours, have declared Islam as the state religion but Indonesia preferred to remain secular. The preamble of 1945 Constitution assures religious freedom by declaring protection and promotion of faith in the Almighty God and endeavoured to create a just civilised humanity. The various governments have been pursuing a religious policy, which respects the right of every religious group and takes into account the feelings of all religious communities. They have officially recognised religions namely, Islam, Protestantism, Catholicism, Buddhism and Hinduism. As a result, there are 26,769 Protestant churches, 13,361 Catholic churches, 34408 Hindu temples, 2552 Buddhist Viharas and 537,837 Muslim mosques. The break up of different religious communities in Indonesia in mid nineties indicated that Muslims comprised 87.2 per cent, Protestants 6 per cent, Catholics 3.5 per cent. Hindus 2 per cent and the Buddhists one per cent. Indonesia gives emphasis on "Unity in Diversity" to unite the people in a common fold. It has heterogeneous, ethnic and linguistic groups.

More than 300 languages are spoken and their culture and life style differ. The majority is of Malay stock, split into dozens of smaller sub-groups, with varying family structures and social systems. The prominent ethnic groups are the Javanese, the Sundanese, the Minhasans, the Bugis, the Makassars and the Balinese. Again there are the Dayaks, the Bataks, and the Dani and the Asmat of Melanesian stock. Various ethnic groups have preserved their customs and traditions and the majority population is of Islamic faith, with sufficient impact of sufism, which came to Indonesia along with the spread of Islam. The opinions differ about who first brought Islam to Indonesia, but it is acknowledged that Sufi saints played the most important role. Traditional Hindu and Buddhist rulers of the era were tolerant of the activities of sufi saints and that approach was reciprocated subsequently when Islam became a powerful force at the government level and allowed Hindu and Buddhist traditions to be amalgamated with the new evolving religion and culture in Indonesia.

It is recorded that when the kings of Sanuidra, Pasai and Perlak of northern Sumatra embraced Islam and established the first Islamic kingdom in the Indonesian archipelago, it paved the path for rulers in other parts of Sumatra and Java to follow suit. The tombstone of the first Islamic ruler, Sultan Malik Al-Saleh of Samudra, dated 1297 had been perused by Ibn Batutta, the Moroccan traveller, who on his way to China in 1341 had stopped at Samudra and became a royal guest of the then ruler. Marco Polo, who visited Perlak earlier in 1292 had also referred to the existence of Samudra as an Islamic state. The projection based on available information suggests that Samudra ruler was under the impact of Sufism. Such observations, however are opposed by a section of the intellectuals who argue that Islam came to Indonesia through Muslim traders from Persia and Gujarat and there are some who say that Arab missionaries (Egypt, Hejaz or Hadramut) had introduced Islam in Indonesia. Whatever may be the reality, but nobody can refute the impact of sufism on art and culture, namely the *Wayang*, myths and folklores, poems and songs, the Islamic calendar, ceremonies and festivals, etc. sufi saints understood that Javanese were very fond of art, so they inserted Islamic teachings in the stories of Ramayana and Mahabharata to be played in *Wayang*. They created new myths, stories, poems and songs, which had local names, local languages but Islamic teachings. A sufi saint, Walisongo led the sufi movement in the 15th century and became very popular in Java with Islamic ideologies. His strategy of adopting local stories, local heroes and myths were adopted by the Sufi saints in other parts of the archipelago. Thus, proper atmosphere was created and the people started accepting Islam without any holy war or bloodshed. Here it is important to remember that the different islands and regions in Indonesia had different traditions, culture and myths and when they accepted Islam, they accepted it with them. As a result, Islam did not remain a monolithic force as in other parts of the world. There are thus different types of Islamic people spread all over Indonesia.

Political Problems

Indonesia is faced with numerous problems of different types, but we may point out only the political problems outstanding. The archipelagic concept as enunciated by the founding fathers are losing its importance and *Panchaseela* doctrine, especially its third principle "Unity of Indonesia" has been endangered. The separatist movement in Aceh and Irian Jaya are too serious to be ignored. East Timor, which had been annexed after a military action in 1975 has already broken away through a referendum in 1999, and similar demands are articulated by separatists in Aceh and Irian Jaya.

Again Indonesia, was a protagonist of "Unity in Diversity" (Bhineka Tunggal Eka), where intra-ethnic and inter-ethnic relations were harmonious on the eve of its independence. But the experiences of the past few years have shown that there is ethnic tension now. The Chinese, who have traditionally been involved in business and trade and who have prospered, are made victims of looting, arson, rape, riots and humiliation since 1998. Anti-Chinese riots have been taking place and the worst affected areas are Medan, Titipatan, Solo and Samarinda. The hooligans argue that the Chinese are responsible for spiralling price rise and the economic crisis. In February 1998, the riots in Medan were serious enough to compel some ethnic Chinese to leave their houses. Twelve Chinese owned shops had been torched and dozens of buildings damaged at Kendari in Sulawesi.

The Christians are also not feeling safe as riots have taken place against them at Ambon and Maluku. The lumpens are let loose with the tacit support of the Islamic groups.

Again the religion has come in the path of Megawati Sukarnoputri's candidature as President of Indonesia. Though she is a popular leader and daughter of the Father of the Nation, her credentials to uphold Muslim values are questioned because of her genealogy. When her candidature for Presidency was considered, there were lots of debates that her mother and grandmother were Hindus and therefore her Muslim heritage is diluted. The military supported Golkar Party made allegation that Megawati was secretly praying at a Hindu temple in Bali. Another criticism was that she had chosen a majority of non-Muslim candidates for her party, and if appointed the President her conduct would be identical. Finally, since she is a woman, she cannot be appointed the head of the State of a Muslim dominated country. All these opinions prevailed and the MPR did not elect her the President despite the support of PDI, the largest party in MPR with 153 members. Though Abdurrahman Wahid had won only 54 seats, but his support grew rapidly in MPR. Besides other factors, religion played a significant role in mobilising support for him. He got 373 votes in the race for Presidency, whereas Megawati secured only 313. The result was so surprising that there is a demand for directly elected President on the pattern of the US in Indonesia. Needless to say that religion is assuming centre stage and the use of Islam is increasing in the struggle for power. Nahdlatul Ulama (NU), Muhammadiah and Syarikat Islam (IS) have a feeling that they would lose their popular support if they ignore the importance of Islamic religion in socio-economic life. They may be right that Islam is the single most important factor in the unity of the country, but overemphasis is counter-productive as Indonesia has a multi-ethnic and multi-religious society. If the religion is used for power politics, it can generate forces of destabilisation and disintegration and this logic is particularly relevant in Indian and Indonesian context. Darul Islam in Indonesia, for instance, has been advocating Jehad, Islamic purity, and violence. They are influential in Aceh and the result is disastrous. Another debatable issue is the role of the Armed Forces in the politics of the country. Their intrusion in administration and politics had been legitimated with the acceptance *ofdwifungsi* (dual functions). The meaning and significance *ofdwifungsi* were aimed at perpetrating army rule. It was argued that the concern of the armed forces were not simply to look after national defence, but also the actual conduct of the government in the interest of good administration. A powerful myth began to develop that the armed forces had played the principal role in securing independence, that it had done so in the face of obstruction and betrayal by the civilian authorities, and it therefore retained a special right and duty to supervise and take charge of the government. Under the stewardship of Suharto, *dwifungsi* principle became operational and accordingly serving and retired army officers took a wide variety of posts, from that of a cabinet minister down to village head. Though the leading role of the army in the freedom struggle is a historical reality, but at the same time it played some negative role subsequently, that cannot be overlooked.

They had assumed a major role in the economy as the managers of the Dutch enterprises, which had been nationalised in 1957. They took major part in the administrative system and their performances were not satisfactory. They did their best to suppress democratic ethos, which had been cultivated at the time of freedom struggle. When Suharto resigned on 21 May 1998, there were jubilation, but it ushered into an era of political uncertainty and instability, though democracy was restored, but anarchic situation developed in certain areas. For instance, the incidents of violence, riots and vandalism at Aceh, Ambon and Maluku are reprehensible and which is known to the outside world through internet and media. The leaders in the present government have to be highly sensitive to their opinion, without which the task of nation-building, stability and development cannot be promoted.

Instituting inquiry committees, special courts and open hearings against the armed forces might not yield the desired results. For example, the special investigation has implicated some Generals in East Timor massacres in which the name of General Wiranto was mentioned. This was made a pretext to demand the resignation of General Wiranto from the cabinet and the General gracefully resigned. In retrospect, it was found that the conviction was not convincing. General Wiranto is honest and respected and his outer has been disliked by a section of the people and the Armed forces. If the armed forces are offended, it can prove very costly for democratic experiments. Indonesia is also known for corruption in high places. Former President Suharto supported his children to develop business connections, based on privileged access to government contracts, licenses and subsidies. Hutomo Putra Mandala (Tommy) had obtained exclusive rights for the purchase of cloves from farmers. He extracted benefits from monopolies over flour and tin plates.

He also got the coveted post to produce the Indonesian car (Pt Timor Putra Nasional) and establish Sempati Air. Suharto's daughter, Siti Prabowo had got the share in $10 billion project linking Malaysia and Indonesia over the Malacca Straits. Likewise his two other sons Bambang and Sigit Harjojudanto had greatly benefited in business matters because of their genealogy. And the President knew it. The Economist had reported that the members of the Suharto clan could walk into any state bank and demand a loan at favourable terms. This could not be refused and the government always awarded the juicy contracts to Suharto family in the areas of power generation, telecommunications and toll-roads. The political parties had to express their faith in *Panchaseela,* which had been declared a national ideology, which was treated sacred for every Indonesian. The Suharto regime was named *Panchaseela* democracy and the government was responsible for formulation of ideas and interpretation of the *Panchaseela.* The meaning of *Panchaseela* had been stretched too far aimed at prescribing a society modelled on the traditional family, in which parental authority was respected and in which individual interest was subordinate to the community. Political reform had been on the agenda of the government in the post Suharto era. They had decided to lift control over the political parties and thug a multi-party system emerged. All parties were given financial aid from the government and the amount depended on the number of votes received in the elections. They also wanted to activate MPR and DPR by reducing the number of appointed members and increasing their powers in rule making. For instance, although the MPR was declared supreme power through article one of the 1945 constitution, vested with three important tasks, namely, approving the constitution, deciding the guidelines of state policy and election of the President and Vice-President, but its authorities had been eroded. It was authorized to convene a special session whenever necessary but it met only once in five years. Now there is a growing demand that MPR should play an active role in decision-making.

The first step in that direction has been the reduction in the numbers of appointed members and according to 1999 act of the government the members of the MPR are reduced to 700 only instead of 1000. However, the most important aspect of the reform process is that they have decided to restore Article 28 of the 1945 constitution in letter and spirits, which guarantees the right of free assembly and association, of expression of opinion, orally or in writing, to the Indonesian citizens.

Human Rights

Human rights are an important element of civilised society and it has been suppressed in many countries of the Third World, including Indonesia. It has assumed importance in the New World Order and the United States is the ardent advocate of assuring it at the universal level. Though the United Nations general Assembly proclaimed the Universal Declaration of Human Rights in 1948 and emphasised that all human beings are born free and equal in dignity and rights, and endowed with reason and conscience, and should act towards one another in a spirit of brotherhood. This has been ignored very often in course of nation building and modernisation. Though Indonesia has signed the covenants for the Universal Declaration but it has been found lacking in implementing it. Amnesty International published "Indonesia Shock Therapy, Restoring Order in Aceh: 1989-93", and revealed many cases of omission and commission committed by the government. Similarly, there were numerous reports about excesses committed in East Timor, which broke away from Indonesia in 1999. If we go into the genesis of the conflict, we find logic on both sides, namely, the government and the insurgents, but it is human rights that suffer as a result of the conflict. Aceh, situated at the northernmost region of Sumatra, has a distinct culture and history. It has been a strong supporter of Darul Islam movement and views the authority of Central government un-Islamic.

It has been struggling for its own identity and separate nationhood, because the government of Indonesia has not been sensitive to their grievances. The government gave them autonomy in religious and educational affairs after a long struggle in 1959, but it was withdrawn without any rhyme or reason. Though it is rich in iron, oil, gas and coal, it is not given any share in the benefits. At the same time, the government supported migration and transmigration of population to that area which had been disliked. The people in Aceh opposed the presence of new migrants. The continuing conflicts over economic and demographic issues fuelled a separatist movement. In 1976, Hasan Di Tiro established *Gerakan Aceh Merdeka* (Free Aceh movement) and subsequently declared independence. But, this movement was suppressed and Tiro fled to Sweden. It was from Sweden that he announced the formation of Aceh government in exile. The unrest mounted enormously in Aceh in 1989 when National Liberation Front Aceh Sumatra (NLFAS) was established. They mounted onslaughts on the government forces and Amnesty International claimed that 2000 people were killed during 1989-93, and the casualty number had been increasing every year. Similar is the situation in Irian Jaya, where *Organisasi Papua Merdeka* (OPM), also known as Free Papua movement led separatist movement. There has been lot of bloodshed in that province also and the cases of human rights violations are reported. Indonesia gave priority to economic development in the era of new order (1965-98) and that was in tune with International covenant on economic, social and cultural rights (Unga Resolution 2200). In accordance with the Universal Declaration of human rights, the ideal law of free human beings, enjoying freedom from fear and want can only be achieved if the conditions are created whereby every one may enjoy his economic, social and cultural rights, as well as civil and political rights.

Indonesia adopted development programmes for its impoverished population in 1967, when Suharto signed the documents of declaration of world leaders on population. In view of this policy, national family planning programmes were supported and the schemes proved successful in limiting the increase of population, below 3 million population growth annually. Total fertility rate came down to 50% as desired by the government and Indonesian expertise was appreciated in most of the neighbouring countries. But the policy, which proved controversial, was regarding transmigration of the people from densely populated areas to less populated zones. Java and Bali inhabit 65 per cent of Indonesian population. Java alone has 100 million people. This island however occupies only 6.8 per cent of the total land of the country.

Sumatra, which is comparatively bigger in size, has 41 million, Sulawesi 13 million, Nusatenggara 11.5 million, Maluku 11.9 million and Kalimantan has 11 million population. It is known that only 992 out of 17508 islands are mainly populated zones. But, Haryati Soebadio says that 5000 islands are inhabited. There has to be a better management of the inhabited and uninhabited islands to accelerate the pace of development. There is abundance of natural resources in all parts of the country and their exploitation can be facilitated only when there is availability of manpower. Indonesia endeavoured to diversify its population from densely populated areas to new zones. They passed relevant rules in that direction in 1960 and 1973 and transmigrated people from Java to other islands. Initially, 17116 families were settled in Irian Jaya and 8155 in Maluku but a number of people were also transmigrated to Kalimantan, East Timor and Aceh.

Joan Hardejono said that 49772 people were transmigrated in 1979-80,108081 in 1980-81, 123846 in 1981-82, 167477 in 1982-83 and 86298 in 1983-84. As the government supported it, transmigration continued, but it has not resolved the problem of population density in Java. As job opportunities are available mostly in Java, poor and impoverished people continued to come and the problem remains the same.

There has been some omission and commission, while transmigrating the people as alleged by Aceh Merdeka, OPM and some other opposition groups. They stated that the alien population is arbitrarily introduced to change the demographic complexion and this is a matter of intrusion in matters of their human rights. They understand that the transmigrates would alter their indigenous character and usurp their properties. The Javanese speak an alien language and have faith in Islamic religion. But the people in Irian Jaya, Maluku and Ambon are mostly Christians, who allege that Javanese are arrogant with a sense of superiority. The new migrants generally search jobs in oil exploration, mining and forestry department and the local people project this behaviour contrary to their interests saying that ultimately the new transmigrates would deprive them of their resources and wealth. It may prove more suitable and less controversial if the transmigration is directed towards those islands where there is no population at all. As given by the government sources there are more than two-thirds of the uninhabited islands.

The people might not be interested in inhabiting in new areas because of poor living conditions and necessary infrastructure, but the government should take the assistance of the international financial institutions to create necessary conditions for settlement on uninhabited islands of Indonesia. The increasing denudation of forests and logging have to be stopped completely. The forest fires creating smoky haze have to be contained. But Indonesia has the shortage of fire fighting machines. The forest fire in Sumatra and Borneo in 1997 engulfed a large part of Southeast Asia for months. The fire had reached Malaysia, Brunei, Singapore and Australia as well. The smoky haze generated a number of health problems and disrupted tourism and transport systems. A forest fire at Sumatra in March this year caught Malaysia and Singapore as well. The neighbouring countries are alarmed of the recurring forest fire in Indonesia. These developments have grave implications on Indonesian image outside, and therefore the government has to evolve a policy to check fire in its jungles and have to cooperate more closely with the ASEAN regional task force to monitor and stop it.

To conclude, it can be stated that Indonesia has taken commendable steps towards democratisation and liberalisation, but the long impacts of authoritarian rule are yet to be tackled. Threat of the Armed forces remains and it cannot be ruled out that they will not come back. Again ethnic and religious disputes are likely to grow further in Aceh and some other areas, if right steps to minimise corruption and mistakes of the authorities are not taken. However, for a coalition government, which has many partners of different leanings, every new initiative is full of dilemmas. Though Indonesian system has a presidential type of government and five-year tenure of the President is assured, but MPR has been made supreme as per 1945 constitution.

Regional Assertions and Separatist Movements in Indonesia

A more formidable crisis relates to Indonesia's unity and territorial integrity - whether the country can remain together when it is engulfed in violence and threatened by ethnic and religious separatism. Religion, nationalism and feelings of victimization have triggered conflict across the archipelago, and some fear the breakup of the world's fourth most populous nation. Whereas Indonesia has been forced to come to terms with an independent East Timor, it faces ongoing strife in Aceh, Irian Jaya, Kalimantan and elsewhere. These are mainly, but not only struggles for autonomy, if not independence. More than any other province, Aceh is posing the most serious challenge to the unity and integrity of the country. An oil-rich province on the northern tip of Sumatra, Aceh has seen growing demands for a referendum on self-determination in reaction to years of harsh anti-rebel military operations and perceived economic injustices. The Acehnese, like people in many other resource-rich provinces of Indonesia, have long complained about unfair treatment from Jakarta.

In particular, this concerns the lop-sided distribution of national wealth among the regions. Java, they feel, receives a disproportionate portion of the revenue, much of which is earned by other provinces. The national development efforts are largely concentrated on Java, while revenue-earning provinces are perceived to be lagging behind in development. Aceh is also fiercely Islamic and therefore wants to be guided by the Muslim *Sharia* Law. In August last year when there was a recurrence of intensified violence in the area, former President Megawati's trusted security minister, Lt Gen (retd) Bambang Yudhoyono, the current President, branded the Free Aceh Movement (GAM) as 'terrorists', the first time the separatists had been so labeled.

The most recent phase of the conflict in Aceh began in 1999, after the outcome of the East Timor ballot. GAM successes in the field, including cutting the Trans-Sumatra Highway, despite an already high level of TNI activity, led to an escalation of TNI and Brimob operations from mid-2001. GAM is reported to have about 3,500-armed guerrillas in the hills and an active support base of around 10,000. To confront them, the TNI had deployed by April 2003 some 22,000 soldiers in Aceh, along with more than 12,000 paramilitary Mobile Brigade national police and some 10,000 militias, mostly in central Aceh. The Aceh problem is not synonymous with GAM, which was not a factor there until a few years ago, and only later it was blown out of proportion, partly due to the exaggeration by the military. In fact, lately, the GAM factor had become an annoyance to the Acehnese people to the point that its appeal not to fly the Indonesian flag on the last Independence Day was not heeded in most parts of the province. GAM claims it enjoys widespread support from eventually all Acehnese people, while the TNI plays it down, saying that GAM fighters and their supporters account for a few thousand only. Megawati until the beginning of the full-scale and massive military operation was following her predecessor's policy and promised large-scale autonomy, a 70% share of the oil and other revenue to the Acehnese, but ruled out separation as an option. The Indonesian military (TNI) had always insisted on a tough measure against GAM and suggested that the government give GAM until the end of December last year to accept the Law No. 18/2000 on special autonomy, a prerequisite for future dialogues, failing which Aceh would face a harsh military crackdown. But it is well known that even at that time, army generals were putting pressure on the government to sanction a crackdown on the separatist movement. The rebels were gaining strength, especially as it became increasingly clear that direct peace talks during the whole of 2001 and mid-2002 were making little progress.

With 30,000 troops already in the province, there were genuine fears the bloodshed would increase rather than peace being restored. It was in that context of imminent showdown between the government security forces and the GAM that the ceasefire agreement of December 2002 was signed facilitated by the Henry Dunant Centre in Geneva. Despite the ceasefire agreement the ordinary people of Aceh were already skeptical about a peaceful outcome of the process. Despite a dramatic drop in violence during the initial months of the ceasefire agreement, however, the failure to resolve major issues between the two parties and the low credibility of the provincial government had wrecked the prospects for peace. GAM had accepted Aceh's autonomy under Indonesian sovereignty, as a starting point for talks but not as a political end. The government in Jakarta was adamant that autonomy is the final offer but had given the rebels few incentives to work within the Indonesian political system. No less than 10,000 people have already been killed during the longstanding violence in Aceh, including the 10-year military operation, which was lifted in 1998. Both GAM and the Indonesian military deserve blame for the collapse of the peace process, for neither side had shown any genuine interest in making the agreement work. GAM used the peace process to strengthen its forces. TNI used the occasion to prepare the ground for a military onslaught on GAM. It was almost certainly behind the attacks on the Joint Security Committee, which was set-up to monitor both sides' compliance with the December agreement. The blame, however, was on the civilians angry over their failure to stop GAM abuses.

Despite military operations beginning last May, the army has not been able to pacify the region. On the other hand, large numbers of civilians have been displaced from their homes and their livelihood bringing a sense of fear and helplessness to the people of Aceh. Will the military operations resolve the problem of the conflict in Aceh and its people's sense of alienation from the government in Jakarta? The military operation to crush GAM between 1989 and 1999 not only ended in failure, but the human rights abuses perpetrated by the security forces (who have yet to be brought to trial for these crimes) had fostered a sense of fear, distrust-even hatred-towards the government in Jakarta and the military and police. As per the reports in the media, TNI's record in the current operation is no better than in the past. Side by side with the rebels, there have large-scale civilian casualties. The humanitarian sufferings of the ordinary people of Aceh are even worse. The military said 309 rebels have been killed as of 1st July, while 682 have surrendered or been captured. According to the TNI itself, more than 50,000 civilians have fled their homes for tented camps. The actual number of displacement may be even double that number. On November 17, Susilo extended by six months a state of civil emergency in Aceh. The move came as the toll in the 18-month military operation to crush rebels continued to mount, with 11 fresh guerilla fatalities adding to the thousands already killed. The road to peace in Aceh is not through military action, but continues to lie in a negotiated settlement that includes full implementation of the of special autonomy provisions for the province of Aceh. And for this to happen both sides must be prepared to give up their rigid positions. GAM cannot expect a peaceful solution to the conflict unless it is prepared to give up its armed struggle. At the same time the central government is Jakarta also must realize that autonomy is no incentive for GAM to drop support for independence unless it delivers visible benefits. For autonomy to work, it has to be developed in consultation with the people concerned and administered by a responsive, corruption-free government accountable to the people. The new President must be able to convince the people of Aceh and even the international community that every single human rights abuse will be investigated impartially and those responsible will be brought to a very speedy, transparent and open trial. This may not completely heal those scars, but it will definitely go some way in restoring some kind of trust between the Acehnese people and the Indonesian government.

Papua continues to grapple with a limited understanding of the Special Autonomy package. Violence in Papua could escalate, the International Crisis Group warned in a report in September 2002, particularly if the Indonesian military adopted a hard-line approach to the independence movement. The warning came less than two weeks after the killing of three employees of the giant mining company, Freeport, in a well-planned ambush that the military and pro-independence guerrillas had blamed on each other. The report highlighted the role that the struggle over land and resources has played in the conflict, pitting the Indonesian state, and sometimes mining and logging companies, against an independence movement supported by most of the indigenous population. The autonomy package that Jakarta offered in 2001 fell short of local aspirations. To quote Sidney Jones, the ICG's International Crisis Group) Indonesia project Director: "There is a correlation between injustices in the management of management of natural resources and the strength of pro-independence sentiment in Papua. There is little hope for the autonomy option unless Indonesia ends the abusive practices associated with resource exploitation." The ICG noted that the behaviour of the security forces might be the most important factor in easing or exacerbating the conflict. Many Papuans believe that the involvement of the army special forces, Kopassus, in the death of independence leader Theys Eluay in November 2001 was part of a broader strategy to foment unrest in order to justify a crackdown on dissent. Papuan local figures and religious leaders have earlier demanded the government withdraws its non-Papuan troops from the region in an effort to turn it into a 'peaceful zone'. The army, nevertheless, has rejected the suggestion saying: "A separatist movement does exist in Papua. They are also an armed group and against our legitimate government."

The Special Autonomy has not been implemented in the province of Papua. Instead of supporting the implementation of the bill of the Special Autonomy, the President Megawati had issued a new Presidential Decree on the acceleration of the division of the Province into three new provinces in Papua. The central government of Indonesia issued the law of the division of the province of Irian Jaya into three provinces in 1999. However, the law of the division of the province has never been implemented because all the Papuans were united and strongly rejected the central government idea of the division. The rejection was fully supported by the provincial government officials, parliaments, NGOs, religious leaders, and Papuan tribal council. The law issued by the Provincial parliament in Papua then approved the Papuan peoples' rejection. In the year 2000, the central government and the House of Representatives in Jakarta passed the bill of Special Autonomy as response to the Papuans' demand from independence. Through the bill, the name of the province was changed from Irian Jaya to Papua. The division of the Irian Jaya province was not included in the original bill. Despite the strong rejection by the Papuans, the provincial government had accepted the bill, and officially implemented since January 2002. However, the provincial government could not implement the bill, because the central government had yet to approve the establishment of the Papuan People's Assembly *(Majelis Rakyat Papua* or MRP), which was included in the bill of Special Autonomy. So as long as the MRP is not yet established, the bill of the special autonomy cannot be implemented. Instead of supporting the establishment of the MRP in order to implement the Special Autonomy Law, President Megawati had issued the New Presidential Decree on the acceleration of the implementation of the division of the province, which is not included in the bill of the special Autonomy. Under extreme pressure and opposition from the Papuans, the central government had to postpone its plan for division of the province.

Human rights advocates in Indonesia fear a new military campaign in Papua is behind eight recent deaths and has caused up to 5000 people to flee their villages. Several groups have issued statements in recent days blaming the military for a series of incidents in Puncak Jaya regency in the highlands, warning that the military is likely to step up operations. A statement, released in Jayapura and signed by human rights groups Elsham and Kontras, the Legal Aid Foundation and Church groups, details a series of killings and attacks that began on Indonesian independence day, August 17. Human rights groups and churches have called on the new President, Susilo Yudhoyono, to immediately order troops out of Puncak Jaya regency to begin a dialogue with Papuans as he has promised.

Some scholars have suggested that understanding the moral and millennial roots of merdeka is crucial to the success of any initiatives promoting peace and civil society in the region. Brigham Golden, who has studied the Papuan problem in depth, suggested that if 'autonomy' could be socialized and implemented in such a way that fulfils the requirements of the Papuans, the reasons why they want independence, for example, by developing a truth and justice commission, reducing repressive measures by security forces, combating structural racism in the public and private sectors, and giving Papuans tribal institutions a role in the provincial administration, then it could certainly provide a crucial step towards resolving the political deadlock in Papua. To quote: "Merdeka is not simply a request for self-determination in the political sense, but a demand to be in included in reciprocal dialogue with the powers of the globe-and in so doing to gain the dignity of being human. Though tremendously diverse culturally, people throughout Papua seem to share a fundamental belief that the open forum of communication and exchange is the single most important human activity. Indeed to "sit and talk together" *(duduk dan bicara bersama)* is the mode through which relationships are formed and communities are bound together."

The Regional Autonomy Law has now turned out to be a great failure and a stumbling block to smooth decision-making. The aim was noble enough-to give local communities more say over how they are governed and more control over the gold, gas, oil, copper, timber, and other resources extracted from their lands. Under Soeharto, multinationals struck backroom deals in Jakarta to win long-tern concessions, splitting the revenue with Soeharto family members, cronies, and the military. Indigenous people benefited little while their environments were trashed and were crushed when they protested. The autonomy law, which took effect in January 2001, was supposed to end such abuses by giving the country's 26 provincial governments and 300 districts greater control over everything from taxation to public contracts. Each province is now entitled to 15% of oil revenue, 30% of gas revenue, and 80% of the proceeds from mining and forestry on their lands. They also can keep 90% of property taxes collected in their jurisdictions. Some provinces have used their new resources and autonomy well, e.g. Yogyakarta, where Sultan Hamengko Buwono X has used the revenues wisely and fought against corruption and speedily approved projects that used to take more than a year to push through Jakarta. Unfortunately, such regional leaders have turned out to be exception.

Most of the governors who filled the vacuum left by Jakarta's mandarins are army generals, while most district chiefs lack even high-school educations. There are complaints that there is little sign local officials are spending the new funds on public works or development projects. According to some analysts, less than 1% is reaching the poor. It is just stolen at various levels along the way. Instead of empowering people from the province decentralization has turned out to be decentralization of corruption. The drafters of the autonomy law should have taken into account the absence of political institutions, a corrupt bureaucracy and the weak legal system in the provinces before they presented their recommendations to implement the laws. While decentralization had been a positive step on the part of the government, it could not ensure the rules to be transparent and enforced.

A lot more needs to be done to restore the confidence of the people and the outside investors. Indonesia will have to reform its public institutions, especially the civil service and the justice sector, to serve its people and to improve the investment climate. As one report in an economic news magazine (*Business Week*) says: "In industries from telecom to manufacturing to consumer products, managers of multinationals complain of growing harassment at the hands of officials across the country, endless demand for bribes, local officials who disregard contracts signed with Jakarta ministries, state corporations that renege on years-old deals, and outright threats by xenophobic nationalists and increasingly powerful Islamic fundamentalists.... Ill-designed reforms have led to a breakdown of central authority. Indonesia is now a nation of too many bosses-all seemingly determined to advance their own ambitions. Yes, Scenario is gone. But in its attempt to share power, the government has created many Scenarios. The resulting chaos makes it maddeningly difficult to conduct business across far-flung nation. Increasingly, executives complain there are no impartial courts to enforce the laws or contract terms."

Megawati's government had done very little to improve confidence in the judicial system and eradicating corruption. Her reluctance to remove her Attorney General even while corruption charges are established against him has undermined people's trust and confidence in her to be firmness and resolve to eradicate corruption from public life. Recent high profile cases such as the lower court's ruling declaring the local unit of Canada's Manulife bankrupt for not paying a dividend despite the company's sound financial health have only confirmed investor's worst fears. Last year, the International Finance Corporation (IFC) stumbled over what it charged were fictitious creditors blocking its attempt to have a local company declared bankrupt. Subsequently, the IFC suspended its investments in Indonesia while its affiliate, the World Bank, trimmed its lending to Indonesia. Just about every bankruptcy case that went to the Commercial Court ended up disadvantaging foreign investors. All of which helps to explain why foreign companies try to seek justice outside Indonesia whenever possible. Such moves are already bearing fruit. Singaporean and US courts have issued orders to freeze Indonesian assets, something virtually unheard of in the Indonesian local courts. Megawati's administration had failed to prosecute even one large debtor despite her promise that bringing such people to justice would be a top priority when she was sworn in. She was seen by many as following in Soeharto's footsteps of cozying up to large businesses by being too lenient on them.

Leadership Change and the Rising Expectations in Indonesia

Indonesia's historic first direct Presidential election brought an overwhelming victory for Lt. Gen. (retd.) Susilo Bambang Yudhoyono, popularly known as SBY, over the incumbent Megawati Sukarnoputri. SBY has polled 61 per cent against Megawati's tally of 39 per cent, and was inaugurated on 20 October as the country's first directly elected President of most populous Muslim nation and third largest democracy in the world. The Presidential election together with the June parliamentary and Assembly elections have proved that Indonesia's transition to democracy after a stifling 32 years authoritarian rule of the fallen dictator Soeharto, even though slow, is proceeding in a peaceful manner. Despite the skeptics, Indonesia has not dismembered under the pressure of democratic upsurge, and there is every reason to be optimistic about the growth of democracy in Southeast Asia's fulcrum.

Why did Megawati lose to SBY whose army background would have normally made him an unpopular candidate in a period of transition from an authoritarian rule backed by the armed forces, and one who neither did take part in the process toward the fall of Soeharto dictatorship, nor was a serious presidential aspirant until very recently. The reason could be found in her total failure to rise up to the expectations of both the elite and the masses to bring reforms within the political and economic systems that would have not only accelerated the process of democratic transition, but would have also alleviated the sufferings of ordinary people affected by the downturn in its economy; and in her reluctance to address in a meaningful way the problem of endemic corruption in the country. There is widespread feeling amongst the reformers and even amongst her own supporters that Megawati, once a popular opposition leader, had developed signs of authoritarianism and traits of aloofness during her three years as the nation's leader, a tendency that not only undermined her own legitimacy, but also the process toward democracy. Megawati's overwhelming victory in the 1999 elections was possible essentially because she was seen by many as a rallying point of opposition to then president Soeharto's new order. She was a silent symbol of Soeharto's victim of his authoritarian and repressive regime, particularly manifested in the so-called July 27 affair of 1996. Megawati's policies as well as those of her party were viewed by many as betrayal of the very people, the common man, that have voted her, though not directly, to the presidency. Instead of keeping alive the spirit of *reformasi* that calls for greater transparency, accountability and public participation in the political decision-making process, Megawati has been accused of engaging in backroom deals and horse-trading.

Cynicism pervaded the broad spectrum of the political publics about Megawati's ability to provide the necessary leadership in such times of crises and to rule the country, as well as regarding her commitment towards furthering the process of democratic reform. Former student activists who took part in rallies that contributed to the forced resignation of Soeharto openly voice their disappointment and frustration with the new political elites who took the place of the old and suggest that "reform created 'new thieves' who took advantage after the downfall of Soeharto". From the perspective of the reformers, besides the emergence of 'new thieves', the 'old thieves,' and the corruptors in the new order era of Soeharto were still maintaining their important positions in the government, legislative bodies and judiciary. Neither Megawati nor Abdurrahman Wahid, her predecessor, displayed any strong commitment to uncover human rights violations, mainly committed by the TNI. Yet there is a frustration in many that the process of reform and democratization of governance has been limited and too slow to sustain people's patience and faith in democracy. Corruption in public life and arbitrariness on the part of the government are still a common phenomenon. There is lack of sincerity in pursuing old corruption cases and Soeharto has not been brought to the court as yet for his alleged involvement in a number of graft cases. There is no visible improvement of the economic conditions of the people in the street. Ethnic, religious and sectarian violence has not shown any signs of ebbing; on the contrary, the centrifugal and violent forces are raising its head again, the latest being the resumption of killings in Ambon.

Going by Indonesian standards, past and present, to be fair, Megawati's performance was not so unimpressive, as hers was a relatively stable government pursuing a consistent set of economic and political policies throughout its term of office, but these policies, to quote a perceptive analyst of the Indonesian political and economic scene,"... resulted in socio-economic instability in the lives of ordinary people: Employment uncertainty, price uncertainty, uncertainty of access to medicines and hospitals and to higher and vocational education. At the present time, the causes of these uncertainties are not perceived to be the absence of a "strong man" but of the prevalence of culture of self-enrichment, and of rivalry power and resources, among the old parties." The outcome of the April elections, which has brought a hung parliament with none of the major parties receiving a mandate from the people to rule the country. Even though Golkar has emerged as the number one party in terms of its strength in the parliament, its percentage of votes has gone down, however insignificant that percentage might be. The results are surely not an affirmation of the revival of its strength or broadening of its support base among the people. The elections, therefore, have resulted in greater uncertainty in the political process of the country. Now that Susilo Bambang Yudhoyono has become the President in the country's first-ever direct election he will find it hard to take such a fragmented parliament along with him on crucial decisions relating to future political evolution of democracy in Indonesia. The experience of former president Abdurrahman Wahid is a case in point. Notwithstanding his erratic and idiosyncratic behaviour, one of the important reasons for his failure to emerge as an effective president was the lack of support in the parliament from the parties other than his own, PKB, which was only a minority party and could not get the backing of larger parties like the PDI (P) and Golkar. Susilo is already having a tough tome fulfilling his electoral promises. He is facing a deadlock in parliament, which is stopping him from implementing promised reforms. The next few weeks and months will be a key test for the President as he comes under increasing pressure from power-hungry factions. After promising sweeping changes including a crackdown on corruption and economic reforms, SBY is finding he has no room to move, caught between deep divisions in the parliament, the DPR.

On one side of the house is the opposition camp, the Nationhood Coalition, made up of supporters of former President Megawati Sukarnoputri, with the SBY camp, the People's Coalition, on the other side. But the battle lines are drawn not just between these two factions. According to some analysts, there is also a generational struggle going on in the parliament where there is a juxtaposition of the old guard on the one hand, the GOLKAR PDI-P who do not want to let go of their grip on parliament and the new people who are basically, honest people but who do not have a clue how to conduct themselves in a legislative atmosphere and they are positioning themselves in favour of SBY but actually they are not helping him do much either as was evident in the formation of the recent cabinet where SBY's hand was pushed by pressure from these new groups who are quite idealistic and in a way, very naive. Many are worried SBY's tendency to bend with the wind does not bode well for the future.

Implications of Indonesia for Regional Stability and Security

First, while one can perhaps imagine a situation in which other economies in the region perform better than Indonesia for some period of time, it is, however, inconceivable that the region as a whole could prosper in the years ahead without an open, stable and vibrant Indonesia. The impact of political and economic instability in Indonesia has already been felt throughout the region, and even in the coming years will automatically have an effect on the economic development of the whole region, which, in turn, will not only affect the Southeast Asian states' capability to allocate resources to its people, but will also bring uncertainties in the strategic environment of the region. Indonesia's neighbours treat it indulgently out of fear not so much of its strength but of its weakness, and of the specters that evokes: in the short term, economic stagnation; in the long term, waves of refugees, pirate-infested seas and a power vacuum. It is a matter of great concern to everyone using the straits of Malacca for movement of their goods that the incidence of piracy has increased manifold over the last four years and this is generally attributed to Indonesian navy's weakening capacity to patrol the region. Neighbors therefore fear the knock-on effects of prolonged instability in Indonesia.

Second, a political and economic collapse in Indonesia will lead to a major exodus into the neighbouring countries like Malaysia and Singapore, and would undermine their social and economic stability. Indonesia's neighbours are worried. In February 2001, Malaysia's deputy Prime Minister, Abdullah Ahmad Badawi, gave warning of "a new wave of boat people" if things go wrong. In the same month, Malaysia's defence minister, Najib Tun Razak, warned that Indonesia risked 'Balkanization' into warring, splintered territories and posed the biggest security threat in Southeast Asia. "Since the economic crisis, the country (Indonesia) has been experiencing severe instability, with the possible breakup of the state-the Balkanization of Indonesia ... The mind is boggled with the kinds of scenarios that could soon engulf the region, following this," Najib said. He called for international efforts to prevent any break-up of the world's fourth most populous country, an archipelago of 13,000 islands that straddles vital shipping lanes. "The biggest security threat facing the region is the breaking up of Indonesia and we can not allow that to happen," he further said. Malaysia has voiced fears that the political upheaval and ethnic violence in Indonesia are triggering waves of illegal immigration and pose regional social and security concerns. Malaysia had ordered at the time border patrols to be stepped up to stem an expected influx of people fleeing violence in Indonesian-ruled Borneo, an island also shared by Malaysia and tiny Brunei. And then recently the Malaysian government had deported large number of illegal immigrants from Indonesia, which caused some bad blood between the two countries. The governments of Australia and Singapore have similar fears. The conflicts in Aceh and in Maluku while domestic in nature have inevitable consequences on inter-state and regional relations. To escape repression, victimization or unrest, Acehnese or Madurese have fled their territories and entered Malaysia and Singapore complicating their relations with Indonesia. More importantly, as many Acehnese belonging to GAM *(Gerakan Aceh Merdeka)* have been living in Malaysia over the years and the fact their movement for an Islamic slant, has given rise to suspicion about the Malaysian encouragement to Acehnese separatism, resulting in occasional misunderstanding and irritation between Indonesia and Malaysia.

Third, if the Acehnese succeed in their struggle for independence, there are fears as expressed by both the Filipino and Thai foreign ministers in last year's informal summit of ASEAN that it would surely embolden the Pattanis in Thailand and the Moros in the Philippines to push for a similar movement. None of Indonesia's neighbors, therefore, wants to see Indonesia fracture, as it could trigger similar movements elsewhere, as well as add a dangerous element of uncertainty into the region. That is why, all the neighbouring countries of Indonesia in the region as well as major powers, including the United States and Russia have expressed their strong support its territorial integrity and unity of the country.

The prospect of Islamic fundamentalist governments sitting astride stretches of the Straits of Malacca would be a security planner's nightmare. Given the difficulties of patrolling the area, Malaysia and the Philippines also worry that Islamic militants will find it easier to operate in their southern islands. And now the fear of Indonesia, the largest Muslim country in the world, emerging as a safe haven for terrorist networks. Taking advantage of Indonesian Navy's weakness in upgrading its capabilities to patrol the waters in the Malacca Straits, obviously an effect of the financial crunch and a depleting budget, piracy is already on the increase in the region. The International Maritime Bureau (IMB) compiled seven reports of serious incidents on vessels in waters off Indonesia for the last week of October 2004 - a significant rise in an area, which usually sees two or three attacks per week. The 1MB has repeatedly warned of attempts to hijack ships in the Malacca Strait, which runs along the coasts of Indonesia, Malaysia and Singapore and carries half of the World's oil supplies and a third of global trade. Indonesia accounted for more than a quarter of reported pirate attacks in the first six months of the year (50 incidents), according to the 1MB report. Indonesian naval officials, who contribute to three-nation (with Malaysia and Singapore) patrols of the strait, have hinted recently that AI-Qaeda-linked Jemaah Islamiyah militants have plotted to target ships in the hope of using them as floating bombs.

Fourth, Indonesian stability is intimately connected with the peace and regional order in Southeast Asia. Indonesia has the fourth largest population in the world. It has immense natural resources and a strategic location, for it controls all or part of very major waterway between the Pacific and the Indian Ocean. The US Pacific Command transits these "SLOCs" (Sea-Lanes of Communications) in order to support operation in the Gulf. The Japanese need these waterways to transit their oil tankers. More than half of all international shipping trade traverses these waterways. Indonesia made ASEAN possible. ASEAN's formation was a result of Indonesia's adapting a more cooperative approach to its neighbours. One has to cast back a decade or so to see how well Indonesia acted as the region's centre of gravity and a force for progressive change. In the late 1990s it was Indonesia that pushed the warring Cambodian factions into a settlement that ended the long-running conflict in Indochina, which opened the ear up for investment. In the early 1990s it was Indonesia that encouraged the first transactional economic cooperation, which has helped break down barriers to trade within ASEAN. And it was Indonesia's Muslim scholars and intellectuals in the 1990s that first identifies the need for dialogue and reform to head off the rise to Islamic militancy. Ironically, Indonesia made all these constructive contributions to the region and beyond in spite of the authoritarian and repressive domestic political environment. Former President Soeharto, for all his faults, knew the value of international image-building and responsible regional diplomacy. Over the last three decades, ASEAN has developed a pattern of cooperation so strong that it has altered the geopolitics of East Asia. The cohesion among ASEAN countries have added to the stability of the East Asian region by allowing smaller countries to band together to form a counterweight to larger regional powers. Though by far the largest member of ASEAN has remained an organisation of equals. A blow to Indonesia has undermined the integrity of ASEAN as an institution, as well as regional security. An Indonesian instability has also added to the greater incidence of piracy in the waterways of the region, as we have noted earlier. Since much of the world's piracy occurs in Indonesia's shipping lanes, a breakdown of authority has given it free rein. It is easy to see why Colin Powel, America's secretary of State, even before the September 11 incident, had singled out Indonesia as a country that bears close watching. And now with the news of terrorist networks, the United States as well as Indonesia's neighbours want a stronger commitment from it deal with the menace.

And that is why again, the US now does not hesitate to cooperate with the Indonesian military with which it had earlier snapped all links due to its brutal role in East Timor. The US has been a strong supporter of the democratic transition and view the stakes in Indonesia as enormous, for as President Bush has stated, the success of Indonesia, as a pluralistic and democratic state is essential to the peace and prosperity of the Southeast Asian region. One very important element in US policy is seeking enhanced cooperation on security issues and welcomed President Yudhoyono announcement immediately after assuming office that arresting key terrorists is a priority for him and that he would like to enhance international cooperation on terrorism. As the country with the largest Muslim population in the world, Indonesia has a key role to play in demonstrating the virtues of tolerance and mutual respect in a diverse, multi-ethnic polity. The ability of so many Muslims to thieve economically and pursue a democratic, just society shows the way forward for Muslim and multi-religious societies throughout the world. More broadly, without Indonesia, the no-Muslim world finds it hard to imagine Muslim society as tolerant and secular. When the war on terror broke after the 9/11 attacks on New York and Washington, Indonesia was initially held up as the shining example of a pluralistic Muslim society in contrast to the fractured Middle East. But weak government, factional infighting and an appealingly lax legal framework in Indonesia allowed a tiny band of militants to open a new front in the war on terror in Southeast Asia. By being firm and determined, as President Yudhoyono has promised to deal with the menace of extremism and terrorism, Indonesia can again rebuild its international credibility by ensuring security and environment for the international investors to feel safe and in turn promoting economic vitality in the country. This is important, because without Indonesia's presence and responsible leadership, Southeast Asia's chemistry is thrown out of balance and it becomes a region diminished in the eyes of the world. Southeast Asia's future depends on Indonesia and the latter's future depends on President Yudhoyono ability to create a stable Indonesia by fulfilling his electoral promises of combating corruption, providing employment opportunities to the poor and ensuring security through fighting extremism and militancy. In spite of the goodwill of his people and of the neighbours, looking at the tumultuous start of his tenure, one cannot be very optimistic about an Indonesia, which "can put the reckless and tragic interlude behind it."

Maritime Dimension of Security in Southeast Asia

In today's Southeast Asia we are witnessing the emergence of a post cold war order. The region is so diverse in history, culture, religion, colonial heritage and ethnicity that the new regional structure has taken a long time to evolve and is still evolving. There are many new issues and varied perspectives. The final shape of the post cold war system depends not only on the states in the region but also on the policy and role of major players from outside the region, especially the US, Japan and China. At present, at least three trends can be identified: In terms of security matters in general and in maritime security in particular, the region is evolving from a cold war structure to a multilateral framework; from overall military and ideological concerns to economic concerns: and from a preoccupation with conventional security to a focus more on comprehensive security.

There are changing threats and perception of threats of security. Some of the changes are still very volatile and in flux. At the end of the cold wan the states in the region launched a series of multilateral initiatives in order to bolster their national security and stability. APEC was launched and ASEAN was re-vitalised. The membership of the latter was expanded to include the Indo-Chinese states of Cambodia, Laos. Myanmar and Vietnam. While ASEAN is a far cry from the European Union, it does provide a somewhat collective identity and a loose working framework for the Southeast Asian states. ASEAN provides a forum for dialogue not only among its member states but also between its members and non-member states. For example, it engages the major countries in its vicinity, namely Korea. Japan and China in the ASEAN+3 framework. In the field of security, the ASEAN Regional Forum (ARF) goes beyond these three East Asian countries. There are altogether twenty-two nations, including the United States. Russia. Canada and India, to discuss regional security issues. Although it is often criticised as merely a "talk shop," ARF remains the only track one security forum in the Asia-Pacific region. On the track two (or more precisely track 1.5) level there is the Council for Security Cooperation in the Asia Pacific (CSCAP) and its Maritime Working Group. The September 11 terrorist attacks added new impetus to multilateral cooperation among ASEAN military forces. The second annual ASEAN Chiefs of Annies Multilateral Meeting held in early November 2001 agreed for the first time to coordinate anti-terrorist activities through exchanges of information and the setting up of special organisations and communications against cross-border crime. Given the diversity in the region and the recent history of hostility among some of the states, most Southeast Asian states find the presence of the US in the region a stabilising force. Multilateral cooperation is pursued in parallel to and not in the place of US presence. How far multilateralism can go in Southeast Asia and the Asia Pacific, to a certain degree, is also a function of the politics of major countries in the region. With stronger bargaining power, major powers generally prefer to deal with other nations on a bilateral basis. The powers can exert direct influence and fine-tune on the nature of the relationships according to their own need. China, for one, had vehemently opposed a multilateral approach when it first joined the international community. Yet. China's open policy in economic development demanded a high level of participation in the world community. More particularly. China's bid for WTO membership required the support of other nations.

As a result, China has progressively shown more support of multilateralism in the realm of economic cooperation. It has expressed its readiness to establish a free trade zone with ASEAN states in the recent ASEAN+3 meeting. In political and military matters, it often still prefers bilateral negotiation. In the year 2000 alone, China signed four bilateral cooperation agreements (with Indonesia, Myanmar, the Philippines and Singapore). The agreements with the Philippines and Singapore included defence cooperation and exchanges between their respective strategic and security research institutes. While China agreed to workout a code of conduct for the South China Sea with ASEAN, it refused to have the issue discussed in the broader multilateral forum of ARF. The US is another country that has been impatient and dissatisfied with a multilateral process. The Bush Administration frustrated if not angered quite a number of allies and friends by its unilateral action of withdrawing from the Kyoto Memorandum on Global Warming and by its unilateral push for the Theatre Missile Defence (TMD) and National Missile Defence (NMD). The impact of the September 11 terrorist attacks and the need for the US to muster support around the world for its military action against the Taliban made it necessary for Bush and his administration to rally support with allies as well as non-allies. With Secretary of State Colin Powel attending the ARF and Bush attending APEC. there seems to be a renewed acceptance of multilateralism as an effective framework for international politics in the region.

Japan has wanted to play a bigger role in the region. It has done a lot for the region, from the "recycling of yen" to the establishment of the Asian Development Bank; in maritime security, from being the sole contributor to a revolving fund for the safety and environmental security of the Straits of Malacca to the more recent rallying point of coordinated efforts against piracy. However, Japan sways between its desire to lead and tackle the unique problems in the region and its desire to be a team player of world politics. Its response to the Asian financial crisis of 1997 is a case in point. As an analyst observed. "Paradoxically. Japan appears to be both the driving force for monetary regionalism in East Asia and its main opponent... Japan wishes to maintain its status to the region, while at the same time not provoking criticism in Washington" (*Far Eastern Economic Review*, July 12. 2001, p. 29). The comment that "Today, Japan's approach to regionalism, characterised by its preference for hierarchy and its negligence of neighbours' demands, won't work" may provide the clue for success in Asian regionalism: first among equals may be a better leadership style.

Once the cold war was over, the region devoted itself to economic recovery and there were a number of notable successes, first in the Newly Industrialised Economies (NIEs) and later in the "growth triangles" along the hinterland of national boundaries. Such successes brought confidence and higher standards of living to the people. The military, still a powerful group in many of the countries, has also been benefited from the economic growth of the countries with better equipment and amenities. Although there were skirmishes throughout the region, there were no wars. Everyone was dazzled by rapid economic growth. The financial crisis of 1997 came as a shock. It threw most Southeast Asian countries into disorientation and every effort was made to counter the impact of the crisis and to revive the economy. With rapid economic development, there is an increasing need for natural resources. Much of the region's manufacturing and industrial activities depends on the steady supply of low cost energy. Furthermore, most of the Southeast Asian countries are developing nations with very low average income levels. Thus, food security is very important to the maintenance of the quality of life and social stability of these countries. The 1997 financial crisis had a devastating impact on the region. Many countries were strapped with bad debt. Government officials and corrupted politicians were challenged in Southeast Asian states such as Thailand, Malaysia, Indonesia and the Philippines. One consequence was that Suharto and his government were toppled and Indonesia was thrown into social and political chaos. Another consequence was that separatist movements became rampant in both Indonesia and the Philippines. At times, the most important security issue in these two countries was internal law and order. Ultimately, economics remained the crucial instrument to bring about law and order and to turn the tide of events in the region.

Territorial and boundary disputes remain the most explosive maritime security issue in the region. The overlapping claims in the South China Sea tops the list. China/Taiwan and Vietnam claim all the islands and reefs of the South China Sea. Malaysia and the Philippines claim some of the islands closest to their territories. Brunei and Indonesia also have small claims. Most of the Spratlys and other South China Sea islands are too small or semi-submerged to sustain life. The ocean area around the islands is too treacherous to be used as major sea-lanes of communication and transportation. With the exception of brief armed clashes between China and South Vietnam when the latter occupied several islands off its shore, the South China Sea disputes were basically left dormant. It was only after the cold war when countries in the region set forth to exert their territorial sovereignty and exploited their resources from the sea that the territorial disputes in the South China Sea became explosive. An Indonesian initiative has brought all claimants together in a conflict management dialogue for the last ten years.

Issues as emotional as the sovereignty of nations and as enticing as potential ocean resources are not easy to defuse. Overlapping claims among multiple claimants certainly complicate matters, if not making these overlapping claims almost totally impossible to resolve. The greatest tension in recent years, however, is between China and the Philippines over Scarborough Shoal (Huangyan Island). Early this year, a number of confrontations between Chinese fishing boats and the Philippines armed forces took place. Officials on both sides exchanged claims, counterclaims and diplomatic protests but neither country allowed the incidents to disrupt overall bilateral relations. The need for good working relations among the states and the necessity for regional cooperation prevail. Any armed conflict could aversely affect the economic environment and keep other relations on hold. In recent years. China agreed to work with ASEAN to develop a regional code of conduct for the South China Sea. It proved to be a difficult process. To date, significant differences of opinion remain, not only between the ASEAN states and China but also within ASEAN states. Boundary "disputes in other parts of Southeast Asia have seen better though not easier solutions. In most cases, resource-based considerations served as the rationale to compromise. It took years for Thailand and Malaysia to workout their Joint Development Area (JDA) arrangements in the Gulf of Thailand. The area is now, finally producing gas on a commercial scale.

More recently. Thailand and Vietnam agreed to disagree on their overlapping boundary in the Gulf of Thailand, agreed to set up joint naval patrol and are now eyeing the possibility of joint development of gas fields in their vicinity. Cambodia has also asserted pressure on the Thais to have similar agreement over their disputed maritime boundary in the Gulf of Thailand so that they can also start working on some joint development of oil and gas with the Thais. To date, the Thais have found the Cambodian overlapping claims unacceptable and a resolution is still pending. In the Gulf of Tonkin, through a strong political will of the leadership on both sides, Vietnam finally settled its boundary dispute with China at the end of 2000. Sea-lane security in the archipelagos is still a problem. The Philippines has rectified the UN Law of the Sea but according to its Constitution, the Philippines considered the water within the treaty map between the US and Spain as internal waters, not archipelagic waters. Even though it allows passage of ship through its waters, it made no identification of archipelagic sea-lanes for international navigation. As a result, there remains much ambiguity to international navigation rights and obligations through its waters. Indonesia, on the other hand, has followed the Law of the Sea and designated three north-south sea-lanes through its archipelagic waters for international shipping. It has yet to identify any east-west sea-lanes. This lack of official designation of any east-west sea-lane caused some concerns between the US and Indonesia over the transit right of US naval fleet in the mid-1990s. Both sides came to agree that until Indonesia designated the east-west sea-lane, the US fleet would transit through the archipelago according to its customary practice. To date, the east-west sea-lanes have not yet been designated.

With the end of the cold war, most of the conventional maritime security issues, including the explosive issues of overlapping claims in the South China Sea, proved to be unnecessary irritants that leaders of the Southeast Asian governments preferred not to have to deal with. The more earnest issues at hand are non-military in nature. Some of the major ones include piracy, smuggling, environmental security and resource security. All parties concerned agreed that the issues should be tackled but that there were also diverse perspectives and solutions that still needed to be discussed and resolved. Piracy has been rampant in the history of Southeast Asia. The countless islands and numerous waterways in the region provided excellent hideouts and fast get-away routes. Singapore used to be a notorious pirate hideout, but is now a modern state with impeccable law and order. With the passage of time and changes in society and economy in the region, piracy faded into the background. Piracy returns to haunt these waters at the worst of times when law and order is lax. For many years, the region had relatively few cases of piracy.

However, in 2000, the region witnessed a dramatic jump of 56% as compared with 1999, and four and a half times as compared with 1991. While most of the incidents reported by the International Maritime Bureau (IMB) are minor cases of robbery, the violence and brutality of the cases are intensifying. Even organised crime started to get involved. The following table and chart show changes across time and an overview of the geographical locations of the crime committed among countries most prone to piracy. Indonesia and the Philippines were the two countries that were most infested with pirates, and they were the same countries that had a breakdown of law and order caused by social unrest and separatist movements. Because of the increasing seriousness of the piracy issue, quite a number of workshops and conferences were held during the past two years. The atrocity and problems of piracy were well documented. A highlight of some examples of differences in perception that may hamper closer regional cooperation is as follows. As often is the case in regional cooperation in the Asia-Pacific region, sovereignty is a sensitive issue. While no coastal state is against cooperation in eradication of piracy, many are uneasy with the way the International Maritime Bureau (IMB) tried to redefine "piracy." According to the United Nations of Law of the Sea, piracy is "any illegal acts of violence or detention... on the high seas... or in a place outside the jurisdiction of any State..." (1982 UNCLOS. Article 101). Under international law, all states have the right to arrest pirates on the high seas and to punish them according to their own law. In Southeast Asia, vast extent of water falls into the regime of archipelagic waters which are also legally within the territorial sovereignty of the archipelagic state, and are not subject to law regarding piracy on the high seas. But, in reality, most of the acts of "piracy" are committed in straits, ports and anchoring areas within the territorial sea limit of the coastal state. In order to be effective in its act against piracy, IMB defined piracy as "any act of boarding or attempting to board any ship with the intent to commit theft or any other crime and with the intent or capability to use force in furtherance of the act" (2001 Annual Report on Piracy and Armed Robbery Against Ships of the International Maritime Bureau). The re-definition of the term piracy would raise the number of acts of piracy committed and would give rise to a higher profile of the piracy problem. While this would help to alert the world community to the seriousness of the problem, some officials are worried about the possible creeping jurisdiction such re-definition may bring about. It would increase external pressure, if not external interference, on what nations basically consider to be a national law enforcement issue. Japan's offers of assistance, such as enhancement of patrolling capacity and monitoring capacity both in hardware and in training, are welcomed though some nations are uneasy about joint naval patrol with the Japanese navy. Malaysia and Indonesia have expressed that they are unwilling to allow foreign armed vessels into their territorial waters. Southeast Asian nations are small and medium states that often have to take into account the politics and relations of major countries in the region.

Joint naval patrol would introduce the physical presence of yet another major power into the already complex situation in Southeast Asian waters. For easy access of data, transfer of technology, building of capacity and multilateral coordination, some Southeast Asian states would also prefer to have the piracy-monitoring centre, if any, to be established in the region rather than in Japan. The bottom line of the issue is while Southeast Asian countries are sincere in their concern over the menace of piracy they do not consider it a top priority. Furthermore, many see piracy activities as a function of the overall social, economic and political well being of countries and communities in the region. For example, when China was unable to have full control of its coastal area and when corruption and crimes were rampant, there were more piracy activities along its coast, using ports as hideouts. As China's social and economic order improved, piracy statistics correspondingly dropped. Most experts agree that the recent increase in piracy incidents in the Southeast Asian waters, to certain extent, is a function of the social, economic and political disorder in the Indonesian archipelago and its vicinity. Aside from piracy, other crimes at sea are also haunting the region. They include kidnapping and abduction for political and monetary purposes and the smuggling of drugs and goods across national borders. Several high-profile cases of abduction of foreign tourists by the Abu Sayyaf separatists have not only damaged the tourist industry in Southern Philippines but have also affected the islands of Malaysia off East Sabah. Smuggling of goods and illegal drugs is also on the rise. The national security adviser of the Filipino government. Golez: had charged that the "greatest threat" to national security came from Chinese gangs, smuggling illegal drugs into the Philippines. Resource security, especially food security has always been an important stabilising factor for many countries. As Southeast

Asian states turn to nation-building and economic endeavours, the need for resources such as oil and gas becomes a higher and more dominating priority. Energy poor countries such as Thailand are most vulnerable. The search for energy security has led to greater cooperation between Malaysia and Thailand. They shelved their sovereignty rights issue on their overlapping claim in the Gulf of Thailand in order to co-exploit the oil and gas resources there. The success of the joint development project inspired further cooperation among the countries around the Gulf. As an example. Vietnam and Thailand agreed on their overlapping claims and started joint naval patrol of the area. These two countries also are looking at possible joint development of oil and gas resources in that area.

Cambodia also pushed hard on Thailand to have similar arrangements over their common but contested border. Thailand found the Cambodian claim unacceptable and could not agree to disagree. To date, no agreement on the overlapping area has been reached. The concept of energy security has undergone some fundamental changes in recent years. There has been an increasing reliance on natural gas as a main source of energy. Countries turned to a gas pipeline as a way to secure continual supply of energy. Singapore connected a natural gas pipeline from West Natuna. Indonesia and commenced its first production on January 15, 2001. Singapore also signed a contract to connect another gas pipeline from Sumatra. Indonesia. Malaysia too signed a contract to get gas from West Natuna. There is a growing regional integration to ensure regional security of energy supplies. In 1997, the ASEAN Head of States adopted the ASEAN Vision 2020 that called for cooperation "to establish interconnecting arrangements for electricity, natural gas, and water within ASEAN through the ASEAN Power Grid and a ASEAN Gas Pipeline." Such strategies will greatly enhance regional cooperation and energy security. Another resource security issue is more problematic. It is the issue of fishery which is a main source of food security in the region. The need for food and economic income leads to rapid depletion of fish stocks in Southeast Asia, especially in the Gulf of Thailand. With the Exclusive Economic Zone (EEZ) and archipelagic states jurisdictions established by the UNCLOS-III, there are no more high seas in Southeast Asia. Many traditional fishing grounds, formerly free for all to fish, have been changed into either Archipelagic waters or EEZ where the coastal state has the sole jurisdiction over living resources, such as fish. Although UNCLOS-III calls upon the coastal and archipelagic states to respect traditional fishing rights, no proper provision is made in the Southeast Asian waters and fishermen fishing in traditional fishing grounds are often considered to be engaged in illegal fishing. There is also the related issue of fishery disputes, including the passage of fishing vessels through the EEZ of a third country. Thailand has many problems with its neighbours — Malaysia. Myanmar and Cambodia. More recently, the Thais have also had problems with Indonesia for fishing illegally in their EEZ and archipelagic waters. Environmental Security is gaining attention in some parts of Southeast Asia, especially in the straits of Malacca and Singapore. A more important issue concerning navigation in the eyes of Southeast Asian countries, especially Malaysian and Indonesian, is the navigational safety and the environmental security of the straits of Malacca and Singapore. Thousands of ships pass through these straits every year, including some of the world's largest oil tankers. The hazard of navigation through the narrow and shallow waterway is well documented. The Revolving Fund is the only fund existing today that is used to help combat oil pollution in the Malacca and Singapore straits. It was set up with contributions from the Japanese Malacca strait Council. With its funds dwindling, there is no current regional or strategic plan for its replenishment International Maritime Organisation (IMO) has sponsored or co-organised several international conferences in Malaysia and Singapore in recent years to discuss maritime safety and marine pollution in the Straits. The need for greater burden sharing in the maintenance of the Straits was brought up in the 1996 IPS/IMO Conference.

Maritime Dimension of Security in East Asia: Current Scenario

With the growing interdependence of the world, it is hard to imagine a coastal nation that does not, in some important ways, depend on the sea to carry out its essential trade. The idea that the seas are of vital importance to the nations has been addressed eloquently by many scholars and writers. For instance. John N. Moore, a highly respected analyst on naval affairs and associated strategy of sea power, once wrote that for many centuries the majority of countries in the world have depended on the free passage of goods across the sea for their existence. At the regional level. East Asia, which encompasses a huge maritime area, is not an exception. Over the past few years, the East-Asian region has recorded the highest economic growth rate in the world, and one of the fundamental characteristics of this growth is that it is based on seaborne trade.

In East Asia, the heavy dependence on seaborne trade has led to an explosion of shipping carrying exports to other parts of the world as well as within the region itself. Almost all East Asian countries are dependent on the security of the sea lanes of communication (SLOCS), and the protection of merchant shipping both in peace and war times is a task which no country in the region can ignore. While the end of the Cold War and the dissolution of the Soviet Union have reduced or changed the threat to the SLOCS, the drawdown of US forces have tended not only to reduce its capability as principal defender of the SLOCS but also to create discomforting strategic uncertainties. Such a strategic scene has important maritime implications and provides countries in the region with a challenging task of protecting SLOCS. Recently, seeking to protect their coastlines and maritime trade routes from attack. East Asian navies are turning increasingly to submarines that are difficult to detect and armed with weapons that can sink even the largest warship. Recognising this development, the author would like to examine the major sources of threat to SLOCS in East Asia and what should be done to enhance SLOC security, exploring the role of navies.

Perhaps the most powerful factor boosting the importance of the East Asia's maritime environment is the rapid rise in the region's economy. As many data suggest, East Asia has achieved remarkable economic success during the past two decades. In particular, it has recorded the fastest growth rate among all regions of the world since the 1980s. Asia's newly industrialised economies (ANIEs), namely, the Republic of Korea, Taiwan. Hong Kong and Singapore have consistently grown since the 1980s largely because of the successful pursuit of export-led development policies. The newly developing countries in East Asia, such as Thailand, Malaysia. Indonesia and China, have also successfully adopted export-led development strategies following the example of Japan and ANIEs. Accordingly, the pattern of growth of these countries resembles that of the ANIEs. These newly rising East Asian economies have grown much faster than other developing countries in the world in the past 10 years. The World Bank once predicted that by 2020, seven of the world's 10 largest economies (in purchasing power parity terms) would be located in Asia, while only two will be in Europe. The uncertainties about recent regional developments would encourage many to remain somewhat cautious about this prediction. However, the geo-strategic implications of the general trend are profound. The principal source of growth in these economies has been their outward-looking and open-development strategies. Thus, the rapid economic growth of East Asia has been paralleled by an explosion in its external trade. Over the past two decades, for instance, the external trade of East Asia increased nearly twice as fast as world trade in general. As a result, the external trade of this region has already surpassed that of North America. Moreover, the economies of East Asia are growing far more interdependent Trade between the countries in East Asia is growing much faster than their trade with other regions of the world. Clearly, the economies in the region are feeding off each other far more than ever before in order to sustain their high rates of growth. In the late 1990s, it is reported that intra-regional trade in East Asia accounted for more 40 per cent of its total external trade. If East Asia and North America are grouped into one area, namely the Asia-Pacific, the external trade of this enlarged region becomes similar in volume to that of the European Union (EU). It is predicted that during the 21st century, the Asia-Pacific region will account for more than half of the total world trade. It is noteworthy, moreover, that Asia-Pacific international trade already corresponds to more than 60 percent of its overall external trade, similar in proportion to that of the EU. This means, as previously noted, that the Asia-Pacific region has already achieved a degree of trade interdependence and economic integration, generating the highest percentage of world trade volume. A primary consequence is that, because nearly all of tins trade is carried by ship, the growth of shipping tonnages and container loads in the Asia-Pacific has been very rapid and significant. In this regard, it is noteworthy that in 2000 eight of the 10 busiest container ports in the world were located in the Asia-Pacific region.

The speed and sheer mass of this region's economic growth, the rapid rise in the regional economic interdependence, and the concentration of the linkages in vast volumes of the sea traffic highlight the critical importance of shipping in this region. Shipping routes are sometimes rightly described as the arteries of the regional economy. In the Asia-Pacific, an uninterrupted flow of shipping is critical to most regional countries" economic health and prosperity: and to some countries" very survival. The security of shipping or SLOCS is, therefore, an important and increasingly critical strategic interest in this region.

Despite the very importance of the SLOC security in East Asia, it is apparent from a look at the map of the region that the sea lanes are vulnerable, not only because they are proximate to the Asian land mass, but, more importantly, because they pass through the narrow choke points. Maritime traffic from Japan and Korea to the south transits either the Taiwan Strait or the Bashi Channel between Taiwan and the Philippines. Ship sailing from the east coast of Korea or the west coast of Japan must first traverse the Korea Strait. Ships of many nations sailing from the Northern Pacific Ocean to the Indian Ocean or Persian Gulf must either pass through the narrow Strait of Malacca or one of many Indonesian passages. At every one of these choke points, they could face an attack from submarines or aircraft. In the past, the principal threat exerted to the SLOCS in East Asia was obviously that of the Soviet Union. With the end of the Cold War and the dissolution of the Soviet Union, however, such a threat to the SLOCS has been substantially reduced. One should, nevertheless, not be surprised if the security of merchant shipping constitutes a continuing problem. For one thing, there remains the potential for a wide range of low level threats, which include terrorism, piracy, narcotics trade, refugee flows, etc. Obviously such threats are often criminal in nature and do not usually result in destructive confrontation between nations. What is more important, however, is the prevailing strategic uncertainty resulting from the disruption, of the Cold War stability, which could pose a serious threat to the SLOCS in East Asia in the longer term. This development and its maritime implications are something that calls for a careful scrutiny. Indeed, the security of the SLOCS in East Asia is the subject that certainly deserves continued attention.

Currently, there are several major maritime territorial disputes in the seas of East Asia, which can pose threats to the SLOC security in the region. According to the recent opinion poll, conducted by the Far Eastern Economic Review in October 1996. Many Asian people believe that the next war in the region would be over territorial disputes and natural resources There is no doubt that the military confrontation over territory and natural resources necessarily involves the threat or use of sea mines, hence a serious threat to the East Asian sea lanes. On the basis of limited historical experience in East Asia, the coastal state factor could be another major threat to SLOC security in the region. In particular, the potential threats to shipping through international straits could arise from: (a) coastal states' attempts to control freedom of passage for the national security; (b) domestic instability in coastal states; and (c) contention among the neighbouring countries regarding overlapping airtime claims In East Asia, there are a number of straits with international significance. For instance, the Straits of Malacca, the Sunda Strait and the Lombok Strait are the main passage ways between the Indian and the Pacific oceans. The latter two fall into the, archipelagic waters of Indonesia, while the former is part of the territorial sea of Indonesia and Malaysia. In these straits, any attempt to hinder or block passage of ships by coastal states, if the experience of the Suez Canal and the Gulf is any guide, could, pose a threat to SLOC security in the region. In this regard, it is noteworthy that Indonesia has sought to designate three special sea-lanes running in a north-south direction that international shipping could use with minimal restrictions to pass through its archipelagic waters. The extended maritime jurisdictions or the excessive maritime claims by coastal states would be even more risky.

For instance, in 1977, North Korea proclaimed the 50-mile military boundary zone for the purpose of defending its national interest and sovereignty. Its location is up to 50 miles from the baseline of the territorial sea in the East (or the Sea of Japan) and to the boundary line of the economic zone in the Yellow Sea. In this zone (on the sea, in the sea and in the sky), according to the proclamation, acts of foreigners, foreign military vessels and foreign military planes are prohibited and civilian ships and civilian planes are allowed to navigate or fly only with appropriate agreement or approval. In addition, civilian vessels and civilian planes in the zone are not allowed to conduct acts for military purposes or acts infringing upon the economic interests. Thus, the military zone in jurisdictional terms appears even more exclusive than the territorial sea where foreign vessels are entitled to innocent passage. Similarly, China has for more than 30 years announced restrictions in coastal areas well outside its territorial sea for military purposes. Currently, there are two security zones proclaimed by China in the Yellow Sea. One is a Military Alert Zone extending west of a line from the North Korean-China border, at the mouth of the Yalu River, to a point off the Shandong Peninsula. This zone includes the Bo-Hai and legitimately claimed territorial sea as well as an area which other States consider high seas. Entry into the zone is only with the express permission of Chinese authorities. Another is a Military Exclusion Zone in the vicinity of Shanghai. In this zone, entry is forbidden even on innocent passage without specific permission. The idea of establishing the maritime zone for defence or security purposes could be justified as an exceptional measure of self-protection in times of emergency, based on Article 51 of the UN Charter. However, the idea of permanent defence zone is inherently difficult to accept, since such an extended maritime jurisdiction interrupts freedom of navigation.

Piracy is one of the newly emerging sources of threat to SLOC security in the region. In particular, there has been a significant increase in piracy in the region with the Asian financial crisis. According to the data released by the ICC-IMB, two thirds of all the world's reported cases of piracy occur in the Asia-Pacific, with Southeast Asia accounting for a majority of them In East Asia, the piracy attacks, in general, take the form of intruders coming alongside a ship under way, usually during the night, boarding it and then taking possession of whatever cash and negotiable valuables come easily to hand. The notable feature of this type of attack is the degree of skill that is used to board the ship coupled with the fact that violence is not normally used unless resistance is offered. In recent years, three noticeable characteristics may be found in piracy attacks in the region. First, the pirates are becoming increasingly well-equipped. They usually use small speedboats and often have modest radar systems to help them locate their targets. Access to machine guns, mortars and grenade has become easier, heightening the potential for violence during raids. Second, pirates in this region sometimes seize a merchant vessel, dispose of the crew by setting them adrift or even killing them, then bring the stolen ship into port. There the vessel is repainted, given a new name and provided with fake registration documents. Once refurbished, the "phantom ship offers its service in careless cargo owners. Third, pirates in this region are becoming increasingly organised with support networks. That is to say, piracy in the region tends to be more sophisticated and lucrative crimes, supported by organised criminal gang. Hence, some attacks have been masterminded by transnational crime syndicates, who often commit other transnational crimes such as illegal drug trafficking and human smuggling. These are totally new trends and developments as compared to what has been called "Asian piracy" in the past, where ships are boarded and cash and valuables are stolen from the ship's safe and the crew with the minimum of force. Whatever the types, piracy poses real dangers — not only to the lives of crew, but also to other ships in heavily travelled areas (200 ships, half of them oil tankers, enter the Straits of Malacca and Singapore each day). These new trends in regional piracy suggest that such acts of boarding any vessel with the intent to commit theft or other crime, without any doubt, pose a serious threat to SLOC security and have broader implications for regional security.

The East Asian region contains two huge semi-enclosed seas - that is the Yellow/East China Sea encompassing 362,000 square miles, and the East Sea (Sea of Japan) encompassing 445,000 square miles. In terms of marine pollution, the following general observations need to be kept in mind First, the littoral and adjoining areas have the heaviest population concentration in the world. Second, these areas have one of the heaviest concentrations of industry in the coastal zone in the world. Third, this area has a heavy concentration of shipping routes of the world, with its susceptibility to pollution from collision, groundings, discharges from tank clearings, leaks or human error - a major concern. Finally, there is considerable potential for oil and gas in the offshore. With these conditions, the region obviously faces the potential of large-scale deterioration, which could interrupt the navigation of ships. In fact, the coastal waters of the Yellow/East

China Seas already suffer from heavy contamination mainly by pollutants inputs from dangerous cargoes and from the fast growing industrial activities of the littoral states. The East Sea (Sea of Japan) is also showing serious signs of pollution, and large coastal areas, mostly off Japan, are already heavily polluted. It can be easily foreseen that situations will deteriorate unless great care is taken. As the public and national awareness of the importance of environment grows, marine environmental degradation could constitute a serious potential source of threat to SLOCS in the region. In addition to these explained above, there are many other sources of threats to SLOCS in the region which cannot be ignored. As is well known. East Asia-Northeast Asia in particular is an area of high military tension yet one where the littoral states have managed to coexist with relatively few incidents. The existing significant military preparations in the region have the potential to spark open conflict, thus posing a threat to the SLOC security. For instance, China launched over 10 days of guided missiles and heavy artillery tests in the East China Sea just north of Taiwan in August 1995 and in March 1996 respectively, and it seriously threatened SLOC security and safety of civilian aviation.

The best way to maintain the security and safety of SLOCS is to avoid or neutralise the aforementioned possible sources of threat. In practical terms, we need to consult with each other or to establish a cooperative mechanism among regional states, in order to avoid or neutralise the possible threats. Over the past years, there have been various suggestions concerning the means of cooperation to keep SLOCS safe in the region. For instance-the Institute of Strategic and International Studies in Kuala Lumpur has proposed the concept of a Regional Maritime Surveillance and Safety Regime for Southeast Asian waters. This proposal could provide a medium for monitoring illegal activities, sharing information (including surveillance information), combating piracy, enhancing maritime safety and controlling pollution. Indeed, some of this agenda has already moved off the conference table into reality with the July 1992 signing of an anti-piracy accord between Indonesia and Singapore. These countries are now coordinating surveillance and patrolling in the Malacca Straits and adjacent waters. Recently, Rear Admiral (Retd.) Surmihiko Kawamura of Japan made a proposal of establishing an international cooperative SLOC security scheme, placing the US at its core (key strategic player) and having the Asia-Pacific region countries share the responsibilities of the areas and functions in accordance with their capabilities and geographic conditions. In accordance with capabilities and geographic locations of the regional states, Rear Admiral Kawamura suggested the following ideas: (i) maintenance of sea control throughout the Pacific Ocean by the US; (ii) protection of shipping, surveillance and search and rescue (SAR) in regional areas such as the Northeast Pacific, South Pacific or the ASEAN area, etc. by the concerned regional states; and (iii) surveillance of coastal seas and local shipping protection by littoral states. Given the increasing need for the establishment of an international cooperative scheme for SLOC security in East Asia, such a multilateral burden sharing system seems to be very acceptable. To actualise this multilateral cooperative system, however, many political, military and economic difficulties should be removed. In addition to this, establishment of a multilateral cooperative scheme for SLOC security in the post-Cold War era, the urgent task of all regional states in East Asia is to make endeavour to build a stable and secure maritime regime as well as implement maritime confidence-building measures. The stable maritime regime is a prerequisite not only for enhancing security at sea but also for further maritime cooperation among regional states. Along with such efforts to build the stable regime, various maritime confidence and security-building measures should be explored, considering the changing maritime security context.

The following are the most urgent tasks by which regional states should endeavour to strengthen the SLOC security. First, recognising the importance of freedom of navigation to the maintenance of seaborne trade in East Asia, states in the region are encouraged to develop cooperative approaches to the maintenance and protection of sea lanes of communication. Such cooperative approaches might begin with exchanges of information and training in such areas as humanitarian assistance, search and rescue, marine safety,, and maintaining law and order at sea. The exchange of information should include information on likely threats to, or security incidents concerned with sea lanes of communication. In this regard, a recent initiative of the IMB is illustrative of what is possible; it has been instrumental in setting up a Regional Piracy Centre. The Centre, based in Kuala Lumpur, Malaysia acts as an information exchange bureau and works on the basis of mutual assistance and recognises the crucial role of intelligence and information as a policy basis. Second, it is important to enhance the openness and transparency about maritime regime and the practice of regional states with the acceptance of the UN Convention on the Law of the Sea (UNCLOS). It is certain that the Convention has a considerable potential of acting as a confidence-building measure (CBM) within East Asia. The first and perhaps the most significant CBM resulting from UNCLOS is that the Convention assists to clarify the outer limits of coastal state claims to sovereignty and jurisdiction over adjacent maritime areas. A further aspect of UNCLOS as a CBM is the continued emphasis throughout the Convention on maritime cooperation: States are to reach cooperative agreements in determining their maritime boundaries; and they are to cooperate with respect to the utilisation of EEZ. Third, the maritime security context in the region requires measures to reduce risks at sea. Maritime confidence-and security-building measures (MCSBMS) have the objective of reducing the risk of maritime conflicts and misunderstanding or miscalculation of military activities at sea. Such measures include the sharing of naval information and the exchange of personnel as well as more advanced operational measures such as surveillance cooperation or agreements on the prevention at sea between the naval forces.In East Asia, maritime confidence and security building measures could have enormous rewards if they could be put into practice. Bilateral and multilateral naval cooperations for MCSBMs would reduce uncertainty in maritime security environment of East Asia, which will in turn significantly enhance the SLOC security in the region.

Marketing and Consumer Behaviour in East and South East Asia

The extraordinary progress of East and South East Asia (ESEA) has been well documented in both the academic and popular press. The nations individually and collectively have been labelled as "the awakening giants," the sources of a "new world economic order," "the little tiger," "the four tigers," and the period has been hailed as "the Pacific century." The progress is particularly impressive when we consider that immediately after the Second World War (1945) ESEA was a scene of devastation and disorder imbued with potential for further conflict. The notion that the region was "going nowhere" was not simply based on the jaundiced assessment of those without vision but rather the calculated evaluation of the well informed. To accentuate the true nature of the situation Leger (1995, p. 46) uses the example of Korea's per capita GNP that at the time was "roughly equal to that of Haiti, Ethiopia, and Yemen and about a third less than that of India and Pakistan." In the first two decades that followed the Second World War there was little immediate improvement. The region continued to be characterised by the rise of brutal centrally controlled forms of government, civil wars (e.g. Korea, Vietnam), poverty and other damaging forms of internal disorder (e. g., corruption, black markets, insurrections and various forms of political and economic repression). Today, though the process is not complete, and within the region there still exist some of the world's poorest nations, the transformation and the potential are imposing. The full magnitude of the changes is described by Schwab and Smadja (1994, pp. 40-41) as the rise of the "new economic world order" on whose nature they elaborate as follows:

> Perhaps the most spectacular component of the current revolution is the shift in the world economy's center of gravity to Asia. The extraordinary process of fast and steady growth in East Asia since the end of the 1960s has led to an overall redistribution of the world's economic power, the impact and implications of which are just beginning to be felt. In 1960, East Asia accounted for just 4% of world economic output. Today its share amounts to 25%. While GNP in Europe and the Unites States has grown at an average of 2.5% to 3% per year over the past 25 years, many East Asian countries have managed an annual average of 6.5% to 7.5% - a trend that is expected to continue beyond the turn of the century. Between 1992 and the year 2000, 40% of all the new purchasing power created in the world will be in East Asia, and the region will absorb between 35% and 40% of the global increase in imports. East Asian central banks now hold close to 45% of the world's

> foreign reserves, and while the United States and the major European countries keep piling up foreign debt, Japan, Taiwan, Singapore, and Hong Kong are in the remarkable position of not having any.

Indeed, trends suggest that "the 'pacific century' is approaching" (Forbes 1995, p. 24). Initiated by the renaissance of Japan's economic power, and the emergence of the newly-industrialising countries (NICs) as well as the growth of a group of "near NICs", it seems likely that the Pacific will replace the Atlantic ocean as the center of world trade. In essence, ESEA will become the world's most formidable market; the reciprocal relationship between marketing and consumers will be its catalyst. Given this ascent and importance, the purpose of this text is to provide insights to the present conditions and the future trends of marketing and consumer behaviour in the various countries of the region.

As a prelude to the country-specific chapters, it is necessary to address the region as a whole and to extract those aspects that are critical to the explanation of its progress. The contributors, in their presentations for each of the nations, have tended to take a regional perspective. It is not our purpose to reiterate their contributions; we will attempt to distill and to describe the major unifying themes and trends in a conceptual context. But before doing so, two issues should be addressed. The first issue is the question of regional definition and the second is the nature of the statistical data. The alert reader would have already noted that our region description, East and Southeast Asia, is somewhat cumbersome - hence the acronym ESEA - and that we appear to move from Southeast Asia to East Asia to the Pacific Basin, with little apparent distinction. Unfortunately, the literature and common usage are such that this geographic ambiguity cannot be avoided. Many country and region demarcations are possible. Some of these classifications overlap and do not have unique contexts except in those circumstances where they describe a formal alliance or association such as the Association of South East Asian Nations (ASEAN) or Asia-Pacific Economic Cooperation (APEC). Further, the history of the region has been characterised by numerous attempts to form regional alliances, and the existence of contradictory (divisive and unifying) forces. The nations differ on the basis of ethnicity, culture, language, and political and economic systems. Some of the animosities have deep historical roots spanning thousands of years. These animosities may be difficult to overcome, particularly when one notes the fairly recent military hostilities among some of them; the memory of which is deeply ingrained in the national psyches and is always a factor in international relations. The possibility of further territorial disputes is very real. Consider, for example, China with the status of Hong Kong, Taiwan, Macao and the wide ranging dispute over the Spratly islands; border tensions between Myanmar and Thailand, the "Timor question" in Indonesia; the still unresolved Korean conflict; and the Khmer Rouge problem in Cambodia, just to name a few potential flash points. However, the forces for integration and cooperation are also very strong, and are further energised by the pragmatic attitude of the leadership who recognize that true progress can only be achieved through intra regional cooperation. The major trends within the region are toward international accommodation, although the conditions within many nations have not been characterized by political stability and internal turmoil has often been the norm. The movement towards regional integration has been slow but steady and proposals for groupings have been relatively frequent. For these reasons the terminology and acronyms have been numerous and confusing.

The choice we have made is based on the broad grouping of countries that are not only in relatively close geographic proximity, but whose economic and marketing futures are inextricably intertwined. ESEA, therefore, comprises the economically developed nations of Japan, Australia and New Zealand (countries whose futures will increasingly coincide with Asia); the Newly Industrializing Countries or territories (NICs) such a the Republic of Korea (South Korea), Taiwan and Hong Kong; the states of ASEAN (Indonesia, Philippines, Thailand, Malaysia, Singapore, Brunei and Vietnam, and the "observer" cum participant nations, Cambodia, Laos and Myanmar); the evolving socialist economies of the region, the People's Republic of China, Cambodia, Laos, Vietnam, Myanmar, and the Democratic Republic of Korea (North Korea). Also included is Papua New Guinea and the numerous microstates of Oceania.

Natural Resorce Base

The historical basis of national wealth has emanated from natural forces the determining elements of which are location, characteristics and resources. The central location of ESEA within the patterns of world trade as well as the regions vast resources have incited intense competition and colonial exploitation. However, the individual nations vary in the characteristics and extent of their natural resources that form important constraints affecting the economies, markets and consumers. Consider, for example, China's size, topography and arable-land to population ratio, which raise questions about this nation's ability to administer its economy and to feed its people. Singapore on the other hand is densely populated with virtually no natural resources but due to location and a organized, hard working population is rapidly approaching the living standards of the highly-developed nations. Although the regional resources are plentiful and varied, centuries of exploitation and tremendous population pressures have inevitably led to degradation. The condition of the environment presents serious problems in most of the nations and will affect their ability to enhance and to sustain life quality. Further economic progress will lead to greater stresses on air and water quality, traffic congestion, forest and fishery depletion, and soil erosion, thus creating a growth-preservation conundrum for these nations. This is one of the major challenges facing the region.

Existing Political System Government

The second element is "the political system" that - guided by its "ideological" orientation as to the correct nature of the values and structures of the society - will determine the "budget" or financial allocations to various uses and finally will decide the extent of "intervention" in the system. ESEA is a unique crucible of political processes and social change. Within its ambit may be found the extremes of the political spectrum from the democratic (e.g. Australia and New Zealand) to the Stalinist authoritarian (e.g. the Democratic People's Republic of Korea, a.k.a., North Korea). In between one finds various forms of government, some of which have vestiges of military rule (e.g., Indonesia, Thailand and the Republic of Korea, a.k.a., South Korea). Market socialism, market economics under the direction of single party authoritarian rule (e.g., Chinese Communist Party, Vietnamese Communist Party and the State Law and Order Restoration Council of Myanmar (SLORC)) is the new experiment in the region. Although in some cases the progress is slow and faltering it is not a distortion to state that tolerance for personal freedoms is a trend in most parts of the region.

The non-communist nations such as Thailand, South Korea and even Indonesia have moved in the direction toward greater individual freedoms and liberties, which as institutions develop, suggest a more prosperous and peaceful future. The communist/socialist nations, in between periods of repression and motivated by the disintegration of Eastern Europe and the Soviet Union, are also liberalising their institutions and in turn enabling more personal freedoms. Japan provides an interesting departure from the other models. Despite continuous political instability at home it has managed to progress without any apparent damage to its social harmony or economic interests. Irrespective of the trend toward political systems that enable greater personal liberties, the unsettling condition of North Korea, for example, should not be overlooked and further uncertainty within the region may cause problems that could have a negative effect on political reforms and ultimately market development. Nevertheless, the growing pragmatism of the political leadership throughout ESEA suggests that the trend toward liberalization will continue. If the process is managed and the various political transitions occur without open conflict, an auspicious future for the region is assured. It would be a misrepresentation, however, not to state that the region contains some of the most repressive and closed regimes existing in the world today, and these are not simply those labelled "communist". Many of the citizens of ESEA find themselves living in political climates that are not conducive to dissent or the kind of "free" speech enjoyed by some of the more well developed nations with longer democratic traditions. These same climates also affect the marketing and business environments. Government interference beyond the scope of agreed upon conditions, corruption, bribery and unethical business practices, generally, still exist. However, as stated earlier, the movement is toward economic and political systems that are more conducive to expressions of personal liberty and stable business environments. We are reluctant to categorise these trends as "democratic" in the Western sense, but it seems inevitable that further development of economic structures and greater dependence on information technologies will lead to greater freedom of interaction and expression as well as increased levels of trust within these societies.

Existing Economic System and Financial Position

The "economic system" is the third element of the model. Again the nature and influence of this system is determined by three factors: (1) the "ideology," which determines the nature, structure and operation of the system; (2) the "performance" of the system; and (3) the "demand" for the products within the system. The dominant theme in the region is best captured by a headline from *Asian Business* (1992): "The Road to Prosperity Leads to the Market." This headline was designed to describe the process as socialist countries in the region liberalized their economies in an effort to achieve prosperity while retaining power. However, the metaphor is more broadly applicable. Continuing political and economic reform are characteristic of the region as nations attempt to liberalise their economies. China, Vietnam, Cambodia, Laos and Myanmar have, in different ways, sought to liberalise their economic systems and cautiously implemented reforms to move the nations toward the market system. China in particular has been transforming itself from a centrally planned economy into a form of decentralised market system. The moves have been hesitant and often accompanied with clampdowns on dissidents, but despite detractors, economic progress has been made. This spread of economic liberalism, facilitated in part by the collapse of Eastern Europe, has brought these previously isolated nations into the world economy. Other countries, such as Indonesia, the Republic of Korea and Thailand, on whose governments the military retain a strong influence, have shown flexibility in both moving toward civilian government and liberalising the economies. Accompanying this general trend toward the market have been the related trends of privatization, deregulation, and trade and foreign investment liberalisation. Privatization and deregulation have increased the level of internal competition and placed considerable pressure on previously protected institutions such as telecommunications and energy suppliers. While in many parts of the world the attitude to foreign investment is ambivalent, the consistent economic growth in ESEA has been attained through policies to stimulate foreign investment.

Entry of these nations - with their 1.9 billion people - into the international market place has increased competitive pressure for global financial sources. Further, the rise of the vast economic power of the region is not only being fuelled by the big players such as Japan, China and Indonesia, with their exports to Europe and the US, but from within Asia by the four Tigers (Hong Kong, Singapore, South Korea and Taiwan). Indeed, it appears that the time of region-based prosperity is fast approaching. ESEA nations are increasingly looking to their neighbours for sources of funds and conversely for good investment opportunities. Therefore, as they grow wealthy they look to invest in their neighbours and so help them to move towards affluence. Although Japan's influence is well documented newer capital exporters such as Singapore, Malaysia and Hong Kong have also emerged. The consistent high economic growth of these nations has resulted in an increase in their capacity to exert an influence within ESEA and externally. At the present time about half of Asian exports are to other nations within the region. For example, Japan's share of exports to the US has dropped from 40% to less than 33% in ten years because of intensified investment in ESEA. Hong Kong's wealth has influenced the prosperity of the nearby Guangdong province, Taiwan is the biggest investor in Malaysia and Australia the second biggest investor in Indonesia. This welcoming attitude to foreign investment accompanied by a continuing deregulation of trade has resulted in a high degree of interdependence among the economies of the region. Intra regional imports as well as exports were over sixty percent and are growing at a rate of 8.1% per year (Forbes 1995).

This intra regional interdependence is being increased by the pragmatic, innovative search for new ventures that contribute to the prosperity and security of the region. Consider, for example, the recent Singaporean push for a growth triangle and the formation of localised trilateral links. There is also a general recognition for the need to form strategic alliances and other types of partnerships in an effort to gain a technological edge. In conjunction with this trend is the exhortation that executives must look at the market as both region and country specific. There is already considerable posturing and competition for the location of the region's center, both internationally and within nations. Concern, however, has been expressed that trade barriers may be coming down much faster than desired or expected. AFTA (ASEAN Free Trade Area) is in the process of "reducing its trade liberalization period from 15 to 10 years and Asia Pacific Economic Cooperation forum (APEC) intends to abolish all trade barriers by 2010 for industrialized countries and 2020 for all others").

Domestic political realities may even curb this general trend and the progress toward the free trade goals may be uneven, but it seems unlikely that it will be permanently reversed. Indeed these domestic perceptions of internal and external conditions will largely determine the pace of change. For example, the apparent desynchronization of world economic cycles (ESEA has been booming despite a mercurial Japanese economy while Europe always seems to be on the cusp of slipping into recession) has made many of the ESEA nations more self-reliant and confident in themselves. In many respects these nations now see themselves as proactive forces for economic change and development. The implications for the worldwide de-localisation of industrial production have also precipitated another area for concern. On the positive side countries that were previously condemned to simple, labour intensive manufacturing are now able to produce cost-effective and sophisticated high tech products.

Malaysia for example has become the world's leading producer of semiconductors and now discourages labour intensive industries (Schwab and Smadja 1994), thus making the leap to high tech, high productivity, high quality industries and high wages for its citizens. On the negative side countrys that have made the strategic choice to rely on cheap labour as a competitive advantage will likely be forced to rethink and to revise their strategy. The labour cost edge may be retained, in the short term and in relation to some external competition such as US and Europe, but it is not a viable foundation for a sound future within the ESEA region where the flexible corporation may move from Taiwan to China to Vietnam and so on. Further, in some of the countries of the region labour cost advantages seems to vanish in the face of realities (e.g., poor infrastructure, local bureaucracy and "voluntary payments") that accompany daily business operations. Nonetheless, the persistent growth, the size of the population and the inevitable increase of wealth will have a strong impact on the demand for products and services.

Existing Social System, Life and Livelihood Situation

Fourth is the "social system" that consists of "culture," "character," and "interaction." "Culture" determines the most general, enduring set of values within the community. The community may, for example, place a great value on business acumen and education or it may not; it may value conspicuous consumption and wealth accumulation or it may not. "Character" refers to the characteristics of the society, for example, the demographic structure. "Interaction" is used here as a term to indicate the extent to which the society is open or closed; that is, freedom of interaction is afforded to members of society. The following chapters will demonstrate to readers the vast diversity of ESEA. And while some countries are more ethnically homogenous than others (e.g., Korea) within all the nations there exist important differences in, for example, culture, language, and religion, which preclude a simple enumeration. As suggested earlier some of the differences are the sources of animosities that have deep historical roots and that may be difficult to overcome. These differences present challenges to further progress of not only the region but some of the nations themselves.

It is possible that hostilities based on cultural differences and national aspirations could erupt (e.g., Indonesia and the problem of East Timor). However, it is equally true that some of the nations in the region, at least on the surface, present a visible degree of cultural harmony and accommodation (e.g., Singapore and Malaysia). Further, the pragmatism, and the positive cultural attitudes to business and education of some of the cultural groupings suggests that a slow evolution toward cultural reconciliation may be possible. The existence of immigrant groups (e.g., the overseas Chinese) may serve not only, in the economic sense, as a source of investment but more importantly as a cultural bridge between nations.

The desire to minimize the potential for religious conflict (e.g., the high degree of religious tolerance in Australia, New Zealand, and Singapore) is another positive manifestation. Concerning the "character" of the region, there are broad overarching regional tendencies that need to be mentioned. There is little doubt that the size, density and the growth rates of many ESEA nations make them of critical importance to the world. The region may - depending upon which nations are included - contain as much as 60% of the world's population while occupying only about 30% of the total area (23% if Australia and New Zealand are excluded). The region contains the worlds most populous country (China 1,192.0 million people) and seven other nations with populations greater than 40 million people (Indonesia 199.7, Japan 124.8, Vietnam 73.1, Philippines 68.7, Thailand 59.4, Myanmar 45.4, and South Korea 44.6. The average annual population increase varies from 0.3% (Japan) to 2.9% (Cambodia and Laos). Although this latter rate may not seem excessive, when compared to the 0.38% of Europe a stark contrast becomes evident, especially when the enormous population base of ESEA is considered. Although the region contains some of the worlds poorest nations (Cambodia, Laos, Myanmar and Vietnam) also included are several of the world's fastest growing and most powerful economies (China, Hong Kong, Japan, Korea, Singapore and Taiwan). Hong Kong and Singapore are of particular scholarly interest because their progress may illustrate the importance of trade to overcome the problems of population density.

The population of the region is predominantly rural (Australia, Hong Kong, Japan, Singapore and New Zealand are notable exceptions) and there has been a rapid rural - urban drift that strains infrastructure and often leads to a disenfranchised, poor under-class. Other important demographic developments include the emergence of sex and age as determinants of future growth. Women are increasingly likely to be factors in the work force and women's issues generally are likely to become influential when making policy. Regarding age, although the proportion of those over the age of 65 is increasing (particularly in Japan and Singapore) the "youth group" (i.e., those from 15-24 years of age) is also larger than in other parts of the world, thus ESEA overall is younger than other parts of the world. More than half the people are under 25 compared to the US and Europe where the proportion is about a third and a fourth, respectively, so the demographic base for further economic growth also exists. Regional forces that typically affect population changes, include migration patterns, fertility rates, and mortality and life expectancy rates. All are changing and will have an impact on the development of ESEA. Other problems that remain to be resolved include the movement of "guest" workers and refugees. Rising, balanced prosperity for the region may provide the solution to both of these problems.

Existing Knowledge and Education System

The "knowledge system" is the fifth element enumerated. The three components of this system are the extent to which knowledge is well "documented," i.e., the degree to which knowledge in written form, as well as the technological facilities that serve as conduits to knowledge, are readily available; the degree to which it is "independent," i.e., can be relied upon to be objective and free of "ideological" influence; and finally the degree to which guidelines for application ("applicable") may be distilled from the knowledge base. It is this system and the three systems to follow, which present some of the greatest challenges for ESEA. The leadership of the region has recognised that the passing on of "concentrated experience" in the form of recorded knowledge is critical to progress. It is becoming clear that the intra-regional investment needs are going to be accompanied by the development of an intra-regional knowledge base. Indeed, it is the purpose of this text to contribute toward this development. The "education system", presented as element six, consists of "teaching," "research" and "practice." The "practice" component is emphasised because marketing is an applied discipline; a test of the applicability or relevance of "knowledge" is the extent to which research findings are useful and information is taught/learned. Education also is a major challenge facing the region because the present growth has not been based on coordinated and integrated intra-regional educational foundations. Education mimicry has tended to be the norm whereby, often as not, "European models" were adopted. Some - Australia, Hong Kong, Singapore and New Zealand - have used their existing systems to provide the education base for others in the region. In some instances overseas education, whether to the better developed regional institutions or to Europe and North America, has been encouraged. Greater economic development and concomitant need for highly skilled workers will require even greater emphasis on and resource allocation for education and the ESEA governments face some critical decisions in this area.

Other Systems

This leads to the seventh component of the system, which has been labelled "the executive system." Essentially, this refers to the professional practice of marketing. Professionalism depends on the "knowledge" level of the executive population, their "motivation" the extent they actually "implement" modern marketing practices. In many respects the rapid growth in the region is testimony to an adequate understanding of marketing practice. The individual chapters provide ample within-nation evidence of the progress that has been made. There is little doubt that the regional orientation is towards the attainment of greater professionalism in this area. The final component is the "marketing system." This component is shown to consist of "the consumers," "the infrastructure" and "performance." The region possesses some of the most well developed marketing systems in the world - and some of the least well developed. As stated above, the growth of ESEA occurred largely because of foreign investment, cheap labour and export development. Now the region is beginning to see itself as its own market, regionally independent and self-sustaining. This inward or regional focus is partly explained by a substantial consumer base that already exists; when larger numbers of consumers join the middle classes, the ESEA market may dwarf all others. Purchase patterns and consumption practices through out ESEA suggest this transformation is occurring much more rapidly than many observers thought was possible. To achieve fully this potential the infrastructure needs are enormous. Further, and perhaps most importantly, the related specific developments vis-a-vis the marketing mix are critical: without a keen understanding of consumer needs and wants, and the market contexts in which marketers must introduce, promote, distribute, price and support products, marketing efforts are destined to fail. Therefore, trans-regional development will have to include keen awareness of specific markets and consumers and mastery of marketing skills. Moreover, to attain acceptable and sustainable levels of marketing performance, environmental concerns (e.g., the need for clean technology and protection of forests and fisheries), national and regional interests will have to be balanced. The administrative and organisational challenges are immense, and could, without resolution, destroy the potential of ESEA.

The Investment Regime in ASEAN Countries

Within these episodes of evolution and development ASEAN countries have gone through the process of FDI policy changes and legal adjustments to accommodate the changing global legal and economic environment. The pace of investment liberalisation taken by these countries was clearly influenced and affected by the interaction of legal and economic factors in the international sphere, and by a combination of their economic relations outside the region and their own economic policies. The feasibility of a MAI prompts ASEAN countries to adjust their laws and policy to comply with its standard if ASEAN countries would accept a MAI that would establish a new and higher multinational standard of investment liberalisation and protection. This might be seen as an instrument accelerating the process of an open regionalism. Since the 1980s ASEAN countries have embarked on significant reforms of their investment regimes. These investment liberalisation initiatives were undertaken unilaterally. They have occurred due to the recognition of the benefits of a degree of liberalisation and competition in response to change in the international climate, rather than due to the requirements of regional or international agreements. However, by 1995 ASEAN countries were conforming to the Agreement on Trade-Related Investment Measures (TRIMs) to eliminate trade-related performance requirements. Controls of FDI in ASEAN countries, however, remained quite extensive and complex. The policy instruments include the following:

- restrictions on entry and establishment;
- restrictions on the level of foreign ownership permitted;

- special treatment of foreign investors;
- operational restrictions such as local content requirements and minimum export levels;
- investment incentives such as tax concessions.

In addition, there are many other policies that influence FDI such as tariff and other trade barriers, the lack of competition rules and policy, and the degree and type of protection of intellectual property rights.

10

ASEAN-EU-ASEM RELATIONSHIP

ASEAN-EU PARTNERSHIP

The Association of South East Asian Nations (ASEAN) encompasses 10 South East Asian countries. Its key position in the Asia-Pacific region, its dedication to peace and stability in the region and its important economic weight have made ASEAN an essential partner for the European Union in Asia. ASEAN was established on August 8, 1967 in Bangkok, Thailand with the signature of the Bangkok declaration by the five original member nations (Indonesia, Malaysia, Philippines, Singapore, and Thailand). In 1984, Brunei Darussalam was admitted as the sixth member. In 1995, Vietnam also joined ASEAN. Lao People's Democratic Republic and Burma / Myanmar became members in 1997. Cambodia joined in 1999. The Member countries that make up ASEAN have a combined GDP of 656 billion (2002), but there are large economic disparities between the ASEAN members. With a population of some 503 million people, they make up one of the largest regional markets in the world. A significant development for ASEAN took place at the Bali Summit of October 2003: the ASEAN leaders projected the creation of an ASEAN Economic, Security and a Socio-cultural community.

The EU greatly supports this development, considering its first hand experience of the benefits of closer regional integration. The EU is a longstanding dialogue Partner of ASEAN. Co-operation between the EU and ASEAN is based on a Co-operation Agreement (1980) between the EC and member countries of ASEAN: Brunei, Indonesia, Malaysia, Philippines, Singapore, Thailand and Vietnam. Protocols for the accession of Laos and Cambodia to the Agreement were signed in July 2000 but the EU has indicated that it cannot agree to negotiate an extension of this agreement to Burma / Myanmar as long as the situation as regards democracy and human rights in that country does not improve significantly. Burma / Myanmar, therefore cannot participate in EC-ASEAN co-operation actions. In September 2001, the European Commission's presented its Communication "Europe and

Asia: A Strategic Framework for Enhanced Partnerships", which identified ASEAN as a key economic and political partner of the EC and emphasised its importance as a locomotive for overall relations between Europe and Asia. The Commission Communication 'A New Partnership with South East Asia', presented in July 2003, reaffirms the importance of the EC-ASEAN partnership.

Political Dialogue

Political dialogue between the EU and ASEAN firstly takes place at regular Ministerial Meetings. The foreign ministers of both the EU and ASEAN have met for political dialogue every second year since 1978. The 15th ASEAN-EU Ministerial Meeting was held in Jakarta, Indonesia on 10 March 2005. All 25 Member States were represented; Commissioner Ferrero-Waldner represented the European Commission. The meeting underlined by various pro-EU statements of ASEAN Ministers. It is clear that the enlarged EU is more than ever a reference-model for Southeast Asia in their desire for prosperity and stability within Asia. The EU's 'New Partnership with South East Asia' strategy was again confirmed as being at the origin of enhanced relations. The Meeting acknowledged its concrete results; increased support for ASEAN integration by making available EU's proper experience, start of negotiations with Singapore and Thailand on bilateral agreements, concrete joint co-operation in the fight against terrorism, substantial progress under the TREATI (trade) initiative, launch of tri-lateral co-operation, a joint EU-ASEAN visibility strategy, etc. The Meeting took a number of concrete decisions such as the endorsement of the Commission's READI (dialogue instrument for non-trade issues) principle, it approved the Indicative Programme 2005-2006, and agreed meetings of both Informal Coordinating Mechanism (ICM) and Senior Officials (SOM) in the course of this year with a view to step up contacts and prepare the ground for further progress in our relations. The meeting provided the Commission with an occasion to brief the region on the EC's substantial Action Plan for Post Tsunami reconstruction. The Ministers were briefed on the situation in Burma/Myanmar and discussed ways to promote positive developments within the country. Other international issues included Middle-East, Iraq, Korean Peninsula and cross-straits tensions. Furthermore, ASEAN and EU discussed WTO, Kyoto Protocol and Millennium Development Goals.

Trade Relations

In 2003, the EU was ASEAN's second largest export market and the third largest trading partner after the United States and Japan. EU exports to ASEAN were estimated at 39 billion €, while EU imports from ASEAN were valued at 66 billion € . The main exports from ASEAN to the EU are machinery, agricultural products, and textiles. In general, both EU imports and exports of goods to ASEAN between 2000 and 2003 have decreased, largely reflecting global trends, although at a slightly higher rate. In contrast, trade in services during the same period has increased for both EU imports and exports of services with ASEAN. EU FDI flows to

ASEAN are recovering after the fall due to the financial crisis of 97-98. Singapore attracts more FDI than all the other ASEAN countries taken together and was the 4th largest destination for EU direct investment in 2003, after Russia and ahead of China, The EC-ASEAN Joint Co-operation Committee (JCC) promotes and keeps under review the various co-operation activities envisaged in the Co-operation Agreement. An official-level Committee usually meets every 18 months. Sub-committees have been established for Trade and Investment, Economic and Industrial Co-operation, Science and Technology, Forestry, Environment, and Narcotics. The Commission's Regional Indicative Programme for co-operation with ASEAN covering budget years 2005-06 to the amount of 15-20 million reflects the new agenda with ASEAN following the 'New Partnership' communication. The programme was endorsed at the JCC of 26 February 2005 in Indonesia.

EU RELATIONS WITH SOUTH-EAST ASIA

On 9 July 2003, the European Commission adopted a Communication on a "New Partnership with South East Asia", setting out a comprehensive strategy for future EU relations with the region. The strategic priorities identified in the Communication include

1. Supporting regional stability and the fight against terrorism,
2. Human Rights, democratic principles and good governance,
3. Mainstreaming Justice and Home Affairs issues,
4. new dynamism into regional trade and investment relations,
5. development of less prosperous countries, and finally
6. intensifying dialogue and cooperation in specific policy areas, such as economic and trade issues, justice and home affairs matters, science and technology, higher education and culture, transport, energy, environment, and information society.

The Council Conclusions from 2004 showed that Member States agree with the overall strategy. The implementation of the strategy therefore continues, along the suggested lines, both regionally and bilaterally. The policy set out in the Communication remains our agenda for relations with the region. The countries of South-East Asia (Brunei Darussalam, Burma/Myanmar, Cambodia, Indonesia, Laos, Malaysia, the Philippines, Singapore, Thailand and Vietnam) have a total population of 512 million, and an average per capita income of $1,020 (ranging from $260 in Cambodia, through $3,400 in Malaysia, to $29,610 in Singapore). Three countries in the region (Burma/Myanmar, Cambodia, and Laos) are classified as Least-Developed countries by the UN. In political and security terms, whereas the stability in the region is increasing, notably thanks to efforts through the ASEAN Regional Forum, human-rights issues remain an acute concern in several countries in the region, most notably in Burma/Myanmar. Economically, the countries of South-East Asia account for 1.8% of world GNP, and for 5.6% of EU external trade. The region is also a major trade and investment destination for the EU. The EU is currently ASEAN's third largest trading partner and ASEAN's second largest export market after the US. Regional cooperation efforts in South-East Asia have been substantial, since the establishment of ASEAN (the Association of South-East Asian Nations) in 1967. ASEAN's efforts for regional integration have taken a deeper dimension since the 1990s, with the launch of ASEAN Free Trade Area (AFTA), an ASEAN Investment Area (AIA) and the Initiative for ASEAN Integration (IAI) and most lately, in 2003, the so-called Bali concord II which envisages the creation of ASEAN Economic, Security and Social Cultural Communities by 2010.

THE ASIA-EUROPE MEETING (ASEM)

ASEM 5 Summit - Hanoi, 7-8-9 October 2004

39 partners participated in the historic ASEM 5 Summit held in Hanoi between 7th and 9th October 2004. This landmark in Europe-Asia relations welcomed new partners heralding a new stage of development, both consolidating and widening Asia-Europe relation. The Heads of State and Government at the ASEM 5 Summit reviewed international developments and global challenges, and addressed regional developments in Europe and Asia, including the human rights situation in Burma/ Myanmar. A particular focus was on how to deepen the common commitment to a multilateral approach to international relations. The Asia-Europe economic partnership and recent developments at the World Trade Organisation (WTO) were discussed alongside ways to take forward the dialogue of cultures and civilisations. A retreat session was devoted to discussion of the future of ASEM, in particular future enlargements and the key strategic priorities for ASEM.

Key characteristics of the ASEM process include:

- its informality (complementing rather than duplicating the work already being carried out in bilateral and multilateral fora);
- its multidimensionality (devoting equal weight to political, economic and cultural dimensions)
- its emphasis on equal partnership, eschewing any "aid-based" relationship (taken forward under our bilateral relations) in favour of a more general process of dialogue and cooperation
- its high-level focus, stemming from the Summits themselves.

The ASEM 5 Summit was held in Hanoi between 7th and 9th October 2004 with the participation of 39 partners. It marked ASEM's enlargement to the ten new EU Member States as well as to three new countries from the Asean region (Cambodia,

Laos and Burma/Myanmar) that were not yet part of the process. As a result, the ASEM process will now bring together 39 partners from Asia and Europe. As stated in the conclusions of the External Relations Council (GAERC) of 13 September 2004, the participation of Burma/Myanmar was accepted with the expectation that the participation of the Burmese government at the ASEM Summit would be lower than Head of State/Government level. The ASEM 5 Summit also addressed the situation of human rights in Burma/Myanmar. Taking place every two years, alternatively in Asia and Europe, Summits are the most important feature of the process, by giving the main political impetus. ASEM 5 has set the pace and guidelines for the next two years of the ASEM process in the context of enlargement. The ASEM process began in March 1996 with the first Asia-Europe Summit in Bangkok, which brought together the Heads of State and Government of ten Asian countries (Brunei, China, Indonesia, Japan, South Korea, Malaysia, the Philippines, Singapore, Thailand, and Vietnam) and of the fifteen Member States of the EU, as well as the President of the European Commission. The summit established an ongoing process, based on summit-level meetings every second year, regular ministerial meetings (Foreign, Economic and Finance), and more frequent meetings at the senior-official and working level. The second ASEM Summit was held in London in April 1998, the third in Seoul in October 2000 and the fourth was held in Copenhagen (Denmark) on 22-24 September 2002. Since 2001 Ministerial meetings have usually beeb held on an annual basis, following the decision taken at the third Summit in Seoul.

11

ASEAN-Australia-New Zealand Summit and Negotiation

CHAIRMAN'S STATEMENT OF THE ASEAN-AUSTRALIA AND NEW ZEALAND COMMEMORATIVE SUMMIT

Vientiane, 30 November 2004

1. We, Leaders from ASEAN, Australia and New Zealand met on 30 November 2004 in Vientiane, Lao PDR, to commemorate the 30th Anniversary of ASEAN-Australia and ASEAN-New Zealand dialogue relationships in 2004 and 2005 respectively and to set the direction for our future relations.

2. We were gratified that the dialogue partnerships between ASEAN and Australia, and New Zealand have strengthened and matured over the three decades and have contributed to the building of mutual trust and respect, good neighbourliness and interdependence and provided mutual benefits to our peoples. We also noted with satisfaction that our countries have steadily fostered a close, cooperative and multifaceted partnership, including in the areas of security and defence, trade, investment and finance, law and order, development cooperation, education, research, science and technology, tourism, media, culture and the arts, and people to people contacts.

3. We signed a Joint Declaration of the Leaders at the ASEAN-Australia and New Zealand Commemorative Summit. This Declaration will mark the beginning of a new era in our partnerships further intensifying and expanding our cooperation to serve the interests of our peoples and promote peace, stability, sustained development and prosperity in our region.

4. The Leaders of Australia and New Zealand expressed their support for the establishment of the ASEAN Community comprising the ASEAN Security Community, ASEAN Economic Community, and ASEAN Socio-Cultural Community as well as the Vientiane Action Programme (VAP) aimed at further integrating ASEAN and narrowing the developments gaps.

5. We had a very productive and fruitful discussion on regional and international political and economic issues. We agreed to further enhance the ASEAN- Australia and New Zealand economic partnerships by launching negotiations on a Free Trade Agreement (FTA), which will build on the substantial trade and investment linkages already established between ASEAN, Australia and New Zealand. We agreed to commence negotiations on an ASEAN-Australia and New Zealand Free Trade Area in early 2005, to be completed within two years, on the basis of the time frames and the guiding principles agreed by our Economic Ministers.

6. We recognise the importance of the Treaty of Amity and Cooperation in Southeast Asia in building peace and stability in the region and strengthening ASEAN's relationship with its Dialogue Partners. In this connection, the ASEAN Leaders encourage Australia and New Zealand to positively consider acceding to the Treaty in the near future in the spirit of the strong trust and friendship between ASEAN and Australia and New Zealand, and their common desire to contribute to regional peace and stability.

7. We underscored the importance and need to intensify cooperation and capacity building efforts at the bilateral, regional and multilateral levels to combat terrorism and transnational crimes. In this connection, we agreed to strengthen institutional linkages and implement cooperation programmes.

8. The Leaders of Australia and New Zealand agreed to continue their support, including through development cooperation programmes, to ASEAN's economic development and integration efforts as well as to strengthen existing efforts to bridge the development gaps in ASEAN through the Initiative for ASEAN Integration (IAI) and by developing the sub-regional growth areas in ASEAN to promote economic and social development, strengthen the cohesiveness of ASEAN and improve standards of living in the region. They also agreed to continue the Official Development Assistance from Australia and New Zealand to ASEAN, especially the new Member Countries. In this connection, the ASEAN Leaders expressed their appreciation to Australia and New Zealand for their continued assistance.

9. We agreed to strengthen cooperation in human resource development through promoting further education sector linkages through student and youth exchanges and scholarships as well as in preventing and combating the spread of communicable diseases, such as HIV / AIDS, SARS and Avian flu.

10. We agreed to deepen and expand the partnerships based on mutual trust, respect, equality and understanding of each other's cultures and values through people-to-people exchanges among government personnel, educational and academic exchanges, professional exchanges and grassroots interactions.

11. We welcomed the initiatives taken by ASEAN, Australia and New Zealand

to promote a conducive and favourable environment for citizens of ASEAN, Australia and New Zealand who are living, working and studying in each other's territories.

12. The Leaders of Australia and New Zealand agreed to support the early accession of Laos and Vietnam in the WTO.

JOINT DECLARATION OF THE LEADERS AT THE ASEAN-AUSTRALIA AND NEW ZEALAND COMMEMORATIVE SUMMIT

We, the Heads of State/Government of Member Countries of the Association of Southeast Asian Nations (ASEAN), and Australia and New Zealand gathered on 30 November 2004 in Vientiane, Lao PDR for the ASEAN-Australia and New Zealand Commemorative Summit;

Noting that the Summit was taking place during the 30th anniversary year of the dialogue partnership between ASEAN and Australia – ASEAN's first such relationship – and that 2005 would mark the 30th anniversary year of the dialogue partnership between ASEAN and New Zealand;

Recognising that the establishment of the ASEAN-Australia and ASEAN-New Zealand dialogue relations in 1974 and 1975 respectively had paved the way for strengthening of relations, which have contributed to building mutual trust and respect, good neighbourliness and interdependence and provided mutual benefits to our peoples;

Recalling the Joint Statements of the ASEAN Heads of State/Government and Prime Minister of Australia, and the ASEAN Heads of State/Government and Prime Minister of New Zealand on 7 August 1977 and 8 August 1977 in Kuala Lumpur respectively, which demonstrated the mutual desire of ASEAN, Australia and New Zealand to enhance dialogue relations and cooperation;

Acknowledging with satisfaction that our countries have fostered a close, cooperative and multifaceted partnership, including in the areas of security and defence; trade, investment and finance; law and order; development cooperation; education; research, science and technology; tourism; media; culture and the arts; and people to people links; and noting that these linkages are longstanding and have been increasing steadily over time;

Convinced that this record of constructive engagement has laid a strong foundation for a new level of interaction beyond this Summit that will take our partnership to greater heights and closer friendship;

Bearing in Mind the interdependency of the security and prosperity of ASEAN, Australia and New Zealand and that the opportunities and challenges posed by globalisation and the dynamic developments in the region and the world require coordinated and coherent responses at the regional level;

Agreeing on the seriousness of the threat posed by terrorism to the security and prosperity of the region, and of the world in general, and reaffirming our shared determination to prevent, suppress and eliminate terrorism in all its manifestations;

Recognising that the transnational nature of terrorism calls for a comprehensive approach that embraces action on many fronts, including by addressing the economic, social and political factors that create conditions in which extremism can take root and flourish, and noting the contribution that international cooperation on counter-terrorism and relevant development projects can make in this regard;

Recognising the need for close cooperation and coordinated actions to combat transnational crime in order to promote security, peace and stability within our region;

Welcoming the ASEAN-Australia Joint Declaration for Cooperation to Combat International Terrorism signed on 1 July 2004 in Jakarta, and New Zealand's willingness to consider signing a similar Joint Declaration with ASEAN, which will further strengthen security cooperation, in particular on counter-terrorism;

Acknowledging that the proliferation of weapons of mass destruction and their means of delivery poses one of the most serious challenges to international peace and security in our time, and agreeing on the importance of international regional and national efforts to address such proliferation;

Reaffirming the significance of the ASEAN Regional Forum (ARF) as the primary forum for security cooperation in the Asia-Pacific;

Reaffirming our adherence to the principles enshrined in the Charter of the United Nations and other basic principles in international law and in particular, our faith in, and respect for, each other's independence, national sovereignty, territorial integrity, and the principles of non-interference in the internal affairs of other states, renunciation of threat or use of force, peaceful settlement of disputes, equality, and mutual respect and mutual benefit;

Expressing full support for the realisation of the ASEAN Vision 2020 adopted in November 2000 in Kuala Lumpur, and the implementation of the Declaration of ASEAN Concord II (Bali Concord II) signed on 7 October 2003 in Bali leading to the formation of the ASEAN Community comprising the ASEAN Security Community, ASEAN Economic Community, and ASEAN Socio-Cultural Community, as well as the Initiative for ASEAN Integration (IAI) launched in November 2000 in Singapore and the Vientiane Action Programme (VAP) signed on 29 November 2004 in Vientiane aimed at further integrating ASEAN and narrowing the developments gaps;

Recalling the Joint Ministerial Declaration on the AFTA-CER Closer Economic Partnership signed during the 7th AEM-CER Consultations in 2002 in Bandar Seri Begawan; to promote trade, investment and regional economic integration between ASEAN and the CER countries, with a target of doubling trade and investment by 2010;

Recognising the contributions made by Australia and New Zealand through their development assistance programmes to ASEAN and its Member Countries to improve the living standards of the peoples of our region, to promote sustainable development, and to support the realisation of the goals and objectives of the ASEAN Vision 2020, and the Bali Concord II, and to implement the Ha Noi Plan of Action, and the IAI;

Detrmined to nurture our human, cultural and rich natural resources including traditional knowledge and plant variety protection;

Convinced that further broadening and deepening of the three decades of dialogue partnerships will continue to serve the interests of our peoples and is essential for promoting peace, stability, sustained development and prosperity in our region;

Hereby Declare our Commitment to

1. Enhancing Political and Security Cooperation

- Foster strong bonds, good neighbourliness, peaceful co-existence, and prosperity in our region, recognising and respecting the rule of law and justice, as well as the diversity, particularly the differences in development paths, security concerns, values, culture and traditions among countries, and work together to create an environment of tolerance and openness for cooperation and development in the region.
- Cooperate in multilateral fora, in particular the United Nations and the World Trade Organisation, to contribute to the peace, stability, development and prosperity of the region and the world, and to ensure that the benefits of globalisation are equitably shared by all countries, both developed and developing countries as well as the least developed countries.
- Enhance political and security cooperation and partnership through bilateral frameworks, the ASEAN Regional Forum, Asia Pacific Economic Cooperation (APEC) and other regional and international fora.
- Cooperate in areas of disarmament, arm control and non-proliferation of weapons of mass destruction (WMD), their means of delivery and related materials.
- Strengthen international non-proliferation cooperation and efforts including through the United Nations and regional fora.

- Improve awareness, implementation and enforcement multilaterally binding international arm control and non-proliferation instruments and support measures, such as export controls.
- Recognise the importance of the Treaty of Amity and Cooperation in Southeast Asia in building peace and stability in the region and strengthening ASEAN's relationship with its Dialogue Partners. In this connection, ASEAN Leaders encourage Australia and New Zealand to positively consider acceding to the Treaty in the near future in the spirit of the strong trust and friendship between ASEAN and Australia and New Zealand and their common desire to contribute to regional peace and stability.
- Intensify cooperation and capacity building efforts at the bilateral, regional and multilateral levels to prevent, suppress and eliminate international terrorism in all forms and manifestations, and to address the economic, social and political factors that create the conditions which give rise to and nourish extremism.
- Take urgent steps to prevent and combat the menace of transnational crimes such as trafficking in drugs, arms smuggling, human trafficking, particularly in women and children, child sex tourism, cyber crime, international economic crime, sea piracy, money laundering and financing of terrorism, through effective institutional linkages and cooperation programmes.

2. Strengthening Economic Linkages and Financial Cooperation

- Promote growth and development and increase living standards throughout the region, and to further economic integration by launching negotiations on a Free Trade Agreement (FTA), which will build on the substantial trade and investment linkages already established between ASEAN, Australia and New Zealand.
- Build on existing and ongoing cooperation initiatives under the AFTA-CER, CEP, especially in the areas of trade and investment facilitation measures, as well as technical assistance and capacity building among ASEAN, Australia and New Zealand, particularly for the newer ASEAN members.
- Commence negotiations on an ASEAN-Australia and New Zealand Free Trade Area in early 2005, to be completed within two (2) years, on the basis of the time frames and the guiding principles endorsed by our Economic Ministers attached to this Declaration as an Annex.
- Reaffirm and follow through with their commitments as reflected in the agreement reached in Geneva in August 2004 on a framework to guide the

final phase of the Doha Round of World Trade Organisation negotiations recognising the importance of substantial agricultural reform, including the early elimination of all forms of export subsidies, to achieving an acceptable overall outcome in the Doha Round.

- Support the early accession of non-WTO members of ASEAN in the WTO.
- Promote and strengthen cooperation on financial infrastructure and capital market development in order to achieve sustainable growth in the challenging global economy.
- Explore opportunities for a wider cooperation in the field of tourism in areas such as joint promotion, marketing, investment, and manpower development.

3. Consolidating Functional and Development Cooperation

- Cooperate including through development cooperation programmes, to support and facilitate ASEAN's economic development and integration efforts as it strives to realise the ASEAN Community, giving special attention to projects under the IAI and the VAP.
- Strengthen existing efforts to bridge the development gaps in ASEAN by developing the sub-regional growth areas, such as the ASEAN-Mekong Basin Development Cooperation (AMBDC), Ayeyawaday-Chao Phraya-Mekong Economic Cooperation Strategy (ACMECS), Brunei Darussalam-Indonesia-Malaysia-Philippines East ASEAN Growth Area (BIMP-EAGA), Cambodia-Laos-Vietnam Triangle, the Emerald Triangle, Indonesia-Malaysia-Thailand Growth Triangle, and Greater Mekong Sub-region (GMS) to promote economic and social development, strengthen the cohesiveness of ASEAN and improve standards of living in the region.
- Continue Official Development Assistance (ODA) from Australia and New Zealand to ASEAN, especially to the new Member Countries and least developed countries (LDC) of ASEAN in their efforts to narrow the development gaps given the importance, impact and relevance of their past ODA to ASEAN.
- Reinforce mutual cooperation and assistance in human resource development through promoting further education sector linkages student and youth exchanges and scholarships.
- Strengthen cooperation in preventing and combating the spread of communicable diseases, such as HIV/AIDS, SARS and Avian Influenza.
- Encourage the development of new collaborative regional partnerships between Australia, New Zealand and ASEAN members.
- Enhance cooperation in energy security, non-conventional energy, and science and technology.

- Promote cooperation in the field of sustainable agricultural development focusing on human resource development and capacity building, particularly for the least developed countries of ASEAN, in sanitary and phyto-sanitary measures and agricultural standards.
- Promote sustainable development through strengthening cooperation in various areas of the environment protection and management such as biodiversity, chemicals and hazardous waste, forestry and zoology management ASEAN Heritage Parks and cultural heritage and Marine Protected Areas, and water resources management.

4. Promoting People-to-People Contacts and Exchanges

- Deepen and expand partnership based on mutual trust, respect, equality and understanding of each other's cultures and values through people-to-people exchanges among government personnel, educational and academic exchanges, professional exchanges and grassroots interactions.
- Welcome initiatives taken by ASEAN, Australia and New Zealand to promote a conducive and favourable environment for citizens of ASEAN, Australia and New Zealand who are living, working and studying in each others territories.
- Promote awareness and understanding of ASEAN, Australia and New Zealand among our peoples through enhanced cooperation in the areas of public information, media interaction, tourism, language learning, culture, heritage development and grassroots leadership.
- Foster dialogue among cultures and religions as a means for better understanding and friendship among our peoples.

Implementation and Funding Arrangements

- Task our Ministers to continue to identify and implement concrete measures and activities in realising the purposes of this Declaration and to provide, within respective national capacities, resources needed for its implementation.
- Strengthen funding mechanisms for the effective implementation of this Declaration.
- Provide periodic review of the progress made in the implementation of this Declaration utilising existing mechanisms in the dialogue relations.

Signed in Vientiane, Lao PDR, this Thirtieth Day of November in the Year Two Thousand and Four in three originals in the English language.

GUIDING PRINCIPLES FOR NEGOTIATION ON ASEAN-AUSTRALIA AND NEW ZEALAND FREE TRADE AREA (FTA)

The FTA will be mutually beneficial for all parties. With that objective in mind, the negotiations will be guided by the following principles:

(a) The FTA should be comprehensive in scope, covering trade in goods, services and investment.

(b) The objective of the FTA should be to move towards deeper economic integration between the two regions through progressive elimination of all forms of barriers to trade in goods, services and investment; and through trade and investment facilitation and economic cooperation measures.

(c) The FTA should, where relevant, build on members' commitments in the WTO.

(d) Due consideration should be given to the different levels of development and capacity of the Member Countries to participate in comprehensive trade and investment liberalisation. The FTA should therefore include provision for flexibility, including special and differential treatment, especially for the newer ASEAN members.

(e) Recognising the different levels of development among the Member Countries of the two regions, provision should be made for technical assistance and capacity building programs to enable all parties to participate fully and to obtain full benefit from the FTA.

(f) The FTA will be designed to enhance and improve transparency in trade and investment relations between the parties.

(g) The modalities and timeframes of the FTA, including differentiated timeframes for Australia and New Zealand, ASEAN–6 and CLMV, and products, should be settled at an early stage of the negotiations.

(h) The FTA will be open to inclusion of issues not covered by the existing AFTA and CER Agreements, to be agreed by all parties.

(i) The terms of the FTA will be subject to periodic review.

(j) The FTA should be consistent with WTO provisions, including GATT Article XXIV and GATS Article V.

(k) The FTA should draw, as appropriate, on elements of the economic integration agreements of ASEAN and CER. In addition, the elements of any FTAs involving ASEAN Member Countries, Australia and New Zealand may be used as reference points.

(l) AFTA and CER will continue to exist as distinct, functioning agreements, as will the FTAs between ASEAN Member Countries, Australia and New Zealand. No provision in the FTA will detract from the terms and conditions of bilateral and plurilateral FTAs between ASEAN Member Countries, Australia and New Zealand.

The FTA will be fully implemented within 10 years. The negotiations will commence in early 2005 and be completed within two years.

Mr. Kim Hak-Su (July 2000-Present)

Secretary-General Kofi Annan has appointed Kim Hak-Su of the Republic of Korea as Executive Secretary of the Economic and Social Commission for Asia and the Pacific (ESCAP).

Mr. Kim is the Ambassador for International Economic Affairs of the Republic of Korea and a prominent economist. He has vast experience in central banking, development planning, government think-tanks and private sector management, as well as international organizations.

Mr. Kim began his professional career in 1960 as a central bank economist, served as Secretary to the Minister of Commerce and Industry in 1969 and worked for the London Representative Office of the Bank of Korea (1971-73). He joined Daewoo Corporation in 1977 as Executive Director and served ACWOO International Corporation in New York as President.

Mr. Kim worked as Chief Planning Officer and Chief Technical Adviser under the United Nations Department for Technical Cooperation and Development, during most of the 1980s, in island State countries, such as Vanuatu and the Solomon Islands. He joined the Korea Institute for International Economic Policy as a Senior Research Fellow, researching and publishing on issues regarding international economic cooperation during 1989 to 1993.

He served as President of the Hanil Banking Institute before taking up the recent post of Secretary-General of the Colombo Plan, based in Colombo, Sri Lanka (1995-99). He revitalized the 24-member country intergovernment Colombo Plan in Asia and the Pacific, stressing human resources development and focusing on South-South cooperation.

He was appointed Ambassador for International Economic Affairs in June 1999, attending various international meetings as the head of his Government's delegation.

Mr. Kim was born in a rural area of Wonju, Republic of Korea, studied as an undergraduate at Yonsei University, earned a master's degree from Edinburgh University, United Kingdom, and a Ph.D. in economics from the University of South Carolina, United States.

Mr. Adrianus Mooy (1995-June 2000)

Mr. Adrianus Mooy assumed the post of Executive Secretary of the Economic and Social Commission for Asia and the Pacific (ESCAP) on 1 April 1995.

Prior to his appointment, Mr. Mooy was Ambassador of Indonesia to the European Communities in Brussels since 1993. He was Governor of Indonesia's Central Bank, as well as the Governor for Indonesia of the International Monetary Fund, since 1988. In addition, he was the Asian Development Bank's Alternate Governor for Indonesia, as well as for the Multilateral Investment Guarantee Agency in Washington, D.C., during the same five-year period.

Mr. Mooy began his professional career in 1958 in the Faculty of Economics, Gajah Mada University, Yogyakarta, Indonesia, as a Teaching Assistant before continuing his graduate studies at the University of Wisconsin, USA from 1959 to 1965. In 1967, he was appointed Head of the Bureau of Statistics, State Ministry for Economic, Financial and Developmental Affairs, Indonesia. From 1968 to 1969, he served as Head of the Bureau of Domestic Finance, National Development Planning Agency (BAPPENAS).

From 1969 to 1973, Mr. Mooy worked as Economic Affairs Officer at the UN-ECAFE, Bangkok before going back to Indonesia and served as Deputy Chairman for Fiscal and Monetary Affairs, National Development Planning Agency until 1988. Concurrently, Mr. Mooy served as Assistant for Monetary Affairs to the Minister Coordinator for Economic, Financial and Industrial Affairs (EKUIN) from 1978 to 1983; as Executive Secretary of the Monetary Council from 1983 to 1988; and as Assistant for Development Finance to the State Minister for National Development Planning, Indonesia from 1985-88.

Mr. Mooy served as a member of the Indonesian People's Consultative Assembly from 1982 to 1987 and from 1987 to 1992. From 1987 to 1993, Mr. Mooy was a Professor of Economics at the University of Indonesia in Jakarta.

He has been a member of the Indonesian delegation to many international conferences, among them, those within the framework of the Association of South-East Asian Nations (ASEAN) Economic Cooperation, the United Nations Conference on Trade and Development (UNCTAD), the Non-Aligned Movement, and the Intergovernmental Group for Indonesia.

Mr. Mooy holds a Master of Science and a Ph.D. in Economics from the University of Wisconsin, United States. He received his Bachelor of Science in Economics from Gajah Mada University, Yogyakarta, Indonesia.

Mr. Mooy, born on 10 April 1936 in Rote Island, Indonesia, is married with three daughters.

Mr. Rafeeuddin Ahmed (1992-94)

Mr. Rafeeuddin Ahmed, presently the Associate Administrator of UNDP, was the sixth Executive Secretary of the Economic and Social Commission for Asia and the Pacific (ESCAP) from 1992 to 1994. He previously held the post of Under-Secretary-General for International Economic and Social Affairs, while also serving as Special Representative of the Secretary-General for Humanitarian Affairs in South-East Asia. Prior to that, from 1 January 1983, he was Under-Secretary-General for Political Affairs, Trusteeship and Decolonization.

Mr. Ahmed joined the United Nations Secretariat in May 1970 as Secretary of the Economic and Social Council, and from February 1973 served as Director of the Resources and Programme Planning Office in the Department of Economic and Social Affairs. From May 1975, he held the post of Executive Assistant to the Secretary-General until September 1978, when he became Chef de Cabinet.

Mr. Ahmed entered the Foreign Service of Pakistan in October 1955 and held diplomatic posts in Beijing, Cairo and Ottawa. He served as Director for United Nations Affairs and Economic Coordination in the Ministry of Foreign Affairs from February 1968 until joining the Secretariat. While a member of the Permanent Mission of Pakistan to the United Nations from 1965 to 1968, Mr. Ahmed was his country's representative in the Second Committee (Economic and Financial) during the twentieth to the twenty-fourth sessions of the General Assembly.

S.A.M.S. Kibria (1981-91)

Mr. S.A.M.S. Kibria, the current Minister of Finance of Bangladesh, became the fifth Executive Secretary of the Economic and Social Commission for Asia and the Pacific (ESCAP) in 1987.

Before coming to ESCAP, Mr. Kibria had spent more than a quarter of a century as a diplomat. He joined the Pakistan Ministry of Foreign Affairs in 1953 and subsequently held a number of posts in the Pakistan Foreign Service.

Starting as Director-General of the Political Affairs Department in the Bangladesh Ministry of Foreign Affairs, Mr. Kibria became Secretary of the Ministry in charge of administration. In 1973, the Government appointed him as the Bangladesh High Commissioner to Australia, New Zealand and Fiji, based in Canberra.

In 1976, he became the Bangladesh Permanent Representative to the United Nations in Geneva, an assignment which lasted until 1978.

Mr. Kibria returned to Bangladesh in 1978 as Foreign Secretary, serving concurrently in 1979 as the elected Chairman of the Group of 77 Preparatory Committee for UNCTAD V, which was held in Manila. He remained as Foreign Secretary of Bangladesh until joining ESCAP.

Mr. Kibria was educated at the University of Dacca, Bangladesh, the Fletcher School of Law and Diplomacy in Boston, U.S.A. and at the British Foreign Office in London, United Kingdom.

J.B.P. Maramis (1973-81)

Mr. J.B.P. Maramis became the fourth Executive Secretary of the United Nations Economic and Social Commission for Asia and the Pacific (ESCAP) on 1 August 1973.

Previously, he had served with the Government of Indonesia for 22 years in different capacities and, at the time of his appointment to ESCAP, was Indonesia's ambassador to Belgium and Luxembourg and Head of the Indonesian Mission to the European Economic Community (EEC).

As an Indonesian delegate, Mr. Maramis took part in the work of numerous United Nations groups concerned with development issues. In 1970, he became President of the Economic and Social Council (ESCAP's parent body) at a time when the International Development Strategy for the Second United Nations Development Decade 1971-80) was being drawn up.

Mr. Maramis, who was born in Limbung, Indonesia, in 1922, graduated from the University of Leyden, Netherlands, in March 1951. He entered the service of his Government the same year in the Directorate of Economic Affairs of the Ministry of Foreign Affairs and subsequently held a number of posts in the Indonesian Foreign Service.

From 1960 to 1965, Mr. Maramis served as Counsellor in the Permanent Mission of Indonesia to the United Nations and, during that period, was chairman of the Ad Hoc Committee on Co-ordination and Technical Assistance in the United Nations which recommended action that brought about the United Nations Development Programme (UNDP).

In 1969, Mr. Maramis was appointed as Deputy Representative of the Indonesian Mission to the United Nations, and served as the Indonesian representative on the Economic and Social Council. He was Vice-president of the Council in 1969 and President in 1970. In October 1969, he was the Chairman of the "Group of 77" developing countries.

U Nyun (1959-73)

ECAFE's third Executive Secretary, U Nyun, was born in Thaton, Burma in 1910. U Nyun joined the United Nations in 1951 as Chief of ECAFE's Industry and Trade Division and was appointed Deputy Executive Secretary in 1957. He was appointed Executive Secretary in April 1959.

In 1931, he joined the Indian Civil Service, and had a distinguished career in the administrative service of the Government of Burma before joining the United Nations. Among the various posts he held were those of Under-Secretary and Permanent Secretary in the Ministry of Commerce and Industry. He was leader of

Burmese trade missions which concluded trade agreements between Burma and a number of other countries. He also represented Burma at a number of international economic conferences.

He was educated at Rangoon University, Burma, the London School of Economics and Political Science and the School of Oriental Studies of London University, the United Kingdom.

Chakravarthi V. Narasimhan (1956-59)

Mr. Chakravarthi V. Narasimhan of India, became the second Executive Secretary of the United Nations Economic Commission for Asia and the Far East (ECAFE) from 1956 to 1959.

Mr. Narasimhan entered the Indian Civil Service in 1936. After 13 years of service with the Provincial Government of Madras, he joined the Government of India in 1950, and until his appointment to the post of Executive Secretary of ECAFE, he held several important posts in the Indian Ministries of Agriculture and Finance. At the time of his appointment to ECAFE in 1956, he was serving as Joint Secretary in the Economic Affairs Department of the Ministry of Finance.

From January 1959 to March 1961, Mr. Narasimhan was Under-Secretary for Special Political Affairs. Part of this period, he also served concurrently as Associate Managing Director of the United Nations Special Fund (now merged with UNDP).

He was appointed to the post of Chef de Cabinet of the United Nations Secretary-General by the late Dag Hammarskjold in 1961 and continued in that capacity under two more Secretary-Generals, U Thant and Kurt Waldheim, until 15 September 1973.

In addition to heading the Executive Office of the Secretary-Generals, Mr. Narasimhan took over the responsibility for General Assembly Affairs in March 1962. On 1 August 1969, he became deputy Administrator of the United Nations Development Programme (UNDP). He became Under-Secretary-General for Inter-agency Affairs and Coordination at United Nations in October 1973.

Mr. Narasimhan was educated at Madras University, India, and at Oxford University, the United Kingdom.

Dr. P.S. Lokanathan (1947-56)

ECAFE's first Executive Secretary, Palamadai S. Lokanathan of India, was an economist who had made a distinguished career in teaching, government service, and private enterprise, before coming to Shanghai in 1947 to head the office of the United Nations Economic Commission for Asia and the Far East (ECAFE).

Dr. Lokanathan was a member of the Senate of Madras and a member of the

Academic Council of Madras University, where he was Professor of Economics. He was also a member of the Board of Studies in Economics for the Universities of Madras, Travancore, Annamali and Andhra, and Chairman of the Commerce College, Delhi University, Delhi.

While he was still at Madras University, he became a member of the consultative Committee of Economists to the Indian Government; he was also appointed a member of the Labour Advisory Board of the Madras Government, and he was a president of the Economic Association of India.

To a large section of the Indian public Dr. Lokanathan became known as editor of the Eastern Economist which he joined after he worked as editor of the Hindustani Times, also in New Delhi.

ASEAN FOREIGN MINISTERS JOINT COMMUNIQUÉ

"Towards the Harmony, Dynamism and Integration of ASEAN"

38th ASEAN Ministerial Meeting on 26 July 2005

Vientiane, Laos

1. We, the Foreign Ministers of the Association of Southeast Asian Nations (ASEAN), met formally on 26 July 2005 in Vientiane, Lao People's Democratic Republic (Lao PDR), for the first time since the Vientiane Action Programme (VAP), the successor to the Ha Noi Plan of Action (HPA); the ASEAN Security Community (ASC) Plan of Action; and the ASEAN Socio-Cultural Community (ASCC) Plan of Action were adopted at the 10th ASEAN Summit in November 2004 in Vientiane. It was also the first time that Lao PDR hosted our regular annual meeting where we reviewed regional and international political, security, and economic developments, and intra and extra-ASEAN cooperation, including cooperation with our Dialogue Partners as well as wide- ranging issues as we move towards the establishment of an ASEAN Community in 2020 as envisioned in the Declaration of ASEAN Concord II (Bali Concord II) adopted in October 2003 in Bali, Indonesia.

2. The 38th ASEAN Ministerial Meeting was chaired by His Excellency Mr. Somsavat Lengsavad, Deputy Prime Minister and Minister of Foreign Affairs of the Lao PDR.

3. The Honourable Sir Rabbie Namiliu, Foreign Minister of Papua New Guinea, and His Excellency Mr. Jose Ramos-Horta, Senior Minister and Minister of Foreign Affairs of Timor Leste, attended the Opening and Closing ceremonies of the 38th ASEAN Ministerial Meeting as a Special Observer in ASEAN and a Guest of the Chairman of the 38th ASEAN Standing Committee respectively.

4. His Excellency Mr. Bounnhang Vorachith, Prime Minister of the Lao PDR, graced the meeting with a Keynote Address. His Excellency Mr. Bounnhang Vorachith

stated that a key factor leading to the success of ASEAN in the last decades is the harmonious combination of national interests and regional ones. This is the right recognition of the reality that although ASEAN Member Countries are very diverse, they share common interest in peace, stability and prosperity for each country and for the region as a whole. This is the true meaning of the 'Secunity in diversity' of ASEAN and that we should continue our efforts to maintain such a harmonious combination in the process of building our ASEAN Community. Anything contrary to that could affect the basic foundation for the further development of ASEAN. The harmonious combination of national interests and community interests would be much visible by the extent of the ASEAN integration into the process of building the ASEAN Community. While realizing the importance of the ASEAN integration, especially in the economic field in the context of globalization and economic interdependence, ASEAN has adopted the Initiative for ASEAN Integration (IAI), the VAP and other plans of action which are currently being implemented and yielded some preliminary results. One of our immediate priorities is to expeditiously narrow the economic development gap within ASEAN and between ASEAN and other regions. He further stated that with the continuously high oil price, there is a need for ASEAN to pay more attention to the cooperation on energy as previously agreed by the Leaders at the 10th ASEAN Summit. This aims to mitigate the adverse impact on the economy of ASEAN as a whole as well as on the vulnerable economy of ASEAN new member countries, in particular. He noted that one of the energy sectors that can be a benefit to the region on a regular basis is a joint investment in building hydropower dams which would not only supply cheaper energy to the region than the oil based energy but would also enhance closer relations of intra-ASEAN economic development as well as help narrow the economic disparities within ASEAN.

The ASEAN Community

5. We were pleased with the adoption by our Leaders of the VAP, the ASC Plan of Action and the ASCC Plan of Action; the signing of the ASEAN Framework Agreement for the Integration of Priority Sectors; and the progress made in the implementation of programmes and projects building up to the realisation of the ASEAN Community comprising the three pillars of the ASC, AEC, and ASCC as enshrined in the Bali Concord II.

6. We agreed to work towards the establishment of an ASEAN Charter, which will reaffirm the objectives, goals and principles of the ASEAN Community and beyond. In this regard, we agreed on a draft text of the Kuala Lumpur Declaration on the Establishment of an ASEAN Charter, including the establishment of the Eminent Persons Group (EPG), which will be recommended for approval and signature by our Leaders at the 11th ASEAN Summit on 12 December 2005 in Kuala Lumpur, Malaysia.

Vientiane Action Programme (VAP)

7. We expressed our satisfaction with the progress made in the implementation of the VAP, which includes, among others, the signing of the Agreement on the Establishment of an ASEAN Development Fund (ADF) that will, to a great extent, further boost the resource mobilisation efforts to support the financing of the implementation of the VAP and subsequent plans of action to realise the ASEAN Community.

8. We reiterated our commitment to make greater efforts to narrow the development gap among ASEAN Member Countries. In this connection, we called on our Dialogue Partners and friends, as well as regional and international organisations to support us in our efforts to effectively implement the VAP in a timely manner.

Narrowing the Development Gap (NDG) and Initiative for ASEAN Integration (IA)

9. We emphasised the immediate need to bridge the development gap among ASEAN Member Countries, which is crucial for the acceleration of the integration of ASEAN. In the long run, the NDG and IAI will serve as building blocks for the establishment of an ASEAN Community. We noted and highly appreciated the participation of donor countries and institutions that have contributed positively to the implementation of the IAI programme. In the light of the above, we agreed to work even harder to assist the less developed Member Countries and less developed regions in ASEAN to ensure that the integration of ASEAN is carried out in a smooth and unified manner and that the benefits of integration are reasonably shared among the Member Countries. In this connection, we called on our Dialogue Partners and friends, as well as regional and international organisations to support us in our efforts to effectively implement the IAI Work Plan.

ASEAN Security Community (ASC)

10. We were gratified with the significant progress made in the implementation of the ASC Plan of Action, especially those activities that are contained in the VAP. The implementation of the ASC Plan of Action will lead to a peaceful, just, democratic, harmonious and stable ASEAN that is conducive to the sustainable social and economic development in the region as well as strengthen ASEAN's relations with its Dialogue Partners. We therefore called for the continued effective implementation of the programmes and activities under the ASC Plan of Action so as to realise the ASC in a timely manner. The Meeting welcomed the agreement, in principle, to convene the ASEAN Defence Ministers Meeting (ADMM) and a senior defence officials meeting would be convened to prepare for it.

11. We recalled the decision by ASEAN Leaders, through the adoption of the ASC Plan of Action and the VAP, to strengthen our efforts in promoting human

rights in ASEAN. We also recalled decision at the 26th AMM to consider the establishment of an appropriate mechanism on human rights. We noted the work carried out by the non-governmental Working Group for an ASEAN Human Rights Mechanism, including the meeting between the open-ended ASEAN SOM troika and the Working Group at the sideline of the 38th AMM.

Treaty of Amity and Cooperation in Southeast Asia (TAC)

12. We reaffirmed the importance of the Treaty of Amity and Cooperation in Southeast Asia as an instrument of peace, security and cooperation in inter-state relations and were gratified that a growing number of countries outside ASEAN have either acceded or expressed their interest to accede to the TAC. In this context, we welcomed the accessions of the ROK and the Russian Federation during the 10th ASEAN Summit in Vientiane. We also welcomed the accession of New Zealand and Mongolia to the TAC on 29 July 2005. We also welcomed Australia's intention to accede to the TAC and looked forward to its accession to the TAC in Kuala Lumpur in December 2005. We appreciated Timor Leste for its interest to accede to the TAC. To ensure a lasting peace, stability and sustained development of ASEAN, we reiterated our call to other countries to accede to the TAC so as to create a favourable environment conducive for development in the region that will not only be beneficial to ASEAN but all its partners and friends as well.

South China Sea

13. We reaffirmed the importance of the Declaration on the Conduct of Parties in the South China Sea (DoC) signed by ASEAN and China in Phnom Penh in 2002 as an important step towards a regional code of conduct in the South China Sea and has contributed to the peace and stability in the region. We welcomed China's view underscoring that a regional code of conduct in the South China Sea is essential, as conveyed during the 11th ASEAN China Senior Officials Consultations in Shanghai, China, in April 2005.

14. In this connection, we endorsed the establishment of the ASEAN-China Joint Working Group to study and recommend measures to translate the provisions of the DoC into concrete cooperative activities. We looked forward to the 1st Meeting of the Working Group on the implementation of DoC to be held in Manila in August 2005, as a concrete step towards the full implementation of the DoC.

15. We encouraged all parties concerned to continue to exercise of self-restraint and to continue to undertake confidence-building measures that would contribute to the maintenance of peace and stability in the region. In this connection, we took note of the cooperative activities already forged by some concerned parties, which yielded positive results through negotiation and dialogue, in the spirit of mutually beneficial cooperation. We also reaffirmed our commitment to resolve the dispute in the South China Sea through peaceful means in accordance with international

conventions including the United Nations Convention on the Law of the Sea.

Transnational Crimes

16. We commended the work of the ASEAN Ministers Meeting on Transnational Crime (AMMTC) and emphasised the important role of the AMMTC in regional initiatives to combat transnational crimes identified under the Work Programme to implement the ASEAN Plan of Action to Combat Transnational Crime. We also commended the important contributions made by the ASEAN Member Countries to combating transnational crimes as well as the cooperation between ASEAN and the Dialogue Partners in this area through various training programmes and workshops. We looked forward to the convening of the 5th AMMTC on 27-30 November 2005, in Ha Noi, Vietnam. We welcomed the endorsement of the ASEAN Plus Three Concept Plan to implement cooperation in combating terrorism and transnational crime and the efforts of the ASEAN Plus Three countries to develop work programmes to implement cooperation in the specific areas identified.

17. We recalled the adoption by our Leaders of the ASEAN Declaration Against Trafficking in Persons, Particularly Women and Children on 29 November 2004 in Vientiane, Lao PDR. We expressed our commitment to implement the declaration and stressed the importance of developing measures in raising awareness and other capacity building-related activities.

18. We welcomed the Joint Communiqué of the 25th ASEAN Chiefs of Police Conference held on 16-20 May 2005 in Bali, Indonesia.

Counter-Terrorism

19. We expressed outrage at the series of terrorist attacks in the United Kingdom and Egypt that resulted in the loss of innocent lives. We strongly condemn such acts of terror and extend our sympathies to the victims and their families. Such acts of terror will only steel the resolve of the international community to cooperate and defeat the scourge of terrorism.

20. We reiterated our strong condemnation of all acts of terrorism in all its forms and manifestations and emphasised the need to address the root causes of terrorism. We continue to reject any attempt to associate terrorism with any race, region, nationality or ethnic group. In this context, we are fully committed to enhance our cooperative efforts to combat international terrorism at national, regional, and international levels. We looked forward to continuing our determination to enhance coordination and cooperation with the international community in combating international terrorism. We believe this will ensure peace and stability, create an environment conducive to our efforts to attain sustainable development, progress and prosperity in ASEAN. We also reaffirmed that the fight against terrorism should be conducted in accordance with our obligations under international

law and in respect of sovereignty, territorial integrity and the principle of non-interference in the internal affairs of other states.

21. We expressed our appreciation for efforts to enhance capacity to counter-terrorism such as the conclusion of the Treaty on Mutual Legal Assistance in Criminal Matters in November on 29 November 2004 in Kuala Lumpur. We also welcomed the existing network between regional centres, such as the International Law Enforcement Academy (ILEA) in Bangkok, the Southeast Asia Regional Centre for Counter-Terrorism (SEARCCT) in Kuala Lumpur and the Jakarta Centre for Law Enforcement Cooperation (JCLEC) in Semarang, Indonesia. We looked forward to continuing our cooperation in the training of officials involved in counter-terrorism through SEARCCT, JCLEC and ILEA. We welcomed the outcomes of the workshops on International Legal Cooperation under the Bali Regional Ministerial Meeting on Counter-Terrorism coordinated by Thailand.

22. We recalled the adoption of the ASEAN-Japan Joint Declaration for Cooperation to Combat International Terrorism in November 2004 in Vientiane, Lao PDR, and looked forward to the implementation of the activities identified in the Joint Declaration. We also looked forward to the signing of the ASEAN-New Zealand, ASEAN-Republic of Korea, and ASEAN-Pakistan Joint Declarations for cooperation to combat international terrorism in the next few days in Vientiane. We encouraged Canada to consider signing the same declaration with ASEAN.

Treaty on the Southeast Asia Nuclear Weapon-Free Zone (SEANWFZ)

23. We reaffirmed that the 1995 Treaty on the Southeast Asia Nuclear Weapon-Free Zone (SEANWFZ) is extremely important to both confidence-building in Southeast Asia and the non-proliferation of nuclear weapons worldwide. We will continue our efforts to seek ways and means to secure the support of all five Nuclear Weapons States to sign the Protocol to the SEANWFZ. To this end, we expressed our appreciation to China for its readiness to be the first nuclear weapon state to accede to the Protocol to SEANWFZ.

ASEAN Regional Forum (ARF)

24. We reaffirmed ASEAN's role as a primary driving force of the ARF process and the ARF as the primary forum in enhancing political and security dialogue and cooperation in the wider Asia-Pacific region as well as the pivot for building peace and security in the region. We agreed to invite Timor Leste to attend the 12th ARF as the 25th participating country in the ARF and believed that Timor Leste's participation in the ARF would contribute to further enhance political and security dialogue and cooperation in the region.

25. We commended the important progress made in the implementation of the ARF activities, which had to a great extent contributed to political and security

dialogue and cooperation in the Asia-Pacific region. We recognised the need to forge concrete cooperation among the ARF countries in building capacity and capabilities in order to better cope with challenges. We welcomed the ARF's progress towards Preventive Diplomacy (PD) and looked forward to the development of concrete measures in PD.

26. We noted with satisfaction the progress made in the implementation of the agreed ARF activities for the Inter-Sessional year 2004-2005. We agreed to move forward the ARF activities by replacing the Inter-Sessional Support Group on Confidence Building Measures (ISG on CBM) with the ISG on CBM and PD (ISG CBM and PD); to consider developing the concept of the Friends of the ARF Chair; streamline and strengthen working methods of the ARF; and to reactivate the ISM on Disaster Relief. We welcomed Indonesia and the People's Republic of China to co-chair the next ISM on Disaster Relief.

ASEAN Economic Community (AEC)

27. We welcomed the substantial progress made by the ASEAN Economic Ministers in moving towards the realisation of the AEC through measures that reinforce the implementation of its existing economic initiatives; accelerate regional integration in eleven priority sectors; facilitate movement of business persons, skilled labour and talents; and strengthen the institutional mechanism of ASEAN, including improvement of the existing ASEAN dispute settlement mechanism to ensure the expeditious and legally-binding resolution of any economic disputes.

28. In this regard, we noted with appreciation the signing of the ASEAN Framework Agreement for the Integration of Priority Sectors by ASEAN Leaders and the signing of the ASEAN Sectoral Integration Protocols and the Roadmaps for Integration of the Priority Sectors, as well as the Protocol on Enhanced Dispute Settlement Mechanism (DSM) by ASEAN Economic Ministers during the 10th ASEAN Summit in November 2004 in Vientiane. We recognised that this will facilitate the realisation of the aspirations of ASEAN as a single market and a single production base in which there is free flow of goods, services and skilled labour, and a freer flow of capital along with equitable economic development and reduced poverty and socio-economic disparities within and across ASEAN Member Countries.

29. We were pleased to note that steps have been taken to identify new measures for the second phase of the implementation of the integration of priority sectors to further accelerate ASEAN integration to realise the AEC.

30. We also commended the important progress made by Sectoral Ministers in the area of ASEAN economic cooperation, including energy; information communication technology (ICT); transport; tourism; food, agriculture and forestry; minerals; and finance and banking, which has become essential for regional integration.

Sub-regional Cooperation

31. We welcomed the substantial progress made in the sub-regional frameworks of cooperation under the Ayeyawady-Chao Phraya-Mekong Economic Cooperation Startegy (ACMECS), Greater Mekong Sub-region (GMS) programme, and the ASEAN-Mekong Basin Development Cooperation (AMBDC), West-East Corridor, Cambodia, Laos and Vietnam (CLV) Development Triangle, which makes an important contribution to the process of regional integration. We welcomed the successful outcome of the 2nd GMS Summit held in Kunming on 4-5 June 2005 in China.

32. We welcomed the ACMECS Ministerial Retreat held in Thailand in November 2004 which has contributed to the advancement of the process of sub-regional cooperation in reducing the development gaps, thus making contributions to the process of regional integration. We looked forward to the convening of the ACMECS Foreign Ministers' Meeting in Cambodia in August 2005 and the Second ACMECS Summit to be held in Thailand in November 2005, which would help enhance the regional integration process.

33. We noted the progress in the development of the Roadmap for BIMP-EAGA, which serves to increase trade, tourism and investment. We were encouraged by the development in strengthening partnerships with Dialogue Partners. The Northern Territory of Australia has been elevated from observer to plus One Development Partner, China has expressed its intention to become an observer and Japan has conducted the first mission to BIMP-EAGA by visiting Malaysia last year. We welcomed Republic of Korea's announcement to conduct its mission this year.

ASEAN Socio-Cultural Community (ASCC)

34. We were gratified with the adoption of the ASCC Plan of Action by the ASEAN Leaders at the 10th ASEAN Summit. The implementation of the Plan will contribute to the establishment of a caring society, the management of the social impact of economic integration, the enhancement of environmental sustainability and the strengthening of the foundations of regional social cohesion. We therefore called for effective implementation of the programmes and the specific measures under the Plan.

Sectoral Cooperation

Disaster Management

35. We signed on 26 July 2005 the ASEAN Agreement on Disaster Management and Emergency Response, which will provide effective regional mechanisms to mitigate the impacts of natural and human-induced disaster and serve as a joint response to disaster emergencies through concerted national efforts and intensified regional cooperation. We further acknowledged the importance of this agreement to strengthen international efforts towards developing a world-wide early-warning

system for natural and human-induced disasters through, among other things, a multimodal approach, and taking into consideration the internationally agreed framework on the strategy for disaster reduction. We urged for the early operationalisation of an ASEAN Standby Arrangements for Disaster Relief and Emergency Response, which would work in tandem with other similar arrangements.

36. We reaffirmed our commitment to intensify our cooperation as well as with other countries in the areas of emergency relief, rehabilitation and reconstruction; and prevention and mitigation, as called for at the Special ASEAN Leaders' Meeting on the Aftermath of Earthquake and Tsunami in Jakarta in January 2005. We welcomed the results of the Ministerial Meeting on Regional Operation on Tsunami Early Warning Arrangements held in Phuket and the decision to develop a multi-nodal early warning arrangement for the Indian Ocean and the Pacific, and recognised the readiness of the Asian Disaster Preparedness Centre (ADPC) to serve as a focal point working with other centres in the region, such as the ASEAN Earthquake Information Centre (AEIC), ASEAN Specialised Meteorological Centre (ASMC), the ASEAN Disaster Reduction Centre (ADRC), and the Indian Ocean Global Ocean Observing System (IOGOOS).

Environment

37. We welcomed the agreement on the establishment of the ASEAN Centre for Biodiversity (ACB) based in the Republic of the Philippines. The Centre will build on and continue the efforts of the ASEAN Regional Centre for Biodiversity Conservation Project in terms of promoting biodiversity conservation and sustainable use of the region's rich biological resources.

38. We highly appreciate the close and fruitful cooperation among the Mekong River Commission (MRC) member countries during the past 10 years aimed at promoting sustainable management and development of water and related resources for the countries' mutual benefit and the people's well-being in this sub-region.

39. We welcomed the establishment of a Basel Convention Regional Centre for training and technology transfer for Southeast Asia based in the Republic of Indonesia. The Centre will promote and facilitate cooperation among states at the regional level in the field of training and technology transfer regarding the environmentally sound management of hazardous wastes and other wastes and the minimisation of their generation.

40. We commended the efforts taken by the ASEAN Member Countries to address land and forest fires and the resulting transboundary haze pollution, particularly the implementation of the ASEAN Agreement on Transboundary Haze Pollution.

41. We welcomed the ASEAN Declaration on Heritage Parks signed by Ministers

of Environment of all ten ASEAN Member Countries on December 2003 which will generate greater collaboration between ASEAN Member Countries in the preservation of their common natural heritage.

42. We welcomed the efforts made by the ASEAN Member Countries in nominating 22 cities to participate in the Regional Environmentally Sustainable Cities Programme, and to implement the Framework for Environmentally Sustainable Cities (ESC) in ASEAN, which was adopted in December 2003.

Health

43. We were encouraged by the progress achieved in strengthening efforts to prevent and control emerging and resurging infectious diseases such as the Severe Acute Respiratory Syndrome (SARS) and Avian Influenza, especially in enhancing regional coordination mechanisms for early warning and surveillance capacity-building and the establishment of an ASEAN Task Force on Highly Pathogenic Influenza (HPIA) in December 2004.

44. We commended the work of the ASEAN Task Force on AIDS in following up the recommendations of the 7th ASEAN Summit Declaration on HIV/AIDS and the implementation of the ASEAN Work Programme and its review. We believe that ASEAN should have a voice in global forums such as the World Health Assembly (WHA) and participate in global decision-making regarding allocation of funds for HIV/AIDS prevention and control.

45. We expressed our appreciation to all our partners for their support in helping ASEAN implement its priority activities and encourage others to join hands with us in our efforts to prevent and control emerging infectious diseases, and in the fight against HIV/AIDS.

Poverty

46. We welcomed the initiatives and activities to enhance learning among key stakeholders from the government, civil society and the business community to deal with poverty in a comprehensive and integrated manner, and to share and exchange views on how best to mainstream Millennium Development Goals (MDG) processes into normal development functions of governments, and to establish linkages nationally and regionally for mutual support in achieving poverty reduction initiatives.

Culture and Information

47. We welcomed the results of the other areas of ASEAN functional cooperation, including the adoption of a new tagline for ASEAN Ten Nations One Community - at the Meeting of the ASEAN Ministers Responsible for Information (AMRI) in 2004. A number of activities in the culture and information sectors have been

successfully implemented in 2004 to raise ASEAN awareness in as well as outside the Southeast Asia region, such as the 2nd ASEAN Cultural Week held in Vietnam in August 2004, the biennial ASEAN Quiz held in Brunei Darussalam in September 2004 and the ongoing Media Exchange Programmes with our Dialogue Partners. We also welcomed the Art and Cultural scholarship programme for ASEAN Member Countries sponsored by Indonesia in 2004 and encouraged ASEAN's participation for the next scholarship programme to be held in the second half of 2005. We believe that cultural and information activities have played an essential role in bringing ASEAN closer to the people, and thereby further solidifying the foundation to build an ASEAN Community that is bonded by mutual respect and a sense of "we-feeling".

Drugs

48. We welcomed the role of ASEAN Senior Officials on Drug Matters (ASOD) in combating illicit drug trafficking and its increasing cooperation with Dialogue Partners and other regional/international bodies, such as the ASEAN-China Cooperative Operations in Response to Dangerous Drugs (ACCORD), ASEAN-EC Sub-committee on Narcotics, ASEAN Inter-Parliamentary Organisation Fact Finding Committee (AIFOCOM) and United Nations Office of Drugs and Crime Prevention (UNODC).

49. We welcomed the recommendations of the 4th AIFOCOM, held in Luang Prabang, Lao PDR, 9-13 March 2005, which among others, urged all ASEAN Member Countries to formulate an ASEAN Extradition Treaty based on the Treaty of Mutual Legal Assistance (MLA) on Criminal Matters and existing bilateral agreements, and to call upon all ASEAN national parliaments to consider harmonising laws on drug abuse in ASEAN Member Countries.

50. We believed that a Drug Free ASEAN 2015 should be pursued by prevention, treatment and community-based control of drug abuse, including the promotion of alternative development and elimination of illicit drug trafficking. ASEAN Member Countries will undertake close coordination and integrated cooperation, including with Dialogue Partners such as China, Japan and the Republic of Korea, the European Union (EU), India, Australia, and the US. Furthermore, ASEAN Member Countries will promote common perception among law enforcement agencies in combating illicit drug trafficking as well as developing public awareness, especially among young people, concerning the risk of illicit drug abuse and trafficking.

Labour

51. We noted with satisfaction the progress made in ASEAN to address timely labour issues relating to labour mobility and human resource development, such as labour mobility of skilled manpower, strengthening social security, skills recognition arrangements, and HIV/AIDS in the workplace.

Youth

52. We recognised the importance of youth employment issues in the development process and welcomed entrepreneurial initiatives with our Dialogue Partners and through World Bank and International Labour Organisation collaborations.

External Relations

53. We noted with satisfaction the important developments and progress being made in pursuing cooperation with our Dialogue Partners and welcomed steps undertaken by both sides to further advance the mutually beneficial cooperation in various fields.

54. We also took note of the overall progress achieved within the framework of ASEAN Plus Three cooperation. We reaffirmed the importance of the ASEAN Plus Three for the realisation of an East Asian community.

55. We commended the ASEAN Plus Three countries for the overall progress attained in the implementation of the 17 short term-measures of the East Asia Study Group (EASG) adopted by the ASEAN Plus Three Leaders, and encouraged more efforts to implement all the short-term measures by 2007. We noted with appreciation the successful implementation of activities to implement the EASG short-term measures, which includes the forming of the East Asia Business Council; the promotion of networking of cultural heritage of the East Asian countries; the promotion of East Asian studies in the region; the convening of the 2nd East Asia Forum; the 2nd Annual Conference of the Network of East Asian Think-Tanks (NEAT); the collaboration with cultural and educational institutions to promote a strong sense of an East Asian identity and consciousness; the development of information technology jointly to build telecommunications infrastructure and to provide greater access to the internet; establishing poverty alleviation programmes; and the promotion of language programmes for ASEAN Plus Three countries. We welcomed the annual conference of Dean/Directors of Diplomatic Training Institutions of ASEAN Plus Three Countries.

56. We encouraged the implementation of the 9 medium and long-term measures of the EASG. In this regard, we noted with satisfaction the ASEAN Leaders' decision to convene the first East Asia Summit (EAS) on 14 December 2005 in Kuala Lumpur. We reaffirmed our commitment made at the AMM Retreat in Cebu, Philippines on 11 April 2005 to keep the EAS open, outward-looking and inclusive with ASEAN being the driving force. In this context, we welcomed the participation of ASEAN, China, Japan, Republic of Korea, Australia, India, and New Zealand to the first EAS. We commended our Senior Officials for their work on the participation and the modalities of the East Asia Summit which is inclusive and ASEAN-driven.

57. We welcomed the establishment of the Experts Group comprising government officials, scholars and researchers to conduct the feasibility study of the establishment of the East Asia free trade area which will be an integral element of the East Asian community.

58. We noted with satisfaction the broadening and deepening of ASEAN-China cooperation as evidenced by the conclusion of the Plan of Action to Implement ASEAN-China Joint Declaration on Strengthening Strategic Partnership for Peace and Prosperity, the signing of the ASEAN-China Agreement on Trade in Goods, the Agreement on Dispute Settlement, the MOU on Transport Cooperation, the establishment of the ASEAN-China Eminent Persons Group, the organisation of the ASEAN-China Expo in Nanning, the ASEAN-China ICT Week in May 2005 in Beijing, Shanghai and Shenzhen, the ongoing efforts to conclude agreements on trade in services and investment and the MOU on Cultural Cooperation as well as preparation for a two-year implementation plan for the ASEAN-China Plan of Action. We believed that these cooperative activities will further cement ASEAN-China cooperation in the future.

59. We noted the continued efforts to implement the ASEAN-Japan Plan of Action, including in the areas of trade and investments, customs procedures, Small and Medium Enterprises (SMEs), the environment and ICT. We appreciated Japan's active support for the implementation of IAI projects, especially in the area of human resource development, and its support to sub-regional growth areas.

60. We welcome the growing dialogue partnership between ASEAN and the Republic of Korea in the areas of political and security, trade and economic, social and cultural and development cooperation, in particular people-to-people contact in the field of media, youth, culture and the exchange of government officials. We looked forward to the adoption of the Plan of Action to implement the Joint Declaration on Comprehensive Partnership between ASEAN and the Republic of Korea expected to be adopted by the Leaders of ASEAN and the Republic of Korea in December 2005 in Kuala Lumpur.

61. We expressed our appreciation to India for its support in the implementation of the IAI such as the establishment of the Centre for Entrepreneurship Development in the Lao PDR and its agreement to establish similar centres in Cambodia, Myanmar and Vietnam to bridge the development gap among ASEAN Member Countries. We commended the successful ASEAN-India Car Rally organised during the 10th ASEAN Summit. We noted the progress made thus far in the negotiations to establish an ASEAN-India FTA, which is part of the implementation of the ASEAN-India Framework Agreement on Comprehensive Economic Cooperation signed in Bali in 2003. We looked forward to the early conclusion of these negotiations.

62. We welcomed the conclusion, by ASEAN Leaders and the Leaders of the Republic of Korea, India, Australia and New Zealand, of the Joint Declaration on Comprehensive Cooperation Partnership between the Association of Southeast Asia Nations and the Republic of Korea; the ASEAN-India Partnership for Peace, Progress and Shared Prosperity and the adoption of a Plan of Action to implement the partnership; and the Joint Declaration of the Leaders at the ASEAN-Australia and New Zealand Commemorative Summit, respectively, in November 2004 in Vientiane which will chart the future directions of ASEAN's cooperation with them. We looked forward to their effective implementation to elevate ASEAN's cooperation to a higher plane.

63. We welcomed the progress on the implementation of the Trans-Regional EU-ASEAN Trade Initiative (TREATI) to enhance economic cooperation and assist ASEAN in its integration, and the establishment of the ASEAN-EU Vision Group, comprising senior officials, towards enhancing ASEAN-EU relations. We also welcomed the commencement of the Joint Feasibility Study on ASEAN-EU Economic Cooperation, including a possible FTA. In this connection, we noted with satisfaction that the 15th ASEAN-EU Ministerial Meeting adopted in principle the Regional EU-ASEAN Development Initiative (READI) in Jakarta in March 2005 which was subsequently finalised by ASEAN and EC, therefore, providing a new impetus for ASEAN-EU cooperation.

64. We commended the launching of free trade area negotiations with Japan, the Republic of Korea, the ASEAN and Australia and New Zealand Free Trade Area, which will be implemented within ten years.

65. We welcomed the progress the ASEAN-Canada relations, especially with the convening of the ASEAN-Canada Partnership Symposium that was held in February 2005 in Bandar Seri Begawan and the ASEAN-Canada Dialogue in April 2005 in Vancouver. We appreciate Canada's interest to enhance its cooperation with ASEAN in economic areas with the convening of the ASEAN-Canada Trade and Investment Senior Officials Meeting and the ASEAN Business Forum in Toronto in May 2005. We welcomed Canada's commitment to stay engaged with ASEAN by exploring, amongst others, ways in which ASEAN and Canada can promote development cooperation.

66. We looked forward to the inaugural ASEAN-Russia Summit in December 2005 in Kuala Lumpur. We also commended the progress in the negotiations on the ASEAN-Russia Economic and Development Cooperation Agreement and looked forward to its early conclusion.

67. We welcomed the growing trade relationship, economic and development cooperation, political and security cooperation, and cooperation in other areas involving transnational crime, transnational issues, and communicable and emerging diseases between ASEAN and the US. We looked forward to the

development of a strategic partnership between ASEAN and the US to further enhance this relationship in all aspects.

68. We further expressed our appreciation to the United Nations Development Programme (UNDP) for its continued support to ASEAN's integration through its ASEAN-UNDP Partnership Facility 2004-06. We look forward to continuing our partnership and cooperation with the UNDP in supporting ASEAN's integration.

69. We looked forward to the 2nd ASEAN-UN Summit in September 2005 in New York. We believe that the Summit will help elevate ASEAN's relations with the United Nations to a new level.

Developments in Myanmar

70. We have been informed by our colleague, Foreign Minister U Nyan Win of Myanmar that the Government of Myanmar had decided to relinquish its turn to be the Chair of ASEAN in 2006 because it would want to focus its attention on the ongoing national reconciliation and democratisation process. Our colleague from Myanmar has explained to us that 2006 will be a critical year and that the Government of Myanmar wants to give its full attention to the process. We would like to express our complete understanding of the decision by the Government of Myanmar. We also express our sincere appreciation to the Government of Myanmar for not allowing its national preoccupation to affect ASEAN's solidarity and cohesiveness. The Government of Myanmar has shown its commitment to the well-being of ASEAN and its goal of advancing the interest of all Member Countries. We agreed that once Myanmar is ready to take its turn to be the ASEAN Chair, it can do so.

Regional and International Issues

71. We exchanged views on recent regional and international political and security developments, particularly those that affect regional peace, security and stability. Despite the recent terrorist attacks in United Kingdom and Egypt, we were of the view that the overall global security situation remained relatively stable and was marked by a number of positive developments including greater interactions and exchanges between and among countries. We were also of the view that the stable relationship among the major powers is crucial to the region and called upon them to continue to make their contributions to strengthen peace, stability, cooperation and development in the region, and in the world as a whole.

Iraq

72. We underscored that the developments in Iraq remain a cause of great concern. We sincerely hoped for a solution in the foreseeable future that would lead to a durable peace, security, stability and national harmony so that the Iraqi people can truly be the master of their own destiny and country. We welcomed

the International Conference on Iraq that was held in Brussels on 22 June 2005.

Middle East

73. We welcomed the positive developments currently taking place in the Middle East and emphasised the need to carry out the implementation of the Roadmap and the relevant UNSC resolutions. We looked forward to the realisation of the vision of two states - Israel and Palestine - living side by side in peace within secure and recognised borders. We also welcomed the Iraqi and Palestinian elections held this year.

Korean Peninsula

74. We welcomed the recent resumption of the Six-Party Talks and hoped that concerned parties could find solutions acceptable to all sides, towards a nuclear weapon-free Korean Peninsula, on the basis of the principles of mutual respect for sovereignty and equality which will contribute to the maintenance of peace, security and stability in the wider Asia Pacific Region. ASEAN reaffirmed its support to the process and reiterated the potential role of the ARF, as the primary forum for dialogue on peace and security issues in the region, in contributing to the momentum of finding a resolution to the Korean Peninsula issue.

75. We also welcomed the recent resumption of the inter-Korean dialogue. In this regard, we expressed the hope that the dialogue will continue in accordance with the spirit and letter of the 15 June North-South Declaration. We believe that the thawing of inter-Korean relations will be a major step forward in achieving peace and stability on the Korean Peninsula.

ASIAN-AFRICAN SUMMIT 2005 AND THE COMMEMORATION OF THE GOLDEN JUBILEE OF ASIAN-AFRICAN CONFERENCE 1955

76. We noted with satisfaction the outcomes of the Asian-African Summit held in conjunction with the Commemoration of the Golden Jubilee of the Asian-African Conference (1955-2005) on 21-23 April 2005 in Bandung and Jakarta, Indonesia which revitalised the Bandung spirit of the Asian-African Conference of 1955.

77. We support the commitment of Asian-African countries in working toward the realisation of the New Asian-African Strategic Partnership (NAASP) by implementing concrete actions for the benefit and prosperity of our peoples. We also underlined the prominent and leading role of regional/sub-regional organisations in increasing synergy and cooperation in support of the NAASP. In this regard, we agreed to give a mandate to the ASEAN Secretariat to work with other regional/sub-regional organisations in Asia and Africa on issues of interest to ASEAN in supporting the NAASP.

South Summit

78. We welcomed the outcomes of the Second South Summit held in Doha, Qatar, on 12-16 June 2005 in addressing the challenges confronting the South such as poverty, debt burden, trade protectionism, declining Official Development Assistance (ODA), international migration, weak productive and trade capacities, poor infrastructures and volatile commodity export prices and financial flows.

Asia Cooperation Dialogue (ACD)

79. We welcomed the substantial progress being recorded under the framework of the ACD initiated by Thailand as a forum to harness the combined strength of Asian countries with an aim to increase the capabilities and competitiveness of Asian countries by maximising on cultural diversity and abundant resources. We are encouraged by the successful outcomes of the 4th ACD Ministerial Meeting in Islamabad, Pakistan, and welcomed the Islamabad Declaration. We also noted with satisfaction the progress achieved in various areas, for example, the Asian Bond Market Development, Energy Security, and Agriculture.

Forum for East Asia and Latin America Cooperation (FEALAC)

80. We reiterated our continued support to forge links and cooperation between Asia and Latin America in areas of mutual interest including in the political and security, social and culture and economic fields. We recognised the need to enhance cooperation under FEALAC.

Asia-Europe Meeting (ASEM)

81. We congratulated Vietnam for successfully hosting the 5th ASEM Summit in October 2004 in Ha Noi. We welcomed the participation of Cambodia, Lao PDR and Myanmar in the recent expansion of ASEM.

82. We also welcomed the convening of the ASEM Interfaith Dialogue in Bali, 21-22 July 2005, as an important effort to promote greater understanding amongst cultures and faiths.

Asia-Pacific Economic Cooperation (APEC)

83. We commended APEC for exerting its utmost efforts to cooperate, promote and liberalise trade and investment in the Asia-Pacific region. We took note of the progress achieved thus far by APEC member economies towards the Bogor Goals and look forward to the roadmap being developed to guide members to reach the goals by 2010 for industrialised economies and by 2020 for developing economies. We expressed appreciation to the member economies for accommodating the participation of non-APEC ASEAN Member Countries in APEC activities.

Asia-Middle East Dialogue (AMED)

84. We welcomed the convening of the inaugural Asia-Middle East Dialogue

(AMED) in Singapore on 20-22 June 2005. We noted that the sizeable representation of 40 delegations from Asia and the Middle East reflected the deep interest of both regions in strengthening ties. We recognised that AMED was an important first step towards deeper inter-regional engagement to foster mutual understanding and cooperation.

World Trade Organisation (WTO)

85. We welcomed the agreement by WTO members to hold the Ministerial Meeting in Hong Kong in the end of 2005 and reiterated our support to work constructively with other members of the WTO to ensure the successful outcomes of the Ministerial Meeting that is consistent with the goals of the Doha Declaration while, at the same time, we stressed the need for all WTO members to show flexibility and that development-related issues should be the focus of multilateral trade negotiations.

86. We expressed our support for the early accession of Lao PDR and Vietnam into the WTO.

Millennium Development Goals (MDG)

87. We recalled that the MDG adopted in 2000 set clear targets for countries to fulfil in close cooperation with the international community. We noted the slow progress made in the implementation of the MDG and of the upcoming review of the MDG in September 2005. We called on all the concerned parties to fulfil commitments adopted by the recent major international conferences and to enhance the effectiveness of aid through better coordination and harmonisation among the aid-providing countries.

88. We welcomed the convening of the Regional Ministerial Meeting on MDGs in Asia and the Pacific: the Way Forward 2015 to be held in Jakarta, on 3-5 August 2005.

United Nations (UN)

89. We attached importance to effective leadership of the United Nations to address the needs and aspirations of all people, particularly those in the developing world. We welcomed that the Asian-African Ministerial Meeting in Jakarta in April 2005 that generally felt that it would be the turn of the Asian region to occupy the post of United Nations Secretary-General (UNSG) which will become vacant upon the expiry of the term of the current UNSG at the end of 2006. In this regard, we reaffirmed our strong support for the ASEAN candidate from Thailand, Dr. Surakiart Sathirathai, for this important post.

90. We also supported Vietnam's candidature for the presidency of the 33rd UN Food and Agriculture Organisation (FAO).

UN Reform

91. Given its current state of affairs, we recognised the need to reform the United Nations and we agreed that the reforms of the United Nations should be comprehensive in nature and attach greater importance to the reforms of the development-related UN agencies.

Cooperation with Regional Organisations

92. We noted our cooperative relations with the South Asia Association for Regional Cooperation (SAARC) and the Asian-African Sub-Regional Organisations Conference (AASROC) to promote secretariat-to-secretariat level cooperation. We recalled the outcomes of the ASEAN-Gulf Cooperation Council (GCC) and ASEAN-Economic Cooperation Organisation (ECO) Foreign Ministers Meetings in September 2004 in New York where several areas were identified for cooperation between ASEAN, and the GCC and the ECO. We noted that ASEAN is working with the GCC to develop modalities to implement the above identified areas and that the ASEAN Secretariat would be signing a Memorandum of Understanding for cooperation with the ECO Secretariat.

93. We welcomed the signing of the Memorandum of Understanding between the ASEAN Secretariat and the Shanghai Cooperation Organisation (SCO) Secretariat to promote cooperation between the two regional organisations in mutually beneficial areas.

Institutional Matters

94. We commended the work of the ASEAN Senior Officials and the ASEAN Directors-General to streamline and rationalise ASEAN meetings and encouraged them to do even better in the years to come. We expressed our appreciation to the ASEAN Secretariat for its important contribution to the process of ASEAN integration and cooperation. We welcomed the establishment of the Jakarta ASEAN Contact Group to facilitate the coordination among Member Countries on ASEAN cooperation.

39th AMM

95. We elected Malaysia as the Chair of the 39th ASEAN Standing Committee and the Philippines as the Vice-Chair. We looked forward to the 39th ASEAN Ministerial Meeting, the ASEAN+3 Foreign Ministers 313 Meeting, the Post-Ministerial Conferences and the 13th ASEAN Regional Forum to be held on 24-28 July 2006 in Malaysia

STATEMENT BY H.E. MR. SOMSAVAT LENGSAVAD MINISTER FOR FOREIGN AFFAIRS OF THE LAO PEOPLE'S DEMOCRATIC REPUBLIC AS LEAD SPEAKER ON UNITED NATIONS SECRETARY GENERAL'S REFORM PACKAGE IN ITS FINANCIAL ASPECTS AT THE ASEAN MINISTERIAL MEETING

New York, 24 September 1997

Mr. Chairman,

At the outset, let me say how much my delegation and I are pleased to be present here today for the first time in a formal ASEAN Ministerial Meeting, in New York on the occasion of the United Nations General Assembly session. Allow me to assure you, dear colleagues of the full cooperation of the Lao delegation with all our ASEAN friends during the present 52nd General Assembly in the months that lie ahead.

Mr. Chairman,

The Permanent Mission of the Lao People's Democratic Republic to the United Nations has already distributed a discussion paper on United Nations Secretary General's Reform Package in its financial aspects for your kind consideration. You all could have read it. Very briefly, I wish only to say the following.

As already known to all, the United Nations Secretary General H.E Kofi Annan, presented last July, a comprehensive Program for Reform, comprising a series of measures and recommendations. In presenting these measures and recommendations, the Secretary General pointed out that the essential part of and a prerequisite to the success for reform, is the need to put the organisation on a sound financial footing. However, the situation now is that the United Nations continues to be in great financial difficulties. As at 31 August 1997, member states still owe the United Nations 2,6 billion US dollars, with the USA as the largest debtor accounting for 1,5 billions US dollars. Many member States particularly the major contributors, have not paid their dues in full and on time. The Secretary General challenges member States to come up with ideas in order to restore the financial solvency of the organisation. On his part, he proposes that a Revolving credit Fund to be capitalized at a level up to 1 billion US dollars through voluntary contributions, be established by the General Assembly. This idea has prompted a lot of reflections among member States but does not appear to gain support as needed. As a matter of fact, many see this as unrealistic and even there are those who go as far as to say bluntly that they do not wish to pay for those who don't pay.

The Secretary General's idea of establishing a Revolving credit Fund to restore the financial solvency of the organisation, in our view does need further study. While waiting for a more realistic solution, it is essential, as proposed by the Group of 77 and China that all member States, especially the major contributors, discharge their treaty obligations regarding the prompt and full payment without conditions the assessed contributions. By doing so and perhaps only so, that member States could help the Secretary General reform the United Nations.

ASEAN FREE TRADE AREA (AFTA)

ASEAN Free Trade Area (AFTA) is an agreement by the (An association of nations dedicated to economic and political cooperation in southeastern Asia and who joined with the United States to fight against global terrorism) Association of Southeast Asian Nations, of local manufacturing in all ASEAN countries (Ywin, 2003).

When the AFTA agreement was originally signed, ASEAN had six members, namely, (A sultanate in northwestern Borneo; became independent of Great Britain in 1984) Brunei, (A republic in southeastern Asia on an archipelago including more than 13,000 islands; achieved independence from the Netherlands in 1945; the principal oil producer in the Far East and Pacific regions) Indonesia, (A constitutional monarchy in southeastern Asia on Borneo and the Malay Peninsula; achieved independence from the United Kingdom in 1957) Malaysia, (A republic on the Philippine Islands; achieved independence from the United States in 1946) Philippines, (A country in southeastern Asia on the island of Singapore; achieved independence from Malaysia in 1965) Singapore and (A country of southeastern Asia that extends southward along the Isthmus of Kra to the Malay peninsula) Thailand. (A communist state in Indochina on the South China Sea; achieved independence from France in 1945) Vietnam joined in 1995, (A mountainous landlocked communist state in southeastern Asia; achieved independence from France in 1949) Laos and (A mountainous republic in southeastern Asia on the Bay of Bengal) Myanmar in 1997 and (A nation in southeastern Asia; was part of Indochina under French rule until 1946) Cambodia in 1999. AFTA now comprises the ten countries of ASEAN. All the four latecomers were required to sign the AFTA agreement in order to join ASEAN, but were given longer time frames in which to meet AFTA's tariff reduction obligations.

The primary goals of AFTA seek to:

Increase ASEAN's competitive edge as a production base in the world market through the elimination, within ASEAN, of (A government tax on imports or exports) tariffs and non-tariff barriers; and

Attract more (A joint venture between a foreign company and a United States company) foreign direct investment to ASEAN.

The primary mechanism for achieving the goals given above is the Common Effective Preferential Tariff (CEPT) scheme, which established a schedule for phased initiated in 1992 with the self-described goal to increase the "region's competitive advantage as a production base geared for the world market".

The proposal to set up a Free Trade Area in ASEAN was first mooted by the (A native or inhabitant of Thailand) Thai Prime Minister (Click link for more info and facts about Anand Panyarachun) Anand Panyarachun and the Thai proposal was agreed upon with amendments during the ASEAN Seniors Economic Official Meeting (AEM) in (The capital and largest city of Malaysia) Kuala Lumpur. In January 1992, the ASEAN members then signed the Singapore Declaration at the heart of which was the creation of AFTA in 15 years. This is a comprehensive program of tariff reduction in the region, which is to be carried out in phases through the year 2008. This deadline was subsequently moved forward and AFTA became fully operational on January 1, 2003.

The disparity of economic development in the ASEAN countries and difference in political systems, for example, the Philippines follows a (Click link for more info and facts about democratic) democratic system while Vietnam is a (A socialist who advocates communism) communist country, would initially suggest that the region is not exactly an ideal region for economic and political integration. However, Dent (1998) pointed out some factors, which may suggest just the opposite. There are several similarities as well as points of common interest between several of the ASEAN countries. AFTA was established with the aim of eliminating intra-regional tariffs, attracting direct foreign investment and improving the efficiency and competitiveness riff reductions within ASEAN, while leaving members free to set their own tariff levels against non-members. According to this mechanism, tariffs on goods traded within the ASEAN region, which meet a 40% ASEAN content requirement was supposed to be reduced to 0-5% by the year 2002/2003 (2006 for Vietnam, 2008 for Laos and Myanmar, and 2010 for Cambodia).

ASEAN members have the option of excluding products from the CEPT in three cases:

- Temporary exclusions
- Sensitive agricultural products
- General exceptions (ASEAN Secretariat, 2004).

The CEPT scheme covers nearly 98% of all tariff lines in ASEAN. The only products not included in the CEPT Scheme by then, will be those in the General Exceptions category and sensitive agricultural products.

Over the course of the several years, the initial program of tariff reductions was broadened and accelerated and other "AFTA Plus" activities were initiated. This includes efforts to eliminate non-tariff barriers, harmonization of customs nomenclature, valuation, and procedures and development of common produc certification standards among others.

With a population of over 450 million, ASEAN is larger than the (An international organization of European countries formed after World War II to reduce trade barriers and increase cooperation among its members) European Union and companies now can exploit the opportunities presented by an integrated market of increasingly prosperous consumers

Developments as of November 2004

On November 29th, at the ASEAN summit in Laos, the Free Trade Zone timeline was accelerated . The new timeline is described below.

Countries that agree to eliminate tariffs among themselves:

(A sultanate in northwestern Borneo; became independent of Great Britain in 1984) Brunei

(A republic in southeastern Asia on an archipelago including more than 13,000 islands; achieved independence from the Netherlands in 1945; the principal oil producer in the Far East and Pacific regions) Indonesia

(A constitutional monarchy in southeastern Asia on Borneo and the Malay Peninsula; achieved independence from the United Kingdom in 1957) Malaysia

(A republic on the Philippine Islands; achieved independence from the United States in 1946) Philippines

(A country in southeastern Asia on the island of Singapore; achieved independence from Malaysia in 1965) Singapore

(A country of southeastern Asia that extends southward along the Isthmus of Kra to the Malay peninsula) Thailand

Countries, to join in 2012:

(A mountainous republic in southeastern Asia on the Bay of Bengal) Burma

(A nation in southeastern Asia; was part of Indochina under French rule until 1946) Cambodia

(A mountainous landlocked communist state in southeastern Asia; achieved independence from France in 1949) Laos

(A communist state in Indochina on the South China Sea; achieved independence from France in 1945) Vietnam

The ASEAN meeting was observed also by (A communist nation that covers a vast territory in eastern Asia; the most populous country in the world) China, (A republic in the Asian subcontinent in southern Asia; second most populous country in the world; achieved independence from the United Kingdom in 1947) India, (A republic in the southern half of the Korean Peninsula; established in 1948) South Korea, (A constitutional monarchy occupying the Japanese Archipelago; a world leader in electronics and automobile manufacture and ship building) Japan, (A nation occupying the whole of the Australian continent; aboriginal tribes are thought to have migrated from southeastern Asia 20,000 years ago; first Europeans were British convicts sent there as a penal colony) Australia and (An independent country within the British Commonwealth; achieved independence from the United Kingdom in 1907; known for sheep and spectacular scenery) New Zealand.

12

ASEAN-JAPAN-KOREA-CHINA-RUSSIA RELATIONSHIP

CHAIRMAN'S STATEMENT OF THE 8th ASEAN+JAPAN SUMMIT

Vientiane, 30 November 2004

"Strengthening the Dynamic and Enduring ASEAN-Japan Partnership"

1. The 8th ASEAN + Japan Summit was held successfully on 30 November 2004 in Vientiane. The Meeting was chaired by H.E. Mr. Bounnhang Vorachith, Prime Minister of the Lao PDR.

2. We held a fruitful and cordial discussion under the theme of "Strengthening the Dynamic and Enduring ASEAN-Japan Relations". We reiterated the importance of ASEAN-Japan relations, which had contributed to peace, stability, and prosperity in the region and the world.

3. The ASEAN Leaders reiterated that Japan is one of ASEAN's oldest and important dialogue partners and highly valued the support and assistance given by Japan to ASEAN over the last three decades. They called on Japan to continue its strong support to ASEAN's integration, and development.

4. The ASEAN Leaders congratulated Japan on the successful convening of the historic meeting of the ASEAN-Japan Commemorative Summit held in Tokyo last December. We welcomed the signing of the Tokyo Declaration for the Dynamic and Enduring ASEAN-Japan Partnership in the New Millennium and the adoption of the ASEAN-Japan Plan of Action to implement the Tokyo Declaration to strengthen the growing strong and broad-based partnership. In this connection, we noted with satisfaction the Executive Report on the progress of implementation of the Plan of Action and called for closer cooperation at all levels bilaterally, sub-regionally and regionally to further promote the ASEAN-Japan dialogue relations.

5. We exchanged views on a number of regional and international political and economic issues of our mutual concerns. This included the nuclear issue on the Korean Peninsular as well as UN reforms, in particular, those of the Security Council through expanding both permanent and non-permanent categories and working methods. In this connection, we noted the importance of the Six-Party Talks and the need to engage in dialogue to promote mutual confidence. We also shared the view that the Six-Party Talks should be reconvened at the earliest possibility to bring about the common goal of denuclearisation of the Korean Peninsular. We welcomed the important role Japan is playing in the Six-Party Talks.

6. ASEAN Leaders welcomed Japan's accession to the Treaty of Amity and Cooperation in Jakarta in July 2004, which will contribute to the maintenance of peace and stability in the region. We adopted the ASEAN-Japan Joint Declaration for Cooperation on the Fight Against International Terrorism that will further enhance our cooperation in fighting terrorism.

7. We noted the progress on the implementation of the Framework for Comprehensive Economic Partnership (CEP) between ASEAN and Japan signed last year. We acknowledged that the establishment of an economic partnership agreement between Japan and ASEAN Member Countries would help economic growth across ASEAN region. We also agreed that ASEAN-Japan CEP Agreement negotiation should commence in April 2005, and took note of the Economic Ministers' commitment to endeavour to conclude the negotiation within two years from that day.

8. The ASEAN Leaders expressed their appreciation to Japan for its support for the Vientiane Action Programme (VAP) and its assistance in ASEAN's integration through various ASEAN initiatives and projects, namely IAI, Mekong Basin Development, BIMP-EAGA and others, aiming at narrowing the development gaps between the old and new members of ASEAN and human resource development. Japan welcomed the CLMV and the CLV Summits and expressed its support to the implementation of the Vientiane Declaration on Enhancing Economic Cooperation and Integration among Cambodia, Laos, Myanmar and Viet Nam, and the Vientiane Declaration on the Establishment of the Cambodia-Laos-Viet Nam Development Triangle.

9. Taking into account the current high oil price, we supported energy cooperation, in particular, in alternative energy, such as bio-fuels, and hydroelectric power, and stockpiling and energy security. In this regard, ASEAN Leaders encouraged Japan to increase direct investment in Cambodia, Laos, and Myanmar, such as through the construction of hydroelectric power plants and to relocate environmental friendly industries in these three countries in sectors where they enjoyed comparative advantage.

10. We shared the view that there is a need to facilitate the reform of ASEAN-Japan Centre to promote the growing economic partnership between ASEAN and Japan and supported the proposal of Japan for an Eminent Persons Group. We noted the outcome of the ASEAN-Japan Business Dialogue held on 25 November 2004 in Vientiane.

11. The Leader of Japan welcomed the decision reached by ASEAN Leaders to convene the first East Asia Summit (EAS) in Malaysia in 2005. The ASEAN Leaders supported Japan's proposal to host an ASEAN+3 Foreign Ministers Meeting in Kyoto in May 2005 to discuss the concept and modalities of an EAS.

12. The Leader of Japan supported the accession of Laos and Viet Nam to the WTO.

CHAIRMAN'S STATEMENT OF THE 8th ASEAN + REPUBLIC OF KOREA SUMMIT

Vientiane, 30 November 2004

"Deepening ASEAN-Republic of Korea Relationship"

1. The ASEAN Leaders had a productive meeting with H.E. Roh Moo-hyun, President of the Republic of Korea (ROK). We exchanged views on wide ranging regional and international political, security and economic issues.

2. We recalled that the ASEAN-ROK relations began in 1989 and that this year marked the 15th Anniversary of the relationship. We noted with satisfaction that the relations have deepened and widened and many substantive activities have been implemented to support the dialogue partnership and ASEAN's integration efforts. We welcomed the activities and projects by ASEAN and the ROK to commemorate the 15th anniversary to showcase ASEAN-ROK partnership, especially the strong people-to-people contacts between the two sides.

3. The ASEAN Leaders welcomed the ROK's accession to the Treaty of Amity and Cooperation in Southeast Asia, which will not only demonstrate the strong commitment by the ROK to further strengthen political and security engagement with ASEAN to a higher level but will also contribute to regional peace, stability and prosperity.

4. We reaffirmed the importance of the ASEAN-ROK partnership. We signed the ASEAN-ROK Joint Declaration on Comprehensive Cooperation Partnership on this 15th Anniversary of the dialogue relations to further consolidate the partnership and to chart the future direction in the 21st century. We tasked our Ministers to develop a Plan of Action to implement the Joint Declaration for adoption at the next ASEAN-ROK Summit in Malaysia in 2005.

5. We proposed that the ROK consider incorporating ASEAN Studies in the

curriculum of its universities to enable Korean youth to obtain a better understanding of the ASEAN Member Countries and its peoples.

6. We welcomed the recommendations from the ASEAN-ROK Experts Group on the measures to expand two-way trade and investment by liberalising and integrating the markets. We affirmed that the establishment of an ASEAN-ROK Free Trade Area (AKFTA) would be mutually beneficial. In this regard, we agreed to launch the AKFTA negotiations in early 2005 with a goal of having at least 80% of products zero tariff by 2009, and with consideration for special and differential treatment and additional flexibility for new ASEAN Member Countries.

7. Taking into account the current high oil price, the ASEAN Leaders proposed that the ROK work together with ASEAN in defining the global strategy on energy cooperation, in particular, in alternative energy, such as bio-fuels, and hydroelectric power, and oil stockpiling and energy security. In this regard, ASEAN Leaders encouraged the ROK to increase direct investment in Cambodia, Laos, and Myanmar, such as through the construction of hydroelectric power plants.

8. We reaffirmed our commitment to a peaceful and comprehensive solution to the nuclear issue on Korean Peninsular. In this connection, we noted the importance of the Six-Party Talks and the need to engage into dialogue to promote mutual confidence. We also shared the view that the Six-Party Talks should be reconvened at the earliest possibility to bring about the common goal of denuclearisation of the Korean Peninsular. We recognised the important role of the ROK in the Six-Party Talks.

9. The ROK welcomed the signing of Joint Declaration between ASEAN and its other dialogue partners on cooperation to combat terrorism. In this regard, we agreed to further strengthen our cooperation in fighting terrorism.

10. The ASEAN Leaders highly valued the ROK's decision to increase its contribution to the ASEAN-ROK Special Cooperation Fund (SCF) and ASEAN-ROK Future Oriented Cooperation Projects Fund (FOCP) next year, which demonstrates its strong commitment to enhance the dialogue partnership. The ASEAN Leaders also expressed its appreciation to the ROK for its support for the implementation of projects under the Initiative for ASEAN Integration (IAI), and hoped that the ROK will contribute to the implementation of the Vientiane Action Programme (VAP) to assist ASEAN in narrowing the development gaps and accelerating its integration as the whole.

11. The ASEAN Leaders expressed their appreciation to the ROK for its support to bridge the development gaps through cooperation in the sub-regional frameworks, such as the AMBDC, ACMECS, BIMP-EAGA, and GMS to promote economic and social development, and improve living standards of the people in the region.

12. The ROK welcomed and expressed its support to the forthcoming Second East Asia Forum, which will be held in Kuala Lumpur in December 2004. The ROK also welcomed the decision reached by ASEAN Leaders to convene the first East Asia Summit (EAS) in Malaysia in 2005.

CHAIRMAN'S STATEMENT OF THE 8th ASEAN + CHINA SUMMIT

Vientiane, 29 November 2004

"Deepening ASEAN-China Strategic Partnership"

1. ASEAN Leaders held a productive meeting with H.E. Wen Jiabao, Premier of the People's Republic of China. We exchanged views on regional and international political and economic issues of common concern. We also reviewed developments in ASEAN-China relations in recent years. We acknowledged the increasingly important role China has been playing in regional and global affairs.

2. ASEAN Leaders commended China's active and important role in promoting the Six-Party Talks on the nuclear issue on the Korean Peninsular. We noted with encouragement the achievement of the three rounds of the Six-Party Talks. ASEAN Leaders expressed their hope that China would continue to play an important role in the quest for a peaceful and comprehensive solution to the nuclear issue on the Korean Peninsular. We shared the view that there is a need to engage into dialogue to promote mutual confidence and common approach, and that the Six-Party Talks should be reconvened at the earliest possibility to bring about the common goal of denuclearisation on the Korean Peninsular.

3. We expressed our deep concern over the deteriorating situation in Iraq and agreed that the United Nations' leading role in Iraqi post-war construction is important and relevant to the future of the Iraqi people. We are deeply concerned with the situation in the Middle East and called for a peaceful solution to end the violence in this region.

4. We welcomed the accession of the Republic of Korea and the Russian Federation to the Treaty of Amity and Cooperation in Southeast Asia, and encouraged other non-Southeast Asian countries to accede to the Treaty. We shared the view that efforts should be pursued to promote the Treaty as a code of conduct for inter-state relations in the region.

5. ASEAN Leaders reaffirmed their commitment to the One-China Policy and believed that maintaining peace and stability across Taiwan Straits conforms to the common interests of all countries in the region.

6. China commended ASEAN for the signing of the Vientiane Action Programme (VAP), and expressed its support to the implementation of VAP, which will contribute to the realisation of the goals in the ASEAN Vision 2020 and the

Declaration of ASEAN Concord II leading to the establishment of the ASEAN Community comprising 3 main pillars, namely, the ASEAN Security Community (ASC), the ASEAN Economic Community (AEC) and the ASEAN Socio-Cultural Community (ASCC). In this connection, China welcomed the adoption of the ASC Plan of Action and the ASCC Plan of Action and expressed its support in the implementation of activities under the two Plans. China also welcomed the signing of the ASEAN Framework Agreement on the Integration of Priority Sectors and the Protocols, which will support the realisation of the AEC.

7. We agreed to further strengthen cooperation in the non-traditional security field through the implementation of the Joint Declaration of ASEAN and China Cooperation in the Field of Non-Traditional Security Issues signed on 4 November 2002 in Phnom Penh and the ASEAN-China Memorandum of Understanding (MOU) on Cooperation in the field of Non-traditional Security Issues signed on 10 January 2004 in Bangkok. We noted with satisfaction that the Annual Plan for 2004 to implement the MOU has been completed and that ASEAN and China will be working on the Annual Plan for 2005.

8. We adopted the Plan of Action to Implement the Joint Declaration of the Heads of State/Government of ASEAN and China on Strategic Partnership for Peace and Prosperity. We are confident that this Plan of Action would accelerate all-dimensional cooperation between the two sides with a view to consolidating and deepening the ASEAN-China strategic partnership. We also identified a number of priority areas, for implementation, under the Plan, which included energy cooperation, especially alternative clean energy, bio-fuels, and hydroelectric power; SMEs and industrial clustering; public health; science and technology as well as quality supervision, inspection and quarantine inspection.

9. We noted with satisfaction the progress in the implementation of the Framework Agreement on Comprehensive Economic Cooperation between ASEAN and China and agreed to expedite the implementation of the Early Harvest Programme and provide flexibility to the new Member Countries of ASEAN. We welcomed the signing of the Agreement on Trade in Goods and Agreement on Dispute Settlement Mechanism by the ASEAN-China Economic Ministers as part of the implementation of the Framework Agreement on Comprehensive Economic Cooperation as well as the signing of the MOU between ASEAN and China on Transport Cooperation.

10. We agreed to develop comprehensive frameworks for our cooperation in the five key areas, namely agriculture, information and communication technology (ICT), human resource development (HRD), Mekong Basin development and mutual investment.

11. ASEAN Leaders congratulated China for the successful holding of the ASEAN-China EXPO in Nanning earlier this month and welcomed China's plan

to convene an "ASEAN-China Telecommunications Week" in April 2005, in Shanghai. In the area of investment, ASEAN Leaders supported China's project on holding a high-level Seminar on Promoting Investment by SMEs in East Asia in the second half of 2005.

12. The ASEAN Leaders welcomed China's initiative to dispatch young volunteers to ASEAN countries, particularly to CLMV. In this connection, we agreed to further develop this initiative into specific projects taking into account the capabilities of Chinese young volunteers and the needs and requirements of ASEAN Member Countries, especially those of the CLMV.

13. The ASEAN Leaders were supportive of China's proposal for commemorating the 15th anniversary of ASEAN-China dialogue relations and welcomed China's intention to contribute another US$ 5 million to the ASEAN-China Cooperation Fund in 2005.

14. China reiterated its continued support for ASEAN's integration through various development initiatives such as the Initiative for ASEAN Integration (IAI), ASEAN-Mekong Basin Development Cooperation (AMBDC), Brunei Darussalam-Indonesia-Malaysia-Philippines-East ASEAN Growth Area (BIMP-EAGA), and Ayeyawady-Chao Phraya-Mekong Economic Cooperation Strategy (ACMECS).

15. ASEAN Leaders agreed to recognise China as a full market economy and committed not to apply Section 15 and 16 of the Protocol of Accession of the People's Republic of China to the WTO and Paragraph 242 of the Report of the Working Party on the Accession of China to WTO in relation to the trade between each of the ten ASEAN member states and China.

16. We noted with satisfaction the admission of Cambodia, Laos and Myanmar to the Asia-Europe Meeting (ASEM) and expressed appreciation to China for its support for the three ASEAN Member Countries.

17. We expressed our support for Asia's turn to assume the position of United Nations Secretary-General. In this regard, China was pleased to be informed of ASEAN's endorsement of the candidature of H.E. Dr. Surakiart Sathirathai, Minister of Foreign Affairs of Thailand, for this position.

INSTRUMENT OF EXTENSION OF THE TREATY OF AMITY AND COOPERATION IN THE SOUTHEAST ASIA BY RUSSIAN FEDERATION

Whereas the Treaty of Amity and Cooperation in Southeast Asia, which was signed on 24 February 1976 in Bali, Indonesia, was amended by the First and the Second Protocols Amending the Treaty of Amity and Cooperation in Southeast Asia, which were signed on 15 December 1987 and on 25 July 1998 respectively;

Whereas Article 18, Paragraph 3, of the aforesaid Treaty as amended by Article 1 of the aforesaid Second Protocol provides that States outside Southeast Asia may accede to the Treaty with the consent of all the States in Southeast Asia, namely Brunei Darussalam, the Kingdom of Cambodia, the Republic of Indonesia, the Lao People's Democratic Republic, Malaysia, the Union of Myanmar, the Republic of the Philippines, the Republic of Singapore, the Kingdom of Thailand and the Socialist Republic of Viet Nam; and

Whereas the People's Republic of China conveyed its desire to accede to the Treaty in a letter dated 21 March 2003;

Now, therefore, the Governments of Brunei Darussalam, the Kingdom of Cambodia, the Republic of Indonesia, the Lao People's Democratic Republic, Malaysia, the Union of Myanmar, the Republic of the Philippines, the Republic of Singapore, the Kingdom of Thailand and the Socialist Republic of Viet Nam, having considered the said letter, hereby consent to the accession to the Treaty by the People's Republic of China;

Done at Bali, Indonesia, on the Eighth Day of October in the Year Two Thousand and Three.

INSTRUMENT OF ACCESSION TO THE TREATY OF AMITY AND COOPERATION IN SOUTHEAST ASIA BY REPUBLIC OF KOREA

Whereas the Treaty of Amity and Cooperation in Southeast Asia, which was signed on 24 February 1976 in Bali, Indonesia, was amended by the First and the Second Protocols Amending the Treaty of Amity and Cooperation in Southeast Asia, which were signed on 15 December 1987 and 25 July 1998, respectively;

Whereas Article 18, Paragraph 3, of the aforesaid Treaty as amended by Article 1 of the aforesaid Second Protocol provides that States outside Southeast Asia may also accede to the Treaty with the consent of all the States in Southeast Asia, namely Brunei Darussalam, the Kingdom of Cambodia, the Republic of Indonesia, the Lao People's Democratic Republic, Malaysia, the Union of Myanmar, the Republic of the Philippines, the Republic of Singapore, the Kingdom of Thailand and the Socialist Republic of Viet Nam; and

Whereas all the States in Southeast Asia have consented to the accession of the Republic of Korea to the Treaty;

Now, therefore, the Republic of Korea, having considered the aforesaid Treaty as amended by the Protocols, hereby accedes to the same and undertakes faithfully to perform and carry out all the stipulations therein contained.

In witness whereof, this Instrument of Accession is signed by the Minister of Foreign Affairs and Trade of the Republic of Korea.

Done in Vientiane, the Lao People's Democratic Republic, on the Twenty-Seventh Day of November in the Year Two Thousand and Four.

Japan and South Korea

In a move unprecedented in postwar Japan, Prime Minister Junichiro Koizumi made an announcement in September that he would offer the support of the Japanese Self-Defence Forces in America's war against terrorism. In a policy speech to the Diet, late September, Koizumi set the tone for the parliamentary-discussion of anti-terrorist measures stating '"the Sept. 11 terrorist attacks were a despicable attack not only on the United States but also on humanity as a whole" and "our country must make its own efforts to fight terrorism". Stressing that Japan will "cooperate with the international community and take effective measures", the prime minister pledged to implement as soon as possible a seven-point and-terrorism programme.The package included a bill giving legal authorisation for the deployment of Self Defence Forces to provide logistic support, including munitions transportation, for the US led military strikes against terrorists. The bill allows the government to send SDF ships and troops to distant places, such as the Indian Ocean, for the first time in support of direct military operations. The Japanese government has been quick to reassure the immediate neighbours — China and South Korea - that these measures are specifically aimed at bolstering the international coalition against terrorism.

Conspicuous, by its absence as yet , however, has been a similar high-level attempt to build confidence with India, the most prominent of the Indian Ocean and Arabian Sea littoral state with regard to the scope and duration of this naval deployment. This paper argues, (a) any proposal to deploy the SDF in the Indian Ocean region has vital implications for Indian security, and (b) the push for a major role in the Afghanistan crisis needs to be viewed in conjunction with recent Japanese attempts to mediate between India and Pakistan, wherein Japan's overall South Asia policy is increasingly linked to Japan's quest for an enhanced role in international security

Specific Measures

Memories of the Gulf War in 1991 have weighed heavily on Japanese policy-makers in formulating a response to the September 11 terrorist attack on the United States and the subsequent military action in Afghanistan. Indeed. Japan's leaders have acted with the knowledge that they had failed to meet their ally's expectations a decade ago and a similar failure could provide a body blow - perhaps even a fatal one - to the US-Japan alliance. The new legislation allows the SDF to provide logistic and other noncombatant support to the US-led forces, engage in search and rescue activities and carry' out humanitarian relief operations. It eases restrictions on the use of weapons by SDF personnel, allowing them to protect not only themselves, but also those under their care, including refugees and wounded foreign service members. The measures are in striking contrast to the passive stand that Japan took in 1991 during the Gulf War.

At that time, Japan contributed a large sum of money to the US-led multinational force, but provided no physical support. As it turned out, breaking the half-century taboo under the war-renouncing constitution to participate in a war took only a couple of months to achieve. Previously, the Japanese Diet did not enact the Peacekeeping Cooperation Law until one and half years after the Gulf War. Media reports, quoting government sources, suggest that SDF activities to support the US-led strikes on Afghanistan will centre on supply and transport missions carried out by Marine Self-Defence Force (MSDF) vessels. Apparently the Japanese government intends the MSDF supply vessels to transport fuel, food and other supplies to Diego Garcia in the Indian Ocean, that serves as a major logistic base for the US forces.

The Security Council. Japan's top security board which includes Prime Minister Koizumi and other key cabinet members approved a plan on November 8 to dispatch three vessels to the Indian Ocean. The vessels included the supply ship *Hamana* and two destroyers. *Kirisame* and *Kurama*. The mission will focus on intelligence gathering operations and lay the groundwork for a second MSDF task force. While the main task force will be dispatched under the new law enacted for Japan to provide noncombat support for the US-led military action, this three-ship flotilla has been sent under Article 5 of the Defence Agency Establishment Law which allows the government to conduct "necessary investigation and research" ahead of a military operation. More than 1.000 SDF members will take part in the operations. Besides, Japanese Defence Agency officials say that this deployment in the Indian Ocean is open-ended. Six Air Self Defence Force C-130 cargo planes and two multipurpose support planes will also join the operation. The Japanese government had also been very keen to send a top-of-the-line Aegis destroyer to the Indian Ocean. The government had been considering to send the 7,250-ton *Kongo* on an intelligence-gathering mission, but abandoned the plan in the light of a strong domestic opposition along with opposition from its Northeast Asian neighbours.

Asian Security and Japan

The above steps taken by the Japanese government have, however, reinvigorated an analytical and policy debate about the nation's security policy. The most dramatic implication of the support to the US-led war against terrorism is that it significantly extends the perimeter and scope of SDF activities overseas. Under previous legislation enabling Japan-US defence cooperation, geographic guidelines were a major limiting factor; the SDF were to support the US forces only in areas surrounding Japan. The new anti-terrorism law effectively lifts that geographic limit and enables SDF units to conduct activities short of combat operations in the Indian Ocean. In a strategic sense, therefore. Japan is at a turning point. In recent years, Japan's military has begun to bridge the gap between being a self-defence force and a regional military. The transformation was formalised in 1997 when the US-Japan Defence Guidelines were revised and the annual Defence White Paper publicly addressed a regional strategy in "areas surrounding Japan".

In 1999, while taking part in US exercises in Guam. Japan deployed fighter aircraft outside its territory for the first time since World War II. In 2000. Japan's JSDF exercised with other regional forces without the United States. In February 2000, Japan's Foreign Ministry announced that Tokyo was considering to deploy vessels to patrol the Straits of Malacca where shipping had been plagued by piracy. In 2001. Japan for the first time sent officers to observe Cobra Gold, a joint Thai-US military exercise, the largest in the region. In the words of Shunji Yanai, former Japanese ambassador to the United States, "The US wants Japan to help in the Afghan reconstruction process... but I have told a number of US officials that they can't just ask us for money for reconstruction... we will commit ourselves from the peace process stage". Correspondingly. Sadako Ogata, former United Nations High Commissioner for Refugees, has been appointed Prime Minister Junichiro Koizumi's special representative for issues related to Afghanistan.

Ogata will principally coordinate Japan's efforts with other nations and international organisations with regard to humanitarian assistance for refugees, peace negotiations and the eventual reconstruction of Afghanistan after military activities in the region cease. At the same time, the Japanese government has launched a full-fledged study on how Japan can provide aid to Afghanistan in areas such as maintaining public order and rebuilding the nation. Government officials and ruling party members have been calling for a review of the five principles of SDF participation in peacekeeping operations.

Currently, there exists a freeze on activities such as supervision of ceasefires and disarmament. The new antiterrorism law is effective only for two years and does not provide for keeping public order in Afghanistan. "The government should create a permanent law that allows Japan to provide a broad range of support to multinational forces and other organisations based on a UN resolution or other grounds" a senior Foreign Ministry official said, reflecting the general mood in government circles. In this context, it is useful to interpret the US-Japan security alliance both as a tool and a goal. The US-Japan security alliance is a tool in the sense that it provides Japan, with a useful framework within which it could play a larger security role.

It is the goal in the sense that a strengthened alliance with an increased Japanese role would provide Japan's neighbouring countries with reassurance. At a time of declining economic performance, therefore, use of SDF in overseas missions within the broad framework of US-Japan cooperation is a much more cost effective measure to maintain and enhance Japan's position in the international community.

Japan's Self-Defence Forces (SDFs)

Japan's Self-Defence Forces (SDFs) are unwonted in their appellation, characteristics and role as compared with the military forces of other countries. Inaugurated during the Cold War environs half a century ago in July 1954, the SDFs (as the name clearly suggests) were primarily purported to perform the function of solely defending the territory of Japan. Formed initially as the National Police Reserve comprising of about 75,000 personnel, the SDF have indeed come a long way in terms of size, role as well as its level of technology. With a total strength of as many as 239,000 personnel at present, the functions of the SDFs are undergoing shades of transformation in tandem with Japan's incrementally changing security strategy as well as its perception of its own international role.

The strongest bearing on the prescribed role of the Japanese SDFs has been a fallout of the pacifist Constitution of the country, which (under Article 9) calls for the renunciation of war as a sovereign right of the nation and the threat or use of force as a means of settling international disputes and denies the right of belligerency of the state. It is interesting to note that the pacifist Constitution of 1947 clearly states that the state is not to maintain "land, sea and air forces, as well as other war potential." This was the reason why these forces were initially considered unconstitutional by some and restricted themselves to conducting a humanitarian role in providing assistance during natural disasters. However, according to the government position, being a sovereign nation Japan is not denied the inherent right of self-defence. It is in order to possess this minimum level of armed strength necessary for self-defence, that the SDFs are maintained as an armed organisation. In a nutshell, an exclusively defence oriented security policy has been the hallmark of Japan's strategic culture. The Constitution prohibits Tokyo from dispatching its armed forces to foreign land, sea and airspace (overseas deployment) for the use of force, which is considered to be outside the purview of the minimum level of self-defense. The *National Defense Policy Outline FY 1996*, still in force, envisaged a streamlining of the SDFs to make them more compact, enhancing necessary functions and making qualitative improvements to enable them to respond effectively to the changing international situation.

This paper attempts to take a look at the ongoing incremental growth in the scope of the customary role and functions of the SDFs, showing visible elements of change in the post Gulf War era and even more rapidly in the aftermath of the 9/11 crisis. Perhaps the first stride taken in this regard was in 1992, with the passage of the UN Peacekeeping Law to facilitate Japanese forces to participate in UN activities. More recently, following the WTC attacks, marked developments occurred in terms of the passage of laws that expanded the sphere of activities of the SDFs by assigning them new tasks. These developments have to be essentially perceived within the overarching paradigm of Japan's movement towards a 'normal' state.

First Steps Taken - Joining Hands in UN Activities

The Gulf War of 1991 was, in many ways, a turning point in Tokyo's assessment and review of its security construct. The war became a touchstone in Japan's ties with its alliance partner, the US, as well as its contribution to the international order. Barring the dispatch of some minesweepers, Japan chose to restrict its assistance to a financial contribution of US $13 billion. Nevertheless, Japan drew widespread censure for what was termed as mere 'checkbook diplomacy.' Tokyo's inability to dispatch military personnel on the overseas mission for collective self-defence, *as* well as its anti-militarist culture guided its restrained response towards contributing to the war.

The foundations were then laid for a review of both Japan's security policy, as well as augmentation of the role of the SDFs. The landmark passage of the International Peace Cooperation Law or the UN Peace Keeping Law in June 1992 marked the first step taken by the SDF to participate in UN activities over its traditional earmarked duties of protecting Japanese territory and assisting in natural disasters. Consequent to the passage of the law, the gates were opened for Japan's embarkation into several peacekeeping operations undertaken by the UN. It was, however, clear that this kind of cooperation would not include any kind of military activities like supervision of elections, monitoring of ceasefires and inspection of weapons. Assistance in such situations would encompass activities such as provision of medical care and basic amenities like food and clothes. Since then, prominent examples of Tokyo's contribution to peacekeeping initiatives undertaken by the international organisation include Cambodian conflict, East Timor, Haiti and the Golan Heights.

Later, following the WTC attacks in September 2001, Japan passed an amendment to the International Peace Cooperation Law to permit the SDFs engaged in international peace cooperation assignments to use weapons beyond purposes of protecting themselves - to that of protecting the lives of peace cooperation personnel with them on the scene or those who have come under their control while conducting their duties. There has been a reassessment and revision of the role that the Japanese forces are expected to play in UN operations. These changes and alterations are a consequence of the larger role that Japan perceives for itself commensurate with its status in the international community today. In fact, Japan has expressed its desire to become a permanent member of the UN Security Council based on both its significant financial contribution to the organisation, as well as its active participation in UN peacekeeping activities. Prime Minister Koizumi is expected to make an announcement expressing Japan's aspiration on September 21 this year in the UN General Assembly.

Redefinition of the Guidelines of US-Japan Alliance and Role of the SDFs

To put it simply, the guidelines envisaged an expanded role for Japan's forces in the case of any contingency in the defence of not only its own territory, but also in 'areas surrounding it.' This kind of cooperation was to encompass activities like relief, search and rescue, non-combat evacuation operations and provision of rear-area support to US forces including supplies, maintenance and security of US facilities and areas in Japan. In order to support this provision of the revised guidelines, the Japanese Diet passed the Law regarding situations in areas surrounding Japan in August 1999, that authorised the government to undertake, in the case of an unstable situation in 'areas surrounding Japan' rear area support, search and rescue operations and inspection of ships, etc. The Prime Minister requires only a cabinet approval to go ahead with the draft of the basic plan of action to ensure a timely response rather than wait for Dietary approval. However, if the Diet does not grant approval consequently, the course of action is to be suspended. The Director General of the Japan Defence Agency is authorised to specify actions to be included in rear-area support, search and rescue operations in rear-area and ship inspections. The law permits the SDFs to use weapons in cases deemed necessary to protect themselves or those working with them in such operations. A second law was passed to facilitate support to US forces called the Law concerning conduct of ship operations in areas surrounding Japan in 2000.

This law empowered the SDF personnel to conduct ship-inspection operations in its territorial waters or surrounding high seas (including the EEZ) to inspect and confirm cargo and destination of ships (excluding warships) and request, if necessary, a change of route. While conducting these operations, the SDF units are permitted to provide goods and services (like supplies, transportation, repair and medical services) to US forces engaged in activities equivalent to ship operations that contribute to the accomplishment of purposes of the US-Japan Security Treaty.

As a result of the adoption of the revised guidelines, the Japanese forces were to take on a more active role which was not just limited to narrow self-defence purposes. Instead, the revised guidelines solicited greater Japanese participation and taking on new responsibilities (like the provision of rear-area support) in 'areas surrounding Japan' - a phrase that erupted widespread controversy among Tokyo's neighbours like China and Korea on what such an 'area' would encompass. Chinese apprehensions primarily centered around the fact that such a phrase could translate into Taiwan's inclusion into the scope of Japan-US security cooperation.

War on Terror and Japan's SDFs

The September 11 attacks on the WTC and the Pentagon marked the initiation of a new era in international relations. As an ally of Washington, Tokyo was impacted by these events, even as it was cautious not to repeat the 'mistakes' of the Gulf War. However, the impact of the attacks and the subsequent US war on terror in both Afghanistan and Iraq led to changes in the role of the Japanese forces. Following the announcement of a seven-pronged action plan to deal with the situation, Japanese Prime Minister Junichiro Koizumi set up a task force under himself comprising cabinet ministers to take crucial decisions with regard to assistance to the US. Even as the US initiated strikes against Afghanistan, Japan "strongly " supported the Bush administration in its stand on terrorism. At the time of the US action in Afghanistan, Japan dispatched minesweepers, destroyers and 37 Coast Guard cutters that escorted US aircraft carrier *Kitty Hawk* from the Yokosuka naval base on 21 September 2001. The domestic legal framework was set in place to support Japanese actions with the passage of the Anti-terrorism Special Measures Law in November 2001, which paved the way for the dispatch of Japanese SDFs to provide non-combat support to US-led forces engaged in the 'war on terror.' The contents of this kind of cooperation are inclusive of assistance like supply of fuel for ships, transportation of fuel, personnel and goods, repair and maintenance and provision of medical services. The geographical area in which such supply and transportation activities were envisaged included the Japanese territory, Indian Ocean including the Gulf region and related airspace, Diego Garcia and Australian territory. Besides, search and rescue assistance was to be given to victims of terror attacks or if the US or other allied countries request for support and assistance in areas covered by Japan. Also, five ships were dispatched to the Indian Ocean, of which two *(Hamana* and *Towada)* were oil tankers, and three defence ships (the *Kurama, Kirisame* and *Sawagiri).* These ships set sail from the Sasebo naval base for Diego Garcia, which was a prominent base for the US in its attack on Afghanistan to provide rear-area support for refueling American and British ships. This assistance was provided on the plea that such supplies did not constitute exercise of armed force, and was thus permissible. The law, which was stipulated to be effective for a period of two years initially, widened the geographical scope of operations that could be undertaken by the SDF from Japan and areas surrounding it to beyond these borders - overseas, and also permitted the Japanese forces to use their weapons to protect refugees under their care. In April 2004, the Japanese government extended the deployment of SDFs to the Indian Ocean region for six months, even as the maximum number of MSDF vessels supplying fuel and other goods to the US warships in the region would be reduced from five to three due to a relatively lesser requirement of fuel supply in the region now. As per recent estimates, the MSDF has supplied a total of 350,000 kilolitres of fuel on 363 occasions.

Japan's role in the US war on Iraq further drew it closer to its powerful ally, as it emerged a constant source of support to the Bush regime at a time when many countries like France and Germany refused to send troops for the purpose. Despite overwhelming domestic sentiment against the dispatch of troops to the war-torn Iraq, a basic plan defining the scope of the SDF mission was drawn up (under the Law concerning special Measures on Humanitarian and Reconstruction Assistance in Iraq) and the government stood by its decision to send the forces. It was the first time since the end of World War II that Japanese forces had been dispatched to a country still reeling under a situation of war, even though only for a humanitarian mission, like supplying water, transportation, repairing roads and schools and provision of medical facilities, in areas like Samawah. The ASDF has been airlifting personnel and supplies in the area. Two significant factors underscored this dispatch enabled under the Special Measures Law - one, that no area could be lucidly demarcated as "non-combat zone"; and two, no UN sanction backed the US attack at that time. Defending his decision to send troops to Iraq, Koizumi stated, "It can't be said that a nation has fulfilled its duty as a member of the international community if it leaves manpower contributions to other countries out of concern that such a form of assistance poses a risk."

The Japanese government recently announced its decision to keep the SDFs in Iraq as part of the multinational force set up under the UNSC resolution following the handover of sovereignty on June 25, 2004. These preconditions have been set in order to ensure that the Japanese forces are not forced to violate the Constitution by participating in any operation that calls for a use of force. However, the dilemma that could be faced by personnel in the face of a situation of members of the multinational force coming under attack was summed up by a senior GSDF officer who said: "We can't ignore SDF help if a member of the multinational force comes under attack nearby."

The significance of the Japanese decision to send troops to Iraq cannot be understated. The gradual expansion of the scope of the SDF activities during the course of the US war on terror has made Japanese SDFs cross the Rubicon on several fronts. This singular decision along with other developments like the proposed revision of the constitution are bound to have an impact on Japan's security policy in the coming years.

Factors Propelling Changes

What, then, are the major factors that are leading to an augmented role of the Japanese SDFs? Broadly classified, they can be enumerated as being the following:

Emerging Security Concerns of Japan

With a powerful neighbor like China and an uncertain North Korean state in its neighbourhood, Japan's threat perceptions within the region emanate from close quarters. China's rapidly modernising PLA, outstanding territorial issues (like the Senkaku islands dispute) and baggage of history that transcends into other political frictions make the relationship prone to discord. The Taiwan Straits crisis could prove to be another major de-stabilising force in the region around Japan, especially in the case of any kind of military action there. Japan might find itself embroiled in any conflict with which the US is involved, specifically the possible use of Japanese bases in such an event. With North Korea, problems not only revolve around its nuclear programme, but also the issue of abducted Japanese citizens. Pyongyang's rapidly developing military capabilities coupled with severe economic problems only aggravate the element of instability. Coupled with these issues are the frequent cases of North Korean spy ship incursions that Tokyo faces. The North Korean test firing of the *Taepodong-1* missile, that flew over Japanese territory into the Pacific Ocean made the Japanese realise that they were exposed to risks from Pyongyang. Besides, from the Russian front, though the degree of tension has waned to a great degree, the unresolved Northern Islands issue still remains a potential flashpoint.

With all these potential flashpoints in the region, Japan chose to traverse a deviated path from a strictly pacifist posture, and gradually built up its defence capability. Apart from this is the fact that its prominent ally, the US has both encouraged as well as expected Japan to take part in more 'burden sharing' rather than keep the image of being a 'free-rider' on security matters. The augmented role of the SDFs is an intrinsic part of this process of 'normalisation' of Japan to face its security concerns more effectively, in cooperation with the US.

The US Factor

The US-Japan alliance has been the cornerstone of Japan's security structure since the end of the War. However, throughout the course of its development, Washington has made it explicit that it wanted Tokyo to take on a more active role within the partnership. Ties between the two allies reached their nadir at the time of the first Gulf War, when Japan did not live up to the expectations of its partner by providing troops during the conflict. In fact, this element was clearly stated in a report by a bipartisan group led by Richard Armitage in 2000, entitled *The United States and Japan: Advancing Toward a Mature Partnership.* The report called Japan's prohibition against participation in collective self-defence as a "constraint" on alliance cooperation. Besides, it also recommended greater cooperation of all three US armed forces with their Japanese counterparts and removal of Japan's restrains on peacekeeping activities. A recent proposal by Koizumi to revise the Constitution in order to enable the Japanese SDFs to engage in collective self-defence in a step forward by Japan in this regard. Besides, the revised guidelines of 1997 concurrently increased the role of the Japanese SDFs within its ambit. The Japanese Diet has also passed a set of supplementary war bills in June 2004 to counter a foreign military attack, of which one law enables Japan's SDFs to supply provisions to US forces, not just in peacetime but emergencies too. Another law allows the SDFs and US forces in Japan to share goods, including ammunition and services in the case of an attack or probable attack on Japan. These laws have been tailored to dovetail well with the needs of the US-Japan alliance at a time when the US needs Japan, not as a dependent partner, but as a prominent supportive ally.

Domestic Factors

On the domestic front, there is an increased acceptance of the incrementally changing role of the SDFs. In fact, Koizumi had been the first ever sitting Prime Minister to call the SDFs 'military.' Responding to a question in the Upper House Ad Hoc Committee on Military Emergency Legislation of the *Diet*, Koizumi stated that he thought the SDFs were in fact "substantially" a military organisation and will ultimately "receive the honour and status they deserve in the Constitution." A draft prepared by a special team of the Liberal Democratic Party's Research Commission on the Constitution has put forth recommendations that would lead to the SDF being effectively a military organisation. Suggesting an amendment to the Article 9, which prohibits the maintenance of armed forces by Japan, the draft calls for the need to maintain "military forces for self-defense and international cooperation." It also calls for a reinterpretation of the clause on collective self-defense that would enable Japan to exercise the right in case an ally came under attack.

Meanwhile, opposition party, the *Minshuto* (Democratic Party of Japan) has also spoken in favour of revising the Constitution to permit the SDFs to use military force overseas. Voicing the party's position on the issue, *Minshuto* leader Katsuya Okada said that the "Constitution should be revised to allow the SDF to use force overseas as long as there is a UN Security Council resolution." Recent public opinion polls on activities that the SDF should focus on from now on show that while as many as 67.8 per cent people think SDF should focus on disaster relief dispatch, the second priority with a rating of 57.6 per cent has been given to the SDF according national security followed by participation in international peace cooperation efforts.

An Assessment

An assessment of the ongoing modifications in the role of the Japanese SDFs presents an interesting pattern of changes in its features. From being a taboo subject, the ongoing deliberations on the SDF, as well as legal framework being set in place by the Japanese government are all indicative of a greater accommodative understanding on the need to modify the role of these forces. Not only have the self-defence forces moved beyond the geographical limits set for them initially to take an active part in peacekeeping missions abroad, they have been sent overseas to Afghanistan and Iraq without a UN mandate to do so - something that would be unthinkable a few years back. Reflecting a marked shift from a staunch pacifist attitude, the Japanese Coast Guard cutters chased, fought with and sunk a North Korean spy ship that had been spotted in its exclusive economic zone in December 2001. This was not the first such incursion by Pyongyang, but certainly broke ground in terms of response by the Japanese forces. Similarly, the SDF's participation in the multinational force in Iraq has heralded a new chapter for the Japanese troops. The Japanese Maritime Self-Defence Force (MSDF) is the most powerful naval force in the East Asian region, and the MSDF cumulatively with its two corresponding wings, the Air SDF and the Ground SDF, buttressed with the US-Japan security alliance, are capable of preserving and safeguarding Japan's security.

The Japanese government under Prime Minister Koizumi has been instrumental in gearing up these changes. In fact, Koizumi has even called for formulating a permanent law that spells out the principles under which SDFs could be dispatched for overseas missions, instead of a piecemeal response to situations warranting SDF Preliminary reports on the forthcoming national defence strategy also indicate that it would delineate a bigger role for the SDFs. It is expected to call for a revision of the existing force structure in order to offset the cost of deploying the missile defense system, and spell out the key role of the SDF as being in cooperation with the international community to maintain peace and stability, and dealing with new security threats. The recent white paper on defense 2004 issued by the Japan Defense Agency has called for a transfiguration of the SDF into a "more functional force" to meet the new threats and challenges, while at the same time emphasising on the need for more "mobility and flexibility."

13

SOUTH EAST ASIA-SOUTH ASIA-INDIA: CO-OPERATION AND PARTNERSHIP

Southeast Asia and South Asia

By the early centuries of the Christian era, many parts of Southeast Asia and India were a part of the world-trading network. Though this period was marked by the domination of Indian Ocean by Roman trade, it also witnessed the establishment of trade relations between India and Southeast Asia. It has been argued that this relationship further resulted in the colonisation of Southeast Asia, but the argument has been firmly countered in the wake of recent research, which emphasises on the mutual influence, rather than partial view of one-sided influence. In this publication, an attempt has been made to study the process of state-formation vis-a-vis the interplay of trade to examine the role-played by indigenous factors and the influence of 'Indic' elements. It also presents an analysis of relations behind the increased economic activities between India and Southeast Asia from 5-6th century onwards and the resultant socio-political, economic and cultural impact of this relationship on the region.

The sources for the early relationship between India and Southeast Asia are scanty and ambiguous in nature. Southeast Asia has been portrayed and referred as the 'Golden Island' or 'Golden Peninsula' or 'Yavadipa' or 'Suvarnadipa' in the Indian literature from the early centuries A.D. Apart from Ramayana, the Buddhist Jataka fables also mention about Southeast Asia. Chinese records provide a satisfactory, yet still incomplete view of the burgeoning Southeast Asian commerce. In the last few decades, archaeological excavations at various sites in Southeast Asia have resulted in the yielding of various remains, which present a new and different picture of the region. The availability of epigraphic sources and inscriptions at various places has proved to be of great use in reconstructing the history of this region. The various categories of inscriptions found are in Sanskrit, Tamil and indigenous languages. As far as state-formation is concerned, the maritime region has not been well served partly due to paucity of the data, and partly to the fact that most of the scholars dealing with early history of maritime regions are struggling to produce adequate description of the states of the later first millennium AD. The reflections of the Indian ideas, beliefs and religious culture upon the monumental, artistic and literary remains of the early historic states of Southeast Asia made the scholars argue for the colonisation/Indianisation of the region. Coedes argued that the contact with the Brahmana-Buddhist culture of India resulted in the formation of states that were culturally dependent on India. Mabbett argued for the borrowing of ideology and leadership apart from the agricultural technology that made possible the establishment of the first states in the region. This proposition began to be questioned when scholars raised the problem of the identity of the Indian incomers and the circumstances under which they arrived and interacted with the local population. Van Leur argued that the local populace was an active participant in the process. He also argued that necessary political and social skills for state building were acquired from India as these essential ingredients were assumed to be missing in local societies. He continues that the local rulers, having learnt of Indian culture through interaction with Indians on the maritime route, recognised the advantages of certain elements of the Indian civilisation and drew from the Indian tradition for their own benefit. Wolters (1967) stressed the idea of a mutual sharing process in the evolution of Indianised statecraft in Southeast Asia.

The initial contact with the knowledge of Indian cultural tradition came through the Southeast Asian sailors. The local-rulers, recognising the fact that Indian culture provided certain opportunities for administrative and technological advantages *vis-a-vis* their rivals, followed up on these contacts. Thus, the initiative was Southeast Asian, not Indian, and it was a slow process of cultural synthesis rather than Indianisation made possible by the imposition of Hinduism by the influx of the Brahmanas. He continues that Southeast Asian region was characterised by the tribal societies, ruled by chiefs and thus, there was no indigenous sense of kingdom and its supra territorial demands of loyalty among the Southeast Asians themselves. The rulers/chiefs rather than developing state institutions initiated the religious cults to command over the native population. Der Casparis (1983) argued against the proposition of Indianisation of Southeast Asia and its continuity from early centuries of the Christian era to the later times as first contact was made in the peripheral areas, which lacked continuity to central areas (East Kalimantan and 8th century Mataram). He substituted the proposition by a complicated network of relations, both between various parts of each of the two great regions and between the two regions themselves. Apart from South India, Northeastern India (Bengal, Bihar and Orissa) also played an important part and at times, predominated in some regions. Kulke proposed 'convergence hypothesis' to highlight the relative lateness of state-formation in the Eastern and

Southern portions of Indian subcontinent with which Southeast Asia had close contact. He points out that the convergence is well demonstrated in the beginning of temple construction in Java within decades of its inception in south India. Paul Wheatly argued that the early Southeast Asian society was marked by chiefdom, among which the instrumental exchanges characteristic of a reciprocative mode of integration dominated. Entrepreneurial advances associated with developing commerce created social imbalances as 'redistributive exchange' system emerged, for instance, the case of Funan. He holds that several Southeast Asian Societies developed into 'mobilisative sectors' economies, which developed organisational mechanisms for the acquisition, control and disposal of resources in pursuit of collective goals, generally political, and impersonalism took hold. this led to the development of state-institutions and transformation of chief into rulers. The process is detailed but what leads to such changes has not been discussed by Wheatly, as there exist to such changes has not been discussed by Wheatly, as there exist alternative view regarding the nature of early exchange. The important point of his suggestions concerns the potential destabilising effects of partial borrowing of economic and political institutions from other cultures, which may be expected to provoke continuing change with the recipient cultures until a new equilibrium can be established. The importance of trade in political developments and the possibility of archaeological recovery of the phase of transition form lower to higher levels of political integration through the study of evidence from changing trade patterns have begun to be exposed in maritime Southeast Asia. Archaeological sources have supported the argument that long-distance sea trade itself played a key role in stimulating political developments which eventually led to the formation of a state. Christle (1995: 244) divides the maritime southeast Asia into three distinct grouping.

The first grouping covers the end of the pre-historic period in the maritime region (*circa* 5th century BC to 5th century AD), the archaeological remains of which includes megalithic burial sites, inhumation, hoards, boat fragments and settlement sites. The second grouping comprises several sets of early inscriptions on stone found in the region; a few other archaeological remains and some other vague references are found in Chinese records, dating 5th and 6th centuries AD. The third grouping dates 7th to 8th centuries AD, and comprises further collections of inscriptions, some rather more reliable in Chinese and a number of monumental structures and structural remains, assumed to have been produced during this period. Now, it is pertinent to discuss the process of state-formation in few parts of Southeast Asia, as it will help in locating the role of indigenous factors. The two foci of early, state-formation in the maritime Southeast Asia were the Malacca Straits and the Southern sea of the Java shore. These were also the centres of wealth accumulation and trading activities and shared a number of basic political concepts. Political developments occurred in the region owing to the response given by the coastal communities to the same external economic stimuli. The increasing wealth in these two sub-regions was increasingly concentrated in the hands of politically powerful elite who exercised some control over prestige-goods economies. Moreover, the contacts with other regions brought advanced metallurgical techniques and enhanced resource-base of the region. This expansion of economic base of a number of trading communities, possibly in conjunction with increased exposure to more developed political cultures, led to the formation of a series, first of chiefdoms, and then, of nascent states, on the relevant coasts of peninsula and the western islands. It was similar in the case of Funan, which rose on the account of developed trade and port facilities owing to strategic location and supported by an agrarian base. Hall (1949:48,49) argues that Funan may be considered as the first Southeast Asian 'state' as it was an economic centre with an economic base that supported a more sophisticated level of political integration, and acted as the locus of contact between various regional and local marketing networks. Thus, the pre-existing indigenous cultural and ethnic diversity were synthesised with external ideology to create a new systematic higher order cultural base. This is documented in the growing use of Sanskrit in Funan (Sanskrit inscriptions of 3rd century AD), use of Indian vocabulary and technical knowledge.

Thus, trade appears to have been key to economic growth, and control of trade seems to have provided the key to political development. Moreover, trade in this region was the information maximising as it carried a substantial baggage of information and ideas along with material commodities. This suggests that the carriers of most of this trade were the members of maritime Southeast Asian communities rather than outsiders. Here, an important point to be noted is that none of the communities on the East coast of the Indian sub-continent or on the mainland of Southeast Asia, involved in trade at this time, belonged to sophisticated or powerful state and all these communities were in the process of transforming themselves politically. Thus, interaction at this time was on a fairly equal basis. Therefore, it is evident that in the early period before *circa* 200 BC, the above was the case, whereas until 300 AD the other argument of outside stimuli would have been the case.

The economic stimulation came from India and China, whereas the political and cultural stimulation of the region was primarily from Indian subcontinent, probably carried along Buddhist commercial network. The period between *circa* 300 and 600 AD witnessed several fully formed states in this maritime region. Clear differences began to develop during this period between coastal trading states of the Malacca Straits and the increasingly mixed economy. The coastal trading states extended the use of Buddhism as a commercial networking religion, pulling ports of North and West Borneo into their cultural orbit. The elite groups in the states of the Java Sea and their dependencies began to add elements of Hinduism, with its royal and agrarian overtones, to the already existing Buddhist cum 'Megalithic' cultural mix of the ports. They also began to attach farming population of the interior to their coastal centres. Lastly, between seventh and ninth centuries AD, when states in both the sub-regions began to produce literature in the indigenous languages, it is apparent that the old and small states were being increasingly absorbed into larger and more complex political entities. After discussing the process of state-formation in the Southeast Asian region, owing mainly to indigenous factors with the restricted use of Indian elements, it is significant to discuss the trade between the two regions that brought about this interaction and consequent influences. Hall (1985:36-37) has presented four reasons for the growth of this trade. Firstly, historians have theorised that gold became difficult to acquire during this time due to internal disturbances in the central Asian steppe region and slow-down of the flow of Roman gold coins. Consequently, Indian merchants ventured into Southeast Asia looking for the mythical wealth of the "Islands of Gold". Secondly, it was due to revolution in boat construction and navigation techniques, which increased the size of the ships and sailing efficiency. Thirdly, the adequate ideological support provided by Buddhism played a great role as evident in the distribution of outstanding Dipankara statues of Buddha throughout the Southeast Asia. And the last reason was the Chinese interest.

Much of the interaction between Indian and maritime Southeast Asian economies were driven by interest in the trade of the South China Sea and the Eastern Seas of Indonesia. Thus, the Southeast Asian trade was entirely dependent upon the Indian Ocean and South China Sea. In the first three centuries of the Christian era, the trading relations with India is established by the distribution of Roman-Indian Rouletted pottery at a few coasts including North coasts of Java, Bali and the coast of central Vietnam. In the period between *circa* 300 and 600 AD, the volume of Buddhist pilgrimage grew that reflected growing links with India and China. The Southeast Asian trade is well documented after seventh century AD onwards. The seventh and eighth centuries AD witnessed expansion in volume of Asian sea trade involving maritime Southeast, due to Chinese interest and parallel rise in the demand from the prosperous centres on the East coast of India.

The regions that benefited the most were Javanese state of Holing and Malacca Straits port hierarchy of Srivijaya, which also created a bi-polar pattern of trade networking in the archipelago. This was followed by a decline of trade in the late eighth and the ninth centuries owing to the disintegration of the Pallava state in South India. This argument is reinforced not only by epigraphic data from the peninsula and Northeast India, but also by the archaeological evidence that a postage route across Isthmus of Kra was in use for some decades in that century. The period between early tenth and the early thirteenth centuries was marked by an economic boom, benefiting maritime Southeast Asia the most, and it affected sea trade in both the Indian Ocean and the South China Sea. The dominant economic force in the Eastern sector of the Indian Ocean was the grouping of several South Indian merchant associations or manigramam, which operated under the aegis of the expanding Chola Empire. Trade in Southern and Eastern India began to benefit from political consolidation under the Cholas. The maritime trade boom of this period included greater commercial activities; for instance volumes of trade, range of commodities and the number of regular participants were far greater and the region directly involved was far more extensive, and this trade boom was also sustained far longer. The effects on the Indonesian archipelago included increasing carrier of larger volume, lower value cargoes between islands as well as a number of technological and agricultural innovations, particularly in Java and Bali, stimulated by a combination of overseas market opportunities and domestic market pressures. The Chola raids on many Southeast Asian ports including Srivijaya itself seem to be primarily because of the economic interest, rather than mere expansion of territory. Moreover, the effects of these raids appear, for the most part, to have been minimal and transitory. The quantities of Chinese ceramics and other archaeological remains found at the extensive site of Muara-Jambi - which was apparently main port of the state by the eleventh century - indicate that Srivijaya grew increasingly wealthy on trade during the later eleventh and twelfth centuries. The decline of Srivijaya trade after 1028 AD has been countered by Christie (1996:7) as he points to a diplomatic decision by the Chinese court to restrict the burgeoning number of trade missions to port areas.

This may have brought a lull in trade missions but there was no decline in Srivijaya's wealth or power. In the context of the theory of conquest of Kheda, the archaeological remains found at the sites of Sungei Mas and Pengkalan Bujang in Kheda indicate that these ports were engaged in trade in both directions between the tenth and the thirteenth centuries. Although the remains indicate the presence of imported South Indian pottery, the religious remains prove that the port population was largely of local extraction and thus counters the conquest theory. Moreover, there is no evidence that Chola power actually extended to this coast. In Southern India, a series of merchant associations developed powerful networks and vertical monopolies that included from tied manufacturers to private armies. These are of particular interest in relation to trade with Sumatra and the Malaya peninsula, and to Javanese and Balinese responses to the growth in trade during the same period. During the period of 10th to 13th centuries AD, there occurred a shift in focus of merchant associations from the West coasts towards the East, stimulated by increasing trade with the East. It was accompanied by a broadening of the range of commodities involved in trade such as iron, cotton, textile, etc. The effects of these developments on India were seen in the field of the weaving and dyeing industries where introduction of the Draw Loom, spinning wheel and revival of coin minting took place. The Indian trade interests on the Eastern coast of the Indian Ocean is also well reflected in the Tamil language inscriptions and South Indian religious remains found on the Eastern fringe of the Indian Ocean, from Burma down to Sumatra. Many of these inscriptions are bilingual which either bear donations or gifts made to religious centres (Buddhist monasteries and Vishnu and Siva temples) or gives description of trade and the articles of merchandise. These inscriptions also refer to South Indian merchant associations' - Manigramam, actively involved in transit trade bypassing the Malacca Straits, and Nanadesi branch of the Ayyavole. However, most of the thirteenth century Tamil inscriptions do not mention merchant associations, reflecting perhaps the sharp decline in the economic power during this period, also evident from the epigraphic records in the Southern India. Tamil inscriptions and other archaeological remains suggest establishment of the South Indian enclaves to the west of the Malacca Straits. These enclaves were confined to regions accessible directly from the Indian Ocean due to the firm hold of Srivijaya over the groupings. These groupings consisted of mixed personnel of various origins and structures borrowed from Southeast Asian and South Asian societies, which is suggested by evidences from Java and Bali, such as formation of manigramam. It was followed by appearance of local version of manigramam in the major North-coastal parts of both the islands, for example at Julah, which was a predominantly local merchant association, though these local versions also included some foreigners. They were indigenous organisations linked to the local economic system and acted as tax farmers licensed by the rulers. This trend was short-lived. The abandonment of the term may reflect the retreat of organised South Indian groups to the Western edge of the archipelago. At the same time, this fact has to be noted that, in Javanese and Balinese states, the relations between tax-farming merchants and the political leadership were essentially personal, patron-client links.

Individual foreign traders from South India were also present in maritime Southeast Asian ports as merchants and tax-farmers, both before and after the appearance of manigramam in the local inscriptions. The commodities of merchandise included rice, areca nuts, pepper, mysobalans, raw-cotton and cotton-textiles, thread, wax, honey, sandalwood, aloeswood, silk, rose water, yak's tail, camphor oil, civet, horses, elephants, medicinal herbs, semi-precious stones, pearls and metals such as gold, silver, iron, etc. There occurred noticeable changes in the patterns of domestic consumption and production due to large volume of foreign imports and their varied distribution. Another important related aspect is the balance of trade and role of ports at different islands. Although the Malacca Straits port-hierarchy of Srivijaya played an important role in maintaining a largely indigenous hold over the sea-trade links eastwards from the Indian Ocean, partly by forcing powerful South Indian merchant associations to trade on local terms, it was the state of Mataram in Java that played the key role in moulding maritime Southeast Asia's shared economic culture. The state of Mataram played an important role in integrating the long distance sea trade of the ports of Java and Bali into the domestic economies of the two islands that increased the economic influence of the region. In context of influence of Indic elements, it was used as a means of elevating the status of indigenous rulers both in the eyes of their own people and with the visiting Indian merchants whose presence was essential to continue prosperity. The Indian rituals and celestial deities provided the sacro-religious legitimacy to local rulers. The Brahmanas played an important part by performing rituals and concocting genealogies for the local rulers, thus providing legitimacy to the local ruling dynasties By the tenth century, many texts including a few Parvans of the Mahabharata were translated into local languages like Javanese prose. Most of Sanskrit language inscriptions were largely religious in content. The continuing impact of cultural borrowings from India was also reflected in these inscriptions by the heavy use of Sanskrit conceptual vocabulary, the integration of some Indian weights and measures into the local system and the adoption of Sanskrit or Sanskritised names.

The presence of two Buddha statues at Kotachina (Sumatra) points to the influence of Chola sculpture on local building techniques and materials used to build these statues were imported from India. In Kadiri period in East Java, predominance of Vaishnavism is reflected in court poetry of old Javanese literature Another example of Indian influence is the great temple of Angkorvat in Cambodia. Many Indian texts were translated in Southeast Asia like Raghuvamsa of Kalidas. Apart from Buddhist sculpture an Indian affinity is also reflected in the particular form of Tantricism in East Java. Islam in these regions appears to have come from Malabar region of Indian subcontinent, not from the Arab world as has been generally argued. Therefore, it can be argued that the Southeast Asian states borrowed extensively from the broader Indian religious traditions in a manner that suggests a conscious balancing of ideas thought to be useful for the maintenance of power in economies at once agrarian and mercantile. Indian export trade provoked shifts in the habits of consumption that in turn stimulated innovations in the local production. The religious and cultural impact was restricted to the rulers and the elite sections of the society and did not make many inroads into the local level. Thus, it has rightly been argued by Christie (1999:38) that the economic competition and mutual influence rather than forceful confrontation characterised the relations between the Southeast Asia and India. The notion of Indianisation / colonisation of Southeast Asia was the result of a different time when there was a paucity of sources and researches whereas with new researches and discoveries it has been substantially proved that it was a two-way process. The islands of Southeast Asia were already in the process of development and growth, and Indian contacts merely facilitated this process.

Indo-ASEAN Matrix in Current International Relations

On August 9,1965 Singapore, much against the wishes of its leaders, seceded from Malaysia and proclaimed itself as a sovereign independent Republic. Within a month of Singapore's independence, the India-Pakistani conflict of 1965 took place. Singapore was the first country which extended spontaneous support to

India; Malaysia also supported Indian stance in the UN Security Council. On September 9,1965 Lee Kuan Yew declared that Singapore supported India "because India is a friend of Singapore". Naturally the Singapore reaction was widely publicised in the Indian media.

In retrospect, the late 1960's and early 1970's were a period of missed opportunities. Singapore's attempts to befriend India was understandable; India was the undisputed leader of the non-aligned world; Singapore wanted to project the image that it was not a "Third China"; and what is more, the two countries shared the common commitment to secularism and multi-culturalism. Unfortunately Singapore's request that India should assist in the building up of its national army did not elicit a favourable response. The leaders of Singapore believed that its two close Malay neighbours, Malaysia and Indonesia, with whom India had close relations, would not have taken it amiss, if the Singapore armed forces were trained by a friendly, non-aligned country like India. According to informed sources, when Singapore started its national carrier, the Singapore Airlines, the SIA approached Air India for technical and manpower co-operation. When the British bases were wound up, Singapore was keen that India should make use of the dockyard and other facilities for ship building and repair. Once again a golden opportunity to develop Indian stakes in the region was missed.

As far as civilizational states like India and China are concerned, no epoch in history is complete by itself; it is both a continuation and a beginning. Prime Minister Narasimha Rao underscored this basic reality in his famous speech "India and the Asia-Pacific-Forging a new Relationship" in October 1994 at the Institute of Southeast Asian Studies in Singapore. The closer relationship which India seeks today with Southeast Asian countries, especially Singapore, has to be fashioned on twin foundations - the benign interaction of the past and mutuality of interests that exist at present. In its relations with Southeast Asian countries, India has several plus points. Historically Burma, Thailand, Malaysia, Indonesia, Laos and Cambodia have been deeply influenced by Indian political ideas, religion, art and language.

The spread of Indian cultural influences, leading to the cultural enrichment of Southeast Asian countries, constitute a glorious chapter in Southeast Asian and Indian history alike. Indianised Kingdoms like Funan, Sri Kshetra, Pagan, Khemer, Sri Vijaya, Sailendra and Majapahit; the familiar Indo-Sanskritic vocabulary in Thai language and Bahasa Indonesia; architectural monuments like Angkor, pagan, Borobudur and Lara Djonggrong; literary masterpieces like Ramkein, Amaramala, Arjuna Vivaha and Bharata Yudhha, the Wajang Kulit based on the Ramayana and Mahabharata traditions; the living Indian traditions in the island of Bali-all these are testimony to the courage and zeal of Indian princes, priests, poets, merchants and artisans and the ingratiating an assimilable qualities of the peoples of Southeast Asian countries. The spread of Chinese influences in Vietnam was an offshoot of political subjugation and consequent Sinicitation of that country. On the contrary, Indian influences spread into the region in a peaceful way. Except for the solitary incident of Chola invasion of southeast Asia, no other Indian ruler embarked on military expeditions. Secondly, Indian contacts with Southeast Asia did not snap in the thirteenth century. Recent researches in maritime history clearly prove that the Keralites, Tamils and Gujaratis had extensive contacts with Southeast Asia during the medieval period. In fact, in the Islamisation of Indonesia, the Muslims from Gujarat and Malabar, Tamil Nadu and Bengal played decisive roles. Thirdly, Indian historians must reevaluate the concept of "Greater India". The concept was a product of Indian national movement and it gave Indians a sense of pride in their glorious history. At the same time, its leading protagonists, more often than not, adopted a patronising tone and denied Southeast Asian cultures autonomy of their own. Southeast Asian scholars are deeply sensitive and felt hurt because of this attitude of turning a "Nelson's eye" to the rich and virile indigenous cultural traits, which developed in different parts of Southeast Asia, even before contacts with India was established. The last four decades have not seen much improvement in the academic scene. Despite our maritime heritage, few people in India are conscious of the fact that the island of Pu Bresh, located in the Northwest of Sumatra, is only 92 nautical miles away from Indira Point, which is less than the distance between Madras and Tirupati. Similarly, Phuket in Thailand is only 273 nautical miles away from Indira Point, which is less than the distance between Madras and Madurai. The Thais and the Indonesians also share this profound ignorance of geographical realities.

India has land and maritime boundaries with Myanmar, and maritime boundaries with Thailand and Indonesia. These countries are not only our next door neighbours, they have been, as stated earlier, profoundly influenced by India in the cultural sphere. It is interesting to note that historians like K.M. Panikkar, Nilakanta Shastri and RC. Majumdar used the term Southeast Asia to cover both South Asia and Southeast Asia. By accepting the American concept that Southeast Asia - countries stretching from Myanmar to the Philippines - is a different area, we intellectually distanced ourselves from our immediate neighbours. The concept of ocean as a unifying force and focus of regional cooperation has not yet been fully grasped. Take Southeast Asia as an example. Except Laos, which is land locked, all others are maritime countries. Singapore is an island state and Indonesia and the Philippines are archipelagic states. Even within ASEAN, issues relating to maritime cooperation have not received adequate attention.

Historically all members of the Bay of Bengal Community - India, Bangladesh, Myanmar, Thailand, Malaysia, Singapore, Indonesia and Sri Lanka - have witnessed dynamic interaction between maritime trade and cultural evolution. The Bay of Bengal is a composite geographical and ecological unit. It is about the same size as the Mediterranean Sea. The littoral states contain almost one fourth of the world's population. Bay of Bengal is a gift of "mother Nature" and the littoral states can co-operate with one another for common well being. If the littoral states could cooperate in the crucial area of weather forecasting, preventive measures can be adopted and the population could be removed from coastal areas well in advance of nature's fury. Similarly Bay of Bengal is being used by the northeast insurgents in India and the Liberation Tigers of Tamil Eelam (LTTE) in Sri Lanka for illegal smuggling of weapons. This maritime terrorism could easily be contained if the littoral states co-operate with one another. The list can be multiplied. In short, exploitation of living and non-living maritime resources; development of maritime communications; ship building and ship repair; weather forecasting; prevention of pollution and combating of maritime terrorism - these tasks which are the exclusive responsibilities of individual countries at present can best be accomplished through regional co-operation. Unlike the South China Sea, where conflicting territorial claims threaten peace and stability, the Bay of Bengal region is relatively an area of tranquility. India has settled its maritime boundaries with all Southeast Asian neighbours. Agreements were signed with Indonesia in 1974 and 1977; with Thailand in 1978; with Mynamar in 1987; and the trijunction among India, Thailand and Indonesia in 1978. As far as South Asia is concerned, the maritime boundaries with Sri Lanka were demarcated by maritime agreements in 1974 and 1976.

The agreements were based on the principle of equidistance, though in the case of Sri Lanka and Myanmar some concessions were made by New Delhi in the name of good neighbourly relations. The only unsettled maritime border is with Bangladesh. India's keenness to settle the border is not reciprocated by Dacca. What is more, the New Moore island is a subject matter of territorial dispute between the two countries. The increased co-operation, however, suffered a temporary setback following Pokhran II in May 1998. It is, however, necessary to highlight the fact that in the Manila Summit, despite strong pressure from United States, Japan and the European Community, the ASEAN leaders sidestepped the issue of condemning India and Pakistan for the nuclear tests. The Chairman's statement only "expressed grave concern and strongly deplored the recent nuclear tests in South Asia".

In this connection, New Delhi should seriously consider one policy option. Over the years, India has consistently opposed the concept of "nuclear free zone" in different regions. In the context of changed strategic environment in Southeast Asia and the imperatives of improving relations with countries in the region, India should seriously consider endorsing the Treaty of Southeast Asian Nuclear Free Zone (SEANWFZ). The five nuclear powers have taken an ambiguous stand on this proposal. If India supports the concept of SEANWFZ, naturally it would be welcomed by all Southeast Asian countries. The Bay of Bengal Community - as a specific area of regional cooperation - deserves greater attention from academics and policy planners alike. The first welcome step in this direction was the establishment of Bangladesh-India-Myanmar-Sri Lanka-Thailand Economic

Co-operation (BIMSTEC) in June 1998. This is the first organisation of its kind, in which two ASEAN members have come together with three countries of South Asia for economic co-operation. The areas identified for co-operation include communication, infra-structure, energy, trade, investment, tourism and fisheries. It is high time that New Delhi takes the initiative and opens a dialogue with Malaysia, Singapore and Indonesia to form a wider Bay of Bengal Community. By forming such an organisation the "extended neighbourhood", as the Ministry of External Affairs refers to these countries, would rightly become a part of the "immediate neighbourhood". The concept of the Bay of Bengal Community would become the common agenda of all littoral states. The idea of Bay of Bengal Community deserves serious consideration for two additional reasons. First, it would enable India to come out of the India-Pakistan deadlock which had been the course of South Asian Cooperation. Prime Minister Vajpayee's visit to Lahore and the inauguration of Delhi-Lahore-Delhi bus service in February 1999 were illustrations of New Delhi's sincere desire to build bridges with Pakistan which would pave the way for a secure and peaceful South Asia. However the recent Kargil crisis and Pakistan's blatant involvement in the violation of the Line of Control in Jammu and Kashmir have set the clock back as far as the peace process is concerned. What is more, international response had been very favourable to India. Washington, in particular and Beijing, to some extent, had played decisive roles in persuading Pakistan to end its misadventure.

The two countries are of the view that India-Pakistan differences should be resolved through mutual dialogue. The ASEAN has also echoed the same sentiments. In a Joint Communique issued at the end of the recent meeting of the Foreign Ministers, ASEAN has urged India and Pakistan to adhere to the process of dialogue to resolve the "dispute". Second is the China factor. The Southeast Asian countries are today engaged in constructive interaction with China; at the same time, they have, in varying degrees, apprehensions and misgivings about China's long-term intentions and objectives. The Sino-Vietnamese conflict in March 1988 near the Spratlys is a grim reminder that China would take advantage of the vulnerability of its southern neighbours and would even resort to force to buttress its claims. The problem has been rendered complex by the granting of oil exploration licenses by both Hanoi and Beijing in the same areas. In February 1995, China and the Philippines clashed over territorial claims in Mischief Reef. In December 1998 the Filipino and the Chinese navies had another altercation in the same area; in July 1999, tension again erupted following the sinking of a Chinese boat by the Filipino navy.

Despite Beijing's attempts to shelve the territorial claims, discerning observers continue to look at South China Sea as a likely flash point. The fact that China and Pakistan do not belong to the Bay of Bengal community are plus factors; it would definitely reduce strategic dissonance in the region. By the end of the 1950's India's friendship with China (which enabled India to play a significant role in the Geneva Conference, 1954) had not frozen in the snows of the Himalayas. The Indian image in Southeast Asia suffered considerable damage as a result of military defeat in the India-China War, October-November 1962. Though Indian victory in the India-Pakistan War 1971 and the liberation of Bangladesh refurbished India's image to some extent, its impact on Southeast Asia was lessened by two important events, which diametrically changed the international relations in South and Southeast Asia. The first was the Sino-American rapproachement, which culminated in the visit of President Nixon to China in February 1972. Second was the Treaty of Peace, Friendship and Co-operation, which India signed with the Soviet Union in August 1971. While the Treaty was a response to what India perceived as a convergence of interests among Islamabad, Washington and Beijing to the tumultuous developments in the sub-continent, the Southeast Asian countries perceived it as a serious compromise on India's policy of non-alignment. What is more, since the member states of ASEAN viewed Moscow with considerable suspicion, even Indian bonafides were occasionally questioned in ASEAN capitals. As a result, Southeast Asia occupied a low priority for India.

The Indian attitude towards ASEAN, during early years, was also ambivalent. ASEAN came into existence in 1967, when the United States was escalating the Vietnam War. What is more, the original five members were aligned to the West in varying degrees. The Western orientation of ASEAN and the role of the Philippines and Thailand in the Second Indo-China War made New Delhi distance itself from this regional grouping. However, this stance was in sharp contrast to China which condemned ASEAN as "puny counter-revolutionary alliance" and the member states as "US imperialism's running dogs in Southeast Asia". With the acceptance of Zone of Peace, Freedom and Neutrality (ZOPFAN) in November 1971, India felt that it could find commonality of interests with ASEAN. It must however be borne in mind that endorsement of this principle did not imply that the member states of ASEAN shared the same security perspectives. However, in New Delhi's perception, ZOPFAN represented all that India stood for - the acceptance of the principles of non-alignment, and the removal of external influences which would pave the way for the establishment of an area of peace in Southeast Asia. In 1973, at the end of Indonesian Foreign Minister Adam Malik's visit to New Delhi, India made the first explicit reference welcoming ASEAN initiatives. However, the Indo-Soviet Treaty, India's ambivalence on the question of Soviet invasion of Afghanistan, and finally the recognition of the Heng Samrin Government in July 1981 - all these led to estrangement between India and ASEAN. As Kripa Sridharan has pointed out, the period "between 1980-1984 proved to be the most frigid in India-ASEAN relations". New Delhi's attitude towards the Kampuchean crisis was a direct consequence of its assessment of the Sino-Vietnamese differences and the security threat posed to Vietnam by the Pol Pot regime backed by China. What is more, the United States escalated the Sino-Vietnamese differences by supporting China against Vietnam. Hanoi was forced into the Soviet embrace because of Sino-American policies; what is more, the policy of ostracising Vietnam, which was followed by ASEAN, backed by the United States and China, only enhanced Hanoi's dependence on Moscow. The ASEAN did not share this perception. According to ASEAN, Vietnamese invasion of Kampuchea itself was a direct security threat to Thailand, the frontline state. In some ways, Indonesia and Malaysia, shared the Indian perceptions of the Third Indo-China War. Important leaders in Indonesia always had great admiration for Vietnamese struggle for independence. They were also appreciative of Hanoi's attempts to steer clear of the Sino-Soviet rivalry and emerge as a regional power, enjoying autonomy of action vis-a-vis external powers. What is more, Vietnamese antipathy towards China was as strong as that of Indonesia. Jakarta and Kuala Lumpur were suspicious of the long term consequences of China's policy "of fighting Vietnam to the last Khmer soldier". According to Ghazalie Shafie, then Malaysian Foreign Minister, it was in Peking's interest to continue the "leechcraft" so that Vietnam remained weak, disillusioned and internationally ostracised. The unfortunate phase, when "ASEAN-India relations tended to be conditioned by factors extraneous to purely bilateral interaction and overlooked the imperatives of common interest and mutual benefit" is over and an era of co-operative co-existence and begin interaction has begun. India's "Look East policy" coincided with ASEAN's "Look West policy". In 1992, at the Singapore Summit, India was made a Sectoral Dialogue partner.

The potential and success of that partnership was realized soon and in the historic summit in Bangkok in 1995, the decision was taken to elevate India to a Full Dialogue partners. From the Indian point of view, it should be acknowledged that Singapore had played a key role in renewing India's links with ASEAN. Singapore was India's Country Co-ordinator in ASEAN since India became a Sectoral Dialogue partner in 1992. It may be mentioned that ASEAN admitted India, China and Russia together as dialogue partners in the Post Ministerial Conference in Jakarta in July 1996. India was also invited to join the ASEAN Regional Forum (ARF), the ASEAN propelled multilateral security dialogue platform. The significance of India becoming a Full Dialogue partner was highlighted by then Minister for External Affairs I.K. Gujral as follows: "The ASEAN decision to make India a full dialogue partner is based on your far sighted assessment about the political and strategic convergence, acceleration of economic relations and their future potential, and complementarities in areas that were hitherto not evident or remained unexploited... A key objective of India and ASEAN to move from derivative to direct relationship so that there are no distortions, no misperceptions, no ignorance and no intermediation". The post-war developments in Southeast Asia, especially in Singapore, has one positive lesson for India. Southeast Asian countries have made impressive progress in reducing absolute poverty and raising the quality of life of their peoples-better educational facilities, health care, housing and improvement in sanitation. In the Indian situation, even after fifty-two years of independence 423 million people live in absolute poverty, and the rate of literacy is only 61 per cent. Southeast Asian countries were more or less on par with India on the eve of independence; but over the years, thanks to the enlightened policies of their governments, they have made commendable progress. One advantage that Southeast Asian countries had was the defence arrangements with the Western countries which enabled them to keep the defence expenditure to the minimum. The writing on the wall is clear-human development requires a higher priority in India, if India is not to lag behind other developing countries. The accelerated pace of growth is Southeast Asian countries was facilitated by sound infra-structure-power stations, telecommunication facilities, banking and insurance systems and well organised transport system. India hopes to attract huge investments in communications, highways, power generation and development of ports. From an Indian point of view, Singapore has an additional advantage. It is a window to other parts of Southeast Asia. Indian exports, in Singapore dollar terms, grew by 26 per cent during January-November 1998. The balance of trade remains in favour of Singapore at the ratio of 16:5. An important feature of this bilateral trade is the interpret role played by Singapore, with approximately 40 per cent of the trade, both ways, comprising of re-exports.

Another interesting feature of the trade is that the share of manufactured goods is increasing. There is great scope for quantum jump in trade in agricultural produce. In order to attain this objective, India should pay greater attention to quality upgradation, better packaging, introduction of brand names and better transport facilities. The service trade between India and ASEAN is also on the increase. Transport, tourism, aviation, management consultancy, engineering designs and drawing, infrastructure such as roads, power plants and telecommunications-ASEAN countries have been evincing keen interest in developing linkages with India. Indian joint ventures have been in operation in Southeast Asian countries since the early 1960's. Even today the largest concentration of Indian joint ventures is in the ASEAN region. The performance had been mixed, with some outstanding successes and few abysmal failures. In mid-1990's, India had 20 joint ventures with Indonesia with an investment of US $20.26 million; there were 45 joint ventures in Malaysia with an investment of US $30 million; 58 joint ventures companies in Singapore with an investment of US $20 million and 27 joint ventures in Thailand with an investment of US $16.5 million. By 1996, approved direct investments from Southeast Asian countries, in million rupees, were as follows: Singapore-1891.9; Malaysia 129.8; Indonesia (1995)-3133.0; Thailand-414.1; Vietnam 0.3 and the Philippines 2557.5. Joint collaboration, utilising Indian skilled labour and Southeast Asian capital for investment in Third World countries - especially in Vietnam, Laos and Cambodia - is another dimension, which should be pursued. The proposed Making Development project and the trans-Asian railways and roadways can provide opportunities in this direction. The economic crisis in the region indicates that difficult times are ahead for Southeast Asia. From being examples of rapid economic development, these countries are today facing economic stagnation and decline. Growth rates that averaged 8 to 10 per cent per annum over many years have plummeted to negative rates of growth. Economies which had full employment and labour shortage are undergoing increasing unemployment, galloping inflation and flight of foreign capital.

Compounding the situation, the crisis has triggered interethnic tensions and political turbulence, especially in Indonesia. The fractured electoral verdict indicates that Golkar is on its way out and a long spell of political instability will ensue. Religious clashes and violent attacks on the ethnic Chinese are symptomatic of the increasing fissures in social fabric. As Lee Khoon Choy, the former Singapore Ambassador to Indonesia, has summed up: "Indonesia is becoming economically ravaged, spiritually plundered, politically distraught and socially incoherent". The developments in Indonesia, the largest and the most populous in the region, will have profound consequences. It is worth remembering that the main catalyst in the formation of ASEAN were the traumatic developments in Indonesia - the October 1965 coup, the downfall of Sukarno and the emergence of the New Order under Suharto. The Indonesian foreign policy was characterised by its pro-Western orientation, moderation and good neighbourly relations, occasionally even bending backwards, to attain the common goals of ASEAN. The Indonesian commitment to ASEAN has been summed up by Ghazalie Shafie as follows: "ASEAN was liked to a cluster of bamboos, each of which was an independent entity, and which together could withstand turbulent winds; the tallest of the bamboos must always stoop its head. Indonesia is a large country but it has never imposed its will on the ASEAN neighbours". Prolonged instability in Indonesia is bound to have adverse consequences on ASEAN unity. Of equal importance is the continuing strategic fluidity in the region and the likely response of three major external actors - United States, China and Japan. So long as the convergence of interests continue, ASEAN will have the manoeuverability to chart its own destiny. In the keynote address to the recent ASEAN summit, Prime Minister Goh Chok Thong identified the growing tensions among USA, China and Japan as a matter of serious concern. As ASEAN moves ahead into the twenty-first century, fresh challenges will spur the political ingenuity of the new generation of leaders likely to emerge in Southeast Asian countries.

ASEAN-India Partnership for Peace, Progress and Shared Prosperity

We, the Heads of State/Government of Brunei Darussalam, the Kingdom of Cambodia (Cambodia), the Republic of Indonesia (Indonesia), the Lao People's Democratic Republic (Lao PDR), Malaysia, the Union of Myanmar (Myanmar), the Republic of the Philippines (the Philippines), the Republic of Singapore (Singapore), the Kingdom of Thailand (Thailand) and the Socialist Republic of Vietnam (Vietnam), Member Countries of the Association of Southeast Asian Nations (collectively, "ASEAN" or "ASEAN Member Countries", or individually, "ASEAN Member Country"), and the Republic of India (India) gathered in Vientiane, Lao PDR, on 30th November 2004 for the 3rd ASEAN-India Summit;

Adhering to the principles and purposes of the Charter of the United Nations, the Five Principles of Peaceful Co-existence and other universally recognised principles of international law;

Reaffirming our faith in, and respect for, each other's independence, sovereignty, territorial integrity, non-interference in the internal affairs of other states, mutual respect and mutual benefit;

Bound Together by our shared rich and valuable heritage of civilisation, culture, and peaceful economic and social interaction and linkages extending over two millennia as well as by the pluralistic, multi-religious and culturally diverse nature of our respective societies;

Building on the deep and widespread people-to-people linkages and friendship between the Member Countries of ASEAN and India;

Noting with deep satisfaction that the close cooperative and multifaceted partnership, which our countries have fostered, encompassing the political, security, economic, scientific and technological, human resource development, social, cultural and other areas of mutual interest that provides a solid foundation for taking the ASEAN-India partnership to greater heights and new areas;

Determined to optimally utilise our talented and youthful human and rich natural resources, and core competencies in many state-of-the-art technologies and knowledge-based industries;

Convinced that ASEAN-India cooperation serves the essential interests of their peoples and is essential for promoting peace, stability, development and prosperity in Asia and the world;

Aspiring to play a more active role and to meet the political, economic, social and other challenges facing our region in the coming decades, and in helping to shape the world of the 21st century;

Recalling the Joint Statement issued after the 1st ASEAN-India Summit Meeting in Phnom Penh in November 2002 and the agreements and understandings reached during the 2nd ASEAN-India Summit Meeting in Bali in October 2003; and

Attaching great significance to the Framework Agreement on Comprehensive Economic Cooperation between ASEAN and India signed in Bali for realising the full potential of ASEAN-India Regional Trade and Investment Area (RTIA) and economic cooperation.

Hereby commit ourselves to:

- Foster friendship, good neighbourliness, peaceful co-existence and prosperity in the region;
- Promote a long term co-operative partnership based on equality, shared ownership and mutual respect which will enable us to impart synergies to our respective strengths and complementarities to achieve our respective long-term national and regional development goals;
- Cooperate in a coordinated manner to accelerate and mutually reinforce sustainable growth and development of our economies towards shared prosperity, poverty alleviation and reduction of social disparities, to enable our people to enjoy unhindered access to opportunities for development;
- Cooperate in strengthening the UN system, including support for early reforms of the United Nations and the Bretton Woods institutions to make them more democratic and responsive to the priorities of its member states particularly, the developing countries;
- Cooperate in other multilateral fora, in particular the WTO, greater equity and greater benefits from globalisation for the developing countries;
- Jointly address the common challenges to our comprehensive political and economic security, including food, human and energy security;
- Cooperate in combating the menace of international terrorism and other transnational crimes such as trafficking in drugs, arms smuggling, human trafficking particularly in women and children, cyber crimes, international economic crimes, environmental crimes, sea piracy and money laundering, through effective institutional linkages and programmes of cooperation giving priority to information exchange and capacity building;
- Collaborate in areas of general and complete disarmament, and in the non-proliferation of weapons of mass destruction under strict and effective international control;
- Take full advantage of the geographical contiguity of Southeast Asia and India and synergise the strengths of these two significant economic regions to act as powerful engines of growth;
- Give high priority to development of regional infrastructure and road, rail, sea and air transportation links to increase physical connectivity that would facilitate greater movement of goods and people;
- Facilitate travel and tourism between ASEAN and India by developing links of tourist centres to enhance synergies of tourism destinations;
- Promote cooperation in science and technology, in particular information technology and biotechnology, including through joint research and development and commercialisation of new technologies;
- Work through both conventional and innovative trade and economic

arrangements, and full implementation of the ASEAN-India free trade area by 2011 for ASEAN-5 and India, 2016 for the Philippines and India and by 2011 by India and 2016 by the 4 new ASEAN Members Countries, including the early implementation of the Early Harvest Programme, to achieve freer movement of goods, services, investment, and cooperation in other economic areas;

- Reiterate full support for the implementation of the Declaration of ASEAN Concord II, leading to the formation of a more integrated ASEAN Community comprising the ASEAN Security Community, the ASEAN Economic Community and the ASEAN Socio-Cultural Community;
- Cooperate to help bridge the development gap among various regions and countries, including through support to the Initiative for ASEAN Integration and sub-regional growth areas in ASEAN, and cooperation schemes between ASEAN Member Countries and India;
- Promote cooperation in human resource development, through capacity building, strengthening of institutions, training and entrepreneurship development focussing on small and medium enterprises;
- Promote people-to-people exchange involving, among others, parliamentarians, youth, artists, sportspersons and representatives from business, industry, media, academic and think-tank institutions; and
- Preserve our cultural heritage, and promote cultural cooperation for better understanding and friendship among our peoples.

Institutional and Funding Arrangements for Implementation

To realise the objectives of the ASEAN-India Partnership, the following measures will be taken:

- ASEAN and India will implement specific activities and projects as contained in the attached Plan of Action;
- ASEAN and India will strengthen the existing funding mechanisms, including the ASEAN-India Cooperation Fund, for effective cooperation and implementation of the ASEAN-India Partnership and Plan of Action;
- ASEAN and India are committed to providing requisite resources and in accordance with their respective capacities, including mutually exploring effective and innovative external resource mobilisation efforts, to accomplish the various strategies and measures outlined in the Plan of Action;
- The progress made in the implementation of the ASEAN-India Partnership and the Plan of Action will be reviewed by the Senior Officials and the Foreign Ministers of ASEAN and India under the ASEAN-India Dialogue Relations; and

The Plan of Action will be reviewed periodically taking into consideration the dynamic developments in the region and the world.

Signed in Vientiane, Lao PDR this Thirtieth Day of November in the Year Two Thousand and Four in two originals in the English language.

India, ASEAN, and the Indian Ocean

Historical and cultural links between India and the countries of Southeast Asia go back thousands of years and hardly need to be repeated. These ancient linkages, however, provide an ambience and can be built upon. Economically, India and the countries around the eastern part of the Indian Ocean, or the Bay of Bengal, formed a close-knit community. Textiles from the Coromandel coast of India and from Gujarat, and rice and sugar from Bengal were exchanged for spices, silver and gold from Java, Sumatra and the Moluccas, and tin from Malaya. There were large colonies of Indian traders at Malaka, Aceh and at a number of ports in Indonesia. It was this integrated Asian trade which made the Dutch East India company to proceed from Southeast Asia to India, and the English East India company to proceed from India to the Spice Island and Malaka. The point to note is that while the European Companies were always on the look out to create monopolies, the Indian, Indonesian, Polynesian and Chinese traders proceeded on a basis of free trade. This is an interesting commentary on those who try to present free trade as a gift of the developed West or specifically of the US to the rest of the world. The economic symbiosis of India and the Southeast Asian countries was broken with the rise of colonialism, with each colonial power trying to integrate the economy of its colony into its home market. With the end of colonialism, hopes were raised of reviving old ties on the basis of Asian unity, non-alignment and south-south economic cooperation.

These concepts had their own limitations but, before they could be fully explored, the growing Cold War created animosities and suspicions, leading to a set back. As a part of the Cold War scenario, Asia was fragmented into regions - West Asia, Central Asia, South Asia, Southeast Asia, East Asia, etc. The postulate was that each of these regions would work in isolation from each other, enabling the US to establish strategic relations with them according to its convenience and requirements. That this approach did not coincide with the developmental needs of the various regions was of little concern to the Cold War strategists. The rise of NAM and the Group of 77 was a small attempt to reverse this process, but with limited success. A new situation has been created with the end of the Cold War. The attempt of the European countries to establish an European Union, and the growth of economic blocs in various parts of the world had its inevitable impact on Asia. The rapid rise of the economies of many Southeast Asian countries transformed ASEAN from a strategic bloc into more of an economic bloc. However, it was realised that such an economic bloc could not succeed without broadening its horizons from Southeast Asia. Hence, the creation of APEC which also included the US, Japan, China and Australia. India, which had kept out of ASEAN, seeing it only as an US-sponsored strategic bloc, began slowly to reassess its earlier position. This process became more rapid after it embarked on a process of liberalisation in 1991. It showed interest in the membership of the ASEAN, and after some hesitation was accepted as a dialogue partner of APEC and as a full-fledged member of the strategic forum, ARF. India's desire to be a full-fledged member of APEC remains pending. Meanwhile, the recent Southeast Asian melt down has created problems and led to a new situation of flux.

Southeast Asian Melt Down and Recovery

The melt down of 1997 came as a great shock to many of the Southeast Asian countries which had planned and hoped to be able to join the "Rich men's Club" by 2020, without going through a difficult and often painful process of internal change and readjustment. This had also resulted in the growth of a certain superiority complex or an arrogant attitude in dealing with Asian countries outside the ASEAN. Thus, India was almost made to feel a suppliant in its desire to join ASEAN, rather than welcoming its move as a reflection of a healthy desire for outward growth. The lessons of the 1997 melt down have been much debated, with many of the western commentators trying to pin the responsibility to the deficient infrastructure and cronyism of Southeast Asian countries. These have been examined by Dr. Mahathir Mohamad in his book *A New Deal for Asia*, and in his recent address to the Cairo University on the occasion of the 10th Summit of the G-15 countries of which Malaysia is a member. He has rightly emphasised the role of hedge funds, and international currency operators in aggravating the crisis, and the inability or unwillingness of the IMF to see the Asian situation and trying to apply to it uncritically the methods it had adopted to meet the South American crisis. Mahathir has promised to fight "tooth and nail" any new western attempt to hinder Asian development and to bring Asian economies under its domination in the name of globalisation.

Dr. Mahathir's warning is timely because warning bells have been sounded about the prospects of continued economic growth in Southeast Asia. In a recent report, Bill Belchere, Asian Economist at Merill Lynch in Singapore, concluded that "Asia's healing process... appears to be losing momentum". Several economists are lowering their regional growth forecasts by one to two per cent points, to between 3 to 5 per cent next year, and many say a hard landing in the US could cut even deeper.' Equity investors have already pulled billions of dollars out of Thailand, the Philippines, Malaysia and Indonesia. Foreign investments have slowed down considerably. As Malaysia's Deputy Finance Minister, Dr. Shafie Salleh said candidly, the inflow of foreign funds had adopted a watch and wait approach, and were cautious when investing not only in Malaysia but also in Asia as a whole. Many reasons have been cited for this - that on account of the rapid recovery there has hardly been any restructuring so that the banks still have billions of bad debts, and that cronyism is still strong, banks still lending money to those who are politically well connected rather than having means to repay. Thus, a vicious circle has been created - the economy will not really revive till debts are repaid, but debts cannot be repaid till the economy revives. In many cases, there is also a lack of will to repay, hoping for a political bail out. Political uncertainties in the region could also derail economic recovery. Indonesia, which is the most populous country of the region and will have a big influence on the economy of its neighbours, is still in doldrums. Three years after the Asian financial crisis struck, the Indonesian economy is still in limbo, with national debt accounting for more than 80 per cent of its gross national product. This despite an US 46 billion packages from the IMF Of course, twenty years of authoritarian rule and cronyism cannot be overcome in a year's time. Abdurrahman Wahid's valiant effort to establish a democracy based on liberal Islam is being hampered by fundamentalist groups encouraging religious conflict in the name of *jehad*, ethnic tensions, separatism, difficulties in reducing the political and economic clout of the army, and corruption in high places. While internal difficulties are real enough, it is seen that the Southeast Asian recovery was largely based on growing exports to the US. This, in turn, had a large component of electronic goods and computer hardware, which have reached a saturation point. Heavy dependence of Southeast Asian countries on the US for their exports and in their economy.

Dr. Mohammed Arif, Executive Director, Malaysian Institute of Economic Research, agrees that the near term prospect of Southeast Asian countries "is dependent on the happenings in the US and Japan" and that a downturn in the US economy would affect those economies that are heavily dependent on the US market, and that "it is Malaysia that will be affected most, given the composition of its exports to the US Nor will Japan be able to compensate for the US slowdown since the Japanese economy "remains sedated". While hard decisions regarding internal restructuring will have to be taken by the countries of the region, the role of India - both on account of its geographical position, size of economy and its foreign orientation - cannot be underestimated. At the outset it should be noted that India remained largely unaffected, both by the Southeast Asian meltdown and by the sanctions imposed upon it following its nuclear explosions in Pokharan in May 1998. The Indian economy grew 7.5 per cent in 1996, declined to 5 per cent in 1997, but grew to 6.8 per cent in 1998 and 6.4 per cent in 1999. It is expected to grow 7 per cent in 2000. This shows both the strength of the Indian infrastructure, and the determination by successive governments of deciding its own priorities, adopting a step by step strategy towards liberalisation rather than the leap through strategy enunciated and pressed by the IMF and tried with disastrous results by Russia following the break-up of the Soviet Union. Second, despite India's wide ranging poverty - even now 35 per cent of India's population is still below the poverty-line, it should be remembered that India has a huge internal market with a middle class of 200 millions with considerable purchasing power. Thus, India today is one of the emerging big market. It is this which brought the US President Bill Clinton to India, and made him dance in a village square in Rajasthan. Of course, we do not expect Dr. Mahathir or Gus Dur (Abdurrahman Wahid, President of Indonesia) to do likewise. But it is necessary for the leadership in these and other Southeast Asian countries to note the strength and opportunity provided by the Indian market and the ability and will of successive Indian governments to withstand external pressure considered harmful to national developmental efforts or self-respect. As it is, it is South Korea which has seen the potential of the Indian market before many others.

It has established a definite share in the car market of India for which global giants from Western countries and Japan are competing. South Korea has also established itself in the field of consumer electronics. In 1995, Malaysia had 39 joint ventures in operation or under implementation while Singapore had 37. These have not grown significantly since then. However, Singapore, South Korea are the only East Asian countries which have tried seriously to tap the Indian market. Like India, China is also an emerging big market and has a growing trade with ASEAN. But it is not argued that India or China should be seen as a substitute or replacement of the Western market. There is no turning back from globalisation. What is being argued is the need for diversification, and of the advantage of neighbourhood markets both on account of cost benefit and in many cases acceptability on account of shared cultural values. There is an opinion in some quarters in some Southeast Asian countries that the desire of India as also of China of wanting closer relations with Southeast Asian countries and join ASEAN was in reality a devise to "latch on" to these countries, and to assert their leadership over them. Speaking for India, it might be said that even during Nehru's time when India was in a stronger position *vis-a-vis* Southeast Asian countries, India never tried to assert a leadership role.

As it is, perhaps Dr. Mahathir and Gus Dur, if and when he overcomes the internal problems in Indonesia, might be in a better position to provide leadership to ASEAN and to countries beyond. India's desire to come out of the artificially created cage of South Asia is based not only on history, and a part of its growth, but also a realisation of the limits of SAARC. The very size of India and its large economy created fears in the minds of many neighbouring countries of South Asia which India has, to some extent, been able to dispel. Pakistan's insistence of treating Kashmir as a core issue and unwillingness to undertake meaningful steps towards liberalising trade relations among SAARC countries till the core issue had been resolved according to its lights has also made India look outside South Asia to the rapidly growing countries of Southeast Asia. Dr. Mahathir, who has been an advocate of the "look east" policy for Malaysia and other Asian countries since 1981, has put forward the concept of an East Asian Economic

Compact (EAEC) whereby Japan, South Korea and China are made economic partners of ASEAN.

This concept of 10 + 3 appears to us in India to be a flawed one which could create a serious strategic and economic imbalance in the region. Just as Dr. Mahathir has warned against the western economic domination, an East Asian or Japanese-Chinese economic domination would be equally dangerous. Economic autonomy within the framework of globalisation needs to be carefully maintained. Recent developments have added to the strategic importance of ASEAN, and of Indonesia, Singapore, Malaysia in particular. They are the essential link between the Indian Ocean and the South China Sea and the Pacific Ocean on account of their control over the Malaka, Sunda and Lombok Straits or choke points. Oil has considerable bearing on geopolitical configurations. In a recent paper in *Foreign Affairs* Amy Jaffe and Robert Manning have postulated that by the year 2010, Asia will obtain 90 per cent of its oil imports from the Persian Gulf while Middle East oil will contribute less than 5 per cent of America's oil consumption. Even if these figures may be exaggerated, the importance of Middle East oil for the rapidly growing Asians economies including East Asian economies will increase greatly, as also of Indonesia and Malaysia with their growing resources of oil and gas.

The question of safeguarding sea-lanes in the Indian Ocean including piracy has also attracted attention. Bearing all these factors in mind, the group of 10 + 3 should be broadened to include India, thus forming a 10 + 4. Although the 10 + 3 group is an economic group, and Japan joined it reluctantly for fear of US opposition, it has obvious political and strategic connotations. Since strategy today includes economic development, it would be illogical to exclude India from an economic grouping with a strong strategic potential. To expand its economic horizon, India put forward the concept of an IOR-ARC which already includes 21 countries including Indonesia, Singapore and Thailand from Southeast Asia. But this association is too broad, and would perhaps take decades to fructify.

Thus, it is a long term goal. For the realisation of immediate objectives, India set up in June 1998 a smaller regional organisation (BIMSTEC) consisting of Bangladesh, India. Myanmar, Sri Lanka and Thailand. On account of internal difficulties in many of the concerned countries, even this association has not made much progress. There is some thinking that BIMSTEC should be broadened to include Malaysia, Singapore and Indonesia, thus constituting a Bay of Bengal Community (BOBCOM). Such a community would revive old relations between littoral countries bordering the Bay of Bengal which historically played a role similar to that played by the Mediterranean Sea. However, building blocs by themselves are no more than means of promoting more meaningful relations between the countries constituting the bloc. If meaningful relations can be built, they would provide a surer basis for the emergence of a bloc. Building economic and cultural relations between India and Southeast Asian countries has made less progress during the last few years than had been visualised. While FICCI has made a study of the import-export regions and rules of investment in Indian Ocean Rim countries, trade between India and Southeast Asian countries has stagnated. India can provide a market for oil and gas, minerals, computer goods, electrical goods in addition to the traditional goods from countries of Southeast Asia. What India can sell in return is not as clear. May be information and knowledge industries are one field, as also machinery for intermediate level industries, as also defence equipment for beefing up the security needs of the countries of the region.

New Vistas for Cooperation

While the strengthening of economic and strategic ties have their own logic and takes time, what can perhaps be done immediately is to strengthen ties between India and Southeast Asian countries in the fields of education and professional studies. India can train and strengthen the infrastructure of Southeast Asian countries in the fields of medicine, management studies, marine sciences, and information technology. The Manipal Academy of Higher Education, a Deemed University has, under the dynamic leadership of its President, Dr. Ramdas M. Pai, started a programme of inducting 150 students from Malaysia who would do their training partly in India and partly in Malaysia, and would get a medical degree from Manipal. Such programmes need to be expanded. Basic sciences and human and social sciences can also be included. Exchange of students and teachers, and participation of research programmes and academic symposia need to be expanded.

In this, not only governments and institutions and organisations in India such as the University Grants Commission, the Indian Council of Social Science Research, the Indian Council of Historical Research, the National Institute of Oceanography, etc., can play a role and interact with their counterparts, non-governmental organisations, such as the Society for Indian Ocean Studies, which includes a whole range of eminent people from marine sciences, education, international relations, defence, etc., can also play a role. The involvement of these agencies would also help in improving the visibility of Southeast Asian countries in India, and of India in Southeast Asian countries. As at present, negative features, such as communal or race riots, or caste wars as in Bihar are reported in the Southeast Asian press about India. In India, too, pride of place about Malaysia in the Indian press was the Anwar Ibrahim sodomy trial. But things are improving. Thus, recently *Times of India* editorially welcomed Dr. Mahathir's speech at Cairo at the occasion of the G-1 5 meeting warning against mindless globalisation, while the *Hindu* has been regularly following developments in Indonesia. The ocean has often been seen as a factor which divides. But all our history shows that the eastern part of the Indian ocean, the Bay of Bengal as it is called, was a great unifying factor. It played the same role in Asia to some extent, as the Mediterranean in South Europe. These ancient linkages have to be revived, adopting what Dr. Mahathir's calls, "a step by step" approach.

PLAN OF ACTION TO IMPLEMENT THE ASEAN-INDIA PARTNERSHIP FOR PEACE, PROGRESS AND SHARED PROSPERITY

1. Political and Security Cooperation

1.1 Political

1.1.1 Foster closer cooperation and consultation between our delegations on reforming and democratising the United Nations and the institutions under the United Nations System by making them more reflective of the contemporary realities, and especially in the World Trade Organisation and other Bretton Woods institutions, so as to articulate the aspirations of the developing countries for equitable treatment and representation of their views;

1.1.2 Consult and cooperate on regional and international political and security issues of mutual interest and concern;

1.1.3 Promote norms and practices by ensuring the participation and involvement of women in consultations and peaceful settlement of disputes, particularly those reflected under the Treaty of Amity and Cooperation in Southeast Asia for consultations and peaceful settlement of disputes;

1.1.4 Cooperate closely in opposing the threat of weapons of mass destruction and on disarmament issues with the objective of total elimination of all weapons of mass destruction, including nuclear weapons; and

1.1.5 Strengthen the regional security dialogue and cooperation through the ASEAN Regional Forum for the maintenance of regional peace and stability.

1.2 Terrorism and Other Transnational Crimes

1.2.1 Strengthen and expand effective cooperation to combat international terrorism and other transnational crimes including through the existing ASEAN Ministerial Meeting on Transnational Crimes (AMMTC);

1.2.2 Build institutional linkages for intelligence and information sharing, exchange of information, and cooperation in legal and enforcement matters;

1.2.3 Develop joint training programmes and use regional organisations for technical assistance to effectively fight terrorism and other transnational crimes such as money laundering, drug trafficking, trafficking in persons, particularly of women and children, arms smuggling, cyber crimes, international economic crime and sea piracy;

1.2.4 Exchange ideas and jointly promote best standards and practices and explore ways to safeguard the sovereign rights of the parties, the common maritime boundaries, and shared maritime environment;

1.2.5 Explore developing anti-terrorism cooperation and assistance packages, covering among others, immigration controls, customs cooperation, land, air and sea safety;

1.2.6 Encourage accession to all relevant international counter-terrorism conventions and protocols and implement relevant UN resolutions on counter-terrorism;

1.2.7 Cooperate closely in opposing the threat of weapons of mass destruction especially in the context of such weapons falling into the hands of terrorists; and

1.2.8 Explore other avenues of cooperation between ASEAN and India taking into consideration the Work Programme to Implement the ASEAN Plan of Action to Combat Transnational Crimes.

2. Economic Cooperation

2.1. Trade and Investment

2.1.1 Establish ASEAN-India Regional Trade and Investment Area (RTIA) covering trade in goods, trade in service and investment as outlined under the Framework Agreement for Comprehensive Economic Cooperation;

2.1.2 Encourage participation of trade and industry representatives in the Business Summits and trade fairs held in India and ASEAN countries with special incentives for the participation of Cambodia, Laos, Myanmar, and Vietnam;

2.1.3 Promote and facilitate cross flows foreign direct investment into ASEAN countries and India through cooperation between investment promotion agencies, dissemination of information on investment policies, rules and procedures, and linkages between investors and local entrepreneurs;

2.1.4 Establish sectoral linkages involving business and industries to promote business interaction in specific sectors of industries;

2.1.5 Maximise the synergies for promoting trade in goods and services, as well as in investment flows between ASEAN and India, and identify barriers to trade in services, with a view to addressing them, in accordance with the level of development of each participating country; and

2.1.6 Work towards establishing bilateral Agreements between Member Countries of ASEAN and India for Investment Promotion and Protection and Double Taxation Avoidance.

2.2. *Customs Cooperation*

2.2.1 Enhance trade facilitation by streamlining customs procedures, formalities and practices in accordance with international conventions and best practices;

2.2.2 Encourage development of on-line linkages of India and ASEAN countries with regard to Certificate of Origin; and

2.2.3 Provide technical assistance and capacity building to the CLMV Countries to upgrade their customs capacity.

2.3. *Standards and Conformance Cooperation*

2.3.1 Establish linkages between national standards and conformity assessment bodies and technical regulators for mutual recognition of conformity assessment procedures and results and capacity building;

2.3.2 Facilitate the exchange of information on standards and conformity assessment procedures in relation to the regulatory requirements of Member Countries of ASEAN as well as India for easy access by the regulatory bodies and exporters in the participating countries through identification of contact points;

2.3.3 Set up technical cooperation in capacity building in the area of accreditation and certification bodies and laboratories;

2.3.4 Establish export and import inspection systems in line with internationally accepted good regulatory practices; and

2.3.5 Promote technical assistance in the area of standards and conformance to CLMV Countries.

2.4. *Finance*

2.4.1 Improve financial stability, among others, through voluntary swap arrangement;

2.4.2 Enhance regional monetary and financial cooperation;

2.4.3 Develop and promote an Asian bond market;

2.4.4 Further develop capital market infrastructure in areas of legal and regulatory and supervisory framework and cross border trading clearance settlement;

2.4.5 Enhance financial sector links between ASEAN and India;

2.4.6 Explore various ways to enhance trade financing in the region; and

2.4.7 Assist ASEAN Countries, particularly CLMV in the development of their capital markets.

2.5. *Transport and Infrastructure*

2.5.1 Expedite completion of India-Myanmar-Thailand trilateral highway and extension to Laos and Cambodia;

2.5.2 Encourage private sector participation in highway projects and port and coastal shipping projects in India and in the development of roads and railways in the Member Countries of ASEAN;

2.5.3 Strengthen cooperation in the field of shipping through, among others, the formation of ASEAN-India maritime association to provide an institutional basis to coordinate and enhance ASEAN-India cooperation in marine transport; and

2.5.4 Strengthen ASEAN-India air connectivity by working towards progressively greater liberalisation of air services between ASEAN and India.

2.6. *Energy*

2.6.1 Promote and develop trade and investment interest in gas-related projects;

2.6.2 Promote and develop trade and investment interest in the electricity sector, and pursue an integrated and coordinated development programme to establish compatibility of electricity grids, and work towards liberalisation of power trade among ASEAN Member Countries and India;

2.6.3 Develop and strengthen institutional linkages between ASEAN Centre for Energy (ACE) and India to cooperate on R&D into energy efficiency and renewable energy, and to establish programmes of cooperation; and

2.6.4 Promote sustainable and optimal utilisation of renewable energy, coal and new hydrocarbon projects, and cooperate in energy policy and planning, energy efficiency and conservation, as well as in the establishment of institutional linkages for developing other programmes of cooperation.

2.7. *Science and Technology*

2.7.1 Information and Communication Technology

2.7.1.1 Bridge the digital divide among and within our countries and use the synergies between our hardware and software capabilities for strengthening the IT industry in the region;

2.7.1.2 Set up Advanced Institutes of Information Technologies in different ASEAN countries, in particular CLMV for facilitating the building up of ICT capabilities;

2.7.1.3 Organise regular meetings of IT Ministers in ASEAN and India including with the IT Ministers of Indian states to facilitate exchange of experiences;

2.7.1.4 Strengthen institutional cooperation in the ICT infrastructure connectivity between ASEAN and India to accelerate the IT trade between ASEAN and India;

2.7.1.5 Promote and facilitate ICT workshops and training in the developments of ICT capacity building;

2.7.1.6 Promote human resource cooperation through various training courses, e-Learning, seminars, workshops as well as exchange of visits among IT experts;

2.7.1.7 Promote the development of an ASEAN-India broadband high speed optical fibre network and promote information flow and the application of new technology in the region; and

2.7.1.8 Exchange programmes among government officials of ASEAN and India in the areas of rural development and poverty eradication that will help provide additional income to rural households and improve the quality of lives. For example:

(i) visits and training programmes on good practices in rural development and poverty eradication;
(ii) R&D on rural products such as handicrafts, leather-based crafts and beads works.

2.7.2 *Research and Development and Technology Management*

2.7.2.1 Promote joint R&D and technology development in areas having potentials for commercial applications with the involvement of public and private sector, through, among others, the formation of strategic alliances between ASEAN and Indian enterprises;

2.7.2.2 Cooperate in the field of technology management, on issues, covering IPR management, technology forecasting, technology assessment, technology inter-mediation in areas such as materials science, marine technology, microelectronics design and processing, and multimedia;

2.7.2.3 Establish a Technology Transfer Network, to facilitate the pooling of information on the availability of technologies and experts with the enterprises/ R&D organisations in the region; and

2.7.2.4 Support ASEAN's environmental programme and activities under its Environmentally Sustainable Cities Initiative by organising seminars and workshops to share India's experiences in lowering urban air pollution and use of alternative fuel.

2.7.3. *Space Technology Applications and Biotechnology*

2.7.3.1 Develop a medium to long term programme of cooperation in the field of space technology promoting collaboration in its applications for broadcasting and telecommunication, effective management of natural resources and environment, disaster mitigation and weather forecasting;

2.7.3.2 Establish an ASEAN-India Biotechnology Network to encourage cooperation in the field of plant biotechnology for crop improvement; and

2.7.3.3 Develop an inventory of the region's bio-resources and joint research on issues relating to animal biotechnology, bio-informatics and regulatory issues concerning biotechnology.

2.8. *Human Resource Development*

2.8.1 Increase the number of fellowships for ASEAN students, especially to those from CLMV countries to pursue higher education in India;

2.8.2 Set up Software Development and Training Centres in the CLMV countries and provide DoE (Design of Experiments) accreditation to these training centres;

2.8.3 Establish facilities for teaching English language in select Member Countries of ASEAN especially in the CLMV countries;

2.8.4 Promote closer collaborations between universities in ASEAN and India through the ASEAN University Network;

2.8.5 Work towards developing a comprehensive ASEAN-India Programme for Capacity Building for better coordination and monitoring; and

2.8.6 Support the CLMV Countries to upgrade their education systems through implementation of curricula for kindergarten, primary, secondary and tertiary education.

2.9. *Sharing Experience on Managing Development*

2.9.1 Hold regular meetings of the ASEAN-India policy makers and Network of Think Tanks (AINTT) to facilitate exchange of development experiences; and

2.9.2 Institute fellowships for promoting studies on ASEAN-India relations.

2.10. *Pharmaceuticals and Health*

2.10.1 Share experiences and capability in developing quality generic pharmaceuticals industry, to make medicines more affordable to people;

2.10.2 Cooperate in joint production of diagnostic and therapeutic supplies for HIV/AIDS, vaccines such as, but not limited to, BCG, anti-venin, equine rabies, anti-hepatitis and anti-tetanus, serum vaccines, generic drugs and traditional medicines like Ayurveda and Herbal medicines; and

2.10.3 Address health related issues having bearing on countries in the region, especially in light of emerging diseases such as SARS and avian flu.

2.11. Commodities, Agriculture, Horticulture and Food Processing

2.11.1 Develop closer interaction between the Ministries related to Agriculture, Horticulture and Commodities in the ASEAN Member Countries and India to initiate joint actions on issues of common interest.

2.12. Small and Medium Enterprises (SMEs)

2.12.1 Develop joint programmes in capacity building aimed at strengthening the capacities of SMEs on both sides;

2.12.2 Share on a regular basis policy and other experiences in the promotion of a dynamic, networked, and competitive SME sector;

2.12.3 Encourage collaboration in the formation and linkages of associations of small-scale industries and other non-government organisations through training of personnel, and information dissemination;

2.12.4 Foster supply and subcontracting linkages and partnerships involving SMEs from ASEAN and India as well as other firms within and outside the region through trade missions, study visits and other network-building activities;

2.12.5 Collaborate in the joint development and compilation of system toolkit packages and other materials for training in enterprise organisation and management skills, including financial reporting and business plan preparations, technology upgrading, quality maintenance and assurance, ISO standard certification;

2.12.6 Promote various associations of small-scale industries and other business organisations in support of ASEAN-India SME development and linkages;

2.12.7 Organise Indian technology exhibitions in new Member Countries of ASEAN with a focus on machinery and equipment for small scale and rural industries; and

2.12.8 Establish SME Service Centres in ASEAN countries, in particular CLMV and virtual SME Service Centres for ASEAN and India SMEs.

3. Social and Cultural Cooperation

3.1. Social

3.1.1 Promote cooperation and regional commitment on the poverty alleviation efforts and for achieving Millennium Development Goals, including sustainable development;

3.1.2 Create a Forum for sharing of experiences in labour market liberalisation and addressing issues relating to mobility of skilled labour between ASEAN and India;

3.1.3 Promote dialogue between Government officials and civil societies of ASEAN and India in the field of rural development, poverty alleviation, women empowerment, and issues concerning protection to children against exploitation, gender equality and old age care; and

3.1.4 Encourage home stay facilities.

3.2. *Tourism*

3.2.1 Promote and facilitate more tourism flow;

3.2.2 Consider establishing a high level cooperation mechanism between relevant tourism authorities;

3.2.3 Consider reciprocal arrangements where possible for relaxing existing visa regulations and extending travel concessions to ASEAN and Indian tourists;

3.2.4 Promote cultural and rural tourism through joint tourism packages, including Eco-Tourism, adventure tourism, sports tourism, religious circuit tourism, by utilising their geographical diversity; and

3.2.5 Promote budget tourism packages by using multi-modal transport, including luxury coaches and ferry services.

3.3. *Culture*

3.3.1 Promote greater awareness and appreciation of each other's traditional and contemporary cultures through establishment of an autonomous ASEAN-India Foundation (AIF) to facilitate exchange and linkage programmes in the areas of creative and performing arts, cultural education, conservation and management of cultural and archaeological heritage, cultural enterprises and creative industries;

3.3.2 Institutionalise regular exchange of views of Culture Ministers to promote better understanding of cultural diversity and in formulation of cultural policy in the context of globalisation;

3.3.3 Encourage regular interaction among cultural workers of ASEAN and India aimed at fostering deeper cultural reflection;

3.3.4 The AIF may also provide for ASEAN-India Civil Societies' Forum to discuss and exchange, experiences on preserving traditional cultural values from the negative impacts of the process of trade liberalisation and globalisation. Among the concerns of the forum will be the ways to increase dissemination of local cultural contents among the youth and other efforts aimed to strengthen healthy national identity among them; and

3.3.5 Work together to prevent the illegal smuggling of cultural heritage so as to make these valuable objects stay within jurisdiction of its rightful owner.

3.4 People-to-People Contacts, Media, Entertainment, and Sports

3.4.1 Facilitate greater interaction between media of ASEAN and India for reducing the information gaps;

3.4.2 Establish ASEAN-India Parliamentarians' Forum to provide for regular interaction; and

3.4.3 Works towards organising ASEAN-India Games.

4. Institutional and Funding Arrangements for the Implementation of the Plan of Action

4.1 Draw up specific work programmes, if necessary, to implement the various actions and measures outlined in this Plan of Action;

4.2 India will provide technical support to the ASEAN Secretariat in implementing the Plan;

4.3 Strengthen existing funding mechanisms for effective coordination and implementation of this Plan;

4.4 Provide requisite resources in accordance with their respective capacities, exploring effective and innovative resource mobilisation to accomplish the various 'strategies and measures outlined in the Plan;

4.5 Conduct regular review of the Plan through existing mechanisms such as the meeting of the Foreign Ministers of ASEAN and India, the ASEAN-India Senior Officials Meeting, the ASEAN-India Joint Cooperation Committee, the ASEAN-India Working Group to ensure consistency with the priorities of the ASEAN-India dialogue relations and to incorporate new and urgent areas of cooperation given the dynamic regional and global developments; and

4.6 Submit a progress report of the implementation of the Plan of Action to the annual ASEAN-India Summit through the meeting of the Foreign Ministers of ASEAN and India.

INDIA'S INTEREST IN SOUTH EAST ASIA

The major thrust of the domestic policies of India and ASEAN were entirely different. India endeavoured to establish socialistic pattern of society and thus nationalisation, democratisation, secularisation became the prevailing norm. On the other hand, ASEAN countries supported privatisation and open market system. They provided incentives to investors and welcomed transnational corporations and technologies. The ASEAN growth rates were high at 6 to 8 percent and it was projected as a trojan horse of success. The ASEAN model attracted their former adversaries like Vietnam to join it. Vietnam's admission was followed by Laos, Myanmar and Cambodia and hence all the ten countries of Southeast Asia became the partners in ASEAN. Promotion of free trade was welcomed and rapid steps were taken to hastern the face of globalisation. However, the economic development of the region was suddenly jolted after the financial crisis of 1997-98. The investors started withdrawing their deposits and thus there was acute shortage of foreign currencies. This crisis taught the value of state control on financial institutions and also that of constant monitoring over it. Hence Indian economic system proved relevant in the changed context.

India and Southeast Asia admit convergence of interests in economic, political and security matters. It faced reverses in the SAARC and ASEAN regions initially. It evolved new initiatives to strengthen partnership with countries in Southeast Asia and Far East in the post Cold War era and called it "Look East Policy".

It was identified as Central to India's foreign policy in the entire Asia-Pacific. India's look east had three-pronged approach. First, to renew political contacts with the ASEAN partners; second, to increase economic interaction (trade, investment, science and technology, tourism etc) and third, to forge defence links with ASEAN partners as a means to enhance political and strategic interests and understanding. Indian think-tanks are reviewing the notion of economic security self-reliance and national interests in light of developments in the post-cold war era.

As a nation of one billion people, India cannot afford to remain a marginal player in the global economy, as measured for instance by our share in world trade or income. Commensurate with her size and civilizational characteristics, India is willing to assume greater role in global affairs and world economy. Look East policy is endeavoured to fulfil those aspirations and it has evoked positive response in the ASEAN region. The meaning and contents of Look East policy was decided by Narasmiha Rao himself during his tenure as the Prime Minister of India (1991-95). His speech delivered on 8 September 1994 in Singapore was a milestone to influence the opinion of Southeast Asians where he spoke about endogenous and exogenous nature of the problems, which were a matter of common concern and common interests, and they were

(a) interpretations of sovereignty, whether over the oceans, in outer space, over territory, resources etc.;

(b) frictions arising out of differing cultural perceptions - as we witnessed in the case of Michael Fay;

(c) massive needs and demands of relatively underdeveloped populations and migratory tendencies, with no respect for national boundaries;

(d) confrontational postures on a broad range of fundamental issues related to trade barriers, currency stabilisation, international aid and investment flows;

(e) intensification of the debate over linkages between issues such as human rights, labour-laws, environmental protection and resource management, liberal information flows etc. in political and economic relationships.

Southeast Asian countries were also looking for suitable answers to aforementioned issues but Indian premier pointedly articulated "the increasing tendency on the part of dominant powers to assume that they can not only define the means, but even the ends, of collective international endeavour. This has been revealed in the form of intrusive prescriptions in the areas of social regulation, dissemination of knowledge, technological development and even domestic administration. The worst part of this tendency is that on closer scrutiny, it can be easily shown to be based on unsympathetic half-knowledge, and not unoften even total ignorance. He further stated that worldwide criminal networks of drug trafficking: smugglers, terrorists, money launderers and other such elements who have no stake in peace and real prosperity but manage to suborn Governments to ensure the furtherance of their own interests." The opium growing golden triangle is located in Southeast Asia and clandestine sale of illegal drugs and narcotics are endemic. The issue of human rights record in Indonesia, Burma, Vietnam, Laos and the Philippines are very often criticized and the demands for more democratization are advocated.

The spratlys are being claimed by the Chinese and the possession of Vietnam, Malaysia and the Philippines in that region are questioned. Besides there are some religious groups sponsoring terrorism. The organisations like Jemaah Islamiyah are inspired by Al Qaida, and they have trained terrorist groups in the name of Islam. They have suicide squads and sophisticated weapons to attack their targets. Aceh in Indonesia, Mindanao in the Philippines and Patani in Thailand are in the grip of Islamic terrorists but people in certain areas in Malaysia are also supporting fanatics. There has been attacks on public places and various governments are faced with a dilemma on how to tackle them. As they take the help of religion to legitimate their violence (Jehad), they are supported by some of their co-religionists.

Indeed it is delicate to address the issue of terrorism based on religion and this is a pretext for the United States to advise them about certain measures. India and Southeast Asia are sensitive to prescriptions given by the Western world to tackle their domestic problems. They have their indigenous way to address them and show full faith in dialogue and negotiations for conflict resolution. They believe that the problem of terrorism is a temporary phenomenon and it would wither away in due course. However, there is consensus on the fact that terrorists are inhuman and enemy of the civilised world. They are bound to be contained effectively in due course because the people in general demand peace and development. Indian perspective of outstanding problems of common concern for the region complimented Southeast Asian opinion. India was invited to be a sectoral partner of ASEAN in 1992 and full dialogue partner in 1995. The sectoral partnership was to promote trade, investment and tourism relations, but dialogue partnership had a broad agenda for cooperation. It had security, political, economic and cultural areas of cooperation. In 1996, India became a member of ASEAN Regional Forum (ARF) aimed at confidence building, conflict resolution and preventive diplomacy. It was guided by ASEAN stand on the question of East Timor during 1998-99. India had been an active member of the ARF and has worked together with ASEAN in several areas including search and rescue, sea piracy and disaster relief, helping to further advance the ARF process. India has acceded to ASEAN's Treaty of Amity and Cooperation (TAC) this October, which would further promote regional peace and stability especially when it shares ASEAN's fundamental principles of non-interference, respect for each other's territorial integrity and sovereignty and resolving disputes in a peaceful manner. This would move India to the inner circle of ASEAN. Collaboration in the international fora to realise the aspirations of the developing world will increasingly feature as another facet of ASEAN-India relations, given India's leading role in supporting the cause of the developing world. Economic relations too have significantly improved. In so far as India is concerned, in less than four years from 1992, our two-way trade has more than doubled; in 1996-97, it stood at US$6 billion and crossed the target of US$10 billion in the year 2002. From negligible investments in 1992, investment approvals from ASEAN upto 1997 were in excess of US$5 billion.

In the reverse direction, ASEAN accounts for a significant proportion of Indian investments abroad. Significantly, the region has emerged as a promising growth area in trade, investments, joint ventures, tourism, etc. The two-way trade constitutes about 6 percent of India's total trade. India's principal ASEAN trading partners are Indonesia, Singapore, and Malaysia. With others, the trade is gradually picking up. India's exports to ASEAN grew by 37.9 percent in 2002-2003 and the value stood at US$4.65 billion. The main items of Indian exports comprise of gems and jewellery, drugs and pharmaceuticals, electronic goods, meat and meat products, sugar, cotton yarn fabrics, wheat, spices and finished leather. India's imports from ASEAN stood at US$4.8 billion in 2002-03 witnessing a rise of 18 percent since 2001-02. the main items of Indian imports include vegetable oils, electronic goods, newsprint, natural rubber, pears and precious stones, and wood and wood products. The FDI inflow into India from ASEAN in 2002 stood at US$85 million. Over the period from 1992-2003, ASEAN accounted for about 3.55 percent of the total FDI inflow into the country. Sector, wise, power and oil refinery, telecom, electrical equipment, and IT have received the largest share of ASEAN investments. Now, pharmaceuticals, biotechnology, and the Info Tech are turning out to be the promising areas for ASEAN investments. State wise, Singapore, Malaysia and Indonesia are the top three investors. The total FDI inflow to the ASEAN countries from India during 2002 stood at US$182 million. The main recipients of the funds were Indonesia, Malaysia, and Singapore. An obvious and natural extension of India's economic space, it was perceived, was ASEAN, which had emerged as a significant and promising growth area of the world. With a combined population of nearly 400 million and a land area larger than India's, ASEAN's GDP is in the region of US$ 400 billion; its exports, already significant, have grown steadily and are in the region of US$220 billion; it is an important destination for foreign investments and a major source of investments abroad. India is exploring communication routes from New Delhi to Hanoi through construction of railways and highways. Tamu-Kalewa-Moreh road has been constructed and direct trade and transit facilities have been increased with the ASEAN. India is a member of BIMST-EC (Bangladesh, India-Myanmar-Sri Lanka-Thailand Economic Cooperation) in which Nepal and Bhutan have recently joined. BIMST-EC is endeavoured to promote close cooperation of South Asian with Southeast Asian region. India is also supporting Mekong-Ganga cooperation in which India and five ASEAN countries, namely Cambodia, Laos, Vietnam, Burma and Thailand are associated. The decision of India, Thailand and Burma to build a road linking Thailand to India through Myanmar is bound to promote Indian trade with the countries in the Mekong region and beyond. The ASEAN-India Business council (AIBC) and India-ASEAN Economic cooperation committee (AIECC) are exploring trade and investment relations and they indicate a large potential for future cooperation. The trading ties with ASEAN countries are increasing but it is not commensurate with the vast potentials as focussed in India-ASEAN summit meetings, which has been held twice so far.

India's Trading Ties with ASEAN Countries

(Figures for 2002-03 in US$ million)

Country	*Exports*	*Imports*	*Total*
Singapore	1434.32	1445.31	2879.63
Malaysia	752.90	1477.14	2230.04
Indonesia	832.70	1391.86	2224.56
Thailand	716.60	22.76	739.36
Philippines	475.80	124.67	600.47
Vietnam	339.90	9.35	369.25
Myanmar	75.60	338.77	414.37
Cambodia	19.99	0.61	20.60
Laos	1.58	0.14	2.73
Brunei	4.48	0.32	4.81
Total	4653.88	4830.92	9484.80

Source: Commerce Ministry of India.

The first summit was held in Cambodia in 2002 and the second was held in Indonesia in 2003. The ASEAN has reiterated the faith that partnership with India has been conceived as a ongoing effort to create interdependence and linkage with a country with a large and liberalising market as well as a democratic and pluralistic polity which could respond positively to ASEAN's aspirations. Indian Prime Minister, Atal Bihari Vajpayee attaches great importance to emerging relations with the ASEAN and has participated in the summit meetings with a range of ideas to promote cooperation in economic and strategic areas. Some of the recognised sectors that India has advocated for cooperation are science and technology, biotechnology, information technology, space technology application, financial services, human resource development and education, etc. Indian Prime Minster, while attending the second India-ASEAN summit, had projected shining India in the following words, "Over the last 12 years, the Indian economy has maintained an average annual growth of over 6 percent, which is better than that of most other countries." Our interest rates are falling, inflation has been kept down, and foreign exchange reserves are growing rapidly. India remained unaffected by the Asian financial crisis a few years ago. We have targeted an 8 percent growth over the next five years. As our economic base is large, there is considerable untapped potential for India's continued - and even accelerated -economic growth. Perceptions shape decisions. Often they are flawed. Sometimes, they are incomplete. The rich cultural diversity and spiritual traditions of India are well known, but they constitute only one aspect of India. There is another India, the India of the 21st Century, which is still not so well known, with its many strengths:

> "One, an inherently strong economy driven primarily by indigenous skills and domestic enterprise."

Two, a growing and accessible domestic market, with import and investment barriers falling away. To take just one random example of the growth of the market: in the last few months, it has been absorbing about 2 million mobile phones a month. Import duties are moving towards ASEAN levels, and sectorial caps on foreign investment are rising. Three, a rich pool of human resources – English speaking, with R&D skills, technological training and managerial capabilities. Four, some special capabilities in state-of-the-art technologies. India is one of only three countries – the others are USA and Japan- to have idigenously designed and manufactured super computers. It is one of only 6 countries, which can bild and launch its own satellites. Five, global leadership in technologies of the knowledge Economy. India's pre-eminent position in IT and IT enabled services has led global companies to set up captives in India or to out source their operations to quality Indian service providers. Six, a sound and transparent financial system, with well-managed banking and insurance sectors, and vibrant capital markets. Our paperless, computer-driven National Stock Exchange is the third largest in the world, in terms of number of annual transactions. India is today a country on the move. We are experiencing many revolutions simultaneously. There is, of course, the IT revolution. This in turn has unleashed a socio-cultural revolution, which has empowered hundreds of millions of our citizens, strengthening our democracy and stimulating our creativity." Vajpayee stated further that "it is this India that seeks to partner ASEAN in this era of globalisation. India's trade and economic interaction with the ASEAN countries has been steadily growing, but not fast enough. A year ago at the First India-ASEAN Business Summit, I had said that the India-ASEAN trade of less than 10 billion dollars does not do justice to our combined population of one and a half billion people, producing a trillion and a half dollars worth of goods and services annually. Our trade has since grown by about 25 percent, but my comment remains valid." He said that "Non-Asians view Asia as the principal market of the future. But it will also emerge as a manufacturing hub and, global provider of services. In the next 10 years, as the population of the devleoped world ages, a younger and better-educated workforce will emerge in Asia to fill the breach. This generation will drive the future growth of the global economy. Asian countries should work towards strengthening their mutual synergies, so that they are strategically placed to derive maximum benefit from emerging opportunities.

The India-ASEAN partnership should energise this process to move us closer to our shared goal of making this truly the Asian century." India's position at the intersection of Asia's main cultural and geopolitical zones has implications for ASEAN since developments in India would have an impact on the region. India shares maritime borders with Thailand and Indonesia, and with the enlargement of ASEAN, India is now the immediate neighbour of Myanmar, sharing a 1600 kilometre border. India possesses nuclear capabilities and a modern naval force. With its dynamic economic growth and superiority in engineering and sciences, India is expected to play an important role in maintaining the peace, stability and prosperity of Asia. India is committed to its relations with ASEAN since it believes in a shared destiny with the region and wants to identify with it. The strengthening of its relations with ASEAN and East Asia is seen as a success of its "Look East" Policy promulgated in 1991. The realisation of the ASEAN-India Summit in November 2002 was an important milestone in its "Look East" Policy. Mr. S. Pushpanathan, Head of External Relations Cell in ASEAN Secretariat (Jakarta) has stated that "Medical research and pharmaceuticals have been identified as areas for closer cooperation between ASEAN and India. In medical research, cooperation could focus on the prevention of communiciable diseases.

In pharmaceuticals, ASEAN would be keen to work with India on strengthening ASEAN's capacity and competitiveness in the manufacturing of pharmaceuticals, traditional medicines and biological products, facilitating access to affordable medicines." India's pharmaceutical market is expected to grow from US$6 million in 2002 to about 25 billion in 2010 with the reduction in manufacturing costs, the introduction of new technologies, a growing middle class, competitive markets and better research and development. India is expected to gain a substantial global generics market share. ASEAN investors could take advantage of the opportunities by investing in this sector, focusing on joint manufacturing of pharmaceutical products, which could help reduce the import costs of such products.

Tourism cooperation holds great potential given the historical, religious and cultural affinities between India and ASEAN, and the growing purchasing power of the Indian middle class. There were some 750,000 Indian visitors to ASEAN in 2000, making up only 2 percent of total visitor arrivals in our region, while ASEAN visitors accounted for less than 5 percent of India's total visitor arrivals.

Considering the projected demand and opportunities, the private sectors of both sides could look at better promotional and marketing activities to boost tourism, including pilgrimage tourism. Besides economic interaction, a range of activities in cultural, political and strategic areas are projected. Southeast Asia has emerged as anothet hub of terrorism. There are a number of terrorist groups in the region which has had links with Al Qaida formed in 1987 by Osama bin Laden. Their way of thinking and style of operation are inhuman and violent. Their act of bombing tourist resorts in Bali in 2002 shocked the people everywhere.

Their network in Indonesia and the Philippines are adversely affecting the image of ASEAN as a heaven for peace and stability. The bombing of Davao airport in March 2003 and Bali blast in October 2002 were masterminded by Abu Sayyaf group in the Philippines and Jemaah Islamiyah in Indonesia respectively. Kumpulan Militan Malaysia (KMM) has also got assistance from Al Qaida to support terrprist activities. Laskar Jihaad under Jaafar Umar Thalib in Indonesia has been actively supporting the rise of radical Islam and has been responsible for several incidences of violence in Ambon.

Moro Islamic Liberation Front (MILF) and Abu Sayaff group in the Philippines are supporting terrorist activities in Mindanao. Jemaah Islamiyah under Abu Bakar Bashir, is believed to have command, control and communication structures to guide their trained militia, and they are keen to force the creation of Islamic state in different parts of Southeast Asia. India, on its part, is witnessing the menace of terrorism in Kashmir and areas in the border regions adjoining Burma. Most of them have transnational support and they are posing substantive threat to issues of peace and development. India and ASEAN have collectively resolved to Sign Declaration for cooperation to combat terrorism on 8 October 2003. The declared objectives of the declaration are two fold:

(a) The participants reaffirm the importance of having a framework for cooperation to prevent, disrupt and combat international terrorism through the exchange and flow of information, intelligence and capacity-building.

(b) The participants emphasize that the purpose of this cooperation is to enhance the efficacy of those efforts to combat terrorism.

International terrorism would increasingly figure as an important area for ASEAN-India cooperation due to developments in India and ASEAN. Both sides want to ensure a peaceful and stable region to conduct economic activities and cooperation besides contributing to the international fight against terrorism. A declaration will be concluded this October to formalise ASEAN-India cooperation in addressing terrorism and related crimes. India-ASEAN cultural relations have also improved. Being the birth place of Lord Buddha, India is an area of intense academic interests. There are various places in India connected with Southeast Asian literature and there are a number of people who want to visit them. ASEAN understanding of India and vice versa have increased. Indian Council of Cultural Relations (ICCR) is offering fellowship to students from ASEAN countries and ASEAN-India Fund in supporting lecture series from eminent persons in India and vice versa. The government agencies at the ASEAN level are sincere in promoting understanding and partnership feeling. However, it would prove strategically useful if the department of Southeast Asian studies of Jawaharlal Nehru University, which has produced hundreds of M.Phil and Ph.D. on Southeast Asia, where dozens of students from Southeast Asia have worked, is strengthened on the pattern of Singapore Institute of Southeast Asian Studies, better perspectives for new ideas and initiatives would emerge. To conclude India-ASEAN relations are bound to grow if Asia-Pacific will be the hub of economic activities in the 21st Century. They have to work together closely to face the challenges and revive the affluence of the Subarnabhumi, wherein both were closely connected.

CHAIRMAN'S STATEMENT OF THE 3rd ASEAN + INDIA SUMMIT

Vientiane, 30 November 2004

"Deepening ASEAN-India Partnership"

1. The ASEAN Leaders had a productive meeting with H.E. Dr. Manmohan Singh, Prime Minister of the Republic of India. They congratulated Prime Minister Singh for his assumption of the Prime Ministership, and welcomed him to the ASEAN-India Summit for the first time.

2. We held a productive meeting on various issues of mutual interest, including regional and international political and economic issues, ways to deepen ASEAN-India partnership and the future direction of the relations.

3. We recognise the growing and active role of India in major international economic and political affairs in the United Nations, its agencies and other multilateral fora. We agreed to cooperate in major regional and international fora for mutual benefit and to add a stronger voice and ensure equitable share of

benefits for the developing countries. We noted India's foreign policy initiatives to forge closer and friendlier relations with the major powers and others.

4. The Leader of India welcomed the adoption by the ASEAN Leaders of the Vientiane Action Programme (VAP) to realise the goals of the ASEAN Vision 2020 and the Declaration of ASEAN Concord II. India expressed its support to the implementation of activities and projects under the VAP.

5. We acknowledged that the pluralistic and multi-cultural nature of our societies depended on the spirit of tolerance, peaceful co-existence and mutual respect for our diversity. We agreed that strengthening of our relations, rooted in long-standing and close historical and cultural ties, serves the fundamental interests of our peoples.

6. We expressed satisfaction on the progress made in ASEAN-India relations since the last two ASEAN-India Summits held in Cambodia in 2002 and Indonesia in 2003. We signed the "ASEAN-India Partnership for Peace, Progress and Shared Prosperity" and adopted its Plan of Action to expand and deepen our partnership and our cooperation in the new century.

7. We acknowledged that the signing of Partnership, India's accession to the Treaty of Amity and Cooperation in Southeast Asia, the adoption of the ASEAN-India Joint Declaration for Cooperation to Combat International Terrorism reflected our determination and commitment to move forward the relationship in a substantive, comprehensive and purposeful manner contributing to regional peace and stability, and shared economic prosperity and development.

8. We noted with satisfaction the progress made thus far in the negotiations of the ASEAN-India Trade Negotiating Committee to establish an ASEAN-India free trade area (FTA), which is part of the implementation of the ASEAN-India Framework Agreement on Comprehensive Economic Cooperation signed in Bali last year. We look forward to the early conclusion of these negotiations. We recognise that the ASEAN-India FTA would create new opportunities for strengthening and enhancing economic, trade and investment cooperation in the two regions.

9. We noted that ASEAN and India have agreed to an interim Rules of Origin for Early Harvest Programme (EHP). The Interim Rules of Origin will be based on a general rule of 40% of value-added with the ASEAN-proposed list of minimal processes, subject to reasonably short list of products where product specific rules will be negotiated and mutually agreed in time for the implementation of the EHP by 1 April 2005. The details of the Rules of Origin will be worked out by the ASEAN-India Trade Negotiating Committee.

10. The ASEAN Leaders expressed their sincere appreciation to India for its support and unilateral concessions to the CLMV and hoped that the CLMV would

enjoy further continued cooperation and assistance from India with a view to effectively bridging the development gap among ASEAN members and between ASEAN and the outside world. In this connection, India offered to provide concessionary loans for social and development projects.

11. The ASEAN Leaders welcomed the convening of the Third ASEAN-India Business Summit held on 19-21 October 2004 in India and was pleased with the outcomes of the said Summit. We also noted the progress in implementing India's offer on Open Sky policy made at our last Summit in Indonesia.

12. We noted that regional trade arrangements in South, Southeast Asia and East Asia served as building blocks towards wider economic and development cooperation in Asia and acknowledged that ASEAN and India, working in partnership, could contribute immensely to linking these regional trade arrangements together to promote Asia's economic growth and prosperity.

13. The ASEAN Leaders expressed their appreciation to India for its support in the implementation of the projects under the Initiative for ASEAN Integration (IAI), in particular, its support to establish an Entrepreneurship Development Centre (EDC) in each CLMV, aimed at promoting capacity building in the areas of entrepreneurship and skilled labour development, and fostering SMEs, trade and investment in the respective countries and the region. The first EDC was opened in Vientiane during the 10th ASEAN Summit and similar EDCs will be opened in Cambodia, Myanmar and Vietnam in 2005.

14. The ASEAN Leaders welcomed India's continued support to ASEAN Member Countries in capacity building, particularly human resource development. The ASEAN Leaders welcomed the proposals of the Leader of India to further enhance cooperation in the areas of information and communications technology, space technology and application, including remote sensing, agriculture, and health and pharmaceuticals.

15. The ASEAN Leaders congratulated India for initiating and successfully organising the ASEAN-India Car Rally, which commenced on 22 November 2004 in Guwahati, India and will end in Batam, Indonesia. We officially flagged off the rally in Vientiane on 30 November 2004 and noted that the rally has already generated public awareness of ASEAN-India relations and would promote connectivity, especially road transport and enhance trade, investment, tourism and people-to-people links between the ASEAN Countries and India. The ASEAN Leaders took note of India's proposal to jointly organise the rally on a regular basis.

India and Southeast Asia: Ensuring Regional Services

With the recent visit of the Indian prime minister to Southeast Asia, fifth in less than three years, and signing of a clutch of agreements with the Association of Southeast Asian Nations (ASEAN) on a range of issues covering counter-terrorism, accession to the ASEAN Treaty of Amity and Cooperation (TAC), a kind of code of conduct on how inter-state relations are conducted, and importantly a framework agreement to create an India-ASEAN free trade and investment area agreement by 2016, New Delhi has not only placed, what was beginning to be written off as one of those non-starters, the Look East policy, is on top of the country's foreign policy agenda, but also has sent the clearest political signal that it places high premium on this region. India is already member of the ASEAN Regional Forum (ARF), a Dialogue Partner and Summit member of ASEAN since 1995 and 2002 respectively. These institutional arrangements will ensure that top Indian leaders would be frequent visitors for regular interaction with ASEAN and its member countries. Simultaneously, India is also in the process of finalizing bilateral free trade agreements with two ASEAN member states, that is Thailand and Singapore. One of the three facets of the Look East policy that was initiated in the early 1990s is related to strategic issues (the other two being economic and political.) Although much of the current attention is focused on economic aspects, it may be useful to remember that it was defence/security-linked issues, to be precise maritime-related, that in fact compelled India to formulate a new policy toward Southeast Asia and those gradually propelled the policy to encompass the other aspects.

In the following, the article traces the involvement of Indian military in Southeast Asia, the role the Indian Navy played in the genesis of the Look East policy in the 1980s, the strategic and defence relations that India has built since then with a number of Southeast Asian nations, and finally explore prospects for cooperation in the maritime sphere between India and Southeast Asia keeping in view the evolving maritime security environment in the region. It is argued that, for a variety of reasons, a great opportunity is available for the Indian Navy to play a vital and unique role in the waters around Southeast Asia. It may be remembered that peace, stability and prosperity of Southeast Asia is in India's interest simply because India's relations with that region prospered whenever it remained free of political and economic turmoil. In the realm of security, India and its armed forces can contribute substantially to the promotion of peace and stability in the region.

Connected as such with one of the oldest and most prominent trade routes, India's association with Southeast Asia can be traced back to the ancient times. While the flourishing economic and cultural links were disrupted during the colonial interlude, it was during the freedom struggles in India and in many countries of Southeast Asia that led to the rediscovery of each other. It may indeed come as a surprise that Southeast Asia was the region in which India was most involved in the heady days of its independence and soon after. Much before India attained independence in August 1947, Indian leadership envisioned the future importance of Southeast Asia and India's involvement. Even the strategic significance of Southeast Asia caught the attention of a leading Indian strategic thinker who argued that the "Gulf of Malacca is like the mouth of crocodile, the Peninsula of Malaya being the upper and the jutting end of Sumatra being the lower jaw. The entry to the Gulf can be controlled by the Nicobars and the narrow end is dominated by the island of Singapore." The Indian nationalist leaders convened the Asian Relations Conference in New Delhi in March 1947 primarily to express solidarity with the freedom struggles all across Southeast Asia. Equally important was the Special Conference on Indonesia that was held in January 1949, which was attended by 15 nations, to express support to the Sukarno-led armed struggle against the Dutch colonial rule. In fact it has been argued that freedom struggles especially in Indonesia and Vietnam provided major inputs in shaping the nascent Indian foreign policy in the late 1940s. Interestingly, the Indian military trained the armed forces of Indonesia after it became independent, and Indonesia was the only country outside the Commonwealth with which the Indian Navy held joint exercises.

Despite geographical proximity to Southeast Asia, sharing its maritime boundary with at least Indonesia, Thailand and Myanmar (India's second longest border, land and maritime together, is with Myanmar), the closeness of Andaman and Nicobar Islands in the Bay of Bengal to Southeast Asia than to mainland India, and the fact that southern Indian tip is astride some of the most critical sea lanes of communication in the Indian Ocean connecting Southeast Asia (and East Asia) with West Asia and Europe through which nearly 40 percent of the world's trade passes through, Southeast Asia was hardly a foreign policy priority to New Delhi till about a decade back.

It was amidst developments in the 1980s such as the Vietnamese military intervention to overthrow the dreaded Pol Pot in Cambodia, strong exception ASEAN took to this, India's recognition of the Vietnam-installed regime, the expansion of the India Navy came under considerable focus because of perceptions that India along with the former Soviet Union and Vietnam might take concerted moves to check growing Chinese influence in Southeast Asia, particularly after the Soviets gained a foothold at Cam Ranh Bay naval base in Vietnam. The spectre of another Cold War-motivated conflict in Southeast Asia was looming large in the minds of ASEAN leaders. Coinciding with this was the so-called Indian military build-up, especially its acquisition of certain high profile naval ships and systems.

It may be useful to recall some reactions that emanated especially from Southeast Asia. Although the first reaction came as far back as mid-1986 when Indonesia protested against reported Indian moves to a new naval base in the Andaman and Great Nicobar Islands, criticism of the Indian Navy reached its peak in the late 1980s and early 1990s. Indonesia was more explicit in June 1989. In a meeting held in New Delhi, Indonesia's then Naval Chief, Admiral Rakefendo, formally conveyed to the Indian officials his government's concern over the Indian naval expansion. According to a Time report, "In Jakarta an army colonel described his government as 'concerned' about India's long-term intentions of Indian naval expansion.

The main reason, he explained, why Indonesia was planning to build a large naval base on Sumatra was that it would provide quick access to the Bay of Bengal. Malaysian reaction was relatively more moderate. According to a former Malaysian Defence Minister, India's growing military might to project power well beyond its borders has caused "some concern and alarm in East Asia and Western Pacific ... India must show its neighbours, including Malaysia and other countries in Southeast Asia, that it does not have any ambitions to interfere in regional affairs."

From an ASEAN point of view, a possible Indian naval role in the waterways that pass through Southeast Asia connecting Bay of Bengal with East Asia was of major concern, particularly given the close proximity of India's newly expanded and upgraded base on the Andaman island, called Fortress Andaman (FORTRON). These straits are important international sea lanes of communication that form the main link between the Indian and Pacific Oceans. As noted, because of its close links with the former Soviet Union and Vietnam, it was feared that India along with these two could undermine the Chinese role, and to a lesser extent, even the American role in Southeast Asia.

ASEAN's second worry was a possible clash of maritime spheres of influence between India and China. It was reported that "the Indian military officials in private have suggested that an understanding should be reached with China to delineate naval spheres of influence between the Indian Ocean and the South China Sea. Indian strategic cooperation could extend eventually to member-countries of the Association of Southeast Asian Nations (ASEAN) and Vietnam in an effort to check Chinese encroachment into Southeast Asia." India's image as a fast growing military power trying to extend its influence beyond South Asia remained even after drastic changes in international security.

Even while the Cold War had decisively wound up by the early 1990s, India was looked upon by some ASEAN states as one of the strong competitors to project its power into Southeast Asia and possibly fill the power vacuum that would inevitably ensue after the superpower withdrawal. Acquisition of certain equipment, such as the second aircraft carrier from the UK, a nuclear-powered submarine on lease, TU-142 MR long-range maritime reconnaissance aircraft, modern Kilo-class conventional submarines from the former Soviet Union, and the expansion of naval facilities at the Andamans in Bay of Bengal, was seen to be an attempt to acquire power projection capabilities and an ability to control crucial Malacca and other straits in the region. By the time the Cold War was beginning to wind down, different kind of concerns started cropping in Southeast

Asia in the light of Soviet withdrawal from Vietnam and American intent to downsize its presence in the Philippines.

It was argued that, with the sudden withdrawal of the super powers, it would create a power vacuum in the region and the Asian great powers, such as China, Japan and India, would vie with each other to fill that void. Once again, possible Indian motives and its military potential to extend its reach into Southeast Asia became subject of considerable debate. These were the circumstances that compelled policy makers in New Delhi to undertake concerted moves firstly to allay the fears in Southeast Asia and secondly to wriggle out of the negative image that got built up. A series of events such as the end of the Cold War, establishment of a new government in New Delhi under the leadership of P.V. Narasimha Rao, the domestic economic doldrums and later the opening up of the Indian economy, etc., came in quite handy to put in place a new policy framework. Although Rao has been credited with for the Look East policy, one can trace the roots of the policy to the initiatives Indian Navy took in the late 1980s. Economic exigencies and political compulsions later were added incentives to re-look at Southeast Asia afresh.

Once the Cold War came to an end, it became imperative for India to dispel fears about its military expansion in an otherwise traditionally non-hostile ASEAN region, lest face the risk of further marginalisation. Also, Southeast Asia itself witnessed a sea change in the political atmosphere in the region. The Cambodian issue was no longer contentious and Vietnam was perceived as an ally rather than an enemy by ASEAN. India as a military power in the emergent Asian balance of power could no longer be ignored. Contrary to the previous perception, the Southeast Asian nations began to look upon India as a power that could play a kind of "balancing role".

On the other hand, it was in India's interest to ensure that Southeast Asia would not be dominated especially by China once it became obvious that the superpowers were going to build-down their presence, which coincided with a similar thinking within Southeast Asia. The upshot of convergence of interests of India and Southeast Asia was the genesis of a new strategic interaction with several of ASEAN nations. Critical remarks with regard to the ambitions of the Indian Navy were replaced by many instances of greater defence cooperation between India and Southeast Asia. A number of confidence building measures (CBMs) that India undertook and greater appreciation of Indian maritime threats by the Southeast Asian countries created a new era of cooperation which began to transcend beyond the naval contours.

Perhaps, the most important were the joint naval exercises India started holding periodically with Indonesia, Malaysia and Singapore since late-1991 near the Andamans. The Indian Naval chief claimed that the ship visits and communication exercises should dispel the apprehensions about any Indian ulterior motives in

Southeast Asia. Equally significant were the defence ties that were being forged between India and many Southeast Asian countries. It was reported that during the visit by Malaysian Defence Minister Najib Tun Abdul Razak in March 1992, a wide-range of defence ties was discussed. Prime Minister Mahathir Mohamad indicated in an interview that the level of cooperation between Malaysia and India would be upgraded with the Malaysian decision to buy the Russian MiG-29 fighter aircraft. He explained that India could extend service and training facilities and supply spare parts.

India and Malaysia signed a Memorandum of Understanding on defence cooperation in February 1993 which, though primarily meant to train Malaysian air force personnel, was fairly broad-ranging to include joint development of certain defence systems of common interest. India expanded facilities at MiG-29 assembly factory to meet the Malaysian demand and at least 100 pilots and ground-supporting staff were trained as part of this MoU, although not much progress could take place with regard to joint development. Malaysia was keen to train its marine commando forces and service its naval boats in India, and have regular exchanges between the navies. Similarly, Kuala Lumpur also expressed interest in the Indian HAL-built *Dornier* 228 Maritime Patrol Craft and HAL-built *Chetak* helicopters for search and rescue and *Cheeta* light utility helicopters.

India's cooperation with Singapore that began in 1993 is probably the deepest. A Singapore proposal for an agreement for the training of its naval and other areas of defence cooperation, which had been pending since 1994, was reportedly cleared by the Indian defence minister in late 1998. Singapore's main interest seems to train its naval personnel in the Indian naval establishment.

Singapore is the only country that has the rare distinction of gaining access to the training facilities at Cochin's Southern Naval Command, in addition to other training facilities. More significant are the anti-submarine warfare exercises India and Singapore have started to hold since 1996 at India's Eastern Command. Apart from joint naval exercises between the two navies, Singapore has already made of India's missile testing range at Chandipur to test out its guns and some missiles in its inventory. Singapore also faces problems regarding the training of its air force crew who earlier used to use the American facilities in the Philippines.

Singapore has already been using Australia, but the Indian option is also being pursued. India has also imported a few patrol boats from Singapore. A number of bilateral defence cooperation activities have been formalized by signing a defence cooperation agreement recently. Thailand too has recently expressed interest in holding joint naval exercises with the Indian Navy. After acquiring the aircraft carrier, Thailand too has turned to India train its naval personnel as the Indian Navy is the only Asian navy that has a long experience of operating carriers. Thai pilots have been trained to operate Sea Harriers in India. Though strictly not in the realm of defence, Thailand has been keen on developing nuclear energy and has in fact broached the idea during the Indian Prime Minister's visit in April 1993 for the supply of a nuclear research reactor. India has signed a defence cooperation agreement with Vietnam in 1994 in an attempt to upgrade the strategic dialogue and understanding between the two countries. Although Vietnam has been downsizing its military quantitatively, its equipment is almost entirely supplied by the former Soviet Union, which urgently needs upgradation or replacement. Recently Vietnam has contracted to acquire a squadron of SU-27 Flankers from Russia, but upgradation of large number of MiG-21 fighters has been on the cards. India would be in a position to help Vietnam in this regard once its own MiG-21 fighters are upgraded in Russia (which India is expected to do under Russian licence). Similarly, there have indications that Vietnam is interested to build up its navy with Indian help in the coming years. However, so far there is no evidence of any concrete cooperation in defence hardware. Joint naval exercises and visits by the senior officers of the Indonesian Navy to the Andaman and Nicobar Islands naval sites, which were Indonesians' major concern, have dispelled earlier fears. Beyond the usual exchange of visits of senior officers, there was very little substantive cooperation till an agreement was signed during the Indian prime minister's visit in January 2001. As part of the 'Agreement on Cooperative Activities in the field of Defence', an Indian defence company, Bharat Electronics Limited, was supposed to supply spare parts for a radar system and other equipment for the Indonesian armed forces, but failed to do so because of some technical-legal complications.

It certainly is a major setback as far India's strategic relations with Indonesia is concerned especially in view of the fact that after more than five decades that defence level contacts were established. Similarly, the earlier anticipated cooperation in aerospace industry also failed to materialise. More recently, for the first time the navies of India and Indonesia have begun to undertake joint patrolling in the Malacca Straits primarily aimed at curbing piracy. As part of the defence cooperation agreement, India is involved in training the Laotian army. Even the Philippines has expressed interest to cooperate with India in the field of defence. Both Defence Minister and the Under Secretary of Defence of the Philippines visited the Indian naval ships, two destroyers and a missile corvette, during a port call at Manila. Quoting observers conversant with the Filipino naval needs, a newspaper report commented that "India had already figured in the calculations of the Philippines as a possible source for the procurement of naval vessels... there is a possibility of the Philippines now looking at India, among others, for the purchase of patrol boats and missile corvettes."

Yet another facet of Indian naval diplomacy is the annual congregation of Bay of Bengal navies, India, Bangladesh, Sri Lanka, Indonesia, Malaysia, Singapore and Thailand, near the Andamans, called the Milan. It was a unique initiative India started in early 1995 involving so many navies of the neighbouring countries. Apart from naval exercises, this event includes coordination of search and rescue operations at sea and establishment of inter-operability with other navies. This is followed by seminars at Port Blair on marine environmental protection and pollution control, disaster relief operations and protection of exclusive economic zones. In the recent past, much of the activity is centered around exchange of personnel for training purposes especially with Singapore, Malaysia, Indonesia and even Myanmar, and periodic naval exercises. An interesting feature after the 911 incidents is the Indian Navy's presence and participation in escort and joint patrolling activities in the Andaman Sea region. Apart from escorting US ships carrying supplies to Afghanistan for counter-terrorism effort, the navies of India and Indonesia have started bilateral joint patrolling along the Malacca and other Straits of Southeast Asia. The Indian Navy is also actively involved in the protection of sea lanes of communication.

Maritime Security Environment in India and South-East Asia

There are a number of maritime security issues that deserve not just a close examination but also greater cooperation among all those concerned with these problems. Many of these cannot be addressed by individual nations but need concerted multilateral action in a cooperative fashion. While many of the Southeast Asian nations have serious limitations given the small sizes of their navies, India has two advantages: its geographic location and possessing the largest navy in the Indian Ocean littoral with a dedicated coast guard service. India is also better placed because there are no maritime disputes pending with any of its Southeast Asian neighbours. Some of the maritime issues where the Indian Navy can take an active part are briefly discussed below.

Security of sea lanes of communication from the Bay of Bengal all the way up to the Sea of Japan, including the strategically important South China Sea, has once again emerged as a vital aspect, especially because of growing fears of terrorist attacks. If civilian aircraft can be used to a devastating effect, super tankers carrying oil can also be used to create havoc at the ports and near the choke points to cause serious damage and disrupt trade. For instance, the straits of Southeast Asia and the South China Sea region are the world's second busiest international sea lanes. "More than half of the world's supertanker traffic passes through the region's waters. More than half of the world's annual merchant fleet tonnage passes through the Straits of Malacca, Sunda, and Lombok, with the majority continuing on into the South China Sea. Tanker traffic through the Strait of Malacca leading into the South China Sea is more than three times greater than Suez Canal traffic, and well over five times more than the Panama Canal. Virtually all shipping that passes through the Malacca and Sunda Straits must pass near the Spratly Islands." It may be noted that the sea lanes in the region carry the most critical elements for the very survival of the economies of large industrialised nations such as Japan and South Korea (now increasingly China), i.e., energy from West Asia. The other dimension in a way related to the above is the security of sea lanes, which has emerged as a major menace in the last few years is piracy because this region is most prone to piracy on the high seas. According to the International Maritime Bureau (IMB), reported incidents of piracy attacks tripled since the early 1990s. In 1999, the IMB's Piracy Reporting Centre (PRC) in Kuala Lumpur tracked 285 piratical attacks-an increase of more than 40 per cent compared to the previous year. In 2002 reported incidents of piracy attacks in this region were 216. While there is slight drop in numbers but they are becoming deadlier. Joint patrolling and concerted action in a multilateral fashion involving regional navies is the only way this problem can be addressed. Indonesia, Malaysia and Singapore, for instance, are already undertaking joint anti-piracy activities, but it is limited to a small geographic area. Moreover, there are severe constraints because of their limited naval capabilities. India and Indonesia too have begun jointly patrol the region and that arrangement can be further extended to other ASEAN nations and others in Northeast Asia. Regular intellectual exercises, such as the conference of the regional navies/coast guards of the Asia Pacific that was held in Tokyo in March 2000 would help in forging cooperation as well as in evolving effective strategies to combat piracy.

South China Sea

The strategically located islands of Spratly and Paracel in the South China Sea have been subject of dispute over sovereignty by several countries with claims varying in degrees and nature. The existence of large quantities of oil and gas reserves may be proven right or wrong, the piracy issue may be tackled, the shipping may not get disturbed after all, but no one can deny the fact that the control of these islands offers enormous strategic importance. Particularly if these islands came under the control of China, the entire security calculus would undergo a radical change. Till this issue is settled peacefully, closer naval links with India would be useful while negotiating with a large neighbour like China. The drug producing 'golden triangle' being in the vicinity, the region is a major international conduit for drug trafficking. The other problem interlinked to this is the spread of small arms and light weapons.

The black and grey markets for these weapons especially in the Indochina region and on the borders of Thailand have been principal source of supply for many insurgency movements in Southeast Asia, India and Sri Lanka. There have been several instances of the Indian Navy and coast guard intercepting the movement of weapons. In February 1998, in a combined operation involving the army, air force and navy, a huge consignment of light weapons was seized in a 48-hour operation, code named "Operation Leech", in the Andaman Sea, which would probably have landed up in northeast India. It was confirmed that the arms consignment had its origin somewhere in Southeast Asia. There are variety of other maritime-linked issues of common concern and interest that can be addressed by close cooperation and collaboration such as search and rescue, pollution at sea, disaster management, and a number of others. For instance, the Indian Navy assisted the Indonesian Navy for hydrographic survey of the waters off Sabang (Indonesia) from April 30, 2001 to May 19, 2001. Similar exercises can be undertaken with other nations as well.

The Look East policy has emerged one of the priority areas of India's foreign policy and a flurry of visits by top leaders and signing of a number of agreements at the regional level with ASEAN and at the bilateral level with its member states will ensure that New Delhi will remain deeply engaged with this region. The relationship between India and Southeast Asia is evolving into a multifaceted one encompassing economic, political and strategic aspects. In the maritime dimension, the Indian Navy is in a position to play a unique role in promoting India's relations with Southeast Asia. Apart from being the largest navy in the Indian Ocean littoral, it has other vantage points as well, which it can take full advantage of. The Cold War strategic divide and the suspicions that some Southeast Asian countries harboured have given way to close cooperation.

The very same Indian Navy is now perceived to be a major stabilizing force, which can contribute to regional peace and stability. It is about time the Indian Navy grabbed this historic opportunity to undertake an activist role in the sphere of maritime security. There are a number of issues in the maritime sector that the Indian Navy and Coast Guard can play an important role in cooperation with Southeast Asia. Straits of Southeast Asia are one of the busiest in terms of shipping and they are also most prone to piracy attacks. Especially after 9/11 terrorist attacks, terrorist threat to disrupt trade has gone up considerably. Search and rescue, tackling pollution at sea, assistance in hydrographic surveys, etc., are other areas cooperation can be forged. It is important that the Indian Navy continues regular interaction through bilateral and where possible multilateral naval meets and exercises with their counterparts in Southeast Asia. Periodic seminars and conferences, exclusive studies and other intellectual exercises will greatly help in identifying not only areas of cooperation in the maritime field but also ways of achieving them.

OVERVIEW OF ASEAN-INDIA RELATIONS TILL DATE

As part of the Council's effort to provide the most comprehensive "business briefing" on ASEAN in the global economy, the Council is pleased to announce the creation of an ASEAN-India section to our website. This section, similar to our ASEAN + 3 page, will provide information and resources to track ASEAN's growing strategic engagement in the areas of trade, investment, and defense with India. This addition to our programming reflects our continued belief that understanding ASEAN well, requires understanding the evolution of ASEAN's links with Asia (ASEAN + 3, India and bilateral links with Japan).

US awareness about India's emergence as global competitor in information technology and one of Asia's leading growth engines has grown in recent years. However the Council believes that the level of understanding about the growing connections between India and ASEAN and their implications for the US business community in the region have yet to be fully developed.

The Council recognizes that the ASEAN-India relationship has the potential to be one of Asia's most strategic intra-regional dynamic relationships. Hence, as we continue to monitor ASEAN's engagement with the plus three countries (Japan, Korea and China), we will look to provide perspectives on how regional trends in ASEAN and developments in Asia are influenced by ASEAN's growing ties with India.

On June 29th, 2006 India and Singapore today took a major step forward in boosting their bilateral ties by signing a Comprehensive Economic Cooperation Agreement (CECA). The agreement is an integrated package liberalizing the trade in goods and services and an agreement on investments. It also has pacts for cooperation in customs, science and technology, education, e-commerce, intellectual property and media. The two sides signed a Bilateral Investment Protection Agreement, a double taxation avoidance agreement.

List of Indian-ASEAN Summit Meetings

- ASEAN-India Partnership for Peace, Progress and Shared Prosperity Agreement, 3rd ASEAN-India Summit, Nov 30, 2004
- Emerging Asian Trends in India-ASEAN Relations
- ASEAN-India ties entering a new phase
- India-ASEAN Senior Officials Meeting, May 20-21, 2003, New Delhi
- ASEAN-India: on the threshold of a new era in partnership
- Joint Statement of the First ASEAN-India Summit: ASEAN-India Cooperation in the 21st Century First ASEAN-India Summit, Phnom Penh Cambodia, Nov 5, 2002
- ASEAN-India Dialogue, Jan. 26 2002, Kuala Lumpur, Malaysia
- Joint Press Release The 1st Meeting of the ASEAN-India Joint Sectoral Cooperation Committee, The 1st Meeting of the ASEAN-India Joint Sectoral Cooperation Committee Bali, Indonesia, Jan 7-8, 1994

Indian-ASEAN Business and Economic Trends

- Framework Agreement on Comprehensive Economic Cooperation between the Association of Southeast Asian Nations and The Republic of India
- India-ASEAN partnership
- PM of India inaugural address at the Second India-ASEAN Business Summit, September 4, 2003, New Delhi

- Foreign Minister Speech at the Second India-ASEAN Business Summit, September 4, 2003, New Delhi
- India-ASEAN FTA
- India-ASEAN Trade Statistics

Indian-ASEAN Science, Defense and Security Relations

- ASEAN-India Strategic Engagement: Singapore-India Synergy
- ASEAN-India Joint Declaration for Cooperation to Combat International Terrorism
- Overview of India and ASEAN Scientific Cooperation
- Indian and ASEAN Eminent Persons Lecture Series
- India-ASEAN Cooperation in Information and Communication Technologies: Issues and Prospects

Indian and ASEAN Based Resources on Indian-ASEAN Ties

- Research and Information System for the Non-Aligned and Other Developing Countries
- South Asia Analysis Group Institute of Southeast Asian Studies
- India's Ministry of Foreign Affairs
- India's Observer Research Foundation
- Bridge-Singapore
- ASEAN Secretariat and India
- Federation of Indian Chambers of Commerce and Industry
- Confederation of Indian Industry.

Part III

ASEAN Sectoral Integration Protocols and Roadmaps

14

TRANSPORT, TRAVEL AND TOURISM SECTORS

ASEAN Sectoral Integration Protocol for Automotives

The Governments of Brunei Darussalam, the Kingdom of Cambodia, the Republic of Indonesia, the Lao People's Democratic Republic (hereinafter referred to as "Lao PDR"), Malaysia, the Union of Myanmar, the Republic of the Philippines, the Republic of Singapore, the Kingdom of Thailand and the Socialist Republic of Vietnam, Member States of the Association of South East Asian Nations (hereinafter collectively referred to as "ASEAN" or "Member States" or singularly as "Member State");

Recalling the Declaration of ASEAN Concord II (Bali Concord II) issued in Bali, Indonesia on 7 October 2003, pursuant to which ASEAN is committed to deepen and broaden its internal economic integration and linkages with the world economy to realise an ASEAN Economic Community;

Desiring that the ASEAN Economic Community will result in ASEAN becoming a single market and production base, turning the diversity that characterises the region into opportunities and business complementation to make ASEAN a more dynamic and stronger segment of the global supply chain;

Noting that as a first step towards the realisation of the ASEAN Economic Community, the Leaders have signed the ASEAN Framework Agreement for the Integration of Priority Sectors on 30th November 2004 in Vientiane, Lao PDR (hereinafter referred to as the "Framework Agreement");

Having carried out an initial round of negotiations and concluded the roadmap for the full integration of the automotive sector in ASEAN,

Have agreed as follows:

Article 1: Objective

The objective of this Protocol is to spell out measures as in the Roadmap referred to in Article 2 to be taken by Member States on a priority basis so as to enable the progressive, expeditious and systematic integration of the automotive sector.

Article 2: Measures

1. The integration measures to be pursued are grouped into two broad categories, taking into account existing agreements or earlier relevant committed measures, namely:

(a) Common measures which cut across all priority sectors; and

(b) Specific measures that are of direct relevance to the automotive sector.

2. All categories of measures shall be pursued in parallel.

3. SEOM may conduct additional negotiations, as and when necessary, to consider new integration measures for the sector.

Article 3: Emergency Measures

1. Article 6 of the Common Effective Preferential Tariff (CEPT) Agreement on Safeguard Measures shall be applied to this Protocol.

2. Where emergency measures are taken pursuant to this Article, immediate notice of such action shall be given to the Ministers responsible for ASEAN economic integration referred to in Article 19 of the Framework Agreement, and such action may be the subject of consultations pursuant to Article 22 of the Framework Agreement.

Article 4: Appendices

1. The Roadmap for Integration of Automotive Products Sector shall be Appendix I to this Protocol and shall form an integral part of it. The negative list in relation to the automotive sector shall be Appendix II to this Protocol.

2. Additional measures other than those identified in the Appendix I may be introduced, as and when deemed necessary through an amendment pursuant to paragraph 2 of Article 5 of this Protocol.

Article 5: Final Provisions

1. Member States shall undertake the appropriate measures to fulfill the agreed obligations arising from this Protocol.

2. The provisions of this Protocol may be modified through amendments mutually agreed upon in writing by all Member States.

3. This Protocol shall enter into force on 31 August 2005. Notwithstanding the specified date of entry into force, Member States undertake to carry out the obligations which arise prior to the date of entry into force of this Protocol in accordance with the timelines indicated in the Framework Agreement for the Integration of Priority Sectors and the Roadmap for Integration of Automotive Products Sector attached to this Protocol.

4. This Protocol shall be deposited with the Secretary-General of ASEAN, who shall furnish a certified copy to each Member State.

In witness whereof, the undersigned, being duly authorised thereto by their respective Governments, have signed the ASEAN Sectoral Integration Protocol for Automotives.

Done at Vientiane, Lao PDR on 29 November 2004, in a single copy in the English language.

ROADMAP FOR INTEGRATION OF AUTOMOTIVE PRODUCTS SECTOR

1. Objective

The objectives of integrating the automotive sector are:

- Strengthen regional integration efforts through liberalization, facilitation and promotion measures to ensure full integration of the automotive sector by 2010.
- Promote private sector participation.

2. Measures

This roadmap includes issues specific to the automotive industry sector, as well as horizontal issues cutting across all sectors. Suggested measures are:

I. Measures for increasing intra-ASEAN Trade and Investment
   - Tariff Elimination
   - Non-Tariff Measures (NTMs)
   - Custom Cooperation
   - Effective Implementation of AICO and CEPT Scheme
   - Improvement of Rules of Origin
   - Standards and Conformance
   - Future investment
   - Improvement of Logistics Services

II. Measures for increasing ASEAN Automotive Industry's Technological Capabilities
   - Enhancing ASEAN Car Manufacturing Capability

III. Measures for improving human resources capability
- Training and Skill Certification System

3. Coverage

The scope of products includes passenger cars, commercial cars, special purpose vehicles, motorcycles, parts / components for both two wheelers and four wheelers.

ASEAN SECTORAL INTEGRATION PROTOCOL FOR AIR TRAVEL

The Governments of Brunei Darussalam, the Kingdom of Cambodia, the Republic of Indonesia, the Lao People's Democratic Republic (hereinafter referred to as "Lao PDR"), Malaysia, the Union of Myanmar, the Republic of the Philippines, the Republic of Singapore, the Kingdom of Thailand and the Socialist Republic of Viet Nam, Member States of the Association of South East Asian Nations (hereinafter collectively referred to as "ASEAN" or "Member States" or singularly as "Member State");

Recalling the Declaration of ASEAN Concord II (Bali Concord II) issued in Bali, Indonesia on 7 October 2003, pursuant to which ASEAN is committed to deepen and broaden its internal economic integration and linkages with the world economy to realise an ASEAN Economic Community;

Desiring that the ASEAN Economic Community will result in ASEAN becoming a single market and production base, turning the diversity that characterises the region into opportunities and business complementation to make ASEAN a more dynamic and stronger segment of the global supply chain;

Noting that as a first step towards the realisation of the ASEAN Economic Community, the Leaders have signed the ASEAN Framework Agreement for the Integration of Priority Sectors on 30th November 2004 in Vientiane, Lao PDR (hereinafter referred to as the "Framework Agreement");

Having carried out an initial round of negotiations and concluded the roadmap for the full integration of the air travel sector in ASEAN,

Have agreed as follows:

Article 1: Objective

The objective of this Protocol is to spell out measures as in the Roadmap referred to in Article 2 to be taken by Member States on a priority basis so as to enable the progressive, expeditious and systematic integration of the air travel sector.

Article 2: Measures

1. The integration measures to be pursued are grouped into two broad categories, taking into account existing agreements or earlier relevant committed measures, namely:

(a) Common measures which cut across all priority sectors as specified in the Framework Agreement; and

(b) Specific measures that are of direct relevance to the air travel sector.

2. All categories of measures shall be pursued in parallel.

3. The ASEAN Transport Ministers (ATM) through STOM and its relevant Working Group(s) may conduct additional negotiations, as and when necessary, to consider new integration measures for the sector.

Article 3: Appendices

1. The Roadmap for Integration of Air Travel Sector shall be Appendix I to this Protocol and shall form an integral part of it.

2. Additional measures other than those identified in the Appendix I may be introduced, as and when deemed necessary through an amendment pursuant to paragraph 2 of Article 4 of this Protocol.

Article 4: Final Provisions

1. Member States shall undertake the appropriate measures to fulfill the agreed obligations arising from this Protocol.

2. The provisions of this Protocol may be modified through amendments mutually agreed upon in writing by all Member States.

3. This Protocol shall enter into force on 31 August 2005. Notwithstanding the specified date of entry into force, Member States undertake to carry out the obligations which arise prior to the date of entry into force of this Protocol in accordance with the timelines indicated in the Framework Agreement for the Integration of Priority Sectors and the Roadmap for Integration of Air Travel Sector attached to this Protocol.

4. This Protocol shall be deposited with the Secretary-General of ASEAN, who shall furnish a certified copy to each Member State.

In Witness Whereof, the undersigned, being duly authorised thereto by their respective Governments, have signed the ASEAN Sectoral Integration Protocol for Air Travel.

Done at Vientiane, Lao PDR on 29 November 2004, in a single copy in the English language.

ROADMAP FOR INTEGRATION OF AIR TRAVEL SECTOR

1. Objective

The objective of this initiative is to advance the full liberalisation of air transport services in ASEAN, to achieve the ASEAN Leaders' vision of Open Sky in the ASEAN region. This Roadmap will build upon the Roadmap for ASEAN Competitive Air Services Policy adopted by the Ninth ATM Meeting in Yangon, Myanmar in October 2003. The Roadmap will complement the overall policy goals of the Action Plan for ASEAN Air Transport Integration and Liberalisation to be adopted at the Tenth ATM in Phnom Penh, Cambodia in November 2004.

2. Measures

This Roadmap provides concrete actions that ASEAN Member Countries shall pursue to achieve greater and significant air transport liberalisation in ASEAN, through a staged and progressive implementation. This roadmap includes issues specific to (a) Liberalisation of air freight services; and (b) Liberalisation of scheduled passenger services. In the implementation, two or more ASEAN Member Countries who are ready can negotiate, conclude and sign implementing agreements/ arrangements in line with the ASEAN-X Formula, on a plurilateral, multilateral or sub-regional basis. The other Member Countries could join in the implementation when they are ready. ASEAN Member Countries can also conclude more liberal bilateral arrangements for air services liberalisation. ASEAN Member Countries shall be provided flexibility with regard to the implementation of the proposed timeline for the specific measures.

3. Coverage

The liberalisation measures will cover the movement/carriage of both passengers and cargo or freight by air transport.

ASEAN SECTORAL INTEGRATION PROTOCOL FOR TOURISM

The Governments of Brunei Darussalam, the Kingdom of Cambodia, the Republic of Indonesia, the Lao People's Democratic Republic (hereinafter referred to as "Lao PDR"), Malaysia, the Union of Myanmar, the Republic of the Philippines, the Republic of Singapore, the Kingdom of Thailand and the Socialist Republic of Viet Nam, Member States of the Association of South East Asian Nations (hereinafter collectively referred to as "ASEAN" or "Member States" or singularly as "Member State");

Recalling the Declaration of ASEAN Concord II (Bali Concord II) issued in Bali, Indonesia on 7 October 2003, pursuant to which ASEAN is committed to deepen and broaden its internal economic integration and linkages with the world economy to realise an ASEAN Economic Community;

Desiring that the ASEAN Economic Community will result in ASEAN becoming a single market and production base, turning the diversity that characterises the region into opportunities and business complementation to make ASEAN a more dynamic and stronger segment of the global supply chain;

Noting that as a first step towards the realisation of the ASEAN Economic Community, the Leaders have signed the ASEAN Framework Agreement for the Integration of Priority Sectors on 30th November 2004 in Vientiane, Lao PDR (hereinafter referred to as the "Framework Agreement");

Having carried out an initial round of negotiations and concluded the roadmap for the full integration of the tourism sector in ASEAN,

Have agreed as follows:

Article 1: Objective

The objective of this Protocol is to spell out measures as in the Roadmap referred to in Article 2 to be taken by Member States on a priority basis so as to enable the progressive, expeditious and systematic integration of the tourism sector.

Article 2: Measures

1. The integration measures to be pursued are grouped into two broad categories, taking into account existing agreements or earlier relevant committed measures, namely:

(a) Common measures which cut across all priority sectors; and

(b) Specific measures that are of direct relevance to the tourism sector.

2. All categories of measures shall be pursued in parallel.

3. SEOM may conduct additional negotiations, as and when necessary, to consider new integration measures for the sector.

Article 3: Appendices

1. The Roadmap for Integration of Tourism Sector shall be Appendix I to this Protocol and shall form an integral part of it.

2. Additional measures other than those identified in the Appendix I may be introduced, as and when deemed necessary through an amendment pursuant to paragraph 2 of Article 4 of this Protocol.

Article 4: Final Provisions

1. Member States shall undertake the appropriate measures to fulfill the agreed obligations arising from this Protocol.

2. The provisions of this Protocol may be modified through amendments mutually agreed upon in writing by all Member States.

3. This Protocol shall enter into force on 31 August 2005. Notwithstanding the specified date of entry into force, Member States undertake to carry out the obligations which arise prior to the date of entry into force of this Protocol in accordance with the timelines indicated in the Framework Agreement for the Integration of Priority Sectors and the Roadmap for Integration of Tourism Sector attached to this Protocol.

4. This Protocol shall be deposited with the Secretary-General of ASEAN, who shall furnish a certified copy to each Member State.

In Witness Whereof, the undersigned, being duly authorised thereto by their respective Governments, have signed the ASEAN Sectoral Integration Protocol for Tourism.

Done at Vientiane, Lao PDR on 29 November 2004, in a single copy in the English language.

ROADMAP FOR INTEGRATION OF TOURISM SECTOR

1. Objectives

The objectives of this initiative are to:

- Achieve full integration of the Tourism sector across all ASEAN Member Countries in moving towards the end-goal of an ASEAN Economic Community as directed by Leaders at the Bali Summit in October 2003.
- Strengthen regional integration efforts through liberalisation, facilitation, and promotion measures to ensure full integration of the Tourism sector by 2010.
- Enhance competitiveness of tourism sector within ASEAN in order to promote ASEAN as a single tourism destination.
- Promote private sector participation and out-sourcing programme within ASEAN.

2. Measures

The integration measures include both common issues cutting across all sectors and specific issues to the tourism sector.

3. Coverage

The sub-sectors subject to services liberalisation appear as Attachment 1.

No.	*Measures*	*Implementing Body*	*Time Line*
	COMMON ISSUES		
I	**Liberalisation of Trade in Services**		
1	Member States shall accelerate the liberalisation of trade in services earlier than 2020. This could be achieved through:		
	—Setting clear targets and schedules of services liberalisation for each priority sector and each round towards achieving freer flow of trade in services by 2010; and	Coordinating Committee on Services (CCS) and Coordinating Committee on Investment (CCI)	on-going
	—The application of the ASEAN-X formula		
2	Accelerating the development of Mutual Recognition Arrangements (MRAs);	CCS	before 2008
3	Promotion of joint ventures and cooperation, including in third country markets	CCS and CCI	on-going
II	**Facilitation of Travel in ASEAN**		
4	Harmonise procedures for the issuance of visas to international travelers	Directors-General of Immigration Departments and Heads of Consular Affairs Division of the Ministries of Foreign Affairs (DGICM)	31 December 2004
5	Provide visa exemption for intra-ASEAN travel by ASEAN nationals		2005
III	**Trade and Investment Promotion**		
6	Intensify intra- and extra-ASEAN joint promotion efforts regularly	CCI; ASEAN Chambers of Commerce and Industry (ASEAN-CCI); and relevant Industry Clubs/ Associations	on-going
7	Organise regular private sector initiatives to undertake:	CCI; ASEAN Business Advisory Council	on-going
	—undertaking more efficient joint ASEAN facilitation and promotion measures to promote FDI ASEAN selling-buying missions; and	(ASEAN-BAC); and ASEAN-CCI	
	—promotional activities to assist CLMV countries		
8	Undertake more effective joint ASEAN facilitation in promotion		on-going

No.	*Measures*	*Implementing Body*	*Time Line*
	measures and develop new sources of inward foreign direct investments, particularly from potential countries such as the People's Republic of China, India and the Republic of Korea		
IV	**Human Resource Development**		
9	Develop and upgrade skills and capacity building through joint trainings and workshops	Senior Labour Officials Meeting (SLOM)	on-going
	SPECIFIC ISSUES		
V	**Acceleration of the liberalisation of tourism sector**		
10	Eliminate the limitations on market access and national treatment to achieve freer flow of trade in tourism sector	CCS	31 December 2010
VI	**ASEAN Tourism Promotion and Marketing**		
11	Encourage the private sector to engage in a joint promotion and marketing of ASEAN tourism activities such as the launching of the ASEAN Hip Hop Pass	ASEAN Tourism Association (ASEANTA)	beginning April 2004
12	Provide diverse ASEAN tourist attractions by promoting a collective tourism package to include, among others, the main markets of China, Japan, Republic of Korea and India	Task Force on ASEAN Tourism Marketing	by 2005
13	Member countries collectively use Visit ASEAN Campaign Logo in exhibitions, media, and publication in their campaigns to promote ASEAN as a single tourism destination		by 2004
14	Collectively organise an ASEAN Tourism Area in international tourism fairs to continuously promote ASEAN as a single tourism destination		31 December 2005
15	Work towards the televised promotion of ASEAN by Leaders as a single destination for tourism and investment.		regularly
16	Set up criteria for an ASEAN Tourism Heritage site and procedures for an ASEAN Heritage Award	National Tourism Organisation (NTO) of Thailand	before ATF 2005
VII	**Tourism Investment**		
17	Provide incentives in the development of tourism infrastructure so	ASEAN NTOs	beginning December 2004

No.	Measures	Implementing Body	Time Line
	as to encourage private investment to ASEAN countries		
18	Provide support and facilitate implementation for the tourism projects approved under the ASEAN Pioneer Project Scheme (APPS)	Focal Points / NTOs and ASEAN BAC	beginning 2005
19	Undertake a study to identify tourism areas that can be attractive for investment and measures to be pursued to promote investment in tourism	NTOs and CCI	by 2005
20	Develop and implement eco-tourism project to promote investment in tourism	NTO Thailand	beginning 2005
VIII	**Tourism Standards**		
21	Establish ASEAN tourism standards, by initially working on the development of hotel standards that would focus on environmental management certification system of hotel	ASEAN NTOs	by 2005
IX	**Human Resource Development**		
22	Establish ASEAN minimum competency standards for tourism professionals	Task Force on Tourism Manpower Development	31 December 2005
23	Establish a Tourism Resource Management and Development Network		31 December 2004
24	Strengthen HRD activities through the development of an intra-ASEAN curriculum covering exchange programme, cross-training, and cross-certification activities	ASEAN NTOs	beginning 2004
25	Initiate a study to establish and strengthen collaborative networks among all tourism-related stakeholders and to create ASEAN Databank to facilitate the growth of tourism	Asian Development Research Forum (ADRF) and Thailand Research Fund (TRF)	30 June 2005
X	**Facilitation of Travel in ASEAN**		
26	Study the feasibility of developing some types of visa facilitation for non-ASEAN travelers traveling within ASEAN	DGICM	beginning 2005

15

Natural Resource-based Sectors: Fisheries, Agriculture, Rubber & Wood

ASEAN SECTORAL INTEGRATION PROTOCOL FOR FISHERIES

The Governments of Brunei Darussalam, the Kingdom of Cambodia, the Republic of Indonesia, the Lao People's Democratic Republic (hereinafter referred to as "Lao PDR"), Malaysia, the Union of Myanmar, the Republic of the Philippines, the Republic of Singapore, the Kingdom of Thailand and the Socialist Republic of Viet Nam, Member States of the Association of South East Asian Nations (hereinafter collectively referred to as "ASEAN" or "Member States" or singularly as "Member State");

Recalling the Declaration of ASEAN Concord II (Bali Concord II) issued in Bali, Indonesia on 7 October 2003, pursuant to which ASEAN is committed to deepen and broaden its internal economic integration and linkages with the world economy to realise an ASEAN Economic Community;

Desiring that the ASEAN Economic Community will result in ASEAN becoming a single market and production base, turning the diversity that characterises the region into opportunities and business complementation to make ASEAN a more dynamic and stronger segment of the global supply chain;

Noting that as a first step towards the realisation of the ASEAN Economic Community, the Leaders have signed the ASEAN Framework Agreement for the Integration of Priority Sectors on 30th November 2004 in Vientiane, Lao PDR (hereinafter referred to as the "Framework Agreement");

Having carried out an initial round of negotiations and concluded the roadmap for the full integration of the fisheries sector in ASEAN,

Have Agreed as follows:

Article 1: Objective

The objective of this Protocol is to spell out measures as in the Roadmap referred to in Article 2 to be taken by Member States on a priority basis so as to enable the progressive, expeditious and systematic integration of the fisheries sector.

Article 2: Measures

1. The integration measures to be pursued are grouped into two broad categories, taking into account existing agreements or earlier relevant committed measures, namely:

(a) Common measures which cut across all priority sectors; and

(b) Specific measures that are of direct relevance to the fisheries sector.

2. All categories of measures shall be pursued in parallel.

3. SEOM may conduct additional negotiations, as and when necessary, to consider new integration measures for the sector.

Article 3: Emergency Measures

1. Article 6 of the Common Effective Preferential Tariff (CEPT) Agreement on Safeguard Measures shall be applied to this Protocol.

2. Where emergency measures are taken pursuant to this Article, immediate notice of such action shall be given to the Ministers responsible for ASEAN economic integration referred to in Article 19 of the Framework Agreement, and such action may be the subject of consultations pursuant to Article 22 of the Framework Agreement.

Article 4: Appendices

1. The Roadmap for Integration of Fisheries Sector shall be Appendix I to this Protocol and shall form an integral part of it. The negative list in relation to the fisheries sector shall be Appendix II to this Protocol.

2. Additional measures other than those identified in the Appendix I may be introduced, as and when deemed necessary through an amendment pursuant to paragraph 2 of Article 5 of this Protocol.

Article 5: Final Provisions

1. Member States shall undertake the appropriate measures to fulfill the agreed obligations arising from this Protocol.

2. The provisions of this Protocol may be modified through amendments mutually agreed upon in writing by all Member States.

3. This Protocol shall enter into force on 31 August 2005. Notwithstanding the specified date of entry into force, Member States undertake to carry out the obligations which arise prior to the date of entry into force of this Protocol in accordance with the timelines indicated in the Framework Agreement for the Integration of Priority Sectors and the Roadmap for Integration of Fisheries Sector attached to this Protocol.

4. This Protocol shall be deposited with the Secretary-General of ASEAN, who shall furnish a certified copy to each Member State.

In Witness Whereof, the undersigned, being duly authorised thereto by their respective Governments, have signed the ASEAN Sectoral Integration Protocol for Fisheries.

Done at Vientiane, Lao PDR on 29 November 2004, in a single copy in the English language.

ROADMAP FOR INTEGRATION OF FISHERIES SECTOR

1. Objectives

The objectives of this initiative are to:

- Strengthen regional integration through liberalisation and facilitation measures in the area of trade in goods, services and investments; and
- Promote private sector participation.

2. Measures

This roadmap includes issues specific to the Fisheries products sector, as well as horizontal issues cutting across all sectors which are:

- Measures for increasing intra-ASEAN Trade and Investment
  - Tariff Elimination
  - Non-Tariff Measures (NTMs)
  - Custom Cooperation
  - Effective Implementation of CEPT Scheme
  - Improvement of Rules of Origin
  - Standards and Conformance
  - Future investment
- Improvement of Logistics Services

3. Coverage

The scope of products identified mainly covers

ASEAN SECTORAL INTEGRATION PROTOCOL FOR AGRO-BASED PRODUCTS

The Governments of Brunei Darussalam, the Kingdom of Cambodia, the Republic of Indonesia, the Lao People's Democratic Republic (hereinafter referred to as "Lao PDR"), Malaysia, the Union of Myanmar, the Republic of the Philippines, the Republic of Singapore, the Kingdom of Thailand and the Socialist Republic of Viet Nam, Member States of the Association of South East Asian Nations (hereinafter collectively referred to as "ASEAN" or "Member States" or singularly as "Member State");

Recalling the Declaration of ASEAN Concord II (Bali Concord II) issued in Bali, Indonesia on 7 October 2003, pursuant to which ASEAN is committed to deepen and broaden its internal economic integration and linkages with the world economy to realise an ASEAN Economic Community;

Desiring that the ASEAN Economic Community will result in ASEAN becoming a single market and production base, turning the diversity that characterises the region into opportunities and business complementation to make ASEAN a more dynamic and stronger segment of the global supply chain;

Noting that as a first step towards the realisation of the ASEAN Economic Community, the Leaders have signed the ASEAN Framework Agreement for the Integration of Priority Sectors on 30th November 2004 in Vientiane, Lao PDR (hereinafter referred to as the "Framework Agreement");

Having carried out an initial round of negotiations and concluded the roadmap for the full integration of the agro-based products sector in ASEAN,

Have agreed as follows:

Article 1: Objective

The objective of this Protocol is to spell out measures as in the Roadmap referred to in Article 2 to be taken by Member States on a priority basis so as to enable the progressive, expeditious and systematic integration of the agro-based products sector.

Article 2: Measures

1. The integration measures to be pursued are grouped into two broad categories, taking into account existing agreements or earlier relevant committed measures, namely:

(a) Common measures which cut across all priority sectors; and

(b) Specific measures that are of direct relevance to the agro-based products sector.

2. All categories of measures shall be pursued in parallel.

3. SEOM may conduct additional negotiations, as and when necessary, to consider new integration measures for the sector.

Article 3: Emergency Measures

1. Article 6 of the Common Effective Preferential Tariff (CEPT) Agreement on Safeguard Measures shall be applied to this Protocol.

2. Where emergency measures are taken pursuant to this Article, immediate notice of such action shall be given to the Ministers responsible for ASEAN economic integration referred to in Article 19 of the Framework Agreement, and such action may be the subject of consultations pursuant to Article 22 of the Framework Agreement.

Article 4: Appendices

1. The Roadmap for Integration of Agro-based Products Sector shall be Appendix I to this Protocol and shall form an integral part of it. The negative list in relation to the agro-based products sector shall be Appendix II to this Protocol.

2. Additional measures other than those identified in the Appendix I may be introduced, as and when deemed necessary through an amendment pursuant to paragraph 2 of Article 5 of this Protocol.

Article 5: Final Provisions

1. Member States shall undertake the appropriate measures to fulfill the agreed obligations arising from this Protocol.

2. The provisions of this Protocol may be modified through amendments mutually agreed upon in writing by all Member States.

3. This Protocol shall enter into force on 31 August 2005. Notwithstanding the specified date of entry into force, Member States undertake to carry out the obligations which arise prior to the date of entry into force of this Protocol in accordance with the timelines indicated in the Framework Agreement for the Integration of Priority Sectors and the Roadmap for Integration of Agro-Based Products Sector attached to this Protocol.

4. This Protocol shall be deposited with the Secretary-General of ASEAN, who shall furnish a certified copy to each Member State.

In witness whereof, the undersigned, being duly authorised thereto by their respective Governments, have signed the ASEAN Sectoral Integration Protocol for Agro-Based Products.

Done at Vientiane, Lao PDR on 29 November 2004, in a single copy in the English language.

ROADMAP FOR INTEGRATION OF AGRO-BASED PRODUCTS SECTOR

1. Objectives

The objectives of this initiative are to:

- Strengthen regional integration on through liberalisation and facilitation measures in the area of trade in goods, services and investments; and
- Promote private sector participation.

2. Measures

This roadmap includes issues specific to the Agro-based products sector as well as horizontal issues cutting across all sectors which are:

- Measures for increasing intra-ASEAN Trade and Investment
  - Tariff Elimination
  - Non-Tariff Measures (NTMs)
  - Custom Cooperation
  - Effective Implementation of CEPT Scheme
  - Improvement of Rules of Origin
  - Standards and Conformance
  - Future investment
  - Improvement of Logistics Services

3. Coverage

The scope of products identified mainly covers Agro-based products.

ASEAN SECTORAL INTEGRATION PROTOCOL FOR RUBBER-BASED PRODUCTS

The Governments of Brunei Darussalam, the Kingdom of Cambodia, the Republic of Indonesia, the Lao People's Democratic Republic (hereinafter referred to as "Lao PDR"), Malaysia, the Union of Myanmar, the Republic of the Philippines, the Republic of Singapore, the Kingdom of Thailand and the Socialist Republic of Viet Nam, Member States of the Association of South East Asian Nations (hereinafter collectively referred to as "ASEAN" or "Member States" or singularly as "Member State");

Recalling the Declaration of ASEAN Concord II (Bali Concord II) issued in Bali, Indonesia on 7 October 2003, pursuant to which ASEAN is committed to deepen and broaden its internal economic integration and linkages with the world economy to realise an ASEAN Economic Community;

Desiring that the ASEAN Economic Community will result in ASEAN becoming a single market and production base, turning the diversity that characterises the region into opportunities and business complementation to make ASEAN a more dynamic and stronger segment of the global supply chain;

Noting that as a first step towards the realisation of the ASEAN Economic Community, the Leaders have signed the ASEAN Framework Agreement for the Integration of Priority Sectors on 30th November 2004 in Vientiane, Lao PDR (hereinafter referred to as the "Framework Agreement");

Having carried out an initial round of negotiations and concluded the roadmap for the full integration of the rubber-based products sector in ASEAN,

Have Agreed as follows:

Article 1: Objective

The objective of this Protocol is to spell out measures as in the Roadmap referred to in Article 2 to be taken by Member States on a priority basis so as to enable the progressive, expeditious and systematic integration of the rubber-based products sector.

Article 2: Measures

1. The integration measures to be pursued are grouped into two broad categories, taking into account existing agreements or earlier relevant committed measures, namely:

(a) Common measures which cut across all priority sectors; and

(b) Specific measures that are of direct relevance to the rubber-based products sector.

2. All categories of measures shall be pursued in parallel.

3. SEOM may conduct additional negotiations, as and when necessary, to consider new integration measures for the sector.

Article 3: Emergency Measures

1. Article 6 of the Common Effective Preferential Tariff (CEPT) Agreement on Safeguard Measures shall be applied to this Protocol.

2. Where emergency measures are taken pursuant to this Article, immediate notice of such action shall be given to the Ministers responsible for ASEAN economic integration referred to in Article 19 of the Framework Agreement, and such action may be the subject of consultations pursuant to Article 22 of the Framework Agreement.

Article 4: Appendices

1. The Roadmap for Integration of Rubber-Based Products Sector shall be Appendix I to this Protocol and shall form an integral part of it. The negative list in relation to the rubber-based products sector shall be Appendix II to this Protocol.

2. Additional measures other than those identified in the Appendix I may be introduced, as and when deemed necessary through an amendment pursuant to paragraph 2 of Article 5 of this Protocol.

Article 5: Final Provisions

1. Member States shall undertake the appropriate measures to fulfill the agreed obligations arising from this Protocol.

2. The provisions of this Protocol may be modified through amendments mutually agreed upon in writing by all Member States.

3. This Protocol shall enter into force on 31 August 2005. Notwithstanding the specified date of entry into force, Member States undertake to carry out the obligations which arise prior to the date of entry into force of this Protocol in accordance with the timelines indicated in the Framework Agreement for the Integration of Priority Sectors and the Roadmap for Integration of Rubber-Based Products Sector attached to this Protocol.

4. This Protocol shall be deposited with the Secretary-General of ASEAN, who shall furnish a certified copy to each Member State.

In Witness whereof, the undersigned, being duly authorised thereto by their respective Governments, have signed the ASEAN Sectoral Integration Protocol for Rubber-Based Products.

Done at Vientiane, Lao PDR on 29 November 2004, in a single copy in the English language.

ROADMAP FOR INTEGRATION OF RUBBER-BASE PRODUCTS SECTOR

1. Objectives

The objectives of this initiative are to:

- Strengthen regional integration on through liberalisation and facilitation measures in the area of trade in goods, services and investments; and
- Promote private sector participation.

2. Measures

In bringing greater regional integration, the proposed measures include specific measures that are of direct relevance to the rubber-based products sector, as well as common measures that cut across all priority integration sectors. The integration approaches are premised on:

- Combining the economic strengths of ASEAN member countries for regional advantage;
- Facilitate and promote intra-ASEAN trade and investments;
- Improve the condition to attract and retain manufacturing and other economic activities within the region;
- Promote outsourcing programme within ASEAN; and
- Promote the development of "Made in ASEAN" products and services.

3. Coverage

The rubber-based products cover materials of rubber; tyres, flaps and inner tubes; rubber gloves; and articles of rubber. Details of product coverage appear as Attachment 1.

ASEAN SECTORAL INTEGRATION PROTOCOL FOR WOOD-BASED PRODUCTS

The Governments of Brunei Darussalam, the Kingdom of Cambodia, the Republic of Indonesia, the Lao People's Democratic Republic (hereinafter referred to as "Lao PDR"), Malaysia, the Union of Myanmar, the Republic of the Philippines, the Republic of Singapore, the Kingdom of Thailand and the Socialist Republic of Viet Nam, Member States of the Association of South East Asian Nations (hereinafter collectively referred to as "ASEAN" or "Member States" or singularly as "Member State");

Recalling the Declaration of ASEAN Concord II (Bali Concord II) issued in Bali, Indonesia on 7 October 2003, pursuant to which ASEAN is committed to deepen and broaden its internal economic integration and linkages with the world economy to realise an ASEAN Economic Community;

Desiring that the ASEAN Economic Community will result in ASEAN becoming a single market and production base, turning the diversity that characterises the region into opportunities and business complementation to make ASEAN a more dynamic and stronger segment of the global supply chain;

Noting that as a first step towards the realisation of the ASEAN Economic Community, the Leaders have signed the ASEAN Framework Agreement for the Integration of Priority Sectors on 30th November 2004 in Vientiane, Lao PDR (hereinafter referred to as the "Framework Agreement");

Having carried out an initial round of negotiations and concluded the roadmap for the full integration of the wood-based products sector in ASEAN,

Have agreed as follows:

Article 1: Objectives

The objective of this Protocol is to spell out measures as in the Roadmap referred to in Article 2 to be taken by Member States on a priority basis so as to enable the progressive, expeditious and systematic integration of the wood-based products sector.

Article 2: Measures

1. The integration measures to be pursued are grouped into two broad categories, taking into account existing agreements or earlier relevant committed measures, namely:

(a) Common measures which cut across all priority sectors; and
(b) Specific measures that are of direct relevance to the wood-based products sector.

2. All categories of measures shall be pursued in parallel.

3. SEOM may conduct additional negotiations, as and when necessary, to consider new integration measures for the sector.

Article 3: Emergency Measures

1. Article 6 of the Common Effective Preferential Tariff (CEPT) Agreement on Safeguard Measures shall be applied to this Protocol.

2. Where emergency measures are taken pursuant to this Article, immediate notice of such action shall be given to the Ministers responsible for ASEAN economic integration referred to in Article 19 of the Framework Agreement, and such action may be the subject of consultations pursuant to Article 22 of the Framework Agreement.

Article 4: Appendices

1. The Roadmap for Integration of Wood-Based Products Sector shall be Appendix I to this Protocol and shall form an integral part of it. The negative list in relation to the wood-based products sector shall be Appendix II to this Protocol.

2. Additional measures other than those identified in the Appendix I may be introduced, as and when deemed necessary through an amendment pursuant to paragraph 2 of Article 5 of this Protocol.

Article 5: Final Provisions

1. Member States shall undertake the appropriate measures to fulfill the agreed obligations arising from this Protocol.

2. The provisions of this Protocol may be modified through amendments mutually agreed upon in writing by all Member States.

3. This Protocol shall enter into force on 31 August 2005. Notwithstanding the specified date of entry into force, Member States undertake to carry out the obligations which arise prior to the date of entry into force of this Protocol in accordance with the timelines indicated in the Framework Agreement for the Integration of Priority Sectors and the Roadmap for Integration of Wood-Based Products Sector attached to this Protocol.

4. This Protocol shall be deposited with the Secretary-General of ASEAN, who shall furnish a certified copy to each Member State.

In witness whereof, the undersigned, being duly authorised thereto by their respective Governments, have signed the ASEAN Sectoral Integration Protocol for Wood-Based Products.

Done at Vientiane, Lao PDR on 29 November 2004, in a single copy in the English language.

ROADMAP FOR INTEGRATION OF WOOD-BASED PRODUCTS SECTOR

1. Objectives

The objectives of this initiative are :

- Strengthen regional integration on through liberalisation and facilitation measures in the area of trade in goods, services and investments; and
- Promote private sector participation.

2. Measures

This roadmap includes issues specific to the wood-based products, as well as horizontal issues cutting across all sectors. The approaches proposed for the integration for wood-based products are premised on:

- Combining the economic strengths of ASEAN member countries for regional advantage;
- Facilitate and promote intra-ASEAN investments:
- Improve the condition to attract and retain manufacturing and other economic activities within the region;
- Promote outsourcing program within ASEAN; and
- Promote the development of "Made in ASEAN" products and services.

3. Coverage

The scope of wood-based products appears.

16

OTHER SOCIO-ECONOMIC AND INDUSTRY ORIENTED SECTORS: e-ASEAN, ELECTRONICS, TEXTILES, APPAREL AND HEALTHCARE

ROADMAP FOR INTEGRATION OF E-ASEAN SECTOR

1. Objectives

The objectives of integrating the e-ASEAN sector are as follows:

- Liberalisation of trade in ICT products, ICT services and investments;
- Develop, strengthen and enhance the competitiveness of the ICT sector in ASEAN;
- Reduce the digital divide within individual ASEAN Member States and amongst ASEAN Member States; and
- Promote cooperation between the public and private sectors in realising e-ASEAN.

2. Measures

The initiatives build on those already undertaken (such as the elimination of tariffs on ITA1 products for ASEAN-6 countries by 1 Jan 2005), and incorporate additional recommendations in the Bali Concord II, the e-ASEAN Roadmap for Integration of ASEAN (RIA) matrix, and The Singapore Declaration - An Action Agenda, issued at the 3rd ASEAN TELMIN meeting, as well as those gathered from private and public sector representatives from all ASEAN countries.

Full implementation of these recommendations is key for ASEAN to achieve our goal of integrating the e-ASEAN sector by 2010. However they are not meant to be exhaustive, and ASEAN should continue to incorporate other necessary measures as and when appropriate. This roadmap includes issues specific to the e-ASEAN sector, as well as horizontal issues cutting across all sectors.

3. Coverage

This roadmap will cover products in both the e-ASEAN Framework Agreement (ITA1 + 34 items), as well as other ITA products.

ASEAN SECTORAL INTEGRATION PROTOCOL FOR ELECTRONICS

The Governments of Brunei Darussalam, the Kingdom of Cambodia, the Republic of Indonesia, the Lao People's Democratic Republic (hereinafter referred to as "Lao PDR"), Malaysia, the Union of Myanmar, the Republic of the Philippines, the Republic of Singapore, the Kingdom of Thailand and the Socialist Republic of Viet Nam, Member States of the Association of South East Asian Nations (hereinafter collectively referred to as "ASEAN" or "Member States" or singularly as "Member State");

Recalling the Declaration of ASEAN Concord II (Bali Concord II) issued in Bali, Indonesia on 7 October 2003, pursuant to which ASEAN is committed to deepen and broaden its internal economic integration and linkages with the world economy to realise an ASEAN Economic Community;

Desiring that the ASEAN Economic Community will result in ASEAN becoming a single market and production base, turning the diversity that characterises the region into opportunities and business complementation to make ASEAN a more dynamic and stronger segment of the global supply chain;

Noting that as a first step towards the realisation of the ASEAN Economic Community, the Leaders have signed the ASEAN Framework Agreement for the Integration of Priority Sectors on 30th November 2004 in Vientiane, Lao PDR (hereinafter referred to as the "Framework Agreement");

Having carried out an initial round of negotiations and concluded the roadmap for the full integration of the electronics sector in ASEAN,

Have agreed as follows:

Article 1: Objective

The objective of this Protocol is to spell out measures as in the Roadmap referred to in Article 2 to be taken by Member States on a priority basis so as to enable the progressive, expeditious and systematic integration of the electronics sector.

Article 2: Measures

1. The integration measures to be pursued are grouped into two broad categories, taking into account existing agreements or earlier relevant committed measures, namely:

(a) Common measures which cut across all priority sectors; and

(b) Specific measures that are of direct relevance to the electronics sector.

2. All categories of measures shall be pursued in parallel.

3. SEOM may conduct additional negotiations, as and when necessary, to consider new integration measures for the sector.

Article 3: Emergency Measures

1. Article 6 of the Common Effective Preferential Tariff (CEPT) Agreement on Safeguard Measures shall be applied to this Protocol.

2. Where emergency measures are taken pursuant to this Article, immediate notice of such action shall be given to the Ministers responsible for ASEAN economic integration referred to in Article 19 of the Framework Agreement, and such action may be the subject of consultations pursuant to Article 22 of the Framework Agreement.

Article 4: Appendices

1. The Roadmap for Integration of Electronics Sector shall be Appendix I to this Protocol and shall form an integral part of it. The negative list in relation to the electronics sector shall be Appendix II to this Protocol.

2. Additional measures other than those identified in the Appendix I may be introduced, as and when deemed necessary through an amendment pursuant to paragraph 2 of Article 5 of this Protocol.

Article 5: Final Provisions

1. Member States shall undertake the appropriate measures to fulfill the agreed obligations arising from this Protocol.

2. The provisions of this Protocol may be modified through amendments mutually agreed upon in writing by all Member States.

3. This Protocol shall enter into force on 31 August 2005. Notwithstanding the specified date of entry into force, Member States undertake to carry out the obligations which arise prior to the date of entry into force of this Protocol in accordance with the timelines indicated in the Framework Agreement for the Integration of Priority Sectors and the Roadmap for Integration of Electronics Sector attached to this Protocol.

4. This Protocol shall be deposited with the Secretary-General of ASEAN, who shall furnish a certified copy to each Member State.

In witness whereof, the undersigned, being duly authorised thereto by their respective Governments, have signed the ASEAN Sectoral Integration Protocol for Electronics.

Done at Vientiane, Lao PDR on 29 November 2004, in a single copy in the English language.

ROADMAP FOR INTEGRATION FO ELECTRONICS SECTOR

1. Objectives

The objectives of integrating the electronics sector are:

- Develop, strengthen and enhance the competitiveness of the ASEAN Electronics sector and promote ASEAN as an integrated platform in which to do business in electronics;
- Strengthen regional integration efforts through liberalization, facilitation and promotion measures to ensure full integration of the Electronics sector by 2010;
- Promote private sector participation.

2. Measures

This roadmap includes specific measures that are of direct relevance to the Electronics sector, as well as common measures that cut across all priority integration sectors. The integration approaches are premised on:

- Combining the economic strengths of ASEAN member countries for regional advantage;
- Facilitate and promote intra-ASEAN investments;
- Improve the condition to attract and retain manufacturing and other economic activities within the region;
- Promote outsourcing program within ASEAN.

3. Coverage

The scope of products include electronic data processing (EDP) equipment, electrical and electronic home appliances, medical and industrial equipment, telecommunication equipment, communications and radar, automotive electronics, instrumentation and controls, mechanical parts of electronic and electrical products, semiconductor devices (including inputs for the manufacture of semiconductor devices), and other machineries and equipment for the manufacture of semiconductors and printed circuit boards (PCBs).

ASEAN SECTORAL INTEGRATION PROTOCOL FOR TEXTILES AND APPAREL PRODUCTS

The Governments of Brunei Darussalam, the Kingdom of Cambodia, the Republic of Indonesia, the Lao People's Democratic Republic (hereinafter referred to as "Lao PDR"), Malaysia, the Union of Myanmar, the Republic of the Philippines, the Republic of Singapore, the Kingdom of Thailand and the Socialist Republic of Viet Nam, Member States of the Association of South East Asian Nations (hereinafter collectively referred to as "ASEAN" or "Member States" or singularly as "Member State");

Recalling the Declaration of ASEAN Concord II (Bali Concord II) issued in Bali, Indonesia on 7 October 2003, pursuant to which ASEAN is committed to deepen and broaden its internal economic integration and linkages with the world economy to realise an ASEAN Economic Community;

Desiring that the ASEAN Economic Community will result in ASEAN becoming a single market and production base, turning the diversity that characterises the region into opportunities and business complementation to make ASEAN a more dynamic and stronger segment of the global supply chain;

Noting that as a first step towards the realisation of the ASEAN Economic Community, the Leaders have signed the ASEAN Framework Agreement for the Integration of Priority Sectors on 30th November 2004 in Vientiane, Lao PDR (hereinafter referred to as the "Framework Agreement");

Having carried out an initial round of negotiations and concluded the roadmap for the full integration of the textiles and apparel products sector in ASEAN,

Have agreed as follows:

Article 1: Objective

The objective of this Protocol is to spell out measures as in the Roadmap referred to in Article 2 to be taken by Member States on a priority basis so as to enable the progressive, expeditious and systematic integration of the textiles and apparel products sector.

Article 2: Measures

1. The integration measures to be pursued are grouped into two broad categories, taking into account existing agreements or earlier relevant committed measures, namely:

(a) Common measures which cut across all priority sectors; and

(b) Specific measures that are of direct relevance to the textiles and apparel products sector.

2. All categories of measures shall be pursued in parallel.

3. SEOM may conduct additional negotiations, as and when necessary, to consider new integration measures for the sector.

Article 3: Emergency Measures

1. Article 6 of the Common Effective Preferential Tariff (CEPT) Agreement on Safeguard Measures shall be applied to this Protocol.

2. Where emergency measures are taken pursuant to this Article, immediate notice of such action shall be given to the Ministers responsible for ASEAN economic integration referred to in Article 19 of the Framework Agreement, and such action may be the subject of consultations pursuant to Article 22 of the Framework Agreement.

Article 4: Appendices

1. The Roadmap for Integration of Textiles and Apparel Products Sector shall be Appendix I to this Protocol and shall form an integral part of it. The negative list in relation to the textiles and apparel products sector shall be Appendix II to this Protocol.

2. Additional measures other than those identified in the Appendix I may be introduced, as and when deemed necessary through an amendment pursuant to paragraph 2 of Article 5 of this Protocol.

Article 5: Final Provisions

1. Member States shall undertake the appropriate measures to fulfill the agreed obligations arising from this Protocol.

2. The provisions of this Protocol may be modified through amendments mutually agreed upon in writing by all Member States.

3. This Protocol shall enter into force on 31 August 2005. Notwithstanding the specified date of entry into force, Member States undertake to carry out the obligations which arise prior to the date of entry into force of this Protocol in accordance with the timelines indicated in the Framework Agreement for the Integration of Priority Sectors and the Roadmap for Integration of Textiles and Apparel Products Sector attached to this Protocol.

4. This Protocol shall be deposited with the Secretary-General of ASEAN, who shall furnish a certified copy to each Member State.

In witness whereof, the undersigned, being duly authorised thereto by their respective Governments, have signed the ASEAN Sectoral Integration Protocol for Textiles and Apparel Products.

Done at Vientiane, Lao PDR on 29 November 2004, in a single copy in the English language.

ROADMAP FOR INTEGRATION OF TEXTILES AND APPAREL PRODUCTS SECTOR

1. Objectives

The objectives of this initiative are :

- Strengthen regional integration on through liberalisation and facilitation measures in the area of trade in goods, services and investments; and
- Promote private sector participation.

2. Measures

In bringing greater regional integration, the proposed measures include specific measures that are of direct relevance to the textiles and apparel sector, as well as common measures that cut across all priority integration sectors. The integration approaches are premised on:

- Combining the economic strengths of ASEAN member countries for regional advantage;
- Facilitate and promote intra-ASEAN trade and investments;
- Improve the condition to attract and retain manufacturing and other economic activities within the region;
- Promote outsourcing programme within ASEAN; and
- Promote the development of "Made in ASEAN" products and services.

3. Coverage

The textiles and apparel products cover materials of textiles; fabrics; linen; cloth; garments; articles of textiles; and other worn articles.

ASEAN SECTORAL INTEGRATION PROTOCOL FOR HEALTHCARE

The Governments of Brunei Darussalam, the Kingdom of Cambodia, the Republic of Indonesia, the Lao People's Democratic Republic (hereinafter referred to as "Lao PDR"), Malaysia, the Union of Myanmar, the Republic of the Philippines, the Republic of Singapore, the Kingdom of Thailand and the Socialist Republic of Viet Nam, Member States of the Association of South East Asian Nations (hereinafter collectively referred to as "ASEAN" or "Member States" or singularly as "Member State");

Recalling the Declaration of ASEAN Concord II (Bali Concord II) issued in Bali, Indonesia on 7 October 2003, pursuant to which ASEAN is committed to deepen and broaden its internal economic integration and linkages with the world economy to realise an ASEAN Economic Community;

Desiring that the ASEAN Economic Community will result in ASEAN becoming a single market and production base, turning the diversity that characterises the region into opportunities and business complementation to make ASEAN a more dynamic and stronger segment of the global supply chain;

Noting that as a first step towards the realisation of the ASEAN Economic Community, the Leaders have signed the ASEAN Framework Agreement for the Integration of Priority Sectors on 30th November 2004 in Vientiane, Lao PDR (hereinafter referred to as the "Framework Agreement");

Having carried out an initial round of negotiations and concluded the roadmap for the full integration of the healthcare sector in ASEAN,

Have agreed as follows:

Article 1: Objective

The objective of this Protocol is to spell out measures as in the Roadmap referred to in Article 2 to be taken by Member States on a priority basis so as to enable the progressive, expeditious and systematic integration of the healthcare sector.

Article 2: Measures

1. The integration measures to be pursued are grouped into two broad categories, taking into account existing agreements or earlier relevant committed measures, namely:

(a) Common measures which cut across all priority sectors; and

(b) Specific measures that are of direct relevance to the healthcare sector.

2. All categories of measures shall be pursued in parallel.

3. SEOM may conduct additional negotiations, as and when necessary, to consider new integration measures for the sector.

Article 3: Emergency Measures

1. Article 6 of the Common Effective Preferential Tariff (CEPT) Agreement on Safeguard Measures shall be applied to this Protocol.

2. Where emergency measures are taken pursuant to this Article, immediate notice of such action shall be given to the Ministers responsible for ASEAN economic integration referred to in Article 19 of the Framework Agreement, and such action may be the subject of consultations pursuant to Article 22 of the Framework Agreement.

Article 4: Appendices

1. The Roadmap for Integration of Healthcare Sector shall be Appendix I to this

Protocol and shall form an integral part of it. The negative list in relation to the healthcare sector shall be Appendix II to this Protocol.

2. Additional measures other than those identified in the Appendix I may be introduced, as and when deemed necessary through an amendment pursuant to paragraph 2 of Article 5 of this Protocol.

Article 5: Final Provisions

1. Member States shall undertake the appropriate measures to fulfill the agreed obligations arising from this Protocol.

2. The provisions of this Protocol may be modified through amendments mutually agreed upon in writing by all Member States.

3. This Protocol shall enter into force on 31 August 2005. Notwithstanding the specified date of entry into force, Member States undertake to carry out the obligations which arise prior to the date of entry into force of this Protocol in accordance with the timelines indicated in the Framework Agreement for the Integration of Priority Sectors and the Roadmap for Integration of Healthcare Sector attached to this Protocol.

4. This Protocol shall be deposited with the Secretary-General of ASEAN, who shall furnish a certified copy to each Member State.

In witness whereof, the undersigned, being duly authorised thereto by their respective Governments, have signed the ASEAN Sectoral Integration Protocol for Healthcare.

Dibe at Vientiane, Lao PDR on 29 November 2004, in a single copy in the English language.

ROADMAP FOR INTEGRATION OF HEALTHCARE SECTOR

1. Objectives

The objectives of this initiative are to:

- Strengthen regional integration through liberalisation and facilitation measures in the area of trade in goods, services and investments; and
- Promote private sector participation.

2. Measures

The initiatives within incorporate recommendations in the Bali Concord II as well as those gathered from private and public sector representatives from all ASEAN countries.

Full implementation of these recommendations is key for ASEAN to achieve our goal of integrating the healthcare sector by 2010. However they are not meant to be exhaustive, and ASEAN should continue to incorporate other necessary measures as and when appropriate. This roadmap includes issues specific to the Healthcare sector, as well as horizontal issues cutting across all sectors.

3. Coverage

The scope of product coverage for the healthcare sector appears as follows:

No.	*Measures*	*Implementing Body*	*Time Line*
	COMMON ISSUES		
I	**Tariff Elimination**		
1	Eliminate CEPT-AFTA tariffs on all identified products	Coordinating Committee on the Implementation of the CEPT Scheme for AFTA (CCCA)	ASEAN 6: 2007 CLMV: 2012
II	**Non-Tariff Measures (NTMs)**		
2	Establish the Database of ASEAN NTMs to ensure transparency[1]	CCCA	30 June 2004
3	Establish clear criteria to identify measures that are classified as barriers to trade		30 June 2005
4	Establish a clear and definitive work programme for the removal of the barriers.		31 December 2005
5	Adopt the WTO Agreement on Import Licensing Procedures and develop implementation guidelines appropriate for ASEAN.		31 December 2004
III	**Rules of Origin**		
6	Improve the CEPT Rules of Origin by: —making it more transparent, predictable and standardised taking into account the best practices of other Regional Trade Agreements including the rules of origin of the WTO; and —adopting substantial transformation as alternative criteria for conferring origin status.	Task Force on CEPT Rules of Origin (ROO-TF)	31 December 2004

No.	*Measures*	*Implementing Body*	*Time Line*
IV	**Customs Procedures**		
7	Extend the application of the ASEAN Harmonised Tariff Nomenclature (AHTN) for extra-ASEAN trade.	Expert Committee on Customs Matters (ECCM)	on-going
8	Develop a simplified, improved and harmonised customs declaration form.		31 December 2005
9	Ensure full implementation of the Green Lane System for CEPT Products, or similar systems, at entry points of all Member States.		31 December 2004
10	Develop implementation guidelines, as appropriate, for Member States which are not members of the WTO to fulfill the obligations of the WTO Agreement on Customs Valuation		31 December 2004
11	Adopt service commitment (client charter) by ASEAN customs authorities.		31 December 2004
12	Develop the Single Window approach, including the electronic processing of trade documents at national and regional levels	Inter-Agency Task Force on Single Window	31 December 2005
V	**Standards and Conformance**		
13	Accelerate the implementation/ development of sectoral Mutual Recognition Arrangements (MRAs), as appropriate	ASEAN Consultative Committee on Standards and Quality (ACCSQ)	beginning 1 January 2005
14	Encourage domestic regulators to recognise test reports issued by testing laboratories which are already accredited by National Accreditation Bodies in ASEAN that are signatories to ILAC and APLAC MRA		on-going
15	Set clear targets and schedules for harmonisation of standards, wherever required; where international standards are not available, and when requested by industry, align national standards among Member States.		31 December 2005
16	Harmonise and/or develop, wherever appropriate, technical regulations for national application.		31 December 2010
17	Ensure compliance with the requirements, rights and obligations of WTO Agreements on Technical Barriers to Trade and the Application of Sanitary and Phyto-Sanitary Measures		on-going

No.	Measures	Implementing Body	Time Line
18	Explore development of ASEAN policy on standards and conformance to further facilitate the realisation of the ASEAN Economic Community.		beginning 2005
VI	**Logistics Services**		
19	Expedite the development of integrated transport logistics services within ASEAN through: —Promotion of efficient door-to-door cargo transport and cross-border transport facilitation through the expeditious implementation of the ASEAN Framework Agreement on the Facilitation of Goods in Transit, and the ASEAN Framework Agreement on Multimodal Transport; —Improvement of land transport network infrastructures and services to achieve better inter-connectivity, inter-operability and inter-modality with the national, regional and international maritime and air transport gateways; —Strengthening intra-ASEAN maritime and shipping transport services; and —Establishment of enabling and conducive policy environment for increased private sector involvement and/or public-private partnerships in the development of transport infrastructure and the provision and operation of transport logistics facilities and services.	Senior Transport Officials Meeting (STOM)	beginning 2005
VII	**Outsourcing and Industrial Complementation**		
20	Identify and develop specialisation of production processes, research and development (R&D), and testing facilities based on comparative advantages of individual Member States	Working Group on Industrial Cooperation (WGIC), with inputs from the private sector	on-going
21	Develop guidelines to promote outsourcing arrangements among Member States, as applicable.		

No.	*Measures*	*Implementing Body*	*Time Line*
VIII	**ASEAN Integration System of Preferences**		
22	Endeavour to expand the coverage of the ASEAN Integration System of Preferences (AISP) Scheme by including products in the priority integration sectors	CCCA	on-going
IX	**Investments**		
23	Accelerate the opening up of sectors currently in the Sensitive List (SL) by transferring these sectors into the Temporary Exclusion List (TEL) under the Framework Agreement on the ASEAN Investment Area, using the ASEAN-X formula.	Coordinating Committee on Investment (CCI)	beginning 2004
24	Reduce restrictive investment measures in the SL		beginning 2004
25	Complete the progressive elimination of restrictive investment measures in the TEL		on-going[2]
26	Identify programmes and activities to promote investments in ASEAN		31 December 2005
27	Promote manufacturing processes across different ASEAN countries to take advantage of their comparative strengths through:		
	—the establishment of a network of ASEAN free trade zones to facilitate outsourcing activities		beginning 2005
	—undertaking more efficient joint ASEAN facilitation and promotion measures to promote FDI		on-going
28	Promote and facilitate joint/cross border investments in manufacturing activities through:		on-going
	—special incentives, where appropriate, to be given by CLMV for investments from ASEAN		
	—special measures, where appropriate to be given by ASEAN 6 to promote and facilitate relocation of investment to CLMV countries especially for labour intensive manufacturing activities		

No.	Measures	Implementing Body	Time Line
X	**Trade and Investment Promotion**		
29	Intensify intra- and extra ASEAN joint promotion efforts regularly	CCI; ASEAN Chambers of Commerce and Industry (ASEAN-CCI); and relevant Industry Clubs/ Associations	on-going beginning 2005
30	Organise regular private sector initiatives to undertake: —more efficient joint ASEAN facilitation and promotion measures to promote FDI ASEAN selling-buying missions; and —promotional activities to assist CLMV countries	CCI; ASEAN Business Advisory Council (ASEAN-BAC); and ASEAN-CCI	on-going beginning 2005
31	Undertake more effective joint ASEAN facilitation in promotion measures and develop new sources of inward foreign direct investments, particularly from potential countries such as the People's Republic of China, India and the Republic of Korea		on-going
XI	**Intra-ASEAN Trade and Investment Statistics**		
32	Establish an effective system to monitor intra-ASEAN trade and investment through: —provision of updates to the ASEAN Secretariat of the latest trade (goods and services) and investment statistics —preparation of consolidated industry profile, by the respective associations, which among other matters, cover information such as production capacity and product range	Working Group on Statistics; Working Group on Foreign Direct Investment Statistics; and CCCA	on-going
XII	**Intellectual Property Rights**		
33	Expand the scope of ASEAN intellectual property rights cooperation beyond trademarks and patents by including cooperation in copyrights information exchange and enforcement	ASEAN Working Group on Intellectual Property Cooperation (AWGIPC)	31 December 2004

No.	*Measures*	*Implementing Body*	*Time Line*
XIII	**Trade in Services**		
34	Member States shall accelerate the liberalisation of trade in services earlier than 2020. This could be achieved through:		
	—Setting clear targets and schedules of services liberalisation for each priority sector and each round towards achieving freer flow of trade in services by 2010;	Coordinating Committee on Services (CCS) and CCI	on-going
	—Accelerating the development of Mutual Recognition Arrangements (MRAs);		before 2008
	—The application of the ASEAN-X formula; and		on-going
	—Promotion of joint ventures and cooperation, including in third country markets.		on-going
XIV	**Movement of Business Persons, Skilled Labour, Talents and Professionals**		
35	Develop an ASEAN Agreement to facilitate the movement of business persons, including the adoption of an ASEAN Travel Card, taking into account Member States' domestic laws and regulations.	Directors-General of Immigration Departments and Heads of Consular Affairs Division of the Ministries of Foreign Affairs (DGICM)	31 December 2005
36	Develop an ASEAN Agreement to facilitate the movement of experts, professionals, skilled labor and talents, taking into account Member States' domestic laws and regulations	CCS	31 December 2005
37	Accelerate completion of MRAs to facilitate free movement of experts, professionals, skilled labor and talents in ASEAN, taking into account Member States' domestic laws and regulations		31 December 2008
XV	**Facilitation of Travel in ASEAN**		
38	Harmonise procedures for the issuance of visas to international travelers	DGICM	31 December 2004
39	Provide visa exemption for intra-ASEAN travel by ASEAN nationals		2005

No.	Measures	Implementing Body	Time Line
XVI	**Human Resource Development**		
40	Develop and upgrade skills and capacity building through joint trainings and workshops.	Senior Labour Officials Meeting (SLOM)	on-going
	SPECIFIC ISSUES		
XVII	**Investments**		
41	Allow higher share of ASEAN ownership / participation in selected healthcare establish- ments, subject to domestic laws and regulations of each ASEAN country, on an ASEAN-X basis	CCS and CCI	on-going
42	Set up "one-stop centre" in each ASEAN country responsible for facilitating investments, including healthcare projects	CCI	31 December 2008
XVIII	**Standards and Conformity Pharmaceutical Products**		
43	Study the feasibility of an ASEAN Mutual Recognition Arrangement (MRA) for pharmaceutical/ medicinal products	ACCSQ Pharmaceutical Product Working Group (PPWG)	30 December 2005
44	Implement the ASEAN Common Technical Dossier		31 December 2008
45	Harmonise the labelling standards for pharmaceutical/medicinal products		31 December 2006
46	Explore the feasibility of adopting a harmonised placement system for pharmaceutical / medicinal products into the ASEAN markets		31 December 2009
47	To facilitate the approval process, the ASEAN-X formula can be applied. The recognition of the approval proc- ess can only be realised when Mem- ber States fully implement the ACTD		after 31 December 2008
48	Explore the feasibility of implementing a flexible twinning system, where member states voluntarily pair with one or other member states to co-operate in enhancing mutual regulatory capacity and resource development		on-going
49	Formalise a post-marketing alert system for defective and unsafe pharmaceutical/ medicinal products.		31 December 2005

No.	*Measures*	*Implementing Body*	*Time Line*
	Cosmetics		
50	Accelerate implementation of the ASEAN Harmonised Cosmetic Regulatory Scheme (AHCRS), and automatic listing for cosmetics products	ACCSQ ASEAN Cosmetics Committee (ACC)	1 January 2008
51	Formalise a post-marketing alert system for defective or unsafe cosmetic products		31 December 2005
	Medical Device and Equipment		
52	Medical Device and Equipment Working Group to look into integration measures, which includes the following: —Developing a common submission dossier template for product approval in ASEAN —Exploring the feasibility of an abridged approval process for medical devices which regulators of benchmarked countries or recognised regional regulators have approved —Exploring the feasibility of adopting of a harmonised system of placement of medical devices into the ASEAN markets based on a common product approval process —Formalising of a post-marketing alert system for defective or unsafe medical devices or equipment —All ASEAN countries to consider joining the Asian Harmonisation Work Party (AHWP) and work in parallel with the Global Harmonisation Task Force (GHTF) on technical harmonisation efforts	ACCSQ Medical Device and Equipment Working Group	beginning 2005
	Traditional Medicines and Health Supplements		
53	Exchange, review and analyse information on the existing regulatory framework/regime including standard definition, terminologies, and technical infrastructure in Member Countries	ACCSQ Traditional Medicines and Health Supplements Working Group (TMHSWG)	31 December 2006
54	Identify areas for possible harmonisation and MRAs		31 December 2009

No.	*Measures*	*Implementing Body*	*Time Line*
55	Study the existing regulatory frameworks/regime of selected countries and internationally accepted technical guidelines		31 December 2006
56	Enhance the technical infrastructure including mutual confidence in testing and conformity assessment		2004 onwards
57	Formalisation of a post-marketing alert system for unsafe traditional medicine or health supplements		31 December 2007
XIX	**Capacity Building**		
58	More established ASEAN countries to provide training and host attachment programmes for medical and health-related workers from less developed ASEAN member states.	Relevant ASEAN Professional Associations, e.g., ASEAN Association of Radiologists	on-going
59	Provide more exchanges and training for medical and health-related professionals from less developed member states. This is especially necessary for areas of key shortages like specialists and skilled operators of medical equipment MRI and CT scanners		
60	To strengthen cooperation within ASEAN countries in the area of capacity building, i.e., exchange of experts, regulatory infrastructure and human resource development, within available resources	ACCSQ	on-going
61	Member states to consider modelling their technical standards and regulations after ASEAN harmonised technical standards and regulations which is to be evolved from acceptable international or regional technical standards and regulations. This lowers the cost of setting up regulations and is a step towards harmonisation of regulations within ASEAN		
XX	**Movement of Patients**		
62	Minimise visa requirements for intra-ASEAN travel by ASEAN nationals to facilitate cross bosanying persons	CCS and DGICM	31 December 2005

[1] The database on ASEAN NTMs has been completed and posted in the ASEAN Website.
[2] Timelines in accordance with AIA Agreement (ASEAN-6 = 2010; Vietnam = 2013; Cambodia, Laos and Myanmar = 2015)

APPENDICES

APPENDIX—I

COVERED AGREEMENTS

1. Agreement on ASEAN Preferential Trading Arrangements, Manila, 24 February 1977.
2. Agreement on the ASEAN Food Security Reserve, New York, 4 October 1979.
3. Basic Agreement on ASEAN Industrial Projects, Kuala Lumpur, 6 March 1980.
4. Supplementary Agreement of the Basic Agreement on ASEAN Industrial Projects ASEAN Urea Project (Indonesia), Kuala Lumpur, 6 March 1980.
5. Basic Agreement on ASEAN Industrial Joint Ventures, Jakarta, 7 November 1983.
6. Agreement on ASEAN Energy Cooperation, Manila, 24 June 1986.
7. ASEAN Petroleum Security Agreement, Manila, 24 June 1986.
8. Agreement on the Preferential Shortlisting of ASEAN Contractors, Jakarta, 20 October 1986.
9. Supplementary Agreement to the Basic Agreement on ASEAN Industrial Joint Ventures, Singapore, 16 June 1987.
10. Protocol on Improvements on Extensions of Tariff Preferences under the ASEAN Preferential Trading Arrangement, Manila, 15 December 1987.
11. Revised Basic Agreement on ASEAN Industrial Joint Ventures, Manila, 15 December 1987.
12. Agreement Among the Government of Brunei Darussalam, the Republic of Indonesia, Malaysia, the Republic of the Philippines, the Republic of Singapore, and the Kingdom of Thailand for the Promotion and Protection of Investments, Manila, 15 December 1987.
13. Protocol to Amend the Revised Basic Agreement on ASEAN Industrial Joint Ventures, 1 January 1991.
14. Framework Agreement on Enhancing ASEAN Economic Cooperation, Singapore, 28 January 1992.

15. Agreement on the Common Effective Preferential Tariff Scheme for the ASEAN Free Trade Area, Singapore, 28 January 1992.
16. Second Protocol to Amend the Revised Basic Agreement on ASEAN Industrial Joint Ventures, Manila, 23 October 1992.
17. Third Protocol to Amend the Revised Basic Agreement on ASEAN Industrial Joint Ventures, 2 March 1995.
18. Protocol to Amend the Agreement on the Common Effective Preferential Tariff (CEPT) Scheme for the ASEAN Free Trade Area (AFTA), Bangkok, 15 December 1995.
19. Protocol to Amend the Agreement on ASEAN Preferential Trading Arrangements, Bangkok, 15 December 1995.
20. ASEAN Framework Agreement on Services, Bangkok, 15 December 1995.
21. ASEAN Framework Agreement on Intellectual Property Cooperation, Bangkok, 15 December 1995.
22. Protocol Amending the Agreement on ASEAN Energy Cooperation, Bangkok, 15 December 1995.
23. Basic Agreement on ASEAN Industrial Cooperation, Singapore, 26 April 1996.
24. Protocol to Amend the Agreement Among the Government of Brunei Darussalam, the Republic of Indonesia, Malaysia, the Republic of the Philippines, the Republic of Singapore, and the Kingdom of Thailand for the Promotion and Protection of Investments, Jakarta, 12 September 1996.
25. ASEAN Agreement on Customs, Phuket, Thailand, 1 March 1997.
26. Protocol Amending the Agreement on the ASEAN Energy Cooperation, Kuala Lumpur, Malaysia, 23 July 1997.
27. 2nd Protocol to Amend the Agreement on the ASEAN Food Security Reserve, Subang Jaya, Malaysia, 23 July 1997.
28. Protocol to Implement the Initial Package of Commitments Under the ASEAN Framework Agreement on Services, Kuala Lumpur, Malaysia, 15 December 1997.
29. Agreement on the Establishment of the ASEAN Center for Energy, Manila, Philippines, 22 May 1998.
30. Protocol on Notification Procedures, Makati, Philippines, 7 October 1998.
31. Framework Agreement on the ASEAN Investment Area, Makati, Philippines, 7 October 1998.
32. ASEAN Framework Agreement on Mutual Recognition Arrangement (MRAs), Ha Noi, Viet Nam, 16 December 1998.

33. Protocol to Implement the Second Package of Commitments Under the ASEAN Framework Agreement on Services, Ha Noi, Viet Nam, 16 December 1998.
34. ASEAN Framework Agreement on the Facilitation of Goods in Transit, Ha Noi, Viet Nam, 16 December 1998.
35. Protocol on the Special Arrangement for Sensitive and Highly Sensitive Products, Singapore, 30 September 1999.
36. Protocol regarding the Implementation of the CEPT Scheme Temporary Exclusion List, Singapore, 23 November 2000.
37. E-ASEAN Framework Agreement, Singapore, 24 November 2000.
38. Protocol 5: ASEAN Scheme of Compulsory Motor Vehicle Insurance, Kuala Lumpur, Malaysia, 8 April 2001.
39. Protocol to Amend the Framework Agreement on the ASEAN Investment Area, Ha Noi, Viet Nam 14 September 2001.
40. Protocol to Implement the Third Package of Commitments Under the ASEAN Framework Agreement Services, Ha Noi, Viet Nam, 31 December 2001.
41. ASEAN Sectoral Mutual Recognition Arrangement for Electrical and Electronic Equipment, Bangkok, Thailand, 5 April 2002.
42. Protocol to Implement the Second Package of Commitments on Financial Services Under the ASEAN Framework Agreements on Services, Yangon, Myanmar, 6 April 2002.
43. Protocol to Amend the Agreement the Common Effective Preferential Tariff (CEPT) Scheme for the ASEAN Free Trade Area (AFTA) for the Elimination of Import Duties, 31 January 2003.
44. Protocol Governing the Implementation of the ASEAN Harmonized Tariff Nomenclature, Makati, Philippines, 7 August 2003.
45. Agreement on the ASEAN Harmonized Cosmetic Regulatory Scheme, Phnom Penh, Cambodia, 2 September 2003.
46. Protocol to Amend the Protocol Governing the Implementation of the ASEAN Harmonised Tariff Nomenclature, Jeju Island, Korea, 15 May 2004.

APPENDIX—II

WORKING PROCEDURES OF THE PANEL

I. Composition of Panels

1. Panels shall be composed of well-qualified governmental and/or non-governmental individuals, including persons who have served on or presented a case to a panel, served in the Secretariat, taught or published on international trade law or policy, or served as a senior trade policy official of a Member State. In the nomination to the panels, preference shall be given to individuals who are nationals of ASEAN Member States.

2. Panel members should be selected with a view to ensuring the independence of the members, a sufficiently diverse background and a wide spectrum of experience.

3. Nationals of Member States whose governments are parties to the dispute shall not serve on a panel concerned with that dispute, unless the parties to the dispute agree otherwise.

4. To assist in the selection of panelists, the Secretariat shall maintain an indicative list of governmental and non-governmental individuals possessing the qualifications outlined in paragraph 1, from which panelists may be drawn as appropriate. Members may periodically suggest names of governmental and non-governmental individuals for inclusion on the indicative list, providing relevant information on their knowledge of international trade and of the sectors or subject matter of the covered agreements, and those names shall be added to the list upon approval by the SEOM. For each of the individuals on the list, the list shall indicate specific areas of experience or expertise of the individuals in the sectors or subject matter of the covered agreements.

5. Panels shall be composed of three panelists unless the parties to the dispute agree, within ten (10) days from the establishment of the panel, to a panel composed of five panelists. Members shall be informed promptly of the composition of the panel.

6. The Secretariat shall propose nominations for the panel to the parties to the dispute. The parties to the dispute shall not oppose nominations except for compelling reasons.

7. If there is no agreement on the panelists, within twenty (20) days of the decision of the SEOM to establish a panel, at the request of either party, the Secretary-General of ASEAN, in consultation with the SEOM shall, within ten (10) days determine the composition of the panel by appointing the panelists whom the Secretary-General of ASEAN considers most appropriate, and if so relevant, in accordance with any relevant special or additional rules or procedures of the covered agreed or covered agreements which are at issue in the dispute, after

consulting the parties in the dispute. The ASEAN Secretariat shall inform the Member States of the composition of the panel thus formed.

8. Member States shall undertake, as a general rule, to permit their officials to serve as panelists.

9. Panelists shall serve in their individual capacities and not as government representatives, nor as representatives of any organization. Member States shall therefore not give them instructions nor seek to influence them as individuals with regard to matters before a panel.

II. Panel Proceedings

1. In its proceedings the panel shall follow the relevant provisions of this Protocol. In addition, the following working procedures shall apply.

2. The panel shall meet in closed session. The parties to the dispute, and interested parties, shall be present at the meetings only when invited by the panel to appear before it.

3. The deliberations of the panel and the documents submitted to it shall be kept confidential. Nothing in this Protocol shall preclude a party to a dispute from disclosing statements of its own positions to the public. Member States shall treat as confidential information submitted by another Member State to the panel which that Member State has designated as confidential. Where a party to a dispute submits a confidential version of its written submissions to the panel, it shall also, upon request of a Member State, provide a non-confidential summary of the information contained in its submissions that could be disclosed to the public.

4. Before the first substantive meeting of the panel with the parties, the parties to the dispute shall transmit to the panel written submissions in which they present the facts of the case and their arguments.

5. At its first substantive meeting with the parties, the panel shall ask the party which has brought the complaint to present its case. Subsequently, and still at the same meeting, the party against which the complaint has been brought shall be asked to present its point of view.

6. All third parties which have notified their interest in the dispute to the SEOM shall be invited in writing to present their views during a session of the first substantive meeting of the panel set aside for that purpose. All such third parties may be present during the entirety of this session.

7. Formal rebuttals shall be made at a second substantive meeting of the panel. The party complained against shall have the right to take the floor first to be followed by the complaining party. The parties shall submit, prior to that meeting, written rebuttals to the panel.

8. The panel may at any time put questions to the parties and ask them for explanations either in the course of a meeting with the parties or in writing.

9. The parties to the dispute and any third party invited to present its views in accordance with Article 11 shall make available to the panel a written version of their oral statements.

10. The parties to the dispute shall make available to the panel a written version of their oral statements.

11. In the interest of full transparency, the presentations, rebuttals and statements referred to in paragraphs 5 to 8 shall be made in the presence of the parties. Moreover, each party's written submissions, including any comments on the descriptive part of the report and responses to questions put by the panel, shall be made available to the other party or parties.

12. Any additional procedures specific to the panel.

EMERGING ISSUES AND DEVELOPMENTS AT THE REGIONAL LEVEL: TRANSPORT, COMMUNICATIONS, TOURISM AND INFRASTRUCTURE DEVELOPMENT

(Item 7 (d) of the Provisional Agenda)

Report on the Implementation of Commission Resolution 52/6 on Intra-Asia and Asia-Europe Land Bridges

Summary

Within the Asian land transport infrastructure development (ALTID) project, ESCAP has been pursuing activities relating to the formulation of the Asian Highway and Trans-Asian Railway networks which are nearing completion. The emphasis is now shifting towards making the routes operational.

In this regard, activities are being undertaken within the framework given in ESCAP resolution 52/9 of 24 April 1996 on intra-Asia and Asia-Europe land bridges and resolution 48/11 of 23 April 1992 on road and rail transport modes in relation to facilitation measures.

Building on the achievements of the meeting of the transport directors of all United Nations regional commissions held at Cairo in December 1999, ESCAP will develop synergy with the other United Nations regional commissions and more specifically, the Economic Commission for Europe, the Economic and Social Commission for Western Asia and the Economic Commission for Africa in order to look specifically at the development of interregional land and land-*cum*-sea routes between the member countries of each commission.

ESCAP is also making efforts to give to member countries greater ownership of the related activities through the organization of policy-level meetings with the chief executives of the railways of the ESCAP countries as well as the heads of highway administrations. This will also enable the secretariat to put together action plans which reflect the actual needs of its member countries.

ESCAP will continue to develop awareness of the member countries at national and regional levels to secure a higher rate of accession to the conventions listed in resolution 48/11 as an integral part of their infrastructure development planning.

The present report raises a number of issues for consideration by the Commission, including the extension of the implementation period of resolution 52/9 and the adoption of a new resolution with enhanced scope to replace resolution 48/11 and include road transport conventions concerning the work of crews, temporary importation of private vehicles, and the transport of dangerous goods and perishable foodstuffs, and to consider the inclusion of rail transport conventions in that resolution.

I. Progress in the implementation of Resolution 52/9

A. Trans-Asian Railway and Asian Highway

B. Facilitation of land transport at border crossings

C. Refined strategy for the implementation of the ALTID project

II. Main Trust Areas

A. Recommendations of the Committee on Transport, Communications, Tourism and Infrastructure Development at its second session

B. Recommendations of the Meeting of the Heads of Divisions Responsible for Transport of the United Nations Regional Commissions

C. Recommendations of the International Conference on Euro-Asian Transport

D. Improvement of the operational efficiency of land bridges

III. Issues for Consideration

Recognizing the critical role played by transport and communications in the economic and social development of the region and the emphasis increasingly being placed by members and associate members of ESCAP on developing and strengthening intraregional and interregional land transport linkages as part of an integrated regional transport system to sustain growth in international trade and tourism and for the further promotion of regional economic cooperation, the Commission at its fifty-second session adopted resolution 52/9 of 24 April 1996 on intra-Asia and Asia-Europe land bridges.

Resolution 52/9 concerns the implementation of activities under the Asian land transport infrastructure development (ALTID) project, a priority ESCAP project comprising the Trans-Asian Railway and Asian Highway projects, as well as the facilitation of land transport at border crossings, mainly through the implementation of Commission resolution 48/11 of 23 April 1992 on road and rail transport modes in relation to facilitation measures.

In resolution 52/9, the Commission requests the Executive Secretary to report to it biennially on the progress in the implementation of the resolution. The last report on the progress in the implementation of resolutions and major decisions of the Commission in transport, communications, tourism and infrastructure development was considered by the Commission at its fifty-fourth session, held in 1998.

Since then considerable progress has been made in the implementation of resolution 52/9, as indicated in the following sections.

I. PROGRESS IN THE IMPLEMENTATION OF RESOLUTION 52/9

5. The main emphasis of the resolution is on (a) the formulation of the Trans-Asian Railway and Asian Highway networks and the setting up of the related standards and requirements, and (b) facilitation of land transport at border crossings through the implementation of resolution 48/11. The progress achieved so far is discussed below.

A. Trans-Asian Railway and Asian Highway

6. The Trans-Asian Railway network reflects all major intra-Asia and Asia-Europe land bridges. However, the land bridges Northern Europe-Russian Federation-Central Asia-Persian Gulf and North-East Asia-South-East Asia will be the subject of further study to refine the network.

7. The study on the Trans-Asian Railway in the southern corridor as well as the container transport demonstration project (phase I) in the northern corridor, which was undertaken in order to demonstrate the advantages of the rail routes as compared with the related sea routes, was completed in 1999. The findings were considered at the policy-level expert group meetings held in May 1999 at Dhaka and in February 2000 at Bangkok.

8. The Asian Highway network had been formulated for the whole of Asia, with the exception of Bhutan, the Russian Federation and the Korean peninsula. With the completion of the study on a road network connecting China, Kazakhstan, Mongolia, the Russian Federation and the Korean peninsula, the formulation exercise will be complete for the whole of Asia, except Bhutan, which has so far not expressed any interest in joining the Asian Highway project.

9. In addition, the Asian Highway database that was established for the countries of the Association of Southeast Asian Nations (ASEAN) and the South

Asian Association for Regional Cooperation (SAARC) is being expanded to include the countries of the Economic Cooperation Organization (ECO) as a step towards eventual coverage of the entire network. A strategy for upgrading routes and guidelines for the promotion of the Asian Highway was also prepared. Moreover, the strategy for the implementation of the ALTID project has been refined as indicated in section C below.

10. In addition to the progress relating to infrastructure, some improvements were also made in the facilitation of land transport at border crossings, as indicated in section B below.

B. Facilitation of Land Transport at Border Crossings

11. With the completion of the subregional seminars on the benefits of accession to the international conventions listed in Commission resolution 48/11, the main emphasis from 1998 onwards was placed on conducting related national seminars.

12. As a result of all the actions taken, remarkable progress was observed in the countries of Central Asia (see table). Uzbekistan has acceded to all seven conventions listed in the resolution, while Kazakhstan, Kyrgyzstan, Tajikistan and Turkmenistan each became party to four conventions. Armenia and Mongolia each acceded to two conventions and Azerbaijan to one. With its recent accession to an additional convention, the Islamic Republic of Iran is now a party to four conventions. However, much work remains to be done with regard to the accession to conventions and the implementation of resolution 48/11.

13. At national level, one of the next important steps in the implementation of resolution 48/11 will be to carry out related activities in the ECO region within the framework of the ECO/ESCAP/UNCTAD project on international multimodal transport operations in the ECO region, funded by the Islamic Development Bank. Actual implementation of the project is expected to begin in mid-2000.

Table. Status of the accession or being a party to international conventions listed in Commission resolution 48/11, as of 1 March 2000 (click to see the table)

C. Refined Strategy for the Implementation of the ALTID Project

14. In view of the experience gained and some factors which have emerged during the implementation of the ALTID project since 1994, the Commission at its fifty-fourth session, held in 1998, endorsed the refined strategy for the implementation of the project.

15. The refined strategy comprises the following:

(a) Facilitation of land transport at border crossings and maritime transport at ports;

(b) Completion of the formulation of the Asian Highway and Trans-Asian Railway networks covering the whole of Asia, including the missing links;

(c) Formalization of the Asian Highway and Trans-Asian Railway routes/networks;

(d) Improvement of the operational efficiency of the Asian Highway and Trans-Asian Railway routes;

(e) Improvement of transport logistics;

(f) Promotion of the Asian Highway and the Trans-Asian Railway.

16. The approach adopted for implementation of the strategy included the following:

(a) Emphasis on related projects/activities at the subregional and national levels. ALTID-related activities should be coordinated effectively with the related subregional action plans of ASEAN, ECO, SAARC, Bangladesh-India-Myanmar-Sri Lanka-Thailand Economic Cooperation (BIMST-EC) and the ESCAP/ECE (Economic Commission for Europe) Special Programme for the Economies of Central Asia (SPECA);

(b) Cooperation with all other international organizations concerned should be promoted;

(c) A step-by-step approach through the implementation of related projects as part of the ALTID biennial action plans should be a guiding principle;

(d) Monitoring and evaluation of the project should be ensured.

17. In endorsing the refined strategy, the Commission at its fifty-fifth session noted that the implementation of the ALTID project demonstrated clearly the practical importance of the project in facilitating international trade and tourism. The Commission reiterated its strong support for the project as a priority within phase I (1997-2001) of the New Delhi Action Plan on Infrastructure Development in Asia and the Pacific.

18. However, since the components of the refined strategy are rather broad and only limited resources are available, it has become essential to identify the main thrust areas for implementation on a priority basis in the future. To this end, the following sections highlight some of the main thrust areas.

II. MAIN THRUST AREAS

A. Recommendations of the Committee on Transport, Communications, Tourism and Infrastructure Development at its Second Session

19. At its second session, held at Bangkok in November 1999, the Committee requested that the main thrust in the implementation of the ALTID project should

be (a) the completion of the formulation of the Asian Highway and Trans-Asian Railway networks covering the whole of Asia, including the missing links, and (b) the operationalization/improvement of the efficiency of international land transport corridors.

20. The Committee also requested the secretariat to undertake the following activities on a priority basis:

(a) Identification and agreement by ESCAP and ECE, after consultation with member States, on the main Asia-Europe land bridges, with the possible introduction of intermodal and multimodal transport, including the following routes: (i) Western Europe-Russian Federation to the Korean peninsula direct or through Kazakhstan and China, or through Mongolia and China; (ii) Europe-Turkey-Islamic Republic of Iran-South Asia-South-East Asia; (iii) Europe-Turkey-Islamic Republic of Iran-Central Asia-China; (iv) Europe through the Caucasus to Asia (Transport Corridor Europe Caucasus Asia); (v) Northern Europe-Russian Federation-Central Asia-Persian Gulf;

(b) Identification and approval of the main land bridges linking the regions of ESCAP, the Economic and Social Commission for Western Asia (ESCWA) and the Economic Commission for Africa (ECA);

(c) Establishment and dissemination of the Asian Highway and Trans-Asian Railway databases;

(d) Corridor studies along major land bridge routes to identify physical and non-physical barriers and suggest remedial measures;

(e) Active promotion of the Asian Highway and Trans-Asian Railway, using a brochure on the Asian Highway that was published in 1999 as an example;

(f) Formalization of the Asian Highway and Trans-Asian Railway networks through coordination by ESCAP and in close consultation with member governments to promote coordinated development;

(g) Implementation of Commission resolution 48/11 and the Convention on Facilitation of International Maritime Traffic, 1965, as amended;

(h) Establishment of special working groups for the operationalization of major land bridges;

(i) Organization of demonstration runs of international trains along the major land bridges;

(j) Coordination with and support for the ad hoc Asian railway chief executives' meeting to be held in the second part of 2000 and the ad hoc meeting of heads of highway administrations;

(k) Introduction/improvement of information systems for international traffic.

21. With regard to the facilitation of land transport, the Committee urged member countries to nominate focal points and to establish facilitation committees comprising all the ministries and agencies involved, if they had not already done so, and to share experiences in the accession to and implementation of the conventions. It also requested the secretariat to organize further national-level seminars to promote accession to the conventions. The Committee also recognized the need to extend the scope of resolution 48/11 to include road transport conventions on the work of crews, temporary importation of private vehicles, and the transport of dangerous goods and perishable foodstuffs, and to consider the inclusion of rail transport conventions. In this context, the Commission may wish to consider adopting a new resolution with expanded scope to replace resolution 48/11.

22. The Committee noted the value of subregional agreements in facilitating international transport, especially in cases where there were no international conventions or where the issues addressed were only subregional in nature. For issues addressed in conventions, it was recommended that the main text, annexes and protocols should draw upon the international conventions. In that respect, it was recommended that the organizations assisting in drafting those agreements, such as ASEAN and ECO, should cooperate closely in order to ensure consistency among the various agreements, particularly with respect to subregional agreements or transit agreements along certain corridors.

23. The Committee stressed the need to promote further cooperation between ESCAP and other international organizations concerned, particularly ECE, the European Union, the International Union of Railways (UIC), the Organization of Railways Cooperation (OSShD), the International Road Transport Union (IRU), the International Road Federation (IRF) and the World Road Association (PIARC) in the identification and development of the main Asia-Europe land bridges, and establish similar cooperation with ESCWA and ECA for the development of Asia-Middle East-Africa land bridges. A memorandum of understanding between ESCAP and UIC is being prepared. A similar memorandum between ESCAP and OSShD was signed in 1998.

24. The Committee noted with appreciation the activities undertaken by ECE, ESCWA, ASEAN, ECO, ADB and UIC in strengthening transport network linkages and operation and in improving facilitation measures in their respective areas. It expressed satisfaction with the increased level of cooperation between ESCAP, ECE, ECO, ASEAN and the Asian Development Bank (ADB). The cooperation of ESCAP and ECE in the implementation of resolution 48/11 and the SPECA programme was particularly appreciated.

25. The Committee stressed the importance of the second ALTID project assessment, to be carried out in 2001 and endorsed the plan of action for phase IV (2000-01) of the ALTID project, as reflected in document E/ESCAP/CTCTID(2)/2

and Corr.1. This was essential to ensure that activities carried out under ALTID were of practical importance to the countries concerned and that concrete and measurable results were achieved.

B. Recommendations of the Meeting of the Heads of Divisions Responsible for Transport of the United Nations Regional Commissions

26. The first meeting of the Heads of Divisions Responsible for Transport of the United Nations Regional Commissions was held at Cairo in December 1999. The purpose of the meeting was to initiate a dialogue among the five regional commissions on possible land and land-cum-sea transport linkages and to draw up an action plan in order to assist member countries to participate fully in the rapid economic globalization. Present at the meeting were the heads of divisions responsible for transport of ECE, the Economic Commission for Latin America and the Caribbean (ECLAC), ESCAP, ESCWA and ECA.

The meeting identified the major interregional transport links, including those of Asia and Europe, which are indicated below:

Europe-Asia
E91/M55 (Turkey/Syria)
E98/M45 (Turkey/Syria)
E90/M05 (Turkey/Iraq)
CE70-R25 (Turkey/Syria)
E30 (Europe/Russian Federation)
E40/A70 (Europe/Russian Federation/Uzbekistan/Kyrgyzstan/Kazakhstan)
E50/3119/A5 (Europe/Russian Federation/Azerbaijan)
E60/A67 (Europe/Black Sea/Georgia/Azerbaijan/Caspian Sea/Turkmenistan)
E80/A1 (Turkey/Islamic Republic of Iran)
CE10/20 (Europe/Russian Federation Far East)
CE203 (Russian Federation/Kazakhstan/China) (Yekaterinburg/Astana/Drujba/Alataw Pass)
CE30 (Europe/Russian Federation Far East)
CE50 (Europe/Russian Federation/Kazakhstan/China)
CE700 (Russian Federation/Azerbaijan/Central Asia)
CE70 (Turkey/Islamic Republic of Iran/South Asia-South-East Asia)
CE97 (Turkey/Georgia/Azerbaijan)
Asia/West Asia
M10

M40/A2

Khorramschahr-Bastah (M05)

Chareshirin-R10

Khorramshahr/Basrah (R05)

28. The meeting also agreed that the following actions would be necessary:

- Further consultations with the countries concerned in order to finalize the selection of links;
- Traffic forecast studies to identify priority links;
- Studies to assess obstacles at borders, both infrastructure and regulatory;
- Promotion of border-crossing facilitation measures.

Initiatives have already been taken by the secretariat to field missions to the Islamic Republic of Iran and Turkey to undertake consultations with the concerned ministries/agencies regarding the road and rail links between Asia and Western Asia that were identified at the Cairo meeting of transport directors.

29. Furthermore, it was agreed that ESCAP, with contributions from other regional commissions, would prepare an interregional transport cooperation programme to be submitted to potential donors such as the United Nations Development Account. A programme proposal was under preparation when the present document was being finalized. The meeting of all the executive secretaries, held at Bangkok during UNCTAD-X, accorded high priority to the programme proposal.

C. Recommendations of the International Conference on Euro-Asian Transport

30. In connection with the development of Asia-Europe land bridges, and in pursuance of the recommendation of the St. Petersburg Conference, work on the formulation of a joint ESCAP/ECE programme on development of transport links between Asia and Europe is in progress.

31. In this context, the ESCAP Committee on Transport, Communications, Tourism and Infrastructure Development at its second session identified five corridors. Subsequently, the secretariat identified, on a tentative basis, rail and road links between Asia and Europe as reflected in annexes I and II respectively of the present document.

D. Improvement of the Operational Efficiency of Land Bridges

32. Along with the ongoing identification of major Asia-Europe and intra-Asia land bridges, increasing attention is being put by the secretariat on the improvement of their operational efficiency. The study on the Trans-Asian Railway in the southern corridor and the demonstration project (phase I) on development of Asia-Europe

container transport through block trains in the northern corridor completed in 1999 and the SPECA project working group on transport and border crossing could be mentioned as examples.

1. *Trans-Asian Railway in the Southern Corridor*

33. ESCAP in 1995 undertook a preliminary study of the route requirements for the Trans-Asian Railway in the southern corridor within the territories of Bangladesh, India, the Islamic Republic of Iran, Pakistan and Sri Lanka. The detailed study covering five additional countries, namely China, Myanmar, Nepal, Thailand and Turkey, was to re-evaluate and redefine the route network in the corridor to analyse traffic demand as well as technical, operational and commercial requirements and to outline a development plan aiming at operationalization of the identified network.

34. The results of the study were considered by a policy-level expert group meeting held in Dhaka, Bangladesh in May 1999.

35. A major output of the meeting was the adoption of an action plan for the development of the Trans-Asian Railway in the southern corridor of Asia-Europe routes. The plan stipulates immediate, short-term and long-term actions with special reference to the operationalization of the land bridges.

36. The meeting also agreed to establish a special working group on the development and operationalization of the Trans-Asian Railway in the southern corridor. ESCAP was requested to act as coordinator and facilitator in the organization and functioning of the working group. The establishment of the working group is in process in cooperation with UIC.

37. A similar working group was established (with ESCAP participation) in September 1999 for the Trans-Asian Railway route China-Kazakhstan-Russian Federation-Belarus-Poland-Germany. Initial work has already started and a follow up meeting is planned for mid-2000.

2. *Demonstration Project on Development of Asia-Europe Container Transport Through Block Trains in the Trans-Asian Railway Northern Corridor*

38. Similar to the study mentioned above, an important feasibility study on connecting rail networks of China, Kazakhstan, Mongolia, the Russian Federation and the Korean peninsula was completed in 1995. A related expert group meeting was held in October 1995, which strongly supported follow-up work to develop the Trans-Asian Railway northern corridor.

39. Accordingly, a project on the development of Asia-Europe container transport through block trains (phase I) was carried out by ESCAP in cooperation with OSShD. The results of the study were considered by a policy-level expert group

meeting which was held in February 2000 at Bangkok. The objective of the meeting was to determine the concrete steps to be taken. It was decided that the work should be undertaken in two stages. The first stage should aim at demonstration runs of container block trains along all the routes of the Trans-Asian Railway northern corridor, and the second stage should aim at full operationalization of commercial services on all the routes in the corridor.

40. The meeting recommended the establishment of a demonstration project working group for the entire corridor covering all five routes. The main functions of the working group should be to undertake all arrangements for actual demonstration runs. The working group, to be chaired by ESCAP, should work in close cooperation with OSShD and UIC, and should have the active participation of each railway involved. The meeting urged donors to provide financial support for the working group.

41. The meeting also recommended the establishment of a demonstration project national coordinating committee comprising officials from railways, customs, freight forwarders, telecommunications etc. in each country. The committee could be chaired by a high-ranking official responsible for railways who at the same time could represent the country in the working group.

42. The meeting also recommended that the main emphasis in the implementation of the project should be put on the preparation and execution of actual demonstration runs on all the routes under consideration.

43. The Meeting endorsed the phase II activities, which included a number of technical, commercial and organizational activities scheduled for the period 2000-2003.

3. *Special Programme for the Economies of Central Asia Project Working Group on Transport and Border Crossing*

44. The Working Group, with Kazakhstan as the lead country, is expected to play an important role in the development of the land bridges across Central Asia.

45. After launching the joint ESCAP/ECE Special Programme for the Economies of Central Asia (SPECA) in 1998, the Working Group conducted three sessions and adopted in 1999 its work programme for 1999-2000 with the main emphasis on facilitation of land transport at border crossings.

46. Unfortunately Turkmenistan and Uzbekistan did not participate in all the Working Group sessions, thus indicating a major problem in the functioning of the Group.

47. At the request of the Government of Kazakhstan, ESCAP provided in October 1999 advisory services to identify major problem areas in the

operationalization of the Group and to recommend remedial measures.

48. The following major recommendation was made:

In order for the Working Group to be attractive to every SPECA member State as a cooperative arrangement, it must produce concrete results of practical interest to SPECA countries. This could be achieved through the following:

Identification of projects of subregional (SPECA) importance and preparation of the project profiles/project documents for possible funding;

Playing a leading role in solving problems related to transit of shipment through the territory of SPECA countries;

Inclusion of international conferences on land transport and border crossing conducted in SPECA states, as part of the programme of work of the Working Group;

Active participation of the private sector in the activities of the Working Group;

Increased cooperation among the international organizations concerned in the implementation of SPECA-Transport and Border Crossing programme of work.

49. Resource mobilization is apparently a major problem in proper operationalization of SPECA including its Working Group. A clear cut SPECA policy needs to be adopted in this regard by all the members. The issue is being pursued together by the ESCAP and ECE secretariats.

III. ISSUES FOR CONSIDERATION

50. It is quite clear that the implementation of resolution 52/9 is making an important contribution to the development of reliable and efficient land transport linkages to facilitate international trade and tourism.

51. The resolution and the ALTID project enjoy support of 28 countries in Asia and the related activities are being generously funded by the Governments of France, Germany, Japan and the Republic of Korea. The tasks are being carried out in close coordination with ECE, ESCWA, ECA, subregional organizations of ASEAN, ECO, SAARC as well as international organizations concerned, particularly IRU, IRF, OSShD, UIC.

52. Keeping in view the progress made in the implementation of resolution 52/9, the Commission may wish to consider the following issues:

(a) The Commission may wish to endorse the main thrust areas in the implementation of the ALTID project as recommended by the Committee on Transport, Communications, Tourism and Infrastructure Development at its second session, with increasing emphasis on the operationalization/improvement of efficiency of international land transport corridors. In this context the Commission may also wish to urge donor countries and agencies to provide financial and technical support for the implementation of the plan of action for phase IV (2000-01) of the ALTID project (as reflected in the document E/ESCAP/CTCTID(2)/2 and Corr.1) and stress the importance of the second ALTID project assessment in 2001;

(b) The Commission may wish to consider adopting a new resolution with expanded scope to replace resolution 48/11, to include road transport conventions concerning the work of crews, the temporary importation of private vehicles, and the transport of dangerous goods and perishable foodstuffs, and to consider the inclusion of rail transport conventions (paragraph 21);

(c) The Commission may wish to support the recommendations of the heads of divisions responsible for transport of the United Nations regional economic commissions at their meeting held in December 1999 at Cairo, particularly those relating to Asia-Europe and Asia-West Asia links as presented in the document under considerations (paragraph 27);

(d) The Commission may wish to stress the importance of early completion of the formulation of the joint ESCAP/ECE programme on development of transport links between Asia and Europe. It may also wish to take note of the preliminary identified Asia-Europe rail and road links as reflected in annexes I and II to the present document;

(e) The Commission may wish to stress the importance of implementing recommendations

(f) The Commission may wish to express its gratitude to the Governments of France, Germany, Japan and Republic of Korea for their generous support in the implementation of resolution 52/9;

(g) In view of the importance of resolution 52/9 in facilitating international trade and tourism, the Commission may wish to prolong its period of implementation with a renewed call for a report on its implementation to be submitted to the Commission for its consideration every two years;

(h) The Commission may wish to provide additional guidance on the implementation of resolution 52/9.

GLOSSARY

Army of the Republic of Vietnam (ARVN). The military ground forces of the South Vietnamese government (Republic of Vietnam) until its collapse in April 1975. ARVN originated in the Vietnamese military units raised by French authorities to defend the Associated State of Vietnam in the early 1950s. During the Second Indochina War, it grew to over 1 million men and women organized into eleven army divisions (plus specialized units, such as Rangers and Special Forces) deployed in four Corps Tactical Zones (redesignated as Military Regions in 1971).

Asian Development Bank (ADB). Established in 1966, the ADB assists in economic development and promotes growth and cooperation in developing member countries. Membership includes both developed and developing countries in Asia and developed countries in the West.

Association of Southeast Asian Nations (ASEAN). Founded in 1967 for the purpose of promoting regional stability, economic development, and cultural exchange. ASEAN's founding members were Indonesia, Malaysia, the Philippines, Singapore, and Thailand; Brunei joined ASEAN in 1984.

Baba Chinese. Descendants of marriages between Chinese men and Malay women, many of whom moved to Singapore from Malacca in the early nineteenth century. Although mixed parentage gradually disappeared through marriage with Chinese immigrants, the Babas usually spoke Malay or English as their first language and identified more closely with Singapore and Malaya than with China. After establishment of Straits Settlements in 1826, their descendants also came to be known as Straits Chinese.

Bahasa Indonesia. The Indonesian national language, also known as Indonesian; an Austronesian language reported to be modelled on Riau Malay and 80 percent cognate with Standard Malay.

Black Flag Forces. A band of mostly Chinese adventurers who fled to northern Vietnam after the collapse of the Taiping Rebellion (1851-64) in China. They eventually placed themselves at the service of the imperial court in Hue and fought the French forces in the 1883-84 Tonkin campaign.

Boat People. Refugees who fled Vietnam by sea after 1975. Many fell victim to pirate attacks in the Gulf of Thailand, drowned, or endured starvation and dehydration as a result of their escape in ill-equipped and undersized vessels. Those who reached safety in neighboring Southeast Asian countries were accorded temporary asylum in refugee camps while awaiting permanent resettlement in industrialized Western nations willing to accept them.

Bodhisattva. One destined to become a Buddha (enlightened one); a person who has achieved enlightenment, but who defers achieving nirvana in order to help others achieve it.

Bonze. A general term for a Buddhist monk (as opposed to the more specific *bhikku*, meaning an ordained monk).

Bushido. Literally, the way of the warrior (samurai), a term applied to the principles of loyalty and honor; a code of stoic endurance, scorn of danger and death, religious worship of country and sovereign, and proper social relationships; an aesthetic life-style.

Cao Dai. Indigenous Vietnamese religion centered in Tay Ninh Province, southern Vietnam. It was founded and initially propagated by Ngo Van Chieu, a minor official who, in 1919, claimed to have had a series of revelations. The faith grew under the leadership of Le Van Trung, its first "pope" or Supreme Chief, chosen in 1925. Doctrinally, the religion is a syncretic blend of Christianity, Buddhism, Taoism, Confuciancism and Western nineteenth-century romanticism. Before the fall of Saigon, the Cao Dai had about 1 to 2 million adherents.

Ch'ondogyo. Teachings of the Heavenly Way, an indigenous monotheistic religion stressing the equality of man and the unity of man and the universe. Formerly Tonghak, Ch'ondogyo had approximately 27,000 followers and 66 churches in South Korea in 1988.

China Proper. Used broadly to mean China within the Great Wall, with its eighteen historic provinces. Divisible into two major, sharply contrasting regions, north China and south China. The dependencies on the north and west—Manchuria (now usually referred to as northeast China), Mongolia, Xizang (Tibet), and Xinjiang or Chinese Turkestan—were known in the imperial era as Outer China.

Chinese People's Political Consultative Conference (CPPCC). A quasi-constitutional united front organization that provides an institutional framework for interaction between party and state leaders and representatives of mass groups and democratic parties. Members include distinguished scholars, educators, and intellectuals, key representatives of religious and minority nationality groups, and leading members of political parties loyal to the Chinese Communist Party during the anti-Guomindang years. The first CPPCC convened in 1949, the second in 1954, the third in 1959, the fourth in 1964, the fifth in 1978, and the sixth in 1983, the seventh was scheduled for 1988. The CPPCC's 1949 Common Programme served as the law of the land until superseded by the 1954 state constitution.

Chua. A lord or prince. The hereditary title used by the Trinh and Nguyen families, who ruled Vietnam in the name of the emperor during the later Le Dynasty in the sixteenth through the eighteenth centuries.

Chuch'e (juche). The political ideology promulgated by Kim Il Song. The application of Marxism-Leninism to the North Korean experience based on autonomy and self-reliance.

Class struggle. In Marxist terms, the conflict waged by the masses of the workers and the oppressed under the leadership of the communist party against the privileged, oppressive, and property-owning ruling class. Until late 1978, class struggle was the official line of the Chinese Communist Party.

Co Mat Vien. An advisory council set up by Emperor Minh Mang following the rebellion of Le Van Khoi in the 1830s.

Colombo Plan. Founded in 1951 and known as the Colombo Plan for Cooperative Economic Development in South and Southeast Asia until it was expanded in 1977 and called the Colombo Plan for Cooperative Economic Development in Asia and the Pacific. It is an arrangement that permits a developing member country to approach a developed member country for assistance on a one-to- one basis. Assistance may be technical or in the form of capital or commodity aid.

Comintern. Short form for Communist International or the Third International, which was founded in Moscow in 1919 to coordinate the world communist movement. Officially disbanded in 1943, the Comintern was revived as the Cominform (Communist Information Bureau) from 1947 to 1956.

Committee for Coordination of Investigations of the Lower Mekong Basin. Established in 1957 under the sponsorship of the United Nations Economic and Social Commission for Asia and the Pacific, the Committee aims to develop water resources in the lower Mekong basin through improvements in hydroelectric power, irrigation, flood control, watershed management, and navigation. Its membership is limited to Laos, Thailand, and Vietnam.

Commonwealth of Nations. Often referred to as the British Commonwealth, the Commonwealth is formally an association of forty-nine sovereign, independent states that acknowledge the British monarch as symbolic head of the association. Commonwealth membership is expressed in cooperation, consultation, mutual assistance, and periodic conferences of national leaders.

Communist International (Comintern). Founded in Moscow in 1919 to coordinate the world communist movement, the Comintern was officially disbanded in 1943. Also called the Comintern or Third International, it was founded in Moscow in 1919 to coordinate the world communist movement. Officially disbanded in 1943, the Comintern was replaced from 1947 to 1954 by the Cominform (Communist Information Bureau), in which only the Soviet and the ruling East European communist parties (except for Yugoslavia, which was expelled in 1948) and the French and the Italian communist parties were represented. The Cominform was dissolved in 1956.

Communist Party of Malaya (CPM). Known as the Malayan Communist Party (MCP) until the 1960s. Founded in Singapore in 1930 with a predominantly Chinese membership, the party carried out armed resistance to the Japanese during World War II. From 1948 to 1960, its military arm, the Malayan Peoples Liberation Army, practiced guerrilla warfare in the rural areas of peninsular Malaya with the support of underground organizations in Malaya and Singapore. In the late 1980s, an estimated 500 guerrillas and the party leadership maintained themselves in the jungles of the Malaysian-Thai frontier.

Comprador. Vietnamese communist term (used originally in China to mean purchasing agent) applied disparagingly to the middleman who extracts a profit without engaging in economic production, that is, a "comprador capitalist." The term is also applied to an entrepreneur in Cholon, Ho Chi Minh City's predominantly Chinese sister city.

Confrontation (Konfrontasi). Indonesia's 1963-66 effort to disrupt the new state of Malaysia, which Indonesian leaders regarded as a front for a continued British colonial presence in Southeast Asia.

Consultative Group on Indonesia (CGI). Formed after the March 1992 demise of the Inter-Governmental Group on Indonesia. Except for the Netherlands, the membership is the same as IGGI.

Council for Mutual Economic Assistance (Comecon). Also abbreviated CEMA and CMEA, the organization was established in 1949 to promote economic cooperation among socialist bloc countries and is headquartered in Moscow. Its members in the 1980s included the Soviet Union, Bulgaria, Czechoslovakia, East Germany, Hungary, Poland, Romania, Cuba, Mongolia, and Vietnam.

Danwei (work unit). The basic-level organization through which party and government officials control social, political, and economic behavior of residents. The *danwei* typically controls the allocation of housing, grain, edible oil, and cotton rations; the issuance of permits to travel, to marry, and to bear or adopt children; and permission to enter the army, party, and university and to change employment.

Demarcation Line. Established under the Korean armistice agreement of 1953; marks the actual cease-fire line between South Korea and North Korea.

Democracy Wall. A wall in the Xidan district in Beijing where, beginning in December 1978, in line with the party's policy of "seeking truth from facts," activists in the democracy movement recorded news and ideas, often in the form of big-character posters. These activists were encouraged to criticize the Gang of Four and previous (failed) government policies, but the wall was closed in December 1979 when the leadership and the communist party system were being criticized along with past mistakes and leaders. The shutdown coincided with suppression of political dissent.

Democratic Centralism. A system through which the people influence the policies of the government and party members influence the policies of the party; while the government and party maintain centralized administrative power to carry out the policies demanded by their constituents. Within both representative and executive organizations, the minority must abide by the decisions of the majority, and lower bodies must obey the orders of the higher level organizations. The concept, derived from the organizing principles of the Communist Party of the Soviet Union, was called for as early as 1928 by Mao Zedong.

Democratic parties. Eight political parties that have been loyal to the communist government since 1949. They are China Association for Promoting Democracy, China Democratic League, China Democratic National Construction Association, China Zhi Gong Dang (Party for Public Interest), Chinese Peasants' and Workers' Democratic Party, Jiusan (September Third) Society, Guomindang Revolutionary Committee, and Taiwan Democratic Self-Government League.

Emergency. The 1948-60 communist insurgency in peninsular Malaya and Singapore; most active between 1948 and 1951.

European Economic Community (EEC). Originally established by the 1957 Treaty of Rome and sometimes referred to as the Common Market, an association of twelve West European nations with common economic institutions and policies toward trade with non-Community nations. One of three communities; besides the EEC, there are the European Coal and Steel Community and the European Atomic Energy Community, collectively known as the European Community.

Expert. Term usually juxtaposed with "red". Denotes special knowledge or skills, or both, relating to economic management, science, and technology. Cadres are required to be both red and expert, the emphasis on one or the other depending on the current political milieu.

First Indochina War (1946-54). The anticolonial conflict, also known as the Viet Minh War, between France and the Viet Minh, a Vietnamese communist-dominated coalition of Indochinese nationalist elements led by veteran revolutionary Ho Chi Minh. The French defeat at Dien Bien Phu in May 1954 marked the final episode of the war. The conflict was brought to an end officially by the Geneva Conference of July 1954 and its resulting agreements.

Five Principles of Peaceful Coexistence. Mutual respect for each other's territorial integrity and sovereignty; mutual nonaggression; mutual noninterference in each other's internal affairs; equality and mutual benefit; and peaceful coexistence. Originated with a 1954 agreement between Zhou Enlai and India's Jawaharlal Nehru.

Five Relationships. The Confucian concept of ideal social relationships, formulated by classical Chinese philosophers such as Mencius (372-289 B.C.), which states that there should be affection between father and son, righteousness between ruler and minister, attention to their separate functions between husband and wife, proper order between old and young, and faithfulness between friends.

Food and Agriculture Organization (FAO). A United Nations specialized agency established in 1945 to raise living standards and increase the availability of agricultural products.

Four Cardinal Principles. Socialism; dictatorship of the proletariat; supporting the party leadership; and Marxism-Leninism-Mao Zedong Thought. In vogue in China since 1979.

Four Modernizations. The core of a development strategy aimed at turning the country into a relatively advanced industrialized nation by the year 2000. The modernizations are those of agriculture, industry, science and technology, and national defense. The concept was embodied first in the Third Five-Year Plan (1966-70), launched in earnest by Zhou Enlai at the Fourth National People's Congress (1975), and adopted as the official party line at the Third Plenum of the Eleventh Central Committee (December 1978).

Fretilin. Revolutionary Front for an Independent East Timor (Frente Revolucionária do Timor Leste Independente); a guerrilla movement seeking the independence of East Timor. Fretilin was established in 1974.

Gang of Four. Term used by the post-Mao leadership to denote the four leading radical figures—Jiang Qing (Mao's fourth wife), Zhang Chunqiao, Yao Wenyuan, and Wang Hongwen—who played a dominant political role during the Cultural Revolution decade (1966-76) until Mao's death in September 1976 and their arrest several weeks later. Their "antiparty" deeds are often linked with Lin Biao, an early leader of the Cultural Revolution, who also has been discredited.

General Agreement on Tariffs and Trade (GATT). Negotiated in 1947 among twenty-three original signatories who were members of the United Nations Economic and Social Council and went into effect January 1, 1948, as an interim arrangement pending the ratification of the proposed International Trade Organization. GATT functions as a multilateral treaty aimed at promoting the expansion of international trade on a nondiscriminatory basis. As of 1992, 101 nations, including Indonesia, had acceded to the GATT.

Generalized System of Preferences (GSP). A policy promoted by the United Nations Conference on Trade and Development under which developed countries grant tariff exemptions to imports from developing countries. The United States GSP programme was authorized by the International Trade and Tariff Act of 1974 and was extended by the International Trade and Tariff Act of 1984. Singapore "graduated" from the United States GSP programme as of January 1, 1989, as it was no longer considered a developing country.

Golkar. Golongan Karya (Functional Groups); the ruling political parties; a federation of groups within society, such as peasants, workers, and women.

Great Leap Forward. A drive to increase industrial and agricultural production following the suspension of Soviet aid and the desire to catch up with the advanced nations of the world. The campaign was conceived by Mao Zedong in late 1957, adopted by the National People's Congress in 1958; it continued through 1960. Emphasis was placed on accelerated collectivization of agriculture, national self-sufficiency, and labor-intensive methods. The campaign resulted in widespread waste of resources and was partially responsible for famine in 1960 and 1961.

Gross Domestic Product (GDP). The value of domestic goods and services produced by an economy in a given period, usually a year. Only output of goods for final consumption and investment is included, as the value added by primary or intermediate processing is assumed to be represented in the final prices (2) Gross domestic product plus income from overseas investments and wages minus earnings of foreign investors and foreign workers in the domestic economy.

Group of 77. Founded in 1964 as a forum for developing countries to negotiate with developed countries for economic aid, by the 1980s its membership had expanded from the original 77 nations to include the 127 members of the Nonaligned Movement.

Group of Fifteen. Group of Third World countries that participated in the Conference on International Economic Cooperation, held in several sessions between December 1975 and June 1977; it has continued to meet and add additional members since 1977. The group in 1992 included nineteen members: Algeria, Argentina, Brazil, Cameroon, Egypt, India, Indonesia, Iran, Iraq, Jamaica, Mexico, Nigeria, Pakistan, Peru, Saudi Arabia, Venezuela, Yugoslavia, Zaire, and Zambia.

Group of Seventy-Seven. Established in October 1967 with the aim of promoting economic cooperation among developing countries. Indonesia was among the seventy-seven original members. Despite the name, which persists, by 1992 there were 123 members.

Ho Chi Minh Trail. An intricate network of jungle trails, paths, and roads leading from the panhandle of northern Vietnam through Laos and Cambodia into the border provinces of southern Vietnam. At the height of the Second Indochina War, it was a major resupply artery for Hanoi's armed forces operating in South Vietnam.

Hoa Hao. Indigenous Vietnamese religion centered in An Giang Province, southern Vietnam. It was founded in the 1930s by Huynh Phu So, the son of a village elder in Chau Doc Province. Doctrinally, the faith is a variant of Mahayana Buddhism, but allows no intermediary between man and the Supreme Being. Before the fall of Saigon in 1975, the Hoa Hao had more than 1 million adherents.

Hundred Flowers Campaign. Also Double Hundred Campaign. Party-sponsored initiative to permit greater intellectual and artistic freedom. Introduced first into drama and other arts in the spring of 1956 under the official slogan "Let a hundred flowers bloom, let the hundred schools of thought contend." With Mao's encouragement in January 1957, the campaign was extended to intellectual expression and, by early May 1957, was being interpreted as permission for intellectuals to criticize political institutions of the regime. The effect was the large-scale exposure and purge of intellectuals critical of party and government policies.

Indochina Federation. A political concept, never fully realized, joining the three Indochinese states into a confederation, first proposed at the Indochinese Communist Party Central Committee meeting in October 1930. The government of France resurrected the term in 1946 to describe a limited internal self-government granted to the states of Vietnam (including Cochinchina), Laos, and Cambodia. In the 1980s, the term was used disparagingly by some observers and analysts to categorize Vietnam's military presence in, and influence over, Laos and Cambodia.

Inter-Governmental Group on Indonesia (IGGI). An international group of lenders established in 1967 by the Netherlands to coordinate multilateral aid to Indonesia. The other members included the Asian Development Bank, International Monetary Fund, United Nations Development Programme, World Bank, Australia, Belgium, Britain, Canada, France, Germany, Italy, Japan, New Zealand, Switzerland, and the United States. In March 1992, Indonesia announced that it was rejecting further IGGI aid as long as the Netherlands chaired the organization. IGGI was replaced by the Consultative Group on Indonesia.

International Monetary Fund (IMF). Established along with the World Bank in 1945, the IMF is a specialized agency affiliated with the United Nations and is responsible for stabilizing international exchange loans to its members when they experience balance of payments difficulties.

International Telecommunications Satellite Organization (INTELSAT). Established by two international agreements concluded at Washington, D.C. in August 1971, and effective in February 1973, INTELSAT was formed to carry forward the development, construction, operation, and maintenance of the global commercial telecommunications satellite system. In the 1980s, there were 109 signatory member nations and 30 nonsignatory user nations.

Jawi-Peranakan. Malay term for the descendants of marriages between Indian Muslim men and Malay women.

Juku. Privately established schools that teach either academic or nonacademic subjects. Academic *juku* offer tutorial, enrichment, remedial, and examination preparatory classes that supplement regular school work. Most hold classes after school and/or on weekends.

Kebatinan. An amalgam of animist, Hindu-Buddhist, and Islamic (especially Sufi) mystical elements that combine to form Javanese mysticism. As a body of belief, *kebatinan* is officially recognized in the 1945 constitution and is administered by the Department of Education and Culture rather than by the Department of Religious Affairs. Also known as *kejawen*, *agama Jawa*, or Javanism.

Khmer Rouge. The name given to Khmer communists by Prince Sihanouk in the 1960s. Later (although a misnomer) it was applied to the Cambodian insurgents of varying ideological backgrounds who opposed the Khmer Republic of Lon Nol. Between 1975 and 1978 it also became an informal designation for the regime of Democratic Kampuchea, whose leaders were the radical Pol Pot faction of the Kampuchean (or Khmer) Communist Party. After the Vietnamese invasion of Cambodia in December 1978, the Khmer Rouge became one of the three components of the Coalition Government of Democratic Kampuchea that contested the Vietnamese presence and the Hanoi- installed regime of the People's Republic of Kampuchea.

Khwan. Body-spirit or life-soul, generally thought to reside in the head; illness and death follow loss of the *khwan*.

Long March. The 12,500-kilometer-long trek made by the Red Army in the face of the Guomindang's "annihilation campaigns." Began in October 1934 in Jiangxi Province and ended in October 1935 in Shaanxi Province. Some 100,000 persons left the communist base area in Jiangxi but only about 28,000 arrived in Yan'an, Chinese Communist Party headquarters for the next decade. It was during the Long March that Mao Zedong gained his preeminent role in the party.

Luang. Title of distinction designating that its bearer is in royal service.

Mao Zedong Thought. Sayings and writings of Mao that served as a major source of national ideology until his death in 1976 and since then have undergone a cautious but critical reappraisal. By 1980 the meaning of the term had expanded to include the collective thoughts of all key party leaders.

Mass Line. Term for party policy aimed at broadening and cultivating contacts with the masses of the people and to accentuate the leadership role of the Chinese Communist Party.

Mass Movement. Derived from the concept of "mass line". Party-directed campaign designed to mobilize the masses in support or execution of major policies. Such movements were characteristic of the 1950s through the 1970s and were controlled and coordinated by permanent mass organizations.

Missing-in-action (MIA). United States military term for servicemen who remained unaccounted for at the end of the Second Indochina War. In the 1980s, rumors persisted that some MIAs were still alive and had been detained involuntarily in Vietnam after the war.

National People's Congress. Highest organ of the state, elected in accordance with the principles of democratic centralism. As of 1987, six congresses had been held, the first (1954), second (1959), third (1965), fourth (1975), fifth (1978), and sixth (1982), the seventh was scheduled for 1988; annual sessions were held most years except during the Cultural Revolution. The Standing Committee is the permanent organ of the National People's Congress and functions between annual sessions.

Neighborhood. Term in general use in China for the urban administrative unit usually found immediately below the district level, although an intermediate, subdistrict level exists in some cities. Also called *streets* (administrative terminology varies from city to city). Neighborhoods encompass 2,000 to 10,000 families. Within neighborhoods, families are grouped into smaller residential units of 100 to 600 families and supervised by a residents' committee; these are subdivided into residents' small groups of fifteen to forty families.

New Culture Movement. Refers to the period between 1917 and 1923, which was marked by student and intellectual ferment and protests against the warlord government. Culminated in the May Fourth Movement of 1919.

New Economic Zones. Population resettlement scheme undertaken in southern Vietnam after 1975 to increase food production and alleviate population pressure in congested urban areas, especially Ho Chi Minh City (Saigon). The sites selected for resettlement previously had been undeveloped or had been abandoned in the turbulence of war.

Newly Industrializing Economics (NIEs). A category of economies of nations or other political entities that experienced rapid industrial expansion and concomitant growth in their per capita GNP in the 1981s.

Nihon (or Nippon). Japanese term for Japan, based on the two Chinese ideographs (*riben* in pinyin romanization), meaning source of the sun. The official pronunciation, as designated by the Ministry of Education, Culture, and Science, is Nippon (or in full, Nippon Koku—Nippon country). The common pronunciation in everyday usage, however, is Nihon (Nihon Koku). The use of the term "Nihon" antedates Prince Shotoku's seventh-century reference to himself as the Son of Heaven of the Land of the Rising Sun and possibly dates from the establishment of the Nihon-fu (Japan Office) in the Yamato colony in southern Korea that served as a liaison office of the Yamato court to the Chinese court, probably as early as the sixth century. Marco Polo (or his scribe) referred to present-day Japan as Cipingu (Ribenguo in pinyin romanization), which has variously appeared as Cipangu, Jipangu, and Jipan, from which the current spelling of Japan undoubtedly descends.

Nonaligned Movement (NAM). Formed as the result of a series of increasingly structured nonaligned conferences, the first of which met at Belgrade, Yugoslavia in September 1961, the NAM's purpose is to insure the sovereignty and territorial integrity of nonaligned nations. In the 1980s, there were 127 member nations.

One country, two systems. A policy originating in the early 1980s that promotes reunification of Hong Kong, Macao, and Taiwan with the mainland and offers them a high degree of autonomy as special administrative regions of China. Through separate agreements with Britain and Portugal, Hong Kong and Macao are to revert to Chinese control in 1997 and 1999, respectively.

Overseas Chinese. Term usually used to refer to any person of Chinese origin living abroad on a permanent basis, without regard to his or her current citizenship. Overseas Chinese minorities are concentrated principally in Southeast Asia but are also found in other parts of Asia, the Middle East, Europe, North America, South America, and the Caribbean. Overseas Chinese have long been important to the government in power in China as a source of business contacts and of financial and moral support from abroad. The majority of foreign investment in China is by overseas Chinese, and more than 90 percent of all foreign tourists who visit China are overseas Chinese. Also used in China to refer to persons living in China who have returned from sojourns abroad.

Pancasila. The state philosophy based on five interrelated principles: belief in one supreme God; just and civilized humanitarianism; nationalism as expressed in the unity of Indonesia; popular sovereignty arrived at through deliberation and representation or consultative democracy; and social justice for all the Indonesian people. The Pancasila was announced by Sukarno on June 1, 1945. From Sanskrit: *panca* (five) and *sila* (principle).

Parrot's Beak. The part of the Cambodian province of Svay Rieng that juts into the southern Vietnamese provinces of Tay Ninh and Long An. During the South Vietnamese and United States incursion into Cambodia in 1970, and again during the Vietnamese invasion that drove the Khmer Rouge from power in 1978, the area was the scene of heavy fighting.

People's Action Party (PAP). Singapore's dominant political party, which has controlled the government by winning every general election since 1959.

People's Army of Vietnam (PAVN). The military forces of the Democratic Republic of Vietnam (until 1976) and, after reunification, of the Socialist Republic of Vietnam. During the Second Indochina War, PAVN bore the brunt of the fighting against the United States military forces in Vietnam, but was consistently able to recoup its losses and infiltrate units south by means of the Ho Chi Minh Trail. Failing to topple the Saigon government during the Tet Offensive of 1968, PAVN undertook its first conventional invasion of South Vietnam in the Easter Offensive of 1972. This attempt ended in defeat, but PAVN's next effort, the Spring Offensive of 1975, quickly overran the ineffectual ARVN resistance and toppled the Saigon government, thereby bringing to a close the Second Indochina War.

People's Commune. Formerly the highest of three administrative levels in rural areas in the period from 1958 to 1982-85, when they were replaced by townships. Communes, the largest collective units, were divided in turn into production brigades and production teams. The communes had governmental, political, and economic functions.

Phi. General term for a variety of spirits believed to have power over human beings. Specific kinds of spirits may have particular names.

Phra. Traditional princely title prefix designating that its bearer is a relative of the king; functional title given to holders of ranks in the civil administration below that of *phraya;* honorific for monks or persons and objects having religious associations.

Phrai. Generic term for commoners, variously translated as servant, serf, or, incorrectly, as slave. The *phrai* was bound to the land in the service of a *nai* under the *sakdi na* system.

Phraya. Traditional princely title conferred on holder of second highest rank in the civil government and on viceroys of tributary states. Sometimes seen as *phrajaa* or *phya*.

Phumphaek. Six areas into which Cambodia was divided in 1973.

Pribumi. Literally, an indigene, or native. In the colonial era, the great majority of the population of the archipelago came to regard themselves as indigenous, in contrast to the nonindigenous Dutch and Chinese (and, to a degree, Arab) communities. After independence the distinction persisted, expressed as a dichotomy between elements that were *pribumi* and those that were not. The distinction has had significant implications for economic development policy.

Produced Nation Income (PNI). A measure of an economy's material production that excludes income generated by the service sector and depreciation on capital equipment. It is used to measure controlled or communist economics where accounting procedures may ignore the service sector as "unproductive."

Production Brigade. Formerly the intermediate administrative level in the people's commune system, the organizational structure of the collective sector in agriculture. The highest level was the commune; the lowest, the production team. Most brigades were transformed into townships or villages in the period from 1982 to 1985. (*See also* people's commune, production team, townships, villages.)

Production Team. Formerly the basic accounting and farm production unit in the people's commune system. Production teams were largely disbanded during the agricultural reforms of 1982-85. In the administrative hierarchy, the team was the lowest level, the next higher levels being the production brigade and people's commune. Typically the team owned most of the land and was responsible for income distribution. Since 1984 most teams have been replaced by villages. (*See also* people's commune, production brigade, village.)

Putonghua. The common spoken language; also called *guoyu* (national language). The official spoken language of China, used in its various forms by more than 70 percent of the population. The People's Republic government started promoting *putonghua* in 1956 for use in schools, the cultural arena, and daily life as a means of bringing about the standardization of the language used by the Han nationality. *Putonghua* is based on the northern dialect, and uses Beijing pronunciations as its standard.

Red Guards. Generally used to refer to young people—primarily students—in their teens and twenties who began in May 1966 to support the leftist intraparty struggle then emerging against Liu Shaoqi and others. They made world famous the "little red book," *Quotations from Chairman Mao,* and were known for their use of big-character posters during the Cultural Revolution. Acting under the leadership of Mao and his radical adherents, Red Guards were the "soldiers" and the vanguard of the Cultural Revolution. The term Red Guard was derived from the early days of the Chinese Communist Party's armed struggle.

Rehabilitation. A practice dating from the early years of the Chinese Communist Party. Denotes the reinstatement in positions of responsibility of former government and party officials and military personnel who had been accused of wrongdoing. Rehabilitations sometimes take place posthumously to clear a former leader's name and reputation.

Repelita (Rencana Pembangunan Lima Tahun). A five-year economic development plan: Repelita I (FY 1969-73), Repelita II (FY 1974-78), Repelita III (FY 1979-83), Repelita IV (FY 1984-88), and Repelita V (FY 1989-93).

Responsibility System. A practice, first adopted in agriculture in 1981 and later extended to other sectors of the economy, by which local managers are held responsible for the profits and losses of the enterprise. This system partially supplanted the egalitarian distribution method, whereby the state assumed all profits and losses.

Revisionism. As used by communists, term refers to political, economic, and social tendencies that stray to the right of orthodox Marxism-Leninism. The Chinese communists long insisted that these tendencies were counter-revolutionary and that internal and external enemies (such as the Soviet Union) were infected by this negative phenomenon.

Riel. The Khmer Republic's currency unit, divided into 100 sen. Since October 29, 1971, its exchange rate has been adjusted by the National Bank of Cambodia according to market fluctuations; the initial rate, set on October 29, 1971, was 140 riels to US$1. Past exchange rates have been 35 riels to US$1 (January 1955 to August 1969) and 55.4 riels to US$1 (August 1969 to October 1971, following devaluation).

Ronin. Originally, a "wave person," or a masterless samurai who has left the service of his lord, either by choice or forced circumstances, and serves others with his bold and sometimes desperate deeds. In contemporary Japan, a student who has failed the entrance examination to the institution of choice and has chosen to spend an additional year or more in study to take the examination again.

Ruble. The Soviet Union's currency unit. In June 1987, its value was approximately 0.64 rubles to US$1.

Rupiah (Rp). Basic unit of currency. The exchange rate was fixed at Rp415 to US$1 from 1971 to 1978, when the rupiah was devalued to Rp625. Thereafter, the rate has floated slightly, although two major devaluations occurred in 1983 and 1986, bringing the exchange rate to Rp1,641 at the end of 1986. A policy of more gradual depreciation at about 5 percent per year has been followed through 1992. In November 1992, the exchange rate was valued at Rp1,881 per US$1, or Rp1 = US$.00018. The rupiah is made up of 5, 10, 25, 50, and 100 coins and 100, 500, 1,000, 5, 000, and 10,000 notes. UPDATE.

Sangha. Ascetic community within which a man can improve his karma; brotherhood of Buddhist monks; the Theravada Buddhist clergy.

Santri. Orthodox Muslims. In the Javanese context, the *santri* are also sometimes referred to as *putihan* (white ones), an allusion to their purity, especially as contrasted to *abangan* Javanese.

Search and Destroy Missions. Offensive military operations undertaken by United States combat units in Vietnam to find and neutralize the enemy, especially when the enemy's strength and disposition had not been fixed precisely. The capture and holding of territory during such operations was not a priority.

Second Indochina War (1954-75). Armed conflict that pitted Viet Cong insurgents native to southern Vietnam and regular PAVN units with Chinese and Soviet logistical and materiel support on one side against ARVN, United States, and smaller forces from the Republic of Korea (South Korea), Australia, Thailand and New Zealand on the other. Most of the ground fighting occurred in southern Vietnam. However, part of the conflict also involved an intensive air war over North Vietnam and Laos from 1965-73 and combat between competing indigenous forces in Laos and Cambodia.

Sharia. Muslim law, based on the Quran and precedents established by early Muslim jurists.

Shia (or Shiite). A member of the smaller of two great divisions of Islam. The Shias supported the claims of Ali and his line to presumptive right to the caliphate and leadership of the Muslim community, and on this issue they divided from the Sunnis in the first great schism of Islam. Later disagreements have produced further schisms among the Shias. Shias revere twelve imams, most of whom are believed to be hidden from view.

Shifting Cultivation. A traditional method of agriculture characterized by the rotation of fields rather than crops, the use of short cropping periods and long fallow periods, and the maintenance of fertility by allowing natural vegetation to regenerate on fallow land. Clearing of new or previously cropped land is often accomplished by cutting and burning vegation. Also known as slash-and-burn or swidden agriculture. Thai term is *tam rai*.

Siam. Official name of the Thai kingdom from 1855 to 1939 and again from 1946 to 1949. Used conventionally in European sources from the late sixteenth century for the kingdom of Ayutthaya and later the kingdom of Bangkok, hence the term Siamese to describe their inhabitants.

Siamese. Inhabitants of Siam. Historically used by Mon and Khmer to distinguish Tai-speaking settlers in the Chao Phraya Valley from those in other regions. The term was extended in conventional usage to inhabitants of Siam. Between 1939 and 1946 and since 1949, Thai and not Siamese has been employed to describe the dominant ethnic group of Thailand and Central Thai to denote the Thai of the Chao Phraya Valley.

Singapore Dollar (S$). Singapore's monetary unit, which in late 1989 had an exchange rate of US$1 to S$1.94.

Sino-Thai. Term used by observers of Thailand for persons of Chinese and Thai ancestry. It does not apply to a clearly delineated, cohesive group; some such persons have been essentially assimilated into Thai society; others (usually with a recent Chinese forebear) have not.

Socialist Education Movement. Inaugurated in September 1962 at the Tenth Plenum of the Eighth National Party Congress Central Committee as a mass ideological campaign for both party cadre and the general population. The movement was patterned along the lines of the Yan'an rectification campaign of 1942-45 and was intended to increase ideological "correctness" and consciousness, especially in regard to reversing "capitalist" and "revisionist" tendencies perceived in social and economic life. The Socialist Education Movement, which continued at least until 1965, is considered a precursor of the Cultural Revolution.

Straits Chinese. Chinese born in the Straits Settlements in the nineteenth and early twentieth centuries and more oriented to Southeast Asia than to China. They often spoke Malay or English as their first language.

Straits Settlements. Trading ports along the Strait of Malacca that were under direct British rule during the colonial period in contrast to the Malay States, which retained their native rulers. Governed from 1826 as part of British India, the Straits Settlements became a crown colony in 1867. Although the major Settlements were Singapore, Penang, and Malacca, the Straits Settlements also included Dindings, south of Penang, and Labuan Island, off the northern coast of Borneo.

Tai. A family of languages spoken in Southeast Asia and southern China including Thai ; by extension the peoples speaking languages of that family.

Thai. A national of Thailand; one or more persons of the (region- ally varied) ethnic group dominant in Thailand; the (dialectically varied) language of the Thai people, one of several grouped in Tai family of languages; also used adjectivally.

Tonghak. Literally, Eastern learning, an indigenous religious movement founded by Ch'oe Che-u in the early 1860s, which spearheaded a popular, anti-foreign rebellion in 1894-95. Later renamed Ch'ondogyo.

Total Defence. Singaporean national defense strategy calling for a small but well-equipped military force backed by trained reserves and an extensive civil defense organization.

United front. Chinese Communist Party strategy that attempts to utilize an organization or movement for the purpose of building a consensus and an organized following for party-supported programmes and goals. Historically, the term is associated with the Guomindang-Chinese Communist Party first united front (1923-27) and second united front (1937-45).

Value-Added Tax. A tax levied on the value added income of a firm, defined as the difference between total sales revenue and costs of intermediate inputs, such as raw materials, used in the production process.

Viet Cong. Contraction of the term Viet Nam Cong San (Vietnamese communists), the name applied by the governments of the United States and South Vietnam to the communist insurgents in rebellion against the latter government, beginning around 1957. The Vietnamese communists never used the term themselves, but referred to their movement as the National Front for the Liberation of South Vietnam (also known as the National Liberation Front), formally inaugurated in December 1960.

World Bank. Informal name used to designate a group of four affiliated international institutions: the International Bank for Reconstruction and Development (IBRD), the International Development Association (IDA), the International Finance Corporation (IFC), and the Multilateral Investment Guarantee Agency (MIGA). The IBRD, established in 1945, has the primary purpose of providing loans at market-related rates of interest to developing countries at more advanced stages of development. The IDA, a legally separate loan fund but administered by the staff of the IBRD, was set up in 1960 to furnish credits to the poorest developing countries on much easier terms than those of conventional IBRD loans. The IFC, founded in 1956, supplements the activities of the IBRD through loans and assistance designed specifically to encourage the growth of productive private enterprises in the less developed countries. The MIGA, founded in 1988, insures private foreign investment in developing countries against various noncommercial risks. The president and certain officers of the IBRD hold the same positions in the IFC. The four institutions are owned by the governments of the countries that subscribe their capital. To participate in the World Bank group, member states must first belong to the International Monetary Fund.

Yamato. Refers to the country of Japan or things Japanese, such as *yamato-e* (Japanese painting) and to the ancient court from which the imperial family arose. The Yamato court was situated either in modern Nara Prefecture, from the early fourth century A.D., or in northern Kyushu, starting perhaps in the early third century A.D.

Yobiko. A type of private school that specializes in preparing high-school graduates for university-entrance examinations, often through intensive full-time programmes.

Bibliography

Alagappa, Muthiah. 1995. "Contestation and Crisis, " Political Legitimacy in Southeast Asia: The Quest for Moral Authority. Muthiah Alagappa, ed. Stanford: Stanford University Press. Pp. 54-65.

Alagappa, Muthiah. 1995. "Seeking a More Durable Basis of Authority, " Political Legitimacy in Southeast Asia: The Quest for Moral Authority. Muthiah Alagappa, ed. Stanford: Stanford University Press. Pp. 293-334.

Allen, Jim. 1976. "Comment on 'An Evolutionary Approach to the Southeast Asian Cultural Sequence," *Current Anthropology*, 17.2:227-228.

Amore, Roy C. 1981. "Have Stories, Will Travel: How Buddhism Won the Southeast," in Southeast Asia: Women, Changing Social Structure, and Cultural Continuity. Geoffrey Hainsworth, ed. Ottawa: University of Ottawa Press. Pp. 150-55.

Anderson, Gerald H., ed. 1968. Christ and Crisis in Southeast Asia. New York: Friendship Press.

Arnold, Fred, and Nasra M. Shah. 1986. Asian Labor Migration: Pipeline to the Middle East. Boulder, Colorado: Westview Press.

Atkinson, Jane Monnig, and Shelly Errington, eds. 1990. Power and Difference: Gender in Island Southeast Asia. Stanford: Stanford University Press.

Attygale, R.C.L. 1961. "Social Change and the Idea of Excellence in Tropical Asian Society," World Yearbook of Education. London: Evans. Pp. 181-88.

Aung-Thwin, Michael. 1985. Pagan: The Origins of Modern Burma. Honolulu: University of Hawaii Press.

Baker, Christopher. 1981. "Economic Reorganization and the Slump in South and Southeast Asia," Comparative Studies in Society and History, 23.3:325-49.

Barker, Randolph, Bobert W. Herdt, with Beth Rose. 1985. The Rice Economy of Asia. Washington, D.C.: Resources for the Future.

Barnes, R.H. 1995. "Introduction," in Indigenous Peoples of Asia. R.H. Barnes, Andrew Gray, and Benedict Kingsbury, eds. Ann Arbor: Association for Asian Studies, Monograph and Occasional Paper Series, No. 48. Pp. 1-12.

Bastin, John, ed. 1967. The Emergence of Modern Southeast Asia: 1511-1957. Englewood Cliffs, N.J.: Prentice-Hall.

Bauer, Christian. 1984. A Guide to Mon Studies. Clayton, Australia: Monash University, Centre of Southeast Asian Studies, Working Paper No. 32.

Bayard, Donn. 1983. "The Development of Metallurgy in Southeast Asia: A Reply to Loofs-Wissowa," *Journal of Southeast Asian Studies*, 14.1:12-17.

Benda, Harry J. 1965. "Political Elites in Colonial Southeast Asia: An Historical Analysis," Comparative Studies in Society and History, 7:233-51.

Bentley, G. Carter. 1986. "Indigenous States of Southeast Asia," Annual Review of Anthropology, 15:275-305.

Bernatzik, Hugo Adolf. 1970. Akha and Miao: Problems of Applied Ethnography in Farther India. Alois Nagler, trans. New Haven: Yale University Press.

Bernet Kempers, A.J. 1988. The Kettledrums of Southeast Asia: A Bronze Age World and Its Aftermath. Rotterdam and Brookfields: A.A. Balkema, Modern Quarternary Research in Southeast Asia, Vol. 10.

Bhattacharya, D.K. 1976. "Comment on 'An Evolutionary Approach to the Southeast Asian Cultural Sequence," *Current Anthropology*, 17.2:229-30.

Bonacci, Mark A. 1991. Senseless Casualties: The AIDS Crisis in Asia. Washington, D.C.: International Voluntary Services.

Bradley, David, ed. 1985. Language Policy, Language Planning, and Sociolinguistics in Southeast Asia. Canberra: Australian National University, Department of Linguistics, Research School of Pacific Studies, Papers in Southeast Asian Linguistics, No. 9.

Brand, A. 1976. "Trade and the Patrimonial State: Weber and Van Leur," The Developing Economies, 14.1:21-36.

Brandon, James R. 1967. Theatre in Southeast Asia. Cambridge, Mass.: Harvard University Press.

Bray, Fracesca. 1986. The Rice Economies: Technology and Development in Asian Societies. Oxford: Basil Blackwell.

Bresnan, John. 1994. From Dominoes to Dynamoes: The Transformation of Southeast Asia. New York: Council on foreign Relations.

Briggs, Lawrence P. 1949. "The Appearance and Historical Usage of the Terms Tai, Thai, Siamese and, Lao," *Journal of the American Oriental Society*, 69.2:60-73.

Briggs, L.P. 1951. "The Syncretism of Religions in Southeast Asia, Especially in the Khmer Empire," *Journal of the American Oriental Society*, 71:230-49.

Brocheux, Pierre, ed. 1981. Histoire de l'asie du sud-est: rJvoltes, rJformes, rJvolutions. Lille: Presse Universitaires de Lille.

Brown, David. 1994. The State and Ethnic Politics in Southeast Asia. London: Routledge.

Brown, Rajeswary Ampalavanar. 1994. Capital and Entrepreneurship in Souh-East Asia. New York: St. Martin's Press.

Brown, Roxanna M. 1988. The Ceramics of South-East Asia: Their Dating and Identification. 2nd. edition. Singapore: Oxford University Press (Oxford in Asia Studies in Ceramics).

Brown, Russel E. 1968. Doing the Gospel in Southeast Asia. Valley Forge: Judson Press.

Bunker, Emma C. 1972. "The Tien Culture and Some Aspects of Its Relationship to the Dong-Son Culture," In Early Chinese Art and Its Possible Influence in the Pacific Basin. Noel Barnard, ed. New York: Intercultural Arts Press. Pp. 291-332.

Buss, Andreas. 1984. "Max Weber's Heritage and Modern Southeast Asian Thinking on Development," *Southeast Asian Journal of Social Science*, 12.1:1-15.

Buss, Andreas. 1986. "Max Weber's Heritage and Modern Southeast Asian Thinking on Development," Religion, Values and Development in Southeast Asia. Bruce Matthews and Judith Nagata, eds. Singapore: Institute of Southeast Asian Studies. Pp. 4-21.

Carroll, Theodora Foster. 1983. Women, Religion and Development in the Third World. New York: Praeger.

Catlin, Amy and Dixie Swift. 1987. Textiles as Texts: Arts of Hmong Women from Laos. Los Angeles: The Woman's Building.

Centre d'Etude du Sud-Est Asiatique, UniversitJ Libre de Bruxelles. 1967. Education et de'veloppement dans le Sud-Est l'Asie/Education and Development in Southeast Asia. Brussels: Editions de l'Institut de Sociologie, UniversitJ Libre de Bruxelles.

Chamberlain, James R. 1991. "MPne: A Tai Dialect Originally Spoken in NghL An (NghL Tinh), ViLtnam," *Journal of the Siam Society*, 79.2:103-123.

Chang, Kwang-chih. 1962. "Major Problems in the Culture History of Southeast Asia," Bulletin of the Institute of Ethnology, Academia Sinica, 13:1-23.

Chesnov, Ia. V. 1976. "On the Southeast Asian Cultural Sequence," *Current Anthropology*, 17.4:756-57.

Chiranan Prasertkul. 1989. Yunnan Trade in the Nineteenth Century: Southwest China's Cross-Boundaries Functional System. Bangkok: Institute of Asian Studies, Chulalongkorn University.

Chlenov, M.A. 1976. "Comment on 'An Evolutionary Approach to the Southeast Asian Cultural Sequence," *Current Anthropology*, 17.2:320-31.

Christie, Clive J. 1996. A Modern History of Southeast Asia: Decolnization, Nationalism and Separtism. London: I.B. Tauris.

Clad, James. 1989. Behind the Myth: Business Money and Power in Southeast Asia. London: Hyman.

Clammer, John. 1984. "Secularization and Religious Change in Contemporary Asia," *Southeast Asian Journal of Social Science*, 12.1:49-58.

Clammer, John. 1985. "Weber and Islam in Southeast Asia," *Journal of Developing Societies*, 1:224-36.

Clammer, John. 1987. "Urban Anthropology in Southeast Asia: A Brief Overview," *Contributions to Southeast Asian Ethnography*, 6:3-12.

Coe, Michael D. 1961. "Social Typology and the Tropical Forest Civilizations," *Comparative Studies in Society and History*, 4.1:65-85.

Cohen, Myron L., ed. 1992. Asia: Case Studies in the Social Sciences: A Guide for Teaching. Armonk, N.Y.: M.E. Sharpe.

Colchester, Marcus. 1995. "Indigenous Peoples' Rights and Sustainable Resource Use in South and Southeast Asia," in Indigenous Peoples of Asia. R.H. Barnes, Andrew Gray, and Benedict Kingsbury, eds. Ann Arbor: Association for Asian Studies, Monograph and Occasional Paper Seris, No. 48. Pp. 59-76.

Coomraswamy, Ananda K. 1965. History of Indian and Indonesian Art. New York: Dover.

Connor, Walker. 1969. "Ethnology and the Peace of Southeast Asia," World Politics, 22.1:52-86.

Cowan, C. D., and O. W. Wolters, ed. 1976. Southeast Asian History and Historiography: Essays Presented to D. G. E. Hall. Ithaca, New York: Cornell University Press.

Crouch, Harold, and Zakaria Ahmad, eds. 1985. Military-Civil Relations in South-East Asia. Kuala Lumpur: Oxford University press.

Cushman, Jennifer, and Wang Gungwu, eds. 1988. Changing Identities of the Southeast Asian Chinese since World War II. Hongkong: Hongkong University Press.

Dalby, Andrew. 1993. South East Asia: A Guide to Reference Material. London: Hans Zell Publishers, Regional Reference Guides, no. 2.

Davidson, Jeremy H. C. S., and H. Cordell, eds. 1982. The Short Story in South East Asia: Aspects of a Genre. London: School of Oriental and African Studies.

Davidson, Jeremy H. C. S. 1982. "The Modern Short Story in South East Asia: An Introduction," in The Short Story in South East Asia: Aspects of a Genre. London: School of Oriental and African Studies, University of London. Pp. 1-28.

Dhaninivat, Prince. 1967. "Thai Migrations," Symposium on Historical,

Archaeological and Linguistics Studies on Southern China, South-East Asia, and the Hong Kong Region. F.S. Drake, and Wolfram Eberhard, eds. Hong Kong: Hong Kong University Press. Pp. 43-48.

Dingwall, Alastair. 1995. Traveller's Literay Companion: South-East Asia. Brighton: In Print.

Dixon, Chris. 1991. South East Asia in the World-Economy: A Regional Geography. Cambridge: Cambridge University Press.

Dissanayake, Wimal, ed.. 1994. Colonialism and Nationalism in Asian Cinema. Bloomington: Indiana University Press.

Djiwandono, J. Soedjati, and Yong Mun Cheong, eds. 1988. Soldiers and Stability in Southeast Asia. Singapore: Institute of Southeast Asian Studies.

Dodd, William Clifton. 1923. The Tai Race: Elder Brother of the Chinese. Cedar Rapids: The Torch Press.

Donkin, R. A. 1976. "Comment on 'An Evolutionary Approach to the Southeast Asian Cultural Sequence," *Current Anthropology*, 17.2:231.

Downing, Bruce T., and Douglas P. Olney, eds. 1982. The Hmong in the West: Observations and Reports. Minneapolis: University of Minnesota, Southeast Asian Refugee Studies Project, Center for Urban and Regional Affairs.

Drake, F.S., and Wolfram Eberhard, eds. 1967. Symposium on Historical, Archaeological and Linguistics Studies on Southern China, South-East Asia, and the Hong Kong Region. Hong Kong: Hong Kong University Press.

DuBois, Cora. 1949. Social Forces in Southeast Asia. St. Paul: University of Minnesota Press. (Reprinted, Cambridge: Harvard University Press, 1959).

Dulong, Claude. 1958. Asia Jaune, Asia Rouge. Paris: Flammarion.

Durand, Maurce, and Nicole Louis. 1967. "Etude des systPme d'Jducation dans les diffJrentes zones de l'Asie du Sud-Est," in Education et de dJveloppement dans les Sud-Est l'Asie. Pp. 62-82.

Dutt, Ashok K., ed. 1985. Southeast Asia: Realm of Contrasts. 3rd rev. ed. Boulder, Colorado: Westview Press.

Eade, J.C. 1989. Southeast Asian Ephemeris: Solar and Planetary Positions, A.D. 638-2000. Ithaca, NY: Cornell University, Southeast Asia Program.

Elson, Robert E. 1992. "International Commerce, the State and Society: Economic and Social Change," The Cambridge History of Southeast Asia. Volume Two, The Nineteenth and Twentieth Centuries. Nicholas Tarling, ed. Cambridge: Cambridge University Press. Pp. 131-96.

Embree, Ainslie T., and Carol Gluck, eds. 1994. Asia in Western and World History. Armonk, N.Y.: M.E. Sharpe.

Embree, John F. and W.L. Thomas, Jr. 1950. Ethnic Groups of Northern Southeast Asia. New Haven: Yale University Southeast Asia Studies.

Emerson, Rupert. 1954. "Paradoxes of Asian Nationalism," Far Eastern Quarterly, 13:131-42.

Emerson, Rupert. 1971. "Post-Independence Nationalism in South and Southeast Asia: A Reconsideration," Pacific Affairs, 44.2:173-92.

Endicott, Kirk, Thomas N. Headland, and Pranab Ganguly. 1987. "Negrito Religions," in The Encyclopedia of Religion. Mircea Eliade, ed. New York: Collier Macmillan Publishers. Vol. 10, pp. 347-49.

Esposito, John L., ed. 1987. Islam in Asia: Religion, Politics, and Society. New York and Oxford: Oxford University Press.

Everett, Ray H. 1927. "International Traffic in Women and Children," *Journal of Social Hygiene*, 13:269-88.

Fisher, Charles A. 1964. Southeast Asia: A Social, Economic and Political Geography. London: Methuen and Co.

Fischer, Joseph. 1964. Universities in Southeast Asia: An Essay in Comparison and Development. Columbus, Ohio: Ohio University (International Education Monographs, #6).

Flatz, Gebhard. 1965. "Hemoglobin E in Southeast Asia," in Felicitation Volumes of Southeast Asian Studies Prsented to His Highness Prince Dhannivat. Bangkok: the Siam Society. Vol. I, pp. 91-106.

Forest, Alain, Yoshiaki Ishizawa, and Leon Vandermeersch, eds. 1991. Cultes Populaires et Societes Asiatiques: Appareils cultuels et appareils de pouvoir. Paris: Editions L'Harmattan and Tokyo: Sophia University.

Fox, James J. 1987. "Southeast Asian Religions: Insular Cultures," in The Encyclopedia of Religion. Mircea Eliade, ed. New York: Collier Macmillan Publishers. Vol. 13, pp. 520-30.

Fraser-Lu, Sylvia. 1989. Silverware of South-East Asia. Singapore: Oxford University Press.

Fryer, Donald W. 1970. Emerging Southeast Asia: A Study in Growth and Stagnation. New York: McGraw-Hill.

Furnivall, J.S. 1943. Educational Progress in Southeast Asia. New York: Institute of Pacific Relations.

Furnivall, J.S. 1945. "Some Problems of Tropical Economy," in Fabian Colonial Essays. R. Hinden, ed. London: Allen and Unwin. Pp. 167-71.

Geddes, William Robert. 1976. Migrants of the Mountains: The Cultural Ecology of the Blue Miao (Hmong Njua) of Thailand. Oxford: Clarendon Press.

Geddes, W. R., ed. 1987. Asian Perspectives in Social Science. Honolulu: University of Hawaii Press for the Seoul National University Press, the Institute of Social Sciences, International Studies Series No. 6.

Gesick, Lorraine, ed. 1983. Centers, Symbols, and Hierarchies: Essays on the Classical States of Southeast Asia. New Haven: Yale University Southeast Asia Studies.

Ghose, Rajeshwari, ed. 1987. Protest Movements in South and Southast Asia: Traditional and Modern Idioms of Expression. Hong Kong: University of Hong Kong, Centre of Asian Studies.

Ginsburg, Norton, Bruce Koppel, and T.G. McGee, eds. 1991. The Extended Metropolis: Settlement and Transition in Asia. Honolulu: University of Hawaii Press.

Glover, I.C., ed. 1992. Southeast Asian Archaeology 1990.. Hull: University of Hull, Centre of South-East Asian Studies.

Gokhale, Balakrishna G., ed. 1966. Asian Studies One: A Collection of Papers on Aspects of Asian History and Civilization. Bombay: Popular Prakashan.

Golay, Frank H. 1976. "Southeast Asia: The 'Colonial Drain' Revisited," in Southeast Asian History and Historiography: Essays Presented to D.G.E. Hall, ed. by C.D. Cowan and O.W. Wolters. Ithaca, New York: Cornell University Press. Pp. 368-87.

Golay, Frank H., Ralph Anspach, M. Ruth Pfanner, and Eliezer Ayal. 1970. Underdevelopment and Economic Nationalism in Southeast Asia. Ithaca, New York: Cornell University Press.

Goldschmidt, Ed. and E. J. Kunkel. 1971. "The Structure of the Peasant Family," American Anthropologist, 73:1058-1076.

Goloubew, Victor. 1932. "Sur l'origine et la diffusion des tambours mJtalliques," Praehistorica Asiae Orientalis (Hanoi: Imprimerie de lExtrLme-Orient), 1:137-50.

Gombrich, Richard. 1987. "Buddhist Cultic Life in Southeast Asia," in The Encyclopedia of Religion. Mircea Eliade, ed. New York: Collier Macmillan Publishers, Vol. 15:463-67.

Goodman, Grant K., ed. 1991. Japanese Cultural Policies in Southeast Asia during World War II. New York: St. Martin's Press.

Gorman, Chester F. 1971. "The Hoabinhian and After: Subistence Patterns in Southeast Asia during the Late Pleistocene and Early Recent Periods," World Archaeology, 1:300-20.

Gosling, L. A. Peter, ed. 1979. Population Resettlement in the Mekong River Basin. Chapel Hill, N.C.: University of North Carolina at Chapel Hill, Department of Geography (Studies in Geography No. 10).

Gosling, L. A. Peter. 1983. "Changing Chinese Identities in Southeast Asia: An Introductory Review," in The Chinese in Southeast Asia, Vol. 2: Identity, Culture, and Politics. Linda Y. C. Lim, and L. A. Peter Gosling, eds. Singapore: Maruzen Asia, Economic Research Centre and Centre for South and Southeast Asian Studies. Pp. 1-14.

Groslier, Benard Philipe. 1960. "Our Knowledge of Khmer Civilization: A Re-Appraisal," *Journal of the Siam Society*, 48.1:1-28.

Guennou, Jean. 1986. Missions JtrangPres de Paris. Paris: Fayard.

Gunasekaram, S. 1987. "Demographic Problems of Southeast Asia," in Southeast Asia Affairs 1987. Singapore: Institute of Southeast Asian Studies. Pp. 45-62.

Gunatilleke, Godfrey, Neelan Tiruchelvam, and Radhika Coomraswamy. 1983. Ethical Dilemmas of Development in Asia. Lexington, MA: Lexington Books, D. C. Heath.

Guyot, James F., and Ann Ruth Willner, eds. 1970. "Military Elites in Southeast Asia," *Journal of Comparative Administration*, Special Issue, November.

Hagesteijn, RenJe. 1989. Circles of Kings: Political Dynamics in Early Southeast Asia. Sydney and Wellington: George Allen & Unwin and Dordrecht, Holland/ Providence, R.I.: Foris Publications.

Hainsworth, Geoffrey B., ed. 1982. Village-level Modernization in Southeast Asia: The Political Economy of Rice and Water. Vancouver: University of British Columbia Press.

Hall, D.G.E. 1981. A History of South-East Asia. Fourth edition, New York: St. Martin's Press.

Hall, Kenneth R. 1985. Maritime Trade and State Development in Early Southeast Asia. Honolulu: University of Hawaii Press.

Hall, Kenneth R. 1992. "Economic History of Early Southeast Asia," The Cambridge History of Southeast Asia. Volume One, From Early Times to c. 1800. Nicholas Tarling, ed. Cambridge: Cambridge University Press. Pp. 183-75.

Hall, Kenneth R., and John K. Whitmore, eds. 1976. Explorations in Early Southeast Asian History: The Origins of Southeast Asian Statecraft. Ann Arbor: University of Michigan Center for South and Southeast Asian Studies (Michigan Papers on South and Southeast Asia, 11).

Han, Sang-bok, ed. 1986. Asian Peoples and Their Cultures: Continuity and Change. Seoul: Seoul National University Press.

Han, Sang-bok. 1986. "Introduction: Anthropological Studies on Asian Peoples and Their Cultures," Asian Peoples and Their Cultures: Continuity and Change. Sang-bok Han, ed. Seoul: Seoul National University Press. Pp. 1-12.

Hanks, Lucien M. 1972. Rice and Man: Agricultural Ecology in Southeast Asia. Chicago: Aldine-Atherton.

ul Haq, Obaid. 1986. "Islamic Resurgence: The Challenge of Change," in Islam and Society in Southeast Asia. Taufik Abdullah and Sharon Siddique, eds. Singapore: Institute of Southeast Asian Studies. Pp. 332-48.

Harley, J.B., and David Woodward. 1994. The History of Cartography, Volume 2, Book 2: Cartography in the Traditional East and Southeast Asian Societies. Chicago: University of Chicago Press.

Harris, David R. 1976. "Comment on 'An Evolutionary Approach to the Southeast Asian Cultural Sequence," *Current Anthropology*, 17.2:231-32.

Hart, Donn V., comp. 1980. Theses and Dissertations on Southeast Asia Presented at Northern Illinois University: An Annotated Bibliography. DeKalb, Il: Northern Illinois University, Center for Southeast Asian Studies (Bibliographical Publication, 6).

Hart, Gillian. 1989. "Agrarian Change in the Context of State Patronage," in Agrarian Transformations: Local Processes and the State in Southeast Asia. Gillian Hart, Andrew Turton, and Benjamin White, eds. Berkeley and Los Angeles: University of California Press. Pp. 31-49.

Hart, Gillian, Andrew Turton, and Benjamin White, eds. 1988. Agrarian Transformations: Local Processes and the State in Southeast Asia. Berkeley and Los Angeles: University of California Press.

Hartman, John F. 1986. "The Spread of South Indic Scripts in Southeast Asia," Crossroads, 3.1:6-20.

Hassan, M. Kamal. 1986. "Some Dimensions of Islamic Education in Southeast Asia," in Islam and Society in Southeast Asia. Taufik Abdullah and Sharon Siddique, eds. Singapore: Institute of Southeast Asian Studies. Pp. 40-79.

Hatch, Martin. 1987. "Music and Religion in Southeast Asia," in The Encyclopedia of Religion. Mircea Eliade, ed. New York: Collier Macmillan Publishers. Vol. 10, pp. 191-94.

Hauser, Philip M., Daniel B. Suits, and Naohiro Ogawa, eds. 1985. Urbanization and Migration in ASEAN Development. Honolulu: University of Hawaii Press; distributed for the National Institute of Research Advancement, Tokyo.

Hayden, Brian. 1976. "Comment on 'An Evolutionary Approach to the Southeast Asian Cultural Sequence," *Current Anthropology*, 17.2:232-33.

He Zhao Fa. 1983. "The Study of Southeast Asia in China Today," in The Southeast Asian Evironment. Douglas R. Webster, ed. Ottawa: University of Ottawa Press (Proceedings of the Annual Conference of the Canadian Council for Southeast Asian Studies). Pp. 221-29.

Heidhues, Mary F. Somers. 1983. Politik in Shdostasien: Grundlagen und Perspektiven. Hamburg: Institut fhr Asienkunde (Mitteilungen des Instituts fhr Asienkunde Hamburg, 136).

Heine-Geldern, Robert. 1956. Conceptions of State and Kingship in Southeast Asia. Ithaca, N.Y.: Cornell University Southeast Asia Program (Data Paper Number 18).

Henry, George. 1986. "A Proposal for a General Computer-Based Romanization for Southast Asian Indic-Derived Scripts," Crossroads, 3.1:62-79.

Herbert, Patricia, and Anthony Milner. 1989. South-East Asia Languages and Literatures: A Select Guide. Honolulu: University of Hawaii Press for the South-East Asia Library Groups.

Hewison, Kevin, Richard Robison, and Garry Rodan, eds. 1993. Southeast Asia in the 1990s: Authoriatarianism, Democracy and Capitalism. St. Leonards, N.S.W.: Allen and Unwin.

Heyzer, Noeleen. 1986. Working Women in Southeast Asia: Development, Subordination, and Emancipation. Philadelphia: Open University Press.

Heyzer, Noeleen, James V. Riker, and Antonio B. Quizon. 1995. Government-NGO Relations in Asia: Prospects and Challenges for People-Centered Development. New York: St. Martin's Press.

Higgott, Richard, and Richard Robison, eds. 1985. Southeast Asia: Essays in the Political Economy of Structural Change. London: Routledge and Kegan Paul.

Higgott, Richard, and Richard Robison. 1985. "Introduction," to Southeast Asia: Essays in the Political Economy of Structural Change. Richard Higgott and Richard Robison, eds. London: Routledge and Kegan Paul. Pp. 1-15.

Higgott, Richard, Richard Robison, with Kevin J. Hewison and Garry Rodan. 1985. "Theories of Development and Underdevelopment: Implications for the Study of Southeast Asia," in Southeast Asia: Essays in the Political Economy of Structural Change. Richard Higgott and Richard Robison, eds. London: Routledge and Kegan Paul. Pp. 16-62.

Higham, C.F.W. 1976. "Comment on 'An Evolutionary Approach to the Southeast Asian Cultural Sequence," *Current Anthropology*, 17.2:233.

Higham, Charles. 1988. The Archaeology of Mainland Southeast Asia. Cambridge: Cambridge University Press.

Hirschman, Charles. 1994. "Population and Society in Twentieth-Century Southeast Asia," *Journal of Southeast Asian Studies*, 25.2:381-416.

Hirschman, Charles, Charles F. Keyes, and Karl Hutterer, eds. 1992. Southeast Asian Studies in the Balance: Reflections from America. Ann Arbor: Association for Asian Studies.

Hitchcock, M.J., V.T. King, and M.J.G. Parnell, eds. 1992. Tourism in South-East Asia. London and New York: Routledge.

Ho Kuang-chung. 1967. "Chinese Literature in South-East Asia," Symposium on Historical, Archaeological and Linguistics Studies on Southern China, South-East Asia, and the Hong Kong Region. F.S. Drake, and Wolfram Eberhard, eds. Hong Kong: Hong Kong University Press. Pp. 300-305.

Hobart, Mark. 1986. "Introduction: Context, Meaning, and Power," in Context, Meaning, and Power in Southeast Asia. Mark Hobart and Robert H. Taylor, eds. Ithaca, N.Y.: Cornell University Southeast Asia Program, Studies on Southeast Asia. Pp. 7-20.

Hobart, Mark, and Robert H. Taylor, eds. 1986. Context, Meaning, and Power in Southeast Asia. Ithaca, N.Y.: Cornell University Southeast Asia Program, Studies on Southeast Asia.

Hooker, M. B., ed. 1986. The Law of Southeast Asia. Vol. 1: The Pre-Modern Texts. Singapore: Butterworths.

Horowitz, Donald L. 1985. Ethnic Groups in Conflict. Berkeley and Los Angeles: University of California Press.

Houmphanh Rattanavong. 1990. "Regarding What One Calls the Thai," in Proceedings of the 4th International Conference on Thai Studies, 11-13 May, 1990. Kunming: Institute of Southeast Asian Studies, Vol. 1, pp. 162-175.

Howard, Michael C. c1994. Textiles of Southeast Asia: An Annotated and Illustrated Bibliography. Bangkok: White Lotus.

Hsh Yhn-ts'iao. 1967. "Notes on the Studies of Ancient Malaya," Symposium on Historical, Archaeological and Linguistics Studies on Southern China, South-East Asia, and the Hong Kong Region. F.S. Drake, and Wolfram Eberhard, eds. Hong Kong: Hong Kong University Press. Pp. 172-75.

Huffman, Frank E. 1985. Bibliography and Index of Mainland Southeast Asian Languages and Linguistics. New Haven: Yale University Press.

Hugo, Graeme, Chan Kwok Bun. 1990. "Conceptualizing and Defining Refugee and Forced Migrations in Asia," Southeast Asian *Journal of Social Sciences*, 18.1:19-42.

Huq, Muhammad Shamsul. 1965. Education and Development Strategy in South and Southeast Asia. Honolulu: East-West Center Press, 1965.

Hurst, Philip. 1990. Rainforest Politics: Ecological Destruction in South-east Asia. London and New Jersey: Zed Books.

Hhsken, Frans, and Jeremy Kemp, eds. 1991. Cogation and Social Organization in Southeast Asia. Leiden: KITLV press.

Hutterer, Karl L. 1976. "An Evolutionary Approach to the Southeast Asian Cultural Sequence," *Current Anthropology*, 17.2:221-27, 237-42.

Hutterer, Karl L. 1977. "Reinterpreting the Southeast Asian Palaeolithic," in Cultural-Ecological Perspectives on Southeast Asia. William Wood, ed. Athens, Ohio: Ohio University Center for International Studies, Papers in International Studies, Southeast Asia Series, No. 41. Pp. 9-20.

Hutterer, Karl L. 1979. "'Roots': Prehistory and Environment," in An Introduction to Indochinese History, Culture and Life. John Whitmore, ed. Ann Arbor: Center for South and Southeast Asian Studies, University of Michigan. Pp. 11-18.

Ichimura, Shinichi, ed. [1977] c1976. Southeast Asia: Nature, Society, and Development: Contributions to Southeast Asian Studies. Honolulu: University Press of Hawaii, Monographs of the Center for Southeast Asian Studies, Kyoto University, 9.

Ichimura, Shinichi. [1977] c1976. "Introduction: Interdisciplinary Research and Area Studies," Southeast Asia: Nature, Society, and Development: Contributions to Southeast Asian Studies. Shinichi Ichimura, ed. Honolulu: University Press of Hawaii, Monographs of the Center for Southeast Asian Studies, Kyoto University. 9. Pp. 1-12.

Ileto, Reynaldo. 1992. "Religion and Anti-colonial Movements," The Cambridge History of Southeast Asia. Volume Two, The Nineteenth and Twentieth Centuries. Nicholas Tarling, ed. Cambridge: Cambridge University Press. Pp. 197-248.

Irwin, E. 1937. With Christ in Indochina: The Story of Alliance Missions in French Indochina and Eastern Siam. Harrisburg: Pennsylvania Christian Public.

Itty, C. I., ed. 1984. Searching for Asian Paradigms: Contributions of Youth to the Promotion of Social Goals and Cultural Values in the Development Process. Bangkok: Asian Cultural Forum on Development.

Iwata, Keiji. 1968. "Village Shrines in the Mainland Southeast Asia," in Folk Religion and the Worldview in the Southwestern Pacific. N. Matusumoto and T. Mabuchi, eds. Tokyo: Keio Institute of Cultural and Linguistic Studies, Keio University, Minatoku, Tokyo. Pp. 47-53.

Iyer, Pico. 1988. Video Night in Kathmandu and Other Reports from the Not-So-Far East. New York: Alfred A. Knopf. (New York: Viking, 1989).

Jackson, Karl D. 1985. "Post-Colonial Rebellion and Counterinsurgency in Southeast Asia," In Governments and Rebellions in Southeast Asia. Chandran Jeshurun, ed. Singapore: Institute of Southeast Asian Studies, Regional Strategic Studies Programme. Pp. 3-52.

Jamieson, Neil L. 1984. "Toward a Paradigm for Paradox: Observations on the Study of Social Organization in Southeast Asia," *Journal of Southeast Asian Studies*, 15.2:320-29.

Janse, Olov. 1958. Archaeological Research in Indo-China. Bruges: St. Catherine Press.

Janse, O. 1967. "Notes on Some Complex Problems Raised by Excavations in South-East Asia," Symposium on Historical, Archaeological and Linguistics Studies on Southern China, South-East Asia, and the Hong Kong Region. F.S. Drake, and Wolfram Eberhard, eds. Hong Kong: Hong Kong University Press. Pp. 26-28.

Jeshurun, Chandran, ed. 1985. Governments and Rebellions in Southeast Asia. Singapore: Institute of Southeast Asian Studies, Regional Strategic Studies Programme.

Johns, A.H. 1976. "Islam in Southeast Asia: Problems of Perspective," in Southeast Asian History and Historiogrpahy: Essays Presented to D.G.E. Hall, ed. by C.D. Cowan and O.W. Wolters. Ithaca, New York: Cornell University Press. Pp. 304-320.

Johns, A.H. 1987. "Islam in Southeast Asia," in The Encyclopedia of Religion. Mircea Eliade, ed. New York: Collier Macmillan Publishers. Vol. 7, pp. 404-22.

Jomo K.S., ed. 1997. Southeast Asia's Misunderstood Miracle. Boulder, Colorado: Westview.

Jones, E.L. 1991. "A Framework for the History of Economic Growth in Southeast Asia," Exploring Southeast Asia's Economic Past. G.D. Snooks, A.J.S. Reid, and J.J. Pincus, eds. Melbourne: Economic History Society of Australia and New Zealand, Australian Economic History Review, Vol. XXXI, No. 1. Pp. 5-19.

Jones, Gavin W., ed. 1984. Women in the Urban and Industrial Workforce: Southeast and East Asia. Honolulu: University of Hawaii Press, Distributed for the Development Studies Centre, Australian National University.

Jones, Gavin W. 1988. "Urbanization Trends in Southeast Asia: Some Issues for Policy," *Journal of Southeast Asian Studies*, 19.1:137-54.

Jones, Gavin W. 1994. Marriage and Divorce in Islamic South-East Asia. Oxford: Oxford University Press.

Kachorn Sukhabanij. 1957. "The Thai Beachhead States in the 11th-12th Centuries," Sinlapakn, 1.3, and 1.4; reprinted with concurrent pagination.

Kammerer, Cornelia Ann, and Nicola Tannebaum, eds. 1996. Merit and Blessing in Mainland Southeast Asia in Comparative Perspective. New Haven: Yale

University, Yale Southeast Asia Studies, Monograph 45.

Karim, Wazir Jahan, ed. 1995. 'Male' and 'Female' in Developing Southeast Asia. Oxford and Washington, D.C.: Berg Publishers.

Karim Wazir Jahan. 1995. "Introduction: Genderising Anthropology in Southeast Asia," 'Male' and 'Female' in Developing Southeast Asia. Wazir Jahan Karim, ed. Oxford and Washington, D.C.: Berg Publishers. Pp. 3-10.

Karim Wazir Jahan. 1995. "Bilateralism and Gender in Southeast Asia," 'Male' and 'Female' in Developing Southeast Asia. Wazir Jahan Karim, ed. Oxford and Washington, D.C.: Berg Publishers. Pp. 35-74.

Kathirithamby-Wells, J. 1992. "The Age of Transition: The Mid-Eighteenth to the Early Nineteenth Century," The Cambridge History of Southeast Asia. Volume One, From Early Times to c. 1800. Nicholas Tarling, ed. Cambridge: Cambridge University Press. Pp. 572-19.

Kathirithamby-Wells, Jeyamalar. 1993. "Restraints on the Development of Merchant Capitalism in Southeast Asia before c. 1800," Southeast Asia in the Early Modern Era: Trade, Power and Belief. Anthony Reid, ed. Ithaca, N.Y.: Cornell University Press. Pp. 123-48.

Katz, Nathan. 1987. "Buddhism and Politics in Sri Lanka and Other Theravda Nations Since 1945," in Movements and Issues in World Religions: A Sourcebook and Analysis of Developments since 1945—Religion, Ideology and Politics. Charles Wei-hsun Fu, and Gerhard E. Spiegler, eds. New York: Greenwood Press. Pp. 157-76.

Katz, Nathan, and Stephen D. Sowle. 1987. "Theravda Buddhism and Marxism in the Postward Era," in Movements and Issues in World Religions: A Sourcebook and Analysis of Developments since 1945—Religion, Ideology and Politics. Charles Wei-hsun Fu, and Gerhard E. Spiegler, eds. New York: Greenwood Press. Pp. 417-62.

Kemp, Jeremy, ed. 1990. Peasants and Cities, Cities and Peasants: Rethinking Southeast Asian Models. Overveen: ACASEA.

Kempers, A.J. Bernet. 1988. The Kettledrums of Southeast Asia: A Bronze Age World and Its Aftermath. Rotterdam and Brookfelds: A.A. Balkema, Modern Quarternary Research in Southeast Asia.

Keyes, Charles F. 1979. "Buddhist Economics in Practice," in Visakha Puja B.E. 2522 (1979). Bangkok: Annual Publication of the Buddhist Association of Thailand. Pp. 19-25.

Keyes, Charles F. 1981. "Southeast Asian Tribal Religion," in Abingdon Dictionary of Living Religions. Keith Crim, Roger A. Bullard, and Larry A. Shinn, eds. Nashville: Abingdon. Pp. 709-713.

Keyes, Charles F. 1983. "Merit-Transference in the Kammic Theory of Popular Therava-da Buddhism" in Karma: An Anthropological Inquiry. Charles F. Keyes and E. Valentine Daniel, eds. Berkeley: University of California Press. Pp. 261-86.

Keyes, Charles F. 1983. "Introduction," to Symposium on "Peasant Strategies in Asian Societies: Moral and Economic Approaches," *Journal of Asian Studies*, 62.4:753-68.

Keyes, Charles F. 1987. "Buddhist Pilgrimage in South and Southeast Asia," The Encyclopedia of Religion, Mircea Eliade, general editor. New York: Macmillan, vol. 11. Pp. 347-49.

Keyes, Charles F. 1987. "Tribal Peoples and the Nation-State in Mainland Southeast Asia," In Southeast Asian Tribal Groups and Ethnic Minorities: Prospects of the Eighties and Beyond. Benedict O'G. Anderson, et al. Cambridge, Massachusetts: Cultural Survival, Inc., Cultural Survival Report, 22.. Pp. 19-26.

Keyes, Charles F., ed. 1991. Reshaping Local Worlds: Rural Education and Cultural Change in Southeast Asia. New Haven: Yale University Southeast Asia Studies.

Keyes, Charles F. 1991. "Christianity as Indigenous Religion in Southeast Asia," Social Compass, 38.2:177-200.

Keyes, Charles F. 1996. "Being Protestant Christian in Southeast Asia," *Journal of Southeast Asian Studies*, 27.2:280-92.

Kherian, GrJgoire. 1967. "Instruction de la femme, condition de l'Jvolution et de la croissance," in Education et dJveloppement dans le Sud-Est de l'Asie. Pp. 49-59.

Khin Thitsa and Signe Howell. 1983. Women and Development in Southeast Asia, I. Papers. Canterbury, Kent: University of Kent, Centre of South-East Asian Studies (Occasional Paper No. 1).

Kingsbury, Benedict. 1995. "'Indigenous Peoples' as an International Legal Concept," in Indigenous Peoples of Asia. R.H. Barnes, Andrew Gray, and Benedict Kingsbury, eds. Ann Arbor: Association for Asian Studies, Monograph and Occasional Paper Seris, No. 48. Pp. 13-34.

Kirsch, A. Thomas. 1973. Feasting and Social Oscillation: Religion and Society in Upland Southeast Asia. Ithaca, N.Y.: Cornell University, Southeast Asia Program (Data Paper No. 92).

Kirsch, A. Thomas. 1990. "The Quest for Tai in Tai Context: Forethoughts and Afterthoughts," Crossroads, 5.1:69-79.

Kitagawa, Joseph M., and Frank Reynolds. 1976. "Theravada Buddhism in the

Twentieth Century," in Buddhism in the Modern World. Heinrich Dumoulin and John C. Maraldo, eds. New York: Collier Books. Pp. 43-64.

Klein-Hutheesing, Otome. 1995. "Gender at the Margins of Southeast Asia," 'Male' and 'Female' in Developing Southeast Asia. Wazir Jahan Karim, ed. Oxford and Washington, D.C.: Berg Publishers. Pp. 75-97.

Kleindienst, Maxime R. 1976. "Comment on 'An Evolutionary Approach to the Southeast Asian Cultural Sequence," *Current Anthropology*, 17.2:233-34.

Koch-Isenburg, Ludwig. 1966 [1963]. The Realm of the Green Buddha: A Thrilloing Expedition into the Strange Exotic Lands of Tropical Asia. Translated from the German by Richard and Clara Winston. New York: Pyramid Books.

Kondapi, C. 1951. Indians Overseas, 1838-1949. Madras: Oxford University Press.

Korff, Rhdiger. 1996. "Global and Local Spheres: The Diversity of Southeast Asian Urbanism," *Sojourn: Journal of Social Issues in Southeast Asia*, 11.2:288-313.

Koson Srisang. 1984. "Ethics and Politics," in Searching for Asian Paradigms: Contributions of Youth to the Promotion of Social Goals and Cultural Values in the Development Process. C. I. Itty, ed. Bangkok: Asian Cultural Forum on Development. Pp. 43-56.

Kratoska, Paul, and Ben Batson. 1992. "Nationalism and Modernist Reform," The Cambridge History of Southeast Asia. Volume Two, The Nineteenth and Twentieth Centuries. Nicholas Tarling, ed. Cambridge: Cambridge University Press. Pp. 249-324.

Krausse, Gerald H., ed. 1988. Urban Society in Southeast Asia. Vol. 1: Social and Economic Issues; Vol. 2: Political and Cultural Issues. Hong Kong: Asian Research Service, Asian Studies Monograph Series.

Krause, Gerald H., ed. 1988. Urban Society in Southeast Asia. Volume II: Poltical and Cultural Issues. Hong Kong: Asian Research Service, Asian Studies Monograph Series.

Kress, Jonathan H. 1976. "Comment on 'An Evolutionary Approach to the Southeast Asian Cultural Sequence," *Current Anthropology*, 17.2:234.

Krzyzaniak, Lech. 1976. "Comment on 'An Evolutionary Approach to the Southeast Asian Cultural Sequence," *Current Anthropology*, 17.2:234.

Kuhlke, Hermann. 1978. The Davaraja Cult. Translated from the German by I.W. Mabbett. Ithaca, N.Y.: Cornell University, Southeast Asia Program, Data Paper, No.108. (Orig. published in German in 1974.)

Kulke, Hermann. 1986. "The Early and Imperial Kingdom in Southeast Asian History," in Southeast Asia in the 9th to 14th Centuries. David G. Marr, and A. C. Milner, eds. Singapore: Institute of Southeast Asian Studies and the Research School of Pacific Studies, Australian National University. Pp. 1-22.

Kunstadter, Peter, ed. 1967. Southeast Asian Tribes, Minorities and Nations. 2 vols. Princeton: Princeton University Press.

Kunstadter, Peter. 1967. "Introduction," in Southeast Asian Tribes, Minorities and Nations, Peter Kunstadter, ed. 2 vols. Princeton: Princeton University Press. Pp. 3-72.

Kunstadter, Peter, E.C. Chapman, and Sanga Sabhasri, eds. 1978. Farmers in the Forest: Economic Development and Marginal Agriculture in Northern Thailand. Honolulu: The University Press of Hawaii (East-West Center Book).

Lafont, Pierre-Bernard. 1971. "GJnies, Anges et DJmons en Asie du Sud-est," en GJnies, Anges et DJmons. Paris: Ed. du Seuil, Sources Orientales VIII. Pp. 343-82.

Lafont, Pierre-Bernard, ed. 1976. Asie du Sud-Est Continentale, Vols. 2 and 3. Paris: L'Asiath'eque.

Lafont, P.B., ed. 1989. Les frontiPres du Vietnam: Historie des frontiPres de la peninsule indochinoise. Paris: Editions l'Harmattan.

Lafont, P.B. 1989. "La notion de frontiPre dans la partie orientale de la pJninsule indochinoise," Les frontiPres du Vietnam: Historie des frontiPres de la peninsule indochinoise. P. B. Lafont, ed. Paris: Editions l'Harmattan. Pp. 11-24.

Laurentin, RenJ. 1971. Flashes sur l'ExtrLme-Orient. Paris: Le Seuil.

LL ThBnh Kh^i. 1967. "ProblPmes gJnJraux de l'Jducation et du dJveloppement en Asie," in Education et dJveloppement dans le Sud-Est de l'Asie. Pp. 13-28.

Leach, E.R. 1954. Political Systems of Highland Burma. Cambridge: Harvard University Press. (Reprinted, with a new introductory note by the author, in London: London School of Economics and Political Science and G. Bell and Sons, Ltd. [1964]; and Boston: Beacon Press [1965].)

LefJvre-Pontalils, Pierre. 1892. "Etude sur quelques alphabets et vocabulaires ThaVs," T'oung Pao, 3:39-64/.

Legge, John D. 1976. "Southeast Asian History and the Social Sciences," in Southeast Asian History and Historiogrpahy: Essays Presented to D.G.E. Hall, ed. by C.D. Cowan and O.W. Wolters. Ithaca, New York: Cornell University Press. Pp. 388-404.

Legge, J.D. 1992. "The Writing of Southeast Asian History," The Cambridge History of Southeast Asia. Volume One, From Early Times to c. 1800. Nicholas Tarling, ed. Cambridge: Cambridge University Press. Pp. 1-50.

Lent, John A. 1995. Asian Popular Culture. Boulder: Westview.

Lester, Robert C. 1973. Therevada Buddhism in Southeast Asia. Ann Arbor: University of Michigan Paperback.

Li Fang Kuei 1977. A Handbook of Comparative Tai. Honolulu: The University Press of Hawaii.

Lieberman, Victor. 1993. "Local Integration and Eurasian Analogues: Structuring Southeast Asian History," Modern Asian Studies, 27.3:475-72.

Liefer, Michael, ed. 1995. Dictionary of Modern Politics of South-East Asia. New York: Routledge.

Lilley, Rozanna. 1990. "Afterword: 'Ethnicity' and Anthropology," Ethnic Groups across National Boundaries in Mainland Southeast Asia. Gehan Wijeyewardene, ed. Singapore: Institute of Southeast Asian Studies. Pp. 173-84.

Lim, Linda Y.C. 1983. "Chinese Economic Activity in Southeast Asia: An Introductory Review," in The Chinese in Southeast Asia, Vol. 1: Ethnicity and Economic Activity. Linda Y. C. Lim, and L. A. Peter Gosling, eds. Singapore: Maruzen Asia, Economic Research Centre and Centre for South and Southeast Asian Studies. Pp. 1-29.

Lim Pui Huen. 1981. "Library Needs for Southeast Asian Studies," A Colloquium on Southeast Asian Studies. Tunku Shamsul Bahrin, Chandran Jeshurun, and A. Terry Rambo, eds. Singapore: Institute of Southeast Asian Studies. Pp. 145-70.

Lim Teck Ghee. 1988. "Non-Government Organizations and Human Development," in Reflections on Development in Southeast Asia. Lim Teck Ghee, ed. Singapore: Institute of Southeast Asian Studies. Pp. 160-191.

Ling, Trevor. 1993. Buddhist Trends in Southeast Asia. Singapore: Institute of Southeast Asian Studies.

Ling, Trevor. 1993. "Introduction," Buddhist Trends in Southeast Asia. Trevor Ling, ed. Singapore: Institute of Southeast Asian Studies. Pp. 1-5.

Lingat, Robert. 1937. "Vinaya et droit laVques: Jtudes sur les conflits de la loi religieuse et de la laVque dans l'Indochine hinayaniste." Bulletin Icole FranHaise d'ExtLme-Orient, 37:415-77.

Lingat, Robert. 1951. "La conception du Droit dans l'Indochine Hinyaniste," Bulletin Icole FranHaise d'ExtrLme-Orient, 44:XX-XX.

Luce, Gordon H. 1970. Old Burma-Early Pagn. Locust Valley, New York: J.J. Augustin Publisher.

Mabbet, Ian W. 1969. "Devaraja," *Journal of Southeast Asian History*, 10.2:202-23.

Mabbet, Ian W. 1977. "The 'Indianization' of Southeast Asia: Reflection on the Historical Sources," *Journal of Southeast Asian Studies*, 8.2:143-61.

Mabbet, Ian W. 1977. "Varnas in Angkor and the Indian Caste System," *Journal of*

Asian Studies, 36.3:429-42.

Mabbet, Ian W. 1985. "A Survey of the Background to the Variety of Political Traditions in Southeast Asia," in Patterns of Kinship and Authority in Traditional Asia, I.W. Mabbett, ed. London: Croom Helm. Pp. 69-84.

Mabbet, Ian W. 1986. "Buddhism in Champa," in Southeast Asia in the 9th to 14th Centuries, David G. Marr and A.C. Milner, eds. Singapore: Institute of Southeast Asia Studies; and Canberra: Research School of Pacific Studies. Pp. 289-313.

MacAndrews, Colin, and Chia Lin Sien, eds. 1982. Too Rapid Rural Development: Perceptions and Perspectives from Southeast Asia. Athens, OH: Ohio University Press.

McCoy, Alfred W., and Alan A. Block, eds. 1992. War on Drugs: Studies in the Failure of U.S. Narcotics Policy. Boulder: Westview.

McGee, T.G. 1967. The Southeast Asian City. A Social Geography of the Primate Cities of Southeast Asia. London: G. Bell and Sons, Ltd.; New York: Praeger.

Mackie, Jamie. 1992. "Changing Patterns in Big Business in Southeast Asia," Southeast Asian Capitalists. Ruth McVey, ed. Ithaca, N.Y.: Cornell University Southeast Asian Studies. Pp. 161-90.

Mackie, Jamie. 1993. "A Political Overview of Southeast Asia," in Southeast Asia Affairs 1993. Singapore: Institute of Southeast Asian Studies. Pp. 3-21.

McNeely, Jeffery A., and Paul Spencer Wachtel. 1988. Soul of the Tiger: Searching for Nature's Answers ih Southeast Asia. New York: Athena Books of Paragon House. (Reprinted, Honolulu: University of Hawaii Press).

McVey, Ruth. 1981. "Islam Explained: Review Article," Pacific Affairs, 54.2:260-87.

McVey, Ruth, ed. 1992. Southeast Asian Capitalists. Ithaca, N.Y.: Cornell University Southeast Asian Studies.

McVey, Ruth. 1992. "The Materialization of the Southeast Asian Entrepreneur," Southeast Asian Capitalists. Ruth McVey, ed. Ithaca, N.Y.: Cornell University Southeast Asian Studies. Pp. 7-34.

Malalgoda, Kitsiri 1970. "Millennialism in Relation to Buddhism," Comparative Studies in Society and History, 12.4:424-41.

Manderson, Lenore, ed. 1986. Shared Wealth and Symbol: Food, Culture and Society in Oceania and Southeast Asia. Cambridge: Cambridge University Press.

Marr, David G., and A. C. Milner, eds. 1986. Southeast Asia in the 9th to 14th Centuries. Singapore: Institute of Southeast Asian Studies and the Research School of Pacific Studies, Australian National University.

Marten, Gerald G., ed. 1986. Traditional Agriculture in Southeast Asia: A Human Ecology Perspective. Boulder, Colorado: Westview Press. Published in Cooperation with the East-West Center Environment and Policy Institute.

Marten, Gerald G. 1986. "Traditional Agriculture and Agricultural Research in Southeast Asia," in Traditional Agriculture in Southeast Asia: A Human Ecology Perspective. Gerald G. Marten, ed. Boulder, Colorado: Westview Press. Published in Cooperation with the East-West Center Environment and Policy Institute. Pp. 326-40.

Matthews, Bruce. 1986. "Buddhism, Modernization and National Purpose," Religion, Values and Development in Southeast Asia. Bruce Matthews and Judith Nagata, eds. Singapore: Institute of Southeast Asian Studies. Pp. 51-60.

Mathews, Bruce, and Judith Nagata, eds. 1986. Religion, Values and Development in Southeast Asia. Singapore: Institute of Southeast Asian Studies.

Matisoff, James A. 1983. "Linguistic Diversity and Language Contact," in Highlanders of Thailand. John McKinnon and Wanat Bhruksasri, eds. Kuala Lumpur: Oxford University Press. Pp. 56-86.

Matisoff, James A. 1991. "Sino-Tibetan Linguistics: Present State and Future Prospects," Annual Review of Anthropology, 20:469-504.

Matras-Troubetzkoy, Jacqueline, and Christian Taillard, ed. 1980. Cheminements: Ecrits offerts B Georges Condominas. Paris: L'Ecole des Hautes Etudes en Sciences Sociales (Asie de Sud-Est et Monde Insulindien, no. 1-4, vol 11).

Maxwell, Robyn J. 1987. Southeast Asian Textiles: The State of the Art. Clayton, Victoria: Monash University, Center for Southeast Asian Studies, Working Papers, No. 42.

Meillet, A., et M. Cohen, eds. 1924. Les langues du monde. New ed., 1952. Paris.

Melchor, Alejandro, Jr. 1985. "Insurgency Movements in Southeast Asia: A Perspective," In Governments and Rebellions in Southeast Asia. Chandran Jeshurun, ed. Singapore: Institute of Southeast Asian Studies, Regional Strategic Studies Programme. Pp. 55-66.

Miettinen, Jukka O. 1993. Classical Dance and Theatre in South-East Asia. Singapore: Oxford University Press.

Milgram, Lynne, and Penny Van Esterik, eds. 1994. The Transformative Power of Cloth in Southeast Asia. Toronto: The Museum for Textiles and the Canadian Council for Southeast Asian Studies.

Mus, Paul. 1975. India Seen from the East: Indian and Indigenous Cults in Champa. Translated by I.W. Mabbett and ed. by I.W. Mabbett and David P. Chandler. Melbourne: Monash University, Centre of Southeast Asian Studies (Monash Papers on Southeast Asia, No.3), 1975. (Originaly published as "Cultes indiens et indige'nes au Champa," Bulletin de l'Ecole FranHaise d'ExtrLme-Orient, 33:367-410, 1933)

Muzaffar, Chandra. 1986. "Islamic Resurgence: A Global View," in Islam and Society in Southeast Asia. Taufik Abdullah and Sharon Siddique, eds. Singapore: Institute of Southeast Asian Studies. Pp. 5-39.

Nash, Manning, et al. 1966. Anthropological Studies in Theravada Buddhism. New Haven: Yale University, Southeast Asia Studies (Cultural Report Series, No.13).

Neher, Clark D., and Ross Marlay, eds. 1995. Democracy and Development in Southeast Asia: The Winds of Change. Boulder: Westview Press.

Neill, Stephen C. 1987. "Christianity in Asia," in The Encyclopedia of Religion. Mircea Eliade, ed. New York: Collier Macmillan Publishers, Vol. 3, pp. 418-423.

Ness, Gayl D., and Hirofumi Ando. 1984. The Land is Shrinking: Population Planning in Asia. Baltimore: Johns Hopkins University Press.

Nguyen Huu Chao. 1967. "Planification et financement de l'Jducation en Asie du Sud-Est," in Education et dJveloppement dans le Sud-Est de l'Asie. Pp. 29-48.

Nhat Tien, Duong Phuc, and Vu Thanh Thuy. 1981. Pirates on the Gulf of Siam: Report from the Vietnamese Boat People Living in the Refugee Camp in Songkhla-Thailand. 2nd ed. San Diego: Boat People S.O.S. Committee.

Nrrland, Irene, Sven Cederroth, and Ingela Gerdin, eds. 1986. Rice Societies: Asian Problems and Prospects. Riverdale, Maryland: Curzon press, The Riverdale Company, Scandianavian Institute of Asian Studies, Studies on Asian Topics 10.

Nordhold, Nico Schulte, and Leontine Visser, eds. 1995. Social Science in Southeast Asia: From Particularism to Universalism. Amsterdam: VU University Press for Centre for Asian Studies Amsterdam.

Noss, Richard B., ed. 1984. An Overview of Language Issues in South-East Asia, 1950-1980. Singapore: Oxford University Press.

Olsen, Edward A., and Stephen Jurika, Jr., eds. 1986. The Armed Forces in Contemporary Asian Societies. Boulder, Colorado: Westview Press.

O'Neil, Thomas, with photographs by Michael Yamashita. 1993. "Mekong River," National Geographic, February. Pp. XX-XX.

Ong Choo Suat, ed. 1986. Southeast Asian Cultural Heritage: Images of Traditional Communities. Singapore: Institute of Southeast Asian Studies, Programme on the Cultural Heritage of Southeast Asia.

Osborne, Milton. 1988. Southeast Asia: An Illustrated History. Expanded edition. Sydney, Wellington, Boston: Allen & Unwin.

Osborne, Milton. 1995. Southeast Asia: An Illustrated History. 5th ed. Sydney: Allen & Unwin.

Oshima, Harry T. 1987. Economic Growth in Monsoon Asia. Tokyo: University of Tokyo Press. (Distributed by Columbia University Press)

Owen, Norman G., ed. 1987. Death and Disease in Southeast Asia: Explorations in Social, Medical and Demographic History. Singapore: Oxford University Press. Publication of the Asian Studies Association of Australia.

Ownby, David, and Mary Somers Heidhues, eds. 1993. "Secret Societies" Reconsidered: Perspectives on the Social History of Early Modern South China and Southeast Asia. Armonk, N.Y. and London: M.E. Sharpe.

Parkin, Robert. 1991. A Guide ot Austroasiatic Speakers and Their Languages. Honolulu: University of Hawaii Press, Oceanic Linguistics Special Publication, No. 23.

Parnwell, Michael, and Raymond Bryant, eds. 1996. Environmental Change in South-East Asia. New York: Routledge.

Paton, D.M. 1965. "Christian Missions in Asia," in Asia: A Handbook. G. Wint, ed. London: Antony Blond.

Patra Sukontasarp, et al., eds. 1982. Proceedings: Second Asian Workshop on Child and Adolescent Development. Bangkok: Burapasilpa Press for Behavioral Science Research Institute, Sri Nakharinwirot University, Bangkok.

Patya Saihoo. 1981. "Southeast Asian Studies in Thailand," A Colloquium on Southeast Asian Studies. Tunku Shamsul Bahrin, Chandran Jeshurun, and A. Terry Rambo, eds. Singapore: Institute of Southeast Asian Studies. Pp. 134-44.

Pauker, Guy J. 1985. "Government Responses to Armed Insurgency in Southeast Asia: A Comparative Examination of Failures and Successes and Their Likely Implications for the Future," in Governments and Rebellions in Southeast Asia. Chandran Jeshurun, ed. Singapore: Institute of Southeast Asian Studies, Regional Strategic Studies Progamme. Pp. 71-97.

Peacock, James L. 1978. Muslims Puritans: Reformist Psychology in Southeast Asia Islam. Berkeley and Los Angeles: University of California Press.

Pelzer, Karl J. 1978. "Swidden Cultivation in Southeast Asia: Historical, Ecological, and Economic Perspectives," in Farmers in the Forest. Peter Kunstadter, E.C. Chapman and Sanga Sabhasri, eds. Honolulu: The University Press of Hawaii. Pp. 271-286.

Peterson, Jean Treloggen. 1977. "The Merits of Margin," in Cultural-Ecological Perspectives on Southeast Asia. William Wood, ed. Athens, Ohio: Ohio University Center for International Studies (Papers in International Studies, Southeast Asia Series, No. 41). Pp. 63-73.

Pfanner, David, and J. Ingersoll. 1962. "Theravada Buddhism and Village Economic Behavior," *Journal of Asian Studies*, 21:341-61.

Picard, Michel, and Robert E. Wood. 1997. Tourism, Ethnicity and the State in Asian and Pacific Societies. Honolulu: University of Hawaii Press.

Pinkerton, John. 1811. A General Collection of the Best and Most Interesting Voyages and Travels in All Parts of the World. London: Longman, Hurst, etc.

Pinto, Fernao Mendes. 1989. The Travels of Mendes Pinto. Rebecca D. Catz, ed. and trans. Chicago: University of Chicago Press.

Postlethwaite, T. Neville, and R. Murray Thomas, eds. 1980. Schooling in the ASEAN Region: Primary and Secondary Education in Indonesia, Malaysia, the Philippines, Singapore, and Thailand. New York: Pergamon Press.

Pryor, R.J., ed. 1979. Migration and Development in Southeast Asia: A Demographic Perspective. Kuala Lumpur: Oxford University Press.

Queen, Christopher S., and Sallie B. King, eds. 1996. Engaged Buddhism: Buddhist Liberation Movements in Asia. Albany: State University of New York Press.

Rambo, A. Terry. 1981. "Environment and Development: The Place of Human Ecology in Southeast Asian Studies Programmes," A Colloquium on Southeast Asian Studies. Tunku Shamsul Bahrin, Chandran Jeshurun, and A. Terry Rambo, eds. Singapore: Institute of Southeast Asian Studies. Pp. 185-94.

Raybeck, Douglas. 1983. "Chinese Patterns of Adaptation in Southeast Asia," in The Chinese in Southeast Asia, Vol. 2: Identity, Culture, and Politics. Linda Y. C. Lim, and L. A. Peter Gosling, eds. Singapore: Maruzen Asia, Economic Research Centre and Centre for South and Southeast Asian Studies. Pp. 15-33.

Reed, Robert B., ed. 1990. Patterns of Migration in Southeast Asia. Berkeley: University of Clfiornia, Center for South and Southeast Asian Studies.

Reid, Anthony. 1983. "Introduction," Slavery, Bondage, and Dependency in Southeast Asia. Anthony Reid, ed. New York: St. Martin's Press. Pp. 1-43.

Reid, Anthony, and David Marr, eds. 1979. "Bibliographical Appendix: Southeast Asian Historical Writing," in Perceptions of the Past in Southeast Asia, ed. by Anthony Reid and David Marr. Singapore: Heinmeann Educational Books (Asia) for the Asian Studies Association of Australia. Pp. 401-25.

Reynolds, Craig J. 1992. "Authenticating Southeast Asia in the Absence of Colonialism: Burma," Asian Studies Review, 15.3:141-51.

Reynolds, Frank. 1972. "Buddhism and the Anthropologists: Some Comments Concerning Recent Works on Southeast Asia," History of Religions, 11.3:303-314.

Reynolds, Frank E. 1981. "Toward a History of Religions in South and Southeast Asia: Some Reflections on the Work of Paul Mus," Religious Studies Review, 7.3:220-33.

Reynolds, Frank E., and Regina T. Clifford. 1980. "Buddhism and National Integration," in Transitions and Transformations in the History of Religions. Frank E. Reynolds and Theodore M. Ludwig, eds. Leiden: E. J. Brill. Pp. 56-90.

Richter, Linda K. 1989. The Politics of Tourism in Asia. Honolulu: University of Hawaii Press.

Richter, Linda K. 1990. "Exploring Theories of Female Leadership in South and Southeast Asia," Pacific Affairs, 63.4:524-40.

Rigg, Jonathan. 1991. Southeast Asia: A Region in Transition; A Thematic Human Geography of the ASEAN Region. London: Unwin Hyman.

Robinson, Richard, Kevin Hewison, and Richard Higgot, eds. 1987. Southeast Asia in the 1980s: The Politics of Economic Crisis. Sydney, London and Boston: Allen & Unwin.

Robinson, Richard, Kevin Hewison, and Garry Rodan, eds. 1995. Southeast Asia in the 1990s: Authoritarianism, Democracy and Capitalism. Sydney: Allen & Unwin.

Roff, William R., ed. 1987. Islam and the Political Economy of Meaning: Comparative Studies of Muslim Discourse. Berkeley and Los Angeles: University of California Press.

Rooney, Dawn F. 1987. Folk Pottery in South-East Asia. Singapore: Oxford University Press.

Rowland, John. 1992. Two Transitions: Indochina 1952-1955, Malaysia 1969-1972. Centre for the Study of Australia-Asia Relations, Griffith University.

Ruey Yih-fu. 1967. "A Study of the Miao People," translated and summarized by V.T. Tang, Symposium on Historical, Archaeological and Linguistics Studies on Southern China, South-East Asia, and the Hong Kong Region. F.S. Drake, and Wolfram Eberhard, eds. Hong Kong: Hong Kong University Press. Pp. 49-58.

Rhluand, Jhrgen. 1992. Urban Development in Southeast Asia: Regional Cities and Local Government. Boulder, CO: Westview.

Russell, Susan D., ed. 1989. Ritual, Power, and Economy: Upland-Lowland Contrasts in Mainland Southeast Asia. DeKalb, IL: Northern Illinois University, Center for Southeast Asian Studies, Monograph Series on Southeast Asia, Occasional Paper, No. 14.

Sandhu, Kernial Singh. 1981. "Southeast Asian Studies: Some Unresolved Problems," A Colloquium on Southeast Asian Studies. Tunku Shamsul Bahrin, Chandran Jeshurun, and A. Terry Rambo, eds. Singapore: Institute of Southeast Asian Studies. Pp. 15-27.

Sardesai, D.R. 1989. Southeast Asia: Past and Present. 2nd edition. Boulder: Westview Press.

Sarkisyanz, Manuel. 1970. "The Social Ethics of Buddhism and Socio-Economic Development in South-East Asia," Asian and African Studies, pp. 7-21.

Sastrapratedja, M. 1984. "The Crisis of Religion as a System of Legitimation," *Southeast Asian Journal of Social Science*, 12.1:16-24.

Scalapino, Robert A., Seizaburo Sato, and Jusuf Wanandi, eds. 1986. Asian Political Institutionalization. Berkeley: University of California, Institute of East Asian Studies, Research Papers and Policy Studies 15.

Schecter, Jerome. 1967. The New Face of Buddha: The Fusion of Religion and Politics in Contemporary Buddhism. London: Victor Gollancz; New York: Coward-McCann.

Scott, James C. 1976. The Moral Economy of the Peasant: Rebellion and Subsistence in South-east Asia. New Haven: Yale University Press.

Scott, James C., and Benedict J. Tria Kerkvliet, eds. 1986. Everyday Forms of Peasant Resistance in Southeast Asia. London: Frank Cass.

Scott, James G. 1918. "Indo-Chinese Mythology," in The Mythology of All Races. John A. Mac Culloch and Louis H. Gray, eds. Boston: Marshall Jones. Vol. XII, pp. 247-357, 429-30, 448-50. (Reprinted, New York: Cooper Square Publisher [1964], Vol. XII.)

Sears, Laurie J., ed. 1993. Autonomous Histories, Particular Truths: Essays in Honor of John R.W. Smail. Madison: University of Wisconsin, Center for Southeast Asian Studies, Monograph No. 11.

Sears, Laurie J. 1993. "The Contingency of Autonomous History," Autonomous Histories, Particular Truths: Essays in Honor of John R.W. Smail, Laurie J. Sears, ed. Madison: University of Wisconsin, Center for Southeast Asian Studies, Monograph No. 11. Pp. 3-35.

Sebeok, Thomas A., ed. 1967. Current Trends in Linguistics: Linguistics in East Asia and South East Asia. The Hague: Mouton. Vol. II.

Selimkhanov, I. R. 1984. "The Tin Problem of Southeast Asia and Its Use in the Bronze Metallurgy of Ancient Azerballan," in Southeast Asian Archaeology at the XV Pacific Science Congress. Dunedin, New Zealand: University of Otago, University of Otago Studies in Prehistoric Anthropology, Volume 16. Ed. by Donn Bayard. Pp. 270-77.

Sesser, Stan. 1993. The Lands of Charm and Cruelty: Travels in Southeast Asia. New York: Alfred A. Knopf. Paper if available.

Shaffer, Lynda Norene. 1995. Maritime Southeast Asia, 300 B.C. to A.D. 1528. Armonk, New York: M.E. Sharpe.

Shamsul Bahrin, Tunku, Chandran Jeshurun, and A. Terry Rambo, eds. 1981. A Colloquium on Southeast Asian Studies. Singapore: Institute of Southeast Asian Studies.

Sharp, Lauriston. 1962. "Cultural Continuities and Discontinuities in Southeast Asia," *Journal of Asian Studies*, 22.1:3-12. (Reprinted in Man, State and Society in Contemporary Southeast Asia. Robert O. Tilman, ed. New York: Praeger, 1969. Pp. 45-54.)

Shiratori, Yoshiro. 1957. "A Question of the Ancient History of Thai," Abstracts of Paper [presented at the 9th Pacific Science Congress, Bangkok, 1957), pp. 22-23.

Shorto, H.L. 1979. "The Linguistic Protohistory of Mainland South East Asia," with comment by D.T. Bayard in Early South East Asia: Essays in Archaeology, History, and Historical Geography. R.B. Smith and W. Watson, eds. Kuala Lumpur: Oxford University Press. Pp. 273-80.

Sirisena, W.M. 1978. Sri Lanka and South-East Asia: Political, Religious and Cultural Relations from A.D. c. 1000 to c. 1500. Leiden: E.J. Brill.

Smail, John R.W. 1961. "On the Possibility of an Autonomous History of Modern Southeast Asia," *Journal of Southeast Asian History*, 2:72-102. (Republished in Autonomous Histories, Particular Truths: Essays in Honor of John R.W. Smail, Laurie J. Sears, ed. Madison: University of Wisconsin, Center for Southeast Asian Studies, Monograph No. 11, 1993, pp. 39-70.)

Smith, Bardwell L., ed. 1978. Religion and Legitimation of Power in Thailand, Laos, and Burma. Chambersburg, Pa.: Anima Books.

Snodgrass, Adrian. 1985. The Symbolism of the Stupa. Ithaca, NY: Southeast Asia Program, Cornell University Press.

Snooks, G.D., A.J.S. Reid, and J.J. Pincus, eds. 1991. Exploring Southeast Asia's Economic Past. Melbourne: Economic History Society of Australia and New Zealand, Australian Economic History Review, Vol. XXXI, No. 1.

Solheim, Wilhelm G., II. 1967. "Two Pottery Traditions of Late Prehistoric Times in South-East Asia," Symposium on Historical, Archaeological and Linguistics Studies on Southern China, South-East Asia, and the Hong Kong Region. F.S.

Drake, and Wolfram Eberhard, eds. Hong Kong: Hong Kong University Press. Pp. 15-22.

Solheim, Wilhelm G., II.. 1987. "Archaeology and Anthropology in Southeast Asia," *Journal of Southeast Asian Studies*, 18.2:175-81.

Sombat Chantornvong and Thak Chaloemtiarana. 1981. "Promising but Reluctant: Southeast Asian Studies in Thailand," A Colloquium on Southeast Asian Studies. Tunku Shamsul Bahrin, Chandran Jeshurun, and A. Terry Rambo, eds. Singapore: Institute of Southeast Asian Studies. Pp. 171-84.

Somsak Phansomboon. 1957. "A Bioseriological Consideration of the Migration of the Thai Race: A Preliminary Report of a New Concept," *Journal of the Siam Society*, 45.2:55-63.

Spae, Joseph J. 1974. "Asian Religious Values and Development," in Religon and Development in Asian Societies. Colombo: Marga Publications. Pp. 74-88.

Stange, Paul. 1992. "Religious Change in Contemporary Southeast Asia," The Cambridge History of Southeast Asia. Volume Two, The Nineteenth and Twentieth Centuries. Nicholas Tarling, ed. Cambridge: Cambridge University Press. Pp. 529-84.

Stargardt, Janice. 1986. "Hydraulic Works and South East Asian Politics," in Southeast Asia in the 9th to 14th Centuries. David G. Marr, and A. C. Milner, eds. Singapore: Institute of Southeast Asian Studies and the Research School of Pacific Studies, Australian National University. Pp. 23-48.

Steinberg, David J., ed. 1971. In Search of Southeast Asia: A Modern History. New York: Praeger. (Reprinted, Honolulu: University of Hawaii Press, 1985.)

Stivens, Maila 1991. Why Gender Matters in Southeast Asian Politics. Clayton, Victoria: Monast University, Monash Papers on Southeast Asia.

Stockwell, A.J. 1992. "Southeast Asia in War and Peace: The End of European Colonial Empires," The Cambridge History of Southeast Asia. Volume Two, The Nineteenth and Twentieth Centuries. Nicholas Tarling, ed. Cambridge: Cambridge University Press. Pp. 329-86.

Stoler, Ann Laura. 1991. "Carnal Knowledge and Imperial Power: Gender, Race, and Morality in Colonial Asia," Gender at the Crossroads of Knowledge: Feminisst Anthropology in the Postmodern Era. Micaela di Leonardo, ed. Berkeley and Los Angeles: University of Califonria Press. Pp. 51-101.

Stoler, Ann Laura. 1992. "Rethinking Colonial Categories: European Communities and the Boundaries of Rule," Colonialism and Culture Ann Arbor: Nicholas B. Dirks, ed. The University of Michigan Press, The Comparative Studies in Society and History Book Series. Pp. 319-52.

Strong, John S. 1991. The Legend and Cult of Upagupta: Sanskrit Buddhism in North India and Southeast Asia. Princeton: Princeton University Press.

Su Chung-jen. 1967. "Places in South-East Asia, the Middle East, and Africa Visited by ChLng Ho and His Companioins, A.D. 1405-1433," Symposium on Historical, Archaeological and Linguistics Studies on Southern China, South-East Asia, and the Hong Kong Region. F.S. Drake, and Wolfram Eberhard, eds. Hong Kong: Hong Kong University Press. Pp. 198-211.

Subrahmanyam, S. 1986. "Aspects of State Formation in South India and Southeast Asia, 1500-1650," The Indian Economic and Social History Review, 23.4:357-77.

Sukhumbhand Paribatra, M. R., and Chai-Anan Samudavanija. 1984. "Factors Behind Armed Separatism: A Framework for Analysis," In Armed Separatism in Southeast Asia. Lim Joo-Jock and Vani S., eds. Singapore: Institute of Southeast Asian Studies, Regional Strategic Studies Programme. Pp. 30-48.

Sullivan, Gerard, and S. Gunasekaran. 1993. "The Role of Ethnic Relations and Educaion Systems in Migration from Southeast asia to Australia," Sojourn, 8.2:219-49.

Supang Chantavanich and E. Bruce Reynolds, eds. 1988. Indochinese Refugees: Asylyum and Resettlement. Bangkok: Chulalongkorn University, Institute of Asian Studies, Asian Studies Monographs No. 039.

Suryadinata, Leo, ed. 1997. Ethnic Chinese as Southeast Asians. Singapore: Institute of Southeasts Asian Studies.

Swearer, Donald K. 1987. "Buddhism in Southeast Asia," in The Encyclopedia of Religion. Mircea Eliade, ed. New York: Collier Macmillan Publishers. Vol. 2, pp. 385-400.

Swearer, Donald K. 1987. "Folk Buddhism," in The Encyclopedia of Religion. Mircea Eliade, ed. New York: Collier Macmillan Publishers. Vol. 5, pp. 374-378.

Swearer, Donald K. 1995. The Buddhist World of Southeast Asia. Albany: State University of New York Press.

Szanton, David L. 1981. "Southeast Asian Studies in the United States: Towards an Intellectual History," A Colloquium on Southeast Asian Studies. Tunku Shamsul Bahrin, Chandran Jeshurun, and A. Terry Rambo, eds. Singapore: Institute of Southeast Asian Studies. Pp. 72-87.

Tam Siu-Mi, and David Y. H. Wu. 1988. "Minorities Policy in the People's Republic of China: Its Implications in Southeast Asia," *Southeast Asian Journal of Social Science*, 16.2:78-95.

Tambiah, Stanley J. 1977. "The Galactic Polity: The Structure of Traditional Kingdoms in Southeast Asia," Annals of the New York Academy of Sciences, 293:69-97.

Tambiah, Stanley J. 1978. "The Buddhist Conception of Kingship and Its Historical Manifestations: A Reply to Spiro," *Journal of Asian Studies*, 37.4:801-809.

Tanabe, Shigeharu, ed. 1991. Religious Traditions among Tai Ethnic Groups: A Selected Bibliography. Bangkok: Ayutthaya Historical Study Centre.

Tanaka, Yozo, Minako Mori, and Yoko Mori. 1992. "Overseas Chinese Business Community in Asia: Present Conditions and Future Prospects," Rim: Pacific Business and Industries, 2:2-24.

Tandurp, Anders. 1995. "World War and Village War: Chaning Patterns of Rural Conflict in Southeast Asia, 1945-1955," in Imperial Policy and Southeast Asian Nationalism, 1930-1957, ed. by Hans Antl'v and Stein Trnnesson. Richmond, Surrey: Curzon Press. Pp. 170-190.

Tannebaum, Nicola, and Cornelia Ann. 1996. "Introduction," Merit and Blessing in Mainland Southeast Asia in Comparative Perspective. Cornelia Ann Kammerer and Nicola Tannebaum, eds. New Haven: Yale University, Yale Southeast Asia Studies, Monograph 45. Pp. 1-19.

Tarling, Nicholas, ed. 1992. The Cambridge History of Southeast Asia. Volume One, From Early Times to c. 1800. Cambridge: Cambridge University Press.

Tarling, Nicholas. 1992. "The Establishment of the Colonial RJgimes," The Cambridge History of Southeast Asia. Volume Two, The Nineteenth and Twentieth Centuries. Nicholas Tarling, ed. Cambridge: Cambridge University Press. Pp. 5-78.

Taylor, John G., and Andrew Turton, eds. 1988. Sociology of "Developing Societies" in Southeast Asia. London: Macmillan.

Taylor, R.H., ed. 1996. The Politics of Elections in Southeast Asia. Washington, D.C.: Woodrow Wilson Center Press and Cambridge: Cambridge University Press.

Tepper, Elliott L., ed. 1980. Southeast Asian Exodus: From Tradition to Resettlement. Ottawa: Canadian Asian Studies Association.

Terwiel, B.J. 1994. "Rice Legends in Mainland Southeast Asia: History and Ethnography in the Study of Myths of Origin," in "Rice in Southeast Asian Myth and Ritual." Anthony R. Walker, ed., Contributions to Southeast Asian Ethnography, 10:5-36.

Thomas, M.M. 1966. The Christian Response to the Asian Revolution. London: S.C.M. Press.

Thompson, Virgina and Richard Adloff. 1948. Cultural Institutions and Educational Policy in Southeast Asia. New York: I.P.R. Secretariat.

Thompson, Virginia, and Richard Adloff. 1950. The Left Wing in Southeast Asia. New York: William Sloane Associates, for the International Secretariat, Institute of Pacific Relations.

Thompson, Virginia. 1947. Labor Problems in Southeast Asia. New Haven: Yale University Press.

Thompson, Virginia, and Richard Adloff. 1955. Minority Problems in Southeast Asia. Stanford: Stanford University Press, Issued underthe auspices of the International Secretariat, Institute of Pacific Relations.

Tilman, Robert O., ed. 1969. Man, State, and Society in Contemporary Southeast Asia. New York: Praeger.

Tollefson, James W. 1991. Planning Language, Planning Inequality: Language Policy in the Community. London: Longman.

Trocki, Carl A. 1992. "Political Structures in the Nineteenth and Early Twentieth Centuries," The Cambridge History of Southeast Asia. Volume Two, The Nineteenth and Twentieth Centuries. Nicholas Tarling, ed. Cambridge: Cambridge University Press. Pp. 79-130.

Truong, Thanh-Dam. 1990. Sex, Money and Morality: Prostitution and Tourism in Southeast Asia. London: Zed Books.

Tucker, Richard P., and J. F. Richards. 1983. Global Deforestation and the Nineteenth-Century World Economy. Durham, N. C.: Duke University Press.

Turley, William S., ed. 1985. Confrontation or Coexistence: The Future of ASEAN-Vietnam Relations. Bangkok: Chulalongkorn University, Institute of Secruity and International Studies.

Turnbull, C.M. 1992. "Regionalism and Nationalism," The Cambridge History of Southeast Asia. Volume Two, The Nineteenth and Twentieth Centuries. Nicholas Tarling, ed. Cambridge: Cambridge University Press. Pp. 585-45.

Turton, Andrew, and Shigeharu Tanabe, eds. 1984. Historical and Peasant Consciousness in South East Asia. Osaka: National Museum of Ethnology (Senir Ethnological Studies, 13).

Ulack, Richard, and Gyula Pauer. 1988. Atlas of Southeast Asia. New York: Macmillan.

United Nations. UNESCO. 1966. Curriculum, Methods of Teaching, Evaluation and Textbooks in Primary Schools in Asia. Bangkok: UNESCO Regional Office of Education in Asia.

United Nations. UNESCO. 1970. "Reforms and Reorganization in Education in the Asian Region," Bulletin of the UNESCO Regional Office for Education in Asia, 4.

Van Esterik, Penny. 1995. "Rewriting Gender and Development Anthropology in

Southeast Asia," 'Male' and 'Female' in Developing Southeast Asia. Wazir Jahan Karim, ed. Oxford and Washington, D.C.: Berg Publishers. Pp. 247-60.

Vatikiotis, Michael R.J. 1996. Political Change in Southeast Asia. London and New York: Routledge.

Wain, Barry. 1981. The Refused. New York: Simon & Schuster.

Wang Gungwu. 1979. "The Study of the Southeast Asian Past," in Perceptions of the Past in Southeast Asia. Anthony Reid and David Marr, eds. Singapore: Heinemann Educational Books, Published for the Asian Studies Association of Australia. Pp. 1-8.

Wang Gung-wu. 1981. Community and Nation: Essays on Southeast Asia and the Chinese. Kuala Lumpur: Heinemann Educational Books (Asia) for the Asian Studies Association of Australia, Southeast Asia Publications Series, No. 6.

Warren, Carol. 1985. "Class and Change in Rural Southeast Asia," in Southeast Asia: Essays in the Political Economy of Structural Change. Richard Higgott and Richard Robison, eds. London: Routledge and Kegan Paul. Pp. 128-46.

Waterson, Roxana. 1990. The Living House: An Anthropology of Architecture in South-East Asia. Singapore: Oxford University Press.

Watson, Keith. 1976. "The Education of Racial Minorities in South East Asia with Special Reference to the Chinese," *Compare*, 6.2:14-21.

Watson, Keith. 1980. "Missionary Education in Asia: Lesson from the Past—Challenge for the Future," *Spectrum*, 12.3:4-9.

Watson, Keith. 1982. "The Contribution of Mission Schools to Educational Development in South East Asia," in Education in the Third World. Keith Watson, ed. London and Canberra: Croom Helm. Pp. 71-87.

Weatherbee, Donald E. 1986. "U.S. Perspectives on ASEAN and Regional Security," United States-Thailand Relations. Berkeley: University of California, Institute of East Asian Studies, Research Papers and Policy Studies, 20. Pp. 215-30.

Wheatley, Paul. 1975. "Satynrta in Suvaradvpa: From Reciprocity to Redistribution in Ancient Southeast Asia," in Ancient Civilization and Trade. Jeremy A. Sabloff and C.C. Lamberg-Karlovsky, eds. Albuquerque: University of New Mexico Press. Pp. 227-283.

Wijeyewardene, Gehan, ed. 1990. Ethnic Groups across National Boundaries in Mainland Southeast Asia. Singapore: Institute of Southeast Asian Studies.

Wijeyewardene, Gehan. 1990. "Introduction: Definition, Innovation, and History," Ethnic Groups across National Boundaries in Mainland Southeast Asia. Gehan Wijeyewardene, ed. Singapore: Institute of Southeast Asian Studies. Pp. 1-13.

Winks, Robin W., and James R. Rush, eds. 1990. Asia in Western Fiction. Manchester: Manchester University Press.

Wolters, O.W. 1994. "Southeast Asia as a Southeast Asian Field of Study," *Indonesia*, 38:1-17.

Wong Hoy Kee, Francis. 1973. Comparative Studies in Southeast Asian Education. Kuala Lumpur: Heinemann Educational Books (Asia), Ltd.

Wood, Robert E. 1980. "International Tourism and Culture Change in Southeast Asia," *Economic Development and Culture Change*, 28.3:561-582.

Wood, Robert E. 1984. "Ethnic Tourism, The State, and Cultural Change in Southeast Asia," in "Tourism and Ethnicity," Special Issue of Annals of Tourism Research. Charles F. Keyes and Pierre van den Berghe, eds., 11.3:353-374.

Woodward, Mark R., and Susan D. Russell. 1989. "Introduction: Transformations in Ritual and Economy in Upland and Lowland Southeast Asia," in Ritual, Power, and Economy: Upland-Lowland Contrasts in Mainland Southeast Asia. Russell, Susan D., ed. DeKalb, IL: Northern Illinois University, Center for For Southeast Asian Studies, Monograph Series on Southeast Asia, Occasional Paper, No. 14. Pp. 1-26.

Wu, David Y. H. 1988. "Introduction: The Issues of National Policies and Minority Cultures in Southeast Asia," *Southeast Asian Journal of Social Science*, 16.2:1-5.

Yamamoto, Tadashi, ed. 1995. Emerging Civil Society in the Asia Pacific Community: Nongovernmental Underpinnings of the Emerging Asia Pacific Regional Community. Singapore: Institute for Southeast Asian Studies and Tokyo: Japan Center for International Exchange.

Yao Souchou. 1987. "Ethnicity: The Symbolic and Political Dimensions," *Sojourn*, 2.2:169-77.

Yip Yat Hoong, ed. 1973. Roles of Universities in Local and Regional Development in Southeast Asia. Singapore: Regional Institute of Higher Education and Development.

Yong Mun Cheong. 1992. "The Political Structures of the Independent States," The Cambridge History of Southeast Asia. Volume Two, The Nineteenth and Twentieth Centuries. Nicholas Tarling, ed. Cambridge: Cambridge University Press. Pp. 387-466.

Yoshihara Kunio. 1988. The Rise of Ersatz Capitalism in South-East Asia. Singapore: Oxford University Press.

INDEX

A

N

O

P

R

S